BUSINESS AND GOVERNMENT

Dr. Francis Cherunilam

M.A., M.B.A., D.D.P., Ph.D.

(Formerly Director,
School of Management Studies,
Cochin University of Science & Technology,
Cochin - 682 022.
and
Professor and Chairman, Marketing Area, IIMK).
e-mail: cherunilam@gmail.com

Himalaya Publishing House

ISO 9001:2008 CERTIFIED

First Edition	:	1982	Tenth Revised Edition	:	1998
Second Edition	:	1984	Eleventh Revised Edition	:	1999
Third Edition	:	1986	Twelfth Revised Edition	:	2000
Fourth Edition	:	1988	Thirteenth Revised Edition	:	2003
Fifth Edition	:	1990	Fourteenth Revised Edition (Silver Jubilee Year Edition)	:	2007
Sixth Edition	:	1992			
Seventh Revised Edition	:	1993	Fifteenth Revised Edition	:	2012
Eighth Revised Edition	:	1996	Sixteenth Edition	:	2013
Ninth Revised Edition	:	1997	Seventeenth Revised Edition	:	2017

Published by : Mrs. Meena Pandey for **Himalaya Publishing House Pvt. Ltd.,**
"Ramdoot", Dr. Bhalerao Marg, Girgaon, **Mumbai - 400 004.**
Phone: 022-23860170, 23863863; **Fax:** 022-23877178 .
E-mail: himpub@vsnl.com; **Website:** www.himpub.com

Branch Offices :

New Delhi : "Pooja Apartments", 4-B, Murari Lal Street, Ansari Road, Darya Ganj, New Delhi - 110 002. Phones: 011-23270392, 23278631; Fax: 011-23256286

Nagpur : Kundanlal Chandak Industrial Estate, Ghat Road, Nagpur - 440 018. Phones: 0712-2738731, 3296733; Telefax: 0712-2721215

Bengaluru : Plot No. 91-33, 2nd Main Road Seshadripuram, Behind Nataraja Theatre, Bengaluru - 560020. Phones: 08041138821, 09379847017, 09379847005

Hyderabad : No. 3-4-184, Lingampally, Besides Raghavendra Swamy Matham, Kachiguda, Hyderabad - 500 027. Phones: 040-27560041, 27550139; Mobile: 09390905282

Chennai : New No. 48/2, Old No. 28/2,Ground Floor, Sarangapani Street, T. Nagar, Chennai - 600 012. Mobile: 09380460419

Pune : First Floor, "Laksha" Apartment, No. 527, Mehunpura, Shaniwarpeth, (Near Prabhat Theatre), Pune - 411 030. Phones: 020-24496323/24496333; Mobile: 09370579333

Lucknow : House No. 731, Shekhupura Colony, Near B.D. Convent School, Aliganj, Lucknow - 226 022. Mobile: 09307501549

Ahmedabad : 114, "SHAIL", 1st Floor, Opp. Madhu Sudan House, C.G. Road, Navrang Pura, Ahmedabad - 380 009. Phone: 079-26560126; Mobile: 09377088847

Ernakulam : 39/176 (New No. 60/251), 1st Floor, Karikkamuri Road, Ernakulam, Kochi - 682011, Phones: 0484-2378012, 2378016; Mobile: 09344199799

Bhubaneswar : 5, Station Square, Bhubaneswar - 751 001 (Odisha). Phone: 0674-2532129; Mobile: 09338746007

Kolkata : 108/4, Beliaghata Main Road, Near ID Hospital, Opp. SBI Bank, Kolkata - 700 010. Phone: 033-32449649; Mobile: 09883055590, 07439040301

DTP by : Sudhakar Shetty

Printed at : Geetanjali Press Pvt. Ltd., Nagpur, on behalf of HPH.

PREFACE TO THE SEVENTEENTH EDITION

With this edition, my first book is completing three-and-a-half decades of journey. It has been very exciting as well as challenging to chronicle the business-government interface over the last seven decades since the Independence. To begin with, the greatest challenge was to formulate a framework of the scope of the book which hardly had any model available. Taking stock of the historical developments of the three-and-a-half decades since Independence to 1982, the year of the publication of this book, and presenting them comprehensively and concisely was a herculean task for a novice at a fairly young age and at a time when data sourcing was too difficult. Since the publication of the first edition, the engagement became constantly monitoring the developments and suitably modifying the work for new editions.

The overwhelming response, to this work since the very beginning instilled in me the required confidence and enthusiasm for the subsequent works, including the flagship publication *Business Environment: Text and Cases* which in fact is a much broader and enlarged version of *Business and Government*. By His grace and the blessings of the academic community, it has been an academic journey fast forward and I have been able to do nearly sixty books.

I would like to place on record my deep indebtedness to the Himalaya Publishing House for the constant encouragement. And I bow down before the academic community for the enormous encouragement I have been getting.

Dr. FRANCIS CHERUNILAM

Cochin,
3rd January, 2017

PREFACE TO THE FIRST EDITION

Business and Government is a subject to growing importance and interest, for the government control over the material resources, regulation of private business and public ownership of business have been expanding. With the emergence of new problems and the aggravation of the existing ones, the government has been arming itself, justified or not, with more and more powers of control. This book provides a critical review of the economic and business policies of the government and the various control measures adopted to implement them.

This book covers the syllabi of the *Business and Government* of the Business Administration courses of institutes of management and universities in India. It is expected that it will be useful also for the students of Economics, Commerce, Planning, Public Administration, etc. Special attention has been devoted for treating the subject matter in such a way that even those who do not have an academic background of Economics or Management will be able to easily understand the various topics dealt within the book.

The enormous encouragement I have received from my teacher and associates charged me with the spirit and enthusiasm to proceed with this work with more vigour and seriousness. I am at a loss as to how to express the deep sense of gratitude I owe to them. It is not possible to mention their names here. I must, however, express my special thanks to Mr. Joy Sebastine, Department of Political Science, St. Philomena's College, Mysore, who reviewed the manuscript of some of the chapters and gave valuable suggestions. The author alone is responsible for the errors, mistake and shortcomings that may be there.

It must mentioned here that as the government policies and controls are subject to frequent changes or modifications, no book on this subject can be up-to-date. Constructive criticisms and suggestions to improve the book are welcome.

Dr. FRANCIS CHERUNILAM

CONTENTS

CHAPTER

1

Business and Government – An Introduction

It is widely recognised that "the two most powerful institutions in society today are business and government; where they meet on common ground – amicably or otherwise – together they determine public policy, both foreign and domestic for a nation".[1]

Historically, the role of the government in respect of business varied considerably in kind and degree, from *laissez faire* and mercantilism to conventional communism characterised by centralised planning and almost state monopoly. The last six-and-a-half decades or so, the period since the end of the II World War and the coming into being of World Bank – IMF and GATT (the forerunner of WTO), have witnessed several shifts, evolutionary to revolutionary, in the approach, policy and mode of government intervention in business across the world. The economic crisis that swept across the world around 2008 once again demonstrated the economic stabilisation role of the government.

The last few decades have witnessed a move from Marx to market in Communist countries while several market economies became more marketised by privatisation and liberalisation.

The government, however, plays a very important role in the modern economy. Even the modern capitalist or market economies are mixed or regulated systems. In such economies "a substantial share of the nation's product goes to satisfy public wants, a substantial part of the private income originates in the public budget, and public tax and transfer payments significantly influence the state of private income distribution".[2]

Moreover, the budget policy affects the level of employment and prices in the private sector. Thus, the present day capitalist economy is a mixed system, including a sizable and virtually important sphere of public economy along with the market sector.

As the Musgraves remark, "the prevalence of government may reflect the presence of political and social ideologies which depart from the premises of consumer choice and decentralised decision-making. But this is only a minor part of the story. More important, there is the fact that the market mechanism alone cannot perform all economic functions. Public policy is needed to guide, correct and supplement it in certain respects. It is important to realize this fact since it implies that the proper size of the public sector is, to a significant degree, a technical rather than an ideological issue."[3] A variety of reasons explain why this is the case, including the following:

1. The contractual arrangements and exchanges needed for the market operation cannot exist without the protection and enforcement of a governmentally provided legal structure.
2. The claim that the market mechanism leads to efficient resource use *(i.e.,* produces what consumers want most and does so in the cheapest way) is based on the condition of the competitive factors and product markets. This means that there must be no obstacles to free entry and that consumers and producers must have full market knowledge. Government regulation or other measures are needed to secure these conditions.
3. Even if all barriers to competition were removed, the production or consumption characteristics of certain goods are such that these goods cannot be provided through the market. Problems of "externalities" arise which lead to "market failure" and require solution through the public sector.
4. The rate of discount used in the valuing of future (relative to present) consumption may differ as seen from a public and a private point of view.
5. The market system, especially in a highly developed financial economy, does not necessarily bring high employment, price level stability, and the socially desired rate of economic growth. Public policy is needed to secure these objectives.
6. Social values may require adjustments in the distribution of income and wealth, which results from the market system and from the transmission of property rights through inheritance.

As the Musgraves further remark, "to argue that these limitations of the market mechanisms call for corrective of compensating measures of public policy does not prove, of course, that any policy measure which is undertaken will in fact improve the performance of economic system. Public policy, no less than the private policy, can err and be inefficient."[4]

Since the Great Depression, there has been an increase in the stabilisation, allocation and distribution functions performed by the governments of the predominantly market economies. However, the extent of State control and the types of control may vary widely between nations depending upon the nature and stage of development of the economy, the behaviour of the private sector, the political philosophy, social attitude, and administrative system, etc.

There is hardly any country in the world, the economy of which is not in one way or other influenced by the State activities.

Even in the market economies, State ownership of enterprises and even the whole of certain industries is not uncommon. The public utilities in these countries are either under strong State control or owned by the State. There had also been a tendency in some of these countries to nationalise certain critical industries as well as to own enterprises in important industries. This was true of the members of the European Economic Community (EEC), Canada, etc. However, since the late 1970s, the trend has been privatisation.

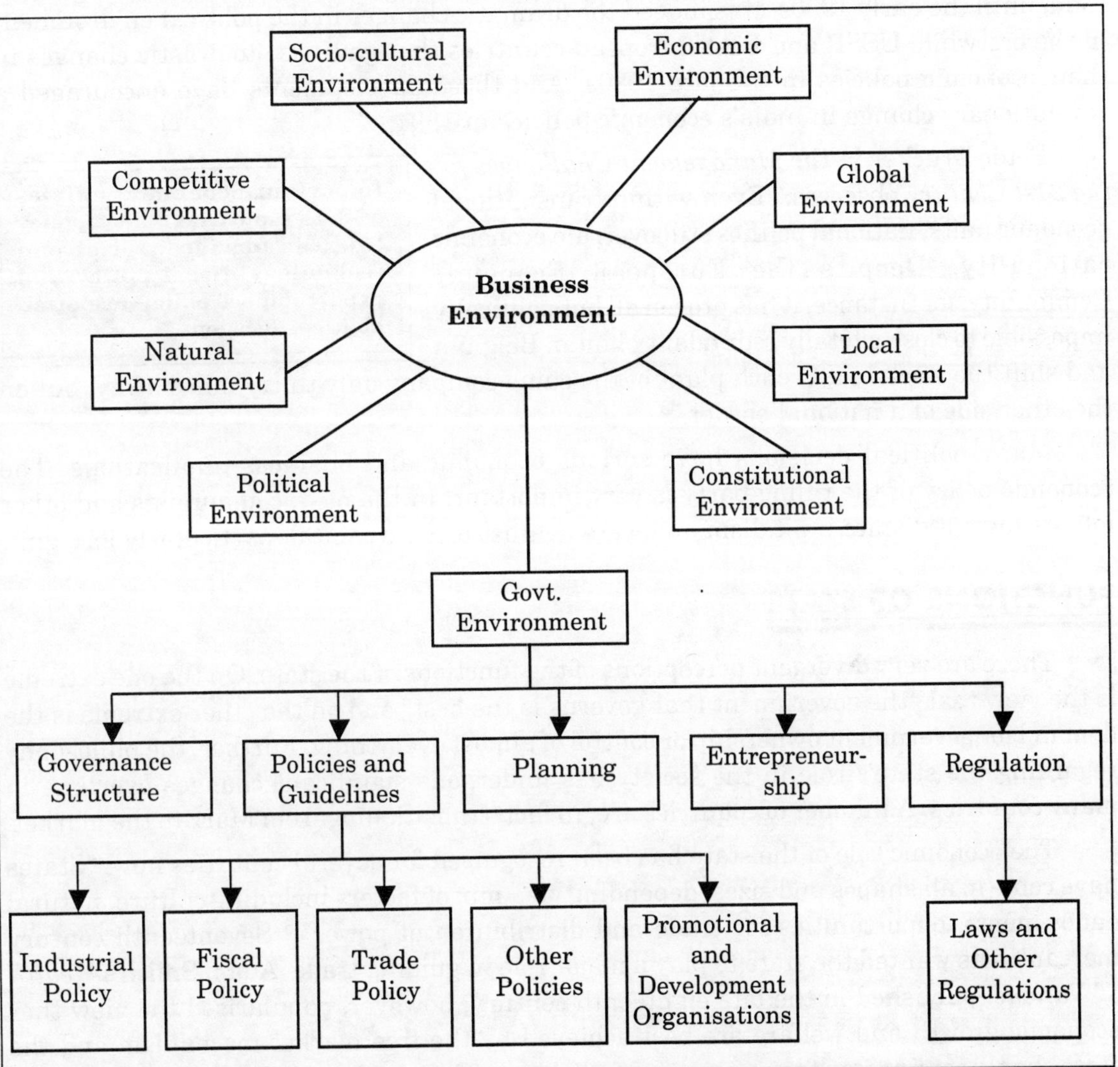

Fig. 1.1: Business and Government — A Component of Business Environment

It is often politics that determines economic and business policies highlights the critical importance of the political environment to business. The political environment includes factors such as the characteristics and policies of the political parties, the nature of the Constitution and government system and the government environment encompassing the economic and business policies and regulations. These factors may vary as considerably between different nations, between different provinces of the same nation and also overtime.

Major economic policy decisions often have political underpinnings. The adoption, in the early 1950s, of the principle of *socialist pattern of society* as the socio-economic philosophy by the Congress party, which ruled India until 1995, except for a brief period (1977-1980), was mainly responsible for the public sector dominated development strategy followed in India until the early 1990s. It is indeed the dramatic changes in the political environment in the erstwhile USSR and East European countries that gave rise to drastic changes in their economic policies in the late 1980s. And these developments have encouraged a revolutionary change in India's economic policies in 1991.

Important economic policies such as industrial policy, policy towards foreign capital and technology, fiscal policy and export-import policy are often political decisions.

Peter Drucker in the *Management Challenges for the 21st Century* observes: "Even within transnational economic units, national politics still overrule economic rationality. Despite the European Economic Community, for instance, it has proven all but politically impossible to close a totally redundant plant in Belgium and shift the work to a French plant of the same company only thirty miles away, but on the other side of a national border."[5]

Many political decisions have serious economic and business implications. The economic policy of the ruling party is very important. In the past, communists and other leftists favoured state capitalism and were against private capital, particularly foreign.

FUNCTIONS OF STATE

There are very divergent perceptions of the functions of the state. On the one extreme is the view that "the government that governs is the best" and on the other extreme is the demand for government ownership or control of almost everything. Further, the philosophy regarding the state's role in the society has undergone significant changes overtime in many countries. A number of countries are, in fact, transitioning from Marx to the market.

The economic role of the state has been recognised for several centuries now. "States have come in all shapes and sizes, depending on a mix of factors including culture, natural endowments, opportunities for trade and distribution of power".[6] Seventeenth century mercantilists wanted the state to play a major role in guiding trade. Adam Smith's *Wealth of Nations,* published in the late eighteenth century, however, popularised the view that economic growth and welfare are best achieved by the free market mechanism and the state should confine itself to certain core functions such as law and order, defence, etc., and enforcement of contracts, essential for the proper functioning of the market economy. "But even then, state intervention went on to play a vital, catalytic role in the development and growth of markets in Europe, Japan and North America."[7] Even in the United States, which is regarded as the citadel of market economy, State has been playing an active role in the development of several industries/sectors.

BOX 1.1: STATE AND GOVERNMENT: SOME CONCEPTS

State, in its wider sense, refers to a set of institutions that possess the means of legitimate coercion, exercised over a defined territory and its population referred to as society. The state monopolises rule making within its territory through the medium of an organized government.

The term *government* is often used differently in different contexts. It can refer to the process of governing, to the exercise of power. It can also refer to the existence of that process, to a condition of "ordered rule". "Government" often means the people who fill the positions of authority in a state. Finally, the term may refer to the manner, method, or system of governing in a society: to the structure and arrangement of offices and how they relate to the governed. While keeping these distinctions in mind, we also use the terms *state* and *government* colloquially and sometimes interchangeably — as they are often used in discussion and writing around the world.

Government is normally regarded as consisting of three distinct sets of powers, each with its assigned role. One is the *legislature,* whose role is to make the law. The second is the *executive* (sometimes referred to as "the government"), which is responsible for implementing the law. The third is the *judiciary,* which is responsible for interpreting and applying the law.

Classifications of government are many but have tended to concentrate on two criteria; the arrangement of offices, which is more narrow in conception, and the relationship between government and the governed.

The first classification is based on the relationship between the executive and the legislature. In a *parliamentary* system, the executive's continuance in office depends on its maintaining the support of the legislature. Members of the executive are commonly also members of the legislature. A prime minister may be the most powerful member of the executive, but important decisions within the executive are usually made collectively by a group of ministers. In a *presidential* system the executive's position is independent of the legislature. Members of the executive are not normally also members of the legislature, and ultimate decision-making authority within the executive lies with one person, the president.

The second classification concentrates on the distribution of power between levels of government. In a *unitary* state, all authority to make laws is vested in one supreme legislature whose jurisdiction covers the whole country. Local legislatures may exist, but only with the sufferance of the national legislature. In a *federal state,* local legislatures are guaranteed at least a measure of autonomous decision-making authority. In a *confederation,* a group of sovereign states combine for specified purposes, but each state retains its sovereignty.

Courtesy: World Bank: *World Development Report,* 1997.

In most modern economies the state's regulatory role is now broader and more complex than ever before, covering such areas as the environment and the financial sector, as well as more traditional areas such as monopolies. The design of regulation needs to fit the capability of state regulatory agencies and the sophistication of markets, and give greater emphasis to personal responsibility.

The first half of the twentieth century witnessed an increase in the state intervention in the economy. The Russian Revolution of 1917 and the consequent establishment of communist rule in the USSR had great influence across the globe on the thinking of the state's role. The *Great Depression* in USA (which eventually spread to other countries), that set in with the *Wall Street* collapse of 1929 and assumed terrific proportions in the early 1930s, brought to fore the important role the state has in a capitalist economy. Shortage of entrepreneurship and other development resources and ideological flavour encouraged many developing countries to assign a very important role to the state in the socio-economic system.

The post Second World War paradigm "coalesced around three basic themes, all of which commanded broad, if not uniform, agreement. This three-pillared consensus remained largely undisturbed until the first oil price shock of 1973. First was the need to provide welfare benefits to those suffering from transitory loss of income or other deprivation. Second was the desirability of a mixed public-private economy, which would often mean nationalising a range of strategic industries. Third was the need for a coordinated macroeconomic policy, on the grounds that the market alone could not deliver stable macroeconomic outcomes that were consistent with individuals' objectives. In time, the goals of macroeconomic policy were made explicit: full employment, price stability, and balance of payments equilibrium.

States thus took on new roles and expanded existing ones. "By mid-century the range of tasks performed by public institutions included not only wider provision of infrastructure and utilities, but also much more extensive support for education and health care."[8]

A reversal of this trend set in the 1980s. Communism collapsed in the USSR and East Europe. China started economic reforms in the late 1970s and widely opened the economy for foreign investment in the eighties. Privatisation caught on at an amazing speed in many developed market economies and developing economies.

However, the government expenditure as a percentage of the GDP increased substantially in the developed and developing countries. In the OECD countries (developed countries) total government expenditure as a percentage GDP increased from about 10 per cent in the beginning of the 20th century to nearly 20 per cent in 1960 and to nearly 50 per cent in 1995. In India, the total budgetary transactions of the Central and State Governments and Union Territories amounted to about 32 per cent of the GDP in 2004-05.

Classification of Functions of State

Functions of the state varies from basic minimum requirements to active participation in several other sectors. Figure 1 classifies the functions of government along a continuum, from activities that will not be taken at all without state intervention, to activities in which the state plays an active role in coordinating markets or redistributing assets.

- The basic functions include the pure public goods such as the provision of property rights, macroeconomic stability, control of infectious diseases, safe water, roads, and protection of the destitute. In many countries the state is not even providing these. Recent reforms have emphasized economic fundamentals, but social and institutional (including legal) fundamentals are equally important to avoid social disruption and ensure sustained development.
- Going beyond these basic services are the intermediate functions, such as management of externalities (pollution, for example), regulation of monopolies,

and the provision of social insurance (pensions, unemployment benefits). Here, too, the government cannot choose, but only how best to intervene, and government can work in partnership with markets and civil society to ensure that these public goods are provided.

- States with strong capability can take on more-activist functions, dealing with the problem of missing markets by helping coordination. East Asia's experience has renewed interest in the state's role in promoting markets through active industrial and financial policy.[9]

	Addressing market failure			***Improving equity***
Minimal functions	*Providing pure public goods* Defence Law and order Property rights Macroeconomic management Public health			*Protecting the poor* Anti-poverty programmes Disaster relief
Intermediate functions	*Addressing externalities* Basic education Environmental Protection	*Regulating monopoly* Utility regulation Anti-trust Policy	*Overcoming imperfect information* Insurance (health, life, pensions) Financial Regulation Consumer Protection	*Providing social insurance* Redistributive pensions Family allowances Unemployment insurance
Activist functions	*Coordinating private activity* Fostering markets Cluster initiatives			*Redistribution* Asset redistribution

Fig. 1.2: Functions of the State (Adopted from World Bank, *World Development Report*, 1997)

Reinvigorating the State's Capability

Reinvigorating the state's capability can be achieved through the following:[10]

☞ ***Rules and Restraints:*** Mechanisms for enforcing the rule of law, such as an independent judiciary, are critical foundations for sustainable development. Along with appropriate separation of powers and the presence of watchdog bodies, they also restrain arbitrary behaviour.

☞ ***Competitive Pressure:*** Competitive pressure can come from within the state bureaucracy, through recruitment of civil servants on the basis of merit. It can come from the domestic private sector, through contracting out for services and allowing private providers to compete directly with public agencies. Or it can come from the international marketplace, through trade and through the influence of global bond markets on fiscal decisions.

- ***Voice and Partnership:*** The means to achieve transparency and openness in modern society are many and varied — business councils, interaction groups, and consumer groups, to name a few. Institutional working arrangements with community groups can contribute to greater state effectiveness by giving citizens a greater voice in the formulation of government's policies. And partnerships between levels of government and with international bodies can help in the provision of local and global public goods.

The State, Institutions, and Economic Outcomes

The State sets the formal rules — laws and regulations — that are part and parcel of a country's institutional environment. These formal rules, along with the informal rules of the broader society, are the institutions that mediate human behaviour. But the state is not merely a referee, making and enforcing the rules from the sidelines; it is also a player, indeed often a dominant player, in the economic game. Everyday, state agencies invest resources, direct credit, procure goods and services, and negotiate contracts; these actions have profound effects on transactions costs and on economic activity and economic outcomes, especially in developing economies. Played well, the state's activities can accelerate development. Played badly, they will produce stagnation or, in the extreme, economic and social disintegration. The state, then, is in a unique position: not only must it establish, through a social and political process, the formal rules by which all other organisations must abide; as an organisation itself, it, too, must abide by those rules.[11]

TABLE 1.1 : IMPACT OF STATE

Ways of State Promoting Development	***Harmful Impact of State***
• By providing a macro-economic and a micro-economic environment that sets the right incentives for efficient economic activity.	• The wrong kind of rules can actively discourage the creation of wealth. For example, the state may penalize private wealth by distorting prices-through an overvalued currency, for example, or by creating agricultural marketing boards that tax farmers' output and give them little in return.
• By providing the institutional infrastructure- property rights, peace, law and order, and rules — that encourages efficient long-term investment, and	• Even if the rules themselves are benign, they may be applied by public organizations-and their employees-in a harmful fashion. They may, for example, impose huge transactions costs, in the form of red tape or bribery, on entrepreneurs setting up new businesses or restructuring old ones.
• By ensuring the provision of basic education, health care, and the physical infrastructure required for economic activity, and by protecting the natural environment.	• But potentially the largest source of state-inflicted damage is uncertainty. If the state changes the rules often, or does not clarify the rules by which the state itself will behave, businesses and individuals cannot be sure today what will be profitable or unprofitable, legal or illegal, tomorrow. They will then adopt costly strategies to insure against an uncertain future — by entering the informal economy, for example, or sending capital abroad–all of which impede development.

Courtesy: World Bank, *World Development Report, 1997.*

Economic Roles of Government

As pointed out earlier, the government plays an important role in almost every national economy of the world.

Governments normally play four important roles in an economy, *viz.*, regulation, promotion, entrepreneurship, and planning.

While the state control of economy is a universal phenomenon, the extent and nature of the control vary widely between nations, depending upon the nature and stage of development of the economy, the behaviour of the private sector, the political philosophy, social attitudes, administrative system, etc.

As stated above, the extent and nature of these roles in a given situation depend on a number of factors. Some salient features of these roles are outlined below:

Regulatory Role: Government regulation of the business may cover a broad spectrum extending from entry into business to the final results of a business. The reservation of industries to small-scale, public and cooperative sectors, licensing system, etc., regulate the entry. Regulations of product mix, promotional activities, etc., amount to regulation of the conduct of business.

Results of business operations may be regulated by such measures as ceilings on profit margins, dividend, etc. The State may also regulate the relationship between enterprises. Examples of this include restrictions on intra-corporate investments, inter-locking of directors and appointment of sole selling agents.

Government regulation of the economy may be broadly divided into direct controls and indirect controls.

Indirect controls are usually exercised through various fiscal and monetary incentives and disincentives or penalties. Certain activities may be encouraged or discouraged through monetary and fiscal incentives and disincentives. For instance, a high import duty may discourage imports and fiscal and monetary incentives may encourage the development of export-oriented industries.

The direct administrative or physical controls are more drastic in their effect. The distinguishing characteristic of direct controls is their discretionary nature. They can be applied selectively from firm-to-firm and industry-to-industry, at the discretion of the State.

Regulation of the business had been rampant in the developing countries. Since the late 1980s, however, a deregulation trend has set in. This has drastically transformed the competitive environment and has given an impetus to globalisation.

Promotional Role: The promotional role played by the government is very important in developed countries as well as in the developing countries. In developing countries, where the infrastructural facilities for development are inadequate and entrepreneurial activities are scarce, the promotional role of the government assumes special significance. The State will have to assume direct responsibility to build up and strengthen the necessary development infrastructures, such as power, transport, finance, marketing, institutions for training and guidance and other promotional activities.

The promotional role of the State also encompasses the provision of various fiscal, monetary and other incentives, including measures to cover certain risks, for the development of certain priority sectors and activities.

Entrepreneurial Role: In many economies, the State also plays the role of an entrepreneur — establishing and operating business enterprises and bearing the risks. A number of factors such as socio-political ideologies; dearth of private entrepreneurship; neglect of certain sectors, like the unprofitable sectors, by the private entrepreneurs; absence of or inadequate competition in certain segments and the resultant exploitation of consumers, etc., have contributed to the growth of State owned enterprises (SOEs) in many countries.

There was a tendency in many developing countries to assign a dominant place to the public sector. Public sector dominance was usually established in capital-intensive projects like steel, capital goods, petrochemicals and fertilisers for which investment requirements were very large and the expected private returns, at least in the short-run were too low to provide an incentive for private profitability. In many cases even when the private sector was prepared to undertake the risk and invest. State ownership of such industries existed for one reason or other.

> **Since the 1980s many governments have resorted to privatisation, in varying degrees, and have redefined the role of the public sector.**

Planning Role: Especially in the developing countries, the State plays a very important role as a planner.

The importance of planning to a less developed economy was often emphasised by Jawaharlal Nehru, the chief architect of Development Planning in India. He rightly observed: "Whatever it may be in other countries, in underdeveloped countries like ours, which have to develop fairly rapidly, the time element is important and the question is how to use our resources to the best advantage. If our resources are abundant it will not matter how they are used. They will go into a common pool of development. But where one's resources are limited, one has to see that they are directed to the right purpose so as to help to build-up whatever one is aiming at."

> **The scope of private business depends, to a large extent, on the economic system which indeed is rooted in political philosophy.**

Economic Systems

At one end, there are the free enterprise/market economies or capitalist economies, and at the other end are the centrally planned economies or communist countries. In between these two are the mixed economies. Within the mixed economic system itself, there are wide variations. The freedom of private enterprise is the greatest in the market economy, which is characterised by the following assumptions:

1. The factors of production (labour, land, capital) are privately owned, and production occurs at the initiative of the private enterprise.
2. Income is received in monetary form by the sale of services of the factors of production and from the profits of the private enterprise.

3. Members of the free market economy have freedom of choice insofar as consumption, occupation, savings and investment are concerned.
4. The free market economy is not planned, controlled or regulated by the government. The government satisfies community or collective wants, but does not compete with private firms; nor does it tell the people where to work/or what to produce.

The completely free market economy, however, is an abstract system rather than a real one. Today, even the so-called market economies are subject to a number of government regulations. Countries like the United States, Japan, Australia, Canada and member countries of the EEC are regarded as market economies.

The communist countries had, by and large, a centrally planned economic system. Under the rule of a communist or authoritarian socialist government, the state owned all the means of production, determines the goals of production and controls the economy according to a central master plan. There was hardly any consumer sovereignty in a centrally planned economy, unlike in the free market economy. The consumption pattern in a centrally planned economy is dictated by the State.

China, East Germany Soviet Union, Czechoslovakia, Hungary, Poland, etc., had centrally planned economies. However, recently several of these countries have discarded communist system and have moved towards the market economy.

In between the capitalist system and the centrally planned system falls the system of the mixed economy, under which both the public and private sectors co-exist, as in India. The extent of State participation varies widely between the mixed economies. However, in many mixed economies, the strategic and other nationally very important industries were fully owned or dominated by the State. This tendency has been changing.

The economic system, thus, is a very important determinant of the scope of private business. The economic system and policy are, therefore, a very important external constraint on business.

Trends in Political/Economic Philosophies/Outlook

While there are no radical differences in the philosophies of major political parties in some countries, the situation is quite different in some others. The government system in a number countries, including several countries which are making rapid economic progress and having liberal policies towards foreign capital and technology, is not very democratic. That does not mean that they are not good to make business with. As a matter of fact, in several such countries the procedures are simpler and decisions are quicker than in some of the democratic countries.

Until the political and economic changes ushered in the late 1980s and in the early 1990s in the Eastern Europe, and erstwhile USSR, these countries were a separate block by themselves with several common characteristics. Private enterprises were very limited and State trading, particularly counter trade, was the rule. There were a lot of restrictions on imports and foreign business. This did not, of course, mean that the communist system was insurmountable for multinationals or other foreign firms. Under such a system, in several instances, winning over the top brass of the party or government was a strategy to obtain business. It may be noted that although companies like PepsiCo were kept out of India they were going better with countries like USSR.

In the past, public sector was assigned a very important role in many non-communist, particularly the developing, countries too. In India, *for example,* where the industrial policy wanted the public sector to gain *control over the commanding heights* of the economy limited the scope of the private enterprise, both domestic and foreign. Even in areas where foreign capital was allowed, there was ceiling on the foreign equity participation.

Further, in the past, foreign firms in many developing countries were under the fear of nationalisation.

The clock, however, has turned a full circle in most of the communist and many other countries. Privatisation has progressed at an amazing speed. The erstwhile communist countries and the Peoples' Republic of China where the communist party is still in power, are on the rapid road from Marx to the market. As a result there has been an influx of foreign investment to these countries.

> **As against the past suspicion of and antagonism against foreign capital and technology, a large number of the developing countries, including the former commu-nist ones, are in a competition to woo foreign capital and tech-nology.**

Although the trend of the direction of government policies across the world appears to be broadly one of convergence, there are lots of differences in the restrictions and regulations of business, scope of foreign business, trade policies, procedures, incentive systems and so on.

Coalition governments of different political parties are becoming common. Sometimes, the constituents of the coalition are parties with very different economic ideologies, making the scenario complex or confusing/uncertain.

Some political leaders are so powerful that they wield enormous control over the party. The vision and ideology of such leaders have stupendous implications for business. *For example*, Chandra Babu Naidu, the Chief Minister of Andhra Pradesh was popularly known as the Chief Executive Officer (CEO) of the State because of his perspective vision for the development of the State. His contribution to the industrial and economic transformation of the State is commendable.

Changes in the nature of State's role or extent of State's involvement in the economy can affect the business environment. When public sector was assigned a major role in the industrial development and industrial licensing was very widely applicable, the Central Government in India had an imposing position in deciding the location of projects and type and size of enterprises. However, the substantial reduction in the role of the public sector and delicensing drastically changed, the situation and now State Governments have a much greater role and freedom than in the past in the industrial development, including promotion of FDI.

> **There is a universal trend towards political decentralisation. This indicates some shifts in the power centres firms have to deal with.**

The number of politically independent nations has been on the increase as a result of the splitting up of what was once a single country into several ones. A major reason for this is the rise of what Naisbitt calls tribalism which is defined as "the belief in fidelity to ones' own kind, defined by ethnicity, language, culture, religion, or, (now) the profession".[12] Universally, the desire of ethnic groups to become independent of the supremacy of others is growing. Naisbitt observes that democracy greatly magnifies and multiplies the assertiveness of the tribes; repression does the opposite. And the anguished drama of the tribalism is most pronounced where they are repressed the most brutally. According to Naisbitt, it may be a long time before there are 1,000 countries in this world, but by the middle of this century we should be close to that number because:[13]

Hostilities between some countries affect business of firms even in third countries. Arab nations, *for example,* did not do business with firms having dealings with Israel. These countries even insisted that third country firms who wanted to do business with them must produce an Israel boycott certificate. Because of the political ties with Israel, the US government had adopted countervailing laws to prevent the US firms from complying with this boycott. Sometimes, there are also economic sanctions.

GOVERNMENT AND LEGAL ENVIRONMENT

Several aspects of the government environment have already been referred to in the preceding sections of this chapter. A detailed description of the governments role in the economy is given in the next chapter.

In most countries, apart from those laws that control investment and related matters, there are a number of laws that regulate the conduct of the business. These laws cover such matters as standards of product, packaging, promotion, ethics, ecological factors, etc.

In many countries, with a view to protecting consumer interests, regulations have become stronger. Regulations to protect the purity of the environment and preserve the ecological balance have assumed great importance in many countries.

Some governments specify certain standards for the products (including packaging) to be marketed in the country: some even prohibit the marketing of certain products. In most nations, promotional activities are subject to various types of controls. Several European countries restrain the use of children in commercial advertisements. In a number of countries, including India, the advertisement of alcoholic liquor is prohibited. Advertisements, including packaging, of cigarettes must carry the statutory warning that "cigarette smoking is injurious to health". Similarly, baby foods must not be promoted as a substitute for breast feeding. In countries like Germany, product comparison advertisements and the use of superlatives like *best* or *excellent* in advertisements is not allowed. In the United States, the Federal Trade Commission is empowered to require a company to provide sufficient evidence to substantiate the claim concerning the quality, performance or comparative prices of its products.

Many countries today have laws to regulate competition in the public interest. Elimination of unfair competition and dilution of monopoly power are the important objectives of these regulations.

There are a host of statutory controls on business in India. Although the controls have been substantially brought down as a result of the liberalisation, a number of controls still prevail.

Certain changes in government policies such as the industrial policy, fiscal policy, tariff policy, etc., may have profound impact on business. Some policy developments create opportunities as well as threats. In other words, a development which brightens the prospects of some enterprises may pose a threat to some others. *For example,* the industrial policy liberalisations in India have opened up new opportunities and threats. They have provided a lot of opportunities to a large number of enterprises to diversify and to make their product mix better. But they have also given rise to serious threats to many existing products by way of increased competition; many seller's markets have given way to buyer's markets. Even products which were seldom advertised have come to be promoted very heavily. This battle for the market has provided a splendid opportunity for the advertising industry.

SUMMARY

The State, *i.e.,* the government, plays a very active role in all economies, including the market economies, *albeit,* the extent and nature of State intervention vary widely between nations.

Functions of the state varies from basic minimum requirements to active participation in several other sectors. The functions of government may be classified along a continuum, from activities that will not be taken at all without State intervention to activities in which the State plays an active role in coordinating markets or redistributing assets.

The economic roles of Government may be classified into four categories. *Figure 1.3* gives a summary view of the important functions and economic roles of the State.

Functions of Government	*Economic Roles of Government*
Basic Functions These include the pure public goods such as the provision of property rights, macroeconomic stability, control of infectious diseases, safe water, roads, and protection of the destitute.	**Regulatory Role** Regulation may cover a wide spectrum extending from entry into a business through the conduct of the business to final results of the business, and also the exit. Regulation is very important for the proper functioning of a market economy.
Intermediate Functions These, include matters such as management of externalities (*e.g.:* pollution), regulation of monopolies, and the provision of social insurance (pensions, unemployment benefits).	**Entrepreneurial Role** Direct participation of government in business was very common particularly in the socialist and developing countries. Reasons included ideological and dearth of private entrepreneurship and capital. Privatisation, however, has become widespread since the mid-1980s.
Activist Functions These involve measures to stabilize and promote markets and to redistribute assets/income.	**Planning Role** The national necessity for proper utilisation of scarce resources and prioritization of development objectives and ideological reasons have made this an important role of governments in the developing and socialist countries.
	Promotional Role This is also more important in developing countries than in the developed because speedy development of the industry and commerce and the economy requires the development of the infrastructure, including facilitating organisations.

Fig. 1.3: Functions and Economic Roles of Government

REFERENCES

1. Marshall E. Dimock, *Business and Government,* New York: Holt, Rhinemann and Winston Inc. 1960, p. 1.
2. R. A. Musgrave, *The Theory of Public Finance,* Kogakusha Ltd., Tokyo, 1959, p. 3.
3. R. A. Musgrave and P. B. Musgrave, *Public Finance in Theory and Practice,* McGraw-Hill Kogakusha Ltd., Tokyo, 1976, p. 5.

4. *Ibid.*, p. 6.
5. Peter F. Drucker.
6. World Bank, *World Development Report,* 1997, p. 19.
7. *Ibid.*, p. 21.
8. *Ibid.*, p. 22.
9. *Ibid., pp.* 26-27.
10. *Ibid.*, p. 28.
11. *Ibid.*, p. 30.
12. John Naisbitt.
13. *Ibid.*

☆☆☆

CHAPTER

2

BUSINESS AND GOVERNMENT IN INDIA

ECONOMIC ASPECTS AND IMPLICATIONS OF THE INDIAN CONSTITUTION

The Indian Constitution incorporates a number of matters that are economically very significant and have far-reaching implications. The socio-economic and political objectives of the Indian Republic and the basic guiding principles of state functioning have been clearly laid down in the *Preamble* to the Constitution, the *Fundamental Rights* and in the *Directive Principles of State Policy*. The Constitution also outlines the economic powers and responsibilities of the Union Government and the State Governments. In fact, a number of constitutional amendments, including the first amendment, were effected to enable the state to implement its economic policies and programmes.

The economic responsibility bestowed on the state by the Indian Constitution is so enormous that it provides scope for great government interference in the functioning of the economy and business.

It is indeed paradoxical that though the government, in the past, had proclaimed that certain policy measures had been taken and laws had been enacted to give effect to certain constitutional provisions, some of these very policies have been given up or reversed and Acts repealed since the liberalisation ushered in 1991, while those constitutional provisions continue unchanged.

The Preamble

The Preamble to the Indian Constitution states that,

THE PEOPLE OF INDIA have solemnly resolved to constitute India into a SOVEREIGN SOCIALIST, SECULAR, DEMOCRATIC REPUBLIC to secure to all its citizens:

JUSTICE, social, economic and political;

LIBERTY of thought, expression, belief, faith and worship;

EQUALITY of status and of opportunity;

and to promote among them all —.

FRATERNITY assuring the dignity of the individual and the unity and integrity* of the Nation.

[*The words "Socialist Secular", and "and integrity" were inserted by the Constitution (42nd Amendment) Act, 1976.]

The Preamble of a statute conveys the general object and intention of the legislature in enacting it. Although not an essential feature, whenever a Constitution contains a Preamble, it expresses the political, religious and socio-economic values which it envisages to promote. But, it does not control the meaning and scope of the other provisions of the Constitution. However, the Preamble may be a guide when the statute is vague. Otherwise, full effect should be given to the express words of the enactment.

The Preamble to the Indian Constitution lays down that the attainment of social, economic and political *justice,* and *equality of* status and of opportunity should be among the most important basic guiding principles of the functioning of the State. As if this were not enough, the Constitution was amended in 1976 to add, among other things, that India should be a socialist State. In fact, as early as December 1954, the Indian Parliament had accepted the *socialist pattern of society* as the objective of social and economic policy. To give this objective more prominence, it was incorporated in the Preamble to the Constitution in 1976 under the controversial 42nd Amendment.

The Fundamental Rights

It has been claimed that the Indian Constitution offers all citizens, individually and collectively, the best fruits of democracy and those basic freedoms and conditions of life which alone make life significant and productive. The rights enumerated in Part III of the Constitution cover a wide range and are declared to be fundamental and justiceable.

As the Preamble conveys the general object and intention of the Constitution and would be a guide in the interpretation of a statute when it is vague, the Preamble to the Indian Constitution gives some indications of the need and scope for State intervention in the functioning of the economy with a view to discharging its duties and responsibilities for the realisation of economic and associated objectives.

The theory of fundamental rights implies limited government. It aims at preventing the government and the legislature from becoming totalitarian, and in doing so it affords the individual an opportunity for self-development. But these rights are not absolute; they are subject to limitations imposed by the State in order to secure rights for all individuals or to promote the greater interests of the community or the State, or to serve the needs of a planned society.

The Fundamental Rights enumerated in Part III of the Constitution are:

1. Right to Equality
2. Right to Freedom
3. Right against Exploitation
4. Right to Freedom of Religion
5. Cultural and Educational Rights
6. Right to Constitutional Remedies.

The Constitution had also guaranteed, under Article 19(1)*(f)*, the Fundamental Right to Property; and Article 31 had prohibited the deprivation of property of any person save by authority of law; and for the deprivation of property compensation had been payable. But, in 1976, the 44th Amendment of the Constitution abolished the fundamental right to property by deleting Articles 19(l)*(f)* and 31. However, Article 300 A of the new Chapter IV added to Part XII of the Constitution provides that "no person shall be deprived of his property save by authority of law". Thus, though the right to property is no longer a fundamental right, it has been retained as a Constitutional Right.

The Fundamental Rights also have economic significance.

The Right to Equality prohibits discrimination against any citizen on grounds of religion, race, caste, sex or place of birth. In public employment, it ensures equality of opportunity to all citizens. This is, however, subject to certain limitations, such as the right of the state to reserve posts for backward classes which, in the opinion of the state, are not adequately represented in the services.

The Constitution guarantees the "citizens the fundamental right to freedom to practise any profession, carry on any occupation, trade or business. This right is subject to reasonable restrictions in the interest of the general public. Under the First Amendment to the Constitution (1951), the State is empowered to make laws relating to professional or technical qualifications necessary for practising any profession or carrying on any trade, business, industry or service, whether to the exclusion, complete or partial, of citizens or otherwise.

The Fundamental Right against Exploitation prohibits traffic in human beings, and beggary and other forms of forced labour; and any contravention of this provision shall be an offence punishable in accordance with the law. However, this does not prevent the State from imposing compulsory service for public purposes. In imposing such services, the State shall not make any discrimination on grounds of religion, race, caste or class.

A very important thing to be noted is that this power of the State to impose reasonable restrictions in the public interest had resulted in a remarkable increase in the statutory control over the business and a substantial expansion of the entrepreneurial or participative activities of the State. Consequently, there has been an abridgement of the economic liberty of the citizens embodied in Article 19(l) (g).

The Fundamental Rights enumerated in the Constitution guarantee a number of economic rights to the citizens; but at the same time, the State has the power to impose reasonable restrictions on such rights in the public interest.

Fundamental Duties

By the 42nd Amendment of the Constitution, adopted in 1976, Fundamental Duties of the citizens have also been enumerated. These enjoin upon a citizen among other things, to abide by the Constitution, to cherish and follow noble ideals which inspired our national struggle for freedom, to defend the country and render national service when called upon to do so and to promote harmony and spirit of common brotherhood amongst all people of India transcending religious, linguistic and regional or sectional diversities.

The Directive Principles

The Directive Principles of State Policy is a unique feature of India's Constitution. The Directive Principles are in the nature of directions to the legislature and executive that they should exercise their authority in such a manner as to ensure due respect for, and observance of these principles. Although these directives are not justiceable, the courts cannot altogether avoid taking cognizance of them.

The Directive Principles are the imperative basis of State policy and the Constitution directs the State to apply these principles in making laws.

The Directive Principles that are economically very significant are quoted below:

(*a*) The State shall strive to promote the welfare of the people by securing and protecting as effectively as it may a social order in which justice, social, economic and political, shall inform all the institutions of the national life [Article 38(1)].

(*b*) The State shall, in particular, strive to minimise the inequalities in income, and endeavour to eliminate inequalities in status, facilities and opportunities, not only among individuals but also amongst groups of people residing in different areas or engaged in different vocations [Article 38(2)].

(*c*) The State shall, in particular, direct its policy towards securing:

1. That the citizens, men and women equally, have the right to an adequate means of livelihood.
2. That the ownership and control of the material resources of the community are so distributed as best to subserve the common good.
3. That the operation of the economic system does not result in the concentration of wealth and means of production to the common detriment.
4. That there is equal pay for equal work for both men and women.
5. That the health and strength of workers, men and women, and the tender age of children are not abused and that citizens are not forced by economic necessity to enter a vocation unsuited to their age or strength.
6. That children are given opportunities and facilities to develop in a healthy manner and in conditions of freedom and dignity and that childhood and youth are protected against exploitation and against moral and material abandonment (Article 39).

(*d*) The State shall ensure that the operation of the legal system promotes justice, on a basis of equal opportunity, and shall, in particular, provide for legal aid, by suitable legislation of schemes or in any other way, to ensure that opportunities for securing justice are not denied to any citizen by reason of economic or other disabilities (Article 39-A).

Sections of Article 39 were quoted as the basis of several government policies and Acts.

(*e*) The State shall take steps to organise village panchayats and endow them with such powers and authority as may be necessary to enable them to function as units of self-government (Article 40).

(*f*) The State shall, within the limits of its economic capacity and development, make effective provision for securing the right to work, to education and to public assistance in cases of unemployment, old age, sickness and disablement, and in other cases of underserved wants (Article 41).

(*g*) The State shall make provision for securing just and humane conditions of work and for maternity relief (Article 42).

(*h*) The State shall endeavour to secure, by suitable legislation or economic organisation or any other way, to all workers, agricultural, industrial or otherwise, a living wage, conditions of work ensuring a decent standard of life and full enjoyment of leisure and social and cultural opportunities and in particular the State shall endeavour to promote cottage industries on an individual or cooperative basis in rural areas (Article 43).

(*i*) The State shall take steps, by suitable legislation or in any other way, to secure the participation of workers in the management of undertakings, establishments or other organizations engaged in any industry (Article 43-A).

(*j*) The State shall promote with special care the educational and economic interests of the weaker sections of the people, and, in particular, of the scheduled castes and the scheduled tribes, and shall protect them from social injustice and all forms of exploitation (Article 46).

(*k*) The State shall regard the raising of the level of nutrition and the standard of living of its people and the improvement of public health as among its primary duties and, in particular, the state shall endeavour to bring about prohibition of the consumption, except for medicinal purposes, of intoxicating drinks and of drugs which are injurious to health (Article 47).

(*l*) The State shall endeavour to organise agriculture and animal husbandry on modern and scientific lines and shall, in particular, take steps for preserving and improving the breeds, and prohibiting the slaughter of cows and calves and other milch and draught cattle (Article 48).

(*m*) The State shall endeavour to protect and improve the environment and to safeguard the forests and wildlife of the country (Article 48-A).

These Directive Principles make quite clear how important is the economic responsibility bestowed on the State by the Constitution.

Through constitutional amendments, new directives were added to provide a greater socialist orientation to development. For instance, in 1978, by the 44th Amendment, a new clause was added to Article 38; and this new clause contains a directive to strive to minimise the inequalities in status, facilities and opportunities. The 42nd Amendment incorporated a new Article, 43-A, to direct the State to take suitable steps to secure workers' participation in management.

There have been many occasions when the Directive Principles and Fundamental Rights have been in conflict with each other. In the early days, the Supreme Court held that the Fundamental Rights were a sacrosanct part of the Constitution and nothing, including the Directive Principles, could override them. But the view that the Fundamental Rights should be subordinated to the Directive Principles gained ground in later years.

While asking the *Lok Sabha* to refer the Constitution (Fourth Amendment) Bill to the Select Committee, Prime Minister Nehru declared that the Fundamental Rights must subserve the Directive Principles. In the *Keshwanand Bharti vs. State of Kerala,* Justice Mathew observed that "in building up a just social order, it is sometimes imperative that the Fundamental Rights should be subordinated to Directive Principles. Economic goals have an uncontestable claim for priority over ideological ones on the ground that excellence comes only after existence. It is only if men existed that there can be fundamental rights."

The Directive Principles of State Policy enunciated in the Indian Constitution provide an enormous scope for government intervention in the functioning of the economy.

However, quite interestingly, although state control of the economy had been deepened and widened as if it were a Constitutional requirement, this trend has been reversed since 1991 while the same Preamble and Directive Principles are held sacrosanct.

Freedom of Trade, Commerce and Intercourse

According to Article 301 of the Constitution of India, trade, commerce and intercourse throughout the territory of India shall be free. This freedom, however, is not without restrictions.

The freedom guaranteed by Article 301 is in the widest terms and applies to all forms of trade, commerce and intercourse. It is subject only to restrictions specified in Article 302 to 305 and the freedom to carry on trade, commerce and intercourse throughout India guaranteed under Article 301 cannot be taken away by an executive action.

According to Articles 302 to 305, the State can impose reasonable restrictions on the freedom expressed by Article 301. Accordingly, Parliament may impose such restrictions on the freedom of trade, commerce or intercourse between one State and another or within any part of the territory of India as may be required in the public interest. The States Governments are empowered to impose any tax on goods imported from other States if similar goods in the State are subject to similar tax so as not to discriminate between goods so imported and goods manufactured or produced in that State.

Separation of Powers

Separation of powers is an important feature of the Indian Constitution, "the separation of powers contemplates the idea that the governmental functions must be based on a tripartite division of legislature, executive and judiciary. Each organ should be separate, distinct and sovereign in its own allocated sphere and it should not exercise the functions assigned to another."[1] As Chief Justice Subba Rao observed in the *Golak Nath vs. State of Punjab,* "the Constitution demarcates the jurisdiction of these organs minutely and expects them to exercise their respective powers without overstepping their limits. They should function within the spheres allotted to them. No authority created under the Constitution is supreme; the Constitution is supreme and all the authorities function under the supreme law of the land".[2]

Division of Power

India's Constitution distributes the items for legislation among three lists:

- Union List
- State List
- Concurrent List.

The respective jurisdictions of the Union and the States and their mutual relations have been clearly defined in the Indian Constitution.

The Union has exclusive power to make laws on all matters in the Union List and the States have exclusive powers to make laws in the State List. Except for the Union Territories, the Centre cannot normally legislate on any matter included in the State List. Parliament can, however, do so if the Council of States recommends by at least two-thirds majority that such legislation is in national interest; if two or more States mutually agree that this should be done for such States and to implement treaties or international agreements or conventions.

Both the Union and States can legislate on matters in the Concurrent List. However, in case of any conflict between the Union laws and State laws, the Union laws shall prevail. Further, the Union has exclusive power to make laws on any matter not enumerated in the Concurrent List or State List.

Expansion in State Intervention

The first four decades of planning witnessed an expansion of State intervention in the economy. The Constitution was amended a number of times. The Constitution of India, which came into force in 1950, was first amended in the very next year. By the First Amendment of the Constitution, the State has been empowered to impose restrictions on the right of citizens to carry on any trade, business, industry or service with a view to enabling the State to undertake any scheme of nationalisation or prescribing the professional or technical qualifications necessary for practising any profession or carrying on any occupation, trade or business.

The brief account of the economic significance of the Indian Constitution given above makes it abundantly clear that the State has to shoulder a very heavy responsibility to attain the egalitarian goals set forth in the Constitution. Any responsibility should have commensurate authority also. Over the years, the Government has assumed enormous powers of control over the economy. How effectively and judiciously these powers have been exercised, and how satisfactorily the problems have been solved are different questions.

> **The State has, from time-to-time, acquired increasing powers to control private activity and enlarge its own ownership and management of the economy.**

The Government has been very active in playing all the four important economic roles.

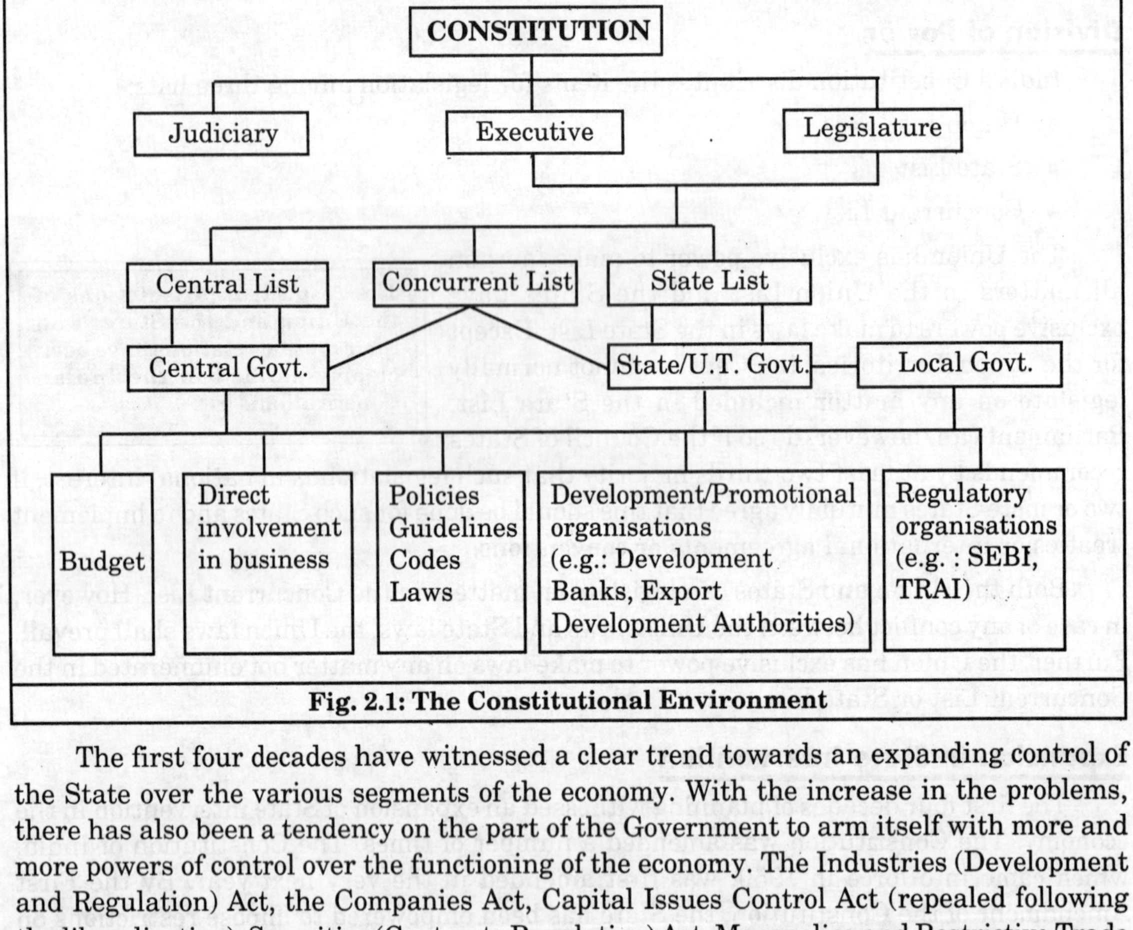

Fig. 2.1: The Constitutional Environment

The first four decades have witnessed a clear trend towards an expanding control of the State over the various segments of the economy. With the increase in the problems, there has also been a tendency on the part of the Government to arm itself with more and more powers of control over the functioning of the economy. The Industries (Development and Regulation) Act, the Companies Act, Capital Issues Control Act (repealed following the liberalisation), Securities (Contracts Regulation) Act, Monopolies and Restrictive Trade Practices Act, Essential Commodities Act, Prevention of Blackmarketing and Maintenance of Supplies of Essential Commodities Act, Conservation of Foreign Exchange and Prevention of Smuggling Activities Act, Foreign Exchange Regulation Act (replaced by the Foreign Exchange Management Act in 2000), Imports and Exports (Control) Act [replaced by the Foreign Trade (Development and Regulation) Act in 1992], etc., provide the Government with sweeping powers of control over industry and commerce, so much so that Government cannot escape the responsibility for any shortfalls, drawbacks, or imperfections in these sectors of vital importance to the economy.

There are quite a good number of industrial and labour laws which regulate employer-employee relations, working conditions, wages, bonus, labour welfare and social security, etc.

The commercial banking sector was brought under the effective control of the Reserve Bank of India by the Banking Companies Act of 1949 and the Amendment Acts of 1956 and 1962, the Banking Laws (Miscellaneous Provisions) Act, 1963, etc. The Securities and Exchange Board of India (SEBI) regulates the capital market.

Indirect controls have also been playing their part in serving the national development goals. Various quantitative and qualitative monetary weapons have been deployed from time-to-time to regulate the economy, mainly to control prices. A number of fiscal and monetary incentives have been offered to encourage the growth of such priority sectors as the export industry, small industry and small business. Monetary, fiscal, financial and physical incentives have been provided for the accelerated development of the backward regions. Fiscal and monetary policies have also been employed, as disincentives to discourage certain undesirable or inessential activities. The direct controls had considerably grown in importance.

No less important than the regulatory role is the promotional role of the Government in India. Being a mixed economy, the State has to provide the necessary facilities for the growth of the private sector. Our industrial policy has assigned an important role to the private sector in a number of industries. State's promotional role include development of infrastructural facilities, fostering of institutions, to provide financial aid and developmental support to business.

The expansion in the entrepreneurial/participative role of the state was been very spectacular. The public sector has grown substantially, both vertically and horizontally. The total investment in the Central Government industrial enterprises has grown from ₹ 29 crores spread over 5 units on April 1, 1951, to ₹ 3,24,632 crore in 240 units in 2002. In some industries, the public sector gained an absolute or near monopoly, and it had a commanding position in a number of basic and heavy industries. However, as pointed out earlier, the economic liberalisation has seriously affected the public sector dominance.

Both fresh investments and nationalisation have contributed to the growth and expansion of the public sector. More than 90 per cent of the commercial banking sector came to be in the hands of the State. Successive nationalisations — the nationalisation of the Imperial Bank and the establishment of the State Bank of India, in 1955, the nationalisation of 14 major private banks in 1969 and another six in 1980 — have been mainly responsible for it. The insurance business in the country, too, had been nationalised. The dawn of the present century has witnessed the move towards privatisation/ divestment.

Apart from monopoly in the field of railway transport, communications and air transport, the public sector accounted for a considerable share in shipping and road passenger transport. In the energy sector, the public sector had virtual monopoly in coal mining, exploration and refining of petroleum and in the generation and supply of electricity.

At one time, the public sector corporations accounted for about one-tenth of the country's total foreign trade. Imports and exports of certain important items are *canalized* through public sector agencies.

As a consequence of the liberalisation, however, privatisation/divestment has been spreading.

The public distribution system has been expanded to remove the imperfections in the distribution of essential goods and to protect the interests of the vulnerable sections. The Government has been playing a major role as a planner. The Planning Commission was set up in 1950 and the First Five Year Plan was launched in 1951 with the objective of achieving a rapid rise in the standard of living of the people by an efficient exploitation of the resources of the country, increasing production and offering opportunities to all for employment in the service of the community. Our Five-Year Plans place special emphasis on improvements in the living conditions of the poor. The objective of distributive justice has been given added emphasis in the later Plans.

A significant aspect of Indian planning is the respect for democratic and property rights, unlike in the centrally planned economy. In Indian planning, there has been the balancing of the various economic elements and a sort of a fusion of the public, private and joint sectors, heavy and light industries, and big, medium, small and cottage industries.

In short, as Rosan observed[3], unquestionably, the Indian government held the levers that determined the levels of output of all large and medium-sized firms by: (1) its own direct production of a wide variety of inputs and final products; (2) its grant, or refusal, of permission to private firms to produce new items or to expand production; (3) its provision of capital funds, and control of security issues by private firms; (4) its control of access to foreign exchange; and, (5) its control of imports.

There has, however, been a very significant relaxation of these controls since 1991.

BOX 2.1 : THE EVOLUTION OF THE ROLE OF THE STATE IN INDIA

When India became independent in 1947, income per capita had been stagnating for half a century, and modern industry was minimal.

The Nehru years, 1947-64. India's first Prime Minister, Jawaharlal Nehru, saw industrialisation as the key to alleviating poverty, and a powerful State with a planned economy as essential, if the country was to industrialise rapidly, accelerate public saving and investment, and reduce the role of foreign trade and achieve self-sufficiency. Unlike many East Asian countries, which used State intervention to build strong private sector industries, India opted for State control over key industries. Believing the potential of agriculture and exports to be limited, Indian Governments taxed agriculture by skewing the terms of trade against it and emphasizing import substitution. They saw technical education as vital for industrialisation.

Garibi Hatao, 1966-77. Under Prime Minister Indira Gandhi, two major shifts took place in the role of the State. First, the neglect of agriculture was reversed through State activism in subsidising new seeds and fertilisers, agricultural credit, and rural electrification. The green revolution took off, and by the mid-1970s India was self-sufficient in grain. The second shift was the tightening of State control over every aspect of the economy. Under the slogan of *garibi hatao* ("abolish poverty"), banks were nationalised, trade was increasingly restricted, price controls were imposed on a wide range of products, and foreign investment was squeezed. The State achieved a stranglehold on the economy. Yet growth of gross domestic product (GDP) failed to accelerate, remaining at 3.3 per cent a year during this period.

The spending boom and rising fiscal deficits, 1977-91. Between 1977 and 1991, most stringent controls on imports and industrial licensing were gradually relaxed, stimulating industrial growth. The government expanded anti-poverty schemes, especially rural employment schemes, but only a small fraction of the rising subsidies actually reached the poor. Competition between political parties drove subsidies up at every election. The resulting large fiscal deficits (8.4 per cent of GDP in 1985) contributed to a rising current account deficit. India's foreign exchange reserves were virtually exhausted by mid-1991, when a new government headed by Narasimha Rao came to power.

The reform phase, since 1991. Rising interest payments on India's foreign debt meant that neither the Central Government nor the State Governments could continue to finance both subsidies and heavy public investment. The former won out, and the government began to woo private and foreign investment. Thus, impending bankruptcy drove the reform process and changed the state's role from that of principal investor to that of facilitator of entrepreneurship. This shift was expected to free up government finances for more social spending, but in practice the fiscal crunch prevented a significant increase.

Rao's government abolished most industrial and import licensing, devalued the rupee, drastically reduced import tariffs, liberalised the financial sector and foreign investment, and allowed private investment in areas previously reserved for the government.

The new coalition governments that came to power in 1996 and thereafter has by and large sustained these reforms.

Thus, the old national consensus on socialism has given way over the course of a few years to a new consensus on liberalisation. But formidable challenges remain. Most parties agree on the need for reform, yet no party is eager to retrench surplus labour, close unviable factories, or reduce subsidies. The reforms so far are a positive step but must be extended and accelerated if India is to catch up with the East Asian tigers.

Courtesy : World Bank, *World Development Report, 1997.*

AN EVALUATION OF THE CONTROL REGIME IN INDIA

Planned development has enabled India, undoubtedly, to achieve significant progress in several spheres. However, the fact remains that the achievements in many areas have been much below the potential targets. The rate of growth and the pace of development, in general, were slow due to the deficiencies and drawbacks of the development policies, regulatory measures and implementation.

The policy of limiting the role of the private sector, particularly of the so-called large houses, has contributed in no small measure to the shortages and high prices of several goods and services that the nation suffered for a long period.

In view of the dearth of entrepreneurial activities, investible funds and expertise in the private sector in the early days of development, assigning the public sector a very important role in the development process was inevitable. However, establishing exclusive monopoly or a predominant position for the public sector in many industries where private sector was capable of making progress, in fact ran counter not only to the objective of faster growth but also to some of the other social objectives.

The over-enthusiasm to encompass almost the whole gamut of economic activities by the public sector resulted in the State not being able to pay sufficient attention and resources for the development of certain critical sectors. The policy of barring the private sector from such critical sectors compounded the infrastructural problems.

The injudicious expansion of the public sector has created serious problems of public finance. It has increased the unproductive expenditure due to the swelling of the bureaucratic set up. State Governments are burdened with the mounting losses of their enterprises, many of which are in the non-priority areas. Although many Central Government enterprises have been incurring huge losses, the central public sector as a whole has been making profits because of the enormous profits generated by enterprises in monopoly sectors like oil. The public sector has become notorious for time and cost overruns, overstaffing and general inefficiency.

> **The MRTP regulation, industrial licensing, indiscriminate reservation of items for the small-scale sector, overemphasis on import substitution, highly restrictive policy towards foreign capital, technology, etc., have retarded competition, decelerated growth and contributed to the foreign trade gap.**

The licensing system in India, introduced as an instrument to help achieve some of the objectives of the industrial policy, not only failed to achieve its purpose but also produced several negative effects. Prof. Jagadish Bhagwati, an economist of international repute, in his Sir Purshotham Thakurdas Memorial Lecture in 1987 observed: "In essence, the industrial licensing system which had grown into a Frankenstein, that few of us foresaw in the early 1950s when we gave it birth, had degenerated into a series of arbitrary, indeed inherently arbitrary, decisions where one activity would be chosen over another, simply because the administering bureaucrats were so empowered to choose some of them. Some of them even came to rationalise and believe in the social virtues of the system that gave them these absurd powers."[4]

There is a strong general feeling that not only that there were too many controls and overlapping of policies but also, as a World Bank expert points out, the principle of Indian policy was to elaborate rules (and exceptions) to them, which are not only detailed and specific, but also subject to wide discretion.

The protection of the small-scale sector too has had adverse effects on the exports.

Similarly, the overemphasis on import substitution as a development strategy and as a means to help achieve trade balance and the lack of appreciation of the export development potentials have had severe adverse effects on the export development. While foreign exchange was available even for indiscriminate import substitution, genuine needs of the export sector were overlooked. "Thus, in the mid-fifties, while export industries like jute and cotton textiles were denied foreign exchange for their much-needed modernisation, a much too liberal approach was followed in India in allocating foreign exchange to many non-essential industries in the name of import substitution".

Import substitution and the associated protection of domestic industries had other adverse effects too. The sheltered domestic market acted as a deterrent to efficiency improvement and thus the "prospects of newly established industries becoming at some stage earners of foreign exchange are further diminished".

There is a widespread impression that the price controls in India discouraged investment and production leading to corruption and black marketing.

The controlled regime in India have had a number of adverse effects. The liberalisation process that started in 1991 and which still continues and the resultant accelerations of growth are an acknowledgement of this fact.

SUMMARY

The role of the Government in India is guided and governed by the principles and provisions of the Indian Constitution. Of particular significance are the *Preamble* to the Constitution which indicates the objects and intention of the Constitution, the Fundamental Rights which imposes limitations on State's power, the Directive Principles of State Policy which suggest numerous socio-economic welfare responsibilities for the State, separation of powers of judiciary, executive and legislature and division of power and responsibility between the Union and the States.

The Government control over the Indian economy grew enormously in the first four decades since Independence. Since 1991, India has been passing through a process of decontrols and economic reforms. This implies a redefinition of the role of the State.

There has been a global trend towards decentralisation of power and responsibility. It has been true of India too to some extent. The Central Government's role in industrial development has significantly diminished as a result of the delicensing and substantial reduction in the role of the public sector. Now it is left to the States to play an active role in the industrial development by creating a conducive environment for the development of industries, including attracting foreign investment.

REFERENCES

1. D. Rajeev, "Separation of Powers and Judicial Activism: Tradition versus Modernity," Cochin University Law Review, 1997, p. 329.
2. Cited by Rajeev, *ibid.*, p. 331.
3. George Rosan, *Industrial Change in India,* Allied Publishers Ltd., Allahabad, p. 15.
4. Cited by D.J. Kanvinde, "New Thrust in Industrial Policy and Emerging Challenges for the Banking System", *State Bank of India Monthly Review,* May 1988, pp. 235-6.

☆☆☆

CHAPTER 3

INDUSTRIAL POLICY

There is no other economic policy in India which has so dominantly determined the pattern and direction of development of the economy as the Industrial Policy. To a large extent, the Industrial Policy reflected the socio-economic and political ideology of development. Indeed, the Industrial Policy Resolution of 1956, the fundamental principles of which reigned until 1991, was described by some people as the Economic Constitution of India.

The Industrial Policy indicated the respective roles of the public, private, joint and cooperative sectors; small, medium and large-scale industries and underlined the national priorities and the economic development strategy. It also expressed government's policy towards foreign capital and technology, labour policy, tariff policy, etc., in respect of the industrial sector. In short, the industrial development, and thereby the economic development to a very significant extent, has been guided, regulated and fostered by the industrial policy.

The Industrial Policy of Government of India and the regulatory measures introduced to achieve the policy objectives had been matters of severe controversy. While the industrialists and many others in India and abroad and many foreign governments and international development organisations regarded the policy as too restrictive and the regulations and procedures too cumbersome and perplexing, the leftists in India had been demanding a more restrictive regime.

The industrial policy and regulation had grown more and more restrictive until about the mid-seventies. Having realised the deleterious effects of the restrictive regime, the 1980s saw a very slow process of liberalisation. In tune with the economic reforms ushered in 1991, the Industrial Policy too underwent a drastic change.

The era deregulation ushered in by the Narasimha Rao government in 1991 is an open acknowledgement of the failure of the control regime to deliver the goods. The Indian planners were fascinated and influenced by the Russian model so that the development strategy in India was directed towards creating *socialist pattern of society*. It is interesting to note that, following the introduction of political and economic reforms in the erstwhile USSR, the Soviet newspaper *Izvestia,* which observed that many elements of the Indian economic system were borrowed from the Soviet model, stated that the main culprit for the present economic crisis in India was the obsolete economic system based on socialism.

The following pages provide the salient features of the industrial policy of India up to 1991, very briefly, and the new policy. A detailed account of the policy until 1991 is available in the old editions of the author's *Business and Government* and *Business Environment*.

INDUSTRIAL POLICY UP TO 1991

The industrial policy of India prior to the liberalisation ushered in 1991 was characterised by the following features:

Reservation of Industries

1. Future development of most of the import industries was exclusively reserved for the public sector.
2. Manufacture of a large number (over 850 in 1991) of items was reserved for the small-scale sector.

Dominance of Public Sector

In the early decades, the policy of the Government was to ensure that the public sector gained control over the commanding heights of the economy.

The *Industrial Policy Resolution of 1948,* established public sector monopoly/near monopoly in 9 industries.

The *Industrial Policy Resolution of 1956,* brought out in the light of the adoption by the Parliament of the *socialist pattern of society* as the national goal and the Second Five Year Plan model which gave emphasis to the basic and heavy industries, further expanded substantially the role of the public sector.

Future development of 17 most important industries was exclusively reserved for the public sector (Schedule A). Further, public sector was assigned priority for establishment of new units in 12 most important of the remaining industries (Schedule B). See *Annexure 11.1* for the list of industries in Schedules A and B.

The public sector also established its monopoly or dominance in several other industries which did not belong to any of the above two categories of industries. This was done by the government by not giving licence to the private enterprises or by nationalisation.

Entry and Growth Restrictions

There were a number of entry and growth restrictions on the private sector (particularly on the large firms and foreign firms) even in respect of industries where the private sector was allowed. A licence was mandatory for establishing new units' with investments above a specified limit, for manufacturing new products and for substantial expansion of existing undertakings.

Large firms (having assets, including those of interconnected undertakings, of ₹ 100 crore or more) and dominant undertakings (*i.e.,* those having a market share of 25 per cent or more) had to obtain clearance under the Monopolies and Restrictive Trade Practices (MRTP) Act, in addition to the industrial licence, for establishing new undertakings, substantial expansions and manufacture of new items. There were also restrictions on import of capital goods, etc.

Restrictions on Foreign Capital and Technology

The scope of use of foreign capital and technology was limited. Even in industries where foreign capital was allowed, it was normally subject to a ceiling of 40 per cent of the total equity, although exceptions were allowed in certain cases. Operations of foreign companies in India and issue of securities abroad by Indian companies were regulated under the Foreign Exchange Regulation Act (FERA), 1973.

INDUSTRIAL POLICY LIBERALISATIONS

On July 24, 1991, Government of India announced substantial modifications to the industrial policy, characterised by a revolutionary change from the policy of the previous era.

This policy, which is referred to even today as the *new* Industrial Policy, has enormously expanded the scope of the private sector by opening up to the private sector most of the industries which had been reserved for the public sector and substantially dismantling the entry and growth restrictions. Adjectives such as 'dramatic', 'revolutionary', 'drastic' etc. have been used to describe the nature of the change in the industrial policy.

BOX 3.1: INDUSTRIAL POLICY: THE PRIME MOVER OF LIBERALISATION

The new industrial policy, which heralded the economic reforms in India, has reduced the industrial licensing requirements, removed restrictions on investment and expansion, and facilitated easy access to foreign technology and foreign direct investment, besides throwing open all but a few industries to the private sector. This policy has been made more and more liberal by subsequent modifications.

The salient features of the new industrial policy are the following:

Objectives

The major objectives of the new Industrial Policy package are:

1. To build on the gains already made.
2. To correct the distortions or weakness that may have crept in.
3. To maintain a sustained growth in productivity and gain full employment.
4. To attain international competitiveness.

It has been stated that the pursuit of these objectives will be tempered by the need to preserve the environment and ensure the efficient use of available resources. All sectors of industry, whether small, medium or large, belonging to the public, private or cooperative sectors will be encouraged to grow and improve on their past performance.

Redefinition of the Role of Public Sector

The role of the public sector was redefined and the scope of the public sector has been drastically abridged.

The number of industries reserved for the public sector was reduced to eight and it was later pruned, in stages, to two (atomic energy and railway transport).

The policy also seeks selective privatisation and withdrawal of the public sector from industries which do not conform to its redefined role. See the chapter on public sector for more details.

Expansion of the Scope of Private Sector and Dismantling of Entry and Growth Restrictions

The scope of private sector has been expanded enormously by drastically reducing the number of industries reserved for the public sector and by substantially dismantling the barriers to entry and growth.

Delicensing: All but 18 industries were freed from licensing. The number was later reduced, in stages, to a few. The industries subject to industrial licensing account for only a very small share of the value added in the manufacturing sector.

TABLE 3.1: INDUSTRIAL POLICY CHANGES

Pre-1991 Policy	Current Policy
Industrial licensing was the rule	Licensing is an exception
Public sector monopoly/dominance in strategic, basic and heavy industries	All but two industries are open to the private sector
MRTP Act restrictions on entry and growth of large companies	No such restrictions
Foreign investment allowed only in select industries, that too subject to, normally, a ceiling of 40% of total equity and prior permission.	Foreign investment allowed in a large number of industries, including up to 100% of equity in many of them. Automatic route available subject to specified conditions.
Restrictive policy towards foreign technology	Very liberal policy towards foreign technology
Reservation of large number of products for small scale sector	Reservation list is being pruned.

Removal of MRTPA Restrictions: Most of the provisions of the MRTP Act pertaining to concentration of economic power (i.e., those requiring prior permission for establishment of new undertaking, substantial expansion, manufacture of new items and mergers and acquisitions) were scrapped.

Dereservation

The number of items reserved for exclusive manufacture by the small-scale sector has been drastically reduced. The number of reserved items at the beginning of 2007 was 239 compared to 873 in 1984. The policy of reserving industries for the exclusive development by the public sector has also been largely done away with.

Liberalisation of Foreign Investment

The policy towards foreign capital and technology has been modified very significantly and progressively liberalised. FDI is allowed in all industries, except industries falling in a small negative list, in varying levels, ranging from 26 per cent to 100 per cent of the total equity.

Since 1992-93, the Indian stock market is open for investment by Foreign Institutional Investors (FIIs) and Indian companies satisfying certain conditions may access foreign capital market by *Euro issues.* The chapter on *foreign capital and technology* provides more details.

Related Measures

The industrial policy reforms have been supplemented and reinforced by reforms in related areas.

> **Industrial policy liberalisation is just one, but very important, component of economic reforms in India.**

Progressive integration of the Indian economy with the global economy has been acknowledged as one the objectives of the *Exim Policy.* The import policy has been made more liberal by drastically reducing the tariff levels and quantitative restrictions and by procedural reforms.

Rupee was made partially convertible on current and later it was made fully convertible. Measures have been initiated to move towards capital account convertibility.

The Capital Issues Control Act and the office of the Controller of Capital Issues were scrapped and free pricing of capital issues was introduced. Financial sector, including the capital market, has undergone very significant reforms.

Price controls have been gradually eased out.

Several restrictions imposed in respect of foreign investment, like phased manufacturing programme, foreign exchange balancing, etc., have been, by and large, removed.

EVALUATION OF THE INDUSTRIAL POLICY LIBERALISATION

The economic reforms ushered in since 1991 are revolutionary indeed in comparison with the policy and procedural reforms hitherto attempted in India. It, undoubtedly, is a bold step in the direction of freeing the Indian industry from the shackles of abortive and crippling controls.

Although further policy changes and reform are needed, changes already introduced, if implemented in real earnest, will certainly provide a considerable growth impetus. However, real debureaucratising is a challenging task. The bureaucracy has a tendency to attempt to defeat the measures aimed at deregulations.

A strong mandate and political will and bold administrative measures are essential for implementing several of the proposals. The government, however, often shows signs of confusion and lack of boldness on the face of opposition from trade unions, politicians and bureaucrats. There will certainly be strong opposition from these groups to protect their vested interests. For example, in the face of the strong opposition from the trade unions, the government's stand on privatisation has not been clear. In our country the might of the organised minority often gets prominence over the rights and welfare of the unorganised majority.

The policy environment now in India is much more conducive for both domestic and foreign investments than in the past. However, there are now a host of countries trying to woo foreign investment with much more conducive economic environment than in India. Further, cultural factors also tilt the balance in favour of other nations as far as foreign investment is concerned. Further, foreign business still regard the policy and procedural system in India perplexing. Even many Indian entrepreneurs feel that the policy/procedural and development environments in countries like China are much superior to that in India and a number of them prefer to locate production bases abroad. The development of the infrastructural sector has been tardy in India even after the liberalisation. Because of these factors one should not expect wonders out of the belated measures.

However, for the first time the domestic industry has been given a considerable leeway to prove its mettle. This dynamism coupled with an enhanced external collaboration and competition should be expected to provide a considerable momentum for development. At the same time, the government should strive to remove the remaining lacunae and to implement the proposed reforms in letter and spirit.

Although the economic policy liberalisation of 1991 came in for scathing criticism by the opposition parties, when these parties drew up their election manifestoes in April 1996, their anti-liberalisation stand was conspicuous by its inconspicuousness. More interestingly, when the short-lived BJP government and the United Front Government that followed announced their economic policies, they amounted not only to endorsing the liberalisation policy ushered in by the Congress Government under Narasimha Rao but also to carrying forward the process of deregulation and decontrol to achieve faster economic growth. The economic policy of the United Front (UF) government as expressed in the Common Minimum Programme (CMP), which observed that there was no substitute for growth, and that the country's GDP needed to grow at over seven per cent in the next 10 years in order to abolish endemic poverty and unemployment, stated that the UF government is committed to faster economic growth. The document on the CMP observed that further deregulation and decontrol might be required in the agricultural, industrial and other sectors to accelerate economic development. In short, India's economic liberalisation is almost unanimously accepted by all political parties so that it is irreversible.

The Union Budget 2001-2002 was hailed for initiating the second generation reforms. Whichever political party or combine comes to power in future, the difference will be, at the most, in its fine-tuning. In other words, the major differences between the political parties in India will no more be related to economic policies or ideologies; the differences will pertain rather to ethnic and related factors (including the issue of secularism and regional factors). The ubiquitous support to liberalisation seen now is due to the good liberalisation can do for the economic development of the country. Developments since 1991 have demonstrated the growth and competitive impulses that the liberalisation can generate. There is also a lot of lessons to be learnt from the Chinese experience of liberalisation.

Merits of the Liberal Industrial Policy

1. The opening up of the industries exclusively reserved for the public sector to the private sector paved the way for faster growth of these industries by increased investment and expanded entrepreneurship.
2. The liberalisation of foreign investment policy has helped to step up the investment in a number of industries, including several vital sectors.
3. The FII has invigorated the Indian capital market.
4. An important impact of the liberalisation is the faster development of the infrastructural sector driven by private investment, both domestic and foreign.

   However, the pace of infrastructure development is still quite unsatisfactory and this will be a major constraint in speeding up pace of overall development.
5. The removal of restrictions on entry and growth has been helping companies to rationalise their business portfolio and product mix, improve efficiency and to achieve faster growth.
6. The liberalization, by delicensing, scrapping of MRTP restrictions and privatisation, has paved way for business consolidation, helping achievement of scale economies and efficiency improvements.

> **Liberalisation has facilitated substantial increase in investment, growth of entrepreneurship and expansion of the industrial sector, imparting considerable dynamism to the economy as a whole.**

7. As implied in some of the points mentioned above, the new industrial policy enables corporates to restructure their portfolios, adding new business and/or exiting some of the old businesses.
8. The easy access to foreign technology, capital goods, intermediates and raw materials help improve the competitiveness of the Indian firms.
9. The increase in competition and the scope for global sourcing (as mentioned above) have increased the competitiveness of Indian firms. This is significantly

encouraging globalisation of Indian firms, as is evinced by the increase in exports, setting up of greenfield enterprises abroad and overseas mergers and acquisitions.

10. The increase in competition has helped to improve the efficiency and competitiveness of public sector enterprises.
11. The growth of large firms is encouraging growth of small-scale and medium-scale units by ancillarisation and outsourcing. Many such firms are getting technological and managerial support from the large firms, both domestic and foreign.
12. One of the greatest advantages of liberalisation is the benefits the consumer derive from the increasing competition. What were seller's markets in the past have been becoming buyer's markets.

Consumers benefit from competition in the following ways:

(*a*) Choice of goods and services has increased fabulously.

(*b*) There is very substantial improvement in product quality and features.

(*c*) Competition keeps a lid on prices.

(*d*) Firms are becoming more and more innovative, introducing new and improved products.

(*e*) After-sales service is becoming more and more important.

(*f*) What were seller's markets in the past have been becoming buyer's markets, increasing the bargaining power of buyers.

(*g*) Consumers are now getting much better credit and other facilities and incentives.

Demerits of the Liberal Industrial Policy

1. Competition between unequals. Relatively small Indian firms have to compete with large foreign firms with huge resources and vast experiences.
2. The pattern and direction of development are determined mostly by market forces rather than by larger national interests.

Several important social aspects are ignored by liberalisation. Indian industry also suffers from absence of a level-playing field.

3. Unfair competition. Large firms, particularly multinationals, may engage in unfair competition to the detriment of small and medium firms. The nation needs to effectively implement the Competition Law to check this.
4. Increasing presence of foreign firms would cause drain of income from India to abroad. (At the same time, the increasing presence of Indian firms would have the opposite effect).
5. Ecological Deterioration. Delicensing could result in indiscriminate industrial location and resources depletion, causing ecological problems and heavy social costs.

6. Demonstration effect and conspicuous consumption. The flood of all sorts of goods from all parts of the world and the marketing tactics (including unscrupulous) foster demonstration effect and encourage conspicuous consumption.
7. Increasing FII investment would mean that the Indian stock market is increasingly influenced by foreign players. This would also mean spanning away of profits of Indian firms by foreign players.

Measures for Improvement

Government needs to take certain measures to make the environment more conducive for faster and healthy development of the industry and economy. These include:

1. Rationalisation of policies and procedures to usher in more transparency and ease of doing business.
2. Ensuring a level playing field to put the Indian firms on equal footing with their foreign counterparts.
3. Effective implementation of the Competition Act to safeguard the Indian firms and consumers from unfair competition.
4. Policies and regulations for ecological protection.

Further reform of the policy and regulatory environment is required in several spheres.

5. Effective control over imports and smuggling to ensure that foreign goods enter the Indian market strictly as per government policies and regulation only.
6. Effective monitoring and control of the imports through Free/Preferential Trade Agreement.
7. Adequate protection to Indian firms from unhealthy and unfair competitions. Wherever needed, infant industry protection shall be accorded on a rational basis.
8. Measures to improve the infrastructure and common support to the industries.
9. Reform of the administrative system to make it more efficient and business friendly.
10. It shall be compulsory that foreign firms operating in India (except small trading and the like) list on Indian stock exchange so that Indian public can also share the prosperity of business of these firms.
11. Foreign goods shall be subject to rigorous quality and other mandatory checks.

States' Industrial Policies

Until the economic liberalisation ushered in 1991, the Union Government played the dominant role in the industrial development of India, particularly by its investment in public enterprises and industrial licensing. However, now the State Governments can have a much greater role than in the past for industrial development. Almost all States now have their own industrial policies. States' industrial policies mainly aim at development of infrastructure and identifying industries suitable for the State and giving incentives. Readers are advised to get the latest industrial policy of the State from the official website.

SUMMARY

Until 1991, the industrial policy of India was characterized by a monopoly or dominant role for the public sector in strategic basic and heavy industries; preference for small-scale units and reservation of a large number of items for the SSI sector; preference for cooperative sector and joint sector in several areas; a host of entry, growth, and operational and functional restrictions on the private sector; and a very restrictive attitude towards foreign capital and technology.

Industrial policy liberalisations have greatly benefitted the Indian economy and helped India to emerge as a very fast growing and dynamic economy.

The industrial policy announced in July 1991 along with other economic policy changes and measures ushered in a process of economic reforms in India. Now there are no entry and growth restrictions on the private sector, except in a very small number of industries. The policy towards foreign capital and technology has been substantially liberalised. Imports have been very significantly liberalized; quantitative restrictions on imports, by and large, have been removed.

As a result, the industrial sector has become very dynamic, competition has increased substantially benefitting the economy and consumers. Economic growth rate has increased significantly. Indian economy which has been the second fastest growing in the world is expected to emerge as the fastest growing economy in the near future.

However, several measures are needed to guard against the deleterious effects of liberalisation.

ANNEXURE 3.1

SCHEDULES TO INDUSTRIAL POLICY RESOLUTION, 1956

Schedule A

(Industries reserved for the public sector)

1. Arms and ammunition and allied items of defence equipment.
2. Atomic energy.
3. Iron and steel.
4. Heavy castings and forgings of iron and steel.
5. Heavy plant and machinery required for iron and steel production, for mining, for machine tool manufacture and for such other basic industries as may be specified by the Central Government.
6. Heavy electrical plant including large hydraulic and steam turbines.
7. Coal and lignite.
8. Mineral oils.
9. Mining of iron ore, manganese ore, chrome ore, gypsum, sulphur, gold and diamond.
10. Mining and processing copper, lead, zinc, tin, molybdenum and wolfram.
11. Minerals specified in the Schedule to the Atomic Energy (Control of Production and Use) Order, 1953.
12. Aircraft.
13. Air transport.
14. Railway transport.
15. Ship-building.
16. Telephones and telephone cables, telegraph and wireless apparatus (excluding radio receiving sets).
17. Generation and distribution of electricity.

Schedule B

(Industries where public sector had priority in establishing new unit)

1. All other minerals except "minor minerals" as defined in Section 3 of the Minerals Concession Rules, 1949.
2. Aluminium and other non-ferrous metals not included in Schedule 'A'.
3. Machine tools.
4. Ferro-alloys and tool steels.
5. Basic and intermediate products required by chemical industries such as the manufacture of drugs, dyestuffs and plastics.

6. Antibiotics and other essential drugs.
7. Fertilisers.
8. Synthetic rubber.
9. Carbonisation of coal.
10. Chemical pulp.
11. Road transport.
12. Sea transport.

☆☆☆

CHAPTER 4

IDRA AND INDUSTRIAL LICENSING

A policy can be effectively implemented and the objectives achieved only if the Government has the power to take the measures required for this purpose. It is with this purpose that the Industries (Development and Regulation) Act was passed in 1951. Until the economic liberalisation ushered in 1991, the entry into business, growth and expansion of firms were regulated by licensing exercised by the Central Government under this Act.

INDUSTRIES (DEVELOPMENT AND REGULATION) ACT

The Industries (Development and Regulation) Act, 1951, amended from time-to-time, is one of the most effective weapons the Government possesses to regulate the development and to control the activities of the industrial sector.

> **The IDRA brought under Central control the development and regulation of a number of industries, the activities which affect the country as a whole and the development of which must be governed by economic factors of national importance.**

Objectives

The main object of the Act is to provide the Central Government with the means to implement their Industrial Policy. Thus, the principal objective of the IDRA is to empower the Government:

- To take necessary steps for the development of industries.
- To regulate the pattern and direction of industrial development.
- To control the activities, performance and results of industrial undertakings in the public interest.

Main Provisions

> **The IDRA empowers the Central Government to take promotional and regulatory measures for the orderly development of the industrial sector.**

The IDR Act contains provisions to realise the above objectives. Some of the salient features of the Act are the following:

Development Measures: The Act provides for the establishment, by the Central Government, of a *Central Advisory Council,* consisting of representatives of the owners of industrial undertakings, employees, consumers, primary suppliers, etc., for the purpose of advising the Central Government on matters concerning the development of the industries.

It also provides for the establishment, for any scheduled industry or group of scheduled industries, a *Development Council* consisting of members representing the interests of the owners, employees, consumers, etc., and persons having special knowledge of matters relating to the technical or other aspects of the industries, for purposes such as recommending measures for improving the performance of the industries.

Regulation of Entry and Growth: The IDR Act empowers the Central Government to regulate the development of industries by means of licensing with suitable exemptions as decided by the Government. Accordingly, the entry into a business or the expansion of an existing business may be regulated by licensing.

Supervision and Control: The Government, under this Act, can make a full and complete investigation if it is of the opinion that — *(a)* in respect of any scheduled industry or undertaking, there has been or is likely to be a substantial fall in the volume of output, or a marked deterioration in the quality of output or an unjustifiable rise in the price of the output; *(b)* any industrial undertaking is managed in a manner highly detrimental to the scheduled industry concerned or to the public interest.

Consequent upon the investigation as mentioned above, the Government is empowered to issue such directions to the industrial undertaking or undertakings for all or any of the following purposes, namely,

(*i*) regulating the production of any article or class of articles by the industrial undertaking or undertakings and fixing the standards of production,

(*ii*) requiring the industrial undertaking or undertakings to take such steps as the Central Government may consider necessary to stimulate the development of the industry to which the undertaking or undertakings relates or relate,

(*iii*) prohibiting the industrial undertaking or undertakings from resorting to any act or practice which might reduce its or their production, capacity or economic value, and

(*iv*) controlling the prices, or regulating the distribution, of any article or class of articles which have been the subject matter of investigation.

The Act also provides that any direction of the above nature may be issued by the Central Government at any time when a case relating to any industry or industrial undertaking or undertakings is under investigation. Such a direction shall have effect until it is varied or revoked by the Central Government.

For the purpose of ascertaining the position of working of any industrial undertaking or for any other purpose mentioned in the Act, or the rules made thereunder, any person authorised by the Central Government in this behalf can (*a*) enter and inspect any premises; (*b*) order the production of any document, book, register or record in the possession or power of any person having the control of or employed in connection with any industrial undertaking; and (*c*) examine any person having the control of, or employed in connection with, any industrial undertaking.

Takeover of Management: The power of control entrusted to the Central Government under the IDRA extends to that of the takeover of the management of the whole or any part of an industrial undertaking which fails to comply with any of the directions mentioned above. The Government can also takeover the management of an undertaking which is being managed in a manner highly determined to the scheduled industry concerned or to public interest.

Further, the Central Government can takeover the management of industrial undertaking owned by a company under liquidation, with the permission of the High Court, if the Government is of the opinion that the running or restarting the operations of such an undertaking is necessary for the maintaining or increasing the production, supply or distribution in the public interest.

In respect of the industrial undertaking, the management of which has been taken over by the Government, the IDRA empowers the Government to take steps, in appropriate cases, to liquidate or reconstruct the company concerned in the public interest.

Price and Distribution Controls: For securing the equitable distribution and availability at fair prices of any article or class of articles relatable to any scheduled industry, the Central Government is empowered by the Act to control its/their supply, distribution and price.

Exemptions: The Central Government is empowered to exempt any industrial undertaking or class of industrial undertakings or any scheduled industry or class of scheduled industries from all or any of the provisions of the Act in certain cases in the public interest.

INDUSTRIAL LICENSING

> **Licensing was regarded as an important means to help achieve the desired pattern of industrialisation to serve the socio-economic development objectives.**

The Industries (Development and Regulation) Act, 1951, empowers the Central Government to regulate the establishment and certain activities of the industrial undertakings by means of licensing. The licensing provisions of the IDRA may apply to industrial undertakings set up by any person or authority including the Government.

A licence is a written permission from the Government to an industrial undertaking to manufacture specified articles included in the Schedule to the Act. If a new company has to be formed, the industrial licence in the first instance, is issued in the name of the applicant, and later when the company has been formed, the necessary endorsement to that effect will be made in the licence.

A licence contains particulars of the industrial undertaking, its location, the articles to be manufactured, its capacity on the basis of the maximum utilisation of plant and machinery, and other appropriate conditions which are enforceable under the Act. It is also subject to a validity period within which the licensed capacity should be established.

Prior to the economic liberalisation ushered in 1991, the licensing was a means to help achieve some of the objectives of the economic policy such as the desired pattern of industrial dispersal, encouraging new entrepreneurs and wider dispersal of industrial ownership, prevention of concentration of economic power, protection and promotion of the small-scale sector, regulation of foreign capital and technology, use of proper technology and scale of economies, achieving demand supply balance, promotion of exports and import substitution, employment generation, etc.

Before the policy liberalisation of 1991, a licence was required for the following purposes: (*i*) Establishment of new undertaking, (*ii*) Manufacture of new item, (*iii*) Substantial expansion of capacity, (*iv*) Continuation of business in certain cases (COB licence), (*v*) Change of location.

Projects involving investment up to specified limits were exempted from licensing, subject to certain conditions. The exemption limit was periodically revised upwards. Before the announcement of the new policy in July 1991, this limit was ₹ 15 crore in non-backward areas and ₹ 50 crore in backward areas.

Industrial Policy Changes

The industrial policy announced in July 1991 has abolished industrial licensing, irrespective of the levels of investment, for all industries except 18 specified industries. There has been subsequent liberalisations.

Now all industrial undertakings are exempt from obtaining an industrial licence to manufacture, except for (*i*) industries reserved for the Public Sector, (*ii*) industries retained under compulsory licensing, (*iii*) items of manufacture reserved for the small-scale sector, and (*iv*) if the proposal attracts locational restriction.

Industries for which industrial licensing is compulsory now are the following:

1. Distillation and brewing of alcoholic drinks.
2. Cigars and cigarettes of tobacco and manufactured tobacco substitutes.
3. Electronic, aerospace and defence equipment: all types.
4. Industrial explosives including detonating fuses, safety fuses, gun powder, nitrocellulose and matches.
5. Hazardous chemicals.
6. Drugs and Pharmaceuticals (according to modified Drug Policy issued in September 1994).

Note: The compulsory licensing provisions would not apply in respect of the small-scale units taking up the manufacture of any of the above items reserved for exclusive manufacture in small-scale sector.

Industrial undertakings exempt from obtaining an industrial license are required to file an Industrial Entrepreneur Memoranda (IEM) with the Secretariat of Industrial Assistance (SIA), Department of Industrial Policy and Promotion, Government of India, and obtain an acknowledgement. No further approval is required.

It is due to reasons of hazardous nature of the product/production, environmental concern, and health and social concerns that some industries are still subject to licensing.

Locational Policy

Industrial undertakings are free to select the location of a project. In the case of cities with population of more than a million (as per the 1991 census), however, the proposed location should be at least 25 kms away from the Standard Urban Area limits of that city unless, it is to be located in an area designated as an "industrial area" before the 25th July, 1991. Electronics, Computer Software and Printing (and any other industry which may be notified in future as "non-polluting industry") are exempt from such locational restriction. Relaxation in the aforesaid locational restriction is possible if an industrial license is obtained as per the notified procedure.

The location of industrial units is further regulated by the local zoning and land use regulations as also the environmental regulations. Hence, even if the requirement of the locational policy stated above is fulfilled, if the local zoning and land use regulations of a State Government, or the regulations of the Ministry of Environment do not permit setting up of an industry at a location, the entrepreneur would be required to abide by that decision.

SUMMARY

Using the provisions of the Industries (Development and Regulation) Act, 1951, the industrial sector was very extensively controlled by the Central Government until 1991. This Act has been regarded as a very draconian one by industrialists, many economists and others. It has been alleged that the Government was obsessed with the scope for regulations, under this *Development* and *Regulation* Act, relegating development to the backburner. The *licence permit raj* gave rise to rampant corruption.

The liberalisation has significantly diminished the importance of this Act. Several people argue that the Act has lost its relevance and, therefore, this Central Act should be repealed. Under the controlled regime, the Central Government had a dominant say on the location of industries. Now that most of the entry and growth restrictions and the reservation of industries for the public sector have been dismantled, it is up to the State Governments to promote industries in the States.

With the economic liberalisation, a lot of responsibility for the development of industries has shifted to the States.

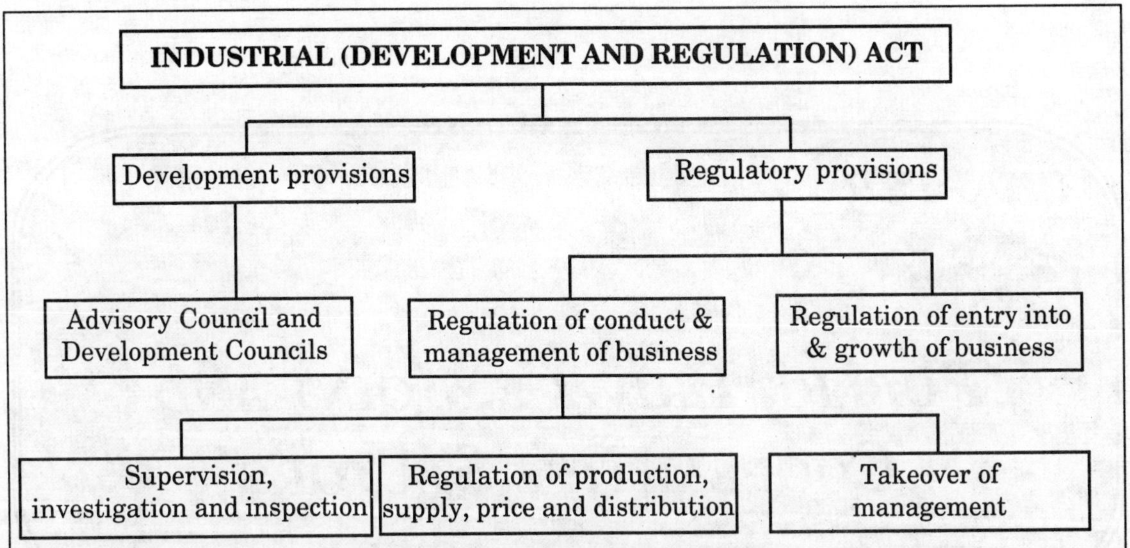

Fig. 4.1: Salient Features of IRDA

☆☆☆

CHAPTER 5

PUBLIC, PRIVATE, JOINT AND COOPERATIVE SECTORS

The mixed economy of India is characterised by the co-existence of public, private, joint and cooperative sectors. The pattern of industrial development of the country has been influenced to a very significant extent by the roles given to these sectors by the industrial policy.

PUBLIC SECTOR

The objective of accelerating the pace of economic development and the political ideology which gave the public sector a dominant role in the industrial development of the nation led to rapid growth of the state owned enterprises (SOEs) sector in India.

Until 1991, the public sector was assigned the dominant role in the development of the basic and heavy industries, with monopoly or near monopoly position in a number of industries.

As the Bureau of Public Enterprises observes, born as the outcome of the conscious policy of the government to speed up the industrialisation of the country with a view to give added impetus to economic growth as well as to achieve certain socio-economic goals as enunciated in the Industrial Policy Resolutions of the government, these enterprises came to cover a wide spectrum of activities in basic and strategic industries like steel, coal, minerals and metals, petroleum, heavy engineering, chemicals, fertilisers and pharmaceuticals, etc., on the one hand, and consumer goods, trading and marketing activities, transportation services, contracts and consultancy services, tourist services, financial services, development of small industries, etc., on the other.[1]

Objectives

The public enterprises which were promoted as an instrument for implementation of the government's socio-economic policies, had a multitude of objectives set for them, *viz.*,

- To help in the rapid economic growth and industrialisation of the country and create the necessary infrastructure for economic development.
- To earn return on investment and thus generate resources for development.
- To promote redistribution of income and wealth.
- To create employment opportunities.
- To promote balanced regional development.
- To assist the development of small-scale and ancillary industries.
- To promote import substitution, save and earn foreign exchange for the economy.

Growth and Performance of Public Enterprises

There had been a phenomenal growth of the public sector since the commencement of planning. In fact, even before the commencement of planning and the adoption of the goal of the *socialistic pattern of society*, the public sector was assigned an important role in the industrialisation and economic development of the country. The *Industrial Policy Resolution of 1948* made it very clear that the manufacture of arms and ammunition, the production and control of atomic energy, and the ownership and management of railway transport would be the exclusive monopoly of the Central Government. It was resolved further that in another six industries the State alone would set up new undertakings. These six industries were: coal, iron and steel, aircraft manufacture, ship-building, manufacture of telephone, telegraph and wireless apparatus, excluding radio receiving sets, and mineral oils.

The *Industrial Policy Resolution of 1956* enlarged the role of the public sector. It stated: "The adoption of the socialist pattern of society as a national objective as well as the need for planned and rapid development require that all industries of basic and strategic importance, or in the nature of public utility services, should be in the public sector. Other industries which are essential and require investment on a scale which only the State, in present circumstances, could provide, have also to be in the public sector. The State has, therefore, to assume direct responsibility for the future development of industries over a wide area." *Schedule A* to the Resolution enumerated 17 industries, the future development of which would be the exclusive right of the Sate. *Schedule B* to the Industrial Policy Resolution, 1956, contained a list of 12 industries which would be progressively State-owned and in which the State would, therefore, generally take the initiative in establishing new units. The Schedules A and B are reproduced in the Annexure to the chapter on *Industrial Policy*.

Out of the 217 operational Central Public Sector Enterprises (CPSEs) 158 made a profit of ₹1,08,435 crore in 2009-10 and 59 enterprises made a loss of ₹15,842 crore.

TABLE 5.1 : GROWTH OF PUBLIC ENTERPRISES			
		Investment (₹ crores)	*Total No. of Enterprises*
1	At the commencement of 1st Plan (1-4-1951)	29	5
2	At the commencement of 2nd Plan (1-4-1956)	81	21
3	At the commencement of 3rd Plan (1-4-1961)	953	48
4	At the commencement of 4th Plan (1-4-1969)	3,902	85
5	At the commencement of 5th Plan (1-4-1974)	6,237	122
6	At the commencement of 6th Plan (1-4-1980)	18,225	186
7	At the commencement of 7th Plan (1-4-1985)	42,811	221
8	At the commencement of 8th Plan (1-4-1992)	1,18,492	237
9	At the commencement of 9th Plan (1-4-1997)	2,01,500	238
10	At the commencement of 10th Plan (1-4-2002)	3,24,632	240
11	At the commencement of 11th Plan (1-4-2007)	4,21,089	244
12	At the commencement of 12th Plan (1-4-2012)	7,29,298	260
13	At the end of March 2015	10,96,057	298

The four decades since the commencement of planning witnessed a substantial growth and expansion of the public sector in India. Investment in industrial undertaking by the Central Government increased from ₹ 29 crore in five units at the commencement of the First Five Year Plan (1951) to ₹ 1,18,492 crore at the commencement of the Eighth Plan (1992) in 237 units. It is further increased to over two lakh crore (₹ 2,01,500 crore) spread over 238 units at the commencement of the Ninth Plan (1997). At the end of March 2010, it was about ₹ 10,96,057 crore in 298 units.

Major part of the Central public sector investment was in the steel, coal, minerals and metals, power and petroleum sectors.

There well over 1,000 State level public enterprises (SLPEs).

The wide range of product and activities of Central public sector enterprises included manufacturing of steel, mining of coal and minerals, extraction and refining of crude oil, manufacture of heavy machinery, machine tools, instruments, heavy machine building equipment, heavy electronical equipment for thermal, and hydel stations, transportation equipment, telecommunication equipment, ships, submarines, fertilisers, drugs and pharmaceuticals, petrochemicals, cement, textile, and a few consumer items — such as bread, newsprint/paper, footwear and contraceptives, operation of air, sea, river and road transport, operation in national and international trade, consultancy, contract and construction services, inland and overseas telecommunication services, hotel and tourists services, etc.

At the beginning of the 1990s, the public sector was dominant in many industries. The PSEs contributed the entire output in the case of petroleum, lignite, copper and primary lead, about 98 per cent of zinc, with over 90 per cent of coal, more than half of steel and aluminium and about one-third of fertilisers. The public sector, thus, came to occupy a commanding position in several critical industries. While setting up of new enterprises was mainly responsible for the fast growth of the public sector, nationalisation of certain industries like coal, copper, insurances, major part of commercial banking sector and a number of sick units has also contributed to this growth.

A significant feature of the public sector investment is the predominance of investment in few crucial sectors, namely, steel, minerals and metals, petroleum, coal and chemicals and fertilisers.

The public sector certainly had a very important role to play in the development of this vast and populous developing economy characterised by dearth of capital, entrepreneurship and technology. However, keeping the private sector completely out of many industries and giving the private sector only a secondary role in many other industries have had severe adverse effects on growth and competition. The new economic policy, characterised by scope for a substantial privatisation, including dereservation of industries for the public sector, in fact, amounts to an acceptance of this.

The performance of many public enterprises has been far from satisfactory. One can, of course, speak of the contribution of the public sector towards GDP, employment generation, exports, etc. The pertinent question, however, is have these contributions been adequate when compared to the massive investments that have gone into the PSEs and at what level of efficiency these enterprises have been operating? Further, to what extent these enterprises, particularly the monopolies, have been customer-friendly?

While the public sector has made very significant contribution to the industrial development of the country, the performance of many PSEs has not been satisfactory.

A large number of PSEs, including several monopolies, have made huge losses. Despite the huge losses incurred by a number of enterprises, the PSEs as a whole could make profits mainly because of the enormous profits made by several public sector monopolies.

Several of the loss making PSEs have been either in non-priority sectors or in sectors where the private sector has proved to be more efficient. A number of loss making units are sick units.

A variety of factors have been identified for the unsatisfactory performance of a large number of public enterprises. While the project formulation has improved over the years, huge cost and time over-runs continued to take place in project implementation. This was on account of problems of land acquisition, procurement of equipment, civil work and other imponderables. Further, the locational and investment decisions in some sectors and projects are observed to have adversely affected performance. It has been noticed that inappropriate location, irrational product-mix and imposed marketing arrangements critically affected the performance of some projects. In the fertiliser sector, choice of technology having been tied to availability of foreign financing had adversely affected their operations. On the other hand, in power sector, excessive investment in generation capacities with incommensurate attention to transmission networks had created serious imbalances. Uneconomical pricing/tariff rates signifying large cross-subsidies reduced the internal resource generation in this sector. This had direct implications for reinvestment on the one hand, and raised demand for power, on the other. These also contributed, among other things, to the heavy losses incurred by most of the State Electricity Boards which continuously failed to realise the three per cent statutory rate of return on assets.

A number of other problems including allocation of resources, delays in the filling up of top-level posts, tight regulations and procedures for investment and restrictions on functional autonomy of the enterprises (*e.g.*, in respect of labour and wage policy), etc., have for long been noticed as serious constraints on PSE operational efficiency.

The public sector is generally criticised for inadequate generation of internal resources.

The Department of Public Enterprises points out that generation of internal resources by public enterprises is constrained by the following factors:

1. Public Sector Enterprises were set up not only for commercial consideration but also for factors such as generation of employment, promoting balanced regional development, etc.
2. Low return on investment on account of price constraints imposed on certain infrastructural goods and services of public enterprises.
3. A number of sick units in the private sector facing closure had to be taken over by the Government and these units form a sizeable part of the Central Public Sector.
4. Number of industries promoted in the public sector with long gestation period.
5. The impact of escalation in the prices of various inputs and periodical wage revision.

Public Sector Policy Changes

After the initial exuberance of the public sector entering new areas of industrial and technical competence, a number of problems have begun to manifest themselves in many of the public enterprises. Serious problems have been observed in the insufficient growth in productivity, poor project management, over-manning, lack of continuous technological upgradation and inadequate attention to R&D and human resource development. The low rate of return on capital invested has inhibited the ability of the public enterprises to regenerate themselves in terms of new investments as well as in new technology development. This resulted in many of the public enterprises becoming a burden rather than an asset to the Government.

A salient feature of the economic reforms is a very substantial reduction in the role of public sector in industry.

It was, therefore, decided to redefine the role of the public sector, in tandem with the economic liberalisation. According to the industrial policy announced on 24-7-1991, the following have been set as the priority areas for growth of public enterprises:

1. Essential infrastructure goods and services.
2. Exploration and exploitation of oil and mineral resources.

3. Technology development and building of manufacturing capabilities in areas which are crucial in the long-term development of the economy where private sector investment is inadequate.
4. Manufacture of products where strategic considerations predominate such as defence equipment.

Accordingly the number of industries reserved for the public sector was pruned to 8. These 8 industries were: *(i)* Arms and ammunition and allied items of defence equipment, defence aircraft and warships, *(ii)* Atomic energy, *(iii)* Coal and lignite, *(iv)* Mineral oils, *(v)* Mining of iron ore, manganese ore, chrome ore, gypsum, sulphur, gold and diamond, *(vi)* Mining of copper, lead, zinc, tin, molybdenum, wolfram, *(vii)* Minerals specified in the schedule to the Atomic Energy (control of production and use) Order, 1958. *(viii)* Railway transport.

The list has been further pruned subsequently and now only atomic energy and railway transport are reserved for the public sector. In May 2001, the sensitive defence production which was hitherto reserved for the public sector was thrown open to the private sector. Foreign investment up to 26 per cent has also been allowed in this sector.

The new industrial policy also indicated that the public sector would withdraw from the following cases:

1. Industries based on low technology.
2. Small-scale and non-strategic areas.
3. Inefficient and unproductive areas.
4. Areas with low or zero social responsibility or public purpose.
5. Areas where private sector has developed sufficient enterprise and resources.

The main elements of the current Government Policy towards Public Sector Undertakings (PSUs) are:

- Bringing down Government equity in all non-strategic PSUs to 26 per cent or lower, if necessary.
- Restructure and revive potentially viable PSUs.
- Close down PSUs which cannot be revived.
- Fully protect the interest of workers.

In order to give thrust to the process of disinvestment in PSUs, a new Department of Disinvestment was set up. The Department is responsible for all matters related to disinvestment of Central Government equity in Central Public Sector Undertakings, implementation of disinvestment decisions and implementation of the erstwhile Disinvestment Commission.

The new Policy also made it clear that the Government will ensure that the public sector is run on business lines as envisaged by in the Industrial Policy Resolution of 1956. It was also decided to close down unviable sick public undertakings.

The Industrial Policy Statement of July 1991 observed that in the 1950s and 1960s, the principal instruments for controlling commanding heights of the economy was investment in key industries. Today, the State has other instruments of intervention, particularly fiscal and monetary instruments.

The post-1991 public sector policy marks a much needed change for accelerating the pace of development by better utilisation of the national resources (including entrepreneurial resources) and for increasing competition and efficiency.

PUBLIC SECTOR RATNAS

More than half of the CPSEs fall into any one of the special categories described as *Maharatna*, *Navratna* and *Miniratna*.

With a view to giving the well-performing CPSEs greater functional and financial autonomy and help them become globally competitive and to emerge as global giants, Government of India initiated a strategy in 1997. It was decided that such PSEs would have freedom to incur capital expenditure, decide upon joint ventures, set up subsidiaries/offices abroad, enter into technological and strategic alliances, raise funds from capital markets (international and domestic) and enjoy substantial operational and managerial autonomy. The Government, after a detailed and in-depth inter-ministerial discussions selected nine PSUs for making them truly world-class entities and it euphemistically named these as *Navaratnas*.

Special statuses, viz., *Maharatna*, *Navratna* and *Miniratna* have been granted to CPSEs on the basis of their strength and certain criteria to accord more autonomy to support their strategic growth and operational efficiency by unleashing their potential.

The nine PSEs that were granted Navaratna status in 1997 were Bharat Heavy Electricals Ltd. (BHEL), Bharat Petroleum Corporation Ltd. (BPCL), Hindustan Petroleum Corporation Ltd. (HPCL), Indian Oil Corporation Ltd. (IOC), Indian Petrochemicals Corporation Ltd. (IPCL), National Thermal Power Corporation Ltd. (NTPC),

Oil and Natural Gas Corporation Ltd., (ONGC), Steel Authority of India Ltd., (SAIL) and Videsh Sanchar Nigam Ltd., (VSNL). Later, the list of Navaratnas was enlarged. At the beginning of 2011, there were 18 of them. Others who joined the list are Bharat Electronics Ltd., (BEL), Coal India Ltd., (CIL), Mahanagar Telephone Nigam Ltd., (MTNL), National Aluminium Co. Ltd., (NACL), Power Grid Corporation of India Ltd., (PGCL), Rural Electrification Corporation Ltd., (RECL), Shipping Corporation of India Ltd., (SCIL), National Mineral Development Corporation Ltd., (NMDCL), and Gas Authority of India Ltd., (GAIL).

The Boards of these PSEs have been broad-based with induction of non-official part-time professional directors. All the measures have been taken with the objective of making the PSEs competitive.

Some of the important decision-making authority delegated by the Government to the Boards of the Navaratnas include the following:

1. To incur capital expenditure on purchase of new items or for replacement, without any monetary ceiling.
2. To enter into technology joint ventures or strategic alliances.
3. To obtain by purchase or other arrangements, technology and know-how.
4. To effect organizational restructuring including establishment of profit centres, opening of offices in India and aboard, creating new activity centres, etc.
5. Creation and winding up of all posts including and up to those of non-Board level Directors, i.e., Functional Directors who may have the same pay scales as that of Board level Directors, but who would not be members of the Board. All appointments up to this level would also be in the powers of the Boards and would include the power to effect internal transfers and redesignation of posts.
6. To structure and implement schemes relating to personnel and human resource management, training, voluntary or compulsory retirement schemes, etc.
7. To raise debt from the domestic capital markets and for borrowings from international market, which would be subject to the approval of RBI/Department of Economic Affairs as may be required and should be obtained through the administrative Ministry.
8. To establish financial joint ventures and wholly-owned subsidiaries in India or abroad subject to certain stipulations.

It was also laid down that these public sector enterprises shall not depend upon budgetary support or Government guarantees. The resources for implementing their programmes should come from their internal resources or through other sources, including the capital markets.

In addition, the government created another category called **Miniratna**. Miniratnas can also enter into joint ventures, set subsidiary companies and overseas offices but with certain conditions. However, as can be inferred from the term, the extent of autonomy which the Miniratnas enjoy is less than that of the Navaratnas. There are two categories of Miniratnas. Category I Miniratnas designation applies to PSEs that have made profits continuously for the last three years or earned a net profit of ₹ 30 crore or more in one of the three years. Category II include those PSEs which have made profits for the last three years continuously and should have a positive net worth. Category I Miniratnas enjoy higher financial autonomy than those in Category II.

A very large number of the PSEs are Miniratnas. Examples include Central Coalfields Ltd., Central Warehousing Corporation Ltd., Chennai Petroleum Corporation Ltd., Cochin Shipyard Ltd., Hindustan Shipyard Ltd., Garden Reach Shipbuilders, Goa Shipyard Ltd., Hindustan Fertilizer Corporation Ltd., Hindustan Organic Chemicals Ltd., HMT (I) Ltd., HMT (MT) Ltd., Hindustan Paper Corporation, etc. There are more than 90 Miniratnas.

In 2009, Government defined a special category of Navaratnas as **Maharatnas**. Navaratnas which satisfy the following criteria are recognized as Maharatnas.

- Having Navaratna Status
- Listed on Indian Stock Exchange with minium public share holding as per SEBI regulations.
- An average annual turnover of more than 25,000 crore during the previous three years.
- An average annual net worth of more than 15,000 crore during the previous three years.
- An average annual net profit of more than 5,000 crore during the previous three years.
- Having significant global presence/international operations.

The six PSEs which got Maharatna status in 2009 are: ONGC, NTPC, SAIL, IOC, BPCL, and, HPCL.

TABLE 5:2: CLASSIFICATION CRITERIA

Miniratna I	Miniratna II	Navratna	Maharatna
◆ Should have made profit for the last 3 years and have a positive net worth ◆ Have not defaulted on loans/interest repayment of the Government ◆ No dependency up on budgetary support or government guarantees ◆ Boards restructured with presence of at least three non-official directors *E.g.*, Ed.CIL, HMT, MECON Ltd	◆ Should have reported profits in the last 3 years with pre-tax profit of ₹ 30 crore or more in any one of the last 3 years ◆ Have not defaulted on loans/interest ◆ No dependency on budgetary support of Government guarantees ◆ Boards restructured with presence of at least three non-official directors *E.g.*, AAI, BEML, Concord, EIL, IRCTC etc.	◆ Should be a Miniratna ◆ Should have 'excellent' very good rating in 3 of the last 5 MoUs ◆ Have secured composite score of 60 or more for 7 identified parameters *E.g.*, BEL, BHEL, BPCL etc.	◆ Should have Navratna status ◆ Listed on Indian stock exchange, with minimum prescribed public shareholding under SEBI regulation ◆ Average annual turnover of over ₹ 25,000 crore in the last 3 years ◆ Average annual net profit after tax of over ₹ 5,000 crore in the last 3 years ◆ Notable global presence or international operations, *E.g.*, Coal India, IOCL, NTPC etc.

ORGANISATION OF PUBLIC ENTERPRISES

Public enterprises in India have been organised in the following forms:

Ministry

For the management of the Indian Railways, there is a full-fledged Ministry of Railways in the Government of India. The Ministry of Railways undertakes and manages all the investments and enterprises connected with the railway transport of the country, and has its own Annual Budget which has to be presented to Parliament and approved by it. The Ministry has a Minister for Railways and the body of management consists of the Railway Board, headed by a Chairman. Besides the Chairman, the Board has three members and a Financial Commissioner. All these five personnel have the status of secretary to the Government of India.

Departmental Undertakings

The Study Team on Public Sector Undertakings has mentioned the following as the principal characteristics of Departmental Undertakings[2].

(*a*) It is financed by annual appropriations from the treasury and all, or a major share, of its revenues are paid into the treasury.

(*b*) It is subject to the budget, accounting and audit controls applicable to government activities.

(*c*) Its permanent staff consists of civil servants, and the conditions of recruitment and service are the same as for other civil servants.

(*d*) It can be sued only by following the procedure prescribed for filing suits against the government.

The Departmental Undertaking is directly subordinate to a Ministry.

The need for secrecy, strategic importance and similar conditions make the departmental form the most suitable form of organisation in certain areas (for defence industry). The ordnance factories, such as the Army Clothing Factory, the Harness and Saddlery Factory, the Gun Carriage Factory and the Ishapore Ordnance Factory under the Ministry of Defence; the Chittaranjan Locomotive Works and the Integral Coach Factory under the Ministry of Railways; and the Posts and Telegraphs under the Ministry of Communications are examples of the departmental form of organisation and management.

While the departmental system ensures effective government control, it suffers from a number of disadvantages, such as too much governmental and political interference, lack of authority and initiative in decision-making, etc.

Government Company

The principal characteristics of the Government Company, as mentioned by the Study Team on Public Sector Undertakings, are the following:[3]

1. It has most of the features of a private limited company.
2. The whole of the capital stock, or 51 per cent or over of it, is owned by the government.
3. All the directors, or a majority of them, are appointed by the government, depending upon the extent to which private capital is participating in the enterprise.
4. It is a body corporate created under a general law, *viz.*, the Companies Act.
5. It can sue and be sued, enter into contract, and acquire property in its own name.

6. Unlike the public corporation, it is created by an executive decision of the government without Parliament's specific approval having been obtained, and its Articles of Association, though conforming to an Act, are drawn up and are revisable by the government.
7. Its funds are obtained from the government and, in some cases from private shareholders, and from revenues derived from the sale of its goods and services.
8. It is generally exempt from the personnel, budget, accounting and audit laws and procedures applicable to government departments.
9. Its employees, excluding those who are on deputation, are not civil servants.

The Industrial Policy Resolution of 1948 had declared that the "management of state enterprises will, as a rule, be through the medium of public corporations under the statutory control of the Central Government, which will assume such powers as may be necessary to ensure this". But most of the public sector undertakings have been organised as companies.

The company form of organisation for public enterprises had come in for much criticism in the beginning. Since the government, in most cases, was the only shareholder, it was said that the provisions of the Company Law did not have much relevance to a government company. Another objection was that the organisation of public enterprises as companies reduced their accountability and diluted audit control. But this criticism was largely met by writing special provisions into the Companies Act in 1956 with regard to the submission of Annual Reports and Accounts and audit by the Comptroller and Auditor General.

The Study Team on Public Sector Undertakings has pointed out that the principal defects generally attributed to a government company are the following:[4]

1. It evades the constitutional responsibilities which a state-owned-enterprise should have to government and Parliament.
2. The law regulating limited companies become a mere fiction because all or most of the functions normally vested in the shareholders and in the management are reserved to government.
3. A meeting of shareholders in the case of a government company is meaningless, for the declaration of profits and the appointments to the Board are naturally reserved to the government.
4. The extent of autonomy that it provides can be materially affected or altered by the executive agencies of the government.

Mainly relying on the above considerations, most of which had emerged from a UN seminar held at Rangoon in 1954 (and later endorsed by another UN seminar held at New Delhi in December, 1959), the Estimates Committee recommended[5] that all wholly state-owned public undertakings should generally be in the form of statutory corporations, and the company form should be an exception to be resorted to only:

1. When the government may have to takeover an existing enterprise in an emergency;
2. Where the state wishes to launch an enterprise in association with private capital; or

3. Where the government wishes to start an enterprise with a view eventually to transferring it to private management.

The government, however, did not accept this recommendation on the ground that the "company form was advantageous in that it allowed the flexibility and autonomy necessary for the successful operation of commercial enterprises and also provided for parliamentary control over the companies under the special provisions of the Companies Act."[6]

The decision taken by the government in 1961 on the recommendations of the Krishna Menon Committee on the form of organisation reads as follows: "Government consider that the form of management of the undertakings should be determined by the requirements of each case. Accordingly, from the point of view of flexibility of operations, the company form of management would be preferable. In some instances, it would be necessary to form statutory corporations, while in a few others, for various reasons, it would be desirable to run the undertakings as departmental organisations."[7]

From the characteristics of the government company mentioned above, it is clear that when the whole capital stock is not owned by the government, it is still generally regarded as a government company provided that the government owns not less than 51 per cent of the capital stock. Such companies are also described as "mixed" or "joint" companies. In such concerns, the government usually enjoys a substantial control of the management. Examples of such companies include Ashok Hotel and Hindustan Shipyard Ltd.

However, there were also examples of the management of the government companies being entrusted to private hands. Hindustan Machine Tools Ltd., Hindustan Shipyard Ltd., Hindustan Housing Factory Ltd., and Indian Telephone Industries Ltd., were, in the beginning, given out to foreign private firms for management.

Public Corporation

The important features of the public corporation (also known as statutory corporation) as mentioned by the Study Team on Public Sector Undertakings are given below:[8]

It is owned by the State.

1. It is created by a special law defining its objectives, powers and privileges and prescribing the form of management and its relationship with government departments.
2. It is a body corporate and can sue and be sued, enter into contracts and acquire property in its own name.
3. Except for appropriations to provide capital or to cover losses, it is usually independently financed; it obtains funds by borrowing either from the government or, in some cases, from the public and through revenues derived from the sale of goods and services, and has the authority to use and re-use its revenue.
4. It is ordinarily not subject to the budget, accounting and audit laws and procedures applicable to government departments.
5. Excluding the officers taken from government departments on deputation, the employees of public corporations are not civil servants, and are not governed by government regulations in respect of conditions of service.

As the Study Team has pointed out, in most democratic countries, the public corporation has been the common form of organisation for public enterprises. "In the United Kingdom, the USA and Canada, the form of public corporation has been adopted. In Italy, the company form has been retained for concerns brought within the public sector; but it is confined to the sub-holding companies and operating units. The two top management institutions that control all the operating units and sub-holding companies are the ENP[9] and IRII[10] and they are statutory corporations. Thus, it is only in India that the government seems to have adopted the method of running companies by directly holding shares in them. In Italy, the state holdings are administered by public corporations which, in turn, hold shares in a number of companies. In India, the government companies have been subjected to both. While it is sometimes claimed that the advantages of the two systems, state managements and private enterprises, have been combined in government companies in India, many witnesses who appeared before us held the view that government companies had merely succeeded in accumulating the disadvantages of both."[11]

Preferring the public corporation to the company, the Team has pointed out that though "from the government pronouncements on the subject it appears that the company form is conducive to greater autonomy, the reports of the Parliamentary Committees indicate the very opposite".[12] In support it has also quoted the following comments made by the Estimates Committee: "The Committee has noticed that in the relations between these undertakings and the Ministry, the former are treated in the same manner as departments and offices of government, controlled and supervised by the secretariat. The state undertakings have thus become adjuncts to Ministries and are Treated more or less on the same lines as any subordinate organisation of office."[13] The Team, therefore, felt that "the setting up of the public corporation will ensure a measure of real autonomy for the public enterprise".[14]

Holding Company

One of the important recommendations of the Study Team has been that integral public authorities should be created for particular sectors of industry and entrusted with the task of the general development of the respective sectors, including the running of undertakings in those sectors and the setting up of new projects. The Team recommended that, to promote this integration, it was necessary to amalgamate public undertakings in such a manner that one integral corporation functioned in each major area of public enterprise, operating the existing units and setting up new projects in the field of the industry entrusted to the corporation.

According to the Study Team, the setting up of the integral public corporation in the industrial and manufacturing field would result in the following advantages.[15]

1. It will end the fragmentation of the industrial effort in the public sector and promote the integration of the efforts to develop each industry in the public sector.
2. It will reduce the span of government control, for many of the functions that are coordinative *per se* will be taken care of at the level of the integral corporation.

3. It will make government control more effective by confining it to a higher level and concentrating it on the few vital and strategic points that the government should control to discharge its responsibility for the formulation of policy and for ensuring that the policy is implemented by the management.
4. It will secure for the management at the operating level greater detachment from direct bureaucratic control and political influence, both of which are inimical to initiative experimentation and vigorous management.
5. It will enable public enterprises to establish otherwise expensive staff organisation in fields like designing and consultancy, cost and management, accounting, industrial engineering, and research.
6. It will lead to better personnel management in public enterprises, and greater uniformity in the terms and conditions of service of the employees.
7. It will enable the corporation to avail of the economies of large-scale operations and to establish common service facilities like training for the particular requirement of the industry and purchase and sales organisations with effectiveness and economy.
8. It will provide much wider prospects to the managerial and technical personnel of public enterprises, increasing the capacity of these enterprises to attract and retain suitable personnel.
9. It will result in a more rational deployment and utilisation of designing and construction engineering personnel and expensive construction equipment.

While each type of organisation has its own advantages and disadvantages, for a particular category of undertakings one form may be more suited than the others.

Suitable Form of Organisation

The recommendations of the Study Team on Public Sector Undertakings regarding the suitable form of organisation are as follows:[16]

1. Industrial and Manufacturing Undertakings: All public undertakings in the industrial and manufacturing field should be entrusted to public corporations, each governing a number of operating units in the same area of industry. It would be advantageous to retain the company form for units in which there is an element of private participation but in such cases, the state-owned shares held in the company should be owned not by the government directly but in the name of the public corporation.

However, the departmental form is generally regarded as the one suitable for undertakings that provide the services that affect the totality of the community or the security of the country.

2. Public Utilities and Services: It has been generally recognised that public utilities and services require greater statutory authority for their operations. Their operations also serve the community in general or a primary need of industry. The public corporation form is, therefore, more suitable for undertakings falling in the category of public utilities and services. The statutes of existing corporations in this category should be revised with a view to ensuring that they are in accord with the needs of autonomy and flexibility.

3. Promotional and Developmental Undertakings: The company form is not suitable for promotional and developmental undertakings. The very nature of these undertakings signifies that the accent is on non-commercial objectives, although the operations are sought to be carried on commercial lines and not on departmental lines. The government may re-examine the desirability of continuing these undertakings as government companies.

4. Commercial and Trading Concerns: A common objective of these undertakings is to act as instruments for the social regulation of trade and business in the field of their operation. Since these undertakings operate in competition with their counterparts in the private sector, there is perhaps some justification for retaining the company form of organisation for these undertakings.

PRICING POLICY IN PUBLIC ENTERPRISES

The public sector pricing policy is an issue that has been widely debated. Should the public sector undertakings earn profits? If they should earn profits, what should be the level of the profits? In areas where there are good prospects for making profits, should they exploit the market to the maximum or should there be a limit to profit rates? Should all the undertakings be run on commercial lines, or is it sufficient if the public sector as a whole makes profit?

If the public sector undertakings are not required to make a profit, what should be the pricing policy? Should it be marginal cost pricing, average cost pricing, or no-profit, no-loss pricing? What should be the factors that should determine the choice of any of the above policies?

These are the basic issues in public sector pricing. An understanding of the important theories of public sector pricing would make some of these issues more clear.

> **Economic, social and political issues affect pricing policy of PSEs.**

Theories of Pricing

Marginal Cost Pricing: Marginal cost pricing refers to the method of setting prices in which price is made equal to the marginal cost of production. The marginal cost pricing implies that the price is set at the point at which the demand curve cuts the marginal cost curve.

The marginal cost pricing theory was first advocated by Professor Harold Hotelling in his article, "The General Welfare in Relation to Problems of Taxation and of Railway and Utility Rates", published in *Econometrica* in 1938. In this article, he argued that, by adopting the marginal cost pricing even if the public utilities ran at a loss which had to be financed by lump sum payments by the state, total economic welfare would be increased by such a pricing policy.

When production is subject to the law of decreasing costs (or increasing returns), the marginal cost price is lower than other prices (average cost price, no-profit, no-loss price, etc.). This lower price enables the poor sections of the society to increase their consumption of public utilities. That is why Hotelling argued that marginal cost pricing would improve economic welfare.

When production is subject to the law of decreasing costs, if marginal cost pricing is adopted, the total revenue will obviously be less than the total cost. It has been argued that this deficit in revenue should be made good by taxing the rich. When this is done, a part of the cost of the public utilities consumed by the poor is paid by the rich. Thus, marginal cost pricing would achieve an income redistribution in favour of the poor and thereby an enhancement in total economic welfare.

But it should be pointed out here that it is not always possible to cover the revenue gap by progressive taxation. In India, and in many developing countries, there is a limit to the amount that can be raised by means of direct taxes. The situation may necessitate higher commodity taxation, which may turn out to be regressive and/or deficit financing. If commodity taxation and deficit financing cause a rise in prices, it is likely to make the plight of the poorest sections more miserable, for the poorest strata usually do not have the economic capacity to consume even the subsidised public utilities. The marginal cost pricing, therefore, sometimes reduces the total economic welfare even under conditions of decreasing costs.

When production is subject to the law of increasing costs (decreasing returns), the marginal cost price represents at higher price than the average cost price or no-profit, no-loss price. Hence, marginal cost pricing under conditions of increasing costs will reduce the total economic welfare, for this higher price will reduce the poor people's consumption of public utilities.

If marginal cost pricing is adopted when production is subject to the law of increasing costs, the enterprise can generate some surplus.

There are some practical difficulties in marginal cost pricing. "Where there are multiple products or services, the determination of detailed costs of each item may be a very costly and complicated affair. There may, as a result, be large economies of administration if services involving unequal costs are charged at a uniform rate. This is the reason why the post office charges the same price for carrying letters from one street to another or from one corner of the country to another.

"The marginal cost cannot be accurately assessed because the factors are indivisible and the various charges on new factor intakes are not the charges on factor use needed for additional increments of output. Marginal costs would be high at points where capacity gets exhausted and for additional production new capacities have to be created. In such cases, the costs incurred at such points are abnormally high and thus the marginal cost cannot be a basis for price fixation.

"If the price is to equal marginal cost, fluctuations in demand and supply would lead to frequent fluctuations in prices, which is not very desirable."[17]

Average Cost Pricing: Average cost pricing refers to the method of setting prices in which price is equal to the average cost of production. Under average cost pricing, the total revenue equals total cost. Average cost pricing, thus, ensures the absorption of the full cost of production into the price.

When calculating the total cost, it is usual to include normal profit in it. Hence, the average cost includes also the normal profit. The average cost price is, therefore, a little higher than the no-profit, no-loss price.

It has been argued that, in the case of the railways, posts and telegraphs, multipurpose projects, etc., the average cost can be more easily calculated than the marginal cost.

Thiemeyer considers the average cost pricing to be fair and just because of the following reasons:[18]

1. Public undertakings are expected primarily to meet needs, that is, to provide an optimum volume of supplies cheaply without seeking any profit.
2. Every purchaser pays the entire cost of the unit or units consumed by him instead of paying only the additional cost of producing these units.
3. Since nobody is required to pay more for the goods he purchases than the amount it actually costs to produce those goods, there is no exploitation.
4. The average cost price is a reliable criterion for investment in many cases.
5. The average cost principle ensures that the entire expenditure of the undertaking is covered and thereby secures the viability and the autonomy of the undertaking.

Under conditions of decreasing costs, the average cost price is higher than the marginal cost price. Hence, the demand for goods or services will be lower if the average cost is the criterion for fixing the price. It will, it has been argued, adversely affect the interests of the consumers.

When production is subject to the law of increasing costs, the average cost is lower than the marginal cost, and hence the average cost pricing will benefit the poor.

The INRICE Theory Committee points out that "the recommendation... that price should be fixed in terms of average unit costs is in practice inapplicable. To take one example, in the transport sector... no satisfactory method of allocating costs according to their origin has yet been found. The problem is at present insoluble on account of practical considerations; moreover, the task of correctly allocating cost elements is fraught with theoretical difficulties of principle, which cannot be overcome by any degree of improvement of the accounting systems of individual economic units and the economy as a whole."[19]

No-Profit, No-Loss Pricing: As the name indicates, the no-profit, no-loss theory holds that the price should be fixed in such a way that there will be neither any profit nor any loss. In other words, the price should just cover all the costs of production.

The average cost price usually includes the normal profit. The no-profit, no-loss price, however, does not provide for normal profit.

Unlike the marginal cost price, the no-profit, no-loss price does not require any subsidy because in this case there is no deficit in the revenue because of the equality between the total revenue and total cost. In other words, there is no need for any "cross subsidisation".

When the price is fixed on the no-profit, no-loss basis, the non-consumers of the commodity or service are not compelled, directly or indirectly, to bear a burden for the benefit of the consumers. At the same time the consumers are given a fair deal, for they bear nothing more than the actual cost of their consumption.

Like the average cost price, the no-profit, no-loss price relieves the state of the burden of mopping up resources to make good the deficit incurred when marginal cost pricing is adopted — when the production is subject to the law of decreasing costs.

Professor Arthur Lewis argues that if the corporation makes a profit or loss, it should be required to adjust its prices so as to eliminate the profit or loss. He advocates this principle on the ground that it will prevent over or under-expansion of the industries concerned and will avoid inflationary or deflationary tendencies.

Profit-Making Pricing: The theory of making profits purports that the prices should be high enough to provide some surplus after absorbing all the costs.

That the public sector enterprises should generate a surplus with which to finance future development plans has been widely accepted today.

Many developing countries have assigned a very important role to the public sector in national development plans. Since the taxable capacity is low and the scope of domestic resource mobilisation through other means is limited, the public sector, which has absorbed large chunks of investment, should be expected to make a significant contribution to the pool of investible funds.

Many economists and planners argued that as the public sector acquired a more prominent position, the role of taxation, deficit, financing, etc., in resource mobilisation should decline and the surplus provided by the public sector should increase. In an economy where the public sector occupies an important position in production and supply, there is good scope for mopping up resources by an appropriate public sector pricing policy. As a matter of fact, in communist countries, most of the financial requirements of the government are met by the surpluses generated by public enterprises through a pricing strategy that serves this purpose.

It may be pointed out here that had the public sector in India generated a reasonable return on the enormous capital investment in them, the pace of economic progress would have been faster. In the absence of a satisfactory level of surpluses from the public sector, we were compelled to put up with more taxes, more deficit financing (which are inflationary in nature) and the slow pace of economic growth.

Indian Public Sector and Profit Objective

> **Making profits to make resources available for investment has been certainly an important objective of the Indian public sector.**

It is quite clear from the plan documents and the pronouncements of people like the Prime Minister that the public sector in India is expected to augment resource availability for national development by making profits. According to the late Prime Minister, Mrs. Gandhi, we advocated the public sector for three reasons: "to gain control of the commanding heights of the economy; to promote critical development in terms of social gain or strategic value rather than primarily on consideration of profit; and to provide commercial surpluses with which to finance further economic development."[20]

A 12 per cent return on investment in the public sector was generally regarded as reasonable.

V. K. R. V. Rao, a well-known economist who was also a Union-Minister and a member of the Planning Commission, pleaded that the pricing policy of the public enterprises "should be such as to promote the growth of national income and the rate of this growth ...Public enterprises must make profits, and the larger the share of public enterprises in all enterprises, the greater is the need for their making profits. Profits constitute the surplus available for savings and investments on the one hand and contribution to national social welfare programmes on the other; and if public enterprises do not make profits, the national surplus available for stepping up the rate of investment and the increase of social welfare will suffer a corresponding reduction... Hence, the need for giving up the irrational belief that public enterprise should, by definition, be run on a no-profit basis."[21]

As the Taxation Enquiry Commission has remarked, "in certain cases, where the state has made a substantial investment, a policy of regulating prices so as to secure an adequate return on the capital invested is not only unobjectionable but may, indeed, be desirable. This is particularly so in the conditions of economically underdeveloped countries, where public enterprise itself, fostered at state expense, may in turn play a role in financing the country's development."[22] The Industrial Policy Resolution, 1956, states: "It is to be expected that public enterprises will augment the revenues of the state and provide resources for further development in fresh fields".

Our Five Year Plan documents have pointed out that the public sector should make a significant contribution to the pool of investible funds by generating commercial surpluses. As one Plan document has observed, "substantial investments have been made in the public sector,... and every effort must be made to ensure that they yield an adequate surplus on the basis of which to plan a further advance. Development has, in due course, to become self-financing; the surpluses from past investments constitute the source for further development. It is important that in choosing their projects for implementation, the Central as well as State Governments keep constantly in mind the needs to get results from these investments as quickly as possible."[23]

The Fourth Plan mentioned that the government had accepted in principle the recommendation of the Committee on the Working of State Electricity Boards (Venkataraman Committee) that the rate of return on capital employed should be raised to 11 per cent per annum on the basis of a phased programme. As regards the irrigation charges, the Plan document cited the important recommendations of the Committee to suggest ways and means of improving financial returns from irrigation projects (Nijalingappa Committee), and underscored the need to mop up resources from the beneficiaries of the irrigation projects. The Plan document further suggested: "Efforts should be directed to raise the rate of returns on capital employed to 15 per cent by industrial and commercial undertakings other than public utilities."[24]

The Fifth Plan also emphasised the need to ensure a reasonable return on public sector investments by improving their operational efficiency. The Draft Five Year Plan, 1978-83, suggested that the Central Government's non-departmental undertakings should aim at earning a return on investment of 10 per cent per annum.

The Sixth Plan has suggested: "Almost all the Central and State enterprises would need to adopt appropriate pricing policies in order to achieve an adequate rate of return on capital employed. Although a substantial revision of tariffs, freight rates and prices had been undertaken in the past, the additional receipts have largely been absorbed by escalation of working expenses due to the revision of emoluments to their employees, rise in input costs, etc. It is, therefore, essential to ensure that the additional resources generated by these enterprises during the Sixth Plan period by way of revision of prices, tariffs, etc., are not eroded by cost increases and that efforts are made simultaneously to secure the maximum feasible improvement in the functioning and efficiency of these enterprises."[25]

The preceding paragraphs make it quite clear that the public sector in India is required to make a profit to step up the level of investment and accelerate the pace of economic progress. This, however, does not mean that each and every enterprise is expected to make a contribution by way of profit.

There are some public enterprises which are not specifically required to operate on commercial basis, while most of the enterprises are expected to generate commercial surpluses. For instance, the agreements between the Government of India, the WHO and the UNICEF require the Hindustan Insecticides and the Hindustan Antibiotics to operate on no-profit, no-loss basis. The ECGC has also been intended to be run on the same principle. Most of public enterprises, including the Road Transport Corporations, Electricity Boards and State Financial Corporations, have been expected to conduct their business on commercial lines.

In short, public enterprises as a whole should generate commercial surpluses to augment the pool of investible funds.

Influences and Guidelines on Pricing Policy

A uniform price for all the public enterprises is ruled out because the nature of goods or services they produce or provide, the production function and the market situations are not uniform.

On the basis of the nature of the business, public enterprises in India may be classified into the following categories:

1. Enterprises engaged in the production or provision of public utilities and services.
2. Enterprises engaged in the production of consumer goods.
3. Enterprises engaged in the production of basic and capital goods.
4. Enterprises engaged in the trading business.
5. Financial enterprises.

The determinants of the pricing policies of these different classes of enterprises, obviously, differ.

The Administrative Reforms Commission has recommended that the following principles should be kept in view in formulating the pricing policies of public enterprises.[26]

1. Public enterprises in the industrial and manufacturing field should aim at earning surpluses to make a substantial contribution to capital development out of their earnings, besides making a contribution to the national exchequer.
2. Public enterprises should in any event pay their way and should not run into losses except in pursuance of the express directive issued by the government in public interest.
3. In the case of public utilities and services, greater stress should be laid on output than on return on investment, the former being extended up to a level at which marginal costs is equal to price.
4. While determining the price structure commensurate with the surpluses expected from them, public enterprises should keep the level of output as near the rated capacity as possible, subject, of course, to the volume of demand for the product.

The Bureau of Public Enterprises is intimately concerned with the problems of pricing. Its main activity is directed towards dealing with specific cases as they arise, rather than with general industry studies. It also issues guidelines to public enterprises on pricing policies. The BPE issued the following guidelines.[27]

1. For enterprises which produce goods and services in competition with other domestic producers, the normal market forces of supply and demand will operate, and their products will be governed by the prevailing market prices.
2. For enterprises which operate under monopolistic or semi-monopolistic conditions, the landed cost of comparable imported goods would be the ceiling. Within this ceiling it would be open to the enterprises to have price negotiations and fix prices at suitable levels. If the landed cost is found or believed to be artificially low, or in other exceptional circumstances it is considered necessary to have higher prices, then the matter should be referred to the Administrative Ministry, the BPE (now DPE), and the Ministry of Finance.
3. Ministries and government departments and public sector enterprises should invariably purchase their requirements from public sector undertakings to the maximum possible extent. Quality requirements and reasonable delivery schedules should of course be enforced, subject to negotiation for agreement on price. Price preference not exceeding 10 per cent will be admissible to public sector undertakings. Where a public sector undertaking requires price preference of more than 10 per cent, the Purchasing Ministry, department or public enter prices should endeavour to reach an agreement by negotiation; where such an agreement is not possible within a reasonable time, the cases have to be submitted to the Cabinet Committee for Economic Coordination. Price preference even up to 10 per cent cannot be permanent or taken for granted.

Every effort should be made to bring down costs and achieve competitiveness.

The pricing policies and practices are profoundly influenced by the competitive situation, the nature of the industry, the supply-purchase relationship with other public enterprises and government departments, etc. "Even a cursory examination of the market conditions under which the public enterprises produce and sell their goods and services would reveal several types of situations. Some enterprises come under a system of price control and regulation, while others operate in the open market; still others operate in international markets. For some enterprises, the Central Government is the sole buyer, others are linked to State Governments and other public enterprises which are their main customers. One can easily see that the managements of public enterprises are not entirely free to set their prices without some constraints."[28]

On the basis of the pricing criteria and practices of different kinds of enterprises, the Bureau of Public Enterprises has made the following broad classifications.[29]

1. Enterprises under a system of price control by the government.
2. Enterprises which sell their products entirely to the government.
3. Enterprises which sell their products mainly to State Government enterprises or to other public sector enterprises.
4. Enterprises selling their products in the international market.
5. Enterprises operating in the open market.
6. Steel.
7. Price fixation by arbitration and award by the government.

Pricing Practices

Some examples of the pricing policies and methods followed by public enterprises are given below:

- ***Administered Prices:*** In the past, prices of certain commodities like steel, coal, oil, fertilisers, etc., were fixed by the government. As a part of the economic reforms, most of the goods have been freed from the administered prices.
- ***No-Profit, No-Loss Prices:*** Some undertakings like the Hindustan Antibiotics price the products on the no-profit, no-loss basis.
- ***Cost-Plus Prices:*** Several enterprises fix prices on a cost-plus basis.
- ***Competitive Prices:*** The liberalisation has increased the relevance of this strategy.
- ***Following the Leader:*** Price decisions of a few public enterprises are based on the behaviour of the leader. For instance, the Kerala Soaps and Oils followed this strategy in respect of some of their products.
- ***Parity Pricing:*** For the products of some of the enterprises which had a monopoly position in the domestic market, parity with the landed cost of the imported product was sought. This was, for instance, true of the Hindustan Shipyard which established the UK parity.

- ***Subsidised Prices:*** Some enterprises which enjoy the benefit of a subsidy from the government sell their products below the cost of production. An example was the price of the contraceptive produced by the Hindustan Latex.
- ***Trade Association Pricing:*** Air-India International, like other international airlines, adopts the fares and freights determined by the International Air Transport Association (IATA). Similarly, the Shipping Corporation of India fixes its prices on the basis of the recommendations of the Shipping Conference.
- ***Discriminatory Pricing:*** Many public enterprises practice price discrimination. This has been true of public sector financial institutions, Electricity Boards and the Railways.

GOVERNMENT AND PARLIAMENTARY CONTROLS OVER PUBLIC ENTERPRISES

It is the general policy, overall performance and decisions with long-term implications that are generally sought to be controlled by the Government and Parliament.

A certain amount of autonomy is a necessary condition for the efficient functioning of any enterprise; and the public enterprises are no exception to this. But public enterprises have been established with public funds to serve social purposes, and hence, there should be public control over them to ensure that they discharge their duties promptly and efficiently and fulfil their objectives. Public control is exercised through the government and Parliament, the representatives of the people. Government and Parliament controls over public enterprises do not mean that the enterprises should not have any autonomy. They should necessarily have a certain amount of autonomy. *Autonomy vs. Accountability* has been, however, one of the unsettled issues in public enterprises.

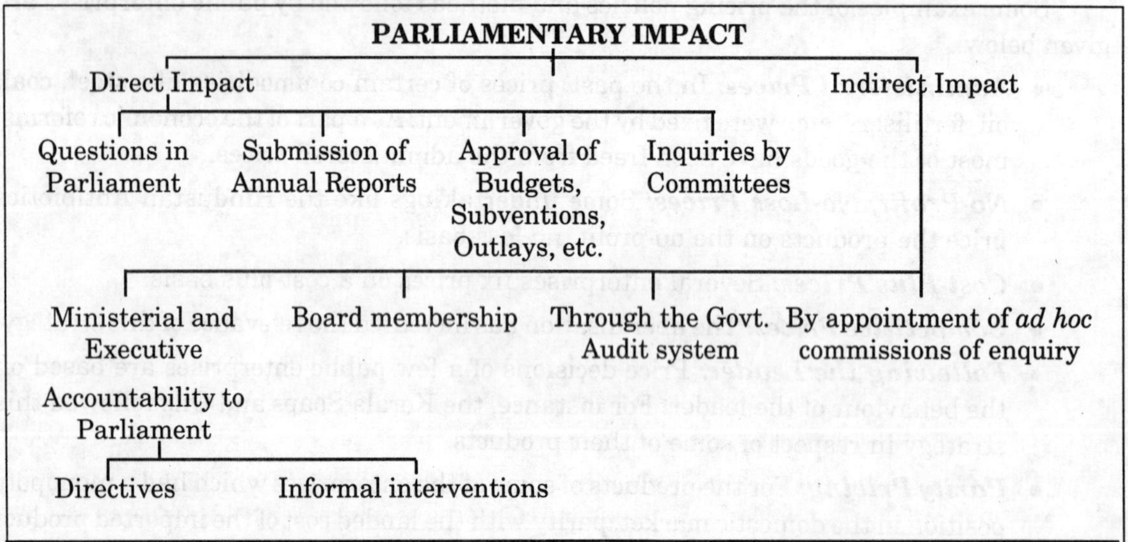

Fig. 5.1: Parliamentary Impact on the Public Sector

(Adopted from the United Nations publication. *Organisation, Management and Supervision of Public Enterprises in Developing Countries* — A Study prepared by V.V. Ramanandhan)

Pandit Nehru observed: "I have no doubt that the normal governmental procedure applied to a public enterprise will lead to the failure of that public enterprise. Therefore, we have to evolve a system for working public enterprises where, on the one hand, there are adequate checks and protection and on the other, enough freedom for that enterprise to work quickly and without delay. Ultimately, it has to be judged by the results, though one cannot judge a government enterprise by financial results alone. In judging big enterprise, one has to judge by final results. Of course, there are checks and audit and all that, but checks come afterwards. The chief man on the top must be able quickly to do what he wants to do."[30]

Government control over public enterprises is usually exercised by giving guidelines and directions for the functioning of the enterprise; appointing the top managerial and administrative personnel like the Chairman, Managing Director and members of the Boards of Directors; requiring government approval for long-term plans, large investments and major policy changes; calling for periodic reports and returns; accounts and audit control, etc. Parliamentary control is exercised by discussions in Parliament and parliamentary committees.

In the early days, the government tended to exercise too much control and only limited powers were delegated to enterprises. However, on the recommendations of the Administrative Reforms Commission, it was decided to reserve only the following well-defined powers for the government.

1. Appointments of chief executives and full-time and part-time members of the Boards of Directors.
2. Sanctioning of capital programmes involving expenditure of a certain magnitude.
3. Approval of five-year annual plans of development and capital budgets.
4. Authorisation of capital to be raised and the conditions thereof.
5. Approval of the revenue budget where a deficit was required to be met by the government.
6. Calling for returns, accounts and other information on the activities of the enterprise.
7. Giving directions to the enterprise on matters involving national security or substantial public interest.

Except the chief executives and members of the Boards of Directors who are appointed by the government, appointments to all-posts are made by the enterprises. Government nominates on the Board of Directors usually two government officials, one representing the administrative ministry and the other representing the Ministry of Finance. These part-time directors, by providing a two-way channel, are expected to facilitate liaison between the government and the public enterprise.

The limit of the expenditure the management of the enterprise can incur by itself without requiring the approval of the government usually varies with the size of the enterprise. All the investments beyond the specified limit require the approval of the Public Investment Board, which is headed by the Secretary (Expenditure) in the Ministry of

Finance. To evaluate the investment proposal, the Public Investment Board can avail of the professional expertise and advice of the Project Appraisal Division of the Planning Commission and the Department of Public Enterprises. The important criteria adopted by the Planning Commission are the relevance of the proposed investment to the overall National Plan, the availability of resources and the social cost-benefit analysis. The Department of Public Enterprises, on the other hand, evaluates the proposal from the point of view of its financial, technical and economic viability. Thus, the Planning Commission's appraisal pertains to the macro aspects and that of the BPE to the micro aspects of the project.

In India, public enterprises are placed under the control of different functional ministries. The ministries have the responsibility to ensure that enterprises under their administrative control function effectively and in a manner conducive to the achievement of the objectives underlying their formation. For this purpose, they lay down, in consultation with the management of the enterprises, their annual targets of production/ turnover, and carry out a periodical appraisal of their performance at review meetings.

Baveja[31] points out that although the government is empowered to issue directives to enterprises to conform to its policies, this is not the normal practice followed except in certain very special cases. The compliance by the enterprises with the policies of the government is achieved by the issue of instructions which are in the nature of guidelines or model rules, and it is left to the judgement of individual enterprises to adopt the suggested course of action with or without adjustments. The guidelines issued by the government relate to various matters, such as personnel and wage policies, general conditions of the service of employees, model conduct rules, economy in the field of construction, and provision of amenities in townships, etc.

Parliamentary Control and Public Accountability

Parliamentary control is a very important aspect of the performance appraisal of public enterprises in India. One of the former Speakers of the Lower House of Parliament, Shri G. V. Mavalankar, once observed: "Merely because the system makes them autonomous, it does not follow that the system can take away the jurisdiction of Parliament for having a full probe into the administration of the autonomous body."[32]

There are three important methods by which Parliamentary control over public enterprises is exercised in India.

1. Holding Debates in Parliament: A debate on the performance or some other issue pertaining to public enterprises may be initiated during the budget debates, or on a discussion of the President's address, or by moving resolutions on any topic, by raising an half-hour discussion on a public undertaking, by moving a motion for adjournment on a matter of public importance, by short discussions on matters of urgent public importance, or "calling the attention" of the House to some urgent matter during discussions on reports of enquiries, or while introducing or amending the statutes of a corporation, or on a presentation of the annual reports.

2. By Interpellation: This means interrupting the proceedings in Parliament and demanding a statement or explanation from the Minister.

There is a practice of setting apart one opening hour of Parliament's meeting time for questions and answers. Members of the House give due notice of their questions to the Ministers and the Ministers concerned give the House the answers which they may prepare with the help of civil servants.

3. By Parliamentary Committees: Special Committees of Parliament, consisting of the members belonging to various parties, examine the various aspects of the functioning of public enterprises.

The CPU

In the earlier years, the Public Accounts Committee and the Estimates Committee of Parliament examined the working of public enterprises. But as these committees were overburdened with work, and also because the criteria for the appraisal of performance of public enterprises had to be different from those applied to the work of the government departments with which these committees were concerned, the Committee on Public. Undertakings was set up in 1964. The members of the CPU are drawn from both the Houses of Parliament. The terms of reference of the Committee are as follows:

(*i*) To examine the reports and accounts of public enterprises.

(*ii*) To examine the reports, if any, of the Comptroller and Auditor General of India on public enterprises.

(*iii*) To examine, in the context of the autonomy and efficiency of public enterprises, if their affairs are managed in accordance with sound business principles and prudent commercial practices, and to exercise such other functions in relation to public enterprises as may be allotted to it by the Speaker from time-to-time.

At the beginning of each financial year, the Committee on Public Undertakings selects for examination-in-depth some 8 to 10 enterprises. These studies cover in great depth every aspect of the working of the enterprises. The secretaries of the administrative ministries, the chief executives of public enterprises and other senior officials are required to appear before the Committee to give oral evidence. The reports of the Committee are presented to the Parliament. An examination of the working of an enterprise by the Parliamentary Committee is essentially in the nature of an evaluation of the performance of that enterprise, and it enables the Committee to make recommendations on how the working of that enterprise may be improved to enable it to discharge more effectively the role assigned to it.[33]

Apart from examining the working of individual enterprises, the CPU undertakes horizontal studies affecting public enterprises as a whole. Some of the horizontal studies of the Parliamentary Committee conducted include foreign collaboration in the public enterprises, financial management, public relations and publicity, personnel policies and the role and achievements of public undertakings.[34]

There is a mechanism available with the Committee to follow-up the implementation of its recommendations. The government is required to furnish the Committee within six months the replies showing the action taken on its recommendations. The replies are further processed by the Committee and a report is submitted to Parliament with the Committee's comments on the government's replies. In the words of Jyotirmoy Basu over the years, this Committee, like its counterpart, the Select Committee on Nationalised Industries in Britain, has become an effective watchdog of Parliament to oversee the functioning of public undertakings and to ensure that they play a stabilising role in the economy of the country.[35]

The annual reports and balance sheets of all the enterprises are required to be laid on the table of both Houses of Parliament within a period of nine months from the close of the accounting year. This provision is contained in the enactments relating to the setting up of statutory corporations as well as in the Companies Act. A consolidated annual report of the working of industrial and commercial undertakings of the Central Government is also required to be placed on the table of the House. It must, however, be noted that Parliament, as a matter of principle, does not generally extend its supervision to matters of day-to-day administration.[36]

The accountability of enterprises is also ensured by a systematic appraisal of their performance by the Audit Boards functioning under the Comptroller and Auditor-General. The accounts of the enterprises are subject to audit by commercial auditors (firms of chartered accountants) appointed on the advice of the Comptroller and Auditor-General. The latter is also authorised to conduct a supplementary or test audit through the Audit Board. These Audit Reports, together with the comments of the Comptroller and Auditor-General, are presented to Parliament and are available for the use of the Committee on Public Undertakings in its examination of the performance of public enterprises.[37]

DEPARTMENT OF PUBLIC ENTERPRISES

The Bureau of Public Enterprises was set up in the Ministry of Finance in 1965 to provide a central focal point of reference and consultation to deal with matters of common interest to public enterprises, like organisational patterns, methods of management, personnel policies, collaboration agreements, project scrutiny and clearance, project and corporate planning, etc. In 1985, the BPE was brought under the Ministry of Industry. In 1990, the BPE was conferred the status of a full-fledged Department and is now known as the Department of Public Enterprises (DPE) in the Ministry of Industry.

The Department of Public Enterprises acts as a nodal agency for all PSEs and assists in policy formulation pertaining to the role of PSEs in the economy as also in laying down policy guidelines on performance improvement and evaluation, financial accounting, personnel management and in related areas. It also collects, evaluates and maintains information on several areas in respect of PSEs. DPE also provides an interface between the Administrative Ministries and the PSEs. In fulfilling its role, it associates itself with other Ministries and organisations and also premier management institutes in the country.

Role and Tasks

The important role and task of the Department are the following:

1. General Policy relating to Public Sector.
2. Matters relating to issue of Presidential Directives and guidelines to Public Sector enterprises.
3. Formulation of policy guidelines pertaining to Public Sector Enterprises in areas like performance improvement and evaluation, financial management, personnel management, board structures, wage settlement, training, industrial relations, vigilance, performance appraisal, etc.
4. Matters relating to reservations of posts in the Public Sector Enterprises for certain classes of citizens.
5. All matters relating to Memorandum of Understanding between the Public Sector Enterprises and the Administrative Ministries/Departments.
6. Matters relating to delegation of powers to Board of Directors.
7. To undertake in-depth studies in respect of significant areas of functioning of Central PSEs.
8. Matters relating to International Centre for Public Enterprises (ICPE).
9. Matters relating to Standing Conference of Public Enterprises (SCOPE).
10. To monitor and evaluate the performance of PSEs and to act as a repository of data and to bring out an Annual Survey for the Parliament.
11. Settlement of disputes among public sector enterprises and between public sector enterprises and Government Departments except disputes relating to tax matters.
12. Advise on establishing new centrally sponsored enterprises including their capital and organisational structure and Memorandum and Articles of Association.
13. All policy matters relating to composition of Board of Director of PSEs, categorisation of top posts, scheduling of PSEs and notification of revised pay scales and DA admissible therein at periodical intervals.
14. Disinvestment Implementation of policy on Public Sector Enterprises.
15. Notify revised scales of pay for Board level executives and the DA admissible thereon at periodical intervals.
16. Coordination of training programmes for managerial personnel in Public Sector Enterprises.
17. Policy relating to deputation of Government officers to PSEs.
18. Assist any committee appointed by the Government to examine any aspect relating to PSEs.
19. Monitoring of performance of sick PSEs and preparing for PMO and Cabinet Secretariat appraising latest development regarding PSEs referred to BIFR.

NATIONALISATION

One of the important contributory factors to the growth and expansion of the public sector was the nationalisation of certain industries as a whole and certain undertakings in some of the other industries.

"Nationalisation is the establishment of the public ownership of the means of production by taking them over from private proprietors or foreign states, and subsequently transferring them to the control of the national government. Nationalisation is a complex process. Since it is initiated by the state, it always reflects changes in the alignment of political forces and interests, and is, therefore, primarily a political move. Since nationalisation brings about a change in the economic position of various groups, classes and forces and entails a redistribution of resources, it has far-reaching economic consequences; which is why, of course, it is undertaken. Naturally, nationalisation also affects social relations and brings about a change in the correlation of social forces. Finally, it affects political and economic relations with other states and groups."[38]

The earlier nationalisations in India had been in the strategic and critical sectors; but later the scope of nationalisation was widened.

The Industrial Policy Resolution of 1948 clearly stated that, "in any emergency, the government would always have the power to takeover any industry vital for national defence", and that the state will not "hesitate to intervene whenever the progress of an industry under private enterprise is unsatisfactory". And there had been a series of nationalisations.

The important objectives of nationalisation were:

1. To have effective control over the strategic and basic sectors of the economy.
2. To put an end to mismanagement by private capitalists.
3. To ensure better utilisation of the productive resources and to serve the genuine needs of the priority sectors and weaker sections.
4. To maintain employment and to safeguard the interests of the workers.
5. To protect the interests of consumers.
6. To take the necessary action for the development of the concerned industry or business.

We may recall here some of the important nationalisations, that took place after independence.

The banking sector witnessed four important nationalisations, including the nationalisation of the Reserve Bank of India in 1949. The Imperial Bank of India was nationalised and the State Bank of India was established in 1955. In 1969, fourteen major commercial banks in the private sector were nationalised. With the nationalisation of another six banks in 1980, more than 90 per cent of the commercial banking business came in the public sector.

The government has also established monopoly in the insurance business. In 1956, life insurance companies and in 1972 general insurance companies were nationalised.

The government acquired the Mazgaon Docks, Mumbai, and the Garden Reach Workshop, Kolkata, in 1960, and the Hindustan Shipyard in 1961.

The coking coal mines were taken over in 1972 and the non-coking mines in 1973. The next three years witnessed the nationalisation of foreign oil companies.

Apart from the nationalisation of certain industries, wholly or partially, individual undertakings in some other industries had also been nationalised to protect the interests of the workers and consumers to fulfil certain other objectives. The National Textile Corporation (NTC), set up in 1968, took over many sick mills. Under the Industries (Development and Regulation) Act, 1951, the government had taken over the management of a number of sick units. Thirteen sick units, earlier managed under the IDRA, were nationalised in 1980.

State Governments, too, have been showing interest in the nationalisation of certain important sectors. Road transport was a common area of nationalisation. Some States like Kerala had nationalised private forests and plantations owned by foreign companies.

The trend of nationalisation of the earlier decades has been reversed by the privatisation of the recent period.

A lot of criticisms have been directed against the performance of the nationalised sectors and undertakings. The nationalised business, by and large, failed to rise up to expectations. Hence, a strong denationalisation (privatisation) trend has set in.

As part of the economic reforms ushered in 1991, Government is trying to correct the past mistake by privatisation. (Also refer to the new public sector policy described elsewhere in this chapter).

PRIVATE SECTOR

In a mixed economy, the private sector, too, has an important role to play. Indeed, it is because of the appreciation of the positive role the private sector can play, and certain limitations of the public sector, that many socialists advocate a mixed economic system. The Industrial Policy Resolution of 1956, which still remained the core of India's industrial policy and which assigned a dominant role to the public sector in a number of vital industries, has made it very clear that, *as an agency for planned national development, in the context of the country's expanding economy, the private sector will have the opportunity to develop and expand.* It is, thus, clear that the adoption of the principle of the socialist pattern of society did not mean the end of the private sector. Instead the private sector was.assigned, and was expected to play, a very important role.

According to the Industrial Policy Resolution, 1956, it was expected that the development of the industries outside the Schedules A & B would be undertaken ordinarily through the initiative and enterprise of the private sector, though it was open to the State to start any industry even in this category. It was "the policy of the State to encourage the development of these industries in the private sector, in accordance with the programmes formulated in successive Five Year Plans, by ensuring the development of transport, power and other services, and by appropriate fiscal and other measures. The state will continue to foster institutions to provide financial aid to these industries, and special assistance will be given to enterprises organised on cooperative lines for industrial and agricultural purposes." While shortcomings still exist, it must be said to the credit of the government that a remarkable progress has been achieved on these lines. It may also be pointed out here that a number of private sector enterprises that already existed in the industries included in the Schedule A have been allowed to develop further.

The Industrial Policy Resolution of 1956 has also made it clear that, "industrial undertakings in the private sector have necessarily to fit into the framework of the social and economic policy of the State and will be subject to control and regulation in terms of the Industries (Development and Regulation) Act and other relevant legislations. The Government of India, however, recognises that it would, in general, be desirable to allow such undertakings to develop with as much freedom as possible, consistent with the targets and objectives of the national plan. When there exist in the same industry both privately and publicly-owned units, it would continue to be the policy of the state to give fair and non-discriminatory treatment to both of them."

The preceding paragraphs give some idea of the government's policy towards the private sector and the industrial spheres open to that sector. Even in the areas where the private sector has been allowed, its operations and development have been regulated by the government in the public interest. The large industrial houses and foreign concerns, particularly, had been subject to a number of checks and controls. Their role had been confined to certain important areas like the heavy investment sector, the core sector, the export sector and backward areas development. The government's policy was to prefer small and new entrepreneurs to large industrial houses in the private sector, wherever possible.

The private sector has been dominant in most of the consumer goods industries. It plays an important role in a number of capital goods industries, too. In a number of important industries, it functions side by side with the public sector.

The joint sector also reflects to some extent the importance of the role of the private sector.

With the new industrial policy announced on July 24, 1991, and modifications introduced thereafter, the role of the private sector has been substantially expanded. Now private enterprises are allowed in all but two industries. Only a very small number of industries are now under industrial licensing (i.e., except in these industries there are no entry and growth restrictions on the private sector). The scope of private sector is increased by the withdrawal of the State from many industries and privatisation (See the section on new public sector policy changes).

The restrictions on large firms and industrial houses and preempting them from many important industries in the past very adversely affected the industrial and economic development.

JOINT SECTOR

The term joint sector refers to the enterprise owned and managed jointly by the private sector and the government/public sector undertakings. The Dutt Committee (Industrial Licensing Policy Inquiry Committee) has defined the concept of the joint sector in the following terms: "The joint sector would, in our view, include units in which both public and private investments have taken place and where the state takes an active part in direction and control."

Formation of Joint Sector Enterprises

Joint sector enterprises may be brought into being by any one of the following ways:

1. The Central Government and private entrepreneurs may jointly set up new enterprises. Sometimes, the Central Government and one or more State Governments together may set up enterprises in partnership with the private sector. (It may be pointed out that the public may also hold shares in joint sector enterprises).
2. State Governments or their industrial development corporations may set up new companies jointly with private partners, involving equity participation by both the partners.
3. Public financial institutions may, through equity participation or conversion of loans or debentures into equity, transform enterprises promoted by private entrepreneurs into joint sector companies.
4. The existing private enterprises may be transformed into joint sector enterprises by the government or government companies acquiring a part of the equity or converting debt into equity or by contributing to an increase in the share capital.
5. The existing public sector companies may be transformed into joint sector enterprises through the sale of some equity shares to private entrepreneurs or the general public. The disinvestments policy of the Government has been, resulting in the transformation of several PSEs to joint sector enterprises.

Industrial investment corporations and industrial development corporations in a number of States have actively promoted joint sector enterprises. In a number of these cases, 26 per cent of the equity is held by the SIIC/SIDC, 25 per cent by private promoter(s) and 49 per cent of the shares are offered to the public.

In pre-independence days, the Princely States of Mysore and Hyderabad had established several industrial enterprises in which equity participation by the general public was permitted. In the years following Independence, a number of companies were floated by the government in collaboration with the private sector by sharing ownership, management and control with them. This form of industrial organisation was found appropriate for the import of foreign technology and capital, as in Cochin Refineries (1963), Madras Refineries (1965), and Madras Fertilisers (1966); for the utilisation of indigenous entrepreneurial and managerial resources, as in Air-India (1947); for the use of organisational capabilities of existing industrial houses, such as the Bird Heilgers group in Bolani Ores (1957); and the mobilisation of financial resources from the public, as in the Gujarat State Fertiliser Company (1965).[39]

Rationale of Joint Sector

> **The joint sector is conceived as a marriage between the managerial expertise of the private sector and the financial resources and social orientation of the public sector.**

It has been viewed as an effective means of achieving a mixed economy. "In a sense, joint sector enterprises represent an application of the concept of mixed economy at the micro level."

The main objectives and advantages of the joint sector are the following:

1. Curbing Concentration of Economic Power: The Dutt Committee advocated the joint sector, viewing it as an important means of curbing the increasing concentration of economic power. The Committee even regarded the joint sector as possibly more effective than licensing in achieving this objective. This was regarded as a very important rationale of the joint sector in the past.

2. Social Control of Industry: Government participation in equity and management is expected to give a social orientation to the enterprise. The joint sector would ensure that the management of industry is conducted according to the overall policies laid down by the government, and that public interest and not merely private profit would guide the operations of the enterprises. "Used effectively and with care, the joint sector can be a more useful instrument than all rules and regulations and penal powers of the state in ensuring that development is according to the plan. The concept of the joint sector has thus the potential, if properly used, to get the best advantages out of the mixed economy which has been accepted in our country as a matter of state policy."[40]

3. Acceleration of Economic Development: The joint sector, by mobilising and augmenting the productive resources, can accelerate the pace of economic development. It enables private entrepreneurs and the State agencies to promote or invest in a greater number of projects than would otherwise be possible. "The resources of the private sector in savings, investments and entrepreneurship can be harnessed in the joint sector with active State help to supplement the efforts made by the State in the public sector without the private profit motive being allowed to vitiate the effort."[41]

4. Promotion of Mixed Economy: It is also expected that the joint sector will promote the mixed economy and help achieve development objectives. "The basic justification of the idea of mixed economy is to harness all the productive forces of society, State as well as private, to the task of economic development with a view to accelerating the process. By allowing the private sector to play its part in the process, the State is able to develop entrepreneurship outside the government, and enlist it to supplement its entrepreneurial role; Similarly, a mixed economy allows the State to take advantage of voluntary savings in society for purpose of investment to supplement the resources it is able to mobilise for this purpose."[42]

5. Broadbasing of Entrepreneurship: Another advantage of the joint sector is that it helps broadbase entrepreneurship by encouraging new and small entrepreneurs. The joint sector enables potential entrepreneurs with small financial resources and less experience to participate in large enterprises as the public sector shares investment and the risk. "Many private entrepreneurs, whose means are not comparable with those of large companies, may come forward and take advantage of joint sector opportunities because the government's support and facilitating roles that are assured to them. There is some evidence of this at the State level, where the industrial development corporations seem to be playing the role of broadbasing entrepreneurship."[43]

COOPERATIVE SECTOR

The co-operative sector, properly organised and functioning, is a real people's sector.

In India, the cooperative sector has been assigned an important role in the development of many sectors. The First Five Year Plan envisaged the cooperative sector to cover a number of vital areas like agriculture, rural and small-scale industry, retail distribution, housing, etc.

Objectives

The cooperative idea took a concrete shape in India for the first time in 1904, when the Cooperative Credit Societies Act — a measure designed to combat rural indebtedness and provide for the registration of credit societies — was passed. Later, in 1912, the Cooperative Societies Act provided for the registration of non-credit societies as well as federations of cooperatives. Since then, the cooperative movement has made progress, especially in the fields of agricultural credit, marketing and processing of agricultural produce, supply of farm inputs and distribution of consumer goods. By far the largest number of societies are in the agricultural credit sector. The primary agricultural credit societies cover over 96 per cent of the rural areas.

The important objectives of the development of the cooperative sector are prevention of concentration of economic power, wider dispersal of ownership of productive resources, active involvement of people in development programmes, augmentation of the productive resources and speedier economic development, liquidation of unemployment and poverty, etc.

State Participation

One of the important aspects of the development of the cooperative sector in India, as in a number of the other countries, is *State participation.*

According to Weerman, the following are the main background factors or influences which lead to a relationship between the state and cooperatives in developing countries.[44]

1. The need to give legal recognition to cooperative societies and to provide for their proper management and supervision in the interest of the movement.
2. The need to safeguard the rights of the people *vis-a-vis* these societies.
3. The need to prevent any abuse or privileges accorded to cooperatives.

4. The need to promote the movement because:
   (*a*) It is, *per se*, desirable and nobody other than the government is likely to take the initiative in promoting it.
   (*b*) It is the best means of national development.
   (*c*) It solves the problem of lack of leadership and local personnel for the diffusion of new ideas and techniques.

The important ways in which the state patronises the co-operative movement in India are: State partnership in the share capital of cooperatives; loans to societies; subsidies and grants; guarantees; contribution to risk fund; tax concessions; legal concessions and sanctions; training and education; help from the Reserve Bank and other banking organisations that help the cooperatives; and supply of government officers on deputation.

Processing and Industrial Cooperatives

Our industrial policy statements have emphasised the role of the cooperative sector in the industrialisation of the country, especially by developing cottage, village and small-scale industries. In the large and medium industries sector, certain agro-industries like sugar, jute and cotton have been considered to be ideally suited for the cooperative sector. At one time the Government of India had also made it a policy that new sugar factories would be allowed only in the public and cooperative sectors.

Today, there are about 45,300 industrial cooperatives with a membership of nearly 2.5 million. The National Federation of Industrial Cooperatives assists in the marketing of the products of member societies.

The structure of processing units established in the cooperative sector conforms to two distinct patterns, namely, (*a*) Units established by independent processing units; and (*b*) Units established as adjuncts to cooperative marketing societies.

Under the first category fall the larger units, such as cooperative sugar factories, spinning mills and solvent extraction plants. Medium and small units, such as rice mills, oil mills, cotton ginning and pressing units, jute baling units, etc., fall under the second category.

The cooperative sector has significant presence in certain industries like cotton textiles, sugar and fertiliser. The Indian Farmers Fertiliser Cooperative Ltd. (IFFCO) is a unique venture of the cooperative movement in India in the field of large-scale fertiliser manufacture.

Storage, Distribution and Marketing Cooperatives

The National Cooperative Development Corporation is responsible for the planning, promotion and financing of the programme of augmenting the storage capacity of the cooperatives at various levels. There are a very large number of rural godowns and marketing godowns. There are also a number of cold storage units.

Cooperatives in India play a significant role in the distribution of agricultural inputs, such as fertilizers, seeds, pesticides, agricultural implements and credit. A large share of the total fertilizers distributed in India are sold through the cooperative distribution system.

The cooperatives have also diversified their activities to cover new lines of business, like the production, processing and distribution of improved agricultural implements and the setting up of agro-service centres. (For the role of cooperatives in the Public Distribution System, see the chapter on *Price and Distribution Controls*).

The cooperative marketing structure consists of a large number of primary cooperative marketing societies, covering all the important agricultural markets in the country.

The National Agricultural Cooperative Marketing Federation (NAFED), which, represents the cooperative marketing societies in the country, promotes inter-State and export trade of farm produce.

Functional Cooperatives

Cooperatives for the weaker sections of society provide increased employment and income opportunities to different sections of the community, such as small and marginal farmers and fishermen. Functional cooperatives for dairy, fishery and poultry mainly relate to the service of the weaker sections.

There are also a very large number of primary housing cooperatives in the country.

Multipurpose Cooperatives

As part of the programme of economic development of tribals, primary cooperatives in tribal areas were reorganised to enable them to function as multipurpose societies providing short, medium and long-term credit to tribals, undertaking collection and marketing of agricultural and minor forest produce, arranging for supply of agriculture inputs as well as essential consumer goods. State level cooperative tribal development corporations/federations have been established in a number of States to serve as apex organisations for the marketing of minor forest produce and consumer goods.

National Level Cooperative Federations: A major development over the past one decade, has been the emergence of national cooperative federations which have added a new dimension to the cooperative infrastructure. With the National Cooperative Union of India at the apex, the other national level cooperative organisations, include the National Agricultural Cooperative Marketing Federation, the All-India State Cooperative Banks Federation, the National Federation of Cooperative Sugar Factories, the National Cooperative Land Development Banks Federation, the National Cooperative Consumer's Federation, the National Federation of Industrial Cooperatives, the All-India Federation of Cooperative Spinning Mills, the National Cooperative Housing Federation, the National Cooperative Dairy Federation of India and the National Federation of Cooperative Urban Banks and Credit Societies.

In the context of a national pattern which is being evolved, the system of workers' participation in management is being introduced in large cooperative industrial units. Special cooperative programmes directed towards increasing employment and income opportunities for the vulnerable sections have been evolved and are being implemented.

The National Cooperative Development Corporation has also extended its activities to cover cooperative programmes for weaker sections.

Problems

While the overall progress of the cooperative movement appears to be striking, there are wide regional disparities. The level of development of agricultural cooperatives is not uniform in all the States.

The cooperative movement in India is very adversely affected by political overshadowing. Many cooperatives are controlled by politicians and/or the economi-cally powerful members.

Many cooperative societies are virtually defunct. Many others are languishing due to financial, organisational and administrative problems.

SUMMARY

On the basis of the ownership pattern, the industrial sector of India consists, broadly, of public, private, joint and cooperative sectors. The development of these sectors was directed by the Industrial policy. The industrial policy until 1991 was characterised by a dominant role assigned to the public sector.

The *Industrial Policy Resolution of 1948,* reserved eight industries to the public sector. The *Industrial Policy Resolution of 1956,* enlarged the role of the public sector by increasing this list to seventeen and earmarking twelve industries to be progressively State-owned and in which the State would, therefore, generally take the initiative in establishing new units.

The four decades until 1991 witnessed a substantial growth and expansion of the public sector in India. Nationalisations also contributed to the growth and expansion of the public sector. The public sector gained control over the commanding heights of the economy. The performance of the public sector, however, was far from satisfactory. The industrial policy announced in 1991, which heralded the economic liberalisation, substantially contracted the role of the public sector. The number of industries reserved for the public sector was reduced to eight and by 2001 May, all industries except atomic energy and railway transport was thrown open to the private sector. Privatisation of public sector units is also an important aspect of the new policy. In short, the industrial development of the country is now left mostly to the private sector.

Besides the public sector, the joint sector and cooperative sectors had been promoted by the Government as a strategy to prevent concentration of economic power in the private sector. With almost all industries open to the private sector without any entry and growth restrictions, the current industrial policy has no specific tenets in favour of the public, joint or cooperative sectors.

Had not the Government suppressed the development potential of the private sector, many Indians companies would have become major players in the global market.

REFERENCES

1. Bureau of Public Enterprises, *Public Enterprises Survey, 1983-84.*
2. Administrative Reforms Commission (A.R.C.), *Report of the Study Team on Public Sector Undertakings,* Manager of Publications, New Delhi, 1967, p. 10.

3. *Ibid.*, pp. 10-11.
4. *Ibid.*, p.13.
5. *Ibid.*, p. 14.
6. *Ibid.*, p. 14.
7. *Ibid.*, p. 14.
8. *Ibid.*, p. 11.
9. *Ente National Idoca buri* (the Great Petroleum Corporation).
10. *Institute per la Ricostruzione Industriale* (Institute for Reconstruction of Industry).
11. A.R.C. *op. cit.*, p. 15.
12. *Ibid.*, p. 18.
13. *Ibid.*, p. 18.
14. *Ibid.*, p. 19.
15. *Ibid.*, pp. 36-37.
16. *Ibid.*, pp. 36-37.
17. Gupta K. R., (Ed.), *Pricing in Public Enterprises,* Atlantic Publishers & Distributors, New Delhi, 1978, p. 9.
18. *Ibid.*, p. 16.
19. *Ibid.*, pp. 16-17.
20. Cited in Government of India, *Public Sector Forges Ahead,* Publications Division, New Delhi, 1975, p. 5.
21. Cited in Gupta K. R., *op. cit.*, p. 19.
22. *Ibid*, p. 19.
23. Government of India, *Third Five Year Plan,* p. 116.
24. Government of India, *Fourth Five Year Plan,* p. 84.
25. Government of India, *Sixth Five Year Plan* (1980-85), p. 63.
26. ARC. *op. cit.*
27. Cited in Khera, S. S., *Government in Business,* National Publishing House, New Delhi, 1977, p. 344.
28. Government of India, *Public Sector Forges Ahead, op. cit.*, p. 18.
29. Cited in Khera S. S., *Government in Business, op. cit.*, p. 318.
30. "Nehru on Public Sector", *Yojana,* January 26, 1981, p. 16.
31. G. C. Baveja, "Relationship of Indian Public Enterprises with Government and Parliament", in *Issues in Public Enterprises Development* (Report of a Seminar organised by the Commonwealth Secretariat and the Government of India, New Delhi, 27th February, 3 March, 1978).
32. *Ibid.*
33. Baveja, *Ibid.*

34. *Ibid.*
35. *Ibid.*
36. *Ibid.*
37. *Ibid.*
38. Kolesov V., *The Public Sector*, Sterling Publishers Pvt. Ltd., New Delhi, 1980, pp. 34-35.
39. Samuel, Paul, Bhattacharya S. K., and Kuchhal S. C., "Joint Sector: Guidelines for Policy", *Economic and Political Weekly,* December 9, 1972.
40. Dutt R. C., "The Joint Sector Organisation", in Chakraborti A. M., (Ed.),.*The Joint Sector,* ICSI, New Delhi, 1974, p. 49.
41. *Ibid.*
42. *Ibid.*
43. Samuel, Paul, *et al., op. cit.*
44. Cited in Purusha Shetty, *State Participation in Corporation* (a Dissertation submitted in partial fulfilment of the requirement for the Degree of Master of Arts in Cooperation, University of Mysore, Mysore, 1981).

☆☆☆

CHAPTER

6

PRIVATISATION AND DISINVESTMENT

A strong reversal of the trend of the statist economic expansion set in globally, since around the 1980, and has become the hallmark of the new wave of economic reforms that has been sweeping across the world. The bold initiatives taken by Prime Minister Margaret Thatcher in the UK have had far reaching impact in the developed economies. Privatisation has been very important integral part of economic reforms in the erstwhile communist countries. Non-communist developing economies too have been carrying out privatisation in varying forms, degrees and measure of success. In short, the trend towards privatisation has been observed in developed and developing economies; in market-oriented and socialist, including communist countries; and cuts across socio-cultural systems. During 1980-92 alone more than 8,500 state-owned enterprises were privatised in over 80 countries.

> **Privatisation marks a shift from dogmatism to pragmatism and amounts to a reversal of a policy assidously pursued for decades.**

Privatisation means transfer of ownership and / or management of an enterprise from the public sector to the private sector. It also means the withdrawal of the State from an industry or sector, partially or fully. Another dimension of privatisation is opening up of an industry that has been reserved for the public sector to the private sector.

Expansion of Public Sector and its Defects

In the 1960s, there was a trend towards nationalisation in Britain. But, since the late 1970s, the trend was towards privatisation by selling State-owned enterprises (SOEs). It indeed became a universal trend.

The rapidity with which the public sector in many countries expanded over roughly in the period from 1960 to 1980, is frequently overlooked. In effect a revolution, a quiet one, occurred in the shifting of resources into the public sector in the decade of the 1970s. In the less developed countries and in many of the poorest countries, the growth of the public sector was characterised by the growth of the parastatal sector — State-owned enterprises. State-owned enterprises had come to account for 10 to 20 per cent of GDP in much of the less developed world, and they were dominant in manufacturing in a great number of countries. What is true for GDP was also true for capital investment. Parastatal enterprises were estimated to be responsible for between 20 and 60 per cent of total investment spending in the less developed world. Regardless of whether socialist or market-oriented, virtually all countries in the 1960s and 1970s saw an expansion of the public sector, and in particular an expansion of state-owned enterprises, across a broad front.[1]

Political overenthusiasm and vested interests caused an indiscriminate expansion of the public sector in many countries and its inherent problems were compounded by irresponsible and inefficient management.

The performance of SOEs in many countries was, by and large, far from satisfactory. They often put large burdens on public budgets and external debt. For example, the net deficit of a sample of SOEs accounted for about 4 per cent of Niger's GDP in 1982. For the seven largest Latin American economies, the combined deficit of SOEs rose from about one per cent of GNP in the mid-1970s to about 4 per cent in 1980-82. One study has found that countries in which SOEs accounted for higher shares of gross domestic investment generally had lower rates of economic growth.[2] In 1997-98, out of the 236 operating Central public undertakings in, India, 100 undertakings had incurred a combined loss of about ₹ 6,541 crore.

The heavy financial burden imposed by the SOEs and the growing public discontent against them due to their inefficiency, indifferent, irresponsible and sometimes even arrogant attitude and lack of concern for the customer needs and corruption, nepotism and squander associated with their organisation and management led to the growing interest in privatisation. As Professor Samuel Paul points out,[3] in country-after-country, unbridled state expansion has led to:

1. Economic inefficiency in the production activities of the public sector, with high costs of production, inability to innovate, and costly delays in delivery of the goods produced;
2. Ineffectiveness in the provision of goods and services, such as failure to meet intended objectives, diversion of benefits to elite groups, and political interference in the management of enterprises; and
3. Rapid expansion of the bureaucracy, severely straining the public budget, causing problems in labour relations within the public sector, inefficiency in government, and adverse effects on the whole economy.

These problems have led many governments to undertake programmes of public sector reform, and pushed by a need to curb public expenditure, to re-evaluate the possibilities for shifting publicly managed activities into the private sector.

The Privatisation Reaction

Privatisation is an inevitable historical reaction to the indiscriminate expansion of the State sector and the associated problems. Even in the 'communist' countries it became a vital measure of economic rejuvenation.

It may be noted that as a result of privatisation the number of people owning shares in Britain almost tripled from 7 to 20 per cent of the adult population between 1978-89. Interestingly, in 1988 Britain experienced a symbolic cross over — for the first time in history more British citizens were holders of shares than were members of unions. Further, as the proportion of shareholders in the total population increases and as the economic lot of the workers and the poor improves, leftist parties increasingly lose their ground. In 1988, for instance, the Labour Party in Britain lost 8 per cent of its members, the biggest exodus since 1981.[4]

Ways of Privatisation

There are different ways of achieving privatisation. "Each country has its own gimmicks. In Britain, the staff of the privatised company have a priority in buying shares, and are entitled to a discount. For instance, 96 per cent of British telecom employees took a share in their company in defiance of the trade union opposition. Although, some of them later sold them (at a higher rate), they derived certain benefits (at least financial ones) from privatisation. The use of the US ESOP (Employees' Share Ownership Plan) practices is another interesting example. ESOP provides for forming special fund which takes bank credit to buy a company's shares and distribute them among employees at the real value or free of charge. The credit is paid back out of the company's profit."[5]

One of the important ways of privatisation is *divestiture,* or privatisation of ownership, through the sale of equity. In countries where there are well functioning capital markets, this entails selling stock to the public. In industrial countries, privatisation has come mainly through divestiture of government economic activities. Among the developing countries, Bangladesh, Chile, Jamaica, Brazil, Peru, Zaire, Pakistan, the Philippines and Sudan offer examples of divestiture.

Divestiture was very substantial in such West European countries as France, Italy, Sweden, the Federal Republic of Germany, and, of course, the champion industrial company privatiser, Britain.

In the Republic of Korea, the government pioneered the establishment of basic industries such as oil refining, steel, and machine tools and then sold them to the private sector once their profitability was established, using the funds raised to pioneer other industries, Brazil created a commission for divestiture in 1981 and Jamaica set up a divestiture committee.

There are a large number of cases where privatisation has taken the form of *denationalisation* or *reprivatisation.* A considerably large number of enterprises were denationalised in countries like Chile, Bangladesh and Pakistan.

> **There is a trend of privatisation of certain functions and activities of public sector organisations.**

Another way of privatisation is *contracting*. Governments may contract out services they have planned and specified to other organisations that produce and deliver them.

Franchising — authorising the delivery of certain services in designated geographical areas — is common in utilities and urban transport. Contracting is common in public works, defence and many specialised services where suppliers compete for contracts and there is no loss of economies of scale, contracting is efficient. But there is scope for corruption in contracting, and long-term contracts tend to encourage monopolistic behaviour by the private supplier. Contracts for road construction and maintenance are common in countries such as Brazil, Colombia, India, and Kenya. In agriculture and urban development in the Philippines and in water supply in the Ivory Coast, private contracts have played an important role.[6]

Another option for the government is to *withdraw* from the provision of certain goods and services leaving them wholly or partly to the private sector.

Privatisation may also take the form *of privatisation of management,* using *leases* and *management contracts.*

Government can shed the burden also by *liquidation* which can be either formal or informal. Formal liquidation involves the closure of an enterprise and the sale of its assets. Under informal liquidation, a firm retains its legal status even though some or all of its operations may be suspended.

Obstacles

When compared to the industrial countries, the progress of privatisation has been slow in the developing countries. As the World Bank points out, governments confront several obstacles, like those mentioned below, when they decide to divest SOEs.[7]

(*i*) Governments usually want to sell the least profitable enterprises, those that the private sector is not willing to buy at a price acceptable to the Government.

(*ii*) Divestiture tends to arouse political opposition from employees who may lose their jobs; from politicians who fear short-term unemployment as a consequences of liquidation or of cost reduction by private owners; from bureaucrats who stand to lose patronage; and from those sections of the public that fear that national assets are being cornered by foreigners, the rich, or a particular ethnic group. Sometimes, the opposition of employees is due to the fact that they will have to bid goodbye to the 'easy going' culture in the public sector and produce results if the enterprise is privatised.

There may be mismatch between the socio-economic rationale of privatisation, government objectives, political opportunism and market realities.

(*iii*) Relatively undeveloped capital markets sometimes make it difficult for governments to float shares and for individual buyers to finance large purchases.

Conditions for Success of Privatisation

Professor Samuel Paul points out that if privatisation is to succeed, in the sense of raising efficiency or effectiveness in the production or delivery of goods and services, the following seven conditions must be met:[8]

First, privatisation cannot be sustained unless the political leadership is committed to it, and unless it reflects a shift in the preferences of the public arising out of dissatisfaction with the performance of other alternatives. Privatisation has in the past worked best when a government was strongly committed to a change, or when a new government vowed to reverse the actions of its predecessors, as has happened in Chile and the United Kingdom. Some governments that had faced severe economic crises, with massive budgetary deficits, had turned to privatisation and divestiture as a part of their adjustment strategy.

Second, any alternative institutional arrangements chosen should not stifle competition among suppliers. Replacement of a government monopoly by a private monopoly may not increase public welfare — there must be a multiplicity of private suppliers. This can be a difficult problem where there are few competent suppliers. Though government may wish to contract out a service, if there are only one or two qualified contractors, the benefits of competition are unlikely to follow.

In this context, most developing countries' systems of regulation need major review and reform. Overregulation of industry discourages private initiative; overregulation of urban land use of building construction retards urban development; and unduly low ceilings on the prices of industrial products and utilities, such as bus transport and electricity, inflate demand and depress the incentives for production.

> **The objective and rationale of privatisation shall be clear and socially and economically justifiable and the process shall be proper and transparent.**

The third, related, condition is freedom of entry to provide goods and services. Long term contracts and franchises limit competition and consumers' choice. In some services that are capital intensive, freedom of entry is difficult to achieve. But in others, such as refuse collection or health services, the public will be better served by several private suppliers competing than by one agency monopolising the market through a long-term contract.

Fourth, public services to be provided by the private sector must be specific or have measurable outcome. Physical construction or utility services, *for example*, can be measured, but most educational services and police protection are not easy to quantify, even though their inputs can be measured. Lack of specificity makes it more difficult to control services provided by the private sector, especially if the public served is illiterate, unorganised, and unassertive. Service delivery by non-governmental organisations or local governments may be more appropriate under these conditions.

Fifth, consumers should be able to link the benefits they receive from a service to the costs they pay for it, since they will then shop more wisely for different services. User charges are one way of establishing this link. The importance of educating consumers and disseminating information to the public cannot be overemphasized here.

Sixth, privately provided services should be less susceptible to fraud than government services if they are to be effective. Services provided through collective or cooperative action at the community level are probably the least susceptible to fraud.

Seventh, equity is an important consideration in the delivery of public services. Broadly speaking, the benefits of privatisation can accrue to the capital owner who supplies the service to the consumer, who receives a more efficient service; and to the public at large, through a reduction in the public sector deficit, and hence in taxes or the rate of inflation, or both. Privatisation will be counter-productive if the ability of the public to pay, determined by the prevailing income distribution, becomes the sole guide for the delivery of services. And, if the benefits of privatisation are likely to be reaped solely by local elites, expatriate groups, or multinational corporations, political resistance to reform is likely to increase.

Benefits of Privatisation

Privatisation benefits the society in several ways. The fact **that** privatisation is an important strategy of economic rejuvenation of even the 'communist' nations is a testimony to the economic role of privatisation.

Countries like the UK have shown how it could help solve the fiscal crisis of the State and to usher in a new industrial democracy. The benefits of privatisation may be listed down as follows:

1. It reduces the fiscal burden of the State by relieving it of the losses of the SOEs and reducing the size of the bureaucracy.
2. Privatisation of SOEs enables the government to mop up funds. Government of India's Budget for 2000-2001 proposed to raise ₹ 10,000 crore during the year through privatisation. (The achievement, however, was dismal as the privatisation plan could not be carried out in real earnest due to various reasons).
3. Privatisation helps the State to trim the size of the administrative machinery.
4. It enables the government to concentrate more on the essential State functions.
5. Privatisation helps accelerate the pace of economic development as it attracts more resources from the private sector for development.
6. It may result in better management of the enterprises.
7. Privatisation may also encourage entrepreneurship.
8. Privatisation may increase the number of workers and common men who are shareholders. This could make the enterprises subject to more public vigilance.

Arguments Against Privatisation

There is strong opposition to privatisation from different corners, based on economic, political, social and management rationale and on vested interests. Some of the important arguments against privatisation are as follows:

1. The public sector has been developed with certain noble objectives and privatisation means discarding them in one stroke.

2. Privatisation will encourage concentration of economic power to the common detriment.
3. If privatisation results in the substitution of the monopoly power of the public enterprises by the monopoly power of private enterprises it will be very dangerous.
4. Privatisation many a times results in the acquisition of national firms by foreign firms.
5. Privatisation of profitable enterprises, including potentially profitable ones, means foregoing future streams of income for the government.
6. Privatisation of strategic and vital sectors is against national interests.
7. There are well managed and ill managed firms both in the public and private sectors. It is not the sector that matters, but the quality and commitment of the management.
8. The capital markets of developing countries are not developed enough for efficiently carrying out privatisation.
9. Privatisation in many instances is a half-hearted measure and therefore it is not properly carried out, with the result that the expected results may not be achieved.
10. In many instances, there are vested interests behind privatisation and it amounts to deceiving the nation. The UNDP's *Human Development Report 1993* observes that in many countries privatisation often has been a 'garage sale' to favoured individuals and groups.

Sins and Pitfalls of Privatisation

Many privatisations have taken place for wrong reasons, under wrong conditions and in wrong ways.

Privatisation does not guarantee unconditional success. Privatisation in many countries has been found to be often fraught with many sins and pitfalls. Dubious objectives, tainted privatisation process, etc., may lead to failure of privatisation.

The commonly observed flaws of privatisation are the following:

1. ***Lack of Proper Strategy:*** An important reason for failure of privatisation is absence of a proper strategy or norms regarding the industries/units to be privatised, the method of privatisation, extent of divestment, selection of buyer/investor, etc.
2. ***Ambiguity of Objectives:*** The real objective of privatisation is another problem. Is it for raising revenue? Is it for making the enterprise competitive? If there are multiple objectives, what is the priority list?
3. ***Connivance:*** Sometimes politicians have hidden objectives behind privatisation. The UNDP Report cited above, points out that in too many cases it has taken place for the wrong reason, under the wrong conditions and in the wrong way.
4. ***Wrong Timing:*** Many privatisation schemes could not get a good price because of the wrong timing. A good price can be obtained if privatisation is done when the performance, market capitalisation and the industry prospects are good. It is

pointed out the *Maruti* could have got a good price had it been privatised when the goings were good.

5. ***Lack of Political Consensus:*** Privatisation is a political process too. As there are opposing views regarding privatisation, there is likely to be some opposition of privatisation. The privatisation of BALCO is a case in point. The government shall try to make clear the need for and objectives of privatisation and shall bring about as broad a consensus as possible.
6. ***Wrong Labour Strategies:*** Most public enterprise have surplus labour, getting rid of which is essential for success of the enterprise. But, to overcome labour resistance to privatisation, often unrealistic promises are given that the labour will not be affected by privatisation. A more open and realistic handling of the labour is needed for making privatisation meaningful. Prospects of retraining and redeployment of the labour are yet to be properly explored in countries like India.
7. ***Lack of Political Will:*** Privatisation is not carried out in real earnest and properly because of lack of political will and/or vested interests. For example, some ministers oppose privatisation of employees under their ministry and some politicians oppose privatisation of undertakings in their constituencies of States.
8. ***Poor Financial Strategies:*** Many privatisations are carried out without a good financial strategy.
9. ***Wrong Environment:*** Mere transfer of ownership does not help improve the performance of an enterprise. Where the market functions poorly and enterprises are still vulnerable to arbitrary government edicts, transferring ownership to the private sector is unlikely to achieve much.
10. ***Prevalence of Monopoly Elements:*** If privatisation results in the conversion of a public sector monopoly to a private sector monopoly, privatisation may not produce much beneficial effects, it could even worsen the situation.
11. ***Problem of Cultural Change:*** Improvement of performance of an enterprise after the privatisation will depend, *inter alia*, on bringing about a change in the work culture and the total enterprise culture. This is no easy task.

Evolution of Disinvestment Policy in India

The policy of disinvestment largely evolved through the policy statements of Finance Ministers in their Budget Speeches. The policy as evolved is enumerated below:

- In the Interim Budget of 1991-92, it was announced that the Government would disinvest up to 20 per cent of its equity in selected PSEs in favour of mutual funds and financial and institutional investors in public sector.
- In the Budget speech of 1992-93, the cap of 20 per cent was reinstated and the list of eligible investors was enlarged to include FIIs, employees and OCBs.
- In April 1993, the Rangarajan Committee recommended disinvesting upto 49 per cent of PSEs equity for industries explicitly reserved for the public sector and over

74 per cent in other industries. But the then Government did not take any decision on the Committee's recommendations.

- In 1996, as per the Common Minimum Programme (CMP), the Budget speech of 1996-97 announced the setting up of Disinvestment Commission for 3 years. CMP also emphasized adding more transparency to the disinvestment process and examine the non-core areas of public sector.
- In the Budget speech of 1998-99, its per cent was announced that the Government shareholding in CPSEs should be brought down to 26 on case-to-case basis, excluding strategic CPSEs where the Government would retain majority shareholding. The interest of workers was to be protected in all the cases. For this purpose, on 16, March, 1999, the Government classified the PSEs into Strategic and Non-Strategic areas. It was decided that Strategic PSEs would be those in areas of:
  - Arms and ammunition and allied items of defence equipment, defence aircraft and warships.
  - Atomic energy (except in the areas related to the generation of nuclear power and applications of radiation and radioisotopes to agriculture, medicine and non-strategic industries).
  - Railway transport.

All other PSEs were to be considered Non-strategic.

- In the Budget speech of 1999-2000, it was announced that the Government would continue to strengthen the Strategic units and "privatizing" the Non-Strategic ones through gradual disinvestment or strategic sale and devise viable rehabilitation strategies for weak units.
- The 2000-01 Budget speech focused on restructuring and revival of viable CPSEs, closure of PSEs which cannot be revived; bringing down Government shareholdings in Non-Strategic CPSEs to 26 per cent or lower, if necessary, and protection of the interest of workers. The receipts from disinvestment would be used for the social sector, restructuring of CPSEs and for retirement of public debt.
- In the *suo motu* statement of 2002, specific aim was given to the Disinvestment Policy — modernization and upgradation of PSEs, creation of new assets, generation of employment and retiring of public debt.
- In the Budget speech of 2003-04, the Government announced details regarding the setting up of Disinvestment Fund and Asset Management Company to hold, manage and dispose the residual holdings of Government.
- In 2004, with the change in the Government, there was a change in the outlook of Disinvestment Policy.

In May 2004, the Government adopted National Common Minimum Programme, which outlined the policy of the Government with respect to the Public Sector.

The UPA Government pledged to devolve full managerial control and commercial autonomy to successful, profit-making companies operating in competitive environment; they won't be privatized. 'Navratna' companies can raise resources from the capital market. Efforts will be made to modernize and restructure sick PSEs.

- It favoured sale of small proportions of Government equity through IPO/FPO without changing the character of PSEs. In regard to this, it approved listing of unlisted profitable CPSEs subject to residual equity of the Government remaining at least 51 per cent and Government retaining the control of management.
- It also constituted the formation of the 'National Investment Fund', where the proceeds from disinvestment of CPSEs would be channelised. 75 per cent of annual income of NIF would be used to finance selected Social Sector Schemes — education, health, employment and the rest 25 per cent to meet the capital investment requirements of profitable and revivable CPSEs.

On 27 January, 2005, the Government approved in principle:

- Listing of currently unlisted profitable CPSEs, each with a Net Worth in excess of ₹ 200 crore, through an Initial Public Offering (IPO) either in conjunction with a fresh equity issue by the CPSE concerned or independently by the Government, on a case-by-case basis, subject to the residual equity of the Government remaining at least 51 per cent and the Government retaining management control of the CPSE.
- Sale of minority shareholding of the Government in listed, profitable CPSEs either in conjunction with a Public Issue of fresh equity by the CPSE concerned or independently by the Government, subject to the residual equity of the Government remaining at least 51% and the Government retaining management control of the CPSE.
- Constitution of a "National Investment Fund"

On 25, November 2005, the Government decided, in principle, to list large, profitable CPSEs on domestic stock exchanges and to selectively sell small portions of equity in listed, profitable CPSEs (other than the Navratnas).

Present Disinvestment Policy

The present disinvestment policy has been articulated in the recent President's addresses to Joint Sessions of Parliament and the Finance Minister's recent Parliament Budget Speeches.

The salient features of the Policy are:

(*i*) Citizens have every right to own part of the shares of Public Sector Undertakings.

(*ii*) Public Sector Undertakings are the wealth of the Nation and this wealth should rest in the hands of the people.

(*iii*) While pursuing disinvestment, Government has to retain majority shareholding, *i.e.*, at least 51 per cent and management control of the Public Sector Undertakings.

Approach to Disinvestment

A salient feature of Government of India's disinvest policy, generally, is to retain at least 51 per cent equity and the management control.

On 5th November, 2009, Government approved the following action plan for disinvestment in profit-making government companies:

(*i*) Already listed profitable CPSEs (not meeting mandatory shareholding of 10 per cent) are to be made compliant by 'Offer for Sale' by Government or by the CPSEs through issue of fresh shares or a combination of both.

(*ii*) Unlisted CPSEs with no accumulated losses and having earned net profit in three preceding consecutive years are to be listed.

(*iii*) Follow-on public offers would be considered taking into consideration the needs for capital investment of CPSE, on a case-by-case basis, and Government could simultaneously or independently offer a portion of its equity shareholding.

(*iv*) In all cases of disinvestment, the Government would retain at least 51 per cent equity and the management control.

(*v*) All cases of disinvestment are to be decided on a case-by-case basis.

Progress of Disinvestment

The disinvestment process began in 1991-92 with sale of minority stake in some PSUs During 1991 to 1999, disinvestment took mostly the form of sale of minority stake in favour of financial institutions.

During 1999-2000 to 2003-04, the thrust was on disinvestment through strategic sale.

Since 2004-05, the focus was mainly on sale of minority stake in the domestic market to the general public in conjecture with issue of fresh equity by the company.

In the last many years, sales of shares of public sector enterprises was seen as an important source of revenue by the Union government. But the realization lagged far behind the targets. While presenting the Union Budget 2016-17, Finance Minister Arun Jaitley stated that the government will soon come out with a comprehensive policy for strategic stake sale that will detail the mode as well as valuation methodology for outright sale of even profit-making companies. He also commented that the previous NDA government led by Atal Bihari Vajpayee had between 1999 and 2004 privatised about a dozen state-owned firms and hotels including Videsh Sanchar Nigam Ltd. (VSNL), Bharat Aluminium Company Ltd. (BALCO), CMC Ltd and Hindustan Zinc Ltd. (HZL). But the policy was buried after the UPA came to power and only minority stake sales was pursued since then.

The total receipt through privatisation till March 2013 amounted to ₹ 1,16,616 crore. The government had raised about ₹ 16,000 crore in 2013-14.

Since the Narendra Modi Government assumed office in 2014, disinvestment policy has assumed a new direction. In 2014-15, around ₹ 24,500 crore was raised by Central Government by selling minority stake in public sector companies. In the Budget for 2015-

16, the finance minister has stated that the government will raise ₹ 28,500 crore by way of strategic stake sale. But the realisation of the target was disappointing. For the financial year 2016-17, the disinvestment target set by the Budget is ₹ 56,500 crore. Of the total budgeted proceeds, ₹ 36,000 crore is estimated to come from minority stake sale in PSUs, while the remaining ₹ 20,500 crore is planned to be generated from strategic sale in both profit and loss-making companies.

Privatisation has gained great importance under the Modi Government.

Recently, NITI Aayog has identified 74 PSUs with respect to disinvestment. Out of this:

- 26: To be closed outright
- 22: Further action to be taken only after revival package is complete
- 10: To be considered for strategic sale/disinvestment
- 6: To be transferred only to states
- 5: To be transferred to states/private firms on long-term lease or otherwise
- 3: To be merged with parent PSUs
- 2: Status quo to be maintained

SUMMARY

Privatisation, which has become a universal trend, means transfer of ownership and/or management of an enterprise from the public sector to the private sector. It also means the withdrawal of the State from an industry or sector, partially or fully. Another dimension of privatisation is opening up of an industry that has been reserved for the public sector to the private sector.

Privatisation is an inevitable historical reaction to the indiscriminate expansion of the State sector and the associated problems. Even in the 'communist' countries it became a vital measure of economic rejuvenation.

The society may benefit from privatisation in several ways. It would help reduce the fiscal burden of the State by relieving it of the losses of the SOEs and reducing the size of the bureaucracy; enable the government to mop up funds; result in better management of the enterprises; encourage entrepreneurship; and help accelerate the pace of economic development as it attracts more resources from the private sector for development. Privatisation may increase the number of workers and common man who are shareholders and this could make the enterprises subject to more public vigilance. Privatisation enables the government to concentrate more on the essential State functions.

The important ways of privatisation are the following:

1. Divestiture, or privatisation of ownership, through the sale of equity.
2. Denationalisation or reprivatisation.
3. Contracting under which Government contracts out services to other organisations that produce and deliver them.
4. Franchising — authorising the delivery of certain services in designated geographical areas — is common in utilities and urban transport.

5. Government withdrawing from the provision of certain goods and services leaving them wholly or partly to the private sector.
6. Privatisation of management, using leases and management contracts.
7. Liquidation which can be either formal or informal. Formal liquidation involves the closure of an enterprise and the sale of its assets. Under informal liquidation, a firm retains its legal status even though some or all of its operations may be suspended.

Governments may confront several obstacles to privatisation. Trade unions and political parties may oppose privatisation. In developing countries, the relatively undeveloped capital markets sometimes makes it difficult for governments to sell shares. Another problem is that governments usually want to sell the least profitable enterprises, those that the private sector is not willing to buy at a price acceptable to the government.

Privatisation will be successful only if certain conditions are satisfied. The policy should be very clear and there should be proper privatisation strategies. Equally important are the commitment and political boldness on the part of the government.

Privatisation is a very important aspect of the economic reforms in India. The Central Government has been reviewing the existing portfolio of public investment with a view to offloading public investment from areas where the following conditions prevail: (*i*) industries based on low technology; (*ii*) small-scale and non-strategic areas; (*iii*) inefficient and unproductive areas; (*iv*) areas with low or zero social responsibility or public purpose; and (*v*) areas where private sector had developed sufficient expertise and resources. Government has also set up a Disinvestment Commission in 1996 for suggesting the modalities for undertaking disinvestment of equities for select PSUs. The Commission has submitted several reports of recommendation. However, the progress achieved has been far from satisfactory, mainly because of lack of commitment and political boldness.

REFERENCES

1. Elliot, Berg, "Privatisation: Development a Pragmatic Approach", *Economic Impact,* 1987/1, pp. 6-7.
2. World Bank, *World Development Report 1987,* World Bank, Washington D.C. 1987, p. 67.
3. Samuel, Paul, "Privatisation and the Public Sector", *Finance and Development,* December, 1985, p: 42.
4. John, Naisbitt and Patricia, Aburdene, *Megatrends 2000,* Avon Books, New York, 1990, p. 162.
5. Alexander, Polyukhov, "Everything for Sale", *New Times,* October 2-8, 1990, p. 31.
6. Samuel, Paul, *op. cit.,* p. 43.
7. World Bànk. *op. cit,* p. 68.
8. Samuel, Paul, *op. cit.,* pp. 44-45.

☆☆☆

CHAPTER 7

MICRO, SMALL AND MEDIUM ENTERPRISES (MSMEs)

The importance of developing micro, small and medium enterprises (MSMEs) has been emphasised by all the industrial policy resolutions and statements and a number of protective and promotional measures have been taken accordingly to support their survival and to encourage their growth. There are about 3.61 crore MSMEs in the country.

The VSI Sector

The village and small industries (VSI) sector in India consists of a very wide spectrum of industries categorised under small, tiny and cottage segments.

> **The VSI sector represents a wide spectrum of production and service activities encompassing a continuum of artisans/handicraft units at one end and modern and technologically sophisticated enterprises with significant investments on the other, producing a wide range of over 7,500 products.**

The VSI sector consists, broadly, of:

- Traditional cottage and household industries (*viz.,* handloom, khadi and village industries, sericulture, handicrafts and coir).
- Modern small-scale industries including tiny units and powerlooms.

While traditional industries are generally artisan based, located mostly in rural and semi-urban areas, involve lower levels of investment in machinery and provide largely part-time employment, modern small-scale units and powerlooms use mostly power operated appliances and machinery, have some technological sophistication and are generally located close to or in the urban areas including large industrial centres. However, as apart of the industrial dispersal policy and rural industrialisation, governments have been encouraging medium small-scale units in rural areas.

There has also been an increase in the variety of products manufactured by the small-scale sector. They have ventured into the manufacture of many new and sophisticated items.

According to the data obtained by the second SSI census, over 80 per cent of the units were proprietary concerns. About 17 per cent were partnerships and limited companies formed less than two per cent of the total number of units.

DEFINITIONS[1]

The first official definition of SSI in India was coined in 1950, in terms of the size of gross investment in fixed assets (plant and machinery, land, building), as well as on the strength of the workforce in the unit concerned. This criterion underwent a number of modifications over the years.

In the latter part of the fifties, the change reflected in defining an SSI unit was mainly a shift from a workforce criterion to an investment criterion. In 1966, the original value in plant and machinery was adopted as the sole norm for defining a unit as small-scale or otherwise.

Similarly, the concepts of ancillary and tiny units were introduced in 1960 and 1977 respectively.

Small Scale Service Establishments (SSSEs) were first classified in 1985 and later redefined in 1991, as Small Scale Service and Business Enterprises (SSSBEs). The definition of Women Entrepreneurs' Enterprise was brought out in 1988 and modified in 1991.

The term Small Scale Industry evokes different meanings for different agencies.

The Planning Commission, Government of India, views the entire Village and Small Industries (VSI) Sector as a part of the SSI sector. The National Sample Survey Organisation under the Central Statistical Organisation (CSO), Government of India, defines the entire industry sector in terms of organised and unorganised segments, as well as in terms of industrial enterprises run by households and non-households. The Central Excise Department, on the other hand, distinguishes SSIs on the basis of the annual turnover of the units (up to a maximum limit of ₹ 30 million). The Reserve Bank of India (RBI) adopts an expanded definition of SSIs which includes traditional industries as well. The industrial policy planners in the Small Scale Industries Board define SSI on the basis of investment in plant and machinery (an upper limit of ₹ 30 million) and cover residual units which do not fall under the assistance programmes of any of the Statutory Boards.

Different segments of SSI have been defined as given below.

Small Scale Industrial Undertaking: An industrial undertaking in which the investment in plant and machinery, whether held on ownership terms or on lease/hire-purchase basis does not exceed ₹10 million is graded as small-scale industrial undertaking.

(The investment ceiling has been revised from time-to-time. It was ₹ 7.5 lakh in 1966 and ₹ 30 million in 1997. An analysis of the quantitative increase in investment ceiling in plant and machinery from the year 1966 to 1997 by segregating the inflation component from the increase in current prices so as to calculate the effective enhancement in real terms shows that: (1) The ceiling of investment in plant and machinery for SSI, in real terms, has remained relatively unchanged from 1966 to 1991. For subsequent years from 1991 to 1996, it would further come down in real terms before increase in the ceiling in 1997. (2) For the most part of the seventies and early eighties, in fact, the upper threshold of investment in plant and machinery for both SSI and ancillary units was below 1970-71 level, in real terms. (3) The revision of the ceiling in 1991 also did not make much of a difference in real terms. (4) It was only the revision in 1997 (to ₹ 30 million) that had provided opportunities for small units to undertake higher investment for technology upgradation, product standardisation, R&D facilities and build competitiveness. However, in 1999 the Government decided to lower the investment ceiling from ₹ 30 million to ₹ 10 million). See the section *Recent Developments* for the latest developments.

Ancillary Industrial Undertaking: An industrial undertaking which is engaged or is proposed to be engaged in the manufacture or production of parts, components, sub-assemblies, tooling or intermediates, or the rendering of services is termed as ancillary undertaking. The ancillary undertaking has to supply or render or propose to supply or render not less than 50 per cent of its production or services, as the case may be, to one or more other industrial undertakings. The investment in plant and machinery, whether held on ownership terms or on lease or on hire purchase, should not exceed ₹10 million.

Tiny Enterprise: A unit is treated as a tiny enterprise where investment in plant and machinery does not exceed ₹ 0.5 million, irrespective of the location of the unit.

Women Entrepreneurs Enterprise: An SSI unit/industry related service or business enterprise, managed by one or more women entrepreneurs in proprietary concerns, or in which she/they individually or jointly have a share capital of not less than 51 per cent as partners/shareholders/directors of private limited company/members of cooperative society is treated as women entrepreneurs' enterprise.

Small Scale (Industry related) Service and Business Enterprises (SSSBEs): Enterprises rendering industry-related service/business with investment up to ₹ 0.5 million in fixed assets, excluding land and building, are called SSSBEs.

Export Oriented Units (EOUs): A unit with an obligation to export at least 30 per cent of its annual production by the end of third year of commencement of production and having investment ceiling in fixed assets — plant and machinery — up to ₹ 10 million is regarded as an EOU.

Organised and Unorganised Sectors: Units in the factory sector are termed as organised sector units. These units are registered under the Factories Act, 1948. The remaining units of the SSI segment and other traditional industries fall under the VSI sector and are termed as unorganised sector units. Such units are not registered under the Factories Act as they employ either less than 20 workers (if power is not used) or less than 10 workers (if the unit is using power) in the industrial unit. In other words, Central Statistical Organisation's (CSO) categorisation of organised and unorganised sector units is based on the criteria of employment in combination with the use/non-use of electric power.

The definition of SSI is linked to the question of ownership. SSI units cannot be controlled or owned by a subsidiary of any other industrial undertaking. This implies that in proprietary/partnership firms, the combined investment of all the units set up by the same proprietor/partners should not exceed the total investment limit fixed for an SSI.

As regards the formation of an SSI as a limited company, the equity investment by other companies in SSIs should not exceed 24 per cent.

Small industry has been subjected to various controls and regulations in terms of the IDR Act, 1951 and other relevant statutes. The restriction on ownership is unique in the Indian context and has been introduced primarily to prevent large companies from obtaining fiscal and other concessions by setting up of SSI units as "fronts". This also discourages the misuse of incentives by establishing more than one SSI unit, in the same line of production, by the same set of entrepreneurs.

Recent Developments

Recent initiatives and measures taken by the Government of India to enable micro, small and medium enterprises (MSME) to enhance their competitive strength, address the challenges of competition and avail of the benefits of the global market include a promotional package and certain legislative measures.

The promotional package seeks to address most of the concerns in the areas such as credit, cluster-based development, infrastructure, technology, and marketing. Capacity building of MSME Associations and support to women entrepreneurs are the other important features of this package.

The Khadi and Village Industries Commission Act, 1956, was amended during 2006-07, introducing several new features to facilitate professionalism in the operations of the Commission as well as field-level formal and structured consultations with all segments of stakeholders.

Micro, Small and Medium Enterprises Development Act, 2006

The Micro, Small and Medium Enterprises Development Act, enacted in 2006 provides the first-ever legal framework for recognition of the concept of "enterprise" (comprising both manufacturing and services) and integrating the three tiers of these enterprises, *viz.*, micro, small and medium. The salient features of this Act are given below.

Under the Act, enterprises have been categorized broadly into those engaged in (*i*) manufacturing, and (*ii*) providing/rendering of services. Both categories have been further classified into micro, small and medium enterprises, based on their investment in plant and machinery (for manufacturing enterprises) or in equipment (in case of enterprises providing or rendering services) as under:

Manufacturing Enterprises: The investment limits of various categories of manufacturing enterprises are as follows:

- **Micro Enterprises:** investment up to ₹ 25 lakh.
- **Small Enterprises:** investment above ₹ 25 lakh and up to ₹ 5 crore.
- **Medium Enterprises:** investment above ₹ 5 crore and up to ₹ 10 crore.

Service Enterprises: The investment limits of various categories of manufacturing enterprises are as follows:

- Micro Enterprises: investment up to ₹ 10 lakh
- Small Enterprises: investment above ₹ 10 lakh and up to ₹ 2 crore.
- Medium Enterprises: investment above ₹ 2 crore and up to ₹ 5 crore.

Other Features: The other important features of the Act include the following:

1. Provision for a statutory consultative mechanism at the national level with wide representation of all sections of stakeholders, particularly the three classes of enterprises, and with a wide range of advisory functions, and an Advisory Committee to assist the Board and the Centre/State Governments.
2. Establishment of specific Funds for the promotion, development and enhancement of competitiveness of these enterprises.
3. Notification of schemes/programmes for this purpose
4. Progressive credit policies and practices
5. Preference in Government procurements to products and services of the micro and small enterprises
6. More effective mechanisms for mitigating the problems of delayed payments to micro and small enterprises
7. Simplification of the process of closure of business by all three categories of enterprises.

SMEs in Other Countries

In India, there exists no definition of medium enterprises and as such, there is no specific definition for small and medium enterprises (SMEs). What prevails here is only the concept of small-scale, ancillary and tiny industry which are related to the historical value of the investment in plant and machinery.

In other countries, SMEs are defined on the basis of both quantitative and qualitative elements, such as, the number of workers employed and/or annual turnover or the level of fixed investment. However, employment is an omnipresent criterion for determining the size of the unit in these countries.

Importance

The khadi, village and small-scale industries have a very important role in the Indian economy characterised by its vast spatial spread, unemployment and underemployment, rapidly rising labour force, capital scarcity, numerous market segments and diverse demand patterns, broad and diverse resource base and supply, predominance of widely scattered numerous village settlements, growing modern large industrial sector giving scope for ancillarisation and so on.

BOX 7.1 : SMALL ENTERPRISES, BIG PART

The SSI sector, as an important segment of the Indian economy, accounts for:

- 8 per cent of the country's GDP
- 95 per cent of the industrial units
- 45 per cent of output in the manufacturing sector
- 40 per cent of total exports
- Employment of about 80 million people.

The distinguishing features and major advantages of these industries, particularly khadi and village industries, are the following:

1. In an economy, like India, characterised by abundant labour supply and the concomitant unemployment and underemployment and rapidly rising labour force, khadi, village and small industries assume special significance because of its high employment potential.
2. Another major advantage is their ability to provide employment in the off-season. To a large number of people, agriculture provides only seasonal employment. Khadi, cottage and some other village industries provide employment opportunities during the off-season and help many households to mitigate their problems during the off-season.
3. Khadi, cottage and certain other village industries provide vast scope for employment of special categories of people like women, children, old-aged, physically handicapped, etc. It is also an avenue for part-time employment for those who are employed elsewhere, either full-time or part-time.
4. Some of these industries provide employment opportunities within the household premises and some others near the place of residence. The locational advantage of these industries are thus, very great.
5. A major advantage of these industries is that the capital-output and capital-labour ratios are comparatively very low. That is, the amount of capital investment required per unit of employment and the capital investment required per unit of output are comparatively very low. In other words, the khadi and village industries in particular and the small-scale units in general maximise employment and output for a given amount of capital. This is of particular importance to a labour-abundant and capital-scarce economies.
6. Because of the low capital-output ratio and low gestation period they promote non-inflationary growth.
7. Khadi and village industries have been found to be of particular help to the weaker sections of the society. The participation of the scheduled castes, scheduled tribes, women and other weaker sections of the society in this sector is significant.

8. These industries promote economising of resource utilisation and conservation of resources. They are expected to ensure maximum utilisation of locally available raw materials by adopting easily adaptable techniques. In some cases, non-conventional raw materials are used, thereby converting waste into wealth.
9. These industries can develop in almost all areas including backward, tribal, hilly and inaccessible areas. They are, thus, helpful in achieving wider spatial dispersal of industrial activities and thereby reducing the regional economic imbalances.
10. They help increase the pace of rural development through the generation of additional employment opportunities and income and through its inputs and output linkages with the other sectors of the rural economy.
11. The small industries have acquired more attention in recent years due to the very less ecological problems they create, compared to the large industries.
12. As khadi and village industries do not use or use only very little electric power or oil, they do not cause energy crisis and foreign exchange crisis.
13. The fact that the village and small industries account for about one-third of our total export earnings shows how important they are to the Indian economy constrained by shortage of foreign exchange.

Development of VISs under the Plans

The government, Central and States, have taken a number of measures to help solve the age-old problems of these industries, such as lack of credit facilities, outmoded methods and techniques, absence of organised marketing, unsatisfactory raw material supply and competition from large-scale units.

All our Five Year Plans and Industrial Policy resolutions/statements have stressed the need to accelerate the development of village and small industries to create large-scale employment opportunities, promote decentralisation and dispersal of industries, achieve diffusion of ownership and prevention of concentration of economic power, promote entrepreneurship, develop agro-based and ancillary industries, improve the skills of artisans and quality of their products, reduce the role of subsidies and to step up the productions of essential articles and those having potential for exports.

Objectives

The main objectives of the development of village and small industries have been the following:

1. To assist in the growth and widespread dispersal of industries.
2. To increase the level of earnings of artisans.
3. To sustain and create avenues of self-employment.
4. To ensure regular supply of goods and services through use of local skills and resources.

5. To develop entrepreneurship in combination with improved methods of production through appropriate training and package of incentives.
6. To preserve craftsmanship and art heritage of the country.

The performance of the small scale sector should be evaluated in the light of the fact that the Plan allocation for this sector has come down from 2 to 4 per cent in the earlier Five Year Plans to about 1.5 per cent.

PROMOTIONAL MEASURES

A number of measures have been taken by the governments, Central and State, to protect this sector from the onslaught of the large sector and to promote its growth.

In the post-reform period, a number of new steps have been initiated by the Government with regard to foreign direct investment, development of infrastructural facilities, establishment of growth centres, export promotion, marketing, etc.

> **Measures taken by the Government from time-to-time, include reservations, upward revision of investment ceilings in the definition, reservation of products for the SSIs, increasing credit flows, preference in Government purchases, modernisation, technology upgradation and improving export performance.**

The important protective and promotional measures include the following:[2]

1. Reservation of Products: Protection has been provided to the small-scale units by the reservation of items for exclusive production in the small scale sector. Over the years there had been an increase in the number of items so reserved, but has significantly reduced it recently.

2. Reservation and Preference in Government Procurement: SSIs have been given protection from competition in the matter of purchases of different products by the DGS&D. A large number of items have been reserved for exclusive purchase from the VSI sector while a number of items have been provided price preference up to 15 per cent over units in the large-scale sector.

3. Infrastructural and Institutional Support: Infrastructural and institutional supports are provided through industrial estates, district industries centres (DICs), Small Industries Service Institute, Khadi and Village Industries Commission (KVIC) and other specialised institutions which provide technical assistance, testing facilities, etc.

4. Machinery on Hire Purchase: The National Small Industries Corporation (NSIC) arranges supply of machines on hire purchase to small-scale units.

5. Marketing Assistance: Marketing assistance including export promotion assistance are provided by institutions such as the NSIC, the Small Industries Development Organisation (SIDO), Handicrafts and Handlooms Export Promotion Corporation, KVIC, etc.

6. Financial Assistance: Financial assistance is provided at concessional terms by commercial banks, state level financial institutions, etc.

In order to step up the flow of assistance to the small sector and to provide a focal point to coordinate at the apex level, the availability of both financial and non-financial inputs required for the orderly growth of this sector, the Small Industries Development Bank of India (SIDBI) was established in 1990.

7. Training: Training for existing and potential entrepreneurs and others associated with the working of the small units are offered by Entrepreneurship Development Institute of India (EDII), Technical Consultancy Organisations (TCOs), financial institutions and commercial banks, management institutes, NSICs, etc.

8. Supply of Raw Materials: Arrangements have also been made for the supply of raw materials, particularly of scarce items, to the small scale units.

9. Promotion of Ancillarisation: The industrial policy also gives importance to ancillarisation. This has been recognised as one of the objective of the public sector industry. One of the factors considered by the government while evaluating application from the private sector for industrial licence was the scope for ancillarisation by the proposed project.

A more detailed account of some of the promotional aspects is given below.

The incentive schemes of the different States are more or less similar across the country because of the tying up of the State schemes with central Government assistance and the tendency of the States to copy the new schemes of others. There is an acute dearth of region specific effective schemes.

Industrial Estates (IE) Programme

With a view to encouraging entrepreneurs to set up small industries and to expand existing units, a programme for the establishment of industrial estates was started in the year 1955. This programme envisaged the following facilities for entrepreneurs: (*i*) the acquisition of suitable land and its development; (*ii*) the construction of factory sheds; (*iii*) the provision of infrastructure like water, electricity, transport, banks, canteens, watch and ward, all-weather approach roads.

The important objectives of this programme were to: (*i*) facilitate the growth of SSIs; (ii) shift industries from congested areas to estate premises; (*iii*) achieve decentralised development in small towns and villages; (*iv*) develop sub-contracting relationship with large industries; (*v*) establish common facility service centres, etc.

This was a centrally-sponsored programme till 1979. Thereafter, it was transferred to the State Industrial Development Corporations (SIDCs). This encouraged, the State Governments, to continue with the development of Industrial Estates/Areas through the SIDCs.

Additional facilities were extended by the different States to entrepreneurs who were setting up new units as well as to those units which were moving out of non-conforming areas and relocating to the developed IEs/Areas. These facilities included subsidy on rent for factory accommodation, allotment of sheds on hire-purchase as well as on outright sale. Other incentives like concessional charges for water and power, exemption from Sales Tax and Octroi (building material, transport subsidy, etc.), were also offered.

EPZs/SEZs Export Industrial Parks

Special incentives for firms, small or large, to undertake manufacturing of export items for export from India have been provided by the Government of India through the establishment of Export Processing Zones (EPZs), recently modified as Special Economic Zones (SEZs) or through 100 per cent export-oriented units (EOUs) set up outside of such zones.

There are also several Technology Parks with focus on specific industries, like the Electronics Hardware Technology Parks (EHTPs), Software Technology Parks (STPs), Bio-Tech Park, Leather Park, etc., with specialized infrastructure, technology back-up and escort services.

Integrated Infrastructural Development Scheme (IID)

Consequent to policy measures for the promotion and strengthening of small and tiny village enterprises announced on 6th August, 1991, the scheme of Integrated Infrastructural Development (IID) (including technological back-up services) in rural/backward areas was announced by the Government of India on 7th March 1994.

The Scheme aimed at augmenting infrastructural facilities in the rural and backward areas with a special emphasis on the linkage between agriculture and industry. The scheme covered centrally developed backward districts other than those covered under the Growth Centre Scheme.

The objectives of the IID Scheme were: (1) To establish approximately 50 IID centres in rural areas/backward districts in the country; (2) To promote SSI and tiny unit clusters with a view to the creation of employment opportunities and to develop exports, (3) To promote stronger linkages between agriculture and industry, (4) To provide Common Service facilities and technological back-up services in selected centres, and, (5) To create/upgrade infrastructure facilities like power, water, telecommunication, etc., in new/existing centres/industrial areas.

Cluster Development

SSIs operating in clusters, derive their strength through a unique state of togetherness. They also benefit from backward and forward economic linkages since such units have similar cultural and social backgrounds, clusters provide an active base for business and social interaction. The economies of agglomeration ensure a network of suppliers that provide raw materials, equipment, machinery, spares, repairs and other services to units, which would otherwise have not been possible. Clusters encourage specialisation in manufacturing processes, inter-firm relationships in production activities, division of labour, sharing of information/experiences. Such an atmosphere provides productivity gains on a continued basis and develops a network of subcontracting between firms.

It has been noticed that clusters have normally emerged for such products as may be produced in a traditional manner and which have no exposure to technology changes, design and manufacturing processes. Initially, units are set up to benefit from the locally available skills, raw materials, etc. Gradually, similar types of industries grow in number by utilising the existing pool of trained workers who shift from one unit and to another. Such clusters classified as *natural clusters.* These centres have grown spontaneously and are not consequent to a policy framework of the government nor that of any other institution for establishing such clusters in specific products.

Because of the advantages of clusters, government and other agencies have been promoting clusters, through the creation of infrastructure, which is accompanied by a range of technical services (designed to cater to a group of units in the local area/industry). Such clusters are termed as *induced clusters.*

The Expert Committee on Small Enterprises (Abid Hussain Committee) observed that "the centre-piece of the new approach is an increasing public-private partnership in setting up support systems for small-scale enterprises. Such public-private partnership would thrive particularly in clusters of small scale enterprises. Agglomeration of SSEs is a source of informational economies, accretion of skills and economies in infrastructure development. As a matter of fact, spontaneous growth of over 300 clusters has already taken place in the country mostly unaided by the State. This growth has been fuelled by access to domestic and international markets and cheap labour. However, further progress in clusters is hamstrung by decrepit infrastructure, environmental degradation, technological obsolescence and meagre skills of the workforce. Worldwide experience confirms that growth in clusters can be buttressed by institutional development, and aided by the abundant provision of services and infrastructure development. The thrust of the future policy for SSEs should be to bolster growth in existing clusters by redirecting current investments in regional development (*i.e.,* backward areas) to such centres of growth which are spreading to less developed regions. The Expert Group therefore recommends that State Governments identify the existing SSE clusters and then promote new types of organisations which are joint ventures between the State Governments or local authorities and business associations in these clusters."

The incentive system for the development of the VSI sector is characterised by several anomalies. It is biased against smallness, labour intensity and rural industrialisation and decentralisation.

Industrial Growth Centres/Schemes

For the promotion of industries in the backward areas, the scheme of establishing Growth Centres was envisaged in 1988 for the establishment of 100 Growth Centres around the country. The criteria for location of centres are as follows: (*i*) Outside 50 kms of cities with a population above 2.5 million; (*ii*) Outside 30 kms of cities with a population of above 1.5 million but below 2.5 million; (*iii*) Outside 15 kms of cities with a population of 0.75 million but below 1.5 million.

The objective of the scheme has been to provide the best of the infrastructure facilities in these Growth Centres nationwide. The other criteria for the establishment of Growth Centres were the proximity to rail heads, National or State highway, access to adequate and dependable sources of water, power, telecommunication facilities, educational and health facilities and sufficient land for the development of housing and for the promotion of tertiary activities. Growth Centres should not lie located in ecologically sensitive areas.

The important prerequisite for the identification of a Growth Centre has been that its sphere of influence should cover an area of 400 to 800 hectares.

INSTITUTIONAL SUPPORT STRUCTURE

There is a network of organisations to support the development of the VSIs.

The Small Scale Industries Board is an apex advisory body constituted by the Government of India to render advice on all the issues pertaining to the SSI sector. The Board was constituted in 1954 to facilitate coordination and provide inter-institutional linkages for the development of the sector. The Union Industries Minister is the Chairman of the Board which consists of State Industries Ministers, select members of Parliament, Secretaries of various departments of Central Government. Heads of financial institutions, industries associations and eminent experts in the SSI field.

The Department of SSI and Agro and Rural Industries (SSI and A&ARI) was created under the Union Ministry of Industry to formulate policy framework and initiate appropriate programmes and schemes for the promotion of SSIs in the country.

The range of functions of the department include the setting up of a network of institutions to render services of a varied nature like, techno-economic and managerial aspects, training, testing facilities, marketing assistance, etc. These activities are supported by a host of other Central/State departments agencies, and autonomous institutions all over the country.

The office of the Development (Commissioner Small Scale Industries), known as the Small Industries Development Organisation (SIDO) was set up in 1951 is the nodal agency for implementation of Central Government policies and plays a constructive role in the strengthening of the SSI sector.

The SIDO functions through a network of Small Industry Service Institutes (SISIs) and a host of other field centres. The major SSI-related activities of SIDO include evolving all India policies and programmes, coordinating policies and programmes of State Governments, liaisoning with different State and Central Ministries, Planning Commission, RBI and Financial Institutions. SIDO also provides a comprehensive range of extension services through allied institutions and monitors Government-sponsored programmes.

At the State level, the Commissioner/Directorate of Industries implement policies for the promotion and development of small-scale, cottage, medium and large-scale industries. The Central policies for the SSI sector serve as the guidelines, but each State evolves its own policy and package of incentives.

The State departments also oversee activities of the field offices, *viz.*, District Industries Centres (DICs), etc. In addition, State Financial Corporations, State Small Industries Development Corporations (SIDCs), and Technical Consultancy Organisations (TCOs) operate at the State level to assist the promotion and development of SSIs. Other regional level agencies include State Infrastructure Development Corporations, State Cooperative Banks, Regional Rural Banks, State Export Corporations, Agro Industries Corporation and Handloom and Handicrafts Corporations. For the purpose of human resources development, there is a network of specialised institutes associated with SIDO. At grassroot level, NGOs play an important role for the development of tiny units.

Industry Associations provide support to the SSI sector and offer with a common platform to raise industry-related issues. Government policies, in recent years, have stressed the increasing role of Industry Associations in the setting up of common facilities and other ventures in the area of technology, marketing and other support services.

Women Entrepreneurs

The importance of the economic development of women takes on an added dimension in India when considered in the context of the prevailing social, legal and economic norms. The Government has, therefore, taken several steps to promote women entrepreneurship.

In view of the initiative shown by women in various economic activities, promotional organisations have been organising special programmes for them. This trend indicates a shift towards a gender-specific approach to such programmes in order to enhance the competence of women in the establishment and management of SSIs.

The 1991 Industrial Policy has envisaged special training programmes to support women entrepreneurs. Accordingly, women entrepreneurs are receiving training through Entrepreneurship Development Programmes (EDPs) conducted by various institutions and organisations both at the Central and State levels.

The SIDO, with its field offices all over the country, has been carrying out development programmes for women entrepreneurs and is providing technical schemes for the setting up of SSI units. In view of changing outlook for the promotion of women enterprises, the SSI Board in 1991 revised the definition of women enterprises by omitting the condition of employing 50 per cent of women workers. This provided a boost to women entrepreneurs to take up businesses and avail of facilities/concessions as are applicable to all SSIs.

The SIDBI, has instituted various developmental initiatives towards promoting women enterprises. The Bank has designed programmes, with a focus on women, *viz.*, Mahila Vikas Nidhi, Mahila Udyam Nidhi, Micro Credit Scheme, Women Entrepreneurship Development Programmes, etc. These programmes have been formulated with the twin objectives of: (*i*) providing training and extension services support to women entrepreneurs through a comprehensive package suited to their skills and socio-economic status; and (*ii*) extending financial assistance on liberal terms, to enable them to set up industrial units in the small scale sector.

Andhra Pradesh has set up an exclusive Industrial Estate For Women Entrepreneurs.

Marketing

Marketing is a major problem area of the VSI sector. This sector generally experiences a lack of resources for sales promotion and advertising. Institutional assistance, therefore, is, often, very much essential for marketing of SSI products.

The marketing infrastructure, as available for SSIs consists of a combination of agencies and incentive schemes such as those mentioned below.

1. NSIC: Registers SSI and tiny units under a single point registration and secures orders for the supply of various stores, on preferential terms tendered by the DGS&D.

2. Sub-contracting Exchanges: There are 16 such exchanges that operate through the Small Industries Service Institutes (SISIs). These exchanges enlist SSIs and identify items for ancillarisation from various Public Sector Undertakings. These offices promote contacts between large and medium-scale industries on the one hand and SSI ancillary units on the other to secure subcontracting jobs.

3. Quality Certification: *(a)* The Bureau of Indian Standards (BIS) sets the standards for different manufactured products and it registers SSIs for the adoption of quality standards as a measure of marketing support, *(b)* SIDO has set up four Regional Testing Centres, which provide testing facilities to SSI units as per BIS standards. In addition, there are a number of field-testing stations extending testing facilities and assistance to SSIs. *(c)* SIDO is operating a scheme to reimburse (up to 75 per cent subject to a maximum of ₹ 0.075 million) the cost of acquiring ISO 9000 certification.

4. Marketing Development Assistance (MDA) Scheme: Ministry of Commerce, Government of India reimburses the expenditure incurred by the SSI delegations that visit foreign countries (60 per cent of the expenditure incurred by the delegation) for the purpose of exploring marketing possibilities. This incentive is extended to admissible items only.

5. Training Programmes for Export Packaging: SIDO in partnership with the Indian Institute of Packaging organizes training programmes for SSI exporters on packaging for exports. Exporters are provided information on the latest packaging standards and techniques in order to boost exports.

6. Organising Exhibitions and International Trade Fairs: For promoting exports, STDO annually participates in selected International Trade Fair and Exhibitions held abroad by the India Trade Promotion Organisation (ITPO). All expenses on space hiring, display, shipment, insurance, handling and clearance, publicity, etc., are borne by SIDO.

7. Export Promotion Councils: The existence of export promotion councils for specific industries provides the SSI member units with a platform for export marketing. A number of Export Promotion Councils are providing marketing infrastructure through procurement of direct orders and distribution of items among member units for production and sale.

These Councils also arrange for quality testing of products, pre-shipment inspection, packaging and sales transactions assistance. These bodies arrange for the participation of member units in various Exhibitions and Trade Fairs.

8. SIDBI's Marketing Finance and Development Department: SIDBI established its Marketing Finance and Development Department (MFDD) in January 1996 to focus attention on marketing-related activities undertaken by the SSI sector. The Bank formulated a comprehensive scheme for providing financial assistance to SSIs enabling them to undertake various marketing activities as also to assist institutions/agencies engaged in strengthening the existing marketing channels and infrastructure for the SSI sector. A special Marketing Assistance Development Fund with sub-allocation for women entrepreneurs has been set up. A number of development and support services have also been undertaken by the Department to assist the marketing efforts of the SSI units.

STATE INDUSTRIAL POLICIES

The State/UT Governments pursue the Central Government industrial policies and assistance is obtained under different centrally sponsored schemes/incentives for disbursement among eligible SSIs. This Central policy framework serves as a guiding principle for States, which evolve respective policies for SSI promotion depending upon the specific requirements of the State. The State Governments also design suitable incentives to encourage existing units to expand/diversify products and support entrepreneurs to establish new units.

In this context, State Governments provide technical and other support services to SSIs through the Directorate of Industries and DICs. The main areas of support and facilities are listed below.

1. To develop and manage industrial areas by respective Industrial Development and Investment Corporation.
2. Financial support services by State financial Corporations (SFCs).
3. Technical guidance by Technical Consultancy Organisations (TCOs).
4. Human resources development by a host of training institutions.
5. Infrastructure development by Infrastructural Development Corporations.
6. Export promotion by Small Industry and Export Corporations.
7. Single Window Assistance by District Industries Centres.

Besides the above, State Governments also offer a range of incentive measures for providing an impetus to industrialisation. These incentives to SSIs are mainly by way of providing land and developed plots/sheds on concessional terms, industrial infrastructural facilities, subsidy on investment (in selected areas) and on generating sets, sales tax and stamp duty exemptions, water supply at reduced rates, seed capital assistance for setting up of units, etc.

KHADI AND VILLAGE INDUSTRIES

Khadi means any cloth woven on handlooms in India from cotton, silk or woollen yarn handspun in India or from mixture of any two or all such yarns.

Industries coming under the purview of Village Industries include: (1) Beekeeping; (2) Cottage match, manufacture of fireworks and agarbatties; (3) Cottage pottery; (4) Cottage soap; (5) Flaying, curing and tanning of hides and skins and ancillary industries connected with the same and cottage leather industry; (6) Ghani oil; (7) Handmade paper; (8) Manufacture of cane-gur and khandasari; (9) Palmgur making and other palm products; (10) Processing, packing and marketing of cereals, pulses, spices, condiments, masalas, etc.; (11) Manufacture and use of manure and methane gas from cow-dung and other waste products (such as flesh of dead animals, night soil, etc.;) (12) Limestone, lime-shell and other lime products; (13) Manufacture of shellac; (14) Collection of forest plants and fruits for medicinal purposes; (15) Fruit and vegetable processing, preservation and canning, including pickles; (16) Bamboo and cane-work; (17) Blacksmithy; (18) Carpentry; (19) Fibre other than coir; (20) Manufacture of household utensils in aluminium; (21) Manufacture of katha; (22) Manufacture of gums and resins; (23) Manufacture of lokvastra; (24) Manufacture of polyvastra; (25) Processing of maize and ragi.

KVIC

The Khadi and Village Industries Commission (KVIC) is a statutory organisation engaged in the task of promoting and developing khadi and village industries with a view to creating employment opportunities in the rural areas and thereby strengthening the rural economy. It was established in 1975 by an Act of Parliament. It is an autonomous body which took over from its predecessor, the All-India Khadi and Village Industries Board, set up in 1953.

The broad objectives that the KVIC has set before it are:

1. the social objective of providing employment;
2. the economic objective of producing saleable articles; and
3. the wider objective of creating self-reliance amongst the people and building up a strong rural community spirit.

The functions of the KVIC are generally to plan, organise and implement programmes for the promotion and development of khadi and village industries. In particular they include:

1. training of persons engaged in production of khadi and village industries;
2. building up reserve of raw materials and implements and supplying them to persons, engaged in the production of KVIs at economical rates;
3. to provide for sale and marketing of khadi and products of village industries and handicrafts;
4. to encourage and promote research in the technique of production of khadi and in the development of village industries, and to provide facilities for study of problems relating to KVIs;
5. to maintain or assist in the maintenance of institutions for the development of KVIs;
6. to undertake, assist or encourage production of khadi or development of village industries;

7. to promote and encourage co-operative efforts among manufactures of khadi and persons engaged in village industries; and
8. for ensuring the genuineness of and for granting certificates to producers of or dealers in khadi or the products of any village industry.

The KVIC have created an organisational base for further development with many State KVI Boards, a large number of registered institutions and industrial cooperatives. KVIC has a very large number of sales outlets in the country. This is a unique national organisation in the country which has its roots in the villages and has wide organisational linkages. Its activities cover numerous villages in the country. A substantial number of beneficiaries belong to the scheduled caste and scheduled tribes and inhabitants in hill and border areas. The participation of women in the activities is also very high.

Integration of small and large industries through ancillarisation is an important feature of industrial development of countries like USA., European countries and Japan. In India, the government policy has been one of encouraging ancillarisation.

ANCILLARY INDUSTRIES

Though all industries are not amenable to ancillarisation, there are a number of industries with scope for considerable ancillarisation. Large industries may benefit from ancillarisation in different ways. One benefit of ancillarisation is the realisation of economies of scale. If the requirement of any item is less than the economic size of production, it stands to gain by purchasing the item from an outside unit of economic size. Further, a large company can relieve itself from the problem of tying up of capital, managerial time, etc., on minor items which can be efficiently produced by ancillaries. The society also benefits from the economies of scale and other efficiencies associated with ancillarisation. As the impact of energy crisis and credit squeeze is comparatively less on small-scale units, ancillarisation offers further advantages to large units in an era of power shortage and financial problems.

Ancillarisation and subcontracting, however, have some problems also. The parts or components supplied by these units may not sometimes be of satisfactory quality. The small units usually do not have the resources for carrying out research and development. Hence, parent units will have to help them to update technology and enforce strict quality control.

Industrial machinery, agricultural and earth moving machinery; machine tools; industrial; scientific and mathematical instruments; locomotives and rolling stock; ships; aircrafts; bicycles; boilers; steam generating plants; steam engine; automotive parts; turbine; internal combustion engine; commercial, office and household equipment; telecommunication equipment; electronics; electrical equipment; packaging items for use in chemicals; some iron and steel industry items are but some fields where there is good scope for ancillarisation.

According to a study conducted sometime ago, the extent of ancillarisation possible in different fields in India is as high as 60 to 90 per cent in transportation industry; 50 to 75 per cent in communications industry and 30 to 50 per cent in prime movers and power based industry. It is 20 to 40 per cent in industrial machinery and machine tools; 15 to 30 per cent in chemicals and pharmaceuticals industry; 10 to 30 per cent in consumption and consumer durable goods industry; and 5 to 10 per cent in basic industry, such as metals, minerals, cement and petroleum. The lowest range is 2 to 10 per cent in wood, paper fibres, glass, ceramics, leather, rubber, etc.[3]

DRAWBACKS AND PROBLEMS

The number of VSI units have increased remarkably. The role of this sector in the Indian economy cannot be underestimated. However, as the Planning Commission observes, some of the important objectives set for the village and small industries sector are yet to be fully achieved.

The dispersal of small-scale units far away from the metropolitan areas and large cities has not taken place to an appreciable extent. Available data indicate that the industrially developed States account for a very large share of the registered small-scale units. Within the developed States, there has been concentration of units in areas which are either metropolitan or large cities or industrial complexes. Although, one may wish a balanced distribution of the units, the small-scale/large-scale linkages, infrastructural and marketing factors and several other reasons contribute to the tendency to concentrate.

Industrial sickness is widespread in the small-scale sector.

Low levels of technology resulting in poor productivity and inadequate returns continue to characterise the traditional industrial sector.

A number of promotional measures designed to develop the VSI sector have not produced the expected results. For example, the Entrepreneurial Development Programme has not made significant progress except in a few States like Gujarat in widening the entrepreneurial base.

It has been pointed out that a number of the registered small-scale units are bogus; they have been registered to avail the credit and other facilities offered to this sector. There is deliberate diversion of resources from the genuine use. Units are deliberately made sick after swindling the credit amount.

Though a number of arguments are put forward in favour of the VSI sector, in a number of cases the VSI units are promoted and sustained at a heavy social cost. The enormous subsidies they are granted, like concessional finance, fiscal incentives, price preferences, etc., have to be borne by the society. It is felt that "it is high time that the Government started to shed its paternalistic attitude to remedy every wrong/weakness through a subsidy, quota, or a scheme and instead attempt to create an enabling environment for people and unleash their entrepreneurial zeal."[4]

The earning levels of a large number of people employed in the VSI sector, especially in the traditional sector, are very low. Unless productivity in this sector increases, there might not be significant improvement in the earning levels.

Available estimates show that the capacity utilisation in different village and small industries is very low.

The major problems of the small-scale units are the following:

Problem of inputs: Inadequacy or non-availability of inputs of proper quality at responsible price is important problem facing a number of units. It is pointed out that the allotment of raw materials by State supply corporations have been very inadequate.

Financial problems: Many small units face financial crisis. Though there has been an increase in the flow of institutional credit to this sector, large part of this has gone to the relatively large units in this sector. The increased flow of institutional funds in favour of the decentralized industrial sector has not covered the artisan sector adequately which continues to depend for a major part of its capital requirements on non-institutional sources, often at exorbitant rates of interest.

Marketing problems: Marketing is a major problem area for the small units in general. Small entrepreneurs, generally, do not have resources and expertise to market their products effectively. Financial constraints do not permit them to offer attractive credit terms and the like, to the marketing intermediaries. The VSI sector is in a weak bargaining position so much so that the intermediaries take advantage of the situation. Though the governments have taken some steps, marketing arrangements for selling of the products of the small units are still quite inadequate.

Competition from the large units: Productivity in the VSI sector is, by and large, not satisfactory. No much progress could be made in the upgradation of technology particularly in the traditional sector. They also suffer from limitations of finance, marketing capability in competing with large enterprises. The increasing global competition poses a big challenge to the VSI units.

Institutional constraints: Though a number of measures have been taken by the Central and State Governments to assist the VSI sector, they have not come up to the expectations. The small entrepreneurs have to cross many hurdles to obtain assistance from them. The District Industries Centres (DICs) have not come up to the expectations. There are many criticisms about the functioning of the organisations meant to assist the VSI sector.

In short, as the Planning Commission observes, low levels of technology resulting in poor productivity and inadequate returns continue to characterize the village and small industries. Coupled with this, the problem of obtaining raw materials of desirable quality at reasonable prices and lack of marketing arrangements for selling their produce at fair prices have deprived the artisans of a good part of the earnings which should have accrued to them.

SUMMARY

Development of village and small scale industries has been given a lot of emphasis in India because of a number of avowed objectives such as promotion of entrepreneurship, generation of employment opportunities, development of decentralized development, prevention of concentration of economic development, utilisation of local resources, protection of interests of artisans, preservation of craftsmanship and heritage of the country, etc.

To support the development of the VSI sector, an elaborate institutional network has been established and several schemes have been introduced to provide infrastructural, financial, technical, operational and marketing assistances. To guard against competition from the large firms, manufacture of a large number of items were exclusively reserved for the SSI sector and SSI units were given preferences in government purchases. They have also been offered several fiscal and monetary incentives.

There is a strong feeling that the policy of exclusive reservation has not contributed to the healthy development of the SSI sector. The Abid Hussain Committee observed, "...instead of focusing on areas that should be the province of the small-scale sector by economic rationale, the SSI policy has traditionally concentrated on exclusive activities for this sector. In this process it has lost sight of the simple but determining logic of market system that it can make business sense for a large company to do anything that can be done more competitively by a small unit. A policy of exclusive reservation for the small-scale industry, therefore, is at best unnecessary and at worst inefficient."

However, the SSI units suffer from a number of problems which include technological, marketing, financial and operational problems. A large number of them are sick/weak, many of which are unviable.

With the liberalisation and globalisation they have come to face increasing competition. This does not mean that the VSI units have no future. Experience of developed economies show that growth of large and small units go hand-in-hand. Efficiency, dynamism and strategy are needed to survive in a competitive environment.

REFERENCES

1. Adopted from SIDBI Report on Small Scale Industries Sector, 1999.
2. The subsections *Promotional Measures, Institutional Support Structure* and *State Industrial Policies* have been adapted from the SIDBI Report on Small Scale Industries Sector, 1999.
3. "Ancillarisation in Indian Industry", *Economic Trends,* 16 July, 1981.
4. James, Manabl, "Strategy for Development of Small Enterprises", *Erudition — The Albertian Journal of Management,* January 2007.

☆☆☆

CHAPTER

8

Industrial Sickness

Industrial sickness is a universal phenomenon. While the industrial sickness is easily manifested in market economies, it may be concealed in economies where the market mechanism does not operate. In a market economy, the competition tests and exposes the strengths and weaknesses of firms and therefore, sickness becomes easily visible.

> **Industrial sickness is a matter of serious national concern because besides affecting the owners, employees, creditors and suppliers, it causes wastage of national resources and social unrest.**

Definition

There are different perceptions of the symptoms and characteristics of industrial sickness. Sickness is a relative concept. Further, "a given sickness manifests itself in several forms, and at a point of time these forms may not throw unambiguous or clear-cut signals. No wonder, then, that sickness is found being understood, interpreted and measured differently by individuals and even by institutions."[1]

"To a layman, a sick unit is one which is not healthy. To an investor, it is one which skips dividends. To an industrialist, it is a unit which is making losses and tottering on the brink of closure. To a banker, it is a unit which has incurred cash losses in the previous year and is likely to repeat the performance in the current and following years."[2] In terms of the definition evolved by the Reserve Bank of India, an industrial unit is regarded as sick if it has incurred cash loss for one year and in the judgement of the bank, it is likely to continue to incur cash loss in the two following years and it has imbalance in its financial structure, such as current ratio being less than 1:1 and worsening debt-equity ratio. The Sick Industrial Companies (Special Provisions) Act, 1985, as amended in 1993, defines a sick industrial company as an industrial company (being a company registered for not less than five years) which has at the end of any financial year accumulated losses equal to or exceeding its entire net worth. The definition is for the purpose of application of the Act which covers only registered companies which have been in existence for at least seven years.

According to the Scheme for Rehabilitation of Small Scale and Non-BIFR Sick Viable Industries, Government of Gujarat, "a unit is considered sick when any of its borrowal accounts has become a *doubtful advance* as defined by the Reserve Bank of India, *i.e.*, principal or interest in respect of any of its borrowal accounts has remained overdue for a period exceeding two-and-a-half years and there is an erosion in the net worth due to accumulated cash losses to the extent of 50 per cent or more of its peak net worth in the preceding two accounting years."

Common symptoms of industrial sickness include failure to pay statutory liabilities like Provident Funds and ESI, contributions, failure to pay timely instalment of capital and interest on loans taken from financial institutions and through public deposits, increase in inventories with a large number of slow or non-moving items, high rate of rejection of goods manufactured, low capacity utilisation and frequent industrial disputes.

Weak Units

It is important to detect sickness at the incipient stage and take necessary remedial measures. The Reserve Bank has, therefore, advised the commercial banks to take remedial measures in respective units at the stage of 50 per cent erosion of their net worth. Such units are termed as weak units to distinguish them from sick industrial companies as defined in the Sick Industrial Companies Act.

An Industrial unit is termed as weak if at the end of any accounting year it has: (*i*) accumulated losses equal to or exceeding 50 per cent of its peak net worth in the immediately preceding five accounting years; (*ii*) a current debt-equity ratio of less than 1:1, and (*iii*) suffers a cash loss in the immediately preceding accounting year.

CAUSES OF SICKNESS

Industrial units may become sick at different stages and due to different reasons. Indeed, some industrial units "are born sick, some achieve sickness and some have sickness thrust upon them."[3]

There are a number of internal and external factors which can cause sickness.

Born Sick: Industrial units born sick are those which are destined for disaster right from their conception due to various causes. A study conducted by the Institute of Economics, Hyderabad, found that 50 per cent of the dead units closed within three years of opening. This proves that these units never had any reasonable survival prospect right from birth.[4]

Any one or more of the following factors may cause the birth of sick units:

1. Lack of experience of the promoters, wrong selection of the project, faulty project planning, etc., may give birth to sick units. The mushroom growth of the so-called consultancy firms has been regarded as a factor contributing to these sorts of problems because the primary interest of such consultancy firms is to make money by selling some ideas or project reports to the aspirants who may, thus, be misguided or made over-enthusiastic. We must also think that the rosy hopes generated by the high-sounding promises and schemes including the self-employment schemes of the financial institutions and other promotional agencies of the Governments also contribute to this unfortunate situation.

2. Paucity of funds and faulty financial management may also cause the birth of sick units. Many new units have been found to be underutilised and the strains of undercapitalisation become evident when the unit becomes operational. In case of some companies, the heavy investment in non-productive capital assets like staff housing projects even before they commence production distorts the liquidity and causes a lot of problems. Problems also crop up due to inadequate provisions for contingencies, faulty fund flow and cash flow estimate, etc.

3. Time and cost overruns sometimes prove to be very disastrous. Particularly in case of large projects, delays in project commissioning due to delay in supply of equipment, both indigenous and imported, slippage in the schedule of civil works, creation of equipment, etc., are not uncommon. Such delays cause cost escalations leading to capital shortage, liquidity problems, hike in the production costs and break-even point, etc.

4. Sickness may arise from locational problems also. It has been observed that "high-technology based units are established in areas without skilled labour or supporting infrastructure; industries based on imported raw materials are founded in regions without adequate transport and communication system".[5]

5. Technological factors like selection of obsolete or improper technology or the technology becoming outdated due to innovations while the project is being executed, sub-standard machinery, wrong collaboration, etc., also cause sickness.

According to the Tiwari Committee, 14 per cent of the large sick units suffered from technical factors and faulty initial planning.

6. Wrong assessment of the market potential or faulty demand forecasting, change in the market conditions, including the change in the consumer tastes and preferences and competitive situation, etc., can also cause birth of sick units.

Achieved Sickness: Industries which achieve sickness are those which fail after becoming operational due to internal causes. Such internal causes which are common are the following:

1. Bad management, which "covers a wide range from inexperience, inefficiency, lack of professional expertise, neglect and internal squabbles to delinquency and dishonesty"[6] is an important cause of industrial sickness. According to the Tiwari Committee Report,

1984, "the factor most often responsible for industrial sickness can be identified as 'management'. This may take the form of poor production management, poor labour management, poor resources management, lack of professionalism, dissensions within the management, or even dishonest management."[7] The Committee found that 65 per cent of the large sick units were affected by this problem.

2. Unwarranted expansion and diversion of resources may also result in sickness. Some concerns tend to expand beyond the resources including managerial capability. Diversion of resources to start new units or to acquire interest in other concerns without due regard to the capability of the unit to provide such funds sometimes lands the unit in trouble.

Personal extravagances and acquisition of unproductive fixed assets like company guest houses, etc., also may contribute to sickness.

3. Poor inventory management in respect of finished goods as well as inputs may land a unit in trouble.

4. Failure to modernise the productive apparatus, change the product mix and other elements of the marketing mix to suit the changing environment is a very important cause of industrial sickness.

5. Poor labour-management relationship and the associated poor worker morale and low productivity, strikes, lockouts, etc., also may ruin the health of a unit to survive.

External Causes: Sickness may be caused also due to factors beyond the control of an industrial unit. Some of these common external factors are the following:

1. Energy crisis arising out of power cuts or shortage of coal and oil have been a serious problem for many industrial units in India.

2. In a number of cases the units are not able to achieve optimum capacity due to shortage of raw materials due to production setbacks in the supply industries, poor agricultural output due to natural reasons, changes in the import conditions, etc.

3. Infrastructural problems like transport bottlenecks also sometimes cause serious problems.

4. It is a general complaint of the industrial circles that the credit squeeze very adversely affects the industrial sector. According to the Tiwari Committee, 24 per cent of the large sick units were affected by shortage of working capital/liquidity constraints.

5. Artificial economic constraints also make their contribution to the growing industrial sickness. Government controls on the product mix and prices caused serious problems for certain industries. Sometimes, it is not possible to automate or rationalise due to unfavourable government policy or labour attitude.

There are, thus, many external and internal factors which can cause industrial sickness. In many cases, sickness is caused by a combination of factors.

Rehabilitation packages suggested by the BIFR for several sick units include such measures as closing down certain divisions or lines of business, modernisation, rationalisation and redeployment of labour force, sale of assets to generate funds, etc. The pity, however, is that a unit which proposes to take such measures before it becomes sick may have to face opposition from the trade unions and even from government/government agencies. And there will be suggestions to take such measures, offer of concessions and the like after the catastrophe has ushered in. Further, the swiftness with which the administrative machinery responds to a grave problem is indicated by the fact that it took three years to establish the BIFR after the Tiwari Committee recommended such a measure! After many years of functioning of the BIFR without producing the expected benefits, there has been a confusion, for quite sometime, as to whether the Sick Industrial Companies Act and the BIFR established under the Act be scrapped or not.

Sometimes the attitude of labour, financial institutions and government which does not allow a unit to take measures, before it becomes sick, to strengthen itself also may cause sickness.

Absence of an appropriate exit policy has significantly contributed to the problem of industrial sickness in India.

PREVENTIVE AND CURATIVE MEASURES

As the Tiwari Committee observes, "Industrial sickness tends to cause loss of production very often leading to unemployment/loss of employment and resulting in blocking of scarce resources of the banks and financial institutions, besides entailing loss of substantial revenue to the exchequer. The magnitude and incidence of industrial sickness are matters of serious concern for the Central and State Governments, Reserve Bank of India, banks and financial institutions not merely due to the above factors, but also because such a trend undermines public confidence in the functioning of the organised sector with attendant repercussions on the overall investment climate in the economy of the country. Several measures have therefore, been taken by the government and financial institutions to detect the symptoms of sickness, and to prevent or cure sickness to the extent possible.

There are some laws which enable the Central Government to monitor and control the functioning of industrial undertakings and to deal with the problem of sickness.

The Companies Act, 1956, empowers the government to collect information from the companies which would enable it to assess the state of affairs of the companies and to take certain measures to prevent mismanagement. The Industries (Development and Regulation) Act, 1951 (IDRA), empowers the government to regulate the management of industrial undertakings, including the takeover of the management or the undertaking. The Sick Industrial Companies (Special Provisions) Act was passed in 1985 to deal with the problem of industrial sickness.

Government endorsed the recommendation of the Chokshi Committee regarding amalgamation of sick units and healthy units and amended Section 72A of the Income Tax Act relaxing the provision relating to carry forward and set off of accumulated business loss and unabsorbed depreciation allowances in case of amalgamation.

In 1981, the government announced certain policy guidelines to deal with industrial sickness. These guidelines required the ministries administratively concerned with various industries to take responsibility for rehabilitation of sick units. Banks and financial institutions were required to strengthen the monitoring arrangement for prevention of sickness.

An important limitation on the ability to tackle sickness arises from the fact that commercial banks may legitimately consider sick units as poor security risks.

A significant policy initiative was the introduction, in June 1987, of liberalised margin money scheme for supplementing the efforts of the State Governments in reducing sickness in the small-scale sector. Under this scheme, the State Governments were to make a matching contribution on a 50:50 basis in providing assistance to sick small-scale units in their rehabilitation.

The Industrial Reconstruction Corporation, later renamed as the Industrial Reconstruction Bank of India, was established to assist the rehabilitation of, mostly, the non-SSI sick units.

In the past, the government tookover the management of a number of sick undertakings under the IDRA, with the objective of reviving them by providing management support and financial assistance through banks and financial institutions. The National Textiles Corporation (NTC) was established to manage the sick textile mills (more than 100 in number) taken over by the Government. However, in due course the government felt that it was a mistake to have gone on taking over sick units and that the government should not be burdened with the mounting losses of the sick units.

Some State Governments like the Government of Gujarat have introduced specific schemes for rehabilitation of sick SSI and non-BIFR sick viable units.

Sick Industrial Companies Act

An important piece of legislation dealing with industrial sickness was the Sick Industrial Companies (Special Provisions) Act, 1985. The objectives of the (SICA), were:

1. The timely detection of sick and potentially sick companies owning industrial undertaking.
2. The speedy determination by a Board of experts of the preventive, ameliorative, remedial and other measures which need to be taken with respect to such companies.
3. The expeditious enforcement of the measures so determined and for matters connected therewith or incidental thereto.

According to the SICA, amended in 1993, a sick industrial company meant an *industrial company (being a company registered for not less than five years) which had at the end of any financial year accumulated losses equal to or exceeding its entire net worth.*

An industrial company was regarded as potentially sick, *if the accumulated losses of an industrial company as at the end of any financial year had resulted in the erosion of fifty per cent or more of its peak net worth during the immediately preceding four financial years.*

Under the Act, the Central Government established a Board for Industrial and Financial Reconstruction (BIFR) to exercise the jurisdiction and powers and discharge the function and duties conferred or imposed on the Board by the Act.

The SICA required the Board of Directors of a sick industrial company to make a reference to the BIFR for determination of the measures to be adopted with respect to the company. The BIFR could direct any operating agency (like the financial institution) to prepare the scheme for revival of the sick unit. The scheme could provide for any one or more of the following measures:

1. The financial reconstruction of the company.
2. The proper management of the sick industrial company by change in or takeover of management of the sick industrial company.
3. The amalgamation of the sick industrial company with any other company, or any other company with the sick industrial company.
4. The sale or lease of a part or whole of industrial undertaking of the sick industrial company.

Where the BIFR was of the opinion that the sick industrial company was not likely to make its net worth exceed its accumulated losses within a reasonable time and that it was not likely to become viable in future and that it was just and equitable that the company should be wound up, it could initiate proceedings with the High Court, for winding up of the company.

There had been all-round criticism against the SICA and the BIFR and it had been felt that they should be scrapped. The SICA was repealed. Revival and Rehabilitation of Sick Companies now come under the Companies Act. See the chapter on Indian Company Law (Chapter 14).

SUMMARY

Sickness is a serious problem that has afflicted the small, medium and large industries and it is a matter of serious national concern because besides affecting the owners, employees, creditors and suppliers, it causes wastage of national resources and social unrest.

Industrial units may become sick at different stages and due to different reasons. Indeed, some industrial units "are born sick, some achieve sickness and some have sickness thrust upon them".

Lack of experience of the promoters; wrong selection of the project; faulty project planning; paucity of funds and faulty financial management; time and cost overruns; wrong location of the project; technological factors like selection of obsolete or improper technology or the technology becoming outdated due to innovations while the project is being executed; sub-standard machinery; wrong collaboration; wrong assessment of the market potential or faulty demand forecasting; change in the market conditions; including the change in the consumer tastes and preferences and competitive situation, etc., can cause birth of sick units.

Firms become sick after becoming operational due to internal causes such as bad management; unwarranted expansion or diversion of resources; poor inventory management in respect of finished goods as well as inputs; failure to modernise the productive apparatus, change the product mix and other elements of the marketing mix to suit the changing environment; and poor labour-management relationship and the associated problems.

Sickness may be caused also due to external factors, *i.e.,* factors beyond the control of an industrial unit, such as energy crisis arising out of power cuts or shortage of coal and oil; failure to achieve optimum capacity due to shortage of raw materials due to production set-backs in the supply industries, poor agricultural output due to natural reasons, changes in the import conditions, etc.; infrastructural problems like transport bottlenecks; credit squeeze; Government controls on the product mix and impossibility to automate or rationalise due to unfavourable government policy or labour attitude.

Absence of an appropriate exit policy has significantly contributed to the problem of industrial sickness in India.

In the past, the Government tookover a large number of sick units, particularly in the textiles industry. Overburdened with their huge financial losses, the Government has given up the policy of taking over sick units.

The Sick Industrial Companies (Special Provisions) Act, was passed in 1985 with the main objectives of timely detection of sick and potentially sick and the speedy determination by a board of experts (BIFR) of the preventive, ameliorative, remedial and other measures which need to be taken with respect to such companies. The SICA and the BIFR miserably failed to achieve their objectives. The Government has announced the decision to repeal this Act.

REFERENCES

1. Sandesara J. C., "Industrial Sickness in India", *The Economic Times,* March 6, 1987, p. 14.
2. Nadkarni V. N., "Sickness in Industry and Its Effect on Banking", *State Bank of India Monthly Review,* June 1983, pp. 245-46.
3. *Ibid.,* p. 246.
4. *Ibid.,* p. 247.
5. *Ibid.,* p. 247.
6. *Ibid.,* p. 247.
7. *Ibid.,* p. 247.

☆☆☆

CHAPTER 9

MONETARY AND FISCAL POLICIES

The Monetary and Fiscal Policies affect the financial sector and the economy in general. They can also be attuned to influence specific sectors or industries or segments.

The Monetary and Fiscal Policies have important influence on the Gross National Product (GNP).

GNP = C + I + G + X

Where:

C = Private consumption expenditure

I = Private investment expenditure

G = Government expenditure

X = Net exports

Three of the components of the GNP, namely C, I and X can be influenced by the monetary policy which can also influence the private consumption and investment spendings and exports and imports.

> **The Government and the Central Bank (i.e., the Reserve Bank, in India) make use of various fiscal and monetary weapons respectively to achieve stability and growth by influencing and regulating the behaviour of the various classes of spenders as savers, consumers and investors.**

The fiscal and monetary policies are also important determinants of business prospects and investment decisions. They can help make the overall economic situation and business prospects bright or check an unwarranted boom or unhealthy demand explosion. They can encourage investment and production in certain priority sectors and discourage them in the non-priority sectors. They are also capable of influencing technological choice and investment and production patterns. In short, the fiscal and monetary policies can influence the aggregate supply and demand and the associated level of employment, wages, interest, rent, prices and profit. Hence, the importance of monetary and fiscal policies.

MONETARY POLICY

Monetary policy may be used to cause changes in the interest rates and money supply and thereby to influence the aggregate demand.

Monetary Policy refers to the use of instruments within the control of the Central Bank to influence the level of aggregate demand for goods and services or to influence the trends in certain sectors of the economy. Monetary policy operates through varying the cost and availability of credit, these producing desired changes in the assets pattern of credit institutions, principally commercial banks. These variations affect the demand for, and the supply of credit in the economy, and the level and nature of economic activities.

The modern economy is regarded as a credit economy in the sense that credit forms the basis of most of the economic activities in such an economy. The level and nature of economic activities such an economy, obviously, are influenced by the cost and availability of credit. The central bank's policies that affect the demand for and the supply of money, therefore, are very important to the industrial and commercial sectors. In a developed economy, credit forms a very important component of money supply.

Measures of Money Stock

A knowledge of the measures of money stock in an economy would help us to understand monetary policy better.

The Reserve Bank of India employs four measures of money stock, namely, Ml, M2, M3 and M4.

M1: The measure of money stock designated by Ml is usually described as the money supply. It is also referred to as narrow money. The components of money supply are currency with the public *(i.e.,* notes in circulation, circulation of rupee coins and circulation of small coins) and deposits (demand deposits with banks and other deposits with the RBI).

Currency with the public forms less than half of the total money supply, whereas the demand deposits constitute more than 50 per cent of the money supply today.

In advanced countries, demand deposits form a major part of the money supply. In India, the proportion of the currency in money supply has been declining. Two decades ago, it formed about three-fourths as against less than 50 per cent today.

M2: M2 is Ml + Post Office Savings Bank Deposits.

M3: M3 is Ml + Time Deposits with the banks. In other words, M3 is money supply plus fixed deposits with the banks. M3 is usually referred to as aggregate monetary resources or broad money.

M4: M4 is M3 plus the total Post Office Deposits.

Monetary Policy and Money Supply

As has been mentioned earlier, money supply comprises currency with the public and demand deposits. Both the monetary and fiscal policies can affect money supply.

The budgetary operations of the Government considerably affect the money supply. If the Government meets its budgetary deficits by borrowing from the Reserve Bank, there will be an increase in money supply, both in currency and bank deposits. The RBI has no control over budgetary operations, though it has opportunities of tendering advice to Government on this matter.

Another source of variation in money supply, over which the RBI's influence is restricted, is the country's international payments position.

Demand deposits are a very important determinant of money supply. As has already been mentioned above, in advanced countries demand deposits form a major part of money supply. In many developing countries, the proportion of demand deposits in money supply has been increasing. This is a trend associated with economic development and improvements in the bankisation and banking habits of the people.

Deposits with banks may originate in two ways — through passive creation or active creation. The former occurs when banks open deposit accounts for customers against the receipt of value either in cash or cheques drawn on other banks. The latter takes place when banks create deposits by extending credits. In the first case, the immediate effect is that there is no addition to the quantum of money, though its distribution may undergo a change; but ultimately it enables the banks to extend credit and thus results in an increase in money. In the second instance, the supply of money is augmented immediately. When a bank extends credit, it would result partly in a rise in deposits either with itself or with other banking institutions. Under the fractional reserve system, the banks can create deposits by a multiple of the reserves, since the payments made with the proceeds of bank loans are eventually redeposited with banks, leading to additional reserve funds.

Central banking instruments of control operate by varying the cost and availability of credit, and these produce desired changes in the assets pattern of credit institutions, principally commercial banks. The item among banks' assets having special significance in this connection is the credit extended by banks to their constituents, which is the sum of what are usually called loans and discounts. The capacity of banks to provide credit depends on their cash reserves (comprising cash in hand and balances with the Reserve Bank), a substantial portion of the reserves being generally held in the form of balances with the Reserve Bank. These increase through a rise in the deposit resources of banks, or by their borrowing from the Reserve Bank, or by sale of their investments. The regulation of credit by the Reserve Bank in essence means regulation of the quantum of the reserves of banks. If the Bank desires to bring about an expansion in credit, it adopts measures to augment the banks' reserves. If credit is to be restricted, it attempts to curtail the reserves.

Instruments of Monetary Policy

The instruments of monetary policy (methods of credit control) may be broadly, divided into:

- General (Quantitative) methods; and
- Selective (Qualitative) methods.

The general methods affect the total quantity of credit and affect the economy generally. The selective methods, on the other hand, affect certain select sectors. In other words, under the selective methods, certain qualitative distinctions are made between different sectors and segments of the economy; and selectivity is applied in regulating the flow of credit.

The statutory basis for the regulation of credit in India is embodied in the Reserve Bank of India Act and the Banking Regulation Act. The former Act confers on the Bank the usual powers available to central banks generally, while the latter provides special powers of direct regulation of the operation of commercial and cooperative banks.

General Credit Controls: There are three general or quantitative instruments of credit control, namely, the Bank Rate, Open Market Operations and Variable Reserve Requirements.

In considering the general methods of credit control, it is important to stress that these are closely inter-related and have to be operated in coordination. All the three instruments affect the level of bank reserves. Open Market Operations and the Reserve Requirements directly affect the reserve base, while the Bank Rate produces its impact indirectly by variations in the cost of acquiring the reserve.

The use of one instrument rather than another at any point of time is determined by the nature of the situation and the range of influence it is desired to wield as well as the rapidity with which the change is required to be brought about. Open Market Operations, for instance, are suited to carry out day-to-day adjustments on even the smallest scale. Changes in Reserve Requirements produce an impact at once and affect the banks generally. The effects of Bank Rate changes are not confined to the banking system and the short-term money market; they have wider repercussions on the economy as a whole.

Bank Rate Policy: The Bank Rate, also known as the Discount Rate, is the oldest instrument of monetary policy. The traditional definition of Bank Rate is that it is the rate at which the central bank discounts or, more accurately, rediscounts — eligible bills. However, today, the term Bank Rate is used in a broader sense and refers to the minimum rate at which the central bank provides financial accommodation to commercial banks in the discharge of its function as the lender of the last resort.

The Bank Rate policy seeks to affect both the cost and availability of credit. The availability depends largely on the statutory requirements regarding the eligibility of bills for rediscounting, and securities for collateral for advances, as also the maximum period for which the credit is available.

As the central bank is the lender of the last resort, a commercial bank which is loaned up can obtain financial accommodation (*i.e.,* loan) from the central bank and re-lend it to its own customers.

An increase in the Bank Rate means an increase in the rate of interest charged by the central bank on its advances to commercial banks. Hence, an increase in the Bank Rate compels commercial banks to raise the rate of interest they charge on their loan and advances to their customers and *vice versa.*

The importance of the Bank Rate lies in the fact that it acts as a pace-setter to all the other rates of interests. In a well-developed money market, like the London Money Market, all the market rates quickly and effectively respond to a variation in the Discount rate.

An increase in the Bank Rate implies an increase in the cost of credit and *vice versa.* The demand for credit usually varies with the variation in the cost of credit. The central bank can, therefore, hope to bring about a contraction in the money supply by raising the Bank Rate and an expansion in the money supply by lowering it.

As per the theory of Bank Rate, an increase in the Bank Rate reduces the extent of borrowings from the money market, the level of inventory holding, investment, employment and prices. A reduction in the Discount Rate has the opposite effects. The central bank may, therefore, attempt to contain an inflationary situation by raising the Bank Rate and fight a depression or recession by lowering it.

Open Market Operations: Open Market Operations refer broadly to the purchase and sale by the Central Bank of a variety of assets, such as foreign exchange, gold, Government securities and even company shares. In India, however, in practice, they are confined to the purchase and sale of Government securities.

Under the Open Market operations, the central bank seeks to influence the economy either by increasing the money supply or by decreasing the money supply.

To increase the money supply, the central bank buys securities from commercial banks and public. For instance, if the Reserve Bank of India buys securities worth ₹ 100 crores, in the first instance the reserves of the commercial banks and currency with the public will increase by ₹ 100 crore. However, the ultimate increase in money supply might be much more than this. When the central bank purchases securities from commercial banks the increase in their reserves might result in a multiple credit creation. Sometimes, the purchase from the public may lead to an increase in the reserves of the banking system and credit expansion if the sellers of securities deposit the receipts with commercial banks. A sale of securities by the central bank has the opposite effects.

Open Market Operations have been employed by the Reserve Bank primarily to assist the Government in its borrowing operations and to maintain orderly conditions in the gilt-edged market. In this process, this instrument has been used to groom the market by purchasing securities nearing maturity to facilitate redemption and to make available on tap a variety of loans to broaden the gilt-edged market. As banker to the Government, it is the duty of the Reserve Bank to create in the gilt-edged market conditions that are favourable to the successful implementation of the Government's borrowing and refunding operations. On the other hand, the Government's loan operations themselves are so arranged as to be in harmony, as general stability of the money and capital markets. Open Market Operations have also been used to provide seasonal finance to banks. In the slack season, banks generally invest their surplus funds in Government securities, which they sell (or against which they borrow) during the busy season, in order to expand credit to industry and commerce, the Reserve Bank being generally ready to deal in these securities.

Variable Reserve Ratios: Commercial banks in every country maintain, either by the requirement of law by or custom, a certain percentage of their deposits in the form of balances with the central bank. The central bank has the power to vary this reserve requirement; and the variation in the reserve requirements affect the credit creating capacity of commercial banks. For instance, if the reserve requirement is 10 per cent, the maximum amount the bank can lend is equivalent to 90 per cent of the total reserves. If the reserve ratio is raised to 20 per cent, the bank cannot lend more than 80 per cent of the total reserves.

The Reserve Bank of India is empowered to vary the cash reserve ratio between 3 per cent and 15 per cent of the total demand and time liabilities. To facilitate the flexible operation of this system, the RBI has also been vested with the power to require the scheduled banks to maintain with it additional cash reserves, computed with reference to the excess of their total demand and time liabilities over the level of such liabilities on the base date to be notified by the Reserve Bank, subject to the proviso that the total reserve to be maintained with the Bank should not exceed 15 per cent of their demand and time liabilities.

In March 2001, the Reserve Bank of India cut the CRR by half a percentage to 7.5 per cent and this was estimated to release over ₹ 4,000 crore to the economy. This indicates the impact that variations in the CRR can have on the money supply and the economy.

SLR: Action has also been taken to prevent banks from offsetting the impact of variable reserve requirements by liquidating their Government security holdings. The Banking Regulation Act has been amended, requiring all banks to maintain a minimum amount of liquid assets which shall not be less than a certain specified percentage of their demand and time liabilities in India, exclusive of the cash balances maintained under Section 42 of the Reserve Bank of India Act in the case of schedule banks, and exclusive of the cash balances maintained under Section 18 of the Banking Regulation Act in the case of non-scheduled banks. This ensures that with every increase in the cash reserve requirements, the overall liquidity obligations are also correspondingly raised.

Selective Credit Regulation: Selective and qualitative credit control refers to regulation of credit for specific purposes or branches of economic activity. While general credit controls operate on the cost and total volume of credit, selective controls relate to the distribution or direction of available credit supplies. It may be mentioned here that some element of selectivity can be imparted to general credit controls also by giving concessions to priority sectors or activities. This has often been done in India.

The aim of selective controls is to discourage such forms of activity as are considered to be relatively inessential or less desirable. Selective credit controls have been used in the Western countries to prevent the demand for durable consumer goods out-running the supply, and generating inflationary pressure. In the USA, they have been used to regulate stock market credit as well. In India, such controls have been used to prevent speculative hoarding of commodities like foodgrains and essential raw materials to check an undue rise in their prices. In addition to selective credit controls, many central banks have acquired powers of direct regulation of the total magnitude, as also the distribution of advances and investments of individual banks as well as of the entire banking system.

Selective credit controls are considered to be a useful supplement to general credit regulation. From available experience, it appears that their effectiveness is greatly enhanced when they are used together with general credit controls. They are designed specifically to curb excesses in selected area without affecting other types of credit. They attempt to achieve a reasonable stabilisation of the prices of particular commodities on the demand side, by regulating the availability of bank credit for purchasing and holding them. It should, however, be noted that prices are determined by the interaction of supply and demand, and that when supply is substantially short, what selective credit controls are likely to accomplish is to moderate the price rise rather than arrest the basic trend.

The Banking Regulation Act confers on the Reserve Bank the power to give directions to banking companies, either generally or to any banking company or group of banking companies in particular, as to —

(*a*) the purposes for which advances may or may not be made;

(*b*) the margin to be maintained in respect of secured advances;

(*c*) the maximum amount of advances or other financial accommodation which, having regard to the paid-up capital, reserves and deposits of a banking company and other relevant considerations, may be made by that banking company to any one company, firm, association of persons or individual;

(*d*) the maximum amount up to which, having regard to the considerations referred to in clause (c) guarantees may be given by a banking company on behalf of any one company, firm, association of persons or individual; and

(*e*) the rate of interest and other terms and conditions on which advances or other financial accommodation may be made or guarantees may be given.

The Reserve Bank is also empowered to issue, from time-to-time, to banking companies generally or to any banking company in particular, such directions as it deems fit in the public interest; or in the interest of banking policy; or to prevent the affairs of any banking company from being conducted in a manner detrimental to the interests of the depositors; or in a manner prejudicial to the interests of the banking company, or to secure the proper management of any banking company generally. The banking companies or the banking company, as the case may be, shall be bound to comply with such directions.

Further, the Reserve Bank may caution or prohibit banking companies generally or any banking company in particular against entering into any particular transaction or class of transactions, and generally give advice to any banking company.

From time-to-time, the Reserve Bank has asked banks in its circular letters to exercise caution in their lending in general, as well as lending against the security of specified commodities and shares.

The techniques of selective credit controls used generally are:

(*a*) Minimum margins for lending against specific securities;

(*b*) Ceilings on the amounts of credit for certain purposes; and

(*c*) Discriminatory rates of interest charged on certain types of advances.

In India, selective credit controls are operated under all the three techniques. While imposing selective controls, care is generally taken to ensure that credit for production, the movement of commodities and exports, is not affected. Selective controls are focused mainly on credit to traders financing inventories.

Moral Suasion: In addition to the above mentioned methods of credit control, both quantitative and qualitative, it may be noted that the use has also been made in this country of moral suasion. Periodically, letters are issued to banks urging them to exercise control over credit in general or advances against particular commodities or unsecured advances. Discussions are also held with bankers for the same purpose. Such discussions between the bank and commercial banks have been frequent. The RBI has been able to build-up over the years good informal relations with banks. Moral suasion, backed as it is by the Bank's vast powers of direct regulation, has proved quite useful. The use of this instrument is facilitated by the concentration of banking business in the hands of the Government.

FISCAL POLICY

Fiscal Policy is that part of Government policy which is concerned with raising revenue through taxation and other means and deciding on the level and pattern of expenditure.

The fiscal policy operates through the budget. The Budget is an estimate of Government expenditure and revenue for the ensuing financial year, presented to Parliament (in case of Union Budget) usually by the Finance Minister. Occasionally, in times of financial crisis, interim Budgets may be introduced later in the year to increase taxation, expenditures, etc. Sometimes, there may be slight modifications in taxation and expenditure without the formality of a revised budget.

> **Fiscal policy can influence the level and pattern of resource allocation/expenditure and the level and pattern of demand.**

The Union Budget

The Constitution of India provides that –

1. No tax can be levied or collected except by authority of law.
2. No expenditure can be incurred for public funds except in the manner provided in the Constitution.

3. The executive authorities must spend public money only in the manner sanctioned by Parliament in the case of the Union and by the State legislature in the case of a State.

An estimate of all anticipated revenue and expenditure of the Union Government for the ensuing financial year is laid before Parliament on the last working day of February every year. This is known as the Annual Financial Statement or the Budget and covers the Central Government's transactions of all kinds in and outside India during the year in which the statement is prepared as well as ensuing year, or the Budget year, as it is known.

All receipts and disbursements of the Union Government are kept under two separate headings, namely, the Consolidated Fund of India and the Public Account of India. All revenues received, loans raised and money received in repayment of loans by the Union Government form the Consolidated Fund. No money can be withdrawn from this Fund except under the authority of an Act of Parliament. All other receipts and disbursements, such as deposits, service funds and remittances go into the Public Account, which is not subject to the vote of Parliament. To meet unforeseen needs not provided in the Annual Appropriation Act, a Contingency Fund of India has also been established under Article 267(1) of the Constitution.

The presentation of the Annual Financial Statement is followed by a general discussion on the Budget in both the Houses of Parliament. The estimates of expenditure from the Consolidated Fund of India are then placed before the Lok Sabha in the form of Demands for Grants. Ordinarily, a separate demand is made for each Ministry. All withdrawals of money from the Consolidated Fund are thereafter authorised by an Appropriation Act passed embodied in another Bill, which is passed as the Finance Act of the Year.

The receipts and expenditure of the Central and State Governments are audited by the Comptroller and Auditor General who is independent of the executive, and his reports on the accounts are submitted to the President/Governor for having them laid before Parliament/State legislature.

The Structure of the Budget: The Budget is divided vertically into revenue (receipts) and expenditure (disbursements). Horizontally, it is divided into revenue account and capital account. The receipts are thus, broken up into Revenue Receipts and Capital Receipts; and disbursements are broken up into Revenue Expenditure and Capital Expenditure.

The revenue expenditure includes all current expenditure of the Government on administration, and the capital expenditure includes all the capital transactions of the Government.

The revenue receipts include revenue from taxes, while capital receipts include market loans, external aid, income from repayments and other receipts, such as income from public undertakings.

State Budgets

Like the Union Government, State Governments, too, have their own budgets. Estimates of receipts and expenditure are presented by the State Governments to their legislatures before the beginning of the financial year and legislative sanction of expenditure is secured through similar procedure.

As in the case of the Union Government, the Constitution has provided for the establishment of a Consolidated Fund, a Public Account and a Contingency Fund for each State.

Finances of the Union and States

The Constitution of India has earmarked separate sources of revenue for the Union and the States.

Sources of Revenue for the Union: The Union List in the Constitution includes the following revenue subjects:

1. Taxes on income other than agricultural income;
2. Duties and customs, including export duties;
3. Duties of excise on tobacco and other goods manufactured or produced in India, except alcoholic liquors for human consumption and opium, Indian hemp and other narcotic drugs and narcotics;
4. Corporation tax;
5. Taxes on the capital value of assets, exclusive of agricultural land, of individual companies; taxes on the capital of companies;
6. Estate duty in respect of property other than agricultural land;
7. Duties in respect of succession to property other than agricultural land;
8. Terminal taxes on goods of passengers carried by the railways, by sea, or air; taxes on railway fares and freight;
9. Taxes other than stamp duties on transactions on stock exchanges;
10. Rate of stamp duty on bills of exchange;
11. Taxes on sale or purchase of newspapers and on advertisements published therein;
12. Fees in respect of any of the matters in the Union List, but not including fees taken in any court;
13. Any tax not mentioned in the State List or Concurrent List.

Sources of Revenue for the State: The State List in the Constitution includes the following revenue subjects:

1. Land revenue, including the assessment and collection of revenue, the maintenance of land records, survey for revenue purposes and records of rights and alienation of revenue.
2. Taxes on agricultural income.
3. Duties in respect of succession to agricultural lands.
4. Estate duty in respect of agricultural land.
5. Taxes on lands and buildings.

6. Taxes on mineral rights, subject to any limitations imposed by Parliament by law relating to mineral development.
7. Duties of excise on the following goods manufactured or produced elsewhere in India: (a) alcoholic liquors for human consumption; (b) opium, Indian hemp and other narcotic drugs and narcotics.
8. Taxes on the entry of goods into a local area for consumption, use or sale therein.
9. Taxes on the consumption or sale of electricity.
10. Taxes on the sale or purchase of goods (other than newspapers).
11. Taxes on advertisements (other than those on newspapers).
12. Taxes on goods and passengers carried by road or inland water ways.
13. Taxes on vehicles, whether mechanically propelled or not, used on roads.
14. Taxes on animals and boats.
15. Tolls.
16. Taxes on profession, trades, callings and employment.
17. Capitation taxes.
18. Taxes on luxuries, including taxes on entertainment, amusements, betting and gambling.
19. Rates of stamp duty in respect of documents other than those specified.
20. Fees in respect of any of the matters in this list but not including fees taken in any court.
21. Fisheries.
22. Forests.
23. Irrigation, water storage and water power.

Concurrent List: The main revenue items in the Concurrent List under the Constitution are:

1. Stamp duties other than duties or fees collected by means of judicial stamps but including rates of stamp duty.
2. Fees in respect of any of the matters in this list but not including fees taken in any court.

The Finance Commission: Under the Constitution of India, a Finance Commission is to be constituted every fifth year or at such earlier time as the President considers necessary to make recommendations to the President as to:

1. The distribution between the Union and States of the net proceeds of taxes which are to be or may be divided between the States of the respective shares of such proceeds;
2. The principles which should govern the grants-in-aid of the revenues of the State in need of such assistance out of the Consolidated Fund of India; and

3. Any other matters referred to the Commission by the President in the interest of sound finance.

The recommendation of the Commission, together with an explanatory memorandum as to the action taken thereon, are laid before each House of Parliament. Eleven Finance Commissions were constituted since the commencement of the Constitution.

IMPORTANCE OF THE BUDGET

There is no other Government measure that affects the whole economy as the Budget. No wonder all sections of the people await the annual Budget with mixed feelings — anxiety, fear and hope.

The importance of functional finance and pump priming are recognised all over the world.

The endeavour of the Finance Minister is to present a Budget which gives maximum support to forces that can move the country forward on the path of growth with stability and social justice. The Budget should set the stage for the achievement of economic and social goals.

In India, today, a substantial part of the GDP is channelled into the Government sector by the Union, State and UT Budgets and disbursed by the Union, State and UT Governments under various development and non-development heads. These indicate the development and distributive importance and implications of the budgetary operations.

There has been a steep increase in the Government expenditures, both in absolute and relative terms.

In a developing economy like India, the Budget policy has to serve the following purposes:

1. Accelerate the pace of economic development by mobilising resources for the public sector and their optimal allocation;
2. Effect improvement in production in the private sector in accordance with the national priorities;
3. Effect improvements in income distribution;
4. Promote exports and encourage import substitution; and
5. Achieve economic stabilisation.

To serve these purposes, apart from the judicious allocation of the budgetary resources, various fiscal incentives and disincentives are also employed by the Budget. An examination of the Budget Proposals will make these very clear.

Certain sectors or industries may be significantly impacted by the budget proposals like tax proposals or budgetary allocations.

In short, both monetary and fiscal operations have repercussions on the whole economy, affecting the price level, the balance of payments, the levels of industrial activity and employment. While the monetary policy influences economic trends, especially investment, through the cost and availability of credit, fiscal policy directly affects the financial resources and purchasing power in the hands of the public. In a country which has adopted a programme of planned economic development, in which the public sector has an important part to play, fiscal policy is concerned largely with effecting structural changes in the economy, while monetary policy aims at regulating investment in the private sector and short-run management of the economy. When economic objectives are set, both monetary and fiscal policies should aim at achieving these objectives. If they are to be successful, a close coordination of monetary and fiscal policies is necessary, for they are complementary and not competitive.

THE FINANCE COMMISSION

Under the Constitution of India, a Finance Commission is to be constituted every fifth year or at such earlier time as the President considers necessary to make recommendations to the President as to:

1. The distribution between the Union and States of the net proceeds of taxes which are to be or may be divided between the States of the respective shares of such proceeds;
2. The principles which should govern the grants-in-aid of the revenues of the State in need of such assistance out of the Consolidated Fund of India; and
3. Any other matters referred to the Commission by the President in the interest of sound finance.

The recommendation of the Commission, together with an explanatory memorandum as to the action taken thereon, are laid before each House of Parliament. So far 14 Finance Commissions have submitted their reports.

SUMMARY

The Monetary and Fiscal Policies are two important instruments employed by the authorities to influence the behaviour and performance of the financial sector and the economy in general. They may also be used to influence specific sectors or industries or segments. In other words, the fiscal and monetary policies are also important determinants of business prospects and investment decisions. They can help make the overall economic situation and business prospects bright or check an unwarranted boom or unhealthy demand explosion. They can encourage investment and production in certain priority sectors and discourage them in the non-priority sectors. They are also capable of influencing technological choice and investment and production patterns.

Monetary Policy refers to the use of instruments within the control of the monetary authority (*i.e.,* the Central Bank of the country- the Reserve Bank of India) to influence the level of aggregate demand for goods and services or to influence the trends in certain sectors of the economy. Monetary policy operates through varying the cost and availability of credit. These variations affect the demand for, and the supply of credit in the economy, and the level and nature of economic activities.

There are, broadly, two instruments of monetary policy (methods of credit control), *viz.,* General (Quantitative) methods; and Selective (Qualitative) methods.

The general methods affect the total quantity of credit and the economy generally. There are three general or quantitative instruments of credit control, namely, the Bank Rate, Open Market Operations and Variable Reserve Requirements.

The Bank Rate, also known as the Discount Rate, refers to the minimum rate at which the central bank provides financial accommodation to commercial banks in the discharge of its function as the lender of the last resort. The lending rate of the commercial banks increase or decrease in accordance with the Bank Rate. The variation in the lending rate affects the demand for credit and, thereby, the money supply. Open Market Operations refer broadly to the purchase and sale by the central bank of a variety of assets, such as foreign exchange, gold, Government securities and even company shares under the Open Market Operations, the central bank seeks to influence the economy either by increasing the money supply or by decreasing the money supply. To increase the money supply, the central bank buys securities from commercial banks and public. A sale of securities by the central bank will have the effect of reducing the money supply. Commercial banks in every country maintain, either by the requirement of law or by custom, a certain percentage of their deposits in the form of balances with the central bank. The central bank has the power to vary this reserve requirement; and the variation in the reserve requirements affects the credit creating capacity of commercial bank.

In considering the general methods of credit control, it is important to stress that these are closely inter-related and have to be operated in coordination. All the three instruments affect the level of bank reserves. Open Market Operations and the Reserve Requirements directly affect the reserve base, while the Bank Rate produces its impact indirectly by variations in the cost of acquiring the reserve. The use of one instrument rather than another at any point of time is determined by the nature of the situation and the range of influence it is desired to wield, as well as the rapidity with which the change is required to be brought about.

The selective methods are intended to affect certain select sectors. In other words, under the selective methods, certain qualitative distinctions are made between different sectors and segments of the economy; and selectivity is applied in regulating the flow of credit. While general credit controls operate on the cost and total volume of credit, selective controls relate to the distribution or direction of available credit supplies. The aim of selective controls is to discourage such forms of activity as are considered to be relatively inessential or less desirable.

The Fiscal Policy is that part of Government policy which is concerned with raising revenue through taxation an other means and deciding on the level and pattern of expenditure.

The fiscal policy operates through the budget. The Budget is an estimate of Government expenditure and revenue for the ensuing financial year, presented to Parliament (in case of Union Budget) usually by the Finance Minister.

The Budget is divided vertically into revenue (receipts) and expenditure (disbursements). Horizontally, it is divided into revenue account and capital account. The receipts are, thus, broken up into Revenue Receipts and Capital Receipts; and disbursements are broken up into Revenue Expenditure and Capital Expenditure.

The revenue expenditure includes all current expenditure of the Government on administration, and the capital expenditure includes all the capital transactions of the Government.

The revenue receipts include revenue from taxes, while capital receipts include market loans, external aid, income from repayments and other receipts, such as income from public undertakings.

Like the Union Government, State Governments too, have their own budgets.

The Constitution of India has earmarked the sources of revenue for the Union and States. Further, under the Constitution of India, a Finance Commission is to be constituted every fifth year or at such earlier time as the President considers necessary to make recommendations to the President as to the distribution between the Union and States of the net proceeds of taxes which are to be or may be divided between the States of the respective shares of such proceeds; the principles which should govern the grants-in-aid of the revenues of the State in need of such assistance out of the Consolidated Fund of India; and any other matters referred to the Commission by the President in the interest of sound finance.

The Budget should strive to give maximum support to forces that can move the country forward on the path of growth with stability and social justice. The Budget should set the stage for the achievement of economic and social goals.

Certain sectors or industries may be significantly impacted by the budget proposals like tax proposals or budgetary allocations. The business community, therefore awaits the budget with a lot of anxiety.

☆☆☆

CHAPTER 10

MONEY AND CAPITAL MARKETS

Money and Capital Markets are two most important components of the Financial Market.

MONEY MARKET

Meaning of Money Market

Money Market is the market for short-term funds, as distinct from the Capital Market which deals in long-term funds.

Sometimes, the term Money Market is used in a very broad sense to include markets for both the short-term, and long-term funds. When the term is used in such a broad sense, Money Market includes, obviously, the Capital Market also. However, when a distinction is drawn between the Money Market and the Capital Market, the former refers only to the market for short-term funds, and the latter for long-term funds. As we draw, in this chapter, a distinction between these two, Money Market should be interpreted as the market for short-term funds.

> **Money Market is a place where the lending and borrowing of short-term funds are arranged and it comprises the short-term credit instruments and the institutions and individuals who participate in the lending and borrowing business. The market for long-term funds is known as capital market.**

In the words of the Reserve Bank of India, a Money Market is a "centre for dealings, mainly of a short-term character, in monetary assets; it meets the short-term requirements of the borrowers and provides liquidity or cash to lenders. It is the place where short-term surplus investible funds at the disposal of the financial and other institutions and individuals are bid by borrowers, again comprising institutions and individuals and also by the government."[1]

Constituents of Money Market

Dr. Lavington divides the money market into inner and outer spheres — the inner constituting "a nucleus of specialised institutions such as the banks, the market for negotiable securities, the bill brokers and the trust and finance companies, and the outer extending beyond this centre, including the work of solicitors, of brokers of securities and the entire system of trade and credit".

The central bank, commercial banks, cooperative banks, savings banks discount houses, acceptance house, etc., are the main constituents of a well developed money market. However, some of these institutions would not be found in some money markets.

The central bank usually occupies a pivotal position in the money market. It is regarded as the 'presiding deity' of the money market. A strong central bank in an organised money market can very significantly influence the conditions and activities of the market. In developing economies like India, organisation and development of a full-fledged money market is one of the prime responsibilities of the central bank.

In developing countries like India, the money market is broadly divided into organised and unorganised markets or sectors. The unorganised segment is by and large outside the control of the central bank and is characterised by lack of uniformity and formality in their business dealings. In India, the indigenous bankers and moneylenders are important constituents of the unorganised money market.

A developed money market consists of certain specialised sub-markets which help the mobilisation of savings by providing fruitful investment opportunities. They are also very helpful in imparting liquidity.

Certain specialised organisations like information bureaus, chambers of commerce, trade associations, etc., help the smooth and efficient functioning of the money market by helping the collection and dissemination of information to industry, trade and commerce.

Functions of Money Market

As the Reserve Bank of India observes, "a well-developed money market is the basis for an effective monetary policy. It is in the money market that the Central Bank comes into contact with the financial sectors of the economy as a whole and it is through varying the liquidity in the market and thereby influencing the cost and availability of credit that the Bank achieves its economic objectives."

The important functions of a well developed money market may be listed down in more precise terms as follows:

1. By providing various kinds of credit instruments suitable and attractive for different sections, a money market augments the supply of funds.
2. Efficient working of a money market helps to minimise the gluts and stringencies in the money market due to the seasonal variations in the flow of and demand for funds.

3. A money market helps to avoid wide seasonal fluctuations in the interest rates.
4. A money market, by augmenting the supply of funds and making them readily available to the legitimate borrowers, helps in making funds available at cheaper rates.
5. A well organised money market, through quick transfer of funds from one place to another, helps to avoid the regional gluts and stringencies of funds.
6. It enhances the amount of liquidity available to the entire country.
7. A money market, by providing profitable investment opportunities for short-term surplus funds, helps to enhance the profit of financial institutions and individuals.

A money market functions like a dam-canal-irrigation system. Like a reservoir it collects and augments the resources and channelises it to the various needed areas.

A well organised money market is an essential condition for the successful operation of the Central Banking Policies. The money market is "the locus of central banking policies for holding the conditions of liquidity within the bounds of what the monetary authorities consider desirable".

THE INDIAN MONEY MARKET

As the Reserve Bank observes, "as in most developing countries, the money market in India comprises two sectors which may broadly be termed as the organised and unorganised markets, with substantially higher rates of interest in the unorganised sector."

The Indian money market consists of two broad sectors, viz., the organised sector (consisting of commercial banks and modern financial institutions) and unorganised sector (consisting of indigenous banks and moneylenders).

The organised market comprises in the first place the Reserve Bank which is "the key constituent of the money market being the residual source of supply of funds and it is this which invests the Bank's operations with great significance", and occupies "a strategic position in the money market",

Then come the commercial banks. They include the public sector banks and other joint stock banks, Indian and foreign.

In the past, quasi-government bodies and large-sized joint stock companies also used to participate in the operations of the money market as lenders, the money lent by them being usually termed 'house money'. In later years, such 'house money' declined to negligible proportions as most of the joint stock companies did not have surplus fund to lend and they were in fact in search of funds which they obtained partly by accepting deposits from the public.

Then there are the financial intermediaries such as call loan brokers and general finance and stock brokers. "The core of the Indian money market is the inter-bank call money market." Although the magnitude of funds dealt in this market is not large in relation to the deposit resources of banks, "perhaps this is the most sensitive sector of the money market". The banks have been directing their demands for accommodation to the Reserve Bank.

According to the Reserve Bank, despite its limitations, "from the point of view of specialisation of functions and organised relationships, the Indian money market may be considered to be comparatively well-developed".

The unorganised sector, which itself is not homogeneous, is largely made up of what are known as "indigenous" bankers. In this market there is no clear demarcation between short-term or long-term finance, in as much as there is usually nothing on the *hundi* (an indigenous bill of exchange) to indicate whether it is for financing trade or providing financial accommodation — in other words, whether it is genuine trade bill or financial paper, by and large, these bills are accommodation bills.

The co-operative credit institutions occupy a somewhat intermediate position between the organised and unorganised sectors of the money market. With the notable increase in the number of commercial bank branches in the rural and semi-urban areas, closer links have been forged between the cooperative credit system and the organised money market, especially with the State Bank and its subsidiaries.

The money market structure in India, loosely knit as it is, is not entirely uncoordinated. The indigenous bankers enjoy rediscount facilities from the commercial banks which in turn have access to the Reserve Bank.

A well-developed money market will have close links with the leading money markets of the world and will be sensitive to the developments in these foreign markets. But the Indian money market was an insular one with little contact with foreign money markets. The money markets of advanced Western countries are characterised by large movements of capital between them. Due partly to the exchange control restrictions on capital movements, there was hardly any movement of funds between the Indian money market and the foreign market. Consequent to the economic reforms ushered in 1991, the Indian market has been getting linked, albeit in a limited way, to the global market.

The money market structure has undergone a change over the years, particularly under the impetus of the economic reforms. Unlike in developed economies where money markets are promoted by financial intermediaries out of efficiency considerations, in India, as in many other developing countries, the evolution of the money market and its structure has been integrated into the overall deregulation process of the financial sector.

The Reserve Bank has gradually developed money markets through a five-pronged effort. First, interest rate ceilings on inter-bank call/notice money, inter-bank term money, rediscounting of commercial bills and inter-bank participation without risk were withdrawn effective from May 1,1989. Secondly, several financial innovations in terms of money market instruments, such as, auctions of Treasury Bills, certificates of deposit, commercial paper and RBI repos were introduced. Thirdly, barriers to entry were gradually eased by (*i*) increasing the number of players (beginning with the Discount and Finance House of India (DFHI) in April 1988 followed by primary and satellite dealers and money market mutual funds), (*ii*) relaxing both issuance restrictions and subscription norms in respect of money market instruments and allowing determination of yields based on demand and supply of such paper, and (*iii*) enabling market evaluation of associated risks, by withdrawing regulatory restrictions, such as, bank guarantees in respect of CPs. Fourthly, the development of markets for short-term funds at market determined interest rates has been fostered by a gradual switch from a cash credit system to a loan-based system, shifting the onus of cash management from banks to borrowers and phasing out the 4.6 per cent 91-day tap Treasury Bills, which in the past provided an avenue for investing short-term funds. Finally, institutional development has been carried out to facilitate inter-linkages between the money market and the foreign exchange market, especially after a market-based exchange rate system was put in place in March 1993.

The changes in the money market structure need to be seen in the context of a gradual shift from a regime of administered interest rates to a market-based pricing of assets and liabilities. The development of money markets in India in the last half of the 1990s has been facilitated by three major factors. First, the limiting of almost automatic funding of the government, largely realised with the replacement of *ad hoc* Treasury Bills (which bore a fixed coupon rate of 4.6 per cent per annum from July 1974, implying a negative real interest rate for most part of the period) by ways and means advances (WMA) at interest rates linked to the Bank Rate and the development of the Government securities market, discussed later in the chapter, permitting a gradual de-emphasis on cash reserve ratio as a monetary policy instrument. Secondly, the development of an array of instruments of indirect monetary control, such as, the Bank Rate (reactivated in April 1997), the strategy of combining auctions, private placements and open market operations in government paper and the liquidity adjustment facility (LAF). Thirdly, the enabling institutional framework was introduced in the form of primary and satellite dealers and money market mutual funds. The monetary authority uses money markets to adjust primary liquidity in the domestic economy and monetary policy is often, in turn, shaped by developments in the money and the foreign exchange markets.

Money Market Instruments and Constituents[2]

The money market instruments in India mainly comprise: (*i*) call money, (*ii*) certificates of deposit, (*iii*) Treasury Bills, (*iv*) other short-term Government securities transactions, such as, repos, (*v*) bankers' acceptances/commercial bills, (*vi*) commercial paper, and (*vii*) inter-corporate funds.

While inter-bank money markets and central bank lending *via* repo operations or discounting provide liquidity for banks, private non-bank money market instruments, such as, commercial bills and commercial paper provide liquidity to the commercial sector.

Call/Notice Money Market: Call and notice money are money dealt for one to 14 days. The period of term money ranges from 14 days to 90 days. This is sometimes a very volatile market and the interest rate is determined by the market forces. This market is of vital importance to banks and financial institutions because of the avenue it provides for investing surplus funds and meeting the deficits. The Inter-bank lending is the major component of this market.

The overnight inter-bank call money market, in which banks trade positions to maintain cash reserves, is the key segment of the money market in India. It is basically an 'over the counter' (OTC) market without the intermediation of brokers. Participation has been gradually widened to include other financial institutions, primary/satellite dealers, mutual funds and other participants in the bills rediscounting market and corporates (through primary dealers) besides banks, LIC and UTI. While banks and primary dealers are allowed two-way operations, other non-bank entities can only participate as lenders. As per the announced policies, once the repo market develops, the call money market would be made into a pure inter-bank market, including primary dealers.

The call money market is influenced by liquidity conditions (mainly governed by deposit mobilisation, capital flows and the Reserve Bank's operations affecting banks' reserve requirements on the supply side and tax outflows, government borrowing programme, non-food credit off-take and seasonal fluctuations, such as, large currency drawals during the festival season on the demand side). At times of easy liquidity, call rates tend to hover around the Reserve Bank's repo rate, which provides a ready avenue for parking short-term surplus funds. During periods of tight liquidity, call rates tend to move up towards the Bank Rate and more recently the Reserve Bank's reverse repo rate (and sometimes beyond) as the Reserve Bank modulates liquidity in pursuit of monetary stability. Besides, there are other influences, such as, *(i)* the reserve requirement prescriptions (and stipulations regarding average reserve maintenance), *(ii)* the investment policy of non-bank participants in the call market which are among the large suppliers of funds in the call market, and *(iii)* the asymmetries of the call money market, with few lenders and chronic borrowers.

Term Money Market: The term money market in India is still not developed. Select financial institutions (IDBI, ICICI, IFCI, IIBI, SIDBI, EXIM Bank, NABARD, IDFC and NHB) are permitted to borrow from the term money market for 3-6 months maturity, within stipulated limits for each institution.

Repos: Repo is a money market instrument, which enables collateralised short-term borrowing and lending through sale/purchase operations in debt instruments. Under a repo transaction, a holder of securities sells them to an investor with an agreement to repurchase at a predetermined date and rate. In the case of a repo, the forward clean price of the bonds is set in advance at a level which is different from the spot clean price by adjusting the difference between repo interest and coupon earned on the security. Repo is also called a ready forward transaction as it is a means of funding by selling a security held on a spot (ready) basis and repurchasing the same on a forward basis. Reverse repo is a mirror image of repo as in the case of former, securities are acquired with a simultaneous commitment to resell.

Repos help to manage liquidity conditions at the short-end of the market spectrum. Repos have often been used to provide banks an avenue to park funds generated by capital inflows to provide a floor to the call money market. During times of foreign exchange market volatility, repos have been used to prevent speculative activity as the funds tend to flow from the money market to the foreign exchange market. The repo rates were reduced with the return of capital flows, which imparted stability to the foreign exchange market.

Commercial Paper: Commercial papers are unsecured promissory notes of short term maturity of highly rated companies, issued to meet working capital requirements. The CP is subject to credit rating by any of the recognized credit rating agencies in India. As the CPs are tradable in the secondary market, including National Stock Exchange, they are regarded liquid.

Commercial Paper (CP) is issued by non-banking companies and all-India Financial Institutions (AIFIs) as an unsecured promissory note or in a dematerialised form at a rate of discount not tied to any transaction. It is privately placed with investors through the agency of banks. Banks act as both principals (*i.e.*, as counter parties in purchases and sales) and agents in dealership and placement. Banks are not allowed to either underwrite or co-accept issue of CP.

Certificates of Deposit: Certificates of Deposit (CD), introduced in June 1989, are essentially securitised short-term time deposits issued by banks during periods of tight liquidity, at relatively high interest rates (in comparison with term deposits). But the transaction cost of CDs is often lower as compared with that of retail deposits. When credit picks up, placing pressure on banks' liquidity, banks try to meet their liquidity gap by issuing CDs, often at a premium. The required amounts are mobilised in larger amounts through CD, often for short periods in order to avoid interest liability over-hang in the subsequent months when credit demand slackens. As banks offer higher interest rates on CDs, subscribers find it profitable to hold CDs till maturity. As a result, the secondary market for CDs has been slow to develop.

Commercial Bills Market: Commercial Bills (Bills of Exchange) are important instruments used to facilitate credit sales. Commercial bills can be discounted with banks and the banks, when they are in need of funds, may rediscount them in the money market.

The commercial bill market in India is very limited. The commercial bills market was constricted by the cash credit system of credit delivery where the onus of cash management rested with banks. The success of the bills discounting scheme is contingent upon financial discipline on the part of borrowers. As such discipline did not exist, the Reserve Bank, in July 1992, restricted the banks to finance bills to the extent of working capital needs based on credit norms. However, in order to encourage the 'bills' culture, the Reserve Bank advised banks in October 1997 that at least 25 per cent of inland credit purchases of borrowers should be through bills.

Money Market Mutual Funds (MMMFs): In April 1992, scheduled commercial banks and public financial institutions were allowed to set up MMMFs, subject to certain terms and conditions. The prescribed restrictions were relaxed subsequently between November 1995 and July 1996 in order to impart more flexibility, liquidity and depth to the market. MMMFs are allowed to invest in rated corporate bonds and debentures with a residual maturity of one year. The minimum lock-in period for units of MMMFs was relaxed from 30 days to 15 days in May 1998. In 1999-2000, MMMFs were allowed to offer 'cheque writing facility' in a tie-up with banks to provide more liquidity to unitholders. MMMFs, which were regulated under the guidelines issued by the Reserve Bank, have been brought under the purview of the SEBI regulations since March 7, 2000. Banks are now allowed to set up MMMFs only as a separate entity in the form of a trust. Currently, there are only three MMMFs in operation.

Treasury Bills: Treasury bills are promissory notes issued by the Central Government to raise short-term funds to bridge short-term mismatches between receipts and expenditures. The RBI which issues the TBs on behalf of the Government does not purchase them before maturity but investors can sell them in the secondary market through the DFHI or get it rediscounted.

CAPITAL MARKET

Capital Market is generally understood as the market for long-term funds. However, sometimes the term is used in a very broad sense to include also the market for short-term funds. For instance, by capital market some people mean "the market for all the financial instruments, short-term and long-term, as also commercial, industrial and Government Paper". When 'Capital Market' is used in such a broad sense, it embraces, obviously, the money market also.

Nature and Constituents

The term Capital Market is often used to refer to the market for long-term loanable funds as distinct from the money market which deals in short-term funds. It should, however, be added that there is no clear-cut distinction between the two markets. Many a time the same institutions receive and supply both short and long-term funds. The money and capital market are in fact inter-dependent, developments and trends in one affecting the other.

The capital market consists of a number of individuals and institutions (including the government) that canalise the supply and demand for long-term capital and claims on capital. The stock exchanges, commercial banks, cooperative banks, savings banks, development banks, insurance companies, investment trust or companies, etc., are important constituents of the capital market.

The capital market, like the money market, has three important components, namely, the suppliers of loanable funds, the borrowers and the intermediaries who deal with the lenders on the one hand and the borrowers on the other.

In the capital market, the supply of funds comes from the individual and corporate savings, institutional investors and surplus of governments. The demand for capital comes mostly from agriculture, industry, trade and the government.

With the emergence of joint stock companies as the predominant form of industrial organisation, developed capital market became a necessary infrastructure for fast industrialisation. Business firms can raise funds from the capital market by issuing shares and credit instruments. Capital market is not concerned solely with the issue of new claims on capital, but also with dealing in existing claims. In fact, marketability, of securities is an important element in the efficient working of the capital market, since investors would be reluctant to make loans if their claims could not be easily disposed of.

The developed countries have comparatively well-developed money and capital markets. But, in the developing countries the capital market, like the money market, is generally underdeveloped.

Importance of Capital Market

The pace of economic development is conditioned, among other things, by the rate of long-term investment and capital formation. And capital formation is conditioned by the mobilisation, augmentation and channelisation of investible funds. The capital market serves a very useful purpose by pooling the capital resources of the country and making them available to the enterprising investors. Well-developed capital markets augment resources by attracting and lending funds on a global scale. The Eurocurrency and Eurobond markets are international finance markets in terms of both the supply and demand for funds.

The increase in the size of the industrial units and business corporations due to technological developments, economies of scale and other factors has created a situation where in the capital at the disposal of one or few individuals is quite insufficient to meet the investment demands. A developed capital market can solve this problem of paucity of funds. For an organised capital market can mobilise and pool together even the small and scattered savings and augment the availability of investible funds. While the rapid growth of capital markets, the growth of joint stock business has in its turn encouraged the development of capital markets.

A developed capital market provides a number of profitable investment opportunities for the small savers.

Nature of the Indian Capital Market

Like the money market, the Indian capital market also consists of an organised sector and an unorganised sector. In the organised market the demand for capital comes mostly from corporate enterprises and government and semi-government institutions and the supply comes from household savings, institutional investors like banks investment trusts, insurance companies, finance corporations, government and international financing agencies.

The unorganised market consists mostly of the indigenous bankers and moneylenders on the supply side. While in the organised sector the demand for funds is mostly for productive investment, a large part of the demand for funds in the unorganised market is for consumption purposes. In fact, many purposes, for which funds are very difficult to get from the organised market, are financed by the unorganised sector. Like the unorganised money market, the unorganised capital market in India is characterised by the existence of multiplicity of interest rates, exorbitant rates of interest and lack of uniformity in their business dealings.

CAPITAL MARKET STRUCTURE

Marketable Securities

- Government Securities
- Corporate Securities
- PSU Bonds
- UTI Mutual Funds

Non-Marketable Securities

- Bank Deposits
- Deposits With Companies
- Loans and Advances of Banks and FIs.
- Post Office Certificates and Deposits

New Issues Market: Players–Original

- Promoters and Directors
- Associates and Friends
- Collaborators
- Employees
- FIs and Banks
- NRIs
- Public

Stock Market Intermediaries

- Brokers
- Jobbers
- Dealers
- Badla Financiers
- Arbitraguers

New Issues Market Players – For Issues

- Merchant Bankers
- Collecting Bankers
- Registrars, Brokers
- Underwriters
- Advertising Agencies
- Printers
- Solicitors
- Sub-Brokers
- Sub-underwriters
- Mailing Agents

Fig. 10.1: Capital Market Structure

EMERGING MARKET STRUCTURE IN INDIA

Recognised Stock Exchanges With Trading Floors 21

- Principal Exchanges
- Regional Exchanges
  - Attached Trading Floors (ATFs)
  - Licensed Dealers (Retail Broking) or Sub-brokers trading in bonds, debentures equities, odd lots, etc., of all companies

Over the Counter Exchange of India

(Computer aided Trading With No Trading Floor)
At Selected Centres
Trading in Equity and debentures of selected companies

National Stock Exchange

Over The Counter Electronic Trading on a National Network System
On National Basis
Institutional Structures
1. Securities Support Corporation
2. National Clearing and Settlement Corporation
3. Central Depository Trust, Whole-sale Debt Segment of Securities, Money Market instruments, debt instruments and tradings in equity shares

Fig. 10.2: Emerging Capital Market Structures in India

(*Figure 10.1* and *Figure 10.2* adopted from V.A. Avadhani, *Indian Capital Market*, Himalaya Publishing House, Mumbai, 1997).

While the activities of the organised market are subject to a number of government controls, the unorganised sector is by and large outside effective government control.

The organised sector has been subjected to increasing institutionalisation. A large chunk of the business of this sector is accounted for by the public sector financial institutions, and there is government control over other segments of the organised capital market.

Development of the Market

The Indian capital market has undergone remarkable changes in the post-independence era. Certain steps taken by the government to place the market on a strong footing and develop it to meet the growing capital requirements of fast industrialisation and development of the economy have significantly contributed to the developments that took place in the Indian capital market over the last five decades or so.

The important facts that have contributed to the development of the capital market in India are the following:

1. Legislative measures: Laws like the Companies Act, the Securities Contracts (Regulation) Act and the Capital Issues (Control) Act, empowered the government to regulate the activities of the capital market with a view to assuring healthy trends in the market, protecting the interests of the investors, efficient utilisation of the resources, etc.

2. Establishment of development banks and expansion of the public sector: Starting with the establishment of the IFCI, a number of development banks have been established at the national and regional levels to provide financial and other development assistance to the entrepreneurs and enterprises. These institutions came to account for a large chunk of the industrial finance.

Thus, an important aspect of the Indian capital market is that a large part of the investible funds available in the organised sector is owned by the government. The new economic policy will change the trend.

3. Growth of underwriting business: There has been a phenomenal growth in the underwriting business, thanks mainly to the public financial corporations and the commercial banks. After the elimination of the forward trading, brokers have begun to take on underwriting risks in the new issue market. In the last one decade the amount underwritten as percentage of total private capital issues offered to public varied between 72 per cent and 97 per cent.

4. Public confidence: Impressive performance of certain large companies encouraged public investment in industrial securities.

5. Increasing awareness of investment opportunities: The improvement in education and communication has created more public awareness about the investment opportunities in the business sector. The market for industrial securities has become broader.

6. Capital Market Reforms: A number of measures have been taken to check abuses and to promote healthy development of the capital market. For details, see the next chapter.

SUMMARY

Money and Capital Markets are two most important components of the Financial Market.

The term Money Market refers to the market for short-term funds, as distinct from the Capital Market which deals in long-term funds. However, sometimes these terms are used very broadly to include markets for both short and long-term funds.

The money market and the capital market have three important components, namely, the suppliers of loanable funds, the borrowers and the intermediaries who deal with the lenders on the one hand and the borrowers on the other. In developing countries like India, the money and capital markets are broadly divided into organised and unorganised markets or sectors. The unorganised segment is, by and large, outside the control of the central bank and is characterised by lack of uniformity and formality in their business dealings. In India, the indigenous bankers and moneylenders are important constituents of the unorganised market. The co-operative credit institutions occupy a somewhat intermediate position between the organised and unorganised sectors of the money market.

The central bank, commercial banks, co-operative banks, savings banks discount houses, acceptance house, etc., are the main constituents of the money market. However, some of these institutions would not be found in some money markets. The central bank usually occupies a pivotal position in the money market. It is regarded as the 'presiding deity' of the money market. A strong central bank in an organised money market can very significantly influence the conditions and activities of the market.

A well-developed money market helps efficient operation of the monetary policy, channelisation of the savings of the society, reduction of seasonal and regional imbalances in the supply of and demand for funds, and reduction of gap between borrowing and lending rates. A money market functions like a dam-canal-irrigation system. Like a reservoir it collects and augments the resources and channelises it to the various needed areas.

The money market instruments in India mainly comprise: (*i*) call money, (*ii*) certificates of deposit, (*iii*) treasury bills, (*iv*) other short-term Government securities transactions, such as, repos, (*v*) bankers' acceptances/commercial bills, (*vi*) commercial paper, and (*vii*) inter-corporate funds.

The capital market serves a very useful purpose by pooling the capital resources and making them available to the enterprising investors. Well-developed capital market augment resources by attracting and lending funds on a global scale.

The capital market consists of a number of individuals and institutions (including the government) that channelise the supply and demand for long-term capital and claims on capital. The stock exchanges, commercial banks, cooperative banks, savings banks, development banks, insurance companies, investment trust or companies, etc., are important constituents of the capital market.

The developed countries have comparatively well-developed money and capital markets. But, in the developing countries the capital market, like the money market, is generally underdeveloped.

The Indian capital market has undergone remarkable changes in the post-independence era. Certain steps taken by the government to place the market on a strong footing and develop it to meet the growing capital requirements of fast industrialisation and development of the economy have significantly contributed to the developments that took place in the Indian capital market over the last five decades or so.

REFERENCES

1. Reserve Bank of India, *Reserve Bank of India: Functions and Working,* RBI, Mumbai.
2. This section is based on Reserve Bank of India, *Report on Currency and Finance, 1999-2000.*

☆☆☆

CHAPTER

11

STOCK EXCHANGE AND ITS REGULATION

Meaning, Importance and Functions

According to the Securities Contracts (Regulation) Act, 1956, *stock exchange means any body of individuals, whether incorporated or not, constituted for the purpose of assisting, regulating or controlling the business of buying, selling or dealing in securities.*

> **Stock Exchange is a market in which securities are bought and sold. It is an essential component of a developed capital market which facilitates mobilisation of investible funds.**

According to this Act, *securities* include (*i*) shares, scrips, stocks, bonds, debentures, stock or other marketable securities of a like nature in or of any incorporated company or body corporate; (*ii*) Government securities; such other instruments as may be declared by the Central Government to be securities; and (*iii*) right or interest in securities.

Stock exchange is regarded as "an essential concomitant of the capitalistic system of economy. It is indispensable for the proper functioning of corporate enterprise. It brings together large amounts of capital necessary for the economic progress of a country. It is the citadel of capital and the pivot of money market.

It provides necessary mobility to capital and directs the flow of capital into profitable and successful enterprises. It is the barometer of general economic progress in a country and exerts a powerful and significant influence as a depressant or stimulant of business activity. It may be defined as the place or market where securities of joint stock companies and of government or semi-government bodies are dealt in."[1]

Speaking in the *Lok Sabha* in connection with his motion for reference of the Securities Contracts (Regulation) Bill to a Joint Committee of the Houses of Parliament in 1955, the Finance Minister made the following observations:[2]

The economic services, which a well constituted and efficiently run securities market can render to a country with a large private sector, operating under the normal incentives and impulses of private enterprises are considerable.

In the first place, it is only an organised securities market which can provide sufficient marketability and price continuity for shares, so necessary for the needs of investors.

Secondly, it is only such a market that can provide a reasonable measure of safety and fair dealing in the buying and selling of securities.

Thirdly, through the interplay of demand for and supply of securities, properly organised stock exchange assists in a reasonably correct evaluation of securities in terms of their real worth. Lastly, through such evaluation of securities the stock exchange helps in the orderly flow and distribution of savings as between different types of competitive investments.

BOX 11.1 : OBJECTIVES AND ROLE OF STOCK EXCHANGE

The objectives and the role of the Bombay Stock Exchange, which have remained the same as enunciated by founding fathers and given as a mandate in 1887 through the charter, highlight the functions and objectives of stock exchanges. These objectives are:

1. To safeguard the interest of investing public having dealings on the Exchange and the members.
2. To establish and promote honourable and just practices in securities transactions.
3. To promote, develop and maintain a well regulated market for dealing in securities.
4. To promote industrial developments in the country through efficient resource mobilisation by way of investment in corporate securities.

The Exchange while providing an efficient market also upholds the interests of the investors and ensures redressal of their grievances, whether against the companies or its own member-brokers. It also strives to educate and enlighten the investors by making available necessary informative inputs.

Dealings on Stock Exchange

Dealings on the stock exchange are subject to the bye-laws and rules of the stock exchange. Stock exchange dealings in India are regulated by the Securities Contracts (Regulation) Act and the Securities and Exchange Board of India (SEBI).

On the trading floor of the stock exchange, dealings are permitted only in the listed securities through the members or their authorised clerks during fixed working hours.

There are two important types of trading on the stock exchange namely *Ready Delivery* contract and *Forward Delivery* contract. The important differences between these two dealings are the following:

Ready delivery contracts, also known as *cash trading* or *cash transactions,* are to be settled either on the same date or within a short period that may extend at best up to seven days. (If the payment and delivery of securities is on the same day or on the next day, it may be called *spot delivery contract)*. As against these, the forward delivery contracts are discharged on fixed settlement days. Ready delivery contracts can be made in respect of all securities, whereas forward delivery contracts are confined to those securities which are placed on the forward list.

Speculation on the Stock Exchange

Stock exchange transactions are made either for the purpose of investment or for speculation. Investment transactions are made with the intention of earning a return on the securities by holding them more or less permanently, whereas speculative transactions are made with the intention of making gains by disposing of the securities at favourable prices.

A stock exchange is characterised by investment and speculative transations. Speculative transactions which seek to profit from price changes provide continuity and volume of business and vigour to the stock exchange.

The nature of the investment transaction and speculative transaction differs. The investment transactions require the actual delivery of securities on the part of sellers and the payment of their full price by the buyers. Speculative transactions, on the other hand, does not involve full payment for and taking delivery of the securities that the speculators have contracted to transfer. As the speculative transactions do not call for the payment of the full price but can be made by the deposit of a fractional part of the price, the volume of speculative transactions usually far exceed that of the investment transactions on any stock exchange. It is, therefore, argued that speculation is necessary to ensure sufficient volume and continuity of business in the stock exchange. However, unregulated speculation is not conducive. Introducing the Securities Contracts (Regulation) Bill, the then Finance Minister Mr. C.D. Deshmukh observed:[3]

"Sceptics may argue that it is impossible for any securities market to function properly because of the undesirable activities of speculators, and yet genuine speculation, which is based on a reasoned forecast of the real value of the investments, represented by the securities which are dealt with on the exchanges, performs a very important function. No stock exchange can operate purely on the basis of investment buying or selling, because "pure" investors in that sense are necessarily few in number and usually possess very limited resources. They cannot provide the requisite volume or continuity of business, which alone would enable a large number of buyers and sellers to trade at all times in the exchanges, and to bring about an adjustment of the relative values of the securities in which they trade, in conformity with their real worth. It is the buying and selling of securities on a large-scale on the basis of reasoned forecasts which alone can give the necessary breadth and continuity to the market. Informed speculation, which takes a reasonable view of future prospects, and thus brings about an appropriate adjustment security values, thus helps not only in the channelling of savings into the most productive lines, but also attracts new savings for investment into particular classes of securities. Too often, unfortunately, speculation in shares and scripts is not based on any reasoned calculation of the prospects of a company, and comes very close to gambling. The basic object of stock exchange reform is, therefore, to regulate speculative activities so that they may not degenerate into gambling; it is not the object of such reform to interfere with investment buying or selling or even with speculation as long as it conforms to the rules of the game."

Types of Speculators: The speculators on a stock exchange may be categorised into the following three (*i*) *Bull:* A bull, also known as *Tejiwalla,* is a speculator who buys shares in the expectation of selling it at a higher price later; (*ii*) *Bear:* A bear, also known as *Mandiwalla,* who sells securities in the expectation of a fall in their prices in future; (*iii*) *Stag:* A stag neither buys nor sells but applies for subscription to the new issues expecting that he can sell them at a premium.

Option Dealing: Option is the right to buy or sell a certain quantity of security at a certain price within a certain time. The option to buy is known as *call option* (or *Teji Sauda)* and the option to sell is known *as Put Option (Mandi Sauda).* The *Put* and *Call* is a double option (known as *Teji-Mandi)* giving the right either to purchase or to sell securities. In an option dealing, a speculator is given the right or option to buy or sell, or both buy and sell, as the case may be on the settlement day or else he will forfeit the option money.

Blank Transfers: Blank transfer means the transfer of a security without specifying the transferee. Although a blank transfer is not by itself, a speculative transaction, it encourages speculation in securities because the same transfer deed without any stamp duty revolves into many sale transactions in securities embodied therein. It also encourages tax evasion.

Carry Over (Badla) Transactions: Carry over or Badla refers to the facility of carry-over of the completion of a forward contract to another/next settlement period any number of times on payment of the badla charge. The badla charge paid by a bull is known as *contago* and that paid by the bear is called *backwardation.*

Organisation of Stock Exchange in India

There were 23 stock exchanges functioning in India including the Over The Counter Exchange of India (OTCEI) and the National Stock Exchange (NSE).

Some of the regional stock exchanges have been bound up. According to the present regulation, stock exchanges which do not satisfy specified criteria will have to wind up. Other regional exchanges have the option to exit.

The Bombay Stock Exchange, which was established in 1875 as "The Native Share and Stockbrokers Association" (a voluntary non-profit making association) is the oldest one in Asia; the Tokyo Stock Exchange was founded only in 1878.

> **The organisational forms of stock exchanges in India differ — voluntary association, public limited company and guarantee company.**

With about 10,000 listed companies, India holds the unique distinction of having the largest number of listed companies in the world. The number of investors is one of the largest in the world.[4]

Since the coming into effect of the Securities Contracts Act, 1956, only those stock exchanges which are recognised by the Government can function in the country. The policy of the Government is that there shall be only one stock exchange in one area. In pursuance of this policy, where more than one stock exchange existed as in Mumbai only one stock exchange was given recognition and the active members of the non-recognised stock exchanges were admitted.

Some stock exchanges like Mumbai, Indore and Ahmedabad are organized as Voluntary Association, some like Kolkata and Delhi are organised as public limited companies, whereas some like Hyderabad, Chennai and Bangalore are guarantee companies.

Each stock exchange is managed by an Executive Committee/Council of Management/ Governing Body to which the Government is empowered to nominate not more than three members. The rules and bye-laws of the stock exchange shall be in conformity with such conditions as may be prescribed by the Government. The Securities Contracts (Regulation) Act empowers the Government also to withdraw the recognition granted to a stock exchange, in the interest of trade or in public interest. Further, in order to deal with abnormal and extraordinary situations which may develop from time-to-time. Government is empowered to supercede a governing body after giving an opportunity to the governing body to be heard in the matter and to appoint in its place any person or persons to perform the functions of the governing body; and to suspend such of the business of a stock exchange under certain circumstances, for such period not exceeding seven days as may be specified, in the interest of trade or in public interest. The period of suspension can be extended from time-to-time, but after the governing body has been given an opportunity of being heard in the matter.

Dealers and brokers dealing outside the area of the recognised stock exchange have to obtain licence from the Government.

Only members and their authorised clerks can enter the trading floor and conduct buying and selling of securities. There are brokers and other intermediaries who assist the buyers and sellers in their dealings.

Members: In the past, only an individual (not a firm or company) could be a member. Now companies can also become members. Multiple membership, *i.e.,* membership in more than one stock exchange is also permitted.

Authorised Clerks: To assist the members for making transactions on the exchange, members are permitted to appoint a fixed number of authorised clerks. The number of authorised clerks varies from one exchange to another. The authorised clerks, as agents of the members, can enter the trading floor and buy or sell on behalf of their employers; but they cannot buy or sell on their own account.

Remisers: The remisers are sub-brokers employed by a member to secure business. The remisers are not permitted to enter the trading floor for exchange dealing. They are meant primarily to secure business from the outsiders. The remisers are very important in securing business because the share brokers are prohibited from making advertisement to solicit business.

Taravaniwalas and Brokers: Indian stock exchange has two categories of members namely Taravaniwalas and brokers. The Taravaniwala in India does the work similar to the *Jobber* in the London Stock Exchange. A jobber is a dealer in securities, while a broker is an agent of a buyer or seller of securities. Jobbers deal only with brokers and not with the public, whereas the broker is a middleman between the jobber and the real buyer/seller. But Taravaniwalas in India have been found to play a double role of broker-cum-dealer.

Clearing House: It is an agency that performs the task of arranging for delivery of securities and their payment by the concerned parties. The clearing house pools together all the bargains made by each member of the stock exchange so as to find out the result position and it traces the ultimate buyers and sellers of securities to put them in touch with each other. The clearing house thus simplifies and expedites the work.

OTCEI

The establishment of the Over The Counter Exchange of India (OTCEI) marked the dawn of a new era in the history of stock exchanges in India. The OTC Exchange is regarded a blessing for the small, both existing and new, companies and for investors, particularly small investors. The OTCEI which was incorporated in 1990 became fully operational in 1992.

> **The OTCEI, promoted by public sector financial institutions which is the first screenbased nationwide stock exchange in India, is of particular importance to small companies and small investors.**

The OTCEI is meant primarily to trade securities of the listed companies, like the other stock exchanges. It is, however, a stock exchange with a lot of differences with those of others. "Although the basic framework of the OTC Exchange is that *of a national market, yet there is no physical location, no counters, no trading ring, no stock exchange building and no hustle and bustle scenes as the conventional stock exchanges.* The buyers and sellers living apart from each other trade in corporate securities over the telephone. The system cuts across urban and rural areas extending the frontiers of the stock market to the entire country. These OTC markets are fully automated exchanges where transactions are completed through a network of telephones/tellers computers right from the first centre to the last centre. In addition, only professional people are authorised to render financial services."[5]

The OTCEI has been promoted jointly by ICICI, UTI, IFCI, IDBI, SBI Capital Markets Ltd., Canara Bank Financial Services Ltd., GIC and LIC. These institutions are sponsor members of this Exchange.

Over The Counter basically implies trading across the counter in scrips which are listed on the OTC exchange.

The term *counter* refers to the location of the member or a dealer of the OTCEI where dealing actually takes place. All the counters trade in all the scrips listed on the OTC Exchange. At every counter, an investor can see the quotes on the PTI-OTC Scan, complete a transaction, as well as ask for investor services. In other words, each counter acts as a trading floor of the OTCEI. Thus, as against a single trading floor in a regular stock exchange, there would be as many trading floors as the number of counters on the OTC Exchange.

Distinguishing Features

The OTCEI has a number of distinguishing features *vis-a-vis* other Stock Exchanges.

1. While other stock exchanges are associations formed by stock brokers, the OTCEI is a company promoted by financial institutions.
2. There are many restrictions on listing on the OTCEI. Several types and categories of companies which are not eligible for listing on a regular Stock Exchange are eligible on the OTCEI. Further, a company listed on any other recognised stock exchange in India would not simultaneously be eligible for listing on the OTC Exchange.
3. The method of price fixation differs between the OTCEI and other exchanges. On the OTC Exchange the pricing of scrips is regulated. The market-makers compulsorily offer buy-sell quotes which are based on proper evaluation of the company. In other Stock Exchanges, the share prices need not necessarily have any relation to the fundamentals. Speculation could cause wide price fluctuations on the regular exchanges.
4. The OTC Exchange is a market for spot deals only.
5. On the OTCEI, the settlement takes place daily, unlike on the other exchanges.
6. The OTC Exchange permits automatic transfer up to 0.5 per cent of a company's equity, whereas in other cases, permission of the companies is required for all transfers.
7. In the OTC Exchange, the spread does not exceed a specific percentage, whereas in a volatile market there is no restriction on spreads.
8. The OTCEI is characterised by a decentralised working with national work. Other exchanges are centralised in nature, members operating from a single location.

OTCEI is the only exchange that allows listing of companies with paid-up capital below ₹ 3 crore. It was set up to aid enterprising promoters is raising finance for new projects in a cost-effective manner and to provide investors with a transparent and efficient made of trading.

Benefits to the Investors

The OTC Exchange offers a number of benefits to the investors. The important advantages of it from the point of view of the investors are:

1. Quick payment of money to the sellers and quick delivery of shares to buyers.
2. Price transparency: On the OTCEI, the investor clearly knows the buying and selling prices, whereas he is not able to know the actual price at which the scrips are bought or sold for him in other stock exchanges.
3. The OTCEI saves the investors from other unscrupulous behaviour of the brokers.
4. Liquidity even for scrips of small and new companies.
5. Fair prices.
6. Simple procedure of buying and selling.
7. Facility to sell even odd lots.

Benefits to the Companies

The OTC Exchange offers certain advantages to the companies also OTCEI is the only exchange that allows companies with less than 3 years track record to tap capital market. The important benefits to the companies are that it:

1. Enables even smaller and less liquid companies to get listed.
2. Facilitate new issues at lower costs.
3. Makes raising capital through issues easy for small, new and closely held companies.
4. Helps create market for scrips of small and new companies.

Listing on the OTCEI

The minimum issued equity capital of a company for eligibility for listing on the OTCEI is ₹30 lakh, subject to a minimum public offer of equity shares worth ₹20 lakh. For companies with an issued equity capital of more than ₹30 lakh but less than ₹3 crore, the minimum public offer should be 40 per cent of the issued capital or ₹20 lakh worth shares in face value, whichever is highest. Companies with an issued equity capital of more than ₹3 crore, seeking listing on the OTCEI will have to comply with the listing requirements and guidelines as are applicable to such companies for enlistment on other recognised stock exchanges.

Any company which wants to list its shares on the OTCEI will have to be sponsored by a sponsor. The responsibilities of the sponsors include appraising the project/company properly, valuing the scrip fairly and promoting its sales.

One of the main functions of the sponsor is *market making, i.e.,* giving two-way (both buy and sell) quotes for the scrip concerned. The sponsor has to do *compulsory market making* for at least three years from the date trading commences. This is intended to provide enforced liquidity for investors. After a period of three years, the sponsor will continue to make market in the scrip till an alternative market-maker is arranged for. A sponsor, who is the *compulsory market-maker* (CMM) may appoint *additional market-maker* (AMM) or dealer. An AMM has to make market in the scrip for at least one year continuously.

Both members and dealers can act as *voluntary market makers* (VMMs) on the OTC Exchange. A VMM has to make market in a scrip for at least three months continuously.

(For more information about the OTCEI, refer V.A. Avadhani, *Investment and Securities Markets in India* (Himalaya Publishing House, Mumbai).

NATIONAL STOCK EXCHANGE OF INDIA

The National Stock Exchange of India (NSEI) was established in 1994 by financial institutions and banks with IDBI as a nodal agency.

NSE operates on the 'National Exchange for Automated Trading' (NEAT) system, a fully automated screen based trading system, which adopts the principle of an order driven market. NSE consciously opted in favour of an order driven system as opposed to a quote driven system. This has helped reduce jobbing spreads not only on NSE but in other exchanges as well, thus reducing transaction costs.

The NSEI has been conceived as a model exchange with a nation-wide electronic screen based "scripless" and "floorless" trading system in securities which is both efficient and transparent and offer equal and nation-wide access to investors.

Till the advent of NSE, an investor wanting to transact in a security not traded on the nearest exchange had to route orders through a series of correspondent brokers to the appropriate exchange. This resulted in a great deal of uncertainty and high transaction costs. NSE has made it possible for an investor to access the same market and order book, irrespective of location, at the same price and at the same cost.

The National Stock Exchange operates mainly in two different segments, *viz., (i)* Wholesale Debt Market, (WDM), and *(ii)* Capital Market (CM).

The WDM is concerned with trading in instruments like Government Securities, PSU bonds, Units 64 of UTI, CDs and CPs by corporate entities (like banks, institutions, brokerage houses).

The CM is concerned with equity and corporate debt instruments by both corporate entities and individuals. It will encourage high net worth corporate trading members with dealer network and short settlement cycles.

Objectives

The NSE has the following objectives.[6]

1. To establish nation-wide trading facility for equities, debts and hybrids.
2. To facilitate equal access to investors across the country.
3. To provide fairness, efficiency and transparency to the securities trading.
4. To enable shorter settlement cycles.
5. To meet international securities market standard.

Features of NSE

The important features of the NSE are the following.[7]

1. The NSE employs a fully automated screen based trading system.
2. It has two segments: the capital market segment and whole sale debt market segment. The capital market segment covers equities, convertible debentures.
3. The NSE market is a fully automated screen based environment. There is no trading floor as is prevalent in the traditional stock exchanges.
4. The market operates with all participants stationed at their offices and making use of their computer terminals, to receive market information, to enter orders and to execute trade.

5. The trading member is the capital market segment are connected to the central computer in Mumbai through a satellite link-up using VSATs (Very Small Aperture Terminals). The trading members in the whole sale debt market segment are linked, through dedicated high speed lines, to the central computer at Mumbai.
6. The NSE has opted for an order driven system. The system provides enormous flexibility to trading members. A trading member can place various conditions on the order in terms of price, time or size. When an order is placed by a trading member, an order confirmation slip is generated. All orders received are staked in price and time priority. The computer system automatically searches for a match and no sooner to the same is found, the deal is struck. If it does not find a match immediately as may happen in the case of less liquid securities, the order is kept pending in the computer unless specified otherwise by the trading member.

TABLE 11.1 : COMPARISON BETWEEN STOCK EXCHANGE, OTCEI AND NSE

	Stock Exchange	*OTCEI*	*NSE*
1. Membership	Individuals, Firms and Corporates	Corporates only	Individuals Firms & Corporates
2. Method of Trading	Floor based	Screen based	Screen based
3. System of Trading	Quote-driven Manual	Code driven Computers linked to central OTCEI through telephone lines	Order driven Computer linked by satellite through VSAT
4. Settlement	T+14	T+3 rolling settlement	Same day to T+5 in WDM. Standard Delivery in Equity market
5. Transparency	NIL	Ensured	Total transparency
6. Intermediary	Jobber needed	Not needed	Not needed

Source: E. Gordon and K. Natarajan, *Capital Market in India* (Himalaya Publishing House, Mumbai).

7. When a trade takes place, a trade confirmation slip is printed at the trading member's work station. It gives details like price, quantity, code number of the party and so on.
8. The identity of the trading member is not revealed to others when he places an order or when his pending orders are delayed. Hence, large orders can be placed in NSE without the fear of influencing the market sentiment.
9. The automated trade matching system secures the best price available in the market to the investor. The trading member can transact a high volume of business efficiently.

Types of Market

The NEAT system has four types of market. They are:

Normal Market: All orders which are of regular lot size or multiples thereof are traded in the Normal Market. For shares which are traded in the compulsory dematerialised mode, the market lot of these shares is one. Normal market consists of various book types wherein, orders are segregated as Regular lot orders, Special Term orders, Negotiated Trade orders and Stop Loss orders depending on their order attributes.

Odd-lot Market: All orders whose order size is less than the regular lot size are traded in the odd-lot market. An order is called an odd-lot order if the order size is less than regular lot size. These orders do not have any special terms attributes attached to them. In an odd-lot market, both the price and quantity of both the orders (buy and sell) should exactly match for the trade to take place. Currently the odd-lot market facility is used for the Limited Physical Market as per the SEBI directives.

Spot Market: Spot orders are similar to the normal market orders except that spot orders have different settlement periods *vis-a-vis* normal market. These orders do not have any special terms attributes attached to them. Currently, the Spot Market is being used for the Automated Lending and Borrowing Mechanism (ALBM) session.

Auction Market: In the Auction Market, auctions are initiated by the Exchange on behalf of trading members for settlement related reasons.

STOCK HOLDING CORPORATION OF INDIA

A new company, namely, the Stock Holding Corporation of India Ltd., (SHCI), was recently established with its registered office in Mumbai, in order to secure efficient post-trade processing services for transactions in securities carried out by the all-India financial and investment institutions (IDBI, ITCI, ICICI, IRBI, LIC, UTI and GIC). SHCI is owned at the outset by the seven sponsoring institutions. It would hold custody of securities of the sponsoring institutions and handle transfer of securities as also collection of dividend/ interest in respect of such securities on their behalf. It was also intended to extend its services to others such as stock-brokers and individual investors after setting up the infrastructural facilities and gaining experience in the field.

REGULATION OF STOCK EXCHANGE

The development of the stock market is directed and the dealings on the stock exchanges are regulated by Government of India in accordance with the Securities Contracts (Regulation) Act, 1956 (SCRA), and the Securities and Exchange Board of India (SEBI) established by the Government.

Securities Contracts (Regulation) Act

The Securities Contracts (Regulation) Act, enacted in 1956, came into force on February 20, 1957.

Objectives of the Act

According to the preamble to the Securities Contracts (Regulation) Act, 1956, (SCRA), the objective of the Act is to *prevent undesirable transactions in securities by regulating the business of dealings in securities and by providing for certain other matters connected with transaction in securities.*

A perusal of the important provisions of the SCRA will indicate that the important objectives of the Act are:

1. To empower the Central Government to regulate the dealings in and functioning of the stock exchange in India.
2. To promote healthy and orderly development of the stock market in India.
3. To prevent unhealthy speculation and other undesirable activities on the stock exchange.
4. To protect the interest of the investors.
5. To provide for reasonable uniformity in respect of the bye-laws and rules of the different stock exchanges in India.

Main Provisions

The Securities Contracts (Regulation) Act, 1956, empowers the Central Government to take appropriate measures to achieve the objectives mentioned above. The important provisions of the Act encompass the authority given to the Central Government, or, in certain cases the SEBI, pertaining to:

1. The grant of recognition or withdrawal of recognition to any stock exchange.
2. Approval of the bye-laws and rules of stock exchanges.
3. Power to direct the stock exchange to make or amend roles and bye-laws in certain cases.
4. Power to make or amend bye-laws or roles for stock exchanges.
5. Monitoring the activities and functioning of the stock exchanges by calling for periodic returns and specific information as and when required and by conducting inquiry into certain matters when the situation so warrants.
6. Power to suspend business of stock exchanges.
7. Power to supersede governing body of any stock exchange on account of specific reasons.
8. Regulation of listing of securities.

Recognition to Stock Exchanges

After the coming into effect of the Securities Contracts (Regulation) Act, 1956, only those stock exchanges which are granted recognition by the Central Government can function in India.

Any stock exchange which is desirous of being recognised may apply to the Central Government in the prescribed manner with the required particulars and a copy of the bye-laws of the stock exchange and the rules relating to the constitution of the stock exchange.

The Central Government may grant recognition to a stock exchange if it is satisfied that the rules and bye-laws of the stock exchange are in conformity with such conditions as may be prescribed with a view to ensure fair dealing and to protect investors. The conditions which the Central Government may prescribe in this respect may relate to (*a*) the qualifications for membership of the stock exchange, (*b*) the manner in which contracts shall be entered into and enforced between members, (*c*) the representation of the Central Government on the stock exchange, and the maintenance of accounts of members and their proper audit. Further, the stock exchange shall be bound to comply with any other conditions which the Central Government may impose in accordance with the Act.

The Act lays down that the Central Government shall not refuse grant of recognition to a stock exchange without giving it an opportunity to be heard and that the reasons for the refusal shall be communicated to the stock exchange in writing.

Only stock exchanges recognised by the Central Government can function in India and the Government can withdraw the recognition in certain cases.

If the Central Government is of the opinion that the recognition granted to a stock exchange should be withdrawn in the interest of the trade or in the public interest, may do so after properly serving a notice on the governing body of the stock exchange and after giving the governing body an opportunity for being heard in the matter.

Consequent to the Securities Laws (Amendment) Act, 1995, a Stock Exchange may establish additional trading floor with the prior approval of the SEBI in accordance with the terms and conditions stipulated by SEBI.

Power of Recognised Stock Exchange to Make Rules Restricting Voting Rights, Etc.

A recognised stock exchange may make rules or amend any rules made by it to regulate the voting rights.

No such rules of a recognised stock exchange made or shall have effect until they have been approved by the Central Government and published by that Government in the *Official Gazette* and, in approving the rules so made or amended, the Central Government may make such modifications therein as it thinks fit, and on such publication, the rules as provided by the Central Government shall be deemed to have been validly made.

The Act empowers the Central Government, subject to certain conditions, direct recognised stock exchanges generally or any recognised stock exchange in particular, as the case may be, to make any rules or to amend any rules already made.

If any recognised stock exchange fails or neglects to comply with any such order within the period specified therein, the Central Government may make the rules for, or amend the rules made by, the recognised stock exchange, either in the form proposed in the order or with such modifications thereof as may be agreed to between the stock exchange and the Central Government.

Bye-laws of Stock Exchanges

Any recognised stock exchange may, subject to the previous approval of the SEBI, make bye-laws for the regulation and control of contracts. The SEBI is empowered, on the basis of a request received from the governing body of a stock exchange or on its own motion, to make or amend any bye-laws in accordance with the SCRA.

Where the governing body of any stock exchange objects to any bye-laws made or amended by the SEBI on its own motion it may apply to the SEBI for a revision of it within specified period. After giving an opportunity to the governing body to be heard in the matter, the SEBI may revise the bye-laws so made or amended.

Power to Obtain Information and to Conduct Inquiry

Every recognised stock exchange shall furnish the Central Government with a copy of the annual report containing all the particulars prescribed. Further, every recognised stock exchange shall furnish to the SEBI such periodical returns relating to its affairs as may be prescribed.

It is also laid down by the Act that every recognised stock exchange and every member of such stock exchange shall maintain and preserve for such periods not exceeding five years, such books of account and other documents as the Central Government may prescribe. These books of account and other documents shall be available for inspection by the SEBI at all reasonable time.

The SEBI is also authorised to call upon any recognised stock exchange or any member of such exchange to furnish any information or explanation relating to the affairs of the stock exchange or the member in relation to the stock exchange.

Besides, the SEBI may call upon a recognised stock exchange or any member thereof to furnish such information or explanation relating to the stock exchange as it may require.

The SEBI is also empowered to appoint one or more persons to make an inquiry in the prescribed manner in relation to the affairs of any of the members of the stock exchange in relation to the stock exchange.

Power to Supersede Governing Body

If the Central Government has sufficient reasons to think that the governing body of any stock exchange should be superseded, it may do so after serving a written notice on the governing body and giving the governing body an opportunity to be heard in this matter. When the governing body is superseded the Government may appoint any person or persons to exercise and perform all the powers and duties of the governing body for such period as may be specified. The Government may vary this period, from time-to-time, by proper notification. The Central Government may call upon the stock exchange to reconstitute the governing body before the termination of this period. These powers are exercisable by the SEBI also.

Power to Suspend Business of Stock Exchange

The SCRA empowers the Central Government to suspend the business of any stock exchange, under certain circumstances, for a period not exceeding seven days in the interest of trade or public interest. The period of suspension may be extended from time-to-time but after the governing body has been given an opportunity of being heard in the matter.

These powers are exercisable by the SEBI also.

Listing of Securities

Listing of securities refers to the sanction of the right to trade the securities on the stock exchange. Only listed securities are allowed to be traded on a stock exchange.

Listing has some advantages.

1. Listing enhances the marketability and liquidity of the security.
2. Another attractiveness of the listed securities is that they command higher collateral value for purpose of bank credit.
3. Listing lends prestige to the security and widens its market.
4. Listed securities enjoy more public confidence as the stock exchange compels the issuer to comply with high standards.
5. Listing provides greater publicity for the company concerned because the prices and their trends in respect of the listed securities are often published by financial and business publications.

A public company desirous of getting its securities listed on a stock exchange shall apply to the stock exchange for this purpose with the required documents such as Memorandum and Articles of Association, copies of all prospectus or statements in lieu of prospectuses issued by the company at any time, etc., and the company shall abide by the conditions of the listing agreement with the stock exchange. Where any stock exchange refuses listing, the company shall be entitled to be furnished with the reasons for that. The company may appeal to the Central Government against the refusal.

SEBI

The establishment of the Securities and Exchange Board of India (SEBI) was a landmark government measure to monitor and regulate capital market activities and to promote healthy development of the market.

> **SEBI has been established to regulate stock market operations for a healthy and orderly development of the market and to protect the genuine interests of the investors.**

The SEBI was constituted in 1988 by a resolution of Government of India and it was made a statutory body by the Securities and Exchange Board of India Act, 1992.

Management

Section 4 of the Act lays down the constitution of the management of SEBI. The board of members of SEBI shall consist of a Chairman, two members from amongst the officials of the Ministries of the Central Government dealing with Finance and Law, one member from amongst the officials of the Reserve Bank of India, two other members to be appointed by the Central Government, who shall be professionals and *inter alia* have experience or special knowledge relating to securities market.

The Act empowers the Central Government to supersede SEBI, if on account of grave emergency, SEBI is unable to discharge the functions and duties under any provisions of the Act, or SEBI persistently defaults in complying with any direction issued by the Central Government under the Act, or in the discharge of its functions and duties under the Act and as a result of such default the financial position of SEBI or its administration has deteriorated, or in public interest.

Objectives

According to the Act, the objectives of SEBI are *to protect the interests of investors in securities and to promote the development of, and to regulate, the securities market for matters connected therewith or incidental therewith.*

Powers and Functions

The SEBI Act casts upon SEBI the duty to protect the interests of investors in securities and to promote the development of and to regulate the securities market through appropriate measures. These measures provide for:

1. Regulating the business in stock exchanges and any other securities market.
2. Registering and regulating the working of stock brokers, sub-brokers, share transfer agents, bankers to an issue, trustees of trust deeds, registrars to an issue, merchant bankers, underwriters, portfolio managers, investment advisers and such other intermediaries who may be associated with securities market in any manner.
3. Registering and regulating the working of collective investment schemes, including mutual funds.
4. Promoting and regulating self-regulatory organisations.
5. Prohibiting fraudulent and unfair trade practices in securities market.
6. Promoting investor education and training of intermediaries in securities market.
7. Prohibiting insider trading in securities.
8. Regulating substantial acquisition of shares and takeover of companies.
9. Calling far information from, undertaking inspection, conducting enquiries and audits of the stock exchanges and intermediaries and self-regulatory organisations in the securities market.
10. Performing such functions and exercising such powers under the provisions of the Capital Issues (Control) Act, 1947, (subsequently repealed) and the Securities Contracts (Regulations) Act, 1956, as may be delegated to it by the Central Government.

> **SEBI has done a very commendable job in regulating the stock exchange transactions and promoting the development of the capital market.**

11. Levying fees or other charges for carrying out the purposes of Section 11 of the Act.
12. Conducting research for the above purpose.
13. Performing such other functions as may be prescribed by the government.

The Board may, for the protection of investors, specify by regulations, the matters relating to issue of capital, transfer of securities and other matters incidental thereto and the manner in which such matters, shall be disclosed by the companies.

The SEBI is also empowered to issue such directions as may be appropriate to certain person or class of persons or company, intermediary or other persons referred to in Section 12 (stock-broker, sub-broker, share transfer agent, banker to an issue, trustee of trust deed, merchant banker, underwriter, registrar to an issue, investment adviser, portfolio manager, etc.) *(i)* in the interest of investors, or orderly development of securities market; or *(ii)* to prevent the affairs of any intermediary or other persons referred to in Section 12, being conducted in a manner detrimental to the interests of investors or securities market; or *(iii)* to secure the proper management of any such intermediary or person.

> **SEBI has also taken several regulatory measures to promote good corporate governance.**

CAPITAL MARKET REFORMS AND DEVELOPMENTS

The number of Stock Exchanges has increased and the capital market has expanded substantially. However, the functioning of the stock exchanges were characterized by many shortcomings with long delays, lack of transparency in procedures and vulnerability to price rigging and insider trading. A number of measures have been taken to overcome these problems. The objectives of these measures, broadly, have been to:

- Provide for effective control of the stock exchange operations.
- Increase the information flow and disclosures so as to enhance the transparency.
- Protect the interests of investors.
- Check insider trading.
- Improve the operational efficiency of the stock exchanges.
- Promote healthy development of the capital market.

Important measures of reform and development include the following:[8]

Free Pricing

Raising of capital from the securities market before 1992 was regulated under the Capital Issues (Control) Act, 1947, which required companies to obtain approval from the Controller of Capital Issues (CCI) for raising resources in the market. New companies were allowed to issue shares only at par. Only the existing companies with substantial reserves could issue shares at a premium, which was based on some prescribed formula. In 1992, the Capital Issues (Control) Act, 1947 was repealed and with this ended all controls relating to raising of resources from the market. Since then the issuers of securities could raise the capital from the market without requiring any consent from any authority either for making the issue or for pricing it. Restrictions on rights and bonus issues have also been removed. New as well as established companies are now able to price their issues according to their assessment of market conditions. However, issuers of capital are required to meet the guidelines of SEBI on disclosure and investor protection. Companies issuing capital are required to make sufficient disclosures, including justification of the issue price and also material disclosure about the 'risk factors' in their offering prospectus. These guidelines have served as an important measure for protecting investor interest and promoting the development of the primary market along sound lines.

Introduction of Book Building

To help overcome the problem of determining the right price at which the market would clear an issue the book building mechanism which introduced in 1995. The Book building mechanism is a method through which an offer price of an Initial Public Offering (IPO) is based on investors' demand. The introduction of book building mechanism gave the issuer the choice to raise resources either through this or the fixed price mechanism. The book building mechanism of floating new capital issues has been devised in such a way that small investors are also able to subscribe to securities at a price arrived at through a transparent process. As the book building process is both time and cost-effective, it is becoming quite popular.

Electronic Trading

Till recently, trading on the Indian stock exchanges took place through open outcry system barring NSE and OTCEI, which adopted screen-based trading system from the beginning *(i.e.,* 1994 and 1992, respectively). At present all other stock exchanges have adopted on-line screen-based electronic trading, replacing the open outcry system.

There are three main advantages of electronic trading over floor-based trading as observed in India, *viz.,* transparency, more efficient price discovery, and reduction in transaction costs. Transparency ensures that stock prices fully reflect available information and lowers the trading costs by enabling the investor to assess overall supply and demand. Owing to computer-based trading, the speed with which new information gets reflected in prices has increased tremendously. The quantity and quality of information provided to market participants during the trading process (pre-trading and post-trading) having significant bearing on the price formation has also improved. Besides, the screen-based trading has the advantage of integrating different trading centres all over the country into a single trading platform. It may be noted that prior to screen-based trading, the very presence of stock markets in different regions implied segmentation of markets affecting the price discovery process. Investors in other locations were, under such conditions, unable to participate in the price formation process at the major stock exchange, namely the BSE. However, with screen-based trading spread across various locations, the process of price discovery has improved in the Indian stock markets. Screen-based trading has also led to significant reduction in the transaction cost since it enabled the elimination of a chain of brokers for execution of orders from various locations at BSE and NSE.

Instruments and Market Participants

The capital market has widened and deepened considerably in the recent years with enlargement of participants and emergence of new instruments. In the Indian capital market, traditionally mainly two instruments were traded, *i.e.,* debt and equity. However, starting from the mid-eighties and especially during the first-half of the nineties, a wide range of innovative/hybrid instruments combining both the features of debt and equity were introduced to suit varied needs of investors and issuers/borrowers. Besides DFIs, PSUs also issued many debt instruments with innovative features.

Markets have also widened with the increase in the number of players, such as, mutual funds and foreign institutional investors.

Improvements in Trading, Clearing and Settlement Systems

The trading, clearing and settlement systems, which had suffered from several bottlenecks, have been considerably improved with measures taken to shorten the settlement cycle through the introduction of rolling settlement system and acceleration of the process of electronic book entry transfer through depository.

Increased Dematerialisation

Safe and quick transfer of securities is an important element for smooth and efficient functioning of the securities market. Apart from the problems involved in the movement of physical security certificates, bad deliveries due to faulty paperwork, theft, forgery, *etc.,* added to the transaction cost and restricted liquidity. To overcome these difficulties, legislative changes were carried out for maintaining ownership records in an electronic book-entry form. Under this mode, securities are transferred in a speedy and safe manner without interposition of issuers in the process, except in few circumstances. In order to catalyse the process of dematerialisation of securities and dematerialised trading, an element of compulsion was introduced by requiring the individual and institutional investors to settle trades compulsorily in dematerialised form in shares of select companies.

Near Elimination of Counterparty Risk

One of the shortcomings of the clearing and settlement process of the Indian stock markets was the absence of a system to reduce counterparty risk. Managing this risk is essential for promoting a safe and efficient market. To provide the necessary funds and ensure timely completion of settlements in cases of failure of member brokers to fulfil their settlement obligations, major stock exchanges have set up Settlement Guarantee Funds. The aggregate corpus of the Fund at the stock exchanges is presently over ₹ 1,000 crore. The NSE has set up a clearing corporation which guarantees settlement of all trades. The clearing corporation, thus, assumes the counterparty risk involved in all the transactions.

All stock exchanges in the country have established clearing houses. Consequently, all transactions are settled through the clearing houses. In the past, while some transactions were settled through the clearing houses, others were settled directly between the members. Routing of transactions through clearing houses has substantially reduced the credit risk in the settlement system.

Circuit Breakers/Price Bands

Circuit breakers were first introduced in 1987 in the US in the wake of sharp fall in the share prices. To contain abnormal price variations, scrip-wise specific daily price bands or circuit breakers in India were introduced in 1995 whereby the trading automatically got suspended if the prices varied either side beyond 8 per cent; further trading was allowed only up to the price band. Price bands, which were originally fixed at 8 per cent, were relaxed in January 2000, whereby a further variation of 4 per cent in the scrip beyond 8 per cent, after a cooling off period of 30 minutes, was allowed. This was made applicable in the case of 100 scrips. In June 2000, for all scrips under compulsory rolling settlement, the price band was relaxed by 8 per cent (from 4 per cent earlier) with half an hour cooling period after the scrip had hit the initial price band of 8 per cent.

While recent experiences in some countries, such as, Brazil, Taiwan and Thailand, showed that circuit filters were successful in slowing down the market momentum, there has been some controversy over the effectiveness of circuit filters over the medium to long-term. Although the circuit filters could have their adverse effects on the process of price formation, they are favoured mainly on the ground that they are the best available tool for containing volatility. This is based on the belief that containing of excess volatility helps to maintain investor confidence in the market.

Structure of Informational Flows

Several measures have been taken to enhance the transparency of the companies. A company offering securities in the Indian capital market is required to make a public disclosure of all relevant information through its offer documents, as indicated earlier. After a security is issued to the public and subsequently listed on a stock exchange, the stock exchange requires the issuing company to make continuing disclosures under the listing agreement. In India, all listed companies are now required to furnish to the stock exchanges and also publish mandated unaudited financial results on a quarterly basis. India is one of the few countries in the world to have a system of quarterly disclosures and it has served a useful purpose in that price-sensitive information on earnings and revenues is now available at greater frequency. The publication of half-yearly corporate results on the basis of limited review by its auditors has also been made mandatory for listed companies. The disclosures of material information, which would have a bearing on the performance/operations of the company, are now required to be made available to the public immediately. Recently, a decision has been taken that the companies would be required to make decisions regarding dividend, bonus and rights announcements or any material event within 15 minutes of the conclusion of the board meeting where the decisions are taken. Following the international practices, companies in India are also required to provide shareholders with cash flow statements in the prescribed format along with the complete balance sheet and profit and loss statement. Companies are also required to furnish to the stock exchanges on a quarterly basis, a statement on the actual utilisation of funds and actual profitability, as against projected utilisation of funds and projected profitability. As part of better corporate governance practices, disclosures about segment reporting, related party transactions and consolidated balance sheet are also expected to be introduced.

Emphasis on Fair Trading Practices

Insider trading has been made a criminal offence punishable in accordance with the provisions under the SEBI Act, 1992. The Regulations define an insider as a person who has access to price-sensitive non-public information with regard to a company. Such a person is prohibited from trading in the securities of such a company under the regulations.

There are now separate regulations in place governing substantial acquisition of shares and takeovers of companies. The regulations are aimed at making the takeover process more transparent and to protect the interests of minority shareholders.

Increasing Integration of Various Segments of Securities Markets

In India, different stock exchanges have so far followed their own practices relating to settlement procedures creating segmentation of the market. While stock exchanges continue to follow different systems, certain developments have resulted in better integration of the various segments of the Indian securities market. The two major stock exchanges, *viz.*, BSE and NSE, have expanded their operations in different locations, thus, providing investors across the country with the facility to trade in the stocks listed/ permitted in these stock exchanges. The Inter-connected Stock Exchange of India Ltd., (ICSI) has been set up as an inter-connected market system and provides its trading members a facility to trade on the national market in addition to the trading facility at the regional stock exchanges. This has integrated the various regional stock exchanges, although the trading activity in the ICSI has not been very significant. Many regional stock exchanges have also become members of BSE and NSE, which further strengthened the integration process of various stock exchanges in the country. Equity market is also increasingly integrating with the Government securities and private corporate sector debt market. The interest rate structure of Government securities and securities issued by the corporate entities is better aligned at present than in the past.

The Impact of the Changing Structure

The changing structure of capital market has had some positive impact on the volatility, liquidity and transaction cost.

SUMMARY

According to the Securities Contracts (Regulation) Act, 1956, *stock exchange means any body of individuals, whether incorporated or not, constituted for the purpose of assisting, regulating or controlling the business of buying, selling or dealing in securities.* Thus, the Stock Exchange is a market in which securities are brought and sold.

Stock exchange is an essential component of a developed capital market. It brings together large amounts of capital necessary for the economic progress of a country.

An organised securities market can provide sufficient marketability and price continuity for shares, so necessary for the needs of investors, and a reasonable measure of safety and fair dealing in the buying and selling of securities. Further, through the interplay of demand for and supply of securities, properly organised stock exchange assists in a reasonably correct evaluation of securities in terms of their real worth. Lastly, through such evaluation of securities the stock exchange helps in the orderly flow and distribution of savings as between different types of competitive investments.

There are 23 stock exchanges functioning in India including the Over The Counter Exchange of India (OTCEI) and the National Stock Exchange (NSE).

The establishment of the Over The Counter Exchange of India (OTCEI) and the National Stock Exchange of India (NSE) added significant new dimensions to the stock exchange system of India.

The OTCEI is a stock exchange with a lot of differences with those of others. "Although the basic framework of the OTC Exchange is that of a *national market, yet there is no physical location, no counters, no trading ring, no stock exchange building and no hustle and bustle scenes as the conventional stock exchanges.* The buyers and sellers living apart from each other trade in corporate securities over the telephone. The system cuts across urban and rural areas extending the frontiers of the stock market to the entire country. These OTC markets are fully automated exchanges where transactions are completed through a network of telephones/tellers computers right from the first centre to the last centre. In addition, only professional people are authorised to render financial services."

In the past, an investor wanting to transact in a security not traded on the nearest exchange had to route orders through a series of correspondent brokers to the appropriate exchange. This resulted in a great deal of uncertainty and high transaction costs. The establishment of the NSE in 1994 has made it possible for an investor to access the same market and order book, irrespective of location, at the same price and at the same cost. The NSE is a nodal exchange with a nation-wide electronic screen-based "scripless" and "floorless" trading system in securities which is both efficient and transparent and offer equal and nation-wide access to investors.

The stock market is directed and the dealings on the stock exchanges are regulated by the Central Government in accordance with the Securities Contracts (Regulation) Act, 1956 (SCRA), and the Securities and Exchange Board of India (SEBI) established by the Central Government.

The objective of the Securities Contracts (Regulation) Act, 1956, (SCRA), is to prevent undesirable transactions in securities by regulating the business of dealings in securities and by providing for certain other matters connected with transaction in securities.

After the coming into effect of the Securities Contracts (Regulation) Act, 1956, only those stock exchanges which are granted recognition by the Central Government can function in India.

The important provisions of the Act encompass the authority given to the Central Government, or, in certain cases the SEBI, pertaining to the grant of recognition or withdrawal of recognition to any stock exchange; approval of the bye-laws and rules of stock exchanges; power to direct the stock exchange to make or amend roles and bye-laws in certain cases; power to make or amend bye-laws or rules for stock exchanges; monitoring the activities and functioning of the stock exchanges by calling for periodic returns and specific information as and when required and by conducting inquiry into certain matters when the situation so warrants; power to suspend business of stock exchanges; power to supersede governing body of any stock exchange on account of specific reasons.

Each stock exchange is managed by an Executive Committee/Council of Management/ Governing Body to which the Government is empowered to nominate not more than three members. The rules and bye-laws of the stock exchange shall be in conformity with such conditions as may be prescribed by the Government. The Securities Contracts (Regulation) Act empowers the Government also to withdraw the recognition granted to a stock exchange, in the interest of trade or in public interest. Further, in order to deal with abnormal and extraordinary situations which may develop from time-to-time. Government is empowered to supercede a governing body after giving an opportunity to the governing body to be heard in the matter and to appoint in its place any person or persons to perform the functions of the governing body; and to suspend such of the business of a stock exchange under certain circumstances, for such period not exceeding seven days as may be specified, in the interest of trade or in public interest. The period of suspension can be extended from time-to-time, but after the governing body has been given an opportunity of being heard in the matter.

Since 1988, the Securities and Exchange Board of India (SEBI) has been playing a very important role in regulating the capital market in India. The objectives of the SEBI are to protect the interests of investors in securities, to regulate the activities of the securities market and promote healthy development of the capital market.

Important measures of reform and development of the capital market include the introduction of free pricing of capital issues; introduction of book building mechanism; introduction of electronic trading, measures to widen and deepen the capital market; improvement in the trading, clearing and settlement systems; promotion of dematerialisation; measures to reduce counterparty risk, introduction of circuit breakers/price bands; measures to increase information flow and to enhance the transparency of the companies; and, ushering in of fair trading practices, including prohibition of insider trading.

Important powers and functions of the SEBI include regulating the business in stock exchanges and any other securities market; registering and regulating the working of stock market intermediaries; promoting and regulating self-regulatory organisations; prohibiting fraudulent and unfair trade practices in securities market; promoting investor education and training of intermediaries in securities market; prohibiting insider trading in securities; regulating substantial acquisition of shares and takeover of companies; and calling for information from, undertaking inspection, conducting enquiries and audits of the stock exchanges and intermediaries and self-regulatory organisations in the securities market.

The functioning of the stock exchanges were characterised by many shortcomings with long delays, lack of transparency in procedures and vulnerability to price rigging and insider trading. A number of measures have been taken to overcome these problems. The objectives of these measures, broadly, have been to provide for effective control of the stock exchange operations; increase the information flow and disclosures so as to enhance the transparency; protect the interests of investors; check insider trading; improve the operational efficiency of the stock exchanges and in general, to promote healthy development of the capital market.

The measures of capital market reforms have had some positive impact on the volatility, liquidity and transaction cost

REFERENCES

1. Kuchhal, S.C., *Corporation Finance: Principles and Problems,* Chaitanya Publishing Co., Allahabad, 1976, p. 261.
2. Cited in the *Reserve Bank of India Bulletin,* October 1956, p. 1025.
3. Cited in the *Reserve Bank of India Bulletin,* October 1956, p. 1025.
4. Anantharaman, T.S., "Emergence of Indian Capital Market", *Cochin Stock Exchange Monthly Bulletin,* February 1995, p. 45.
5. Gordon, E. and Natarajan, K., *Capital Market in India,* Himalaya Publishing House, Mumbai, 1999, pp. 172-3.
6. Adapted from Gordon and Natarajan, *Ibid.,* pp. 173-4.
7. *Ibid.,* pp. 173-4.
8. Most part of this section is adopted from Reserve Bank of India, *Report on Currency and Finance, 1999-2000.*

ANNEXURE 11.1

DERIVATIVES

A derivative is an instrument whose value is derived from the value of one or more *underlying* asset such as commodities, precious metals, currency, bonds, stocks, stock indices, etc. The most common examples of derivative instruments are Forwards, Futures, Options and Swaps.

Trading in derivatives, thus, means trading in instruments such as Forwards, Futures, Options and Swaps.

Forwards and Futures

A forward contract is a customized contract between two parties to buy/sell a specified quantity of a particular instrument or commodity at a specified price at a specified future date. Futures are exchange traded forward contracts, *i.e.,* forward contracts done in organised exchanges like stock exchanges and commodity exchanges.

The major difference between Forward contracts and Futures contracts are the following.[1]

1. Standardized vs. Customized Contract — Forward contract is customized while the future is standardised. To be more specific, the terms of a Forward contract are individually agreed between two counterparties, while Futures being traded on exchanges have terms standardized by the exchange.

   The standardized items in any Futures contract are quantity of the underlying; quality of the underlying (not required in financial Futures); the date and month of delivery; the units of price quotation (not the price itself) and minimum change in price (tick-size); and the location of Settlement.

2. Counterparty risk — In case of Futures, after a trade is confirmed by two members of exchange, the exchange/clearing house itself becomes the counterparty (or guarantees) to every trade. The credit risk, which in case of forward contracts was on the counterparty, gets transferred to exchange/clearing house, reducing the risk to almost nil.
3. Liquidity — Futures contracts are much more liquid and their price is much more transparent due to standardisation and market reporting of volumes and price.
4. Squaring off — A forward contract can be reversed only with the same counterparty with whom it was entered into. A Futures contract can be reversed with any member of the exchange.

If Futures contracts are priced above the spot price, it is known as the *Contango* market. If the Futures price prevails below the spot price, it is known as *Backwardation.*

Option

An option is a contract, which gives the buyer (holder) the right, but not the obligation, to buy or sell a specified quantity of the underlying assets (such as a commodity, currency, or security), at a specific (strike) price on or before a specified time (expiration date). Unlike futures, the purchaser of an option is not obliged to buy or sell at the exercise price and will only do so if it is profitable; if the option is allowed to lapse, the purchaser loses only the initial purchase price of the option (the option money).

The strike or exercise price of an option is the specified/predetermined price of the underlying asset at which the same can be bought or sold if the option buyer exercises his right to buy/sell on or before the expiration day. The price paid by the buyer to the seller to acquire the right to buy or sell is known as the premium.

The one who is obligated to buy (in case of put option) or to sell (in case of call option), the underlying asset in case the buyer of the option decides to exercise his option is known as the option seller/writer. His profits are limited to the premium received from the buyer while his downside is unlimited. The premium fluctuates in response to current market value of the security/exercise price, time period between the strike and the expiry date, supply and demand in the market, etc. The one who buys an option which can be a call or a put option is known as the option holder. He enjoys the right to buy or sell the underlying asset at a specified price on or before the specified time. His upside potential is unlimited while losses are limited to the premium paid by him to the option writer.

An option to buy is known as a *call option* and is usually purchased in the expectation of a rising price: an option to sell is called *a put option* and is bought in the expectation of a falling price or to protect a profit on an investment. Options, like futures, allow individuals and firms to hedge against the risk of wide fluctuations in prices; they also allow speculators to gamble for large profits with limited liability.

When the option's strike price is equal to the underlying asset price, the option is said to be 'at-the-money'. This is true for both puts and calls. A call option is said to be 'in-the-money' when the strike price of the option is less than the underlying asset price. A call option is 'out-of-the-money' when the strike price is greater than the underlying asset price.

The significant differences in Futures and Options are as under:[2]

1. Futures are agreements/contracts to buy or sell specified quantity of the underlying assets at a price agreed upon by the buyer and seller, on or before a specified time. Both the buyer and seller are obligated to buy/sell the underlying asset. In case of options the buyer enjoys the right and not the obligation, to buy or sell the underlying asset.

In case of options the buyer enjoys the right and not the obligation, to buy or sell the underlying asset.

2. Futures contracts have symmetric risk profile for both the buyer as well as the seller, whereas options have asymmetric risk profile. In case of Options, for a buyer (or holder of the option), the downside is limited to the premium (option price) he has paid while the profits may be unlimited. For a seller or writer of an option, however, the downside is unlimited while profits are limited to the premium he has received from the buyer.
3. The Futures contracts prices are affected mainly by the prices of the underlying asset. The prices of options are however, affected by prices of the underlying asset, time remaining for expiry of the contract and volatility of the underlying asset.
4. It costs nothing to enter into a Futures contract, whereas there is a cost of entering into an Options contract, termed as Premium.

Swap

Swap is the means by which a borrower can exchange the type of funds he can most easily raise for the type of funds he wants, usually through the intermediary of a bank. For example, a UK company may find it easy to raise a sterling loan when they really want to borrow Deutsch marks; a German company may have exactly the opposite problem.

A swap will enable them to exchange the currency they possess for the currency they need. The other common type of swap is an interest-rate swap, in which borrowers exchange fixed for floating interest rates. Swaps are most common in the euro-currency markets.

Hedging

Hedging is a mechanism to reduce price risk inherent in open positions. Derivatives are widely used for hedging. A Hedge can help lock-in existing profits. Its purpose is to reduce the volatility of a portfolio, by reducing the risk. Hedging does not mean maximisation of return. It only means reduction in variation of return. It is quite possible that the return is higher in the absence of the hedge, but so also is the possibility of a much lower return.

The basic logic is "If long in cash underlying — Short Future and if short in cash underlying — Long Future". For example, if one has bought 100 shares of Company A and wants to Hedge against market movements, he should short an appropriate amount of Index Futures. This will reduce his overall exposure to events affecting the whole market (systematic risk). In case a war breaks out, the entire market will fall (most likely including Company A). So his loss in Company A would be offset by the gains in your short position in Index Futures.

Some examples of where hedging strategies are useful include:[3]

- Reducing the equity exposure of a Mutual Fund by selling Index Futures;
- Investing funds raised by new schemes in Index Futures so that market exposure is immediately taken; and
- Partial liquidation of portfolio by selling the index future instead of the actual shares where the cost of transaction is higher.

Advantages of Derivatives

As Sanjiv Agarwal observes, the introduction of derivatives in the Indian Capital Market could be seen as an effort to improve the present day mechanics of speculative trading in Forward Scrips. They are more scientific and better suited to fulfil the needs of the market participants and would lead to a mature and efficient market. He points out that derivatives have the following advantages:[4]

1. Derivatives help the market participants to hedge their underlying positions, thereby aiding them in managing their risks. It shall also act as a pro-speculative vehicle for the market traders by providing them a higher degree of leverage and would thereby provide an impetus to the liquidity of the underlying market.
2. Derivatives would insulate the small retail investors from the negative effects of the high speculative activities associated presently with the capital markets. Further, derivatives will provide a genuine risk management tool for the burgeoning institutional players in the Indian Capital Market and the trading members are also corporatising themselves and would be capable of handling sophisticated tools.
3. The major economic benefits of derivatives are that they reduce the risk/increase the willingness to hold the underlying asset; lower transaction costs; enhance the price discovery process; and enhance the liquidity of the underlying asset market.

Index Based Derivatives

As price volatility in individual stocks is very high, futures based on individual stocks are not very common. In India, L.C. Gupta Committee has not mentioned Futures on Individual Stocks as a possible derivative contract. The Index based derivatives is very popular.

The value of an index is derived from the value its underlying. For example, the value of the BSE 30 Sensex, is derived from the value of the 30 shares on which the index is based. These are shares of large well-established and financially sound companies. An index, thus, is an indicator of the broad market. For instance, tracking the changes in the Sensex enables one to effectively gauge stock market movements.

Index based derivatives have several advantages over derivatives based on specific securities. According to the Committee on Derivatives set up by the Securities and Exchange Board of India (SEBI) under the chairmanship of L.C. Gupta, Stock Index Futures are internationally the most popular form of equity derivatives for the following reasons:

1. They provide portfolio hedging facility.
2. There is lesser risk of manipulation of stock index as compared to individual stock prices.
3. Their greater popularity makes them more liquid.
4. Stock index is generally less volatile than individual stock prices.
5. Index futures are cash settled all over the world as the index value is derived from the cash market.

Both the Bombay Stock Exchange (BSE) and the National Stock Exchange (NSE) have launched index futures in June 2000.

According to the sources of the Stock exchange, Mumbai,[5] the Sensex futures would evolve to become the most liquid contract in the country. This is because institutional investors in India and abroad, money managers and small investors use the Sensex when it comes to describing the mood of the Indian Stock markets. Thus, it has been observed that the Sensex is an effective proxy for the Indian stock markets. Higher liquidity in the product essentially translates to lower impact cost of trading in Sensex futures. The arbitrage between the futures and the equity market is further expected to reduce impact cost. Trading in Stock index futures is likely to be predominantly retail driven. Internationally, stock index futures are an institutional product with 60% of the volumes generated from hedging needs. An immense retail participation to the extent of 80-90% is expected in India based on the following factors:

1. Stock index Futures will require lower capital adequacy and margin requirements as compared to margins on carry forward of individual scrips.
2. The brokerage costs on index futures will be much lower.
3. Savings in cost is possible through reduced bid-ask spreads where stocks are traded in packaged forms.
4. The impact cost will be much lower in case of stock index futures as opposed to dealing in individual scrips.
5. The market is conditioned to think in terms of the index and therefore would prefer to trade in stock index futures. Further, the chances of manipulation are much lesser.

The Stock Index Futures are expected to be extremely liquid given the speculative nature of our markets and the overwhelming retail participation expected to be fairly high. In the near future, stock index futures will definitely see incredible volumes in India. It will be a blockbuster product and is pitched to become the most liquid contract in the world in terms of number of contracts traded, if not in terms of notional value. The advantage to the equity or cash market is in fact that they would become less volatile as most of the speculative activity would shift to stock index futures. The stock index futures market should ideally have more depth, volumes and act as a stabilising factor for the cash market. However, it is too early to base any conclusions on the volume or to form any firm trend.

ANNEXURE 11.2

BSE SENSEX

The BSE Sensex, short form of Bombay Stock Exchange Sensitive Index, first compiled in 1986, is a 'Market Capitalization-Weighted' index of 30 component stocks representing a sample of large, well-established and financially sound companies. The index is widely reported in both, the domestic and international, print and electronic media and is widely used to measure the performance of the Indian stock markets.[6]

The BSE Sensex is a benchmark index of the Indian capital market and is considered to be the pulse of the Indian stock markets. As the oldest index of the Indian stock market, it provides time series data over a fairly long period of time.

The objectives of the Sensex are:

To Measure Market Movements: Given its long history and its wide acceptance, no other index matches the BSE Sensex in reflecting market movements and sentiments. Sensex is widely used to describe the mood in the Indian stock markets.

Benchmark For Funds Performance: The inclusion of blue chip companies and the wide and balanced industry representation in the Sensex makes it the ideal benchmark for fund managers to compare the performance of their funds.

For Index Based Derivative Products: Institutional investors, money managers and small investors all refer to the **BSE SENSEX** for their specific purposes. The BSE Sensex is in effect the proxy for the Indian stock markets. Since **SENSEX** comprises of leading companies in all the significant sectors in the economy, we believe that it will be the most liquid contract in the Indian market and will garner a predominant market share.

Criteria for Selection of Scrips for the Sensex

Market Capitalisation: The scrip should figure in the top 100 companies listed by market capitalisation. Also market capitalisation of the scrip should be more than 0.5% of the total market capitalisation of the Index, *i.e.*, the minimum weightage should be 0.5%. Since the BSE Sensex is a market capitalisation weighted Index, this is one of the entry criteria for scrip selection.

Industry Representation: Scrip selection would take into account a balanced representation of the economy. The index companies should be leaders in their industry group with sound management.

Trading Frequency: The scrip should have been traded on every trading day for the last six months. Exceptions can be made for extreme reasons like scrip suspension etc.

Number of Trades: The scrip should be among the top 150 companies listed by average number of trades per day for the last six months.

Volume Traded: The scrip should be among the top 150 companies listed by average volume traded per day for the last six months.

Continuity: Whenever the composition of the Index is changed, the continuity of historical series of Index values is re-established by linking the value of the revised index to its last previous value prior to the review. This is done by changing the base value of the Index to the extent of the percentage change in the market capitalisation of the Index because of the revision. The back calculation over the last one year period would be carried out and correlation of the revised Index to the old Index should not be less than 0.98 to ensure that the historical continuity of the Index is maintained.

The Sensex has historically been the barometer of the Indian capital markets and as such periodic reconstitution becomes mandatory in order to represent the true face of the national economy.

Over the last decades, the Indian economy has undergone a remarkable transition, the relative weightage of different sectors undergoing significant changes. The Sensex was, therefore, reconstructed several times to reflect these changes. The present reconstitutions essentially meant altering some of the stocks that became less prominent and replacing them by new economy stocks. The Index Committee has done so in a manner that maintains continuity so that millions of investors do not have to relearn past peaks and bottom levels. The revamped Sensex captures the Indian economy more realistically.

ANNEXURE 11.3

NSE NIFTY

The S&P CNX Nifty, nicknamed Nifty 50 or Nifty, is the leading stock index of large companies on the National Stock Exchange of India. The Nifty which represents over 20 sectors of the economy and contains 50 diverse stocks, is the flagship index of NSE, the 3rd largest stock exchange in the world in terms of number of transactions (Stock Futures). Some of its purposes include benchmarking fund portfolios, index-based derivatives and Index funds.[7]

The Nifty Index is based upon solid economic research. It is internationally respected and recognized as a pioneering effort in providing simple understanding of stock market complexities. Managed by India Index Services and Products, who have a consulting and licensing agreement with Standard & Poor's, they are the first specialised company focused on the index as a core product in India. A weighted average is used to calculate the Index so changes in the share prices of larger companies have a larger effect.

Some important points regarding Nifty are given below:

- Nifty Index can be used by individuals to track market movements and compare performance of individual companies' *vis-a-vis* market performance.
- Shareholders evaluation of management decisions — performance of a company *vis-à-vis* the market generally reflects the perception of the investor.
- Assist traders and market intermediaries to evaluate performance and sentiments across the market.
- Index funds can replicate Nifty indices to earn market returns.
- Derivative trading — Investors can use Nifty indices for hedging their exposures in the equity markets.
- Benchmarking NAV performances — Nifty is the benchmark for performance of open-ended and close-ended funds.
- It is a simplified tool that helps investors and ordinary people alike, to understand what is happening in the stock market and by extension, the economy. If the Nifty Index performs well, it is a signal that companies in India are performing well and consequently that the country is doing well.

REFERENCES

1. Adopted from the website of Stock Exchange, Mumbai (BSE-Derivatives Segment). bseindia.com is a very good source for information on Derivatives and BSE.
2. *Ibid.*
3. *Ibid.*
4. Sanjiv Agarwal, *Manual of Indian Capital Market*, Bharat Law House, New Delhi, 1997, pp. 484-5.
5. Adopted from the website of Stock Exchange, Mumbai.
6. *Ibid.*
7. Mostly adopted from the website of NSE.

☆☆☆

CHAPTER 12

INDUSTRIAL FINANCE

Finance, which has been aptly described as the "lifeblood" of the industry, is a prerequisite for the mobilisation of real resources to organise production and marketing.

> **Depending upon the nature of the activity to be financed, business requires short-term, medium-term and long-term finance.**

Short-term Finance

Short-term finance usually refers to the funds required for a period of less than one year. Short-term finance is usually required to meet variable, seasonal or temporary working capital requirements.

Borrowing from banks is a very important source of short-term finance. Other important sources of short-term finance are trade credit, instalment credit and customer advances.

Medium-term Finance

The period of one year to five years may be regarded as a medium-term. Medium-term finance is usually required for permanent working capital, small expansions, replacements, modifications, etc.

Medium-term finance may be raised by:

(*i*) Issue of shares

(*ii*) Issue of debentures

(*iii*) Borrowing from banks and other financial institutions

(*iv*) Ploughing back of profits.

Although medium-term financial requirement may be met by issue of shares, this source is of long-term nature.

Long-term Finance

Periods exceeding 5 years are usually regarded as long-terms. Long-term finance is required for procuring fixed assets, for the establishment of a new business, for substantial expansion of existing business, modernisation, etc.

The important sources of long-term finance are:

(*i*) Issue of shares
(*ii*) Issue of debentures
(*iii*) Loans from financial institutions
(*iv*) Ploughing back of profits.

CORPORATE SECURITIES

Corporate securities are instruments by which capital is raised by joint stock companies. There are two classes of corporate securities, namely,

- Ownership securities
- Creditorship securities.

Ownership Securities

Ownership securities are the shares by which the owned capital (also known as risk capital and venture capital) is raised.

Kinds of Shares

The shares of a company may be broadly divided into:

1. Preference shares
2. Equity shares.

Preference Shares

Preference shares are those which have preferential right to the payment of dividend during the lifetime of the company, and a preferential right to the return of capital when the company is wound up.

Preference shares have the following characteristics.

1. The dividend on them is fixed by the Articles of the company.
2. Preference shareholders get their fixed rate of dividend before any dividend is distributed among the other class of shareholders.
3. At the time of winding up the company, the preference shareholders must be paid back their capital before anything is paid to ordinary shareholders.

Kinds of Preference Shares

Cumulative Preference Shares: The cumulative preference shares are entitled to fixed dividends whether there are profits or no profits. If profits are not sufficient to pay dividends in a particular year, the dividends are accumulated and paid in the succeeding year(s) as profits become available for distribution.

Convertible Cumulative Preference Shares: In 1985, Government of India introduced a new type of preference share namely convertible cumulative preference (CCP) share. The entire issue of the CCP shares shall be converted to equity any time between the third and fifth years of the issue. Since the conversion to the equity is compulsory, the CCP shares cannot be redeemed at any stage. The CCP shareholders enjoy the same voting rights as the cumulative preference shareholders. For calculation of debt equity ratio, CCP shares are treated as part of equity. However, for calculation of preference-equity ratio, CCP shares are totally excluded from both categories.

Non-cumulative Preference Shares: Unlike the cumulative preference shares, these shares cannot claim arrears of dividends of any year out of the profits of subsequent years.

Participating Preference Shares: In the case of the participating preference shares, shareholders receive a fixed rate of dividend in priority to ordinary shares and further, the right to participate in the balance of profit in an agreed proportion together with ordinary shareholders.

Non-participating Preference Shares: These shares are entitled to only a fixed rate of dividend; they have no claim in the surplus profit which belongs to ordinary shareholders.

Redeemable Preference Shares: These are shares which can be purchased back by the company. The company reserves its right to call back or purchase these shares at anytime, subject to the provisions of its Articles.

Irredeemable Preference Shares: These are shares that cannot be purchased back by the company.

Equity Shares

All shares which are not preference shares are equity share, also called ordinary shares. Unlike the preference share, equity shares do not have a fixed rate of dividend. Equity shareholders are entitled to dividends only after the dividend claims of the preference shareholders have been met. Similarly, at the time of the winding up of the company, equity shareholders get back their capital only after the capital of the preference shareholders has been paid back. Equity shares are always irredeemable and their holders have normal voting rights.

The Companies Act refers to two types of equity shares, *viz.*, equity share capital —

- With voting rights
- With differential rights as to dividend, voting or otherwise in accordance with such rules and subject to conditions as may be prescribed.

The second type of equity capital mentioned above was included in the Act by the Companies (Amendment) Act, 2000.

The Companies Act provides that a limited company can, if permitted by its Articles of Association, alter its share capital in any of the following ways:

1. It may increase its share capital by the issue of new shares.
2. It may consolidate and divide all or any part of its share capital into shares of a larger amount.
3. It may convert all or any of its fully paid-up shares into stock or reconvert that stock into fully paid-up shares.
4. It may sub-divide the existing shares into shares of lower denomination.
5. It may cancel those shares which have not been taken up and reduce its capital accordingly.

Any of the above alternations can be effected by passing a resolution in the general meeting of the company and requires no confirmation by the court. However, the company shall give notice of any such alterations to the Registrar within thirty days after doing so.

Creditorship Securities

Creditorship securities, which consist of debentures and bonds, are credit instruments which are widely used by companies to raise funds. The capital raised through creditorship securities is known as borrowed capital or debt capital.

Debentures

The term *debenture is* defined as "a document under the company's seal which provides for the payment of a principal sum and interest thereon at regular intervals which is usually secured by a fixed or floating charge on the company's property or undertaking which acknowledges a loan to the company".

Classes of Debentures

1. Redeemable and Irredeemable: From the point of view of redemption, debentures are classified into redeemable and irredeemable. Redeemable debentures are those that will be repaid by the company at the end of a specified period, or on demand, or by installments. Irredeemable debentures are those that are not repayable during the lifetime of the company. Irredeemable debentures are also called perpetual debentures.

2. Mortgage and Simple: From the point of view of security, debentures are classified into mortgage and simple or naked debentures. Mortgage debentures, also called secured debentures, are those which are secured by a charge on the assets or property of the company, whereas simple debentures are those that are not secured by any charge on the assets of the company.

3. Registered and Bearer: From the point of view of records, debentures may be classified into registered and bearer debentures. Registered debentures are those in respect of which the names, addresses and particulars of the holdings of debenture-holders are entered in the Register of Debentureholders. The transfer of a registered debenture cannot be effected without the execution of a regular transfer deed. As against this, the company keeps no such records of bearer debentureholders. Bearer debentures are negotiable by mere delivery of the document.

4. Convertible and Unconvertible: In case of convertible debentures, the holders have the option to convert their debenture holdings into equity shares of the company at a specified rate after a specified period.

NEW ISSUES — MARKETING OF SECURITIES

The securities market may be divided into: *(i)* New Issues Market; and *(ii)* Stock Exchange.

The new issues market is concerned with the floatation of new issues of securities either by new corporations or by existing business concerns. The stock exchange is an organised market where the ownership of existing shares can be transferred from one person or institution to another.

The important methods of the marketing of securities are the following:

Issue to the Public: A public limited company may mobilise funds by selling securities directly to the public as per the provisions of the Companies Act.

The direct placing of the securities is appropriate for companies with a good reputation. It may also be successful if the promoters themselves enjoy a very good reputation.

This method has, however, certain limitations. For a new company with promoters who are not popular and reputed, this method is not advisable because the public may be reluctant to take the risk of investing in such a venture. If the company fails to generate sufficient public response to the issue, its plans may flop.

Private Placement: The term *private placement* refers to the sale of an entire issue of securities by a company directly to one or a few investors, usually financial institutions. Here, the appeal to subscribe to or purchase the securities is made to the investors either directly or through brokers. Insurance companies, investment companies, trust accounts, pension and provident funds, etc., re-suitable institutions with whom the securities can be directly placed for subscription. The growth of institutional investors has increased the scope of private placing.

An important advantage of private placement is the absence of the risk of uncertainty in raising the capital. Moreover, the cost of raising the capital is very low because the commission and other charges are either nil or comparatively low, and no expenditure has to be incurred on issuing a prospectus. The cost of promotion, in general, is very low.

Offer to Special Classes: An established company may raise additional capital by any of the following methods:

Rights Issue: The rights issue is an offer with a pre-emption right to the existing shareholders of the company to further contribute to its share capital. Under the rights issue, new shares are offered to the existing shareholders in certain proportion to their existing share ownership. However, the rights themselves are transferable and saleable in the market.

Issue of Bonus Shares: A company may capitalise its profits or free reserves by the issue of bonus shares to shareholders. Bonus shares are allotted to shareholders in proportion to their respective shareholding.

Offer to the Employees: The issue of shares may be offered to employees. This promotes better industrial relations and higher productivity. *Employees stock option schemes* /issue of *sweat equity* have become very popular in recent years.

Offer to the Customers: This is popular with public utilities. Shareholdings by customers gives them some say in the affairs and functioning of the concern.

Offer to the Creditors: At the time of reorganisation of the capital structure, creditors may be requested to purchase the shares in full settlement of their loans or advances.

Underwriting: The marketing of securities with the support of, or by, underwriting is very popular because this method ensures that the subscription to or sale of the whole of the securities is underwritten.

Underwriting of Securities

The marketing of securities is greatly facilitated by underwriting. An underwriting agreement is defined as "an agreement entered into before the shares are brought before the public that, in the event of the public not taking up the whole of them or the number mentioned in the agreement, the underwriter will, for an agreed commission, take an allotment of such part of the shares as the public has not applied for".

From the point of view of the issuing company, underwriting insures the risk of the public not taking up the required amount of securities. Needless to say that, the facility of underwriting enables the company to raise the required capital; for if the public does not take up the whole of the issue, the balance left is taken up by the underwriter.

Methods of Underwriting

An underwriting agreement may take any of the following three forms:

1. Standing Behind the Issue: Under this method, the underwriter guarantees the sale of a specified number of shares within a specified period. If the public does not take up the whole of the specified amount of the issue, the underwriters standing behind the issue purchase the balance.

2. Outright Purchase: Under this method, the underwriters purchase the issue outright and resell the securities to the investors. The purchase price may be negotiated between the issuer and the underwriter, or may be determined by competitive bidding.

3. The Consortium Method: Under consortium method, also known as the syndicated method, as the name indicates, underwriting is jointly done by a group of underwriters who form a syndicate for this purpose. This method is usually adopted for large issues. The underwriting of large issues by a consortium enables the spread of the risk among the members of the syndicate—no single underwriter bears the entire risk.

Importance and Advantages of Underwriting

Industrial development is fostered, among other things, by the development of the securities market. A good securities market is one of the prerequisites for the growth of joint stock companies. The marketing of securities is necessary for raising the owned capital. Underwriting, therefore, assumes great significance.

> **Underwriters are of great help in ensuring that the company raises the required share capital. Underwriting, thus, plays a very important role in the development of the capital market and in fostering industrial development.**

A public company will have to secure the minimum subscription within the stipulated time after the issue of the prospectus without which the allotment of shares cannot be made; and without the declaration that it has received the stipulated minimum subscription, the company will not be able to obtain the certificate from the Registrar of Companies to commence business. The growth of the underwriting business has been one of the important factors that have contributed to the development of the Indian capital market in the post-independence period.

The underwriting business offers the following advantages to the corporate sector:

1. Underwriting relieves the issuer of the risk of not being able to find buyers for all the issues offered to the public. Thus, the company can be reasonably sure of raising adequate share capital.
2. Underwriters help the company to fulfil the statutory regulations, like securing the prescribed minimum subscription within the stipulated period.
3. Underwriters relieve the issuer of the burden of undertaking the highly specialised function of distributing securities.
4. Underwriters, having expert knowledge of the capital market conditions, can render expert advice to the company on the timing of security issues, the size and type of securities to be issued, the value at which they may be offered, etc.
5. Underwriting business is of enormous assistance in the mobilisation of funds in the capital market because public confidence is enhanced by the underwriting of issues by reputed underwriters.
6. The activities of underwriters help stabilise capital market conditions.

Underwriting offer is similar to insurance business, where the insurer is exposed to risk to the extent of amount insured, but the only gain is the insurance commission. In underwriting, the compensation is underwriting commission.[1]

Underwriting in India

Professional underwriting service has developed in India from the mid-1950s. The Industrial Credit and Investment Corporation (ICICI), established in 1955, has played an important role in the development of professional underwriting service.

A number of factors were responsible for the relative underdevelopment of the underwriting business in the past. Underwriting grows along with the growth of the capital market and industrialisation, and it could not, therefore, grow significantly because of the poor state of the industrialisation and capital market. The conservative attitude of the Indian commercial banks, the absence of specialised institutions like issue houses, investment institutions, financial syndicates as found in Western countries, the preponderance of the *managing agents* who played a multi-faceted role as promoters, financiers, underwriters, managers, etc., of the companies under their group, affected the development of the underwriting business in India.

Underwriting has, however, been developing in the country, particularly after the establishment of the ICICI in 1955. Public sector financial institutions, such as the IFCI, ICICI, IDBI, SFCs, UTI, LIC; commercial banks; investment companies and stockbrokers — all have played an important role in developing the underwriting service.

In India underwriting commission is regulated by statute at a maximum of 2.5 per cent. Similarly, the entry into this business is also regulated by SEBI, whereby only SEBI registered agencies can act as underwriters.

According to SEBI guidelines on investor protection and disclosure dated 11-6-92, underwriting was mandatory for the full it for each issue of capital to the public. This has since been relaxed in view of involved and now the underwriting is optional.

To avoid disputes between the underwriters and issuer company, SEBI has formulated a model underwriting agreement which seeks to standardize the legal relationship between the two parties. It provides clear guidelines for resolving the issues of disputes. It stipulates several norms for the interest of both the parties including the time limit within which, the issue should open from the date of the agreement. It indicates that the time is the essence of agreement. Any failure on the part of any party to adhere to the time limits shall discharge the other party of his obligations. If the prospectus contains untrue statements, the underwriter can terminate the contract prior to the opening of the issue.[2]

INTERNAL FINANCING

(Ploughing Back of Profits)

An important source for fixed and working capital requirements of established companies is the savings generated internally in the form of retained earnings by the process of ploughing back of profits. A profitable company may retain with it a part of the net profits as undistributed profits to strengthen its financial position, or to meet some of the present or future financial requirements. The reserves thus built-up over the years by ploughing back profits may be utilised for the following purposes:

1. Expansion of the undertaking.
2. Replacement of obsolete assets and modernisation.
3. Meeting permanent (regular) or special working capital requirements.
4. Redemption of old debts.

Ploughing back of profits benefits the company, shareholders and society.

Benefits to the Company

The important advantages of retained profit from the point of view of the company are:

1. It enables the company to withstand difficult situations—*for example*, a depression or recession, period of credit squeeze, etc.
2. It enables the company to adopt a stable dividend policy. Sufficient retained earnings enable the company to pay the normal rate of dividend even if, in a particular year, the profit is very little, or the company incurs a loss.
3. Modernisation and expansion programmes will not suffer for want of finance if a company has large retained earnings.
4. Retained earnings can be made use of to set right any shortfalls in the provision for depreciation, bad and doubtful debts, and similar contingencies.
5. The reserves built-up out of undistributed profits may be made use of to retire bonds and debentures, to build up sinking funds, and to redeem debts.
6. Regular or permanent working capital requirements may be met by the surplus retained with the company.
7. It increases the creditworthiness of the company.
8. It may help increase the sales of the company because, as funds cause no problem, it can expand credit sales to a reasonable extent.
9. It reduces the dependence on external sources of finance.

Benefits to the Shareholders

Though the policy of ploughing back part of the profit limits the dividends, from the long-term point of view, it may benefit the shareholders.

The main advantages from the point of view of the shareholders are:

1. It provides a reasonable assurance to shareholders of a stable rate of dividend.
2. The soundness of the company and its stable dividends help appreciate share values.
3. Shareholders stand to benefit from the modernisation and expansion financed by retained earnings.
4. The redemption of debts may also benefit the shareholders.
5. Shareholders will further benefit from the better performance of the company because of its ability to withstand difficult situations and to carry-out timely replacements and improvements.

Benefits to Society

Society, too, may, derive certain benefits if companies favour ploughing back of profits.

1. Modernisation and expansion financed by internal funds benefit society because they improve the supply position and may even reduce the cost of production, for expansion leads to economies of scale and modernisation increases productivity.
2. The increase in corporate investment increases employment opportunities.
3. Internal financing reduces the demand for funds in the capital market. It would, thus, increase the availability of funds for other investors.
4. Society benefits from the stability accorded to the industrial sector by the internal availability of funds.

Dangers of Ploughing Back Profits

Some dangers are associated with indiscriminate policy of ploughing back profits. Some of the possible dangers are:

1. It may lead to concentration of economic power because large retained earnings enable companies to enlarge their business easily by a continual reinvestment of the profits.
2. It gives scope for manipulation. The controlling powers of the company may depress share prices by keeping the dividend rate very low by ploughing back a substantial part of the profit so that they might purchase the shares at low prices and later benefit from a higher dividend and appreciation of the share value due to the rise in the rate of dividends.
3. The top brass of the management may misuse the funds by locking them up in their pet concerns or companies under the same management against the overall interest of the shareholders.
4. It may lead to over-capitalisation if the reserves are capitalised by issuing bonus shares or bonus issues.
5. The ploughing back of profits interferes with the rights and freedom of shareholders. If shareholders get higher dividends, they will be at liberty to distribute their investments as they like, whereas they, especially the small shareholders, do not have any significant say in the investment or utilisation of retained earnings.
6. From the above point of view, it follows that excessive ploughing back of profits may hinder the natural growth of the capital market.

Determinants of Retained Earnings

The following are the three important determinants of retained earning:

Profits: Obviously, the question of the ploughing back of profits does not arise if a company does not earn profits. Normally, a company has to declare a reasonable rate of dividend to satisfy the shareholders and to prevent a depreciation of share values. Hence, only what is left over after paying a reasonable dividend can be ploughed back. Thus, the amount of net profits is an important determinant of internal savings.

Taxation: The rate of corporate taxation is an important determinant of net profits. A high rate of corporate tax imposes limitations on the building up of internal savings.

Dividend Policy: The dividend policy is an important determinant of retained profits. A conservative dividend policy is regarded as necessary to build-up internal savings. Some people advocate a statutory ceiling on dividends to facilitate a greater ploughing back of profits. At times, the government imposed ceilings on dividends.

PUBLIC DEPOSITS

Public deposits is an important source of finance for companies (here the reference is to deposits with non-financial joint stock companies). Public deposits played an important role in industrial finance in the past as well. For instance, in the 1930s, it was an important source for the textile mills of Ahmedabad, Mumbai, Solapur, Bengal and the Punjab. The tea gardens of Bengal and Assam also depended on this source of finance.

Reasons for Popularity

The increasing popularity of public deposits has been mainly due to the following reasons:

1. The rate of interest the companies have to pay on deposits from the public is lower than the interest on bank loans.
2. As the rate of interest offered by the companies have been significantly higher than the rates offered by banks for the same periods, there has been a good public response.
3. Public deposit has been an easier method of mobilising funds than from banks, especially during periods of credit squeeze.
4. To obtain credit from a commercial bank, the company has to satisfy the credit-worthiness of the purpose for which the loan is sought; but in the case of public deposits, there is no such need.
5. It follows from this that public deposits may form a source to finance business activities for which bank finance is not available.
6. A further attractiveness of public deposits from the point of view of the companies is that they are unsecured.
7. Some public sector undertakings have also been drawing upon this source of finance.

Limitations

Public deposits, however, have certain demerits from the point of view of society.

1. As public deposits are unsecured, depositors bear the risk of loss of money in the event of the failure of the company.

2. Public deposits with companies may cause a diversion of resources into non-priority and undesirable areas.
3. Public deposits tend to defeat the objectives of monetary policy, especially a dear money policy. They also distort the planned interest rate structure in the economy.
4. It has been argued by some people that public deposits adversely affect bank deposits. But this argument has been countered by pointing out that if public deposits activate the idle resources in the economy, they would help increase the deposits with commercial banks.

Regulation of Public Deposits

Acceptance of public deposits by companies needs to be regulated in the interest of the depositing public, the efficacy of the monetary policy and resource utilisation. From time-to-time, the Reserve Bank has issued directives regulating public deposits.

These regulations pertain to the ratio of deposits to the paid-up capital and free reserves; the maximum period of deposits; obligation to invest a specified percentage of the deposit in a current or other account with a scheduled bank free from any charge or lien, or in approved securities which shall be used only for the repayment of deposits; filing of periodical returns with the RBI, giving the required information about public deposits/loans; and furnishing of certain specified information on its financial position and its working while issuing advertisements and application forms soliciting deposits.

A Section (58AA) was added by the Companies (Amendment) Act, 2000, with a view to protect the interest of small investors (a small depositor means a depositor who has deposited in a financial year a sum not exceeding twenty thousand rupees in a company and includes his successors, nominees and legal representatives) requires every company, which accepts deposits from small depositors to intimate to the Company Law Board any default made by it in repayment of any such deposits or interest on deposits. No company shall, at any time, accept further deposits from small depositors, unless each small depositor, whose deposit has matured, had been paid the amount of the deposit and the interest accrued thereupon, barring certain exceptions (like a deposit which has been renewed by the small depositor voluntarily).

Further, every company, which has on any occasion made a default in the repayment of a deposit or part thereof or any interest thereupon to a small depositor, shall state, in every future advertisement and application form inviting deposits from the public, the total number of small depositors and amount due to them in respect of which such default has been made.

There is penalty for non-compliance with the provisions relating to the protection of small depositors.

This provision, thus, serves the cause of small depositors and puts the defaulting companies in a clear disadvantageous position. Provision should also have been made in the Act to make public any default in the repayment of the money of other depositors.

SUMMARY

Business enterprises may require short-term, medium-term and long-term capital for different purposes. Table 12.1 indicates the important sources of industrial finance.

TABLE 12.1 : SOURCES OF FINANCE

Short-Term	*Medium-Term*	*Long-Term*
1. Bank Credit	1. Issue of shares	1. Issue of shares
2. Trade Credit	2. Issue of debentures	2. Issue of debentures
3. Instalment Credit	3. Loans from banks and other financial institutions	3. Loans from banks and other financial institutions
4. Customer advances	4. Public deposits (for existing concerns)	4. Ploughing back of profits (for existing concerns)
	5. Ploughing back of profits (for existing concerns)	

Corporate securities are instruments by which a large part of the capital is raised by joint stock companies. There are two classes of corporate securities, namely, ownership securities and creditorship securities.

Ownership securities are the shares by which the owned capital (also known as risk capital and venture capital) is raised. The shares of a company may be broadly divided into equity shares and preference shares. Preference shares are those which have preferential right to the payment of dividend during the lifetime of the company, and a preferential right to the return of capital when the company is wound up. All shares which are not preference shares are equity shares, also called ordinary shares. Table 12.2 lists the different types of securities.

Creditorship securities, which consist of debentures and bonds, are credit instruments which are widely used by companies to raise funds. The capital raised through creditorship securities is known as borrowed capital or debt capital.

TABLE 12.2 : TYPES OF CORPORATE SECURITIES

CORPORATE SECURITIES		
Ownership Securities		**Creditorship Securities**
Equity Shares	***Preference Shares***	***Debentures***
• With voting rights • With differential rights as to dividend, voting or otherwise in accordance with such rules and subject to conditions as may be prescribed.	• Cumulative Preference Shares • Convertible Cumulative Preference Shares • Non-cumulative Preference Shares • Participating Preference Shares • Non-participating Prefer-ence Shares • Redeemable Preference Shares • Irredeemable Preference Shares.	• Redeemable and Irredeemable • Mortgage and Simple • Registered and Bearer • Convertible and Unconvertible.

Companies also meet their financial requirements by ploughing back of profits. A profitable company may retain with it a part of the net profits as undistributed profits to strengthen its financial position, or to meet some of the present or future financial requirements.

Public deposits as a source of finance is popular with companies with good credit rating. It is often cheap finance.

REFERENCES

1. Sanjiv, Agarwal, *Manual of Indian Capital Market,* Bharat Law House, New Delhi, 1977, p. 1200.
2. *Ibid.,* p. 1201.

ANNEXURE 12.1

LEASING

Leasing which is an alternative to selling capital goods is a common thing in business marketing. Basically, leasing is an arrangement between the leasing company or the *lessor* and the user or the *lessee,* the former arranging to buy the capital equipment for the use of the latter. The lessee has to pay the lessor in the form of rentals and the lessor remains owner of the equipment during the specified period.

There are four types of leases, *viz.,*

1. Operating lease
2. Financial lease
3. Sale and lease back transaction
4. Leveraged lease

Operating Lease refers to a short-term lease of an asset for an hour, a day, etc.

The financial lease is for a basic term during which the lease is non-cancellable. The length of this basic period is determined primarily by the economic life of the asset, and is usually shorter than the expected life. This arrangement provides some means by which the company may continue to use the asset after the expiry of the basic lease period, or alternatively a market purchase price is negotiated on the lease termination.

The sale and lease back transaction provides for an arrangement by which an entity that owns a given asset may sell it to the leasing company, and lease it back. This enables the lessee to immediately defreeze the money that it had locked into the original asset, which becomes available to it for working capital or further expansion.

In case of very large assets, a single lessor may not be capable of acquiring it or may not be willing to shoulder the whole risk associated with. Hence, two or more lessors may jointly acquire the asset and lease it to the lessee. Such an arrangement is known as leveraged lease. The leveraged lease is, thus, similar to consortium financing.[1]

Leasing companies claim the following principal advantages for the lessee:[2]

1. Leasing conserves cash flow by providing hundred per cent finance and enables the companies to employ their funds for working capital requirements.

2. Lease obligations are not reported as company's liabilities, whereas loan obligations must be recorded. Consequently, by financing the asset acquisitions with lease, rather than borrowing, a company can report a better debt-equity ratio.
3. Leasing facilities provide certainty and cash flow forecasts as well as budget controls can be more accurate.
4. Leasing, although a firm commitment, is a revenue expense and lease rental, is an allowable expenditure under the Income-tax Act.
5. Leasing also offers additional cost recovery for such contracts which allow recovery of rent, but not interest costs.
6. Formalities to be gone through for obtaining the lease financing are much less than bank or institutional financing arrangements.
7. Leasing facilities are more flexible. Adjustments to rentals schedule can be made to accommodate the special needs of leases.

Haas points out that leasing has the following disadvantages:[3]

In the long-run, leasing usually requires a greater outlay of capital than debt financing does. Thus, the customer may pay more for the same equipment. In addition, although the customer may view lease payments as operating expenses, they are fixed payments that must be met. Lease agreements can be hazardous if the customer is not careful.

Leasing as a financial alternative to equity capital or bank term finance was introduced to the modern world by the United States of America, where it became effective during the 1940s and 1950s. In some of the industrially advanced countries, leasing today plays a very important role in the acquisition of capital goods. It is estimated that in the USA, leasing industry finances about 25 per cent of capital goods acquisition and in the United Kingdom it accounts for about 15 per cent. The leasing industry has taken great strides in the United States.

In India, the leasing industry took roots with the establishment of the First Leasing Company of India Ltd., in Chennai, which started functioning in 1973-74. "The Indian leasing industry grew disjointedly with the First Leasing Company of India Limited operating alone for almost seven years, followed thereafter by several other companies in the late seventies after which a mini entrepreneurial revolution took place."[4] Several public sector institutions like the ICICI, IFCI, State Bank of India, Canara Bank, some SIDCs, etc., have also entered the leasing business, either directly or indirectly.

REFERENCES

1. Farouk, Irani, "Leasing Companies and Banks", *Commerce,* May 28, 1983.
2. These are mentioned in the feature on Leasing Industry, *Commerce,* May 28, 1983.
3. Robert W. Haas, *Business Marketing,* (Boston: PWS-Kent Publishing Company, 1992), p. 634.
4. Farouk, Irani, "Bright Days Ahead", *The Economic Times,* April 28, 1986.

☆☆☆

CHAPTER

13

INDUSTRIAL FINANCIAL INSTITUTIONS

Finance is a prerequisite to mobilise real resources for organizing production. In a developing economy, however, lack of finance is not the only deterrent to economic development. Even when finance is available, other important factors like imperfections in the information flow and dearth of entrepreneurship may come in the way of industrial and economic development. Hence, it is necessary to make finance and other development assistances in a package to take the dormant and developing economies to the take-off stage. Many developing countries, in particular, therefore, set up *Development Banks* rather than institutions which merely provide finance.

"A Development Bank is a multipurpose institution which shares entrepreneurial risk, changes its approach in tune with the industrial climate and encourages new industrial projects to bring about speedier economic growth. The concept of development banking is based on the assumption that mere provision of finance will not help to bring about entrepreneurial development. Successful entrepreneurial banking should include the discovery of investment projects, undertaking the preparation of project reports, provision of technical advice and management services and finally assisting the management of industrial units."[1]

> **The all India institutions, except those specifically meant for the SSIs, assist large and medium scale enterprises and the state level institutions assist small and medium scale enterprises.**

After Independence, starting with the establishment of the Industrial Finance Corporation of India in 1948, a number of development Banks have been set up at all-India and State levels for assisting the development of large, medium and small industries by providing financial and various other promotional assistances.

Types of Institutions

The most important all-India Development Financial Institutions (DFIs) are Industrial Development Bank of India (IDBI), Industrial Finance Corporation of India (IFCI) and Industrial Credit and Investment Corporation of India (ICICI). The Industrial Reconstruction Corporation of India (IRCI) established in 1971 with the main objective of revival and rehabilitation of viable sick units was converted into the Industrial Reconstruction Bank of India (IRBI) in 1985 with more powers and this was again transformed to a new institution called Industrial Investment Bank of India (IIBI).

Besides the above, the All India Financial Institutions (AIFIs) providing industrial finance also include some investment institutions like the Unit Trust of India (UTI), Life Insurance Corporation India (LIC), and the General Insurance Corporation of India (GIC) and its subsidiaries. (These institutions are termed as investment institutions here exclusively from the point of view of their industrial finance function).

Development Banks have been established at the State level too. There is State Financial Corporations (SFCs) and State Industrial Investment/Development Corporation (SIICs/SIDCs) in most of the States.

Financial assistance is provided, directly or indirectly, to the small-scale sector also by National Small Industries Corporation (NSIC), State Small Industries Development Corporations (SSIDCs) and Khadi and Village Industries Commission (KVIC), although financing is only an ancillary function of these organisations.

The Small Industries Development Bank of India (SIDBI), a wholly-owned subsidiary of the IDBI, is an apex institution for promotion, financing and development of industries in the small-scale sector and for coordinating the functions of other institutions engaged in similar activities.

The IDBI is the apex institution which coordinates the activities of various institutions.

A very important source of industrial finance is commercial banks.

Types of Assistance

> **DFIs provide financial and development and promotional assistances.**

Provision of rupee and foreign currency loans, subscription to shares and debentures, underwriting of shares and debentures, guaranteeing of deferred payments and loans are the important types of financial assistance provided by these institutions (some of the institutions do not provide some of these assistances).

Development activities of the DFIs include identifying industrial potentials of different areas; development of entrepreneurship through training and motivation; assistance in project identification, feasibility studies and preparation of project reports; technical and managerial consultancy; seed/risk capital assistance, etc.

Direct assistance from the all-India development banks is normally confined to large projects. Various state level institutions and certain specialised institutions like the National

Small Industries Corporation (NSIC), State Small Industries Development Corporations (SSIDCs), Khadi and Village Industries Commission (KVIC), SIDBI and banks assist small-scale (including khadi and village) units and medium-scale units.

Projects involving very large investment are assisted by the all-India financial institutions through *consortium financing (i.e.,* the project is jointly financed by a group of financial institutions.) In consortium financing, one of the institutions plays the lead role.

The DFIs have sponsored a number of technical consultancy organisations (TCs) and some institutes for entrepreneurial/management development and imparting education/research in capital market.

INDUSTRIAL DEVELOPMENT BANK OF INDIA

The Industrial Development Bank of India (IDBI) was established in 1964 by the Indian Government under an Act of the Indian Parliament, the Industrial Development Bank of India Act, 1964.

The creation of IDBI in particular, and Financial Institutions (FIs) in general, was a considered response to the emergence of broad-based industrial development as an imperative of national policy. This found expression in the gradual evolution, since 1948, of FIs, both at Central and State levels, largely as government owned specialised institutions. These were set up with the principal objective of providing term finance for fixed asset formation in industry. IDBI was entrusted with the additional responsibility of acting as the principal financial institution for coordinating the activities of institutions engaged in the financing, promotion or development of industry.

IDBI was initially established as a wholly-owned subsidiary of Reserve Bank of India. In 1976, the ownership of IDBI was transferred to the Government of India (GoI). The IDBI Act was amended in October 1994 to, *inter alia*, permit IDBI to raise equity from the public, subject to the holding of GoI not falling below 51% of the issued capital.

According to the Bank's Corporate Mission "IDBI's strategic objective is to position itself as India's premier wholesale bank through a full range of wholesale products — lending, capital markets, advisory and risk management — through an integrated group structure".

According to IDBI sources, its strengths lie in:

- Diversified portfolio across different industries, regions and sectors.
- Long-standing business relationships with all major industrial houses.
- Proven core competence in project financing.
- Large balance sheet and sound financials.
- Capacity to take large single party exposure.
- Capacity to leverage.
- Sizeable stock of cost-effective, long-term funds.

- Fairly good retail network with a large investor base.
- Lean organisation with a sizeable pool of qualified, experienced professionals.

Subsidiary Organisations

IDBI has set up a host of subsidiaries and associates with a view to expand the functional reach of the IDBI Group and take advantage of opportunities in a liberalised market economy.

SIDBI: To give focused attention to the needs of small-scale industry, IDBI had set up the Small Industries Development Bank of India (SIDBI) in 1990 as a wholly-owned subsidiary. The SIDBI Act was amended in March 2000, enabling, among other things, the transfer of IDBI shareholding to a maximum 51% from IDBI.

IDBI Capital: A stock broking company, IDBI Capital Market Services Limited (IDBI Capital) was set up in 1993 to provide a range of capital market related services. It commenced operation as a Primary Dealer in November 1999. In the private placement market, it acts as arranger for several institutional and corporate users. IDBI Capital markets public issues of securities through its strong network of agents. As a depository participant, the company offers institutional and retail clients the facility to maintain their investments and securities in electronic form. It also acts as a portfolio manager and manages the investment portfolios of several provident and pension funds. IDBI Capital is one of the primary dealers accredited by RBI to act as a market maker in Government securities.

IDBI Bank: Consequent upon opening up of commercial banking to the private sector, IDBI set up a commercial bank, IDBI Bank Limited in 1994. IDBI Bank offers high technology based top-of-the-line branded products, which have been well received by the market. It is also a leading player in Depository Participation services, enabling customers to hold and trade shares electronically. Consequent upon the initial public offering of the equity share in February 1999, IDBI now holds 57.14% of the equity of IDBI Bank Limited.

INTECH: To take advantage of the emerging business prospects of the IT sector, IDBI set up IDBI Intech Limited (INTECH) in March 2000, to undertake IT-related activities. With the domain knowledge in the financial sector, acquired by its professional staff over the years, and their experience in the development of software for the financial sector, INTECH would capitalise on the business and IT knowledge to offer the IT-related products and services to the IDBI Group and the other organisations in the financial sector.

ITSL: Consequent to amendment of the Debenture Trustee Regulation, 1993, requiring arms length relationship to be maintained between the issuer and the Trustee, IDBI set up IDBI Trusteeship Services Ltd., (ITSL) under the Companies Act, 1956 in March 2001. It proposes to induct an international strategic partner into this venture in due course. The new company would be technology-driven to provide safety, up to date information and professional services to the subscribers and issuers of debentures.

Products

The important products (schemes of assistance) of ISBI are the following:

Project Finance: The objective of this product is to provide long-term finance (Rupee and Foreign Currency Loan) for new projects and expansion, diversification and modernisation of existing projects.

Term loan, underwriting, direct subscription to equity capital and deferred payment guarantee are the types of assistance under the scheme.

Equipment Finance: Equipment finance is available for acquiring specific machinery/ equipment to financially sound companies which have been in operation for a minimum period of 5 years, consistently profit making for last 3 years and dividend paying capacity of not less than two years. Rupee and Foreign Currency Loans are available.

Assistance under the scheme will not be available for acquisition of second hand equipment/machinery, in-house fabrication of equipment/machinery, reimbursement of the cost of the equipment/machinery purchased more than 90 days prior to the date of application; and grassroot projects or major expansion/diversification, which would call for detailed appraisal.

Asset Credit: The objective of this product is to help companies to acquire new machinery/equipment. Financially sound companies which have been in operation for a minimum period of 5 years, consistently profit making for last 3 years and good track record are eligible for assistance under this scheme.

Corporate Loan: This product has been designed to provide for capital expenditure and long-term working capital to financially sound companies with net worth of not less than ₹ 10 crore, having been in commercial operation for 5 years and making profit consistently for last 3 years, besides satisfying certain criteria. Rupee and foreign currency loans are available under this scheme.

Working Capital Loan: The purpose of this scheme is to provide loan component of working capital finance to companies already assisted by IDBI, which are financially sound having a net worth of not less than ₹ 15 crore. Both rupee and foreign currency loans are available under this scheme.

Direct Discounting of Bills: Financially sound companies which have been in operation for at least 3 years and having no defaults to financial institutions can avail this facility for selling machinery/equipment. Assistance up to 100 per cent of the total value (including insurance, taxes and freight) may be provided.

Equipment Lease: Financially sound companies are eligible for financial lease facility for purchase of equipment on lease basis. However, sale and lease back transactions are normally excluded from this facility.

Venture Capital Fund: This has been established to encourage commercial applications of indigenous technologies or adaptation of imported technologies, development of innovative products and services, holding substantial potential for growth and bankable ventures involving higher risk including those in the information technology (IT) sector.

Finance for Medium Scale Industries: IDBI provides Line of Credit (LoC) to all SFCs/SIDCs to finance medium scale industrial units. SSI units are not considered under this scheme.

Bills Rediscounting: The objective of this scheme is to cover or promote sale of indigenous machinery/equipment to commercial establishment or institutions.

Services: IDBI also provides some very important services to promote and develop industries. These include, merchant banking (See the Annexure for details), debenture trusteeship and foreign exchange services.

INDUSTRIAL FINANCE CORPORATION OF INDIA

The Industrial Finance Corporation of India was established in 1948 under the IFCI Act, with the object of making medium and long-term credit more readily available to industrial concerns in India. IFCI was corporatised in 1993 as a part of the financial sector reforms and an initial public offer was made in the same year. Following the successful public issue, IFCI's business volume as well as profits went up significantly, as did its share of fresh sanctions.

Principal Activities

IFCI's financial operations principally include project financing, financial services, and comprehensive corporate advisory services.

Project Financing: Project financing is the core business of IFCI. Financial assistance is provided by way of medium/long-term credit for:

- Setting up new projects
- Expansion/Diversification schemes
- Modernisation/Balancing schemes of existing projects.

Financial Services: IFCI provides assistance tailor-made to meet specific needs of corporates through various specially designed schemes:

- Equipment finance
- Equipment credit, equipment leasing
- Supplier's/buyer's credit
- Leasing and hire purchase concerns
- Corporate loans, short-term loans
- Working capital term loans.

Financial assistance is provided by way of: Rupee loans, loans in foreign currencies, underwriting of/direct subscription to shares and debentures, providing guarantee for deferred payments and foreign loans.

Lending Policies

While overall viability of the project and safety of assistance extended are the fundamental criteria for investment decisions, the board norms followed by IFCI in project financing are given below. However, IFCI adopts a flexible and pragmatic approach in applying these norms, wherever adequate justification exists.

ICICI BANK

The Industrial Credit and Investment Corporation of India Limited (ICICI), which was merged with the ICICI Bank is 2001, was founded by the World Bank, the Government of India and representatives of private industry on January 5, 1955 to encourage and assist industrial development and investment in India. The main objectives of ICICI were the following:

Objectives and Functions

1. Providing assistance in the creation, expansion and modernisation of industrial enterprises;
2. Encouraging and promoting the participation of private capital, both internal and external in such enterprises; and
3. Encouraging and promoting industrial investment and the expansion of investment markets.

Over the years, ICICI has evolved into a diversified financial institution. ICICI's principal business activities include:

1. Medium-term and long-term project financing for the infrastructure and manufacturing sectors,
2. Corporate finance to meet the treasury requirements of Indian companies,
3. Lease finance,
4. A comprehensive range of financial and advisory services.

Diversifications

The liberalisation of the Indian economy in the 1990s offered ICICI an opportunity to provide a wider range of financial services. For regulatory and strategic reasons, ICICI set up specialised subsidiaries in the areas of commercial banking, investment banking, non-banking finance, investor servicing, broking, venture capital financing and state-level infrastructure financing.

ICICI Venture Funds Management Company Limited: With the recent spurt in entrepreneurship in the country, venture capital and private equity capital financing are fast attaining a role of prominence. ICICI, therefore, established the ICICI Venture Funds as a wholly-owned subsidiary. According to ICICI sources, strong parentage and affiliates provide ICICI Venture with access to a broad spectrum of financial and analytical resources.

ICICI Venture seeks to invest in opportunities where its network through ICICI and TCW can create value for all involved.

The Venture's primary investment objective is capital investment through investments by way of equity or equity-related securities in unlisted companies with significant growth potential.

Its investments span a broad spectrum of industries and stages of development. Its main areas of investment are Information Technology; Biotechnology and Life Sciences; Media and entertainment; and Retail Services. ICICI Venture backs companies with a sustainable competitive edge.

ICICI Venture backs companies with a sustainable competitive edge, principally in India, and selectively in cross-border investment opportunities, across all the stages of a company's life cycle.

ICICI Securities and Finance Company Limited: Formed in 1993 when ICICI's Merchant Banking Division was spun-off into a new company, i-SEC today is India's leading Investment Bank and one of the most significant players in the Indian capital markets.

i-SEC endeavours to offer its clients what are probably the widest, most in-depth range of services in the market, with the highest standards of professionalism.

Backed by a strong distribution network, i-SEC is at the forefront of new developments in the Indian debt market. i-SEC Research Reports, Compendia, Updates, I-BEX and Sovereign Bond Index, are sought after by finance, business and reputed publications alike.

The Project Finance Group has helped take strategic projects from the drawing board to financial closure, leveraging the expertise of parent organisations. i-SEC has also executed several assignments in M&A, including business valuations, spin-offs and mergers, for both domestic and overseas clients.

The range of products offered by i-SEC includes (*i*) Corporate Finance — Mergers and Acquisitions, Equity, Bidding (especially for Telecom Projects); (*ii*) Fixed Income — Primary Dealership, Debt Research; (*iii*) Equities — Lead Management, Underwriting, Syndication, Private Equity Placement, Sales, Trading, Broking, Sectoral and Company Research.

ICICI Brokerage Services Limited: Set up in March 1995, ICICI Brokerage Services is a 100% subsidiary of i-SEC. It commenced its securities brokerage activities in February 1996 and is registered with the National Stock Exchange of India Limited and The Stock Exchange, Mumbai.

ICICI Personal Financial Services Limited (ICICI PFS): Formerly *ICICI Credit,* was one of the first four companies to obtain registration as a Non-Banking Financial Company (NBFC) from the Reserve Bank of India (RBI) in 1997.

It is now a focal point for marketing and distribution of all retail asset products for ICICI, including auto loans, consumer durable finance and other financial products. The Company has thus become a critical part of ICICI's retail strategy aimed at offering a comprehensive range of products and services to retail customers.

ICICI Capital Services Limited: ICICI Capital Services Ltd., was incorporated in the name of SCICI Securities Ltd., on September 24, 1994 as a wholly-owned subsidiary of erstwhile SCICI Ltd., with the objective of providing stock broking services to the institutional clients and undertaking activities such as underwriting, primary market placements and distribution industry and company research, etc. After the amalgamation of SCICI with ICICI, it became a wholly-owned subsidiary of ICICI effective from April 1,1996 resulting in the change of name.

The Company is mandated, under review by ICICI, to carry out on its behalf the retail resource raising activities and to provide front office services related to all retail and semi-retail liability products of ICICI. The Company also operates the network of ICICI Centres being set up by ICICI.

The widespread geographical locations of centres, which are well equipped with the necessary infrastructure, have provided the Company with strategic distribution initiatives so as to become one of the top distribution houses in the country.

ICICI Bank: ICICI Bank, the commercial banking outfit of the ICICI Group, was established in 1994.

In October 2001, the ICICI and two of its retail finance subsidiaries — ICICI PFs and ICICI Capital Services Ltd., were merged with the ICICI Bank. It is now India's second largest bank.

DISCOUNT AND FINANCE HOUSE OF INDIA

The Reserve Bank of India, together with public sector banks and financial institutions, has recently set up a company called the Discount and Finance House of India Limited (DFHI), to deal in short-term assets in order to provide liquidity in the money market.

STATE FINANCIAL CORPORATIONS

The State Financial Corporations Act, 1951, has enabled the State Governments to set up State Financial Corporations (SFCs) to function as regional development banks, making a significant contribution to the industrial advancement of their respective States.

The SFCs are meant to finance small and medium-scale industries.

Apart from their share capital, the SFCs depend for financial resources on repayment of loans and income from investments, issue of bonds, refinancing of loans from the IDBI and to a limited extent on borrowings from the RBI, deposits from the public and occasionally loans from the State.

Types of Assistance

Financial assistance from State Financial Corporations takes the following forms:

1. Granting of loans or advances and subscribing to the debentures of industrial concerns.

2. Guaranteeing loans raised by industrial concerns in the capital market or from scheduled banks or state cooperative banks.
3. Guaranteeing deferred payments due from any industrial concern in connection with its purchase of capital goods within India.
4. Underwriting the issues of stocks, shares, bonds or debentures by industrial concerns.
5. Subscribing to the stocks, bonds or debentures of an industrial concern out of the funds representing the special class of share capital subscribed by the State Government and the IDBI in accordance with the provisions of Section 4A of the SFCs Act, 1951.

The SFCs grant loans mainly for the acquisition of fixed assets like land, buildings and plant and machinery.

Sometimes, they also provide loans for working capital margin in combination with loans for acquisition of fixed assets.

SFCs are also providing foreign currency loans to small and medium scale industrial units for import of plant and machinery and/or technical know-how under IDA-World Bank credits to IDBI.

STATE INDUSTRIAL DEVELOPMENT/INVESTMENT CORPORATIONS

Since 1960, many States and Union Territories have set up State Industrial Development Corporations (SIDCs)/State Industrial Investment Corporations (SIICs), with the main object of accelerating the industrial development of the respective States and Union Territories.

The SIDCs/SIICs have been promoted as promotional bodies entrusted with the major task of promoting industries and ensuring balanced regional growth within each State/UT.

For efficiently carrying out the functions of promotion, improvement and development of industries, these Corporations are empowered to plan, formulate and execute industrial undertaking, project or enterprise which is likely to accelerate industrial development. Further, they promote medium/large industrial ventures as joint sector units in collaboration with private entrepreneurs, or as wholly-owned subsidiaries and provide risk capital to new generation entrepreneurs. Various incentive schemes of Central/State Governments are also administered through them.

Functions

These Corporations undertake a wide range of functions. The important functions are:

1. Grant of financial assistance to industrial concerns in the form of:
   (*a*) Direct investment
   (*b*) Loans

(c) Extension of guarantee for loans and deferred payments

(d) Underwriting and subscriptions to the issue of shares, bonds and debentures;

2. Promotion and management of industrial concerns;
3. Provision of industrial sheds/plots; and
4. Promotional activities such as identification of project ideas, selection and training of entrepreneurs, provision of technical assistance during project implementation, etc.

The Corporations in States like Karnataka and Bihar are empowered to undertake special activities like establishing and managing industrial estates, development of industrial areas, generation, transmission and sale of electricity, etc.

INVESTMENT INSTITUTIONS

Unit Trust of India

The Unit Trust of India (UTI), a public sector Mutual Fund was established in 1964. The share capital of the UTI was subscribed by the IDBI, LIC, SBI and its subsidiaries and other scheduled banks and financial institutions.

Sale of units and other savings schemes are the main sources of funds for the Trust.

The main objective of the UTI is to mobilise the savings of the community and channelise them into productive corporate investments so as to provide for growth and diversification of the economy. It is at the same time intended to provide the facility for an equity type of investment to the large and growing number of investors in the small and medium income groups.

The UTI mobilises funds from the public through a number of schemes. The savings thus mobilised is channeled into productive activities by the Trust by investing them in the shares and debentures of industrial concerns.

It is one of the main intentions of the UTI to provide opportunity to investors belonging to small and medium income groups to indirectly participate in the ownership of shares and debentures of joint stock companies.

For small investors, the UTI has been expected to offer the advantages of *(i)* considerably reduced risk since funds are invested in a balanced and well distributed portfolio; *(ii)* the benefit of expert management; *(iii)* a steady income: and *(iv)* liquidity.

The management and performance of the UTI for sometime had been so bad that in by mid-2001 the financial crisis of the Trust became public and it has virtually betrayed the trust of millions of investors.

Life Insurance Corporation of India

Consequent to the decision to nationalise the life insurance business, the Life Insurance Corporation of India was established in 1956 as a wholly-owned corporation of Government of India in order to carry on the business of life insurance and deploy the savings to the best advantage of the policyholders and the community as a whole.

A large part of the funds of LIC is deployed as loans to assist the development of social overheads like housing, rural electrification, water supply and sewerage schemes.

However, LIC provides substantial assistance to the industrial sector.

Besides normal investment operations by way of sale and purchase of securities in stock markets and investment in Government securities, the Corporation has been anticipating with other all-India institutions in extending direct assistance to industries in the form of loan and direct subscription to shares and debentures of industrial concerns.

LIC extends resource support to the term lending institutions by way of subscription to their bonds and thus contributes to industrial financing in an indirect manner.

The Corporation has also helped small and medium industries by granting loans for setting up of industrial estates.

General Insurance Corporation of India

As a member of the consortium of all-India Financial Institutions, the General Insurance Corporation of India and its four subsidiaries (The United India Insurance Co. Ltd., Oriental Fire and General Insurance Co. Ltd., National Insurance Co. Ltd., and New India Assurance Co. Ltd.,) provide assistance to industries in the form of loans, underwriting and direct subscriptions to shares and debentures, placement of short-term deposits with companies, etc.

Besides taking right entitlement and underwriting of debenture issues, GIC, along with LIC and UTI, buys back debentures tendered by individual holders back to companies for encashment after a stipulated period and thus provides liquidity to such long-term financial assets.

INSTITUTIONS FOR SMALL INDUSTRY

There are several institutions specifically to assist the development of the small and village industries.

SIDBI

The Small Industries Development Bank of India Act, 1989, under which SIDBI was established on April 2, 1990, envisages SIDBI to be "the principal financial institution for the promotion, financing and development of industry in the small-scale sector and to co-ordinate the functions of the institutions engaged in the promotion and financing or developing industry in the small-scale sector and for matters connected therewith or incidental thereto".

SIDBI is an apex institution for the small-scale sector.

As an apex institution, SIDBI makes use of the network of the banks and state level financial institutions, which have retail outlets. SIDBI supplements the efforts of existing institutions through its direct assistance schemes to reach financial assistance to the ultimate borrowers in the small-scale sector. Refinancing, bills rediscounting, lines of credit and resource support mechanisms have evolved over the period of time to route SIDBI's assistance through the network of other retail institutions in the financial system. Improved levels of coordination for development of the small-scale sector is also achieved through a system of dialogue and obtaining feedback from the representatives of institutions of small-scale industries who are on the SIDBI's National Advisory Committee and Regional Advisory Committees.

Business Domain

The business domain of SIDBI consists of small-scale industrial units, which contribute significantly to the national economy in terms of production, employment and exports. In addition, SIDBI's assistance flows to the transport, health care and tourism sectors and also to the professional and self-employed persons setting up small-sized professional ventures.

Objectives

Four basic objectives are set out in the SIDBI Charter. They are:

- Financing
- Promotion
- Development
- Coordination

For orderly growth of industry in the small-scale sector. The Charter has provided SIDBI considerable flexibility in adopting appropriate operational strategies to meet these objectives. The activities of SIDBI, as they have evolved over the period of time, now meet almost all the requirements of small-scale industries which fall into a wide spectrum constituting modern and technologically superior units at one end and traditional units at the other.

Operational Emphasis

SIDBI, in its operational strategy, emphasises:

- Enhancement in the flow of financial assistance to SSIs.
- Enhancement in the capabilities of SSIs at all levels, with focus on adoption of improved and modern technology.

The small industries sector in India is dominated by a large number of small units. These microenterprises require special nurturing. SIDBI "has been operating schemes like Single Window Scheme and Composite Loan Scheme.

To ensure that financial assistance is made available to such units on easy terms and with hassle-free procedures. It has been a matter of policy in SIDBI to identify the areas of gaps in credit delivery system and fill them through devising appropriate new schemes and implementing them.

Financial Assistance

SIDBI's assistance now covers:

- Equity
- Term loan (domestic and foreign currency)
- Working capital for inventory, for raw material, through finance against bills receivables and for intangibles.

The purposes for which SIDBI's assistance is provided include new projects, expansion, diversification, technology upgradation, modernisation, quality improvement, environmental management, marketing (domestic and international) and rehabilitation of sick SSIs.

Promotional Orientation

Besides financing, SIDBI provides developmental and support services to SSIs under its *Promotional and Developmental (P&D) schemes.* The focus of such assistance is to ensure:

- Enterprise Promotion
- Human Resource Development
- Technology Upgradation
- Environmental and Quality Management
- Information Dissemination, and
- Market Promotion

As an apex financial institution for promotion, financing and development of industry in the small-scale sector, SIDBI meets the varied developmental needs of the Indian SSI sector by its wide-ranging Promotional and Developmental (P&D) activities.

The P&D initiatives of SIDBI have crystallised over the years and are now oriented to serve rural entrepreneurs and youth, particularly women through programmes to empower them and motivate them to undertake entrepreneurial ventures.

P&D initiatives of the Bank aim at improving the inherent strength of small-scale sector on one hand as also economic development of poor through promotion of microenterprises.

In pursuance of its multifaceted P&D activity, synergistic with its business activities aimed at development of the small industries, SIDBI looks forward to a partnership with NGOs, associate financial institutions, corporate bodies, R&D laboratories, marketing agencies, etc., for national level programmes.

SIDBI has identified the following thrust areas of P&D activities, which are being undertaken in partnership with various institutions, agencies, and NGOs.

SIDBI Foundation for Micro Credit: The SIDBI, an apex financial institution for promotion, financing and development of small-scale industries in India, has launched a major project christened "SIDBI Foundation for Micro Credit" (SFMC) as a proactive step to facilitate accelerated and orderly growth of the microfinance sector in India. SFMC is envisaged to emerge as the apex wholesaler for microfinance in India providing a complete range of financial and non-financial services such as loan funds, grant support, equity and institution building support to the retailing Microfinance Institutions (MFIs) so as to facilitate their development into financially sustainable entities, besides developing a network of service providers for the sector. SFMC is also poised to play a significant role in advocating appropriate policies and regulations and to act as a platform for exchange of information across the sector. Operations of SFMC in the next few years, are expected to contribute significantly towards development of a more formal, extensive and effective microfinance sector serving the poor in India.

Mahila Vikas Nidhi: A trained and skilled woman can earn her livelihood and effectively contribute to the national income. SIDBI operationalises this concept under its Mahila Vikas Nidhi (MVN) programme by assisting accredited NGOs to create training and marketing infrastructure.

Mahila Vikas Nidhi (MVN) is SIDBI's specially designed Fund for economic development of women, especially the rural poor, by providing them avenues for training and employment opportunities.

A judicious mix of loan and grant is extended to accredited NGOs for creation of training and other infrastructural facilities. The basic activity involves setting up of Training-cum-Production Centres (TPCs) by the assisted NGOs to ensure that women are provided with training and employment opportunities.

In addition, activities like vocational training, strengthening of marketing set up for the products of the beneficiary group, arrangements for supply of improved inputs, production and technology improvement are also covered under the MVN scheme. Assistance is given mainly towards capital expenditure and support of a recurring nature is discouraged.

NGOs that have been in existence for at least 5 years, should be registered with properly constituted bye-laws, memorandum and articles of association, governing body, broad-based management and properly maintained accounts and having good track records are eligible for this programme.

Rural Industries Programme: A unique approach for rural industrialisation where the emphasis is on stimulating and helping the potential entrepreneurs to set up small enterprises through consultancy outfit positioned by SIDBI.

Development of viable and self-sustaining enterprises in rural and semi-urban areas has been identified for an intensive thrust by the Bank with a view to addressing problems such as rural unemployment, urban migration, underutilisation of physical resources and skills of rural areas.

The Rural Industries Programme (RIP) of the Bank provides a cohesive and integrated package of basic inputs like information, motivation, training and credit, backed by appropriate technology and market linkages for the purpose of enterprise promotion.

Implementing agencies such as NGOs, development professionals, technical consultancy organisations, etc., are identified and assigned the task of developing RIP. The implementing agency either by itself or by networking with the appropriate agencies, provides the following professional services: identification and motivation of potential entrepreneurs in the rural areas; identifying potential investment opportunities for these entrepreneurs; facilitating skill upgradation; assistance in securing finance from banks and other lending institutions; helping entrepreneurs in selection, sourcing, installation and operation of machinery; arranging market support wherever necessary and guiding entrepreneurs till their units commence commercial production.

SIDBI is encouraging a sub-sectoral approach under RIP to provide necessary technology and marketing linkages as relevant to specific industrial segment and rural clusters.

SIDBI meets part of the manpower cost of the implementing agency, mainly in the form of a performance fee. The fee is linked to units actually grounded by the identified rural entrepreneurs. In deserving cases, the Bank even provides some start-up expenses to the implementing agencies apart from the performance fee.

Entrepreneurship Development Programmes: Entrepreneurship can be developed by training. Towards this end and also to make the Entrepreneurship Development Programmes (EDPs) result-oriented, SIDBI has been supporting suitable agencies to train and guide potential entrepreneurs to set up enterprises.

EDPs aim at training various target groups in entrepreneurial traits so that they obtain adequate information, motivation and guidance in setting up their own enterprises. In order to maintain a homogeneous nature of participating groups, EDPs focus on rural entrepreneurs, women and SC/ST.

The EDPs are normally of 6 weeks duration coupled with proper practical training inputs. Training Agencies specialising in conducting EDPs, Non-Governmental Organisations (NGOs) and specialised technical institutes are extended assistance for conduct of product specific EDPs.

In an effort to attract more professional and result-oriented institutions into the EDP fold, the Bank has made the scheme more performance-oriented by extending reasonable support towards training cost and encouraging the institutions to earn performance fee by grounding units.

Management Development Programmes: Management Development in SSIs has been identified as a crucial area of intervention for the viability, competitiveness and profitability of SSI units especially in the context of present economic transition when the market barriers are gradually being removed. SIDBI took initiative to remedy the shortcoming of HRD in SSI sector by launching two programmes namely Small Industries Management Programme (SIMAP) targeted at qualified unemployed as well as industry sponsored candidates to provide low cost and competent managers to SSI units and Skill-cum-Technology Upgradation Programme (STUP) for owners/managers of SSIs.

Quality Management: SIDBI is also giving due emphasis to creating awareness in the SSI sector regarding the need for quality and environment management. Suitable agencies are appointed to create awareness and assist in implementation of unit specific plan.

As the small-scale sector has been slow to respond to the importance of quality, the Bank launched a major campaign to organise participative workshops all over the country to sensitise the SSI units about the issue and to create awareness about concepts such as

'Total Quality Management' and 'ISO 9000' as also to assist the SSI units in acquiring ISO-9000 certification by making available to them all the major inputs which are required, *viz.*, expert guidance, escort services and finance.

Environment Management: The environment management initiative of the Bank has been launched with the objective to make the SSI units aware of environmental issues and to assist them to acquire a green image by finding solutions to their pollution problems.

The two-pronged approach aims at increasing awareness on the important issues of environment management and supporting the setting up of demonstration projects in homogeneous cluster of SSI units.

The conduct of awareness programmes is entrusted to professional agencies. These agencies conduct interactive and focused programmes, which endeavour to provide solutions to the multifarious problems afflicting SSI units. The objective of this exercise was to educate the SSI units about the environmental regulations, which need to be adhered to, and the steps, which need to be adopted to operate within prescribed norms.

Demonstration projects are implemented by professional agencies by providing select units in homogeneous clusters with escort services. The agency helps in setting up projects which not only reduce pollution levels but also bring-in benefits like improved quality, reduced processing time and material conservation.

NSIC

The National Small Industries Corporation Ltd., which is wholly-owned by the Government of India and meant exclusively for the development of small-scale industries, was established in 1956. The NSCI with its head office at Delhi has regional/ sub-offices in several places. The main functions of the Corporation are the following:

1. Supply of machinery, both indigenous and imported, on hire purchase to help setting up of new small ancillary units and to modernise existing ones.
2. The Corporation's Prototype Development and Training Centres, the sub-centres and the demonstration-cum-training centre at different places develop prototypes which may be transferred along with know-how to manufacturing units for commercial production, and/or renders training in various engineering trades.
3. Under the Raw Materials Assistance Scheme, small-scale units are supplied raw materials — imported and scarce indigenous ones — on a continuing basis, giving them also the benefit of bulk purchases.
4. NSIC helps the marketing of products of small-scale units under the Government Stores Purchase Programme as well as under its Internal Marketing Programme through consortia approach. In the field of export marketing, the Corporation has adopted a 'Single Window' assistance programme.
5. Further, with a view to creating facilities for regular display of products of the small-scale sector. NSIC has put up showrooms-cum-marketing development centres in a number of places in the country.

6. NSIC undertakes small industries projects on turn-key basis and provides total services — from feasibility studies to installation and commissioning of plant.

SSIDCs

State Small Industries Development Corporations have been set up to serve the needs of small-scale industries in the respective States/Union Territories. The SSIDCs have been incorporated under the Companies Act so as to lend them the desired operational flexibility to undertake a variety of activities for the benefit of small-scale industries.

The specific activities undertaken by the SSIDCs include:

1. procurement and distribution of raw materials;
2. supply of machinery to small entrepreneurs on hire purchase basis;
3. management assistance to production units; .
4. operation of seed capital scheme on behalf of the State Governments;
5. construction and management of industrial estates;
6. participating with other institutions in setting up of technical consultancy organisations, and
7. undertaking marketing activities.

In addition to the above, SSIDCs have been providing infrastructural facilities like sheds, godowns and common production facilities, technical and consultancy services, particularly to the unemployed, like preparation of feasibility reports, formulation of project reports and planning for modernisation/diversification of existing product range and implementation of projects. Some SSIDCs have also sponsored industrial potential surveys in some districts to identify viable small-scale projects to be based mainly on locally available raw materials and local demand conditions.

SSIDCs also arrange for marketing of finished products of small industrial units both in domestic as well as international markets under their Marketing Assistance Scheme.

Many SSIDCs are actively associated with the setting up of emporia to assist small-scale units in marketing their products. Such emporia have been set up in metropolitan cities and also places of tourist importance. The showrooms established are consumer goods-oriented and are aimed at ensuring reasonable prices to both the producers and the consumers. Further, SSIDCs also organise and participate in exhibitions in various markets. The products involved are mainly handicrafts, handlooms, ready-made garments, sports goods and the like.

KVIC

The Khadi and Village Industries Commission, established as a statutory organisation under the Khadi and Village Industries Commission Act, 1956, provides various schemes of assistance which cover extension of finance right from the stage of procurement of raw materials, tools and implements to the production of goods and their marketing.

For more information about KVIC, see the chapter on *Village and Small Industries.*

COMMERCIAL BANKS

Commercial Banks are a very important source of finance for the industry. The industrial sector is getting around 50 per cent of the total banks credit.

Particularly, since the major bank nationalisation of 1969, there has been a substantial expansion of the bank branch network and a substantial growth of the bank deposits and credits.

Commercial banks in India had been following the orthodox British line of disfavouring term loans to industries. However, there has been a change in their attitude.

In respect of term finance, the commercial banks, besides providing term credit and subscribing to shares and debentures, indirectly participate in term finance by subscribing to the shares and debentures of financial institutions. Commercial banks also do underwriting of shares and debentures. Some of the banks have merchant banking divisions. Scheduled banks have been permitted to hold in their own investment portfolio shares and debentures of the private corporate sector devolving on them through their underwriting and merchant banking commitments.

The shift in favour of the 'priority sectors' led to a decline in the share of the industrial sector in the total bank credit. Today, the industrial sector accounts for about half of the total bank credit compared to over two-thirds prior to the nationalisation of 1969. This decline in the share has been confined to the medium and large sectors. Small industry is a priority sector and there has been a very significant increase in the proportion of the credit flow to this sector.

SUMMARY

There are a number of institutions at all-India and State levels for assisting the development of large, medium and small industries by providing financial and various other promotional assistances.

The most important all-India Development Financial Institutions (DFIs) are Industrial Development Bank of India (IDBI), Industrial Finance Corporation of India (IFCI), Industrial Credit and Investment Corporation of India (ICICI) and Industrial Investment Bank of India (IIBI). The IDBI is the apex institution which coordinates the activities of various institutions.

Besides the above, national level institutions providing industrial finance also include some investment institutions like the Unit Trust of India (UTI), Life Insurance Corporation India (LIC), and the General Insurance Corporation of India (GIC) and its subsidiaries.

Development banks have been established at the State level too. There are State Financial Corporations (SFCs) and Industrial Investment/Development Corporation (SIICs/SIDCs) in most of the States.

The Small Industries Development Bank of India (SIDBI), a wholly-owned subsidiary of the IDBI, is an apex institution for promotion, financing and development of industries in the small-scale sector and for coordinating the functions of other institutions engaged in similar activities. Financial assistance is provided, directly or indirectly, to the small-scale sector also by National Small Industries Corporation (NSIC), State Small Industries Development

Corporations (SSIDCs) and Khadi and Village Industries Commission (KVIC), although financing is only an ancillary function of these organisations.

A very important source of industrial finance is commercial banks.

Provision of rupee and foreign currency loans, subscription to shares and debentures, underwriting of shares and debentures, guaranteeing of deferred payments and loans are the important types of financial assistance provided by these institutions (some of the institutions do not provide some of these assistances).

Development activities of the DFIs include identifying industrial potentials of different areas; development of entrepreneurship through training and motivation; assistance in project identification, feasibility studies and preparation of project reports; technical and managerial consultancy; seed/risk capital assistance, etc. The IDBI is the apex institution which coordinates the activities of various institutions.

The DFIs have sponsored a number of technical consultancy organisations (TCs) and some institutes for entrepreneurial/management development and imparting education/research in capital market.

As a percentage of GDP, disbursements by financial institutions to industry rose from as low as 0.5 per cent in the first-half of the seventies to 1.4 per cent in the first-half of the eighties, to 2.9 per cent in the first-half of the nineties and further to 3.3 per cent in the second-half of the nineties

TABLE 13.1: INDUSTRIAL DEVELOPMENT/FINANCIAL INSTITUTIONS

All India Institutions (For large and medium industries)	*State Level Institutions (For medium and small industries)*	*Institutions for Small-scale Sector*	*Others*
Industrial Development Bank of India (IDBI) Industrial Finance Corporation of India (IFCI) Industrial Credit and Investment Corporation of India (ICICI) Industrial Investment Bank of India (IIBI) Investment Institutions (UTI, LIC, GIC and subsidiaries)	State Finance Corporations (SFCs) State Industrial Development/ Investment Corporations (SIDCs/ SIICs)	Small Industries Development Bank of India (SIDBI) National Small Industries Corporation (NSIC) State Small Industries Development Corporations (SSIDCs) Khadi and Village Industries Commission (KVIC)	Commercial Banks, Co-operative Banks, Venture Capital Funds, etc.

REFERENCE

1. Prabhakar K. V., "Development Banks — New Trends", *Financial Express,* June 18 and 19, 1981.

ANNEXURE 13.1*

MERCHANT BANKING

"Merchant banks are issue houses rendering such services to industrial projects or corporate units as floatation of new ventures and new companies, preparation, planning and execution of new projects, consultancy and advice in technical, financial, managerial and organisational fields. A number of other functions such as restructuring, revaluation of assets, mergers, takeovers, acquisitions, etc., are also undertaken by them.

A major function of merchant banking is the issue management. The issue can be public issue through prospectus, offer of sale, or private placements, etc."[1]

"According to a notification of the Ministry of Finance, a merchant banker is any person who is engaged in the business of issue management either by making arrangements regarding selling, buying or subscribing to the securities as manager, consultant, adviser or rendering corporate advisory service in relation to such issue management."

Merchant Banking Services

According to the SEBI Guidelines for Merchant Bankers, the authorised merchant banking activities are the following:

1. Issue management, which will *inter alia* consist of preparation of prospectus and other information relating to the issues, determining financing structure, tie-up of financiers and final allotment and/or refund of subscription.
2. Corporate advisory services relating to the issue.
3. Underwriting.
4. Portfolio management services.
5. Managers, consultants or advisers in the issue.

The list of merchant banking services provided by the IDBI, given below, would give an idea of the services rendered by merchant banks.

Corporate Finance

- Project Advisory Services which include:
  - — Review of feasibility, key contracts/structures
  - — Advice on key project contracts
  - — Identifying foreign partners/investors and assistance in evaluation and negotiations
  - — Structuring financing plan and advise on financing options
  - — Financial modelling and sensitivity analysis
  - — Risk analysis and risk allocation
  - — Preparation of project information memorandum
  - — Documentation agency services
  - — Structuring of credit enhancement mechanism

---

* This Annexure is intended only to explain/illustrate the meaning of *Merchant Banking, Mutual Funds* and *Venture Capital.* Those who are interested in the details are advised to refer other publications like *Manual of Indian Capital Market* by Sanjiv Agarwal.

- Policy formulation and evaluation of infrastructure projects
- Project appraisal
- Placement of equity with banks, FIIs, high net worth investors, mutual funds, institutional investors and private equity funds.
- Placement of preference shares and debentures with domestic investors
- Structuring and syndication of bought-out deals
- Coordinating the financial participation of multilateral agencies and international banks
- Arranging buyers' line of credit/suppliers' line of credit/guarantee assistance
- Loan syndication — Rupee and foreign currency from Indian Financial Institutions, banks, multilateral agencies, foreign commercial banks, export credit agencies
- Syndication of structured debt instruments, ECBs and Commercial Papers
- Advice on resolution of inter-creditor issues of offshore lenders (including ECA lenders) and domestic lenders
- Advice on commercial issues of loan/Guarantee documentation, Sponsor documentation, Security documentation.

Issue Management

- Management of public/rights issues of equity, preference shares, convertible, partly convertible and non-convertible debentures including:
  - — Structuring of instruments
  - — Preparation of offer document
  - — Obtaining statutory and other clearances required in connection with the issue
  - — Tying up underwriting and placement through book-building process
  - — Assistance in selection of bankers, brokers, registrars, printers, advertisement agency and other intermediaries
  - — Marketing of the issue
  - — Post-issue activities including finalisation of basis of allotment/refund and listing
  - — Advice on the management of Euro issues
  - — Advice on buyback of securities and management of tender offer
  - — Open Offer Management under SEBI Takeover Code.

Corporate Advisory Services

- — Equity and Business Valuation
- — Advice on Mergers, Acquisitions and Divestitures
- — Advice on Business and Financial Restructuring
- — Privatisation advice
- — Restructuring/rehabilitation advice for weak units
- — Advice on Asset Sale and hive-offs.

Merchant Banking in India

Merchant banking was introduced in India by foreign banks. It was only in the 1970s that Indian banks entered this field.

The following are some of the reasons why specialist merchant banks have a crucial role to play in India:[2]

1. Growing industrialisation and increase of technologically advanced industries.
2. Need for encouragement of small and medium industrialists, who require specialist services.
3. Growing complexity in rules and procedures of the Government.
4. Need to develop backward areas and states which require different criteria.

Institutions engaged in merchant banking, either by themselves or through subsidiaries, in India fall into the following categories:

- Financial institutions like IDBI, IFCI and ICICI.
- Commercial banks — Foreign and Indian (public sector and private).
- Private merchant bankers like DSP, Kotak, etc.

Any person or body proposing to engage in the business of merchant banking would need authorisation by the (SEBI) in their prescribed format.

All merchant bankers are expected to perform with high standards of integrity and fairness in all their dealings. A code of conduct for merchant bankers will be prescribed by SEBI. Within this context, SEBI's authorisation criteria would take into account mainly the following: Professional competence; personnel, their adequacy and quality, and other infrastructure; capital adequacy; and past track record, experience, general reputation and fairness in all their transactions.

MUTUAL FUNDS

A mutual fund is an agency that mobilizes investible resources of, mostly, individuals and invests them in a diversified portfolio of financial assets so as to balance maximization of returns and minimization of risks.

Small investors, particularly, may not have the knowledge, expertise and sufficiency of resources to make prudent, profitable and risk spreading investments. The mutual funds with their intimate knowledge of the investment opportunities and analytical and fund management expertise are therefore, expected to be of great service to the small investors. As James L. Pierce observes, a mutual fund, thus, is "a non-depository, non-banking financial intermediary which acts as an important vehicle for bringing wealth holders and deficit units together indirectly".

According to the SEBI Regulations of Mutual Funds brought out in 1993, a mutual fund is "a fund established in the form of trust by a sponsor, to raise monies by the trustees by the sale of units to the public, under one or more schemes, for investing in securities in accordance with these regulations". In other words, a Mutual Fund (called Unit Trusts in UK) collects money from the public by sale of units and invests them in financial assets like shares, bonds, etc.

Traditionally, the *open-ended* type of mutual fund has been very popular. In the case of the open-ended fund, an investor can buy or redeem *(i.e.,* sell back) units any-time. Open ended schemes, thus, combine, theoretically, return on investment and almost perfect liquidity. In *a close-ended* mutual fund, the corpus of the fund and the duration of the fund are predetermined.

An investor cannot redeem his investment directly from the Fund before the scheme matures. They may however, be traded in the capital market.

The net asset value (NAV) of a fund indicates the worth of the investments made of the fund. The NAV per unit is computed by dividing the net assets of the fund by the number of units outstanding. An NAV of more than the face value indicates capital appreciation and *vice versa.*

The public sector Unit Trust of India (UTI), established in 1964 is the first Mutual Fund in India. The main objective of the UTI is to mobilise the savings of the community and channelise them into productive corporate investments so as to provide for growth and diversification of the economy. It is at the same time intended to provide the facility for an equity type of investment to the large and growing number of investors in the small and medium income groups. For small investors, the UTI has been expected to offer the advantages of *(i)* considerably reduced risk since funds are invested in a balanced and well distribute portfolio; *(ii)* the benefit of expert management; *(iii)* a steady income: and *(iv)* liquidity.

The UTI has grown substantially, launching attractive products suitable to different segments. Its first product, the US-64, an open-ended scheme of the UTI, was very popular because of the fairly high returns and liquidity it offered. However, in 2000 it served a severe blow to the confidence of the small investors, particularly, not only in the UTI but also in the public sector financial institutions and the government itself, when it suspended for sometime the repurchase of the units due to financial crises and the fall in the NAV below the face value. Investments, allegedly, with vested interests and mismanagement led to such a flight.

The Amendment to the Banking Regulation Act in 1993, which empowered the Reserve Bank to permit banks to carry on non-banking businesses such as leasing, mutual funds, etc., gave a fillip to the growth of Mutual Funds. Besides banks, a number of non-banking financial intermediaries (NBFIs), like Jardine Fleming, Birla Mutual Fund, Alliance Mutual Fund, Kothari Pioneer Mutual Fund, etc., are also in the Mutual Fund business in India now.

VENTURE CAPITAL

Development of entrepreneurship demands combination of three vital factors:

- Innovative ideas
- Competency in project preparation and implementation
- Project financing

There may be a many people with good project ideas. These ideas, however, do not get translated into commercially viable practical projects in the absence of the other two factors. Many young technocrats and others with innovative ideas suffer because of this. It is in this context that the Venture Capital can play a crucial role in the industrial development by providing the two missing links.

Venture Capital (VC) has played an important role in the industrial development of USA. The development of the Silicon Valley, in particular, owes a lot the VCs.

Innovative projects, albeit potentially very profitable, are often very risky and, therefore, financiers tend to shy away from such projects. As the VC firms venture into such risky projects, venture capital is also known as *risk capital.*

Venture capital activities have been pioneered in India by AIFIs like ICICI, IDBI and IFCI by setting up Venture Capital divisions or subsidiaries. Venture capital funds have been established by State level institutions, commercial banks and private firms also.

The details of the Venture Capital Fund of the IDBI given below would give some exposure to the characteristics of VC.

VENTURE CAPITAL FUND, IDBI	
Objective	To encourage commercial applications of indigenous technologies or adaptation of imported technologies, development of innovative products and services, holding substantial potential for growth and bankable ventures involving higher risk including those in the Information Technology (IT) Sector.
Eligibility	All industrial concerns defined in Section 2(c) of IDBI Act, 1964. • Ventures, which may not be first in the technology but would be one of the first few offering potential for substantial return. • Venture should normally have innovation content. • Ventures, which deliver traditional products/services in emerging sectors and have sustainable competitive advantage. • Overriding criteria for eligibility will be potential for substantial long-term capital gains.
Target Sectors	IDBI shall target investments in high growth and profitable industry sectors and will exclude mature industries, commodity-type products and highly competitive sectors. The main criteria will be high growth prospects, potential for capital appreciation and clear-cut exit route within a time-frame of 3-5 years.
Nature of Assistance	Equity Term Loan Convertible debt
Extent of Assistance	Finance for capital expenditure, start-up working capital and selectively. for core current assets during commercial operation. Maximum up to 80% of the project cost. IDBI's exposure to be restricted to ₹ 20 crore in each venture.
Project Cost	No upper limit on the cost of the venture.
Promoters' Contribution	Minimum 20% of the cost of the venture, with core promoters' being not less than 10%.

REFERENCES

1. Avadhani V. A., *Investment and Securities Markets In India,* Himalaya Publishing House, Mumbai, 1992, p. 151.
2. *Ibid.,* p. 157.

☆☆☆

CHAPTER 14

INDIAN COMPANY LAW

BRIEF HISTORY OF COMPANY LAW IN INDIA[1]

Indian Company Law has a long history. The Companies Act, 1956, is the successor to the Indian Companies Act of 1913 and is a consolidation of many successive Amendment Acts, statutory rules and principles laid down in decisions of the courts in India and in England. Several Acts were passed from 1850 onwards. The first Act, passed in 1850, was known as the Joint Stock Companies Act. This was followed by two Acts of 1857 and 1860; but the Act of 1866, which followed soon after, repealed all the previous enactments; and this Act itself was repealed in turn by the Act of 1882. This last mentioned Act remained on the statute book up to 1913, though, in the meantime, it was amended several times to meet the demands of the commercial world. The Indian Companies Act of 1913 was passed with the object of consolidating and amending the law relating to trading companies, and was mainly based upon the English Companies Act of 1908, with certain additional provisions to meet the peculiar business conditions obtaining in this country. Since the Indian Act closely followed the English Company Law, the decisions of the English courts under the latter were also generally followed by the courts in India. This Act of 1913, however, did not provide for certain peculiarities of the Indian commercial world, such as the managing agency, and was, therefore, found to be highly unsatisfactory in several respects in the course of its working. Eventually, extensive amendments were introduced in the Act by the Indian Companies (Amendment) Act of 1935, which came into operation on 15th January, 1937. The vast number of amendments introduced by this Act of 1937, however, involved a few omissions; but they were sought to be removed by frequent amendments in the subsequent years.

The Act of 1913 was, however, repealed by the Companies Act of 1956 which was brought into force from 1st April 1956. This Act, while adopting the scheme and most of the provisions of the UK Companies Act of 1948, marked a distinct improvement on the Act of 1913 in several respects and sought to ensure an efficient and honest management of companies governed by the Act.

The Companies Act, 1956, was replaced by the Companies Act, 2013, which is more comprehensive and contemporary than the previous Act. It has introduced several new concepts and regulations.

The Companies Act, 1956, was amended several times, including very significantly sometimes. There was, however, a strong general feeling that the Act needed a thorough overhaul and reformulation, taking into account, in particular, the need to strengthen the corporate governance structure, investor protection and streamlining of procedures. Years of efforts in this direction resulted in the Companies Bill, 2012, which was assented by the President of India on 29th August, 2013, resulting in the Companies Bill, 2012, becoming the Companies Act, 2013.

COMPANIES ACT, 2013 — A SYNOPTIC NOTE

[It may please be noted that this chapter gives only a brief description of what is thought to be important facets of the Act. A bird's eye view of the Act can be obtained from the following three sections of this chapter: *Main Provisions of the Act, Miscellaneous* and *Summary.*]

The Companies Act, 2013, which has replaced the 56 years old Companies Act, 1956, substantially differs from the previous Act in many respects. This landmark law is both more concise and comprehensive compared to the 1956 Act.

The Companies Act, 2013 (CA 2013), has substantially modified the company law in India, reflecting, *inter alia,* a response to the changing business environment. It has 470 Sections and 7 Schedules (compared to 658 Sections and 15 Schedules in the 1956 Act). The current Act has delinked the procedural aspects from the substantive law and provides greater flexibility in rule making *vis-à-vis* the changing business environment. Many facets of the Act are to be explained in the rules prescribed by the Central Government. Interestingly, 74 per cent of the Act provides for delegated legislation as a means of operationalising the provisions as opposed to 16 per cent in the 1956 Act.

The CA 2013 seeks to provide more transparency in corporate governance, enjoins more responsibility and accountability on the Directors of the company, make small companies also to comply with accounting disciplines, protect the interests of small investors and depositors, etc.

It has introduced new provisions or brought about significant changes in the provisions in a number of areas of corporate management and governance. It is claimed that the CA 2013 marks a shift to a more business-friendly corporate regulations and that it would improve corporate governance norms; encourage e-governance; enhance accountability, disclosure norms, compliance and enforcement; raise levels of transparency and protect interests of investors, particularly small investors, and creditors. It is claimed that the Act has ushered in a new era of corporate democracy making a "titanic shift from government control to self-governance."

The CA 2013 has introduced new entities/concepts such as one person company, small company, dormant company, class action suits, registered valuers, serious fraud investigation office etc.

With the CA 2013, India became the first country in the world which has made corporate social responsibility mandatory.

Application of the Act

The Companies Act 2013 applies to the whole of India and to almost all types of companies — it applies not only to companies incorporated under the Companies Act but also to companies incorporated under other Acts, like insurance companies, banking companies, companies engaged in the generation or supply of electricity, except insofar as the provisions of the Companies Act 2013 are inconsistent with the provisions of the respective Act/Acts under which the company was incorporated or has been governed.

Main Provisions of the Act

The main provisions of the Act describe regulations pertaining to the following broad areas.

1. Types of companies and their formation.
2. Public offer and private placement of securities.
3. Issue of different kinds of share capital and debentures.
4. Acceptance of deposits by companies.
5. Management and administration of companies.
6. Declaration and payment of dividend.
7. Accounts of companies.
8. Audit and auditors.
9. Composition of Board of Directors, qualifications and disqualification of Directors, vacation of office by Directors, removal of Directors, duties of Directors etc.
10. Meetings of Board of Directors, powers of Directors and restrictions on powers of directors, Audit Committee etc.
11. Appointment and remuneration of managerial persons.
12. Inspection, inquiry and investigation pertaining to affairs of companies.
13. Compromises, arrangements and amalgamations.
14. Prevention of oppressions and mismanagement.
15. Removal of names of companies from the register of companies.
16. Revival and rehabilitation of sick companies.

17. Winding up of companies.
18. Companies incorporated outside India.

OBJECTIVES OF COMPANIES ACT

The main objective of the Companies Act is to empower the Central Government to regulate the formation of companies by laying down proper norms and compliance requirements and to exercise control over the management of companies to promote healthy development of the corporate sector.

The main objective of the Companies Act is to empower the Central Government to regulate the formation of companies in accordance with certain standards and norms and to control the management of companies by laying down a legal and procedural framework to be adhered to by the companies.

A look at the provisions of the Companies Act indicates that the principal objectives of the Act are to provide:

1. Certain standards and norms and a clear procedure for formation of companies.
2. A comprehensive regulatory framework to provide for honest administration of companies.
3. Norms for adequate, fair and true disclosure of the affairs of companies.
4. Authority to the government to establish various authorities required for the administration of the company law, such as the Registrar of Companies, National Company Law Tribunal and National Company Law Tribunal, Serious Fraud Investigation Office etc.
5. Mechanism for effective investigation into the affairs of any company in respect of which any mismanagement or objectionable practice is suspected.
6. Proper standard of accounting and auditing.
7. Qualifications and norms in respect of appointment of Directors of the Board, powers and responsibilities of the Board, norms regarding Board meetings etc.
8. Protection of interests and rights of shareholders, creditors etc.
9. Prevent insider trading.
10. Regulation of related party transactions.
11. Restrictions on acceptance of deposits by companies.
12. Regulation of compromises, arrangements, amalgamations etc.
13. Prevention of oppression and mismanagement.
14. Norms regarding declaration and payment of dividend.
15. Revival and rehabilitation of sick units.
16. Procedures for winding up of companies.
17. Regulation of issue and transfer of shares and debentures.
18. Enforcement of corporate social responsibility.

CLASSIFICATION OF COMPANIES

Definition of Company

In the words of Lord Justice Lindley, "a company is an association of many persons who contribute money or money's worth to a common stock and employ it in some trade or business, and who share the profit and loss arising therefrom. The common stock so contributed is denoted in money and is the capital of the company. The persons who contribute to it or to whom it belongs are members. The proportion of capital to which each member is entitled is his share. The shares are always transferable although the right to transfer is often more or less restricted". According to Chief Justice Marshall, "a corporation is an artificial being, invisible, intangible, existing only in contemplation of the law. Being a mere creation of law, it possesses only the properties which the charter of its creation confers upon it, either expressly or as incidental to its very existence." Hahlo's *Case Book on Company Law* says that "like any juristic person, a company is legally an entity apart from its members, capable of rights and duties of its own, and endowed with the potential of perpetual succession."

According to the CA 2013, "a company means a company incorporated under this Act or under any previous company law". The Act says that a company formed under the Act may be either a company limited by shares; or a company limited by guarantee; or an unlimited company.

The CA 2013 deals with the following classes of companies.

- Companies limited by shares (subdivided into public, deemed public and private companies)
- Companies limited by guarantee (either with or without share capital)
- Companies with unlimited liability (either with or without share capital)

The Companies Act 2013 also refers to certain special types of companies such as:

- One person company
- Small company
- Dormant company
- Holding and subsidiary companies
- Associate company
- Government company
- Foreign company

According to the Companies Act, there are basically three classes of companies, *viz.*, limited companies, unlimited companies and guarantee companies.

Unlimited Company

A company not having any limit on the liability of its members is termed as unlimited company. The members of an unlimited company are liable, like the partners of a firm, for all its trade debts without any limit.

An unlimited company must have Articles of Association, stating the number of members with which the company is to be registered. An unlimited company may or may not have share capital. As on March 31, 2015, there were 395 unlimited companies.

The High-powered Expert Committee on Companies and MRTP Act, popularly known as the Sachar Committee, observed that "although the present Act provides for the formation of unlimited companies, the latter have hardly had any useful career in the growth and development of the corporate sector. We feel that the concept of a company with unlimited liability of its members does not conform to the corporate concept which necessarily postulates a limited liability. We, therefore, suggest that this type of companies should be abolished from the statue book.... It is also suggested that the existing unlimited companies should be compulsorily required to convert themselves into limited companies." However, even after the significant Amendment Act of 2000 and the replacement of the Companies Act 1956 by the Companies Act 2013, unlimited company continues to have its place in the Indian law.

As on 31st March, 2015, there were 395 companies in India with unlimited liabilities.

Guarantee Company

The liability of the members of a guarantee company is limited by a fixed sum which is specified in the memorandum and beyond which they cannot be called upon to contribute.

The memorandum of a company limited by guarantee shall state the amount up to which each member undertakes to contribute to the assets of the company, in the event of its being wound up, for the payment of the debts and liabilities of a company.

The Sachar Committee observed that "although guarantee companies constitute a very negligible fraction of less than three per cent of the total companies at work in India, they still do have a useful role to play as companies for furthering the objects of commerce, art, science, religion, charity or some other useful objects and usually such a company does not apply its profits or rather income except for these desirable objectives. It is, however, inherent in the very nature of these objectives that such companies be formed as public limited companies, limited by guarantee only and for the purpose enumerated in the present Section 25 of the Act." (Section 25 of the Companies Act 1956 referred to charitable/social purposes)

As on 31st March, 2015, the number of companies limited by guarantees was 6015.

Limited Company

In case of a limited company, the liability of its members is restricted to the amount of share capital subscribed by them or standing in their names, if at any time the company is wound up and the value of its assets is insufficient to meet its liabilities.

There are two important kinds of limited companies, *viz.,*

- Private limited company
- Public limited company.

Private Company

Important features of a private company according to the Companies Act 2013 are the following.

1. The Companies (Amendment) Act 2015 deleted the stipulation of a minimum paid-up capital of one lakh rupees for a private company.
2. The number of members is not more than two hundred (excluding employees and former employees who continue to be members after the employment ceased). Before the coming into effect of the Companies Act, 2013, the maximum permissible number of members of a private company was fifty. Further, earlier there had to be a minimum of two members for a private company. However, the 2013 Act introduced a special category of private company, *viz., one person company.*
3. Its articles restricts the right to transfer its shares.
4. It is prohibited by its articles any invitation to the public to subscribe for any securities of the company;
5. The name of a private limited company shall end with the words "private limited".

At the end of March 2015, there were a total of 952,490 private limited companies in India. 363 of them were government companies.

Public Company

Private companies include both private sector companies and public sector companies. Similarly, public companies include both private sector and public sector companies. About 98 per cent of the public limited companies in India are non-government companies.

According to the CA 2013, a public company means a company:

1. Which is not a private company
2. Companies Amendment Act deleted the stipulation of a minimum paid-up capital of five lakh rupees capital, for a public company.
3. Which has a minimum of seven members (no upper limit).
4. A private company which is a subsidiary of a company which is not a private company shall be deemed to be public company even where such subsidiary company continues to be a private company in its articles.
5. The name of a public limited company shall end with the word "limited".

As on 31st March 2015, there were 63,111 public limited companies in India. 1,054 (less than two per cent of the total) were government companies and the rest non-government companies.

TABLE 14.1 : PRIVATE COMPANY AND PUBLIC COMPANY: A COMPARISON

Requirements/Conditions	Private Company	Public Company
Minimum members	Two (One for OPC)	Seven
Maximum members	200	No limit
Minimum paid-up capital	Not compulsory	Not compulsory
Minimum directors	Two (One for OPC)	Three
Maximum directors	15 (May be increased by Special Resolution)	15 (May be increased by Special Resolution)
Public issue of shares	Not permitted	Permitted
Right to transfer of shares	Restricted by Articles of Association	Permitted
Acceptance of public deposits	Not permitted	Not permitted since Companies Act, 2013

Government Company

According to the CA 2013, Government company means any company in which not less than fifty-one per cent of the paid-up share capital is held by the Central Government, or by any State Government or Governments, or partly by the Central Government and partly by one or more State Governments, and includes a company which is a subsidiary company of such a Government company.

Though the number of Government companies is comparatively small when compared to the number of non-Government companies, they account for a large share of the paid-up capital of all the companies operating in India.

At the end of March 2013, there were 1,381 Government companies in India. 342 of them were private limited companies.

Holding and Subsidiary Companies

According to the Companies Act, "holding company", in relation to one or more other companies, means a company of which such companies are subsidiary companies.

In very simple terms, a company which has control (either managerial or ownership) over another is known as a holding company, and the company so controlled is regarded as a subsidiary company.

A company shall be deemed to be a holding company of another if, but only if, the other is its subsidiary.

A company shall be deemed to be a subsidiary company in any one or more of the following cases:

(*i*) Where one company controls the composition of the Board of Directors of another, the latter becomes a subsidiary of the former.

(*ii*) Where one company holds a majority of the shares in another company, the latter becomes a subsidiary of the former.

(*iii*) Where one company is a subsidiary of another, which is itself a subsidiary of some other company, the first-mentioned company shall also become the subsidiary of the last-mentioned company.

Foreign Company

According to the CA 2013, foreign company means any company or body corporate incorporated outside India which:

(*a*) has a place of business in India whether by itself or through an agent, physically or through electronic mode; and

(*b*) conducts any business activity in India in any other manner.

Chapter XXII of the CA 2013, applies to companies incorporated outside India. If not less than 50 per cent of the paid-up share capital, whether preference or equity, is in Indian hands (individuals or body corporates), the provisions of this Chapter and such other provisions of this Act as may be prescribed shall apply to these companies with regard to the business carried on by it in India as if it were a company incorporated in India.

As on 31-12-2014, there were 4,170 foreign companies in India.

One Person Company

One Person Company (OPC) means a company which has only one person as a member.

The memorandum of One Person Company shall indicate the name of the other person, who shall, in the event of the subscriber's death or his incapacity to contract become the member of the company. 2,238 OPCs were registered until March 2015.

For this, the written consent of this person shall also be filed with the Registrar at the time of incorporation of the One Person Company along with its memorandum and articles. However, this person can withdraw his consent, if he so desires, in such manner as prescribed in the Act. Similarly, member of One Person Company may at any time change the name of such other person by giving notice.

OPC is required to specifically mention the word "one person company" below the name wherever it is used.

The Companies Act provides certain flexibilities to OPC. Some of the relaxations provided to OPC are as under:

- OPC should have minimum one director.
- Where an OPC has only 1 director, the date on which the resolution is signed and dated by such director is considered as the date of the board meeting.
- Provisions of board meeting, quorum and interested director shall not apply to OPC.

- OPC need not hold an AGM.
- Provisions relating to notice, explanatory statement, EGM, quorum, voting, chairman, poll, proxies and postal ballot.
- National Company Law Tribunal's power of calling for EGM does not apply to OPC.
- Financial Statements can be signed by only one director.
- Financial Statements are to be filed with ROC within 180 days from the end of FY.
- OPC can contract with the sole member who is a director.

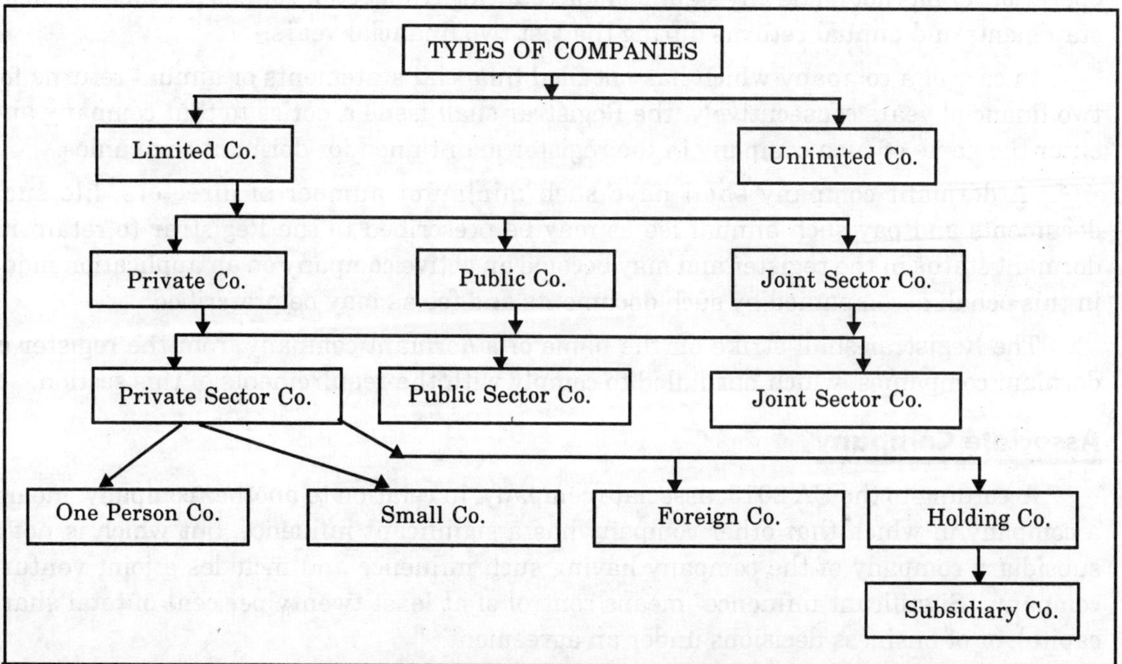

Fig. 14.1: Classification of Companies

Small Company

A small company means a company, other than a public company:

(*i*) paid-up share capital of which does not exceed fifty lakh rupees or such higher amount as may be prescribed which shall not be more than five crore rupees; or

(*ii*) turnover of which as per its last profit and loss account does not exceed two crore rupees or such higher amount as may be prescribed which shall not be more than twenty crore rupees.

Small Company cannot be a holding or a subsidiary company.

The Companies Act provides exemptions to Small Companies from certain requirements relating to board meeting, presentation of cash flow statement and certain merger process.

Dormant Company

> **One person company, small company and dormant company are new terms introduced by the Companies Act, 2013.**

According to the CA 2013, the following types of companies may make an application to the Registrar of Companies in prescribed manner for obtaining the status of a dormant company:

A company formed and registered for a future projector to hold an asset or intellectual property and has no significant accounting transaction.

An inactive company (*i.e.,* a company which has not been carrying on any business or operation, or has not made any significant accounting transaction, or has not filed financial statements and annual returns during the last two financial years.)

In case of a company which has not filed financial statements or annual returns for two financial years consecutively, the Registrar shall issue a notice to that company and enter the name of such company in the register maintained for dormant companies.

A dormant company shall have such minimum number of directors, file such documents and pay such annual fee as may be prescribed to the Registrar to retain its dormant status in the register and may become an active company on an application made in this behalf accompanied by such documents and fee as may be prescribed.

The Registrar shall strike off the name of a dormant company from the register of dormant companies, which has failed to comply with the requirements of this section.

Associate Company

According to the CA 2013, associate company, in relation to another company, means a company in which that other company has a significant influence, but which is not a subsidiary company of the company having such influence and includes a joint venture company. "Significant influence" means control of at least twenty per cent of total share capital, or of business decisions under an agreement.

INCORPORATION OF COMPANY

According to the Companies Act, 2013, a company may be formed for any lawful purpose by the number of persons specified below by subscribing their names/name to a memorandum and complying with the requirements of this Act in respect of registration:

(*a*) seven or more persons, where the company to be formed is to be a public company;

(*b*) two or more persons, where the company to be formed is to be a private company; or

(*c*) one person, where the company to be formed is to be One Person Company (that is to say, a private company),

For incorporation of a company, the promoters of the proposed company shall file with the Registrar of Companies certain specified documents containing the details sought to be provided in the documents. The two most important documents are the Memorandum of Association and the Articles of Association.

Memorandum of Association

The Memorandum of Association is regarded as the *fundamental* document of the company because it contains "the fundamental conditions upon which alone the company is allowed to be incorporated." It is the charter of the company, defining the object of its formation and its operations, and its purpose is to inform its stakeholders its permitted range of enterprise. It is *ultravires* for a company to act beyond the scope of its memorandum, and any departure is invalid and cannot be validated even if assented to by all the members of the company. This indicates that the memorandum should be drawn up with utmost seriousness and care.

The promoters of the company shall subscribe their names to the Memorandum. If a private company is to be formed, at least two persons (one person in respect of a One Person Company) shall, and if a public company is to be formed at least seven persons shall subscribe to the memorandum.

The memorandum of a company shall be in respective forms specified in the Companies Act, 2013. The important information that shall be incorporated in the memorandum includes the following:

(*a*) the name of the company with the last word "Limited" in the case of a public limited company, or the last words "Private Limited" in the case of a private limited company;

(*b*) the State in which the registered office of the company is to be situated;

(*c*) the objects for which the company is proposed to be incorporated and any matter considered necessary in furtherance thereof;

(*d*) the liability of members of the company, whether limited or unlimited.

In the case of a company having a share capital, the memorandum shall provide the following additional information:

(*i*) the amount of share capital with which the company is to be registered and the division thereof into shares of a fixed amount and the number of shares which the subscribers to the memorandum agree to subscribe which shall not be less than one share; and

(*ii*) the number of shares each subscriber to the memorandum intends to take, indicated opposite his name.

Memorandum of Association and the Articles of Association are very important documents to be produced for registration of a company.

The Memorandum of a company limited by guarantee shall state, the amount up to which each member undertakes to contribute to the assets of the company in the event of its being wound up and to the costs, charges and expenses of winding up etc.

The memorandum of One Person Company shall indicate the name of the other person, who shall, in the event of the subscriber's death or his incapacity to contract become the member of the company. (See the subsection *One Person Company* under *Types of Companies* given in an earlier part of this chapter for more information).

The two most important documents are the Memorandum of Association and the Articles of Association.

Conditions regarding the name of the company The name stated in the memorandum shall not be identical with or resemble too nearly to the name of an existing registered company. Further, the use of this name by the company shall not constitute an offence under any law for the time being in force or is undesirable in the opinion of the Central Government.

The Act also makes it clear that a company shall not be registered with a name which contains: (*a*) any word or expression which is likely to give the impression that the company is in any way connected with, or having the patronage of, the Central Government, any State Government, or any local authority, corporation or body constituted by the Central Government or any State Government under any law for the time being in force; or (*b*) such word or expression, as may be prescribed, unless the previous approval of the Central Government has been obtained for the use of any such word or expression.

Articles of Association

The Articles of Association are the rules, regulations and bye-laws for the *internal* management of the affairs of a company. They are framed with the object of carrying out the aims and objects as set out in the Memorandum of Association.

The Articles usually contain provisions relating to such matters as share capital; rights of shareholders and variation of these rights; lien on shares; calls on shares; transfer of shares; conversion of shares into stock; alteration of capital; general meetings and proceedings thereat; voting rights of members, voting and poll, proxies; directors, their appointments, remuneration, qualifications, powers and proceedings; Board of Directors; and so on.

The provisions of the Articles must be in conformity with the Memorandum and the provisions of the Companies Act. The Articles shall be in respective forms specified in the Companies Act, as may be applicable to such company. A company may adopt all or any of the regulations contained in the model articles applicable to such company. In case of any company, which is registered after the commencement of this Act, insofar as the registered articles of such company do not exclude or modify the regulations contained in the model articles applicable to such company, those regulations shall, so far as applicable, be the regulations of that company in the same manner and to the extent as if they were contained in the duly registered articles of the company.

The Articles of a company shall contain the regulations for management of the company. The articles shall also contain such matters, as may be prescribed by law/

regulation. However, a company is free to include such additional matters in its articles as may be considered necessary for its management.

The CA 2013 permits companies to incorporate in the articles provisions for entrenchment as specified in the Act. The articles may be altered only if conditions or procedures as that are more restrictive than those applicable in the case of a special resolution, are met or complied with.

Registration

For the incorporation of the company, there shall be filed with the Registrar within whose jurisdiction the registered office of a company is proposed to be situated, the memorandum and articles with other documents specified in the Act, and fulfilling all the requirement mentioned in the Act. The Registrar on the basis of the documents and information filed shall register all the documents and information and issue a certificate of incorporation in the prescribed form to the effect that the proposed company is incorporated under this Act.

On and from the date mentioned in the certificate of incorporation, the Registrar shall allot to the company a corporate identity number, which shall be a distinct identity for the company and which shall also be included in the certificate. The company shall maintain and preserve at its registered office copies of all documents and information as originally filed.

PROSPECTUS AND ALLOTMENT OF SECURITIES

Issue of Securities by Public Companies

A public company may issue securities, as per the provisions of the Companies Act 2013:

(*a*) to public through prospectus,

(*b*) through private placement, or

(*c*) through a rights issue or a bonus issue.

Only public companies can issue securities to the public. Both public and private companies can raise capital by rights or bonus issues and through private placement.

Issue of Securities by Private Companies

A private company may issue securities, as per the provisions of the Companies Act:

(*a*) by way of rights issue or bonus issue,

(*b*) through private placement.

Public offer includes initial public offer or further public offer of securities to the public by a company through issue of a prospectus, or an offer for sale of securities to the public by an existing shareholder, through issue of a prospectus.

Prospectus

According to the Companies Act, prospectus means any document described or issued as a prospectus and includes a red herring prospectus or shelf prospectus or any notice, circular, advertisement or other document inviting offers from the public for the subscription or purchase of any securities of a body corporate.

Red herring prospectus means a prospectus which does not include complete particulars of the quantum or price of the securities included therein. A company proposing to make an offer of securities may issue a red herring prospectus prior to the issue of a prospectus.

Shelf prospectus means a prospectus in respect of which the securities or class of securities included therein are issued for subscription in one or more issues over a certain period without the issue of a further prospectus.

Matters to be stated in prospectus Prospectus of a public company shall state the following information:

(*i*) details about the company (names and addresses of the registered office of the company, company secretary, Chief Financial Officer, auditors, legal advisers, bankers, trustees, if any, underwriters and such other persons as may be prescribed);

(*ii*) dates of the opening and closing of the issue, and declaration about the issue of allotment letters and refunds within the prescribed time;

(*iii*) a statement by the Board of Directors about the separate bank account where all monies received out of the issue are to be transferred and disclosure of details of all monies including utilised and unutilised monies out of the previous issue in the prescribed manner;

(*iv*) details about underwriting of the issue;

(*v*) consent of the directors, auditors, bankers to the issue, expert's opinion, if any, and of such other persons, as may be prescribed;

(*vi*) the authority for the issue and the details of the resolution passed therefor;

(*vii*) procedure and time schedule for allotment and issue of securities;

(*viii*) capital structure of the company in the prescribed manner;

(*ix*) main objects of public offer, terms of the present issue and such other particulars as may be prescribed;

(*x*) main objects and present business of the company and its location, schedule of implementation of the project;

(*xi*) particulars relating to management perception of risk factors specific to the project; gestation period of the project; extent of progress made in the project; deadlines for completion of the project; and any litigation or legal action pending or taken by a Government Department or a statutory body during the last five years immediately preceding the year of the issue of prospectus against the promoter of the company;

The Prospectus shall provide specified particulars about the company and public issue.

(*xii*) minimum subscription, amount payable by way of premium, issue of shares otherwise than on cash;

(*xiii*) details of directors including their appointments and remuneration, and such particulars of the nature and extent of their interests in the company as may be prescribed; and

(*xiv*) disclosures in such manner as may be prescribed about sources of promoter's contribution.

Reports to be pgrovided with prospectus The prospectus shall also set out the following reports for the purposes of the financial information:

(*i*) reports by the auditors of the company with respect to its profits and losses and assets and liabilities and such other matters as may be prescribed;

(*ii*) reports relating to profits and losses for each of the five financial years immediately preceding the financial year of the issue of prospectus including such reports of its subsidiaries and in such manner as may be prescribed;

(*iii*) reports made in the prescribed manner by the auditors upon the profits and losses of the business of the company for each of the five financial years immediately preceding issue and assets and liabilities of its business on the last date to which the accounts of the business were made up, being a date not more than one hundred and eighty days before the issue of the prospectus;

(*iv*) reports about the business or transaction to which the proceeds of the securities are to be applied directly or indirectly;

Public Offer of Securities to be in Dematerialised Form

According to the CA 2013, every company making public offer; and such other class or classes of public companies as may be prescribed, shall issue the securities only in dematerialised form. Any company, other than those mentioned above, may convert its securities into dematerialised form or issue its securities in physical form in accordance with the provisions of this Act or in dematerialised form.

Allotment of Securities

The Companies Act stipulate certain conditions regarding allotment of securities by companies:

(*a*) the amount stated in the prospectus as the minimum amount has been subscribed and the sums payable on application have been received by the company;

(*b*) the amount payable on application on every security shall not be less than five per cent of the nominal amount of the security or such other percentage or amount, as may be specified by the Securities and Exchange Board by making regulations in this behalf;

(*c*) if the stated minimum amount has not been subscribed and the sum payable on application is not received within a period of thirty days from the date of issue of the prospectus, or such other period as may be specified by the Securities and Exchange Board (SEBI), the amount received shall be returned within such time and manner as may be prescribed.

Listing of Securities in Stock Exchanges

Every company making public offer shall do the needful for the securities to be dealt with in one or more recognised stock exchanges.

The Companies Act lays down every company making public offer shall, before making such offer, make an application to one or more recognised stock exchange or exchanges and obtain permission for the securities to be dealt with in such stock exchange or exchanges. The prospectus shall also state the name or names of the stock exchange in which the securities shall be dealt with.

Further, whenever a company makes any allotment of securities, it shall file with the Registrar of Companies a return of allotment in such manner as may be prescribed.

Private Placement of Securities

Private placement means any offer of securities or invitation to subscribe securities to a select group of persons by a company (other than by way of public offer) through issue of a private placement offer letter.

The offer of securities or invitation to subscribe securities, shall be made to such number of persons not exceeding fifty or such higher number as may be prescribed, [excluding qualified institutional buyers and employees of the company] being offered securities under a scheme of employees stock option as per provisions of the Companies Act, in a financial year and on such conditions (including the form and manner of private placement) as may be prescribed.

SHARE CAPITAL AND DEBENTURES

Kinds of Share Capital

According to CA 2013, the share capital of a company limited by shares shall be of two kinds, namely:

(*a*) equity share capital:

(*i*) with voting rights; or

(*ii*) with differential rights as to dividend, voting or otherwise in accordance with such rules as may be prescribed;

(*b*) preference share capital.

Equity share capital means all share capital which is not preference share capital.

Preference share capital means that part of the issued share capital of the company which carries or would carry a preferential right with respect to:

(*a*) payment of dividend, either as a fixed amount or an amount calculated at a fixed rate; and

(*b*) repayment, in the case of a winding up or repayment of capital, of the amount of the share capital paid up or deemed to have been paid up.

A company may raise capital by issue of shares (equity or preference) and debentures.

The Companies Act prohibits issue of preference shares which are irredeemable. Preference shares are normally liable to be redeemed within a twenty years. However, a company may issue preference shares for more than twenty years for infrastructure projects subject to the provisions of the Companies Act.

Voting Rights

Every equity shareholder shall have a right to vote on every resolution placed before the company. The voting right shall be in proportion to his share in the paid-up equity share capital of the company.

A preference shareholder shall, have a right to vote only on resolutions placed before the company which directly affect the rights attached to his preference shares and, any resolution for the winding up of the company or for the repayment or reduction of its equity or preference share capital. The voting right shall be in proportion to the share in the paid-up preference share capital of the company.

However, if the dividend in respect of a class of preference shares has not been paid for a period of two years or more, such class of preference shareholders shall have a right to vote on all the resolutions placed before the company.

Issue of Sweat Equity Shares

The Companies Act permits the issue of sweat equity shares to directors or employees subject to the conditions specified in the Act. Sweat equity shares is an exception to the prohibition on issue of shares at discount.

Issue of Bonus Shares

A company may issue fully paid-up bonus shares to its members, subject to conditions laid down in the Companies Act, out of:

(*i*) its free reserves;

(*ii*) the securities premium account; or

(*iii*) the capital redemption reserve account:

No issue of bonus shares shall be made by capitalising reserves created by the revaluation of assets.

Alteration of Share Capital

A limited company having a share capital may, if so authorised by its articles, alter its memorandum in its general meeting to:

(*a*) increase its authorised share capital by such amount as it thinks expedient;

(*b*) consolidate and divide all or any of its share capital into shares of a larger amount than its existing shares:

(*c*) convert all or any of its fully paid-up shares into stock, and reconvert that stock into fully paid-up shares of any denomination;

(*d*) subdivide its shares, or any of them, into shares of smaller amount than is fixed by the memorandum, so, however, that in the subdivision the proportion between the amount paid and the amount, if any, unpaid on each reduced share shall be the same as it was in the case of the share from which the reduced share is derived;

(*e*) cancel shares which have not been taken or agreed to be taken by any person, and diminish the amount of its share capital by the amount of the shares so cancelled. Such cancellation of shares shall not be deemed to be a reduction of share capital.

Buyback of Shares

Subject to the provisions of the Companies Act, a company may purchase its own shares or other specified securities out of:

(*a*) its free reserves;

(*b*) the securities premium account; or

(*c*) the proceeds of the issue of any shares or other specified securities.

No buyback shall be made out of the proceeds of an earlier issue of the same kind of shares or same kind of other specified securities.

Issue of Debentures

Debenture is debt instrument issued by companies to raise capital. Following are some of the important provisions of the Companies Act pertaining to issue of debentures.

1. A company may issue debentures with an option to convert such debentures into shares, either wholly or partly at the time of redemption.
2. Companies are prohibited to issue any debentures carrying any voting rights.
3. Secured debentures may be issued by a company subject to such terms and conditions as may be prescribed.
4. A company issuing debentures shall create a debenture redemption reserve account out of the profits of the company available for payment of dividend and the amount credited to such account shall not be utilised by the company except for the redemption of debentures.

MANAGEMENT AND ADMINISTRATION

Some of the important provisions of the Companies Act, regarding Management and Administration of companies are given below.

Register of Members

Every company shall keep and maintain the following registers as specified in the ACT:

> **The Companies Act specifies the records to be maintained by companies, particulars to be provided in annual returns and norms for holding general meetings.**

(*a*) Separate registers of members holding each class of equity and preference shares.

(*b*) register of debenture-holders; and

(*c*) register of any other security holders.

Annual Returns

Every company shall prepare an annual return in the prescribed form containing the particulars as on the close of the financial year. The particulars to be furnished are:

(*a*) its registered office, principal business activities, particulars of its holding, subsidiary and associate companies;

(*b*) its shares, debentures and other securities and shareholding pattern;

(*c*) its indebtedness;

(*d*) its members and debenture-holders along with changes therein since the close of the previous financial year;

(*e*) its promoters, directors, key managerial personnel along with changes therein since the close of the previous financial year;

(*f*) meetings of members or a class thereof, Board and its various committees along with attendance details;

(*g*) remuneration of directors and key managerial personnel;

(*h*) penalty or punishment imposed on the company, its directors or officers and details of compounding of offences and appeals made against such penalty or punishment;

(*i*) matters relating to certification of compliances, disclosures as may be prescribed;

(*j*) details, as may be prescribed, in respect of shares held by or on behalf of the Foreign Institutional Investors indicating their names, addresses, countries of incorporation, registration and percentage of shareholding held by them; and

(*k*) such other matters as may be prescribed.

It is also required that every listed company shall file a return in the prescribed form with the Registrar of Companies with respect to change in the number of shares held by promoters and top ten shareholders of such company, within fifteen days of such change.

Annual General Meeting

Every company, other than a One Person Company, shall hold its annual general meeting every year. Not more than fifteen months shall elapse between the date of one annual general meeting and that of the next. In case of the first annual general meeting, it shall be held within a period of nine months from the date of closing of the first financial year of the company and in other cases, within a period of six months from the date of closing of the financial year.

For a company which has held its first annual general meeting as aforesaid, it is not necessary to hold any annual general meeting in the year of its incorporation.

The annual general meeting shall be called during business hours (between 9 a.m. and 6 p.m.) on any day that is not a National Holiday and shall be held either at the registered office of the company or at some other place within the city, town or village in which the registered office of the company is situated.

If any default is made in holding the annual general meeting of a company, as specified in the Companies Act, the Tribunal is empowered by the Act to call, or direct the calling of, an annual general meeting of the company.

Extraordinary General Meeting

The Board may, whenever it deems fit, call an extraordinary general meeting of the company.

The Companies Act also lays down that the Board shall call an extraordinary general meeting at the requisition made by certain minimum specified members of the company subject to the conditions laid down in the Act. The important conditions are that: In the case of a company having a share capital, the requisition is made by not less than one-tenth of such of the paid-up share capital of the company. In the case of a company not having a share capital, the requisition is made by such number of members who have not less than one-tenth of the total voting power of all the members.

The requisition shall set out the matters for the consideration of which the meeting is to be called and shall be signed by the requisitionists and sent to the registered office of the company.

If the Board does not take adequate measures to hold the meeting so requisitioned within forty-five days from the date of receipt of such requisition, the meeting may be called and held by the requisitionists themselves within a period of three months from the date of the requisition, subject to the provisions of the Act.

The Act specifies how the notice of the general meeting shall be given and the items of information to be annexed to the notice.

Quorum for General Meetings

A shareholder may vote in person attending the annual general meeting, by proxy, postal ballot or by electronic means.

The Companies Act lays down that the quorum for a general meeting, shall be as follows (unless the articles of the company provide for a larger number):

(*a*) in case of a public company: (*i*) five members personally present if the number of members of the company as on the date of meeting is not more than one thousand; (*ii*) fifteen members personally present if the number of members as on the date of meeting is more than one thousand but up to five thousand; (*iii*) thirty members personally present if the number of members as on the date of the meeting exceeds five thousand;

(*b*) in the case of a private company, two members personally present shall be the quorum for a meeting of the company.

If the quorum is not present within half-an-hour from the time appointed for holding a meeting of the company:

(*a*) the meeting shall stand adjourned to the same day in the next week at the same time and place, or to such other date and such other time and place as the Board may determine. If at the adjourned meeting also, a quorum is not present within half-an-hour from the time appointed for holding meeting, the members present shall be the quorum.

In the case of the meeting called by requisitionists, it shall stand cancelled if there is no quorum.

Proxy

Any member of a company entitled to attend and vote at a meeting of the company shall be entitled to appoint another person as a proxy to attend and vote at the meeting on his behalf. However, the proxy shall not have the right to speak at such meeting and shall not be entitled to vote except on a poll, subject to the conditions prescribed by the Central Government.

Vote by Electronic Means

The Central Government may prescribe the class or classes of companies and manner in which a member may exercise his right to vote by the electronic means.

Postal Ballot

The Act also lays down the norms regarding postal ballot.

Report on AGM

Every listed public company shall prepare in the prescribed manner a report on each annual general meeting including the confirmation to the effect that the meeting was convened, held and conducted as per the provisions of this Act and the rules made thereunder.

The company shall file with the Registrar of Companies a copy of this report within thirty days of the conclusion of the annual general meeting as prescribed in the Act.

DECLARATION AND PAYMENT OF DIVIDEND

According to the CA 2013, a company shall declare dividends only out of:

> **A company may declare and pay dividends out of its profits for the year, previous years or free reserves.**

(*a*) (1) the profits of the company for that year after providing for depreciation as specified in the Act, (2) or out of the profits of the company for any previous financial year or years after providing for depreciation.

(*b*) the money provided by the Central Government or a State Government for the payment of dividend by the company in pursuance of a guarantee given by that Government.

(*c*) free reserves, when profits are inadequacy or in any financial year for payment of dividends.

A company may, before the declaration of any dividend in any financial year, transfer such percentage of its profits for that financial year as it may consider appropriate to the reserves of the company.

The Board of Directors of a company may declare interim dividend during any financial year out of the surplus in the profit and loss account and out of profits of the financial year, subject to certain conditions.

The amount of the dividend, including interim dividend, shall be deposited in a scheduled bank in a separate account within five days from the date of declaration of such dividend.

The Companies Act permits the capitalisation of profits or reserves of a company for the purpose of issuing fully paid-up bonus shares or paying up any amount for the time being unpaid on any shares held by the members of the company.

The dividend declared shall be paid or the warrant in respect thereof shall be posted within thirty days from the date of declaration to all shareholders entitled to the payment of the dividend.

According to Companies (Amendment) Act 2015, no company shall declare dividend unless carried over past losses and depreciation in previous year or years are set off against profit for the current year.

Failure to comply with the provisions of the Act pertaining to payment of dividend is punishable.

BOARD OF DIRECTORS

A company being an artificial person, its activities have to be carried out by persons authorised for that purpose. It may be said that the ultimate power rests with the shareholders. However, the responsibility for formulation of strategies for the development of the company and their implementation primarily rests with the Board of Directors, most the Directors being normally elected by the shareholder. The executive authority is usually exercised by the Board of Directors through the various levels of executives appointed by the Board.

Every company, including one person company, shall have a Board of Directors. At least one-third of the Directors of a listed public company shall be Independent Directors and specified class of companies shall have at least one Woman Director.

According to the Companies Act, every company shall have a Board of Directors consisting of individuals as directors. Some important provisions of the Act related to the Board are as follows.

Number of Directors

The number of directors of different categories of companies according to the Companies Act 2013 are as follows:

One Person Company: Minimum one director.

Private Company: A minimum of two and a maximum of fifteen directors.

Public company: A minimum of three and a maximum of fifteen directors.

A private/public company may appoint more than fifteen directors after passing a special resolution.

Woman Director

The CA 2013, for the first time, made it mandatory that certain specified class or classes of companies shall have at least one woman director. Accordingly, every Listed Company/Public Company with paid-up capital of ₹ 100 crore or more/Public Company with turnover of ₹ 300 crore or more shall have at least one Woman Director.

Independent Directors

According to the CA 2013, at least one-third of the total number of directors of a listed public company shall be independent directors (ID) and the Central Government may prescribe the minimum number of independent directors in case of any class or classes of public companies.

An independent director means a director other than a managing director or a whole-time director or a nominee director. Some of the important qualification pertaining to the independent Director are the following: An ID shall be a person: (1) of integrity, possessing relevant expertise and experience; (2) who has not ever been associated with the company or its holding, subsidiary or associate company as a promoter; (3) who is not related to promoters or directors in the company, its holding, subsidiary or associate company; (4) who had or has no pecuniary relationship with the company, its holding, subsidiary or associate company, or their promoters, or directors, during the two immediately preceding financial years or during the current financial year.

Resident Director

The Companies Act 2013 lays down that every company shall have at least one director who has stayed in India for a total period of not less than one hundred and eighty-two days in the previous calendar year.

Director Elected by Small Shareholders

A listed company may have one director elected by small shareholders in such manner and with such terms and conditions as prescribed. In this context, "small shareholder" means a shareholder holding shares of nominal value of not more than twenty thousand rupees or such other sum as may be prescribed.

Additional, Alternate and Nominee Directors

The articles of a company may confer on its Board of Directors the power to appoint any person, other than a person who fails to get appointed as a director in a general meeting, as an additional director at any time who shall hold office up to the date of the next annual general meeting or the last date on which the annual general meeting should have been held, whichever is earlier.

Meetings of Board

The Board of a company shall meet at least four times a year and the interval between two meetings shall not be more than four months.

Number of meetings A new company shall hold the first meeting of the Board of Directors within thirty days of the date of its incorporation.

A company is required to hold a minimum of four meetings of its Board of Directors every year. Not more than one hundred and twenty days shall intervene between two consecutive meetings of the Board.

There is relaxation in the number of meetings in respect of One Person Company, Small Company and Dormant Company. The stipulation in their case is that at least one meeting of the Board of Directors is held in each half of a calendar year and the gap between the two meetings is not less than ninety days.

The conditions regarding the Board meetings is not applicable to One Person Company in which there is only one director on its Board.

Participation of directors in meetings: The participation of directors in a meeting of the Board may be either in person or through video conferencing or other audio-visual means, as may be prescribed, which are capable of recording and recognising the participation of the directors and of recording and storing the proceedings of such meetings along with date and time. However, the Central Government may, by notification, specify such matters which shall not be dealt with in a meeting through video conferencing or other audio-visual means.

Notice of meeting: A meeting of the Board shall be called by giving not less than seven days' notice in writing to every director at his address registered with the company and such notice shall be sent by hand delivery or by post or by electronic means. However, a meeting of the Board may be called at shorter notice to transact urgent business subject to the condition that at least one independent director, if any, shall be present at the meeting. In case of absence of independent directors from such a meeting of the Board, decisions taken at such a meeting shall be circulated to all the directors and shall be final only on ratification thereof by at least one independent director, if any.

Quorum for meeting: The quorum for a meeting of the Board of Directors of a company shall be one-third of its total strength or two directors, whichever is higher. The participation of the directors by video conferencing or by other audio-visual means shall also be counted for the purposes of quorum.

Where a meeting of the Board could not be held for want of quorum, then, unless the articles of the company otherwise provide, the meeting shall automatically stand adjourned to the same day at the same time and place in the next week or if that day is a national holiday, till the next succeeding day, which is not a national holiday, at the same time and place.

Number of Directorship

According to the Companies Act 2013, the maximum number of companies a person can hold office as a director, including any alternate directorship, at the same time is twenty. It is also laid down that the maximum number of public companies in which a person can be appointed as a director shall not exceed ten. For reckoning the limit of public companies in which a person can be appointed as director, directorship in private companies that are either holding or subsidiary company of a public company shall be included.

However, the members of a company may, by special resolution, specify any lesser number of companies in which a director of the company may act as directors.

Powers of Board

The powers of the Board of Directors of a company are derived from the relevant provisions of the Companies Act, the Memorandum or Articles of Association of the company or any valid regulations, including regulations made by the company in general meeting.

> **The Board can exercise all powers and do all acts and things as the company is authorised to do except those powers which can be exercised by the company only in general meeting.**

Powers to be exercised in general meeting Powers which are specified to be exercised or done by the company in general meeting shall be exercised only so. However, no regulation made by the company in general meeting shall invalidate any prior act of the Board which would have been valid if that regulation had not been made.

Powers to be exercised by resolutions passed at meetings of the Board The Board of Directors of a company shall exercise the following powers by means of resolutions passed at meetings of the Board, namely:

(*a*) to make calls on shareholders in respect of money unpaid on their shares;

(*b*) to authorise buyback of securities under section 68;

(*c*) to issue securities, including debentures, whether in or outside India;

(*d*) to borrow monies;

(*e*) to invest the funds of the company;

(*f*) to grant loans or give guarantee or provide security in respect of loans;

(*g*) to approve financial statement and the Board's report;

(*h*) to diversify the business of the company;

(*i*) to approve amalgamation, merger or reconstruction;

(*j*) to take over a company or acquire a controlling or substantial stake in another company;

(*k*) any other matter which may be prescribed.

The Board may delegate any of the powers mentioned above to any committee of directors, the managing director, the manager or any other principal officer of the company or the principal officer of the branch office.

Duties of Directors

1. Subject to the provisions of the CA 2013, a director of a company shall act in accordance with the articles of the company.
2. A director of a company shall act in good faith in order to promote the objects of the company for the benefit of its members as a whole, and in the best interests of the company, its employees, the shareholders, the community and for the protection of environment.
3. A director of a company shall exercise his duties with due and reasonable care, skill and diligence and shall exercise independent judgement.
4. A director of a company shall not involve in a situation in which he may have a direct or indirect interest that conflicts, or possibly may conflict, with the interest of the company.
5. A director of a company shall not achieve or attempt to achieve any undue gain or advantage either to himself or to his relatives, partners, or associates and if such director is found guilty of making any undue gain, he shall be liable to pay an amount equal to that gain to the company.
6. A director of a company shall not assign his office and any assignment so made shall be void.

If a director of the company contravenes the provisions of the Act pertaining to the duties of directors, such director shall be punishable with fine which shall not be less than one lakh rupees but which may extend to five lakh rupees.

Vacation of Office of Director

The office of a director shall become vacant in case:

(a) he incurs any of the disqualifications specified in the Act;

(b) he absents himself from all the meetings of the Board of Directors held during a period of twelve months with or without seeking leave of absence of the Board;

(c) he acts in contravention of the provisions of the Act relating to entering into contracts or arrangements in which he is directly or indirectly interested;

(d) he fails to disclose his interest in any contract or arrangement in which he is directly or indirectly interested, in contravention of the provisions of the Act;

(e) he becomes disqualified by an order of a court or the Tribunal;

(f) he is convicted by a court of any offence, whether involving moral turpitude or otherwise and sentenced in respect thereof to imprisonme t for not less than six months:

(g) he is removed in pursuance of the provisions of this Act;

(h) he, having been appointed a director by virtue of his holding any office or other employment in the holding, subsidiary or associate company, ceases to hold such office or other employment in that company.

If a person, functions as a director even when he knows that the office of director held by him has become vacant on account of any of the disqualifications mentioned above, he shall be punishable with imprisonment for a term which may extend to one year or with fine which shall not be less than one lakh rupees but which may extend to five lakh rupees, or with both.

Where all the directors of a company vacate their offices under any of the disqualifications specified above, the promoter or, in his absence, the Central Government shall appoint the required number of directors who shall hold office till the directors are appointed by the company in the general meeting.

According to the Companies Act, a private company may, by its articles, provide any other ground for the vacation of the office of a director in addition to those specified in the Act.

Vacation of office of a director may also occur due to resignation.

DISQUALIFICATIONS FOR APPOINTMENT OF DIRECTOR

A person shall not be capable of being appointed director of a company, if:

(a) he has been found to be of unsound mind by a court of competent jurisdiction and the finding is in force.

(b) he is an undischarged insolvent.

(c) he has applied to be adjudicated as an insolvent and his application is pending.

(*d*) he has been convicted by a court of any offence involving moral turpitude and sentenced in respect thereof to imprisonment for not less than six months, and a period of five years has not elapsed from the date of expiry of the sentence.

(*e*) he has not paid any call in respect of the company shares held by him, whether alone or jointly with others, and six months have elapsed from the last day fixed for the payment of the call.

(*f*) an order disqualifying him for appointment as director has been passed by a court in pursuance of the provisions of the Act and is in force, unless the leave of the court has been obtained for his appointment in pursuance of that section.

(*g*) he is already a director of a public company which has not filed the annual accounts and annual returns for continuous three financial years or has failed to repay its deposit or interest thereon on due date or pay dividend and such failure continues for one year or more.

A private company, which is not a subsidiary of a public company, may, by its articles, provide that a person shall be disqualified for appointment as a director on any grounds in addition to those specified above.

Board Committees

The Companies Act provides for the constitution of four committees by the Board: Audit Committee, Nomination and Remuneration Committee, Corporate Social Responsibility Committee and Stakeholder Relationship Committee.

The Audit Committee monitors the appointment and performance of the auditors, evaluates reports of auditors, oversees financial transactions of the company and evaluates internal financial controls and risk management system.

Audit Committee

The Companies Amendment Act, 2000, has incorporated the mandatory recommendation of the Birla Committee on Corporate Governance for an Audit Committee for company to act as a catalyst for effective financial reporting, with powers to investigate any activity within its terms of reference and to seek information from any employee. According to this, the major role of the Audit Committee appointed by the Board of Directors is the oversight of the company's financial reporting process and the disclosure of its financial information to ensure that the financial statement is correct, sufficient and credible.

According to the Companies Act, 2013, the Board of Directors of every listed company or any other as may be prescribed, shall constitute an Audit Committee. Important provisions of the Act related to the Audit Committee are the following.

- The Audit Committee shall consist of a minimum of three directors with independent directors forming a majority.
- Majority of members of Audit Committee including its Chairperson shall be persons with ability to read and understand, the financial statement.

Every Audit Committee shall act in accordance with the terms of reference specified by the Board which shall, *inter alia,* include:

(*i*) the recommendation for appointment, remuneration and terms of appointment of auditors of the company;

(*ii*) review and monitor the auditor's independence and performance, and effectiveness of audit process;

(*iii*) examination of the financial statement and the auditors' report thereon;

(*iv*) approval or any subsequent modification of transactions of the company with related parties;

(*v*) scrutiny of inter-corporate loans and investments;

(*vi*) valuation of undertakings or assets of the company, wherever it is necessary;

(*vii*) evaluation of internal financial controls and risk management systems;

(*viii*) monitoring the end use of funds raised through public offers and related matters.

The Audit Committee may call for the comments of the auditors about internal control systems, the scope of audit, including the observations of the auditors and review of financial statement before their submission to the Board and may also discuss any related issues with the internal and statutory auditors and the management of the company.

The Audit Committee shall have authority to investigate into any matter in relation to the items specified in the Act or referred to it by the Board and for this purpose shall have power to obtain professional advice from external sources and have full access to information contained in the records of the company.

Nomination and Remuneration Committee

The Board of Directors of every listed company and such other class or classes of companies, as may be prescribed, shall constitute the Nomination and Remuneration Committee (NRC) consisting of three or more non-executive directors out of which not less than one-half shall be independent directors. The Chairperson of the company (whether executive or non-executive) may be appointed as a member of this Committee but shall not chair the Committee.

Role of NRC

The NRC shall: (*a*) identify persons who are qualified to become directors and who may be appointed in senior management and recommend to the Board their appointment and removal and shall carry out evaluation of every director's performance; and (*b*) formulate the criteria for determining qualifications, positive attributes and independence of a director and recommend to the Board a policy relating to the remuneration for the directors, key managerial personnel and other employees.

(Key managerial personnel means, (*i*) the Chief Executive Officer or the managing director or the manager; (*ii*) the company secretary; (*iii*) the whole-time director; (*iv*) the Chief Financial Officer; and (*v*) such other officer as may be prescribed.)

Prescribed classes of companies shall have a Nomination and Remuneration Committee to identify qualified persons for key managerial positions and recommend policy relating to their remuneration and Stakeholders Relationship Committee to deal with the grievances of security holders of the company.

While formulating the remuneration policy, the Committee shall ensure that: (*a*) the level and composition of remuneration is reasonable and sufficient to attract, retain and motivate directors of the quality required to run the company successfully; (*b*) relationship of remuneration to performance is clear and meets appropriate performance benchmarks; and (*c*) remuneration to directors, key managerial personnel and senior management involves a balance between fixed and incentive pay reflecting short- and long-term performance objectives appropriate to the working of the company and its goals.

Stakeholders Relationship Committee

The Board of Directors of a company which consists of more than one thousand shareholders, debenture-holders, deposit-holders and any other security holders shall constitute a Stakeholders Relationship Committee consisting of a chairperson who shall be a non-executive director and such other members as may be decided by the Board.

The purpose of this Committee is to consider and resolve the grievances of security holders of the company.

(*Corporate Social Responsibility Committee* is described in Chapter 9.)

Prohibition of Insider Trading

The Companies Act prohibits insider trading.

Insider trading means: (*i*) an act of subscribing, buying, selling, or dealing in any security or agreeing to do any of these by any director or key managerial personnel or any other officer of the company either as principal or agent if such a person is reasonably expected to have access to any non-public price-sensitive information in respect of securities of the company.

Communicating any non-public price-sensitive information to any person or counselling about dealing in securities based on such information too is regarded as insider trading.

Price-sensitive information means any information which relates, directly or indirectly, to a company and which if published is likely to materially affect the price of securities of the company.

If any person contravenes the provisions of this section, he shall be punishable with imprisonment for a term which may extend to five years or with fine which shall not be less than five lakh rupees but which may extend to twenty-five crore rupees or three times the amount of profits made out of insider trading, whichever is higher, or with both.

INSPECTION, INQUIRY AND INVESTIGATION

The Companies Act specifies many do's and don'ts for the companies to serve the purpose of the Act for ensuring proper management of companies and healthy development of the corporate sector. It is, therefore, natural that the Companies Act has provisions for the required scrutiny of the affairs of the companies.

Under the Companies Act, the Registrar of Companies is given the power to seek any relevant information or explanation from a company to ascertain facts. He can ask the company to produce any relevant document for his examination and scrutiny. If the registrar is not satisfied with the information or explanation so received, or on a scrutiny of the documents furnished, he is of the opinion that an unsatisfactory state of affairs exists in the company he may call on the company to produce for his inspection such further books of account, books, papers and explanations.

If the Registrar or Inspector appointed to conduct an inquiry feels that any relevant documents are likely to be destroyed, mutilated, altered, falsified or secreted, he may, after obtaining an order from the Special Court for the seizure of such books and papers, enter, with such assistance as may be required, and search, the place or places where such books or papers are kept; and conduct of inspection and inquiry. The provisions of the Code of Criminal Procedure, 1973 relating to searches or seizures shall apply, *mutatis mutandis,* to every search and seizure so made.

The Registrar or inspector shall, after the inspection of the records books of account or an inquiry, submit a report to the Central Government and such report may, if necessary, include a recommendation that further investigation into the affairs of the company is necessary giving his reasons in support.

> **The Registrar can seek any relevant information or explanation from a company to ascertain facts and the Central Government may order an investigation into the affairs of a company if it is felt that an unsatisfactory state of affairs exists in the company which needs to be probed.**

Central Government may order an investigation into the affairs of a company if it is of the opinion that such an investigation is necessary:

(*a*) on the receipt of a report of the Registrar or inspector;

(*b*) on intimation of a special resolution passed by a company that the affairs of the company ought to be investigated; or

(*c*) in public interest,

If an order is passed by a court or the Tribunal in any proceedings before it that the affairs of a company ought to be investigated, the Central Government shall order an investigation into the affairs of that company. For the purposes of an investigation in respect of the references made above, the Central Government may appoint one or more persons as inspectors to investigate into the affairs of the company and to report thereon in such manner as the Central Government may direct.

Serious Fraud Investigation Office

According to the Companies Act 2013, the Central Government shall, by notification, establish an office to be called the Serious Fraud Investigation Office to investigate frauds relating to a company.

Investigation into affairs of Company by Serious Fraud Investigation Office may be initiated (*a*) on receipt of a report of the Registrar or inspector as specified in the Companies Act, (*b*) on intimation of a special resolution passed by a company that its affairs are required to be investigated; (*c*) in the public interest; or (*d*) on request from any Department of the Central Government or a State Government.

REVIVAL AND REHABILITATION OF SICK COMPANIES

Under the Sick Industrial Companies Act (SICA), 1985, an industrial company was regarded as sick if its net worth was completely eroded. This definition of industrial sickness was generally followed until the coming into effect of the Companies Act 2013.

The Companies Act 2013 takes a different view of sickness. Accordingly, a sick company is one which fails to pay the debt. Further, while the Sick Industrial Companies Act dealt with only industrial companies, the current Companies Act is applicable to all types of companies.

Initiation of Reporting of and Determination of Sickness

The authority which deals with sick companies under the Companies Act 2013 is the National Company Law Tribunal.

The tribunal initiates measures for determination whether a company is a sick company on a reference to made by it by any of the following parties who has sufficient reasons to believe that any company has become a sick company:

(*a*) secured creditors of the company representing fifty per cent or more of its outstanding amount of debt;

(*b*) the company itself;

(*c*) the Central Government

(*d*) the Reserve Bank of India;

(*e*) the Government of a State in which all or any of the undertakings belonging to such company are situated;

(*f*) a public financial institution or a State level institution or a scheduled bank which has a financial exposure in the company.

It is laid down in the Act that where a reference of sickness has been made to the Tribunal, (1) the company shall not dispose of or otherwise enter into any obligation with regard to its properties or assets except as required in the normal course of business and (2) the Board of Directors shall not take any steps likely to prejudice the interests of the creditors.

The Tribunal shall determine whether the company is a sick company or not, within a period of sixty days of the receipt of an application regarding sickness.

Revival and Rehabilitation

The authority to deal with sick companies is the NCLT. Sickness may be referred to the Tribunal by secured creditors, Central or relevant State governments, RBI or financiers of the company.

If the Tribunal is satisfied that a company has become a sick company, the Tribunal shall decide, as soon as may be, whether it is practicable for the company to make the repayment of its debts within a reasonable time.

If the Tribunal deems fit that it is practicable for a sick company to pay the debts within a reasonable time, the Tribunal shall, subject to such restrictions or conditions as may be specified, give such time to the company as it may deem fit to make repayment of the debt.

On the determination of a company as a sick company by the Tribunal, any secured creditor of that company or the company may make an application to the Tribunal for the determination of the measures that may be adopted with respect to the revival and rehabilitation of such company.

On the receipt of such an application, the Tribunal shall appoint an interim administrator to convene a meeting of creditors of the company in accordance with the relevant provisions of the Act to consider whether it is possible to revive and rehabilitate the sick company and such other matters, which the interim administrator may consider necessary.

The interim administrator shall appoint a committee of creditors with such number of members as he may determine, but not exceeding seven, and as far as possible a representative each of every class of creditors should be represented in that committee. The interim administrator may direct any promoter, director or any key managerial personnel to attend any meeting of the committee of creditors and to furnish such information as may be considered necessary by the interim administrator.

On consideration of the report of the interim administrator, if the Tribunal is satisfied that the creditors representing three-fourths in value of the amount outstanding against the sick company present and voting have resolved that it is not possible to revive and rehabilitate such company, the Tribunal shall take any one of the following courses of action:

1. Order that the proceedings for the winding up of the company be initiated, or
2. Appoint a company administrator for the company and cause such administrator to prepare a scheme of revival and rehabilitation of the sick company if the Tribunal is of the opinion that by adopting certain measures the sick company may be revived and rehabilitated. (The Tribunal may, if it thinks fit, appoint an interim administrator as the company administrator.)

The scheme prepared by the company administrator shall be placed before the meeting of the creditors of the sick company for their approval. If the scheme is approved by the unsecured creditors representing one-fourth in value of the amount owed by the company to such creditors and the secured creditors, representing three-fourths in value of the amount outstanding against financial assistance disbursed by such creditors to the sick company, the company administrator shall submit the scheme before the Tribunal for sanctioning the scheme:

Where the scheme relates to amalgamation of the sick company with any other company, such scheme shall, in addition to the approval of the creditors of the sick company under this sub-section, be laid before the general meeting of both the companies for approval by their respective shareholders and no such scheme shall be proceeded with unless it has been approved, with or without modification, by a special resolution passed by the shareholders of that company.

The scheme prepared by the company administrator shall be examined by the Tribunal and a copy of the scheme with modification, if any, made by the Tribunal shall be sent, in draft, to the sick company and the company administrator and in the case of amalgamation, also to any other company concerned, and the Tribunal may publish or cause to be published the draft scheme in brief in such daily newspapers as the Tribunal may consider necessary, for suggestions and objections, if any, within such period as the Tribunal may specify.

The Tribunal may make such modifications, if any, in the draft scheme as it may consider necessary in the light of the suggestions and objections received from the sick company and the company administrator and also from the transferee company and any other company concerned in the amalgamation and from any shareholder or any creditors or employees of such companies. The Tribunal shall within sixty days therefrom, after satisfying that the scheme had been validly approved in accordance with this section, pass an order sanctioning such scheme.

WINDING UP OF COMPANIES

Exit of Companies

A company registered under the Companies Act can cease to exist by any one of the following legal methods:

- If a company transfers its undertaking(s) to another company under a scheme of reconstruction or amalgamation, it may be dissolved without winding up, if the court so directs.
- The name of a defunct company may be removed from the Register of Companies by the Registrar.
- A company may be wound up as per the provisions of the Companies Act, 2013.

The Registrar may initiate measures to remove the name of a company from the Register if has reasonable cause to believe that:

(*a*) the company has failed to commence its business within one year of its incorporation;

(*b*) the subscribers to the memorandum have not paid the subscription which they had undertaken to pay and a declaration to this effect has not been filed within the specified period (one hundred and eighty days from the date of incorporation of a company)

(*c*) the company is not carrying on any business or operation for a period of two immediately preceding financial years and has not made any application within such period for obtaining the status of a dormant company under the Companies Act 2013.

Meaning of Winding Up Pennington defines winding up as a process by which the management of a company's affairs is taken out of its directors' hands, its assets are realised by a liquidator, and its debts are paid out of the proceeds of realisation, and any balance remaining returned to its members. At the end of the winding up, the company will have no assets or liabilities. It will, therefore, be only a formal step to have it dissolved, and bring to an end its legal personality as a corporation.

Modes of Winding Up

According to the Companies Act 2013, there are two modes of winding up, *viz.*,

- Winding up by the National Company Law Tribunal
- Voluntary winding up

Winding up by the Tribunal

Circumstances in which a company may be wound up by the Tribunal on petition received under the Companies Act are the following:

(*a*) the company is unable to pay its debts;

(*b*) the company has, by special resolution, resolved that the company be wound up by the Tribunal;

(*c*) the company has acted against the interests of the sovereignty and integrity of India, the security of the State, friendly relations with foreign States, public order, decency or morality;

(*d*) the Tribunal has ordered the winding up of a sick company;

(*e*) fraudulence, misfeasance or misconduct;

(*f*) the company has made a default in filing with the Registrar its financial statements or annual returns for immediately preceding five consecutive financial years; or

(*g*) the Tribunal is of the opinion that it is just and equitable that the company should be wound up.

A petition to the Tribunal for the winding up of a company may be presented by: (*a*) the company; (*b*) any creditor or creditors; (*c*) any contributory or contributories; (*d*) all or any of the persons specified above together; (*e*) the Registrar; (*f*) any person authorised by the Central Government in that behalf; or (*g*) the Central Government or a State Government in specified cases.

Voluntary Winding Up

A company may be wound up by the Tribunal on grounds such as inability to pay debts, sickness, anti-national activities, illegitimate and unfair conduct and mismanagement, special resolution to wind up the company etc.

The circumstances in which a company may be wound up voluntarily are the following:

(*a*) the company in general meeting passes a resolution requiring the company to be wound up;

(*b*) the company passes a special resolution that the company be wound up voluntarily.

The company in general meeting may pass a resolution requiring the company to be wound up voluntarily as a result of the expiry of the period for its duration, if any, fixed by its articles or on the occurrence of any event in respect of which the articles provide that the company should be dissolved.

NATIONAL COMPANY LAW TRIBUNAL AND APPELLATE TRIBUNAL

The Companies Act 2013 has required the Central Government to constitute a tribunal known as National Company Law Tribunal (NCLT) and an Appellate Tribunal known as the National Company Law Appellate Tribunal for hearing appeals against the orders of the Tribunal. The National Company Law Tribunal is often referred to as the Tribunal and the National Company Law Appellate Tribunal is often referred to as the Appellate Tribunal.

With the establishment of these two authorities, the Company Law Board and Board for Industrial and Financial Reconstruction (BIFR) ceased to exist. They would relieve the Courts of their burden while simultaneously providing specialised justice.

Cases under the Companies Act are dealt with by the Tribunal and appeals against orders of the Tribunal can be made to the Appellate Tribunal. Appeals against orders of Appellate Tribunal may be filed to Supreme Court.

The National Company Law Tribunal shall have a President, who shall be a person who is or has been a Judge of a High Court for five years, and the Appellate Tribunal shall have a Chairperson who shall be a person who is or has been a Judge of the Supreme Court or the Chief Justice of a High Court. Both these authorities shall consist of Judicial Members of prescribed qualifications and Technical Members who shall be persons of proven ability, integrity and standing having special knowledge and experience in law, industrial finance, industrial management or administration, industrial reconstruction, investment, accountancy, labour matters, or such other disciplines related to management, conduct of affairs, revival, rehabilitation and winding up of companies.

According to the Act, there shall be constituted such number of Benches of the Tribunal, as may be specified by the Central Government. The Principal Bench of the Tribunal shall be at New Delhi which shall be presided over by the President of the Tribunal.

For the purposes of discharging their functions, the Tribunal and the Appellate Tribunal have the same powers as are vested in a civil court under the Code of Civil Procedure, 1908 while trying a suit in respect of the following matters, namely:

(*a*) summoning and enforcing the attendance of any person and examining him on oath;

(*b*) requiring the discovery and production of documents;

(*c*) receiving evidence on affidavits;

(*d*) subject to the provisions of sections 123 and 124 of the Indian Evidence Act, 1872, requisitioning any public record or document or a copy of such record or document from any office;

(*e*) issuing commissions for the examination of witnesses or documents;

(*f*) dismissing a representation for default or deciding it *ex-parte;*

(*g*) setting aside any order of dismissal of any representation for default or any order passed by it *ex-parte;* and

(*h*) any other matter which may be prescribed.

Any order made by the Tribunal or the Appellate Tribunal may be enforced by that Tribunal in the same manner as if it were a decree made by a court in a suit pending therein. All proceedings before the Tribunal or the Appellate Tribunal shall be deemed to be judicial proceedings. The Tribunal and the Appellate Tribunal shall have the same jurisdiction, powers and authority in respect of contempt of themselves as the High Court has and may exercise, for this purpose, the powers under the provisions of the Contempt of Courts Act, 1971, subject to certain conditions.

Any person aggrieved by any order of the Tribunal may file an appeal to the Appellate Tribunal and any person aggrieved by any order of the Appellate Tribunal may file an appeal to the Supreme Court.

MISCELLANEOUS

Following are some of the important points of the Act not covered above.

Corporate Social Responsibility

With the CA 2013, India became the first country to make spending towards corporate social responsibility mandatory. Accordingly, at least two per cent of the average net profits of the preceding three financial years shall be spent on projects beneficial to the society by companies having:

- net worth of ₹ 500 crore or more; or
- turnover of ₹ 100 crore or more; or
- net profit of ₹ 5 crore or more

Details of the provisions of the Companies Act pertaining to CSR are given in Chapter 9 (*Social Responsibility of Business*) of this book.

Mergers and Acquisitions

The CA 2013 has introduced a fast track and simplified procedure for mergers and amalgamations of certain class of companies such as holding and subsidiary, and small companies after obtaining approval of the Indian government.

The Act permits cross-border mergers, both ways – a foreign company merging with an India company and *vice versa* – with prior permission of RBI.

Class Action Suits

The CA 2013 permits pursuing class action suits (*i.e.,* suits by a group of persons) by members, debenture-holders or depositors. This is an important step towards protecting interests of stakeholders, particularly small investors.

Restrictions on Non-audit Services

The CA 2013 imposes restrictions on auditors on performing non-audit services to the company where they are auditors to ensure independence and accountability of auditor.

Prohibition of Loans to Directors

The CA 2013 prohibits companies from extending, directly or indirectly, any kind of loan/guarantee/security to any of its directors or to any other person in whom the director is interested.

Uniform Financial Year

The CA 2013 has made the financial year uniform for all accompanies (*i.e.,* 1st April –31st March).

National Financial Reporting Authority

The CA 2013 provides for constitution of a National Financial Reporting Authority (NFRA) by Central Government for dealing with matters relating to accounting and auditing policies and standards to be followed by companies and their auditors.

Companies with Charitable Objects

The CA 2013 increased the scope of companies that may be formed with charitable objectives to include sports, education, research, social welfare, protection of environment in addition to the promotion of commerce, arts, science, religion and charity.

Related Party Transactions

The CA 2013 made approval of related party transactions by Audit Committee/Board of Directors at Board meeting mandatory; but Central Government approval for related party transactions is not required now. Related party transactions also require prior shareholder's approval by special resolution for companies having prescribed paid-up capital or transactions exceeding prescribed amounts. Related party transactions shall be disclosed in the Director's Report along with justification thereof.

Prohibition of Acceptance of Public Deposits

Regulations pertaining to public deposits have been significantly amended. After the coming into effect of the CA 2013, no company (other than banking and non-banking financial companies) can accept deposits from the public or renew deposits accepted earlier.

Acceptance of Deposits from Members

However, a company can accept deposits from its members subject to the conditions laid down in the Act. The conditions include passing of a resolution to this effect in general meeting, issuance of a circular to its members indicating the financial position of the company, the credit rating obtained, the total number of depositors and the amount due towards deposits in respect of any previous deposits accepted by the company and such other particulars in such form and in such manner as may be prescribed; depositing not less than fifteen per cent of the amount of its deposits maturing during a financial year and the next year in a scheduled bank in a separate bank account to be called as deposit repayment reserve account; providing deposit insurance as may be prescribed, etc.

Vigil Mechanism

Every listed company or such class or classes of companies, as may be prescribed, shall establish a vigil mechanism for directors and employees to report genuine concerns in such manner as may be prescribed.

The vigil mechanism shall provide for adequate safeguards against victimisation of persons who use such mechanism and make provision for direct access to the chairperson of the Audit Committee in appropriate or exceptional cases. The details of establishment of such mechanism shall be disclosed by the company on its website, if any, and in the Board's report.

E-governance

The CA 2013 permits move towards e-governance. The Act permits maintenance of books of account, deeds, vouchers, writings, documents, minutes and registers maintained on paper or in electronic form. It also permits holding of Board meetings through video conferencing/other electronic mode and voting by shareholders through electronic mode. Serving of documents to companies by electronic mode and filing of documents with the Registrar in electronic mode are permitted. Financial statements are to be placed on company's website.

Secretarial Audit

Secretarial Audit by Company Secretary in practice for listed and prescribed class of companies is now mandatory under the Companies Act. The report of such Secretarial Audit has to be annexed to the Director's report presented in annual general meeting.

The functions of the company secretary include:

(*a*) to report to the Board about compliance with the provisions of this Act, the rules made thereunder and other laws applicable to the company;

(*b*) to ensure that the company complies with the applicable secretarial standards;

(*c*) to discharge such other duties as may be prescribed.

Secretarial standards refers to secretarial standards issued by the Institute of Company Secretaries of India.

National Financial Reporting Authority

The CA 2013 provides for constitution of a National Financial Reporting Authority (NFRA) by Central Government for dealing with matters relating to accounting and auditing policies and standards to be followed by companies and their auditors.

Consolidation of Financial Statements

Consolidation of financial statements is made mandatory for all companies with one or more subsidiaries, whether Indian or foreign. For the purposes of consolidation of financial statements, the expression subsidiary includes associate company and joint venture.

Appointment of Key Managerial Personnel

According to the CA 2013, prescribed class of companies to have whole-time Key Managerial Personnel (KMP). Key managerial personnel refers to:

(*i*) the chief executive officer or the managing director or the manager;

(*ii*) the company secretary;

(*iii*) the whole-time director;

(*iv*) the Chief Financial Officer; and

(*v*) such other officer as may be prescribed.

SUMMARY

The Companies Act, 2013, which has replaced the 56 years old Companies Act of 1956, substantially differs from the previous Act in many respects. The current Act contains many provisions of the previous Act and includes a number of newly incorporated provisions and amended matter.

Some important highlights of the Companies Act, 2013 are given below. A number of important aspects of the Act are given in a summary form in the section *Miscellaneous* above.

Application of the Act

The CA 2013 applies to the whole of India and to almost all types of companies – it applies not only to companies incorporated under the Companies Act but also to companies incorporated under other Acts, like insurance companies, banking companies and electricity companies.

Objective of the Act

The main objective of the Companies Act is to empower the Central Government to regulate the formation of companies in accordance with certain standards and norms and to control the management of companies by laying down a legal and procedural framework to be adhered to by the companies.

Types of Companies

According to the Companies Act, there are basically three classes of companies, *viz.*, limited companies, unlimited companies and guarantee companies.

The CA 2013 introduced some new entities, *viz.*, one person company, small company and dormant company. The first two of these are private companies and last may be public or private.

There are two important kinds of limited companies, *viz.*, private limited company and public limited company.

A private company shall have a minimum paid-up capital of one lakh rupees and the number of members shall not be more than two hundred (excluding employees and former employees who continue to be members after the employment ceased).

A public company shall have a minimum paid-up capital of five lakh rupees and a minimum seven members (no upper limit).

Taking a total view, the CA 2013 deals with the following classes of companies.

- Companies limited by shares (subdivided into public, deemed public and private companies)
- Companies limited by guarantee (either with or without share capital)
- Companies with unlimited liability (either with or without share capital)

The Companies Act 2013 also refers to certain special types of companies such as:

- One person company
- Small company
- Dormant company
- Holding and subsidiary companies
- Associate company
- Government company
- Foreign company

Incorporation of Company

For any lawful purpose, a public company may be formed by seven or more persons, a private company by two or more persons, one person company (which is essentially a private company) by one person.

For incorporation of a company, the promoters of the proposed company shall file with the Registrar of Companies certain specified documents containing the details sought to be provided in the documents. The two most important documents are the Memorandum of Association and the Articles of Association. The Memorandum of Association is regarded as the *fundamental* document of the company which defines the object of its formation and operations. The Articles of Association are the rules, regulations and bye-laws for the *internal* management of the affairs of a company. They are framed with the object of carrying out the aims and objects as set out in the Memorandum of Association.

Corporate Governance

The CA 2013 provides an elaborate legal framework to foster healthy corporate governance. These include:

(*a*) Norms and standards pertaining to the composition of the board of directors, including the stipulations regarding independent director, qualifications and disqualifications for appointment as director, powers of the Board and duties of directors, stipulations regarding Board meetings etc.

(*b*) Provisions regarding norms for accounting, auditors and auditing, preparation and submission of various documents etc.

(*c*) Measures aimed at imparting required transparency about the operations and affairs of the company, including provisions regarding disclosure of information.

(*d*) Regulations regarding related party transactions, inter-corporate investments and loans to directors.

(*e*) Compliance requirements.

Powers to Oversee and Control Management of Companies

The Companies Act has a number of provisions aimed at preventing mismanagement or objectionable activities by companies.

The Act gives powers to the Registrar of Companies to call for information, inspect records books and conduct inquiries into the affairs of companies, conduct inspection and inquiry, search and seize records etc. Further, the Central Government is entitled to investigate into the affairs of any company as per the provisions of the Act.

The Act also provides for the establishment of Serious Fraud Investigation Office by the Central Government. The Central Government may order an investigation into the affairs of any company by the Serious Fraud Investigation Office if the Government is of the opinion that it is necessary to do so.

Winding Up of Companies

There are two modes of winding up, *viz.,* voluntary winding up and winding up by National Company Law Tribunal.

Tribunal and Appellate Tribunal

Cases under the Companies Act is dealt with by National Company Law Tribunal (NCLT), which has replaced the role of High Court in company law matters. The Tribunal, consisting of judicial and technical members, exercise and discharge the powers and functions conferred on it by the Central Government including approval of merger, corporate reorganisation, capital reduction etc. The Tribunal can have such number of Benches as decided by the Central Government.

Appeals against the orders of the Tribunal may be made to the National Company Law Appellate Tribunal and Supreme Court is the authority to consider appeals against orders of the Appellate Tribunal.

Revival and Rehabilitation of Sick Companies

The authority to deal with sick companies under the CA 2013 is the National Company Law Tribunal, which has replaced the role played by the Board for Industrial and Financial Reconstruction (BIFR) established under the Sick Industrial Companies Act (SICA) of 1985 which was repealed in 2003. The CA 2013 covers all types of sick companies whereas the SICA covered only sick industrial companies. While erosion of net worth was the important criterion to decide sickness under the SICA, a company which fails to pay the debt is regarded sick under the CA 2013.

Issue of Securities by Companies

Both public and private companies can raise capital by rights or bonus issues and through private placement. Only public companies can issue securities to the public.

According to the CA 2013, the share capital of a company limited by shares can be of two kinds, namely: (*a*) equity share capital and (*b*) preference share capita.

Prohibition of Insider Trading

The Companies Act bans insider trading (*i.e.,* dealing in securities by any director or key managerial personnel or any other officer of the company having, or reasonably expected to have, non-public price-sensitive information in respect of securities the company). Price-sensitive information is information which is likely to affect the price of securities.

REFERENCE

1. The first two paragraphs of this section are adapted from the *Report of High-powered Expert Committee on Companies and MRTP Acts* (Government of India, 1978).

☆☆☆

CHAPTER 15

PATENTS AND TRADE MARKS

Protection of intellectual property rights has become an issue of wide and serious discussion with the formation of the General Agreement on Trade Related Aspects of Intellectual Property Rights (TRIPs) under the Uruguay Round (UR) Agreement of the GATT (now the WTO).

Intellectual property rights (IPRs) may be defined as "information with commercial value". IPRs have been characterised as a composite of "ideas, inventions and creative expression" plus the "public willingness to bestow the status of property" on them and give their owners the "right to exclude others from access to or use of protected subject matter".

IPRs may be legally protected by patents, copyrights, industrial designs, geographical indications, and trade marks. Special *(sui generis)* forms of protection have also emerged to address specific needs of knowledge-producers as in the case of plant breeder's rights and the protection of layout designs of integrated circuits. A number of countries also have trade secret laws to protect undisclosed information that gives a competitive advantage to its owner.

The UR Agreement on TRIPs covers seven intellectual properties, *viz.,*

1. Copyright and related rights
2. Trade marks
3. Geographical indications
4. Industrial designs
5. Patents

6. Layout designs (topographies) of integrated circuits
7. Undisclosed information, including trade secrets

On copyrights and related rights, the Agreement requires compliance with the provisions of *Bern Convention* to which India is a signatory and the new Copyright Act of India already meets the requirements of the TRIPs Agreement. Trade and Merchandise Marks Act of 1958 was replaced by a new Act, namely, The Trade Marks Act, 1999, so as to provide for the protection of service marks also.

IPRs AND DEVELOPING COUNTRIES

There is a strong view that although the IPRs are intended to encourage R&D, they often provide an opportunity for the developed country firms an opportunity to exploit the developing countries.

Disadvantages/Limitations

The major disadvantages/limitations of a strong the regime of IPRs, as regards developing countries, are the following:

The developing countries, particularly the very poor among them, are ill-equipped for significant R&D. In a world order where the industrial countries are the major producers of technology and developing countries heavily depend on imports of technology, IPRs turnout to be, generally, more beneficial to industrial countries than to developing countries. Developed countries enormously benefit from the benefits of higher prices resulting from the market power provided by IPRs, at the expense of developing countries. While industrial countries gain huge amounts of net transfers from TRIPs, developing countries, including India, are expected to experience net outward transfers on account of TRIPs.

Poor countries have serious limitations to generate intel-lectual property and to efficiently administer IPRs regime.

A strong IPRs regime without adequate safeguards to protect interests of weaker sections can create very serious problems in developing countries. Exorbitant prices will make patented essential drugs beyond the reach of common man.

Developing countries, generally, do not have adequate institutional mechanism and resources to properly administer IPRs regime. For example, a proper competition law and its efficient enforcement are required to combat the potential anti-competitive abuse of IP. While in many industrial countries such abuses are dealt with by general competition law, IPR statutory provisions, or other regulations and guidelines, the developing countries are generally handicapped by the weakness of their regulatory system. A World Bank publication, therefore, cautions that "unless developing countries rapidly establish adequate competition frameworks and regulatory institutions that also address monopoly abuse of IPRs, it is possible that increasing IPR protection could result in welfare losses from monopoly behaviour."[1]

Benefits

Protection of IPRs is not without gains to developing countries.

Stronger IPR protection may encourage investment, both foreign and domestic.

Stronger IPR protection could be expected to give a boost to R&D in countries like India whose potential intellectual capital may be expected to grow in great width and depth.

IPR system provides a great opportunity to developing countries to benefit from protection of indigenous property rights and traditional knowledge. Developing countries hold approximately 90 per cent of world biological resources, which are particularly important in the development of new pharmaceuticals. Mechanisms for sharing the proceeds from commercialising genetic resources can be written into the IPR law, or alternatively, institutions can be built to protect the collective intellectual property rights for traditional knowledge held by cultural groups.

Developing countries are also adversely affected by bilateral agreements on IPRs Since bilateral agreements usually provide for stronger IPRs than TRIPs — which mandates only minimum standards — these agreements may impede the ability of developing countries to implement the flexibility permitted in TRIPs. For example, in 1998 the United States had signed bilateral agreements on IPRs with 21 countries and had included many IPR provisions in science and technology agreements and bilateral investment treaties. In general, the validity of international agreements and standards loses force if bilateral agreements proliferate, superseding the international agreement. The political and economic balance of power does not usually tip in favour of poorer developing countries in negotiating cross-border agreements, and this imbalance is probably accentuated when they enter bilateral agreements.[2]

Experiences and Practices

IPR protection system should take into consideration the socio-economic characteristics and development challenges of the nation.

It is pointed out research in industrial countries does not provide strong evidence that IPRs are necessary to stimulate R&D or innovation in most sectors. Some studies show that a realistically designed IPRs system becomes beneficial after a country has attained a certain level of technological development and R&D capability. Further, an IPRs system becomes beneficial when it incorporates the required safeguards having regard to the conditions and needs of the country. It is observed that although ensuring a core level of IPR protection may increase developing country access to foreign technologies by safeguarding returns for foreign technology producers, excessively strong IPRs can inhibit the diffusion of knowledge. In developing countries, knowledge is built more through access, imitation, and diffusion of foreign technologies rather than only local research. Legitimate ways to transfer technology under some IPR systems such as reverse engineering or inventing around patents are restricted under strong IPRs. The importance of adopting appropriate policies that allow access to technologies can be seen for some East Asian countries in their early stages of development.

This principle is generally followed worldwide, with countries adopting more flexible IPRs at lower levels of per capita income. In Malaysia and Korea, growth in industrial sectors took place under weak IPR regimes, and in later periods governments emphasised incentives for innovation in IPRs as sophisticated local technology sectors developed. Japan introduced patents in the early 20th century after reviewing IPR systems in Europe and the United States. The Japanese system adapted other patent regimes to suit local needs. Emphasis was placed on securing access to foreign technologies, incremental technology development, and diffusion of innovation, through features such as strong anti-trust guidelines for technology licensing and a central licensing office as a countervailing influence on foreign bargaining power pressuring for change in its IPR system.[3]

Maximising Developing Country Benefits from TRIPs

> **Developing countries should take all possible safeguard measures to minimise the adverse effects of TRIPs regulation.**

Having committed to implement TRIPs, to maximize their net gains developing countries need to take advantage of the flexibility built into TRIPs. There are several areas of flexibility within TRIPs that provide the potential for developing countries to maximise benefits by promoting access to technology and preventing anti-competitive abuses while maintaining incentives to innovate, tackle piracy, and still meet TRIPs minimum standards. The *World Development Report 2002* makes the following suggestions in this regard.

Scope and Exclusion: Developing countries can narrow the scope of what falls under IPRs in the following areas in conformity with TRIPs. *First,* developing countries can adopt a narrow interpretation of what constitutes an invention and hence what needs to be patented. For example, Argentina, Brazil, and China have elected not to extend patent protection to software. *Second,* developing countries can take advantage of the TRIPs article that allows limitations and exceptions to copyright. For example, some countries permit unauthorized use for social purposes such as education and scientific research. *Third,* developing countries can avoid patenting life forms and can apply special provisions under TRIPs to exempt public goods from IPR protection. *Finally,* developing countries can expand IPR scope to protect genetic resources, traditional knowledge and folklore, as is promoted by the World Intellectual Property Organization.

Compulsory Licensing: Countries can use compulsory licensing, allowed by TRIPs under some circumstances, to control anti-competitive behaviour that results from IPRs or in national emergencies, such as public health crises. The licence, issued by national authorities, authorises the use of IPR-protected subject matter without the consent of the rights holder, with compensation to the latter to be determined by the government.

Parallel Imports: Parallel imports refers to IPR-protected products imported into a country after being released legitimately in another country. Free trade in IPR-protected goods ensures competition in product markets, reduces prices, and enhances consumer access to new technologies. But trade in IPR-protected products may restrict access to new technologies for developing countries. TRIPs neither endorses nor prohibits parallel imports.

Price Regulation: Some countries regulate price levels and price increases—as is allowed under TRIPs — to ensure that IPRs do not restrict consumer access through excessively high prices, particularly in pharmaceutical products. But price regulations are often fraught with problems.

Competition Law: Anti-competitive abuse of IPRs can be controlled by an effective competition law.

Complementary Actions: The impact of IPRs depends on the broader institutional and policy environment. More liberal trading rules also reduce the risk of monopoly abuse of IPRs by domestic firms. Human capital development is also important; IPRs are more likely to increase technology transfer and encourage domestic innovation in countries with higher levels of human capital.

Another factor is the promotion of national innovation systems. Integration of IPR rules with complementary policies to foster innovation such as public sector research involvement where appropriate can stimulate growth by increasing the commercialization of inventions.

Although, under TRIPS Article 67, industrial country members are obligated to provide technical and financial support for implementing the agreement, only limited assistance has been provided to fulfil this commitment: mostly training and technical assistance in drafting IPR laws. More technical support that is geared toward helping developing countries take advantage of the flexibility allowed in the TRIPS agreement is needed. Concrete financial assistance targets and grants of patents to developing countries (especially for emergency human development needs such as HIV/AIDS treatment) are some of the proposals made for better implementation of Article 67. Others include increased technology transfer assistance and fiscal incentives, such as guaranteed purchase of new drugs for developing countries.

PATENTS

> **Patent is a monopoly right granted by law to use an invention.**

A patent is a legal protection granted for an invention that is new, non-obvious and useful. The patent grants the patent holder the exclusive right to make use or sell the patented products or process. The main purpose of the patent system is to benefit the society. Patents, by providing an opportunity to recoup the cost of invention (which is quite substantial in many cases) and to make profit out of the invention, encourage research and development and thereby contribute to the well-being of the society.

An invention, to be patentable, must satisfy the following three conditions.

- It is new.
- It is useful to the society.
- It is non-obvious to a person possessed of average skill in the art.

Exclusion of an invention from patentability for commercial exploitation is permitted if it is necessary to protect public order or morality, including to protect human, animal or plant life or health or to avoid serious prejudice to the environment. A nation may also exclude from patentability (a) diagnostic, therapeutic and surgical methods for the treatment of humans or animals; (b) plants and animals other than microorganisms and essentially biological process for the production of plants or animals other than non-biological and microbiological process. However, members shall provide for the protection of plant varieties either by patents or by an effective *sui generis* system or by any combination thereof.

Indian Patent Law

Patent protection in India has a long history. Patent protection was introduced in India in the 18th century. Formal patent protection was ushered in by the Patents Act, 1911. The Patents Act, 1970 amended and consolidated the law related to patents.

Some very significant amendments to India's patent law was, however, necessitated by the Agreement on Intellectual Property Rights that emerged from the Uruguay Round of multilateral trade negotiations that brought into being the WTO. Being a member of the WTO, India was obliged to align its patent law with the stipulations under the WTO with effect from January 1, 2005. Accordingly, the Indian Patents Act, 1970 and the Patent Rules 1972 were amended.

The Indian Patents Act, 1970, as amended and effective from January 1, 2005, lays down:

- The eligibility, procedures and conditions for grant of patents
- Inventions and other subjects not patentable
- Rights and obligations of patentee
- Grounds for revocation of patents
- Matters related to working of the patent and compulsory licensing
- Rights of government regarding patented products

1. Grant and Revocation of Patents

The Patents Act lays down the eligibility, procedures and conditions for grant of patents and grounds for revocation of patent.

Under the Act, a patent may be granted to an invention, subject to the provisions of the Act. According to the Act, an "invention" means a new product or process involving an inventive step and capable of industrial application. An "inventive step" means a feature of an invention that involves technical advance as compared to the existing knowledge or having economic significance or both and that makes the invention not obvious to a person skilled in the art.

There is also provision for the grant of patents of addition to the patentee (i.e., granting of patent in respect of any improvement in or modification of an invention which is patented. The grant of patent of addition shall be for a term equivalent to that of the patent for the main invention.

The Act also provides for revocation of patents on certain grounds such as any claim made for the grant of patent has been found invalid, or the Central Government feels that a patent or the mode in which it is exercised is mischievous to the state or generally prejudicial to the public interest.

2. Items not Patentable

A list of inventions and other subjects not patentable is provided in the Patents Act. Some examples of those which are not patentable: Inventions which are frivolous or contrary to public interest; method of agriculture or horticulture; any process of treatment of human beings or animals; plants and animals (other than microorganisms but including seeds, varieties and species and essentially biological processes for production or propagation of plants and animals); a mathematical or business method or a computer program *per se* or algorithms; the mere discovery of a scientific principles or the formulation of an abstract theory or discovery of any living thing or non-living substance occurring in nature; a mere scheme or rule or method of performing mental act or method of playing game; a presentation of information; topography of integrated circuits; an invention which, in effect, is traditional knowledge or which is an aggregation or duplication of known properties of traditionally known component or components.

3. Product Patent

The amended Act provides for grant of product patent. Previously, for food, pharmaceutical and chemical products only process patent was granted. This meant that any body was free to manufacture the same or similar product by a process different from the patented one. This is no more allowed because of the adoption of the product patent.

4. Patent Period

For food, pharmaceutical and chemical products, previously the patent period was 14 years. Now patents are granted for all products for a period of 20 years from the date of application.

5. Rights and Obligations of Patentee

The Act lays down the rights and obligations of patentee. A Patent granted under this Act confers on the patentee the exclusive right to use, make, sell or import the patented process/product. The Act normally prevents third parties from using, making, selling or importing the patented process/product without the consent of the patentee.

The Patents Act makes it clear that patents are not granted merely to enable patentees to enjoy a monopoly but to encourage inventions and to secure that the inventions are worked in India on a commercial scale and to the fullest extent that is reasonably practicable without undue delay; and to make the benefit of the patented invention available at reasonably affordable prices to the public.

6. Working of the Patent

As pointed out above, a patent is granted subject to certain considerations which ensure that it is properly worked in the country to serve the interests of the society. Working of patent means that the patented product is produced in India and made available sufficiently at reasonable prices within reasonable time.

The Act makes it clear that a patent is granted to encourage inventions and to secure that the inventions are worked in India on a commercial scale and to the fullest extent that is reasonably practicable without undue delay; the patent shall not be deemed a monopoly right to import the patented article in to the country. It is also expected that a patent contributes to the promotion of technological innovation and to the transfer and dissemination of technology to the mutual advantage of the producers and users of the technological knowledge.

A patentee is oblighted to produce and make sufficiently available in India the patented product at reasonable price.

7. Compulsory Licensing

The Act provides for compulsory licensing of the patent and revocation of the patent if it is not worked in the country.

A serious concern in India and elsewhere has been that product patents will result in exorbitant prices for drugs, seriously impairing the health and nutritional requirements of the large majority of the population. The considerations regarding the working of patents, laid down in the Act seek to safeguard the public interest in this respect. To protect the interests of the public, Indian Patents Act provides for grant of compulsory licence on ground such as failure to work the patent in the country. Compulsory licensing means grant of licence to third party to work the Patent in the country.

The compulsory licensing sections of the Act are intended to check the abuse of patent rights. They can be invoked if the reasonable requirements of the public with respect to patented inventions have not been satisfied and the patented invention is not available for public at a reasonably affordable price, and if the patented invention is not worked in the territory of India. Section 92 of this law provides for action in case of national emergency, extreme urgency and public non-commercial use, and can be invoked without the grace period of 3 years from grant of patent.

The Act also has a provision for enabling grant of compulsory licence for export of medicines to countries, which have insufficient, or no manufacturing capacity, to meet emergent public health situations (in accordance with the Doha Declaration on TRIPs and Public Health).

8. Parallel Import

The Act also provides for parallel import so that patented product can become available at the lowest international price.

9. Exceptions

The Patents Act also lays down certain exceptions to the rights of the patentee.

Any patented product or process may by made, imported or used by or on behalf of the government for its own use or purpose. The Central Government may also acquire a patent for public purpose, if necessary.

Any patented medicine or drug may be imported by the Government for the purpose merely of its own use or for distribution in any dispensary, hospital or other medical institution maintained by or on behalf of the Government or any other dispensary, hospital or other medical institution specified by the government in public interest.

Any patented process or product may be used or made by any person, for the purpose merely of experiment or research including the imparting of instructions to pupils.

Evaluation

The amendments to the Patents Act has come in for scathing criticism in India. The 1970 Act was regarded as a skilfully drafted piece of legislation which sought to protect the infant drugs and Pharmaceuticals and chemicals industries from foreign monopolies in these fields. The critics fear that the adoption of product patent will enable the multinational drug firms to exploit the Indian consumers. While it is true that patent confers monopoly power on the patentee, in the absence of product patent the patentee does not get sufficient protection.

According to Government sources, the apprehensions that the Patent Amendment will drive up drug prices by ruling out access and availability of medicines at low cost are unfounded. "In the first place, the fact remains that 97 per cent of all drugs manufactured in India are off-patents and so will remain unaffected. These cover most of the life saving drugs, as well as medicines for common ailments. In patented drugs also, in most of the cases there are always alternatives available. Further, the country has 13 Sections under Chapter XVI pertaining to Compulsory Licensing in place; and the Act has strong provisions under Chapter XVII of the Act for outright acquisition of patents to meet national requirements. Besides, there is also the Drug Price Control Order administered by the National Pharmaceuticals Price Authority. With such a framework in place, the concerns and fears relating to rise in drug prices are misplaced. Besides, there are adequate safeguards to protect the interests of domestic industry and the common man from any increase in the prices of drugs."[4]

However, the fact that patented drugs, by and large are vital ones, makes the situation very serious. If he government does not make effective use of the safeguards in the Act to protect the interests of the consumers, their plight could become miserable.

It is also pointed out that, apart from manufacture of drugs, the product patent regime will help the pharmaceutical industry to tap outsourcing of clinical research. By participating in the international system of IPR protection, India, with its vast pool of scientific and technical personnel, and well-established expertise in medical treatment and health care, has unlocked vast opportunities in both exports and outsourcing and has the potential to become a global hub in the area of R&D based clinical research. The Patent

Ordinance also provides adequate safeguards to protect the interest of the domestic industry, and the citizen from any increase in prices of drugs.

The Patent Act needs further fine-tuning. It is observed that we should fine-tune patentability, pre-grant opposition and compulsory licensing, besides providing for revocation of patent as a measure of WTO compatible trade penalty. True the present Act has tightened patentability and pre-grant opposition, but not enough. For one, the pre-grant window is available for a period of six months from the date of publication. This is better than the three months allowed earlier, but not sufficient in view of the 8,000 applications pending. The paucity of time could mean many frivolous cases getting patents and causing damage by the time a post-grant appeal is entertained. A temporary elongation of the pre-grant opposition window to enable examination of the bunched 8,000 applications could be considered, along with a stipulation for swift processing of the objections. In the case of patentability, it would be useful to accept the Mashelkar Panel's recommendation on restricting patentability to new chemical entities and limiting the amplitude of novelty and utility, characteristics that make for patentability, through clear enunciation.

That compulsory license application be allowed three years after the grant of a patent is fine in the normal course. However, a national emergency should not be the only consideration for deviating from this timeframe. Moreover, this application is to be entertained only after the CL applicant has made reasonable efforts to obtain a licence from the patentee over a reasonable period, defined as six months. In effect, three-and-a half-years must pass before a CL application is considered. And there is no saying how long patent office will take to deal with the issue.

TRADE MARKS

Brands and *trade marks,* used very extensively in modern marketing to maintain product identity and to help product promotion, have become very popular terms.

The definitions of some of the important terms given in *Marketing Definitions: A Glossary of Marketing Terms,* published by the American Marketing Association, and the Indian Trade Marks Act, 1999, are given below:

Brand: A brand is a name, term, sign, symbol, or design or a combination of them, intended to identify the goods or services of one seller or group of sellers and to differentiate them from those of competitors.

Brand Name: Brand name is that part of the brand which can be vocalized — the utterable.

Brand Mark: Brand mark is that part of a brand which can be recognized but is not utterable, such as symbol, design or distinctive colouring or lettering.

Trade Mark: A trade mark is a brand or part of a brand that is given legal protection because it is capable of exclusive appropriation.

A trade mark protects the seller's exclusive rights to use the brand name and/or brand mark.

According to the Trade Marks Act, 1999, trade mark means a mark capable of being represented graphically and which is capable of distinguishing the goods or services of one person from those of others and may include shape of goods, their packaging and combination of colours; and

(*i*) in relation to Chapter XII (other than Sec. 107), a registered trade mark or a mark used in relation to goods or services for the purpose of indicating or as to indicate a connection in the course of trade between the goods or services, as the case may be, and some person having the right as proprietor to use the mark; (Chapter XII deals with offences and penalties), and

(*ii*) in relation to other provisions of this Act, a mark used or proposed to be used in relation to goods or services for the purpose of indicating or so as to indicate a connection in the course of trade between the goods or services, as the case may be, and some person having the right, either as proprietor or by way of permitted user, to use the mark whether with or without any indication of the identity of that person, and includes a certification trade mark or collective mark.

According to the Trade Marks Act, certification trade mark means a mark capable of distinguishing the goods or services in connection with which it is used in the course of trade which are certified by the proprietor of the mark in respect of origin, material, mode of manufacture of goods or performance of services, quality, accuracy or other characteristics from goods or services not so certified and registrable as such under Chapter IX (which deals with Certification Trade Marks) in respect of those goods or services in the name, as proprietor of the certification trade mark of that person.

Collective Mark: According to the Trade Marks Act, collective mark means a trade mark distinguishing the goods or services of members of an association of persons, not being a partnership within the meaning of the Indian Partnership Act, 1932 (9 of 1932), which is the proprietor of the mark from those of others.

The Trade Marks Act, 1999

The Indian law relating to trade marks has been amended and consolidated and Trade and Merchandise Marks Act, 1958 has been replaced by The trade Marks Act, 1999.

Objectives

The objectives of The Trade Marks Act, 1999, are to provide for:

- The registration and better protection of trade marks for goods and services
- The prevention of the use of fraudulent marks.

Registrar and Trade Marks Registry

The Controller-General of Patents, Designs and Trade Marks, appointed by the Central Government, is the Registrar of Trade Marks for the purpose of the Trade Marks Act. Further, the Central Government may appoint other officers with such designations as it thinks fit for the purpose of discharging, under the superintendence and direction of the Registrar, such functions of the Registrar under this Act as he may authorise them to discharge.

For the purposes of this Act, there shall be a Trade Marks Registry with its head office at such place as the Central Government may specify. For the purpose of facilitating the registration of trade marks, there may be branch offices of the Trade Marks Registry established at such places as the Central Government may think fit.

The Act also lays down that a Register of Trade Marks shall be kept at the head office of the Trade Marks Registry, wherein shall be entered all details regarding the registered trade marks, (*i.e.*, the names, addresses and description of the proprietors, notifications of assignment and transmissions, the names, addresses and descriptions of registered users; conditions, limitations and such other matter relating to registered trade marks as may be prescribed).

A copy of the register and the other relevant documents shall be kept at each branch office of the Trade Marks Registry.

Registration of Trade Marks

Any person claiming to be the proprietor of a trade mark used or proposed to be used by him, who is desirous of registering it, shall apply to the Registrar in the prescribed manner for the registration of his trade mark.

A single application is enough for registration of a trade mark for different classes of goods and services.

The application shall be filed in the office of the Trade Marks Registry within whose territorial limits the principal place of business in India of the applicant is situated. In the case of joint applicants it shall be filed in the office of the Trade Marks Registry within whose territorial limits the principal place of business in India of the applicant whose name is first mentioned in the application as having a place of business in India is situated.

Where the applicant or any of the joint applicants does not carry on business in India, the application shall be filed in the office of the Trade Marks Registry within whose territorial limits the place mentioned in the address for service in India as disclosed in the application is situated.

Subject to the provisions of this Act, the Registrar may accept the application absolutely or subject to such amendments, modifications, conditions or limitations, if any, as he may think fit, or refuse the application.

In the case of a refusal or conditional acceptance of an application, the Registrar shall record in writing the grounds for such refusal or conditional acceptance and the materials used by him in arriving at his decision.

When an application for registration of a trade mark has been accepted, the Registrar shall cause the application as accepted together with the conditions or limitations, if any, subject to which it has been accepted, to be advertised in the prescribed manner. In certain cases, such advertisement may be made before the acceptance of the application. The purpose of the advertisement is to allow any person who has any opposition to the registration of the proposed trade mark to give proper notice to the Registrar, of opposition to the registration.

If any proper notice of opposition is received, the Registrar shall serve a copy of the notice on the applicant for registration and, within two months from the receipt by the applicant of such copy of the notice of opposition, the applicant shall send to the Registrar in the prescribed manner in counter-statement of the grounds on which he relies for his application. If he does not do so, he shall be deemed to have abandoned his application.

If the applicant sends such counter-statement, the Registrar shall serve a copy thereof on the person giving notice of opposition. The Registrar shall take an appropriate decision after hearing the parties, if so required, and considering the evidence.

On the registration of a trade mark, the Registrar shall issue to the applicant a certificate in the prescribed form of the registration thereof, sealed with the seal of the Trade Marks Registry.

Where registration of a trade mark is not completed within twelve months from the date of the application by reason of default on the part of the applicant, the Registrar may, after giving notice to the applicant in the prescribed manner, treat the application as abandoned unless it is completed within the time specified in that behalf in the notice.

The Registrar may amend the register or a certificate to registration for the purpose of correcting a clerical error or an obvious mistake.

The duration of the registration of a trade mark is ten years, but may be renewed from time-to-time in accordance with the provisions of the Act. The failure to renew the registration may result in the removal of the trade mark from the register.

Where the proprietor of a trade mark claims to be entitled to the exclusive use of any part thereof separately, he may apply to register the whole and the part as separate trade marks. Each such separate trade mark shall satisfy all the conditions applying to and have all the incidents of an independent trade mark.

The Act also provides for registration of several trade marks as a series in one registration, in respect of the same or similar goods or services or description of goods or description of services, which differ in respect of *(a)* statement of the goods or services in relation to which they are respectively used or proposed to be used; or *(b)* statement of number, price, quality or names of places; or *(c)* other matter of a non-distinctive character which does not substantially affect the identity of the trade mark; or *(d)* colour.

The Act also has provisions regarding registration of collective marks and certification trade marks.

Grounds for Refusal of Registration

The Act lists a number of absolute grounds or refusal of registration of trade marks: the trade mark is devoid of distinctive characteristics, it is of such nature as to deceive the public or cause confusion; it is likely to hurt the religious susceptibilities of any class or section; it comprises or contains scandalous or obscene matter; which consists exclusively of marks or indications which have become customary in the current language or in the *bona fide* and established practices of the trade; etc., and relative grounds for refusal (such as identity or similarity with other trade marks) of registration.

The Act also prohibits the registration of names of commonly used and accepted name of any single chemical element or any single chemical compound or international non-proprietary names declared by the WHO.

The Registrar may refuse registration to a trade mark which falsely suggests a connection with any living person, or a person whose death took place within twenty years prior to the date of application for registration of the trade mark, if the applicant does not furnish the consent of such living person or, as the case may be, of the legal representative of the deceased person.

Effect of Registration

The registration of a trade mark gives the registered proprietor of the trade mark:

- The exclusive right to the use of the trade mark in relation to the goods or services in respect of which the trade mark is registered, subject to any conditions and limitations to which the registration is subject.
- The right to obtain relief in respect of infringement of the trade mark in the manner provided by this Act.

No person shall be entitled to institute any proceeding to prevent, or to recover damages, for the infringement of an unregistered trade mark.

Assignment and Transmission

The Trade Marks Act allows the proprietor of a trade mark to assign the trade mark, and to give effectual receipts for any consideration for such assignment. A registered trade mark is assignable and transmissible, whether with or without the goodwill of the business concerned. It may be done in respect either of all the goods or services in respect of which the trade mark is registered or of only some of those goods or services.

An unregistered trade mark may be assigned or transmitted with or without the goodwill of the business concerned.

Associated trade marks shall be assignable and transmissible only as a whole and not separately.

A certification trade mark shall not be assignable or transmissible otherwise than with the consent of the Registrar.

Where a person becomes entitled by assignment or transmission to a registered trade mark, he is entitled to get himself registered as the proprietor of the trade mark, as per the provisions of the Act.

Appellate Board

The Trade Marks Act provides for the establishment of an Appellate Board to be known as the Intellectual Property Appellate Board by the Central Government to exercise the jurisdiction, powers and authority conferred on it by or under this Act.

The Appellate Board shall consist of a Chairman, Vice-chairman and such number of other Members, as the Central Government may, deem fit. The jurisdiction, powers and authority of the Appellate Board may be exercised by Benches thereof. A Bench shall consist of one Judicial Member and one Technical Member and shall sit at such place as the Central Government may specify.

Any person aggrieved by an order or decision of the Registrar under this Act, or the rules made thereunder may prefer an appeal to the Appellate Board in the prescribed manner within three months from the date on which the order or decision sought to be appealed against is communicated to such person preferring the appeal.

Offences and Penalties

Offences under the Act are punishable by imprisonment and fine. Such offences include falsifying and falsely applying trade marks, applying false trade marks and trade descriptions, etc., selling goods or providing services to which false trade marks or false trade description is applied.

SUMMARY

Legal protection of intellectual property rights provide the owners of them the exclusive right to their commercial use, so that they are rewarded for their innovative or marketing ingenuity.

Patent

A patent is a legal protection granted for an invention that is new, non-obvious and useful. The main purpose of the patent system is to benefit the society. Patents, by providing an opportunity to recoup the cost of invention and to make profit out of the invention, encourages research and development and thereby contributes to the well-being of the society.

The Indian Patent Act of 1970 has significant differences from the patent regulation stipulated by the GATT/WTO. The Uruguay Round Agreement imposes more stringent regulations than stipulates more stringent conditions for compulsory licensing of patents, when compared to the Indian law.

It is argued that the acceptance of product patents will strangle the growth of the Indian pharmaceutical industry and the monopolisation of the vital areas of this industry by multinationals will result in sharp increase in drug prices. This fear, however, seems to be exaggerated. Patented drugs account for only a small share of the Indian pharmaceutical market and within the patented drugs segment, more than half of the drugs have other therapeutic equivalents.

While there are strong criticisms against the WTO patent regime on the one hand, there are many who argue that it will be beneficial to India in several ways. This has made several Indian pharmaceutical firms to pay more attention to R&D.

Trade Mark

According to the Trade Marks Act, 1999, trade mark means a mark capable of being represented graphically and which is capable of distinguishing the goods or services of one person from those of others and may include shape of goods, their packaging and combination of colours.

The Indian law relating to trade marks has been amended and consolidated and Trade and Merchandise Marks Act, 1958 has been replaced by The Trade Marks Act, 1999. This Act provides for the registration and better protection of trade marks for goods and services, and the prevention of the use of fraudulent marks.

A registered trade mark is assignable and transmissible, whether with or without the goodwill of the business concerned. It may be done in respect either of all the goods or services in respect of which the trade mark is registered or of only some of those goods or services.

The registration of a trade mark gives the registered proprietor of the trade mark the exclusive right to the use of the trade mark in relation to the goods or services in respect of which the trade mark is registered. This also entitles him to relief in respect of infringement of the trade mark. No person is entitled to institute any proceeding to prevent, or to recover damages, for the infringement of an unregistered trade mark.

The Registrar of Trade Marks for the purposes of this Act is known as the Controller-General of Patents, Designs and Trade Marks.

There is a Trade Marks Registry with its head office at such place as the Central Government may specify. For the purpose of facilitating the registration of trade marks, there may be branch offices of the Trade Marks Registry established at such places as the Central Government may think fit.

Under the Trade Marks Act, an Appellate Board to be known as the Intellectual Property Appellate Board is established by the Central Government to exercise the jurisdiction, powers and authority conferred on it by or under this Act.

Any person aggrieved by an order or decision of the Registrar under this Act, or the rules made thereunder may prefer an appeal to the Appellate Board.

Offences such as falsifying and falsely applying trade marks, applying false trade marks and trade descriptions, etc., and selling goods or providing services to which false trade marks or false trade description is applied are punishable under the Act by imprisonment and fine.

REFERENCES

1. World Bank, *World Development Report 2002*, Oxford University Press, 2002, pp. 146-9.
2. *Ibid.*
3. *Ibid.*
4. "Now for a second dose: Amend The Patent Bill Further", *The Economic Times* (editorial), 28 March, 2005.

☆☆☆

CHAPTER 16

COMPETITION POLICY AND LAW

Competition policy refers to the government policy designed to ensure contestability and fair competition by removing/preventing factors and forces that tend to distort fair competition.

The economic liberalisation has increased the relevance of competition policy. In 1980, less than 40 countries had competition laws; the number has increased to over 100 today. The pace of adoption increased rapidly after 1989, when former centrally planned economies in Central and Eastern Europe introduced comprehensive programmes of investment liberalisation, deregulation, privatisation and competition-law enforcement, and a number of developing countries also adopted competition laws. Moreover, many of these laws have been strengthened over the years, in terms of stricter and broader rules and higher penalties.[1]

> **The objective competition policy and law is to ensure fair competition.**

Fair competition is the hallmark of a free enterprise economy. Economic liberalisation unleashes competitive forces. In the absence of safeguards, this may, however, also provide scope for unfair competition, like powerful competitors crushing small firms through unfair means, collusion, and mergers and acquisitions (M&As) detrimental to competition. Further, there may still be some government policies like reservation for small business, trade restrictions, cross subsidisation, preferences in government procurements, etc., which hamper competition. These call for a competition policy and law.

Competition Policy and Law — Nature and Scope

As Dr. S. Chakravarthy, who was a member of the MRTP Commission and the High Level Committee on Competition Policy and Law puts it, competition policy is essentially understood to refer to governmental measures that directly affect the behaviour of enterprises and the structure of the industry. A coherent and pragmatic competition policy should be capable of enhancing competition in local and national markets. It is an instrument to achieve efficient allocation of resources, technical progress and/consumer welfare and to regulate concentration of economic power detriment to competition with flexibility to adjust to the changing international economic milieu. On a broad note, a well-designed competition policy should govern policies relating to globalisation, liberalisation and deregulation as may have an impact on competition. Of particular importance is the trade policy, which impacts competition on the market significantly –whether positively or adversely — and thus, has to be subservient to competition policy.[2]

Chakravarthy has succinctly drawn up the distinction and relation between policy and law as follows: Competition policy can be regarded as a genus, of which competition law is a specie. The former covers a whole array of executive policies and even approaches, whereas the latter is a piece of legislative enactment having the character of enforceability in a court of law. Government made decisions by way of executive policies and executive guidelines are pronounced in trade policy areas, in terms of which trade is regulated or even liberalised without the promulgation of a law or without the requirement of having to secure the approval of the legislature before applying the same. In policies which are not having the cover of law, there is always the danger of discrimination, abuse of discretion and non-rule based decisions. While one can easily appreciate the difficulties involved in covering and supporting every executive made competition policy by a legislative enactment, it is desirable that there is a codification of the principles the competition law which should act as an umbrella framework for making executive policies. Furthermore, such a competition law should have necessary provisions and teeth, to review any executive policy on the touchstone of competition and also have the power to require the executive to amend its policies, as may be necessary. This will ensure the spirit of competition in the executive policies relating to trade and market.[3]

As an UNCTAD report observes, the main objective of competition laws is to preserve and promote competition as a means to ensure the efficient allocation of resources in an economy, resulting in the best possible choice of quality, the lowest prices and adequate supplies for consumers. In addition to promoting efficiency, many competition laws make reference to other objectives, such as the control of concentration of economic power, promoting the competitiveness of domestic industries, encouraging innovation, supporting small and medium-size enterprises and encouraging regional integration. Some of these additional objectives may sometimes be in conflict with the efficiency objective. The manner in which efforts are made to reconcile these conflicting objectives can be relevant to domestic firms and to the way TNCs are allowed to enter and operate in domestic markets.[4]

> **Competition laws seek to regulate enterprise behaviour and developments that restrict competition.**

Most competition laws deal with enterprise *behaviour* by prohibiting such restrictive business practices as competition-restricting horizontal agreements, acquisitions and abuses of dominant positions, as well as substantially restrictive vertical distribution agreements. In addition, an increasing number of competition laws deals with alterations to the *structure* of markets, through the control of M&As, as well as joint ventures aimed at avoiding the creation of dominant firms, monopolies, or even oligopolies. In some laws, the divestment of 'parts of monopolies is also authorized, to change the structure of markets'.[5]

Most competition laws contain exceptions (basically sectoral) and exemptions (in most cases adopted in respect to categories of practices) to the application of their provisions. These can cover, among others, labour, regulated industries (*e.g.*, telecommunications, defence, agriculture), small and medium-size enterprises, and certain types of cooperative arrangements, including R&D joint ventures. The rationale behind exemptions vary. In some cases (market failures, for example), competition and market forces are not viewed as the best tools leading to the maximization of economic efficiency; rather, direct regulation of prices or entry is used. A number of countries, however, are reviewing the soundness and validity of those across-the-board exemptions. The emphasis is increasingly on applying competition law to all business practices not explicitly imposed on firms by statutory provisions. It is then the task of the competition authority or courts to consider business practices, and focus on those that have the highest probability of anti-competitive effects and the least justification based on efficiency. Usually, such cartel practices as price fixing, collusive tendering and market allocation are prohibited without need for market analysis, while distribution, joint ventures and merger agreements are assessed in a market context and increasingly under a rule-of-reason standard taking into account the efficiencies likely to be achieved and passed on to consumers.[6]

BOX 16.1 : SELECTED RESTRICTIVE BUSINESS PRACTICES ADDRESSED BY COMPETITIVE LAW

There are four main types of business practices that can have anti-competitive effects: practices undertaken by a single firm (when a firm enjoys a dominant position); anti-competitive mergers and acquisitions; horizontal restraints (*i.e.*, arrangements between competitors to restrain competition) and vertical restraints (anti-competitive arrangements between firms along the production-distribution chain). Horizontal and vertical restraints include the following arrangements, which can be undertaken individually or in combination.

	HORIZONTAL RESTRAINTS
Price fixing	Competing suppliers enter into cooperative agreements regarding prices and sales conditions.
Restraint of output	Competing suppliers enter into agreements regarding output and product quality.
Market allocation	Competing suppliers allocate customers amongst themselves, who therefore cannot benefit from competition by other suppliers.
Exclusionary practices	Competing suppliers employ practices that inhibit or preclude the ability of other actual or potential suppliers to compete in the market for a product.

Collusive tendering (bid ragging)	Competing suppliers exchange commercially sensitive information on bids and agree to take turns as to who will make the most competitive offer.
Conscious parallelism	Competing suppliers generally set the same prices, but without an explicit agreement.
Other restraints on Competition	Generally, characterized by suppliers entering into co-operative agreements not to undertake certain actions of competitive value (e.g., advertising).
	VERTICAL RESTRAINTS
Exclusive dealing	A producer supplies distributors and guarantees not to supply other distributors in a given region.
Reciprocal exclusivity	A producer supplies on the condition that the distributor does not carry anybody else's products.
Refusal to deal	A supplier refuses to sell to parties wishing to buy.
Resale price maintenance	A producer supplies distributors only on the condition that the distributor sells at a minimum price set by the supplier.
Territorial restraint	A supplier sells to distributors only on the condition that the distributor does not market the product outside a specified territory.
Discriminatory pricing	A supplier charges different parties different prices under similar circumstances.
Predatory pricing	Suppliers sell at a very low price (or supply intermediate inputs to competitors at excessive prices) in order to drive competitors out of business.
Premium offers or loyalty rebates	A dominant supplier offers discounts or other inducements only to certain parties on the condition they do not sell someone else's products.
Tied selling	Producers force purchasers to buy goods they do not want as condition to sell them those they do want, or force resellers or wholesalers to hold more goods than they wish or need.
Full-line forcing	A supplier requires distributors, for access to any product, to carry all of the supplier's products.
Transfer pricing	May involve over-invoicing or under-invoicing of intermediate inputs between foreign affiliates. Under-invoicing can be used to facilitate predatory pricing.

[a] These may take the form of domestic cartels, import cartels, export cartels and international cartels.

[Reproduced in *World Investment Report 1997* from Boner, Roger Alan and Reinold Krueger, *The Basics of Anti-trust Policy: A Review of Ten Nations and the European Communities*, World Bank Technical Papers Series No. 160, 1991].

Government Policies and Distortions to Competition

Many government polices and regulations designed to serve certain social and economic objectives tend to distort competition. Swaminathan S. Aiyar, has made a pointed reference to the plethora of laws and rules in India that explicitly protect favoured players, reduce competition and give discretion in decision-making to politicians and bureaucrats in the name of public interest. He has observed that public interest is frequently and unabashedly invoked to protect one specific interest group (unionised labour, small scale industries, handloom weavers) with no explanation of how or why the interest of this group transcends all others. He has provided the illustration of restrictive policies which impede competition like reservation of industries for the public sector (Coal, Railways, Postal services, Insurance, Petroleum, etc.), canalisation of exports and imports through the public sector (Petroleum and some agricultural products), the jute packaging, order (compelling fertiliser and cement producers to use jute rather than plastic sacks resulting in leakage of material), reservation of items for the small-scale sector and reservation of items for the handloom sector in support of his contention that many governmental policies are anti-competitive in character. He has also referred to the Industrial Disputes Act which makes it impossible to retrench labour or close units without government permission, even if the units are unviable and to the Urban Land Ceiling Act which inhibits competition in using urban land. In the name of public interest, runs his further argument, protecting job leads to sacrifice of efficiency, raises potential costs and risks and discourages new investment. All governmental policies will have to be viewed through the competition lens to ensure that consumer interest and welfare and economic efficiencies and development dimensions are not pejorated.[7]

It may be noted that the High Level Committee on Competition Policy and Law, appointed by Government of India, recommended removal of several such policy induced distortions as a precondition for competition policy.

> **Many government policies and regulations are competition distorting.**

Even policy measures aimed at promoting competition may have conflicting impacts. As an UNCTAD Report[8] observes, governments rely on several policy tools to ensure that their markets remain contestable and that competition in markets is maintained as far as possible, so that economic growth and welfare are not adversely affected by the inefficient allocation or use of resources. The tools of such policy include trade policy, FDI policy, regulatory policy with respect to domestic economic activity, and competition policy. While the first three comprise rules and regulations that serve several purposes and not only that of maintaining competition with a view to fostering efficiency, the last relates specifically to the rules and regulations — implemented by competition authorities — with respect to arrangements among firms/suppliers and the conduct of individual firm/suppliers, generally but not exclusively, in national markets. It is increasingly recognized that consistency and coherence between the different policies — some of which, as mentioned above, could serve competing objectives — are important. This is reflected in the fact that, in many developing countries, trade liberalisation, FDI liberalisation and domestic deregulation are currently taking place simultaneously. This ensures that the contestability and competition introduced by one set of policies are not undermined by another; but it also makes the pain of adjustment to competition, especially for hitherto protected domestic firms, a problem requiring attention and action by governments.

Interface of FDI and Competition Law

As an UNCTAD Report points out, investment liberalisation and the adoption of competition laws have received impetus from the growth of regional free trade and integration agreements. The European Union, *for example,* includes the institution of a system for ensuring that competition is not distorted in the internal market as one of the means of attaining the basic goals of the Union. When NAFTA was created, Mexico introduced important reforms in its investment legislation and adopted a competition law comparable to that of its NAFTA partners. This process may receive further impetus in the future.

The growing trends of M&As and consolidation increase the importance of competition law.

Cross-border M&As can pose severe threats to competition, both at the time of entry and subsequently. Indeed the threat of monopoly or tight monopoly is potentially the single most important negative effect of cross-border M&As and therefore poses the single most important policy challenge. The challenge, more precisely, is to ensure that policies are in place to deal with those M&As that raise competitive concerns, and they are implemented effectively.[9] It may be noted that in the light of the growing M&As, countries like the United States have further strengthened their competition control system.

Prerequisites for a Competition Policy

Competition process is likely to run smoothly and thus lead to desirable results, only if several prerequisites are met. Micro-industrial governmental policies that may support or adversely impinge on the application of competition policy, according to the High Level Committee on Competition Policy and Law, would include the industrial policy; reservation for the small scale industrial sector; privatisation and regulatory reforms; trade policy, including tariffs, quotas, subsidies, anti-dumping action, etc.; state monopolies policy; and labour policy.

Modifications of many government policies and regulations are needed to prepare the ground for an effective competition policy and law.

There could be serious conflicts between trade policy and competition policy. In this context, therefore, in respect of the above policies, the Committee held the view that the essence and spirit of competition should be preserved while positing the Competition Policy and seeking to harmonise the conflicts between Competition Policy and Governmental Policy. According to the Committee, the Industries (Development and Regulation) Act, 1951 may no longer be relevant except for a matter like regulation of location and environmental protection; there should be no reservation for the small-scale sector of products which are on Open General License (OGL) for imports and there should be a progressive reduction and ultimate elimination of reservation of products for the small-scale industrial and handloom sectors; the economic reforms of liberalisation, deregulation and privatisation need to be further progressed and should be so designed that they strengthen the Competition Policy and *vice versa;* all trade policies should be open, non-discriminatory and rule-bound and they should fall within the contours of the competition principles; all physical and fiscal controls on the movement of goods throughout the country should be abolished; Government should divest its shares and assets in State monopolies and public enterprises and privatise them in all sectors other than those subserving defence and security needs and sovereign functions; all State monopolies and public enterprises will be under the surveillance of Competition Policy to prevent monopolistic, restrictive and unfair trade practices on their part; any form of discrimination in favour of the public sector and government commercial enterprises except where they relate to security concerns must be removed, while at the same time taking care not to create private monopolies out of public monopolies; the Industrial Disputes Act, 1947 and the connected statutes need to be amended to provide for an easy exit to the non-viable, ill-managed and inefficient units subject to their legal obligations in respect of their liabilities; structures like BIPR and the Sick Industrial Companies Act itself may be scrapped; concerns relating to trade dimensions *vis-a-vis* WTO agreements and principles need to be squarely addressed; Urban Land Ceiling Act should be repealed.

All the recommendations of the Committee apply to all industrial and professional enterprises including those in public and private sector.

The Committee suggested that the government while enacting an appropriate Competition Law for the country needs to address the prerequisites as recommended above and that the prerequisites will constitute a foundation over which the edifice of Competition Policy and Competition Law needs to be built.

Contours of Competition Policy

Noting that the focus for most Competition Laws today in the world is in the following three areas, the Committee centred its recommendations on the same.

- Agreement among enterprises
- Abuse of dominance
- Mergers or, more generally, combinations among enterprises.

Agreement Among Enterprises: Horizontal and vertical agreements between firms have the potential of restricting competition. Horizontal agreements refer to agreements among competitors and vertical agreements to an actual or potential relationship of buying or selling to each other.

The Committee recommended that both these types of agreements should be covered by the Competition Law, if it is established that they prejudice competition. Horizontal agreements relating to prices, quantities, bids (collusive tendering) and market sharing are particularly anti-competitive. Vertical agreements like tie-in arrangements, exclusive supply/distribution agreements and refusal to deal are also generally anti-competitive. Agreements that contribute to the improvement of production and distribution and promote technical and economic progress, while allowing consumers a fair share of the benefits should be dealt with leniently. Blatant price, quantity, bid and territory sharing agreements and cartels should be presumed to be illegal.

Abuse of Dominance: Dominance needs to be appropriately defined in the Competition Law in term of "the position of strength enjoyed by an undertaking which enables it to operate independently of competitive pressure in the relevant market and also to appreciably affect the relevant market, competitors and consumers by its actions." The definition needs to be also in terms of "substantial impact on the market including creating barriers to new entrants". The Committee did not consider it desirable to prescribe any arithmetical figure like percentage of market share to define dominance, as a firm with a high market share may conduct business ethically if there is a strong and effective rival in the relevant market and likewise, a firm with a small market share may abuse its market power, if its competitors diffusedly hold the remaining market share.

Abuse of dominance rather than dominance should be the key for Competition Policy/ Law. Abuse of dominance will include practices like restriction of quantities, markets and technical development. Abuse of dominance which prevents, restricts or distorts competition needs to be frowned upon by Competition Law. Relevant market needs to be an important factor in determining abuse of dominance.

Predatory pricing which is defined as the situation where a firm with market power prices below costs so as to drive competitors out of the market is generally prejudicial to consumer interest in the long-run. Instead of always taking an adverse view, it is desirable in the Committee's view that predatory pricing may be treated as an abuse, only if it is indulged in by a dominant undertaking.

By and large, abuse of dominance and exclusionary practices will need to be dealt with by the adjudicating Authority on the rule of reason basis.

Mergers: Mergers need to be discouraged, if they reduce or harm competition. The Committee, however, cautions against monitoring of all mergers by the adjudicating Authority, for the reason that very few Indian companies are of international size and that in the light of continuing economic reforms, opening up of trade and foreign investment, a great deal of corporate restructuring is taking place in the country and that there is a need for mergers, amalgamations, etc., as part of the growing economic process before India can be on an equal footing to compete with global giants, as long as the mergers are not prejudicial to consumer interest.

It is in this context that the Committee recommended that mergers beyond a threshold limit in terms of assets should require pre-notification. The threshold limit suggested is the value of assets of the merged identity at ₹ 100 crore or more and of the group to which merged entity belongs at ₹ 2,000 crore or more, both linked to Wholesale Price Index.

The Competition Law needs to be designed and implemented in terms of the contours enunciated above.

Competition Policy/Law needs to have necessary provisions and teeth to examine and adjudicate upon anti-competition practices that may accompany or follow developments arising out of the implementation of WTO Agreements. In particular, agreements relating to foreign investment, intellectual property rights, subsidies, countervailing duties, anti-dumping measures, sanitary and phytosanitary measures, technical barriers to trade and

Government procurement need to be reckoned in the Competition Policy/Law with a view to dealing with anti-competition practices.

Furthermore the Committee recommended as follows regarding State Monopolies, Regulatory Authorities, Government procurement, Foreign companies, Professions and Standards.

- The State Monopolies, Government procurement and foreign companies should be subject to the Competition Law. The Law should cover all consumers who purchase goods or services, regardless of the purpose for which the purchase is made.
- All decisions of the Regulatory Authorities can bė examined under the touch stone of Competition Law by the Competition Commission.
- Bodies administering the various professions should use their autonomy and privileges for regulating the standard and quality of the profession and not to limit competition. In the competitive and globalised environment there is need to encourage size, growth and international affiliation of professional firms. This should be encouraged and restraints should be removed.
- If quality and safety standards for goods and services are designed to prevent market access, such practices will constitute abuse of dominance/exclusionary practices.

COMPETITION ACT, 2002

The Competition Act, 2002, enacted in 2003, following the recommendation of the High Level Committee on Competition Policy and Law, is a landmark legislation that aims at promoting competition through prohibition of anti-competitive practices, abuse of dominance and regulation of combinations beyond a certain sizes. Certain amendments to this Act were made in 2007 and 2009.

With the coming into effect of the Competition Act, 2002 from September 1, 2009, the Monopolies and Restrictive Trade Practices (MRTP) Act, 1969, was repealed and later the Monopolies and Restrictive Trade Practices Commission was replaced by Competition Commission of India (CCI).

BOX 16.2: WHY THE NEW LAW?

In early nineties, when Government of India undertook widespread economic reforms, Indian enterprises started facing the heat of competition from domestic players as well as from global giants, which called for level playing field and investor-friendly environment. It was felt that the existing Monopolistic and Restrictive Trade Practices Act, 1969 ("MRTP Act") was not equipped adequately enough to tackle the competition aspect of the Indian economy. Hence, need arose for a new Act, shifting the focus from curbing monopolies to encouraging companies to invest and grow, thereby promoting competition while preventing any abuse of market power. Thus, a new competition law, Competition Act, 2002, was enacted in 2003.

Adopted from the Annual Report 2010-11 of Dept. of Company Affairs.

The Competition Act, which extends to the whole of India except the State of Jammu and Kashmir, deals mainly with anti-competitive agreements, combinations and abuse of dominance and it provides for the establishment of a Competition Commission to control these.

Objective

According to the introductory paragraph of the Act, it is an Act to provide, keeping in view of the economic development of the country, for the establishment of a Commission to prevent practices having adverse effect on competition, to promote and sustain competition in markets, to protect the interests of consumers and to ensure freedom of trade carried on by other participants in markets, in India, and for matters connected therewith or incidental thereto.

Main Provisions

Main provisions of the Act pertain to prohibition of anti-competitive agreements; prevention of abuse of dominant position and regulation of combinations. The Act also provides for the establishment of a Competition Commission to take care of these provisions and to protect the interests of consumers.

The Competition Act has essentially four components. The Act:

The Competition Act deals with anti-competitive agreements, abuse of dominant position and M&As detrimental to social interests.

- Prohibits anti-competitive agreements like cartels, which restrict freedom of trade and cause consumer harm by way of limiting production and distribution of goods and services and fixing prices higher than normal.
- Prohibits abusive behaviour of a dominant firm, who through its position of dominance may restrict markets and set unfair and discriminatory conditions.
- Regulates mergers and acquisitions of large corporations in order to safeguard competitive markets.
- Mandates competition advocacy. (With the objective to create awareness on competition issues, the Commission organizes interactive meetings, workshops and seminars, etc., with different regulatory bodies, policymakers, trade organizations, consumer associations and public at large.)

All the four components are inter-related and form an integrated whole. The first three essentially relate to enforcement, while the last one is related to the mandate for promoting competition enshrined in Section 49 of the Act.

Competition Commission and Competition Appellate Tribunal

The Competition Commission of India (CCI), established under the Competition Act, consisting of a Chairperson and six Members, became functional with effect from 1st March, 2009.

The following are the objectives of the Commission.

(*a*) To prevent practices having adverse effect on competition.

(*b*) To promote and sustain competition in markets.

(*c*) To protect the interests of consumers.

(*d*) To ensure freedom of trade.

The overarching aim of the Commission is to make markets work well for consumers using competition as the means. The Commission, in pursuance of its objectives, endeavours to do the following:

- Ensure fair and healthy competition in economic activities in the country for faster and inclusive growth and development of economy.
- Implement competition policies with an aim to effectuate the most efficient utilization of economic resources.
- Develop and nurture effective relations and interactions with sectoral regulators laws in tandem with the competition law.
- Effectively carry out competition advocacy and spread the information on benefits of competition among all stakeholders to establish and nurture competition culture in Indian economy.

The CCI is empowered for imposition of a penalty for contravention of its orders and in certain cases of continued contravention a penalty which may extend to rupees twenty-five crore or imprisonment which may extend to three years or with both.

The CCI is the authority for the administration, implementation and enforcement of the Competition Act. Appeals against the directions/decisions of CCI may be made to the COMPAT.

The Government of India also set up a Competition Appellate Tribunal (COMPAT) on 19th October, 2009, under the provisions of the Competition Act, 2002, to hear and dispose of appeals against any direction issued or decision made or order passed by the Competition Commission of India.

The Competition Appellate Tribunal is empowered to adjudicate on claims for compensation and to pass orders for the recovery of compensation from any enterprise for any loss or damage suffered as a result of any contravention of the provisions of the Act. For implementation of the orders of the Competition Appellate Tribunal as a decree of a civil court. An appeal against the orders of the Competition Appellate Tribunal can be filed to the Supreme Court.

Anti-competitive Agreements

The Act prohibits agreements in respect of production, supply, distribution, storage, acquisition or control of goods or provision of services, which causes or is likely to cause an appreciable adverse effect on competition within India.

According to the Act, agreements or decisions which have any of the following effects shall be presumed to have an appreciable adverse effect on competition:

(*a*) Directly or indirectly determining purchase or sale prices.

(*b*) Limiting or controlling s production, supply, markets, technical development, investment or provision of services.

(*c*) Sharing the market or source of production or provision of services by way of allocation of geographical area of market, or type of goods or services, or number of customers in the market or any other similar way.

(*d*) Directly or indirectly resulting in bid rigging or collusive bidding, shall be presumed to have an appreciable adverse effect on competition.

Further, any agreement amongst enterprises or persons at different stages or levels of the production chain in different markets, in respect of production, supply, distribution, storage, sale or price of, or trade in goods or provision of services, shall be deemed as an agreement in contravention of the relevant provisions of this Act if such agreement causes or is likely to cause an appreciable adverse effect on competition in India. Such agreements include:

The Competition Act prohibits agreements in respect of production or sale of goods and services having appreciable adverse effect on competition.

(*a*) tie-in arrangement;

(*b*) exclusive supply agreement;

(*c*) exclusive distribution agreement;

(*d*) refusal to deal;

(*e*) resale price maintenance,

Abuse of Dominant Position

Section 4 of the Competition Act lays down that no enterprise shall abuse its dominant position. Dominant position means a position of strength, enjoyed by an enterprise, in the relevant market, in India, which enables it to *(i)* operate independently of competitive forces prevailing in the relevant market; or *(ii)* affect its competitors or consumers or the relevant market in its favour.

The following cases are regarded as an abuse of dominant position, *viz.*, an enterprise—

(*a*) directly or indirectly, imposes unfair or discriminatory —

(*i*) condition in purchase or sale of goods or service; or

(*ii*) price in purchase or sale (including predatory price, *i.e.*, price which is kept below the cost with a view to reduce competition or eliminate the competitors) of goods or service.

However, such discriminatory condition or price which may be adopted to meet the competition is excluded from the application of this Section.

(*b*) limits or restricts —

(*i*) production of goods or provision of services or market therefore; or

(*ii*) technical or scientific development relating to goods or services to the prejudice of consumers; or

(c) indulges in practice or practices resulting in denial of market access; or

(d) makes conclusion of contracts subject to acceptance by other parties of supplementary obligations which, by their nature or according to commercial usage, have no connection with the subject of such contracts; or

(e) uses its dominant position in one relevant market to enter into, or protect, other relevant market.

Division of Enterprise Enjoying Dominant Position: According to Section 28 of the Act, the Competition Commissions may order the division of the enterprise enjoying dominant position to ensure that such enterprise does not abuse its dominant position. Such an order may provide for all or any of the following matters, namely:—

(a) the transfer or vesting of property, rights, liabilities or obligations;

(b) the adjustment of contracts either by discharge or reduction of any liability or obligation or otherwise;

(c) the creation, allotment, surrender or cancellation of any shares, stocks or securities;

(d) the formation or winding up of an enterprise or the amendment of the memorandum of association or articles of association or any other instruments regulating the business of any enterprise;

(e) the extent to which, and the circumstances in which, provisions of the order affecting an enterprise may be altered by the enterprise and the registration thereof;

(f) any other matter which may be necessary to give effect to the division of the enterprise.

Prevention of abuse of dominant position by firms is a very important objective of the Competition Act.

Regulation of Combinations

The Act provides for regulation of combination through mergers and acquisitions which causes or is likely to cause an appreciable effect on competition. The Competition Commission has the power to regulate mergers or combinations and to reverse mergers or combinations if it is of the opinion that a merger or combination has or is likely to have an 'Appreciable Adverse Effect' (AAE) on competition in India. The Competition (Amendment) Act, 2007 has mandated pre-merger clearances from CCI to ascertain whether a 'combination' has an 'AAE' on competition within India. Combinations include mergers, amalgamations and acquisition of control, shares, voting rights or assets.

Power to Exempt

The Central Government is empowered to exempt from the application of this Act, or any provision thereof, and for such period as it may specify:

(a) any class of enterprises if such exemption is necessary in the interest of security of the State or public interest;

(*b*) any practice or agreement arising out of and in accordance with any obligation assumed by India under any treaty, agreement or convention with any other country or countries;

(*c*) any enterprise which performs a sovereign function on behalf of the Central Government or a State Government, provided that in case an enterprise is engaged in any activity including the activity relatable to the sovereign functions of the Government, the Central Government may grant exemption only in respect of activity relatable to the sovereign functions.

SUMMARY

With increase in competition in consequent to the liberalisation, Government of India has introduced a competition policy and law, repealing the MRTP Act which sought to control monopolistic, restrictive and unfair trade practices which are prejudicial to public interest, besides regulating the growth and expansion of large firms, including M&As.

The main provisions of the Competition Act, 2002, pertain to prohibition of anti-competitive agreements; prevention of abuse of dominant position and regulation of combinations. The Act provides for the establishment of a Competition Commission of India (CCI) for the administration, implementation and enforcement of the Competition Act. Appeals against the directions/decisions of CCI may be made to the Competition Appellate Tribunal (COMPAT) established under the Act.

REFERENCES

1. UNCTAD, *World Investment Report 1997*, Bookwell, Delhi, 1998.
2. Chakravarthy, S., "Role of Competition Policy in Economic Development and the Indian Experience", *Asian Economic Review*, December 1999, pp. 386-7.
3. *Ibid.*, p. 392.
4. UNCTAD, *World Investment Report 1997*, p. 190.
5. *Ibid.*, p. 190.
6. *Ibid.*, p. 190.
7. Cited by Chakravarthy, *op. cit.*, p. 393.
8. UNCTAD, *World Investment Report 1997*, p. 190.
9. UNCTAD, *World Investment Report 2000*, p. xxvii.

ANNEXURE 16.1

MRTP ACT

The principal law in India to deal with competition was the Monopolies and Restrictive Trade Practices Act, 1969. The MRTP Act, brought into force from 1st June, 1970, was a very controversial piece of legislation. The High Level Committee on Competition Policy and Law, appointed by Government of India, recommended that a new Competition Act may be enacted and the MRTP Act may be repealed. The Government has accepted this recommendation. The MRTP Act has thus become a document of historical value. The salient features of this Act is given here because of the importance with which it reined the industrial sector of the country.

The main objectives of the MRTP Act were (1) Prevention of concentration of economic power to the common detriment, and (2) Control of monopolistic, restrictive and unfair trade practices which are prejudicial to public interest.

As a part of the economic reforms ushered in 1991, the MRTP Act was drastically amended by repealing the provisions of the Act pertaining to concentration of economic power, except the provisions empowering the Government to defuse concentration of economic power to the common detriment. In other words, the main thrust of the MRTP Act now is the achievement of prevention of monopolistic, restrictive and unfair trade practices. Thus, the 'M' has almost been knocked out of the MRTP Act. In other words, large companies have been freed from the MRTPA requirement of prior permission of the government for substantial expansion of existing undertakings, establishing new undertakings and M&As.

In accordance with the provisions of the Act, the Government of India had set up a Commission known as the Monopolies and Restrictive Trade Practices Commission. The MRTP Commission was vested with power to inquire into restrictive, monopolistic and unfair trade practices.

The MRTP Act empowered the Central Government to control and prohibit those monopolistic, restrictive and unfair trade practices that are, or are likely to be prejudicial to the public interest.

A monopolistic trade practice is a trade practice which has, or is likely to have, the effect of unreasonably preventing or lessening competition in the production, supply or distribution of any goods or services; limiting technical development and capital investment to the common detriment; or allowing the quality of goods or services to deteriorate.

A restrictive trade practice is a trade practice which has the effect, actual or probable of restricting, lessening or destroying competition. Such trade practices may tend to obstruct the flow of production or to bring about manipulation of prices or conditions of delivery, etc., to the common detriment.

An unfair trade practice is a trade practice which, for the purpose of promoting the sale, use or supply of any goods or the provision of any services, adopts one or more unfair trade practices (like misleading advertisements) and thereby causes loss or injury to the consumers of such goods or services, whether by eliminating or restricting competition or otherwise.

The Act also empowered the Commission to make any undertaking or person to pay compensation to the party who suffered a loss or damage as a result of the unfair trade practice carried on by the undertaking or person.

The MRTP Act was severely criticized because of its growth defeating provisions. We had a very inept situation of not allowing Indian companies to grow by capacity expansion, establishment of new units or by M&A and because of the short supply importing goods produced by foreign multinationals which were far larger in size than the Indian biggies, spending the scarce foreign exchange.

It is indeed a paradox that laws like the MRTP Act which were designed to prevent monopoly have in effect restricted competition. The MRTP Act has helped lo protect the market position of the large houses by restricting the competition between the large houses.

It is quite evident that the restrictions on the big houses have had many adverse effects — they have retarded competition, decelerated growth in the industrial and consequently in other sectors, and contributed to the foreign trade gap. For example, in the early seventies, having failed to make any headway within India, the only alternative left for the Birlas was to set up firms in other countries and it put up several successful companies in all the ASEAN countries. "This was surely a paradox. The same government which refused us permission to set up manufacturing capacities within the country, allowed us to set up industries outside the country for the same products for which it had said 'no' in India. Thus, we set up a viscose staple fibre plant in Thailand, and started exporting fibre back to India" (Aditya Birla, "State and industry must work together", *Business India*, 30th April, 1988, p. 94.)

☆☆☆

CHAPTER

17

Price and Distribution Controls

Control over price and distribution has been regarded as one of the important means of achieving the socio-economic goals in many planned, especially developing economies. Even market economies have price and distribution controls.

The important factors that call for price and distribution controls in countries like India are short supply of goods and services; unreasonable levels of prices in the free market and the very low levels of income of a large number of people.

Objectives of Price and Distribution Controls

The objectives of price and distribution controls, in general, are to supplement the efforts of other instruments of planning. The specific objectives of the control over price and distribution may be listed as follows:

> **Price and distribution controls aim at preventing abuses by business and to promote the welfare of the vulnerable sections.**

1. Equity or Distributive Justice: Growth with social justice has been accepted as a major objective of development. This implies that the fruits of development should be distributed equitably. But it has been generally accepted that inflation distorts income distribution against the poor. Many a times, the scarcity of "wage goods"— the essential consumer items — leads to blackmarketing, making the life of the poor more miserable. One of the prime objectives of price and distribution controls, therefore, is to protect the vulnerable sections against inflation and shortages, and ensure a reasonable level of consumption for them.

2. Maintain Quality of Goods and Services: Price and distribution controls aim at ensuring the quality of goods and services. For instance, the Industries (Development and Regulation) Act, 1951, the Essential Commodities Act, 1955, etc., empower the Government of India to control the quality of various goods and services.

3. Prevention of Monopolistic, Restrictive and Unfair Trade Practices: Prevention of certain trade practices that are detrimental to the common interest is another major objective of price and distribution controls. In India, the MRTP Act, 1969, seeks to prevent the monopolistic, restrictive and unfair trade practices that are prejudicial to the public interest. This Act, apart from trying to remove certain imperfections in supply, also aims at ensuring that capital investment and technical development are not hampered by such trade practices.

4. Augmentation of Supply: Increasing the supply of goods and services is of paramount importance to reduce the hardships of the people by making goods available at reasonable prices. And this is one of the objectives of the price and distribution controls. Laws like the Industries (Development and Regulation) Act and the Essential Commodities Act contain provisions to prevent unjustifiable reduction in production by industrial undertakings. The public distribution system of the Government of India envisages a comprehensive production-cum-distribution scheme.

5. Enlargement and Smoothening of the Supply System: To remove the imperfections in the supply system in order to ensure the availability of essential goods at reasonable prices to the vulnerable sections in all areas, it is essential to enlarge and strengthen the distribution channels to cover all areas. It is one of the aims of our public distribution system to provide the benefits of its services even to the remote areas and thereby assure social justice.

6. Supply of Inputs to Priority Sectors: Ensuring supply of essential inputs to the priority sectors at reasonable prices is an important objective of the price and distribution controls. For instance, in India, certain industries are accorded priority in the allocation of certain raw materials and intermediate goods which are in short supply. Small-scale industries, export industries, agriculture and other priority sectors have been given credit at concessional terms.

7. Resource Allocation: Control over prices and distribution enables the planning authorities to achieve the desired pattern of resource allocation more easily. Apart from distributing the productive resources as mentioned above, the price and distribution controls can be made use of in other ways also to achieve the objective of resource allocation. To encourage investment in a particular field, it is essential to ensure a remunerative price for the output. For this purpose sometimes price support schemes will have to be adopted. Considerable supply response to prices is noticed in case of certain agricultural commodities. In such cases, deliberate variations in relative prices may be effected to redistribute the area under different crops to obtain a desirable output mix.

8. Prevention of Hoarding and Blackmarketing: Hoarding and blackmarketing have almost become by-products of shortage economy. An effective system of control should prevent the creation of artificial scarcity by the unscrupulous businessmen for profiteering.

Laws like the Prevention of Blackmarketing and Maintenance of Supplies of Essential Commodities, and Essential Commodities Act, are designed to serve this purpose.

9. Control of Inflation and Deflation: As it is abundantly clear from the objectives mentioned above, control of inflation is a principal objective of price and distribution controls. In certain cases, however, prevention of fall in the prices is also the task of these controls. As there is a close inter-relationship between supply and prices, price and distribution policies should mutually support each other to achieve the desired objective.

PRICE POLICY IN INDIA

The price system can be used as a steering mechanism to secure the desired allocation of consumption and production, and thereby the interpersonal and inter-sectoral distribution of income. Hence, it is essential to have a price policy that is comprehensive enough to help achieve the various socio-economic aims. Today, the price policies of various nations aim, in general, at avoiding wide fluctuations in the price behaviour, mobilisation and optimum utilisation of resources by bringing about their rational allocation, providing price incentives for increasing production and redistribution of income in favour of the poor. The nature of price policy a nation should adopt, however, depends on the nature of the economy, objectives of development, the institutional framework, trade and commercial practices and the overall market behaviour.

When the First Five-Year Plan of India was formulated, the planners did not appear to have bothered much about the prices. As the First Plan experienced comparative price stability, the issue of prices was not a major concern while formulating the Second Plan also. But, during the Second Plan period, prices exhibited a disturbing trend and this became a matter of major concern. Hence, a separate chapter on Price Policy was incorporated, for the first time, in the Third Plan document.

The chapter on Price Policy for the Third Plan mainly dealt with the scope and limitations of Price Policy and the constituents of the Price Policy. It stated that the Price Policy in a developing economy should concentrate on two main objectives: *(a)* it must ensure that the movements of relative prices accorded with priorities and targets that had been set in the Plan; and *(b)* it must prevent any considerable rise in prices of essential goods that entered into the consumption of low income groups.

Fiscal and monetary discipline was conceived as the major constituent of price policy. It pointed out that fiscal policy must be directed to mopping up the excess purchasing power which tended to push up demands above the level of available supplies. The quantum of taxation must, in other words, be adequate to keep down consumption to the limits provided for in the Plan. The requirements of public sector investment programme must be met by the transfer of real resources from the public rather than by creation of fresh purchasing power. In other words, fiscal policy in all its aspects must aim at restraining consumption and mobilising savings more effectively.

It was stressed that monetary policy should go hand-in-hand with fiscal policy. Just as the latter should avoid the creation of excess purchasing power through government operations, the former should regulate the pace of credit creation through banks.

The policy also recognised the scope and limitations of the commercial policy in imparting stability to the economy.

While stressing that without adequate fiscal and monetary discipline, other regulatory measures would not have the desired effect, the policy recognised that fiscal and monetary policies by themselves might also not suffice to secure the right relationship between various prices or to prevent undue hardship to low and fixed income groups. "It may be necessary, then, to have physical allocations and direct controls in certain sectors. It will be agreed, for instance, that so long as steel is scarce, it should be distributed between competing uses on the basis of agreed priorities. It may, of course, be essential to raise the price of any commodity that is scarce; but it may not be desirable from an overall point of view to get the highest bidder to get the bulk of the available supplies, leaving the rest to their own devices. If, similarly, there is a shortage of an essential drug, control of prices and distribution at a fair price to genuine users would be the appropriate course of action to adopt. The same reasoning applies to essentials of life like food or cloth. The prices of what may be called basic essentials must be held reasonably stable, in regard to commodities that are less essential, or may be classed as comforts or luxuries, a rise in prices may have to be tolerated. In the case of comfort and luxuries, in fact, an important factor in policy is the need to raise more resources, a rise in their prices does not affect the common man. The techniques of price regulation may vary from commodity-to-commodity; in some cases an increase in production may be the only way to secure a reasonable level of prices. In other cases, buffer stocks, reorganisation of distribution arrangements and some direct controls may be inescapable."

Thus, the Price Policy recognised the importance of fiscal and monetary policies, commercial policy, physical controls, enhancement of supply, etc., in achieving its objectives.

Successive Plans have emphasised the need for achieving price stability and distributive justice. However, the basic objectives and approach enunciated the Price Policy formulated in the Third Plan continued in the successive plans without any remarkable change and more and more measures were taken by the government to realise the objectives. Decontrol of prices and distribution has been a part of the economic reforms ushered in 1991. Price and distribution controls would, however, continue in certain vital areas.

PRICE CONTROLS

A number of measures have been taken to control the prices. These measures include both indirect and direct controls.

Indirect Controls

Indirect controls are exercised mainly through the monetary policy, fiscal policy and commercial (foreign trade) policy.

The term monetary policy refers to the policy of the Central Bank of the country in respect of the cost and availability of credit. The rationale of using the monetary policy to control prices is that there is a very strong direct relationship between money supply and prices. *Ceteris paribus,* an increase in money supply results in an increase in prices and *vice versa*. Hence, a price rise is sought to be arrested by monetary contraction and a fall in prices is dealt with by monetary expansion.

The Reserve Bank of India (RBI) has been employing the Bank (Discount) Rate Policy, Open Market Operations and Variable Reserve Ratio Requirements and various methods of Selective (Qualitative) Credit Control. (See the chapter on *Monetary and Fiscal Policies* for details).

Monetary, fiscal and commercial policies can influence the general price level.

A policy that should go hand-in-hand with the monetary policy to make it effective is the fiscal policy. Fiscal policy refers to the policy of the government in respect of public revenue and public expenditure. Fiscal policy can influence the price level by increasing or reducing the purchasing power of the public. Further, it can affect prices by imposing or removing or varying taxes on commodities or services, and by subsidies. Taxes, like excise duties, sales tax and customs duty, can have a profound impact on the prices of commodities.

Commercial policy has also been used to a certain extent to stabilise the domestic economy. Prices can be kept under control by increasing the supply by importing goods which are in short supply. This has been done for such commodities as edible oils. Further, the government bans the export of certain items the supply position of which is not comfortable within the economy. To prevent an unwarranted fall in the prices, the government may sometimes resort to the deliberate export of certain items.

There are also some other measures such as buffer stock operations which can help avoid wide fluctuations in prices.

Direct Controls

The Central and State Governments in India have armed themselves with a number of Acts to exercise direct control over the functioning of the economy. Laws like the Industries (Development and Regulation) Act, the Essential Commodities Act, the MRTP Act, the Foreign Trade Development and Regulation Act [earlier the Imports and Exports (Control) Act], etc., empower the Central Government to control production, supply, distribution and price in a large number of cases.

Administered Prices

Administered price, a term coined by Lord Keynes, refers to the price which is set consciously by a single decision-making body — like a monopoly firm, a cartel, or a government agency — rather than being determined by the free play or market forces. However, the term administered price often refers to the government determined price.

Adminstered price often refers to the government determined price.

When the market forces of supply and demand are free to interact, the price of a product rises when the supply falls short of the demand and declines when the supply exceeds demand. But under the administered price system, as the price is fixed at a particular level, fluctuations in demand and supply do not cause any price fluctuation. In other words, the administered price is not an equilibrium price. Not only that, the administered price may not reflect the demand and supply conditions; sometimes it may not even absorb the full cost of production.

In India, the price of a number of key commodities were administered by the government. Some key commodities and services such as steel, coal, fertilisers, aluminium and electricity, whose prices were administered, account for about one-fifth of the total weight in the wholesale price index. Thus, in the past the administered price was an important factor affecting the general price level in India. At one time over 70 per cent of the goods and services sold by the public sector enterprises were subject to administered prices. This indicates the importance the administered price had in the Indian economy.

Administered prices were generally fixed on the recommendations of an expert body like the Bureau of Industrial Costs and Prices (BICP) or, in the case of certain public enterprises, on those of specially constituted Inter-Ministerial Committee or Groups. The BICP was later replaced by Tariff Commission.

While recommending prices, the recommendatory body normally goes by the guidelines for price fixation prescribed by the government and, *inter alia*, takes into account the cost of most efficient firms which account for a large percentage of the total output (to ensure a certain level of efficiency in production), the optimal norms of consumption of raw materials and energy as well as capacity utilisation, and provides a fair rate of return which has generally ranged between 10 and 14 per cent on net worth, depending on the differences with respect to factors such as risk, priority, growth prospects, etc. In order to reconcile the interests of consumers as well as producers, a system of retention prices for different producers on the basis of cost of production on one hand and uniform sale prices for consumers on the other had been recommended, and had been in operation in several cases such as steel, fertilisers, cement, etc. Price adjustments had been allowed for changes in major cost components from time-to-time, and a review in depth is undertaken after suitable intervals.

The principle of fair return is relevant to public enterprises as well. However, these enterprises are generally engaged in the provision of infrastructural services or in the manufacture and supply of basic industrial materials such as coal, steel and POL, or agricultural inputs, such as fertilisers; and an increase in their prices generally has a cascading effect. Hence, an attempt had been made to keep down their prices. This, together with managerial deficiencies and other factors, had resulted in inadequate resource generation by the public enterprises, losses in some of them, and a heavy draft on the public exchequer. It also meant the supply of goods and services produced in the public sector at subsidised prices even for non-priority uses, which had the effect of accentuating the imbalances between demand and supply. There was, therefore, a growing realisation that, in the context of continued inflationary pressure at home and abroad, administered prices should not be kept out of tune with other prices without heavy economic cost to the nation.

The principal aim of the administered price system is the protection of the interests of both the producers and consumers. But, in India, in many an instance, the system miserably failed to safeguard the interests of the producer as well as the consumer. Price controls retarded the growth of the concerned industries and increased market imperfections, resulting in persistent commodity shortages and rampant and flourishing black markets.

Industry circles argued that many a times the price was fixed on unrealistic capacity utilisation norms, and that there was a delay in granting price increases to cover cost escalations.

Take the case of the cement industry, for instance. The unrealistic price policy has retarded the growth of the cement industry and the resultant widening of the demand supply gap "has raised the price of cement in the blackmarket to about four times the official price. Government must also recognise that even imported cement costs twice as much as the indigenous product."

In short, the unrealistic price control policy in India, administered by inefficient and corrupt men at various administrative levels, has resulted in growing shortages and rampant blackmarketing, generating enormous black money.

With the advent of the economic reforms, there has been a phasing out of the administered prices.

Dual Pricing

Some commodities like sugar, cotton textiles, paper and aluminium were subject to dual pricing in India in the past.

The system of dual pricing has been designed to allow the weaker sections of the people or the privileged buyers like the government to get the commodity at a lower price. Under dual pricing, a part of the output of an industry may be acquired by the government at a price fixed by it, which is usually lower than the market price, and the remaining part of the output may be sold by the industry at the market price. For instance, under the dual pricing policy for sugar, a part of the total production of sugar was to be sold to the government as levy at the price fixed by the government. The non-levy sugar (the remaining part) was allowed to be sold at the free market price. Sometimes, the free market price went up to three times, the levy price.

The dual pricing system in our country was severely criticised. It was argued that such controls affected capital formation and production in such industries. It is said that the dual pricing system does not always permit the industry to make up for the loss on the levy sales by sales in the free market.

Another criticism is that the system encourages malpractices, blackmarketing, tax evasion, corruption and the generation of black money.

Subsidisation

Prices of certain commodities are directly affected by the policy of subsidisation. Important commodities the prices of which were deliberately kept low by the government subsidies were foodgrains, fertilisers and controlled cloth. Certain export goods also enjoyed the benefit of subsidies.

The principal objective of subsidies is the protection of weaker sections and priority sectors. For instance, foodgrains are subsidised to increase the consumption levels of the vulnerable sections. Certain export goods were subsidised to increase their price competitiveness in the international market so as to increase our foreign exchange earnings.

The steep increase in the outflow from the exchequer by way of subsidies has given rise to the demand for their reduction and even the abolition of certain subsidies. There are two principal arguments for reduction/abolition of subsidies, *viz.*, subsidies eat into the resources for development, and subsidies, as they exist today, cannot be justified on the grounds of economic equity and social justice.

The Essential Commodities Act

The main purpose of the Essential Commodities Act, 1955, was to provide, in the interest of the general public, for the control of the production, supply and distribution of, and trade and commerce in, certain commodities.

The government has listed a number of commodities as essential commodities. For the purpose of this Act, the Central Government may, by a notified order, declare any class of commodity to be an essential commodity.

This Act empowers the Central Government to regulate or prohibit the production, supply and distribution of, and trade and commerce in any essential commodity for securing any of the following purposes:

(*i*) Maintaining or increasing their supplies.

(*ii*) Equitable distribution and availability at fair prices of the commodities concerned.

(*iii*) Securing any essential commodity for the defence of India or the efficient conduct of military operations.

Where an offence under this Act has been committed by a company and it is proved that the offence has been committed with the consent or connivance of, or is attributable to any neglect on the part of, any director, manager, secretary or other officer of the company, such director, manager, secretary or other officer shall also be deemed to be guilty of that offence and shall be liable to be proceeded against and punished accordingly.

The State Governments have issued a large number of orders under this Act inhibiting the free movement of some foodgrains and other agricultural products. In the Budget Speech, 2001-2002, the Union Finance Minister observed that in the changed situation this is undesirable and the Act and therefore, the Government proposed to review the operation of this Act and to remove many of the restrictions on the free inter-state movement of foodgrains and other agricultural products and to prune down the list of essential commodities to the minimum required.

Other Laws to Control Production, Distribution and Prices

Apart from the Essential Commodities Act, there are several Acts which empower the government to control the production, supply, distribution and price of a large number of commodities.

For the purpose of securing the equitable distribution and availability at fair prices of any article or class of articles relatable to any scheduled industry, the Central Government can, under the Industries (Development and Regulation) Act, regulate their production, supply, distribution, trade and price.

The Essential Commodities Act and the Industries (Development and Regulation) Act are supplemented by the Monopolies and Restrictive Trade Practices Act, 1969, the Prevention of Blackmarketing and Maintenance of Supplies of Essential Commodities Act, 1980; the Conservation of Foreign Exchange and Prevention of Smuggling Act, 1947, etc.

THE PUBLIC DISTRIBUTION SYSTEM

A rapid increase in money supply and population and the slow growth in output usually create an imbalance between the demand for, and the supply of, essential consumer items. When the purchasing power of a vast segment of the population is very low, even a slight increase in the prices of wage goods seriously erodes the consumption power of the vulnerable sections. Hence, in a Welfare State, there should be some system to insulate them against such happenings. An important device we have in our country for this purpose is the Public Distribution System (PDS), under which the government makes available essential mass consumption goods at reasonable prices, especially to the poor.

PDS seeks to make essential items easily available at reasonable prices.

Evolution of the PDS in India

Public Distribution System existed in India even before Independence. During the pre-Independence era, the PDS was used as a short-term strategy to meet the war-time needs and famine conditions. With the dawn of planning, it assumed importance as one of the instruments for achieving the objectives of planning.

In the initial stages, the PDS has been pressed into 'off and on' operations, depending upon plentiful and depleted stocks of foodgrains in the country. Since 1956, the supplies of foodgrains under PL 480 programmes compelled the government to evolve a permanent system of a steady outlet for distribution.

In 1957, the Foodgrains Enquiry Committee, under the chairmanship of Mr. Ashok Mehta, recommended the setting up of an organisation for foodgrains' price stabilisation to counteract the fluctuations in their prices by buffer stock operations. The persistent food crisis during the Second and Third Plan periods made the demand for an effective public distribution system more strong. In April 1959, a maiden decision of "State Trading in Foodgrains" was taken by the government. Though the decision seemed to be a remarkable one, it could not be successfully implemented. However, concrete steps for partial state trading were taken after 1963-64, when the country felt an acute shortage of foodgrains.

The emergence of serious inflationary pressures in the early 1970s made a strong demand for an effective civil supplies arrangement. The Department of Civil Supplies was set up in April 1974; in October 1974, this department was converted into the Department of Civil Supplies and Cooperation. As a model department, its function was to assist multi-pronged fiscal, monetary and administrative action on the part of concerned Ministers and Departments of the Central and State Governments to control inflation and to augment the production and distribution of essential commodities. The bringing together of the Civil Supplies and Cooperation highlighted the government's policy to involve the cooperatives more actively in the public distribution system even while taking steps to strengthen the cooperative organisations, more particularly in the productive sectors.

Since 1974, State Governments have also set up their own Civil Supplies Departments to look after the distribution of essential commodities in their respective jurisdiction.

In August 1976, the Department of Civil Supplies and Cooperation was converted into a separate Ministry. The functions of the Ministry of Civil Supplies and Co-operation are two-fold:

(*i*) Those relating to civil supplies and allied matters, which include: (a) monitoring prices, the public distribution system, consumer protection, integrated management of the supply, prices and distribution of certain essential commodities; (b) regulating weights and measures; and (c) control of forward trading.

(*ii*) Those pertaining to cooperation. These include general policy in the field of cooperation, matters relating to national cooperative organisations, cooperative training, education, marketing, processing and consumer cooperation.

On July 1, 1979, the Union Government inaugurated the production-cum-distribution system. The main features of this system are:

(*i*) Every village or a group of villages having a population of 2,000 and above will have a fair price shop. In remote areas, the population coverage would be even less — about 1,000.

(*ii*) Commodity coverage will be extended with a view to strengthening the system.

(*iii*) For the successful implementation of the scheme, effective arrangement will be made for the procurement, including import wherever necessary, and buffer-stocking of the commodities for distribution.

(*iv*) In regard to certain manufactured articles, the Central Government would assist in establishing direct links between the manufacturers and the States and their approved agencies, including cooperatives, for the distribution of such items.

(*v*) Special care will be taken in the production and distribution of the items of basic consumption by the vulnerable sections of society.

In early 1980, the government decided to make the PDS a permanent feature of the economy and an integral part of its price stabilisation policy.

The cooperative sector is assigned an important role in the PDS in India. Besides consumer co-operatives in urban areas, there are very large number of village cooperative societies. At the secondary level, in semi-urban areas, there are several thousands of Agricultural Marketing Societies. Most of these, are engaged in the distribution of consumer articles. At the Central level, the National Agricultural Cooperative Marketing Federation (NAFED) and the National Cooperative Consumers' Federation (NCCF) carry out support price operations, maintenance of reasonable prices of essential items, creation of buffer stocks of surplus production, etc. Thus, the cooperatives have a large base and a great potential to contribute to the successful running of the PDS. But, the co-operatives, too, have their own organisational weaknesses. They have to streamline and strengthen the existing consumer cooperative structure to take up the gigantic task of supplying essential commodities to masses in rural, semi-urban and hilly and tribal areas.

Several states have also established State Civil Supplies Corporations to handle the distribution of essential commodities under the Public Distribution System.

The Indian Public Distribution System (PDS) is probably the largest distribution network of its type in the world. The system is designed to help both the producers and consumers of foodgrains by linking procurement to support prices and ensuring their distribution along with other essential commodities at affordable prices throughout the country. PDS continues to be a major instrument of Government's economic policy for ensuring food security for the poor.

The network of fair-price shops has been expanding over the years. In April 1999 there were about 4.52 lakh ration shops in the country.

Under the PDS the Central Government has assumed responsibility for procurement and supply of essential commodities, *viz.*, wheat, rice, levy sugar, imported edible oils and kerosene, to the State Governments and the Union Territories for distribution at affordable prices to the public. These commodities are made available to the States/UTs at fixed Central Issue Prices (CIP) which are determined by the Central Government and which generally involve subsidies borne by the Central Government. The Central Issue Prices of foodgrains are fixed by the Ministry of Food after taking into account the Minimum Support Price of foodgrains, statutory charges/taxes payable on the Minimum Support Prices and interest charged at the prescribed rate of interest. In the case of other items like sugar, kerosene and imported edible oils, the cost of procurement/production, margins to dealers, transportation incidentals, etc., are included while working out the Central Issue Prices. Some States/UTs also distribute additional items of mass consumption through the PDS outlets.

Targeted Public Distribution System: In June 1997 the Government launched the Targeted Public Distribution System (TPDS) by streamlining the PDS by issuing special cards to the families below the poverty-line (BPL) and selling essential articles under PDS to them at specially subsidised prices. The thrust is to include only the really poor and vulnerable sections of the society such as landless agricultural labourers, marginal farmers, rural artisans/craftsmen such as potters, tappers, weavers, blacksmiths, carpenters, etc., in the rural areas, and slum-dwellers and persons earning their livelihood on a daily basis in the informal sector, like porters, rickshawpullers and handcart pullers, fruit and flower sellers on the pavements, etc., in urban areas.

The TPDS is now in operation in all States/UTs except in Delhi and Lakshadweep.

The PDS, as it operates in our country, has been severely criticised. The major criticism is that the system is inefficient, the supply is not smooth, prompt and sufficient, and the quality of goods supplied is poor. There is a serious allegation that some of the goods of good quality are sold secretly to private traders and low quality goods are sold to the public by the PDS. This needs to be probed into by a competent authority.

In the Performance Appraisal Report (Civil), the Comptroller and Auditor General of India (CAG), has disclosed that the benefits of the public distribution system (PDS) in terms of food availability, income transfer, coverage of the needy and nutrition support did not accrue to the intended sections of society.

The report has pointed out several shortcomings relating to targeting of the beneficiaries, adequacy of food and nutritional security, meagre income transfer to the targeted group, high cost of operations, higher prices charged from the consumers, poor quality and non-existent vigilance system, which adversely affected fulfilment of the envisaged objectives of the PDS.

SUMMARY

Scarcity, market imperfections and social concerns made price and distribution controls as one of the important means of achieving the socio-economic goals in many planned, especially developing, economies. Even market economies have price and distribution controls.

The important factors that call for price and distribution controls in countries like India are short supply of goods and services; an unreasonable level of prices in the free market and the very low levels of income of a large number of people.

The objectives of price and distribution controls, in general, are to protect the interests of the vulnerable sections and to supplement the efforts of other instruments of planning. The price and distribution controls aim at any one or more of the following: Promotion of equity or distributive justice; ensuring the quality of goods and services, prevention of monopolistic, restrictive and unfair trade practices that are prejudicial to the public interest; augmentation of the supply; ensuring the availability of essential goods at reasonable prices to the vulnerable sections in all areas; ensuring supply of essential inputs to the priority sectors at reasonable prices, helping the planning authorities to achieve the desired pattern of resource allocation; prevention of hoarding and blackmarketing; control of inflation and deflation; etc.

The Planning Commission has proposed that the price policy in India, as in developing economies in general, should concentrate on two main objectives: (*a*) it must ensure that the movements of relative prices accorded with priorities and targets that had been set in the Plan; and (*b*) it must prevent any considerable rise in prices of essential goods that entered into the consumption of low income groups. Fiscal and monetary discipline has conceived as the major constituent of price policy. Fiscal discipline in India, however, has been conspicuous by its failure.

The important instruments of price and distribution controls are depicted in Fig. 17.1.

INSTRUMENTS OF PRICE AND DISTRIBUTION CONTROLS

Direct Controls
Controls exercised under laws, like the Essential Commodities Act, IDRA, etc., and the Public Distribution System

Indirect Controls
Controls exercised by policies like Monetary policy, Fiscal Policy, and Trade Policy

Fig. 17.1 : Instruments of Price and Distribution Controls

Ensuring supply of essential commodities at reasonable prices, particularly to the weaker sections and vulnerable areas, is mainly the responsibility of the Ministry of Civil Supplies and Cooperation. The responsibilities of the Ministry relating to civil supplies and allied matters include: *(a)* monitoring prices, the public distribution system, consumer protection, integrated management of the supply, prices and distribution of certain essential commodities; *(b)* regulating weights and measures; and *(c)* control of forward trading.

The Indian Public Distribution System (PDS), which is probably the largest distribution network of its type in the world, is designed to help both the producers and consumers of foodgrains by linking procurement to support prices and ensuring their distribution along with other essential commodities at affordable prices throughout the country. PDS continues to be a major instrument of Government's economic policy for ensuring food security for the poor.

Several states have also established State Civil Supplies Corporations to handle the distribution of essential commodities under the Public Distribution System.

The cooperative sector is assigned an important role in the PDS in India. Besides consumer cooperatives in urban areas, there are very large number of village cooperative societies. At the secondary level, in semi-urban areas, there are several thousands of Agricultural Marketing Societies. Most of these, are engaged in the distribution of consumer articles. At the Central level, the National Agricultural Cooperative Marketing Federation (NAFED) and the National Cooperative Consumers' Federation (NCCF) carry out support price operations, maintenance of reasonable prices of essential items, creation of buffer stocks of surplus production, etc.

The PDS was streamlined and in June 1997 the Government launched the Targeted Public Distribution System by issuing special cards to the families below the poverty line (BPL) and selling essential articles under PDS to them at specially subsidised prices. The thrust is to include only the really poor and vulnerable sections of the society such as landless agricultural labourers, marginal farmers, rural artisans/craftsmen such as potters, tappers, weavers, blacksmiths, carpenters, etc., in the rural areas, and slum-dwellers and persons earning their livelihood on a daily basis in the informal sector, like porters, rickshawpullers and handcart pullers, fruit and flowersellers on the pavements, etc., in urban areas. The TPDS is now in operation in all States/UTs except in Delhi and Lakshadweep.

The administration of the PDS has been far from satisfactory, as it operates in our country, has been severely criticised. The major criticism is that the system is inefficient, the supply is not smooth, prompt and sufficient, and the quality of goods supplied is poor. There is a serious allegation that some of the goods of good quality are sold secretly to private traders and low quality goods are sold to the public by the PDS. The Performance Appraisal Report (Civil), by the Comptroller and Auditor General of India (CAG), has disclosed that the benefits of the public distribution system (PDS) in terms of food availability, income transfer, coverage of the needy and nutrition support did not accrue to the intended sections of society.

Decontrol of prices and distribution has been a part of the economic reforms ushered in 1991. Price and distribution controls would, however, continue in certain vital areas.

☆☆☆

CHAPTER

18

Consumer Rights, Consumerism and Business

An important socio-political environment confronting the business is the growth of consumerism and the legislative measures to protect the consumers. Consumer movement had its conspicuous beginning and development in the United States. There has been a growth of consumer awareness in most countries leading to growth of consumerism and growing demand for consumer protection.

Though consumerism is not well developed in India, there are several consumer organisations in India like the Consumer Guidance Society of India (CGSI), Mumbai, and the Consumer Education and Research Centre (CERC), Ahmedabad, which are doing commendable work. Some of these organisations are very active in conducting product testing and exposing substandard quality and adulteration. The demand for regulatory measures or effective implementation of available measures for consumer protection have been substantiated by the results of such tests. ISI certification of food colours, demanded by the CGSI, is now mandatory. Consumer organisations also play an important role in redressing consumer grievances.

Since 1993, the Consumer Education and Research Society (CERS), sponsored by the CERC, has been performing a very bold and commendable task of comparative testing of consumer goods at their in-house laboratory, and since 1998 its publication *INSIGHT — The Consumer Magazine* has been carrying out test results far and near. The media have been publishing the test findings. These test results enable the consumers to evaluate and compare product of different companies. The manufacturers can, therefore, no longer be complacent.

Consumer movement is growing, *albeit* slowly, in India. It may gather momentum from the growing consumer awareness and the growing feeling that the consumer is ruthlessly exploited and taken for a ride. Many products fail to satisfy the quality requirements and many sellers do not favourably respond to the genuine grievances of consumers.

Many products tests conducted by some consumer organisations have brought to light alarming facts regarding product quality and safety and, they have, therefore, been very vehemently demanding governmental action ensuring quality standards. Consumers have been increasingly taking resort to redressal measures. In short, the business can no more take the consumer for granted.

This does not, however, mean that consumerism is necessarily a problem for the business. Consumerism is, in fact, regarded as an opportunity by consumer-oriented businessmen, as described later in this chapter.

Consumer Rights

Consumers in the advanced countries, obviously, are much more conscious of their rights than in countries like India. In 1962, President John F. Kennedy, and in 1965, President Johnson emphasised the consumer rights and gave an impetus to consumerism in the USA. and other countries.

Important consumer rights include:

1. Right against exploitation by unfair trade practices.
2. Right to protection of health and safety from the goods and services the consumers buy or are offered free.
3. Right to be informed of the quality and performance standards, ingredients of the product, operational requirements, freshness of the product, possible adverse side effects and other relevant facts concerning the product or service.
4. Right to be heard if there is any grievance or suggestions.
5. Right to get the genuine grievances redressed.
6. Right to choose the best from a variety of offers.
7. Right to a physical environment that will protect and enhance the quality of life.

The Consumer Protection Act, 1986, has listed the consumer rights it seeks to protect in India. Details of the Act are given at the end of the Chapter.

BOX 18.1 : RESPONSIBILITIES OF CONSUMERS

Rights do not exist independently. Like a coin which has obverse and reverse, consumer rights have the other side, consumer responsibilities. They are:

1. The consumer should not make vague or general complaints, but have a specific complaint, with supporting information and proof such as a bill.
2. The consumer should try to understand the viewpoint of the seller before making a complaint.

3. In some situations, consumers have to cooperate with the sellers. For instance, in observing a queue, or in a situation of coin shortage using the coupons issued by the bus transport system.
4. Consumers, in asserting their rights, should not inconvenience or hurt other sections of the public. For instance, *Rasta Roko, Satyagraha, Dhama, Bandh,* etc., are ways of expressing one's anger and generating enthusiasm for a cause among general public, but they result in disrupting normal life for others. This is not justified.
5. The consumers should, as a rule, complain against a system and not attack individuals who are incumbents of posts. In most cases, the system or practices call for a change, not individuals. If "A" is removed or transferred from a post, "B" will occupy it, and may be equally helpless in the particular situation to serve consumers!

Courtesy: M.R. Pai, *Guidelines to Consumers — Rights and Responsibilities,* 1987.

(Sponsored in public interest by the Rotary Club of Mumbai)

Exploitation of Consumers

Consumers are, however, by and large, practically denied most of these rights. They are exploited by a large number of restrictive and unfair trade practices. A situation has developed in which the public have become victims of false claims for products blatantly advertised. Behavioural science is extensively applied to marketing to ruthlessly exploit the consumers by stimulating the weak points and soft corners of their mind. Misleading, false or deceptive advertisements are quite common. Many a times, the advertisements deliberately give only half truths so as to give a different impression than is the actual fact. Thus, advertisements may be misleading because things that should be said have not been said, or, because advertisements are composed or purposefully presented in such a way as to mislead. The situation is such that misrepresentations about the quality of a product or the potency of a drug or medicine can be projected without much risk.

As the high-powered Expert Committee on Companies and MRTP Acts, popularly known as the Sachar Committee, points out, fictitious bargains are another common form of deception. Many devices are used to lure buyers into believing that they are getting something for nothing or at a nominal value for their money. Prices may be advertised as generally reduced and cut when in reality the goods may be sold at sellers' regular prices.

Thus, apart from the monopolistic and restrictive trade practices that have the effect of restricting competition and increasing the market imperfections to the common detriment, consumer exploitation through unfair trade practices that mislead or dupe the customers has become widespread. And it is this situation that has largely led to the growth of consumerism.

Consumerism

Philip Kotler defines Consumerism as "a social movement seeking to augment the rights and powers of the buyers in relation to sellers".[1] Boyd and Allen state that "although often abused as a term, consumerism may be best defined as the dedication of those activities of both public and private organisations which are designed to protect individuals from practices that impinge upon their rights as consumers."[2]

In his speech delivered at the 44th Annual General Meeting of *Hindustan Lever, Ltd.* in 1977, the Chairman, Mr. T. Thomas, rightly pointed out: "While the producer has the power or the right to design the product, distribute, advertise and price it, the consumer has only the power of not buying it. One may argue that the producer runs the greater risk in spite of having several rights because the Veto power remains with the consumer. However, the consumer often feels that while he has the power of Veto, he is not always fully equipped to exercise that power in his best interests. This situation may be the effect of lack of information, too much indigestible information or even misinformation from one or several competing producers. This problem facing the consumer has led to 'consumerism'. It is worthwhile to note that consumerism, like several, other social movements, *e.g.*, independence movement Civil Rights movement, etc., has been the result of a social conflict and cannot, therefore, be wished away. It will be with us till the conflict facing the consumer is resolved."

Consumerism, interpreted as a collective endeavour of the consumers to protect their interests, is a manifestation of the failure of the business, including that of the public sector, and the government to guarantee and ensure the legitimate rights of the consumers.

Consumer Protection

For effective consumer protection, a practical response on the part of three parties, for example, the business, the government and the consumers, is essential.

Firstly, the business, comprising the producers and all the elements of the distribution channels, has to pay due regard to consumer rights. The producer has an inescapable responsibility to ensure efficiency in production and the quality of output. He should also resist the temptation to charge exorbitant prices in a seller's market. Many a times, the imperfections on the supply side, like hoarding and blackmarketing, mercilessly gouge the consumer. Hence, a socially responsible producer should see to it that whatever is produced reaches the ultimate consumer in time and at reasonable prices.

As T. Thomas observes, "Restraint is best exercised voluntarily than through legislation which will otherwise become inevitable. Advertising agencies and marketing management have a very important role to play in this respect. By overplaying the claims, they will be cutting the very branch on which they are perched."[3]

Secondly, the Government has to come to the rescue of the helpless consumer to prevent him from being mislead, duped, cheated and exploited. It should also take special care of the vulnerable sections.

The UN Guidelines for Consumer Protection points out that "the governmental role in consumer protection is vital and finds expression through policy-making, legislation and the development of institutional capacity for its enforcement. To provide a legal basis for enforcing basic consumer rights, every country needs to have an irreducible minimum of consumer protection legislation, covering physical safety, promotion and protection of consumers' economic interests, standards for the safety and quality of goods and services, distribution facilities, redress, and education and information programmes. Governments also require the necessary machinery to enforce such legislation." The Guidelines encourage the governments to develop, strengthen or maintain a strong consumer protection policy. In so doing, each government must set its own priorities for the protection of consumers in accordance with its economic and social circumstances and the needs of its population.

The UN Guidelines also calls upon the government to establish distribution facilities for essential consumer goods and services. It is suggested that governments should, where appropriate, consider: (a) Adopting or maintaining policies to ensure the efficient distribution of goods and services to consumers; where appropriate, specific policies should be considered to ensure the distribution of essential goods and services where this distribution is endangered, as could be the case particularly in rural areas. Such policies could include assistance for the creation of adequate storage and retail facilities in rural centres, incentives for consumer self-help and better control of the conditions under which essential goods and services are provided in rural areas; and (b) encouraging the establishment of consumer cooperatives and related trading activities, as well as information about them especially in rural areas.

Further, according to the Guidelines, governments should establish or maintain legal and/or administrative measures to enable consumers or, as appropriate, relevant organisations to obtain redress through formal or informal procedures that are expeditious, fair, inexpensive and accessible. Such procedures should take particular account of the needs of low-income consumers. Governments should also encourage all enterprises to resolve consumer disputes in a fair, expeditious and informal manner, and to establish, voluntary mechanisms, including advisory services and informal complaints procedures, which can provide assistance to consumers. Information on available redress and other dispute-resolving procedures should be made available to consumers.

The motive of private gain tempts business to maximise income by socially undesirable trade practices; and this calls for government intervention. Statutory action to protect the interests of consumers has become quite common. In the United Kingdom, for instance, the Trade Description Act, 1968, prohibits the use of misleading descriptions of goods or services or misleading representation of price reductions. In a number of countries, pro-consumer legislation contains provisions that enable an affected party to seek remedy for compensation for the loss or damage suffered by it at the hands of a person who has indulged in prohibited practices. This is true of the Sherman Act and the Clayton Act of the USA; the Federal Act of Switzerland, the Act Against Restraint of Competition of Spain, the Act concerning Prohibition of Private Monopoly and Maintenance of Fair Trade of Japan, the Trade Practices Act of Australia, the Combines Investigation Act of Canada, etc.

In some countries, statutory bodies are empowered to require the advertiser to substantiate the claims made in the advertisements. For instance, the Federal Trade Commission (FTC) of the United States can seek *affirmative disclosures.* That is, if information in an advertisement is considered insufficient by the FTC, the Commission may require a company to disclose in its advertising some of the deficiencies or limitations of its product or service so that the consumer can judge its negative, as well as, positive attributes. The FTC can also require the advertisers to submit on demand by the Commission data to back-up advertising claims for a product's safety, performance, quality or price comparability. The intent of this *substantiation* is to help consumers make more reasoned choices by having information made available to them. Members of many industry groups, including automobiles, appliances, soaps and detergents, television sets, dentistries, hearing aids, and all over-the-counter drugs have been ordered to provide the Commission with documentation in support of their designated advertising claims. *Corrective advertising* requirements have increasingly been a part of many FTC consent orders. Corrective advertising doctrines are based upon the idea that inaccurate information has already been communicated by advertisers, and that corrective advertising is needed to eliminate the lingering effects of such information.[4]

Thirdly, consumers should accept consumerism as a means of asserting and enjoying their rights. Consumerism should succeed in making the business and the government more responsive to the rights of the consumers. *Consumerism is a social force to (i) make the business more honest, efficient, responsive and responsible, and (ii) pressurise the government to adopt the necessary measures to protect consumer interests by guaranteeing their legitimate rights.*

Peter Drucker has remarked that "consumerism is the shame of the total marketing concept",[5] implying that the concept is not widely implemented. Consumerism reflects not only the failure of the business to widely implement the marketing concept but also the need to give the business policies a social orientation so as to enhance long-run social welfare. As Philip Kotler observes, "consumerism is a clarion call for a *revised marketing concept*".[6] Hence, the original marketing concept has to be broadened to include the societal marketing concept.

"The societal marketing concept calls for customer orientation backed by integrated marketing aimed at generating customer satisfaction and long-run consumer welfare, as the key to attaining long-run profitable volume."[7]

As Kotler points out, "the addition of long-run consumer welfare asks the businessman to include social and ecological considerations in his product and market planning. He is asked to do it not only to meet his social responsibilities but also because failure to do this may hurt his long-run interests as producer."[8] Thus, the message of consumerism is not a setback for marketing but rather points to the next stage in the evolution of enlightened marketing. Just as the sales concept said that sales were all important, and the original marketing concept said that consumer satisfaction was also important, the societal marketing concept has emerged to say that long-run consumer welfare is also important."[9] Hence, he feels that consumerism will be enduring, beneficial, pro-marketing and ultimately profitable. "Consumerism mobilises the energies of consumers, businessmen and government leaders to seek solutions to several complex problems in a technologically advanced society. One of these is the difference between serving consumer desires efficiently and serving their long-run interests. To marketers, it says that products and marketing practices must be found which combine short-run and long-run values for the consumer. It says that a societal marketing is an advance over the original marketing concept and a basis for earning increased consumer goodwill and profits. The enlightened marketer attempts to satisfy the consumer *and* hence his total well-being on the theory that what is good in the long-run for consumer is good for business."[10]

Non-governmental Organisations: NGOs or voluntary organisations have a very important role in consumer protection. Successful consumer movements almost everywhere owe a lot to the efforts of such *consumer advocates.*

It may be noted that one of the stated objectives of the UN Guidelines for Consumer Protection is to facilitate the development of independent consumer groups which should have the freedom to present their views in decision-making processes affecting them. The Guidelines state that consumer organisations should be encouraged to monitor adverse practices, such as the adulteration of foods, false or misleading claims in marketing and service frauds. Business and consumer groups should, also be encouraged by governments to formulate codes of marketing and other business practices to ensure adequate consumer protection. Consumer groups have a role to play as well in undertaking education and information programmes, particularly for low-income populations. Promoting the growth of a strong consumer movement and increasing protection for people in their role as consumers are central aims of Consumers International's work. To this end, it assists newly formed consumer groups in developing countries. Consumers International's independence is guaranteed by strict membership rules — organisations that join must be non-profit making and non-commercial and must operate exclusively in the consumers' interest.

Utility of Consumerism

Well-organised and dynamic consumerism may be expected to produce the following results:

1. Producers and sellers will not take the consumer for granted. When consumers are strong enough to protect their rights, the business will be compelled to shun unfair trade practices.
2. Consumerism will provide feedback for the business. It will enable the producers to understand consumers' grievances, needs and wants. This will assist in the more effective implementation of the marketing concept or the societal marketing concept, depending upon the nature of consumerism.
3. Producers will be able to enlist the support of consumers to minimise the imperfections on the distribution front. Several times the supply position is made worse by hoarding and blackmarketing by traders. Further, many sellers have a tendency to charge a price which is higher than the actual by giving one or other reason. There is no reason why the consumer and producer should not cooperate to get rid of the unscrupulous traders.

(The above points indicate that consumerism is an opportunity for honest and dynamic firms. In fact, quite a few leading businessmen view it so.)

4. Consumerism will make the government more responsive to consumer interests, prompt it to take necessary, statutory measures, and make the required institutional arrangements to safeguard consumer rights.

UN Guidelines for Consumer Protection

After many years of hard lobbying by the International Organisation of Consumer Unions (later renamed as Consumers' International), on 9 April, 1985, the United Nations adopted the Guidelines for Consumer Protection by the General Assembly which provide for enhanced protection of consumers by enunciating various steps and measures around seven themes: (1) Physical Safety, (2) Economic Interests, (3) Standards, (4) Essential Goods and Services, (5) Redress, (6) Education and Information, and (7) Health. The Guidelines also provide for international cooperation in the area of consumer protection. These Guidelines were reviewed from time-to-time by the UN and resolutions adopted to take the issues forward.

Objectives: Taking into account the interests and needs of consumers in all countries, particularly those in developing countries; recognizing that consumers often face imbalances in economic terms, educational levels, and bargaining power; and bearing in mind that consumers should have the right of access to non-hazardous products, as well as the importance of promoting just, equitable and sustainable economic and social development, these guidelines for consumer protection have the following objectives:

1. To assist countries in achieving or maintaining adequate protection for their population as consumers.
2. To facilitate production and distribution patterns responsive to the needs and desires of consumers.
3. To encourage high levels of ethical conduct for those engaged in the production and distribution of goods and services to consumers.
4. To assist countries in curbing abusive business practices by all enterprises at the national and international levels which adversely affect consumers.
5. To facilitate the development of independent consumer groups.
6. To further international cooperation in the field of consumer protection.
7. To encourage the development of market conditions which provide consumers with greater choice at lower prices.

General Principles: Governments should develop, strengthen or maintain a strong consumer protection policy, taking into account the guidelines set out below. In so doing, each government must set its own priorities for the protection of consumers in accordance with the economic and social circumstances of the country, and the needs of its population, and bearing in mind the costs and benefits of proposed measures.

The legitimate needs which the guidelines are intended to meet are the following:

1. The protection of consumers from hazards to their health and safety.
2. The promotion and protection of the economic interests of consumers.
3. Access of consumers to adequate information to enable them to make informed choices according to individual wishes and needs.
4. Consumer education.
5. Availability of effective consumer redress.
6. Freedom to form consumer and other relevant groups or organisations and the opportunity of such organizations to present their views in decision-making processes affecting them.

Governments should provide or maintain adequate infrastructure to develop, implement and monitor consumer protection policies. Special care should be taken to ensure that measures for consumer protection are implemented for the benefit of all sectors of the population, particularly the rural population.

All enterprises should obey the relevant laws and regulations of the countries in which they do business. They should also conform to the appropriate provisions of international standards for consumer protection to which the competent authorities of the country in question have agreed.

Guidelines: The following guidelines should apply both to home-produced goods and services and to imports.

In applying any procedures or regulations for consumer protection, due regard should be given to ensuring that they do not become barriers to international trade and that they are consistent with international trade obligations.

Physical Safety: Governments should adopt or encourage the adoption of appropriate measures including legal systems, safety regulations, national or international standards, voluntary standards and the maintenance of safety records to ensure that products are safe for either intended or normally foreseeable use.

Promotion and Protection of Consumers' Economic Interests: Government policies should seek to enable consumers to obtain optimum benefit from their economic resources. They should also seek to achieve the goals of satisfactory production and performance standards, adequate distribution methods, fair business practices, informative marketing and effective protection against practices which could adversely affect the economic interests of consumers and the exercise of choice in the marketplace.

Consumers should also be protected from such contractual abuses as one-sided standard contracts, exclusion of essential rights in contracts, and unconscionable conditions of credit by sellers.

Standards for the Safety and Quality of Consumer Goods and Services: Governments should, as appropriate, formulate or promote the elaboration and implementation of standards, voluntary and other, at the national and international levels for the safety and quality of goods and services and give them appropriate publicity. National standards and regulations for product safety and quality should be reviewed from time-to-time, in order to ensure that they conform, where possible, to confirm generally accepted international standards. Where a standard lower than the generally accepted international standard is being applied because of local economic conditions, every effort should be made to raise that standard as soon as possible.

Governments should encourage and ensure the availability of facilities to test and certify the safety, quality and performance of essential consumer goods and services.

Distribution Facilities for Essential Consumer Goods and Services: Governments should, where appropriate, consider: *(a)* Adopting or maintaining policies to ensure the efficient distribution of goods and services to consumers; where appropriate, specific policies should be considered to ensure the distribution of essential goods and services where this distribution is endangered, as could be the case particularly in rural areas. Such policies could include assistance for the creation of adequate storage and retail facilities in rural centres, incentives for consumer self-help and better control of the conditions under which essential goods and services are provided in rural areas. *(b)* Encouraging the establishment of consumer cooperatives and related trading activities, as well as information about them especially in rural areas.

Measures Enabling Consumers to Obtain Redress: Governments should establish or maintain legal and/or administrative measures to enable consumers or, as appropriate, relevant organisations to obtain redress through formal or informal procedures that are expeditious, fair, inexpensive and accessible. Such procedures should take particular account of the needs of low-income consumers.

Governments should encourage all enterprises to resolve consumer disputes in a fair, expeditious and informal manner, and to establish voluntary mechanisms, including advisory services and informal complaints procedures, which can provide assistance to consumers. Information on available redress and other dispute-resolving procedures should be made available for consumers.

Education and Information Programmes: Governments should develop or encourage the development of general consumer education and information programmes, bearing in mind the cultural traditions of the people concerned. The aim of such programmes should be to enable people to act as discriminating consumers, capable of making an informed choice of goods and services, and conscious of their rights and responsibilities. In developing such programmes, special attention should be given to the needs of disadvantaged consumers, in both rural and urban areas, including low-income consumers and those with low or non-existent literacy levels.

Consumer education should, where appropriate, become an integral part of the basic curriculum of the education system, preferably as a component of existing subjects.

Consumer education and information programmes should cover such important aspects of consumer protection as the following: *(a)* Health, nutrition, prevention of food-borne diseases and food adulteration; (*b*) Product hazards; (*c*) Product labelling; (*d*) Relevant legislation, how to obtain redress, and agencies and organisations for consumer protection; (*e*) information on weights and measures, prices, quality, credit conditions and availability of basic necessities; and (*f*) As appropriate, pollution and environment.

Governments should encourage consumer organisations and other interested groups, including the media, to undertake education and information programmes, particularly for the benefit of low-income consumer groups in rural and urban areas.

Business should, where appropriate, undertake or participate in factual and relevant consumer education and information programmes.

Consumer Protection and Consumerism in India — Plight of the Indian Consumer

An examination of the important problems facing the Indian consumer would make clear the need for more effective government intervention and consumer movement to safeguard consumer rights.

The following factors make the plight of the Indian consumer miserable:

1. Short supply of many goods and services, especially of essential items, is a very serious problem afflicting the Indian consumer. The demand-supply imbalance has produced all the associated evils of profiteering, hoarding and blackmarketing, corruption, nepotism, irresponsiveness and arrogance towards consumers. Although the situation has improved as a result of the increase in competition due to liberalisation, it is still far from satisfactory.
2. The Indian consumer is also the victim of lack of *effective* or *workable competition*. "Competition among sellers, even though imperfect, may be regarded as effective or workable if it offers buyers real alternatives sufficient to enable them, by shifting their purchases from one seller to another, substantially to influence quality, service, and price. Competition, to be effective, need not involve the standardisation of commodities; it does, however, require the ready substitution of one product for another; it may manifest itself in differences in quality and service as well as in price. Effective competition depends also upon the general availability of essential information; buyers cannot influence the behaviour of sellers unless alternatives are known. It requires the presence in the market of several sellers, each of them possessing the capacity to survive and grow, and the preservation of conditions which keep alive the threat of potential competition from others.... The test of effectiveness and workability in competition among sellers is thus to be found in the availability of buyers of genuine alternatives in policy among their sources of supply."[11] (The above two points should not be confused as one and the same. Short supply refers to quantitative insufficiency, whereas lack of effective competition refers to dearth of enough alternatives.)
3. Many products with which consumers in advanced countries are quite familiar are still new to a very large segment of the Indian consumers. The unfamiliarity of

the consumers with product features makes the sale of substandard, inferior or even defective products easier in India than in advanced countries.

4. Due to low literacy levels and unsatisfactory information flows, the Indian consumers, by and large, are not conscious of all their rights. This encourages irresponsible and unscrupulous business attitudes and tactics.
5. It has been said that the legal process in India is comparatively time-consuming and cumbersome. This discourages the consumers from seeking the redressal of their grievance by means of the judicial process.
6. Consumerism in India is not well organised and developed.
7. Though the public sector had been developed and expanded to serve the public interest by providing effective competition to the private sector, increasing production, improving distribution, etc., it failed to produce benefits that were commensurate with the investment. It is an irony that though consumer welfare is an avowed objective of the public sector, in certain areas the poor performance of the public sector monopolies has made the plight of the consumer more miserable. Some of them have even been charged with unfair trade practices.
8. Though there are a number of laws to safeguard the interests of consumers, they are not effectively implemented and enforced to achieve the objectives.

The above factors call for effective State intervention and consumerism to ensure the rights of consumers.

Government Measures

In India, the Government has taken a number of measures to protect consumer interests. The various Government measures may be classified into *(i)* statutory regulation of private business, and *(ii)* development of the public sector.

Statutory Regulation: Government of India has armed itself with a number of statutory weapons to control the production, supply, distribution, price and quality of a large number of goods and services. It is empowered to regulate the terms and conditions of sale, the nature of trade and commerce, etc. There is a feeling that, "unlike in the West, the Government in India has a large number of controls on industry and is, therefore, in a position to respond more swiftly and effectively than Western Governments. In some ways, our bureaucracy has perfected the art of assuming the guardianship of all interests of the consumers and the vulnerable sections."[12]

Important legislations in this respect include the MRTP Act, Industries (Development and Regulation) Act, Essential Commodities Act, Prevention of Food Adulteration Act, Prevention of Blackmarketing and Maintenance of Supplies of Essential Commodities Act, Trade Marks and Merchandise Marks Act, Sale of Goods Act, Indian Patents and Designs Act, Agricultural Products Grading and Marketing Act, Indian Standard Institute's Certification Act, Standard Weights and Measures Act, Imports and Exports Control Act, Packaged Commodities Order, Price and Stock Display Order, Consumer Protection Act, etc.

There are, thus, a good number of laws to protect consumer interests. But a common complaint is that these laws are not effectively implemented.

The Monopolies and Restrictive Trade Practices Act, 1969, contains provisions to deal with monopolistic, restrictive and unfair trade practices that are prejudicial to public interest.

Growth of Public Sector: There had been a significant growth and expansion of the public sector in India. One of the most important objectives of the public sector was the enhancement of consumer welfare by increasing production, improving efficiency in production and supply, making available goods and services at fair prices, curbing private monopolies and reducing market imperfections, improving the distribution system, and so on. The public sector, in fact, is expected to implement the societal marketing concept.

There is, however, a general feeling that the public sector in India has still a long way to go to realise these objectives. It has established monopolies or near-monopolies in public utilities, whose performance is far from satisfactory.

The irony, further, is that certain laws like the MRTP Act are not applicable to the public sector. As the Sachar Committee has observed, "There is no justification for exempting government and government-controlled/owned undertakings from the provisions relating to control and prohibition of monopolistic and restrictive trade practices and the....provisions relating to unfair trade practices..... The beneficiary of monopoly legislation is the consumer and it is only fair and reasonable that undertakings owned or controlled by the Government should be subject to the same type of rigour and discipline as the private sector undertakings where the interests of consumers are involved."[13]

The government has developed the public distribution system to reduce the hardships of consumers, especially of the vulnerable sections, by making essential consumer goods available more equitably and at fair prices. There is, however, a common complaint that some of the items, especially the foodgrains supplied by the system, are of inferior quality.

Consumerism

Consumerism is still in its infancy in India. There have been occasional mass consumer demonstrations against market imperfections, mainly shortages and exorbitant prices. But several of these demonstrations have been organised with vested political interests and consumer involvement and dedication have been limited. Of course, a number of consumer organisations have been formed in different parts of the country. But with the exception of a very few, they are yet to demonstrate their practical utility. Further, whatever little organised consumer movement there is in India is almost confined to urban areas, leaving the large majority of the Indian consumers high and dry.

A well developed consumerism is essential for the protection of consumer rights. Consumerism has the following important roles to play:

1. ***Consumer Education:*** The consumer is given information about various consumer goods and services. This relates to prices, what the consumer can expect, standard

trade practices, etc. Consumers are also made aware of their rights and responsibilities and the ways of getting the grievances redressed.

2. ***Product Rating:*** In order to guide the consumer in his choice of products, some of the agencies (*for example,* CERS, Ahmedabad) carry out tests and reports the results of such tests.

3. ***Liaison with Government and with Producers:*** Another important role of consumer organisations is to maintain liaison with producers on the one hand and government authorities on the other. As government has a key role in protecting consumer rights, the consumer organisations have an important role to see that government plays its role.

Opportunity for Industry

T. Thomas (former Chairman, Hindustan Lever) observes that consumerism in India has not developed as a social reaction against overselling by industry, as happened in the West. On the contrary, it has been more a reaction to the evil effects of shortages and inflation. Therefore, the industry in India has a unique opportunity to respond to consumerism in a positive manner as outlined below:[14]

1. First of all, marketing must be recognised and practised as something more than sales and distribution. It has to be considered as the company's relationship with the consumer. In the wider context, it can be extended to become a part of the organisation's total responsibility to society. When we talk of the social responsibility of industry, one of its prime social responsibilities is to the consumer through the adoption of sound marketing methods.
2. Yet we cannot be complacent even with good marketing because it is not possible that many manufacturers, including large ones, will always ask all the questions that are relevant to the consumer, particularly with regard to product safety, comparative cost-effectiveness, etc. Consumer movements tend to focus on such questions and may well be seen as an extension of the marketing role. Therefore, industry should cooperate with consumer movements in terms of information on, and education in, the products. Conversely, such information may also educate the consumer in the issues facing the producers, *viz.,* cost of capital, norms of profitability, impact of government policies, etc.
3. Industry will have to invest increasingly in testing the safety of the products in use. It is far better to organise for this than to wait for nasty accidents which will make it all mandatory and exaggerated.
4. Dealing with consumer complaints satisfactorily is yet another responsibility of the industry. Promptness, courtesy and generosity are expected by the consumer with a genuine complaint. Apart from the loss and irritation caused to the consumer, persistent complaints, even if small in number, are often a good indicator of a necessary improvement.

5. Another important role of the industry is in relation to claims made on behalf of the products through advertising. Restraint is best exercised voluntarily than through legislation which will otherwise become inevitable. Advertising agencies and marketing managements have a very important role to play in this respect. By overplaying the claims, they will cut the very branch on which they are perched.
6. Lastly, if industry has to continue to cope with consumerism, it has to invest in R&D because consumer expectations and needs are constantly rising and the constraints on meeting them are changing. To cope with this effectively, industry has to find solution through R&D. It is when consumer needs exceed the industry's ability to meet them that consumerism tends to become menacing. With adequate anticipation by industry, such a situation need not arise.

The above facts indicate that cooperative efforts on the part of consumers, business and the Government are very necessary to protect the rights of the consumers. A well-organised consumerism is needed to make the Government responsive and effective and the business responsible and obliging. To sincere and dynamic business enterprises, consumerism does not pose a threat but offers an opportunity.

Consumer Protection Act, 1986

An important landmark in consumer protection endeavours in India is the Consumer Protection Act, 1986, which provides for a system for the protection of consumer rights and the redressal of consumer disputes.

This Act extends to the whole of India except the State of Jammu and Kashmir, and save as otherwise expressly provided by the Central Government by notification, it applies to all goods and services.

The objective of the Act is to provide for the better protection of the interests of consumers and for that purpose to make provision for the establishment of consumer councils and authorities for the settlement of consumers' disputes and for matters connected therewith.

Consumer Protection Councils

The Act provides for the establishment of a Central Consumer Protection Council by the Central Government and a State Consumer Protection Council in each State by the respective State Governments.

The Central Council shall consist of the Minister in charge of consumer affairs in the Central Government who shall be its Chairman and such number of other official or non-official members representing such interests as may be prescribed. The Council shall meet as and when necessary but at least one meeting of the Council shall be held every year.

The State Council shall consist of such members as may be specified by the State Government by notification from time-to-time.

Objects of Councils: The objects of the Central Council are to promote and protect the rights of the consumers such as:

(*a*) the right to be protected against marketing of goods and services which are hazardous to life and property;

(*b*) the right to be informed about the quality, quantity, potency, purity, standard and price of goods and services so as to protect the consumer against unfair trade practices;

(*c*) the right to be assured, wherever possible, access to a variety of goods at competitive prices;

(*d*) the right to be heard and assured that consumers' interests will receive due consideration at appropriate forums;

(*e*) the right to seek redressal against unfair trade practices or unscrupulous exploitation of consumers; and

(*f*) the right to consumer education.

The objects of every State Council are to protect within the State the rights of the consumers listed above.

Consumer Disputes Redressal Agencies

The Consumer Protection Act provides for a three-tier consumer disputes redressal system encompassing the district, State and national levels. There are, thus, two levels of agencies in the State and one agency at the national level. In other words, the Act provides for the establishment of the following consumer disputes redressal agencies:

(*i*) A *District Forum* in each district of every State. If the State Government deems it fit, more than one District Forum may be established in a district.

(*ii*) A *State Commission* in each State.

(*iii*) *A National Commission.*

The National Commission was established by the Central Government in August 1988. The responsibility for the establishment of the other two agencies, with the prior approval of the Central Government, rests with the respective State Governments.

The District Forum shall consist of (a) a person who is, or has been, or is qualified to be a District Judge nominated by the State Government who shall be its President, (b) a person of eminence in the field of education, trade or commerce, and (c) a lady social worker.

Each State Commission shall consist of a person who is or has been a judge of a High Court, appointed by the State Government (who shall be its President) and two other members who shall be persons of ability, integrity and standing and have adequate knowledge or experience of or have shown capacity in dealing with problems relating to economics, law, commerce, accountancy, industry, public affairs or administration, one of whom shall be a woman.

The National Commission shall consist of a person who is or who has been a judge of the Supreme Court, appointed by the Central Government (who shall be its President) and two other members who shall be persons of ability, integrity and standing and have adequate knowledge or experience of or have shown capacity in dealing with problems relating to economics, law, commerce, accountancy, industry, public affairs or administration, one of whom shall be a woman.

A complaint where the value of the goods or services and the compensation, if any, is less than rupees five lakh is to be dealt with the District Forum; where such value exceeds rupees five lakh but does not exceed rupees twenty lakh it is to be dealt with the State Commission and cases involving more than rupees twenty lakh fall within the jurisdiction of the National Commission. The State Commission will also entertain appeals against the orders of any District Forum within the State. Appeals against the orders of the State Commission can be made to the National Commission. Appeals against the orders of the National Commission can be made to the Supreme Court.

The State Commission is empowered to call for the records and pass appropriate orders in any consumer dispute which is pending before or has been decided by any District Forum within the State, where it appears to the State Commission that such District Forum has exercised a jurisdiction not vested in it by law, or has failed to exercise a jurisdiction so vested or has acted in exercise of its jurisdiction illegally or with material irregularity. The National Commission has similar jurisdiction over the State Commissions.

Consumer Complaints

A complaint, in relation to any goods sold or delivered or any service provided may be filed with the redressal agency by —

(*a*) the consumer to whom such goods are sold or delivered or such service provided;

(*b*) any recognised consumer association, whether the aggrieved consumer is a member of such association or not;

(*c*) one or more consumers, where there are numerous consumers having the same interest; or

(*d*) the Central or State Government.

Remedial Action

If the consumer disputes redressal agency is satisfied that any of the allegations contained in the complaint is true, it shall issue an order to the opposite party directing him to take one or more of the following things, namely:

(*i*) to remove the defect pointed out by the appropriate laboratory from the goods in question;

(*ii*) to replace the goods with new goods of similar description which shall be free from all defects;

(*iii*) to return to the complainant the price, or, as the case may be, the charges paid by the complainant;

(*iv*) to pay such amount as may be awarded by it as compensation to the consumer for any loss or injury suffered by the consumer due to the negligence of the opposite party;

(*v*) to remove the defects or deficiencies in the services in question;

(*vi*) to discontinue the unfair/restrictive trade practice or not to repeat them;

(*vii*) not to offer the hazardous goods for sale;

(*viii*) to withdraw the hazardous goods from being offered for sale;

(*ix*) to provide for adequate costs to parties.

Penalties

If a trader or person against whom a complaint is made or the complainant fails or omits to comply with any order made by a redressal agency, he shall be punishable with imprisonment for any term not exceeding three years or with fine not exceeding ten thousand rupees or with both.

Conclusion

The Consumer Protection Act, 1986, which was modified by the Amendment Act of 1993, is a very important means to protect the consumer rights. However, the effective functioning of the consumer redressal agencies and, consequently, the achievement of its objectives, are hindered by several problems.

The posts of president and/or other members of the fora remaining vacant are not uncommon. Many redressal agencies are not adequately staffed. They also suffer from financial problems.

The Act has been hailed for the timeframe set for the disposal of the cases. In fact, the Act envisages a simple, inexpensive and speedy redressal of consumer grievances related to defective goods, deficient services and unfair and restrictive trade practices. But the problems mentioned above come in the way of expeditious disposal of the cases.

Further, taking recourse to the law is affected by the lack of consumer awareness and education.

One redeeming feature of the Consumer Protection Act is that it applies not only to the private sector but also to the public sector and government agencies. As against this, it may be noted that, the undertakings in the public and cooperative sectors and those undertakings the management of which has been taken over by the Government are exempted even from the provisions dealing with *unfair trade practices* under the MRTP Act.

SUMMARY

Consumers, all around the world, are victims of poor quality, unsafe goods, under-measurement, adulteration and false promises. Indian consumers suffer and lose thousands of crore of rupees every year due to adulteration and quantity deceptions. Further, genuine companies, consumers and governments suffer huge losses due to fake products.

A reaction to these problems has been the growth of consumerism, which may be defined as a collective endeavour of the consumers to protect their interests, is a manifestation of the failure of the business, including that of the public sector, and the government to guarantee and ensure the legitimate rights of the consumers.

International organisations like the United Nations and Consumers' International have a keen interest in fostering consumer protection measures throughout the world. The UN at the persuasion of the Consumers' International has issued a set of guidelines for consumer protection measures.

Fig. 18.1 presents the important factors of consumer protection.

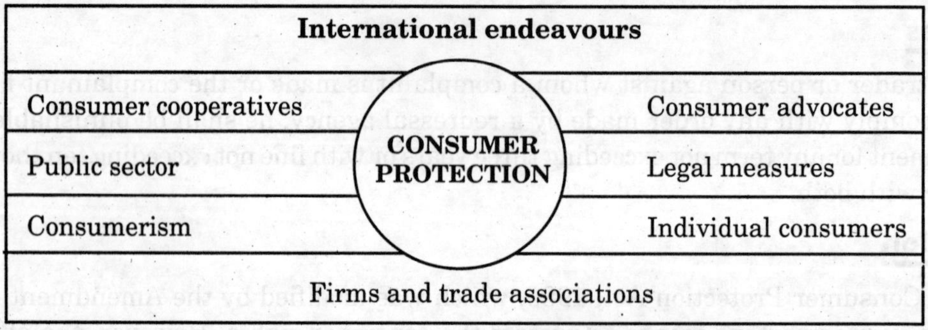

Fig. 18.1: Factors of Consumer Protection

The most important legal measure to protect the consumer rights is the Consumer Protection Act, 1986. This Act provides for the establishment of a Central Consumer Protection Council by the Central Government and a State Consumer Protection Council in each State by the respective State Governments.

The objects of these Councils are to promote and protect the rights of the consumers such as: (*a*) the right to be protected against marketing of hazardous goods and services; (*b*) the right to be informed about the relevant factors about the goods and services so as to protect the consumer against unfair trade practices; (*c*) the right to reasonable choice; (*d*) the right to be heard; (*e*) the right to seek redressal of legitimate complaints; and (*f*) the right to consumer education.

Figure 18.2 depicts the consumer disputes redressal agencies under this Act.

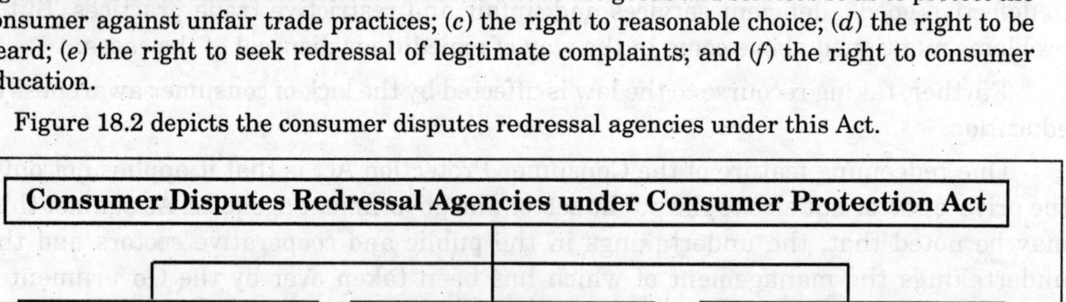

Fig. 18.2 : Consumer Disputes Redressal Agencies Under Consumer Protection Act

If the consumer disputes redressal agency is satisfied that any of the allegations contained in a complaint made to it is true, it shall issue an order to the opposite party directing him to take one or more of the following things, namely: *(i)* to remove the defect from the goods in question; *(ii)* to replace the goods with new goods; *(iii)* to return to the complainant the price, or charges paid by him; *(iv)* to pay compensation to the consumer for any loss or injury suffered; *(v)* to remove the defects or deficiencies in the services in question; *(vi)* to discontinue the unfair/restrictive trade practice or not to repeat them; *(vii)* not to offer the hazardous goods for sale; *(viii)* to withdraw the hazardous goods from being offered for sale; *(ix)* to provide for adequate costs to parties.

Failure to comply with any order made by a redressal agency shall be punishable with imprisonment or fine or both.

REFERENCES

1. Philip, Kotler, "What Consumerism Means for Marketers", *Harvard Business Review,* May-June 1972, p. 49.
2. Harper, W., Boyd Jr., and David, B., Alien. Jr., "Caveat Emptor, Caveat Venditor, Caveat Omnis", in Neelamegham., S., (ed.), *Marketing Management and the Indian Economy,* New Delhi: Vikas Publishing House Pvt. Ltd., 1982, p. 310.
3. From the speech delivered at the 44th Annual General Meeting (1977) of Hindustan Lever Ltd.
4. Rom, Markin, J., *Marketing,* New York, John Wiley & Sons, 1979, pp. 475-76.
5. Cited in Philip, Kotler, "What Consumersim Means for Marketers?" , *op.cit.,* p. 54.
6. Philip, Kotler, *Ibid.,* p. 54.
7. *Ibid.,* p. 54
8. *Ibid.,* p. 55.
9. *Ibid.,* p. 55.
10. *Ibid.,* p. 5.
11. Joel, Dean, *Managerial Economics,* New Delhi: Prentice-Hall of India Pvt. Ltd., (1978), pp. 55-56.
12. From the Chairman's Speech at the 44th Annual General Meeting (1977) of Hindustan Lever Ltd.
13. *Ibid.,* p. 28.
14. For details, see chapter on Price and Distribution Controls.

☆☆☆

CHAPTER 19

LABOUR LEGISLATION

The labour environment is an important determinant of business location and functioning. Factors such as the availability of labour of different skill levels, productivity and cost of labour, flexibility of labour, attitude and behaviour patterns of labour, nature of trade unionism, labour legislation and the effectiveness of their implementation, etc., are important to business. Labour standards, which encompass issues such as child labour, working conditions and labour welfare, wage levels, labour legislation and their implementation, have emerged as an important concern in international business.

> **Labour legislation should provide a framework for protection of rights and interests of employers as well as employees and industrial relations.**

Labour legislation is a very important factor that shapes the labour environment. Protection of the interests of labour was long held as one of the important responsibilities of the State in the democratic countries. However, some recent developments indicate that the Government should intervene to prevent the legitimate rights of consumers, the general public, and employers from being denied by the militant might of organised labour. But many a time there is a tendency to ignore the latter aspect. In the global environment, the cost of such negligence could very high.

The *Directive Principles* in the Constitution of India places a lot of responsibility on the State in respect of labour. The Constitution directs the State to provide work to every citizen who is willing and able to work. Article 42 requires the State to make provision for securing just and humane conditions of work and for maternity relief. Article 43, which is described as the *Magna Carta* of the Indian worker, imposes upon the State the obligation, *inter alia*, to secure, by suitable legislation or economic organisation or in any other way, to all workers, agricultural, industrial or otherwise, work, a living wage, conditions of work ensuring a decent standard of life, full enjoyment of leisure, and social and cultural opportunities.

BOX 19.1 : SECOND NATIONAL COMMISSION ON LABOUR

The Second National Commission on Labour, appointed by Government of India in October 1999, under the chairmanship of Mr. Ravindra Varma, submitted its Report in 2002, i.e., 35 years after the Report of the first National Commission on Labour.

The Terms of References of the Commission were: (i) "to suggest rationalisation of existing laws relating to labour in the organised sector"., and (ii) "to suggest an Umbrella Legislation for ensuring a minimum level of protection to the workers in the unorganised sector".

One of the criticisms of the terms of references to the Commission was that the terms of reference talk of 'rationalisation' of existing laws. The Report of the Commission points out that some critics have tried to create an impression that the word 'rationalisation' means the retrenchment of workers or cutting down the labour force engaged in an industry or plant, and, therefore, indicates an attempt to sanctify 'retrenchment'. According to the Commission, "this is an unwarranted interpretation. In our understanding, rationalisation in this context, means only making laws more consistent with the context, more consistent with each other, less cumbersome, simpler and more transparent."

One of the two main tasks that have been entrusted to the Commission is to suggest Umbrella Legislation for ensuring a minimum level of protection to the workers in the unorganised sector. When the Commission is asked to review legislation and structures that exist in the organised sector and also to make recommendations for legislation and structures in the unorganised sector, it means that the Commission is expected to suggest measures that will cover the problems and needs of the entire workforce in the country.

It was suggested that while conducting the studies, drawing conclusions and formulating the suggestions, the Commission took into account various factors that contributed to the creation of the context in which the Government deemed it necessary to appoint the Commission. The Resolution appointing the Commission itself identified some of these factors as the emerging economic environment: the globalisation of the economy and liberalisation of trade and industry; the rapid changes in technology and their consequences and ramifications; the effects that these changes were likely to have on the nature and structure of industry, on methods and places of production, on employment and the skills necessary to retain employability and mobility; and the responses that are necessary to acquire and retain economic efficiency and international competitiveness. The Resolution also desired that while considering the demands of international competitiveness, the Commission took into account the need to ensure a minimum level of protection and welfare to labour, to improve the effectiveness of measures relating to social security, safety at places of work and occupational health hazards; to pay special attention to the problems of women workers, minimum wages, evolving a healthy relation between wages and productivity; and to improve the efficiency of the basic institutional framework necessary to ensure the protection and welfare of labour.

Another set of factors sharpening the need for an urgent review of the existing laws in the organised sector and of the inadequacy of laws and structures in the unorganised sector, arose from the experiences that all social partners — entrepreneurs, workers and the State and Central Governments — have had, of the way the existing laws have worked during the last few decades. All three partners have complained that the laws, as they exist, are unsatisfactory. All three wanted a comprehensive review, and a comprehensive reformulation of the legal framework, the administrative framework and the institutional structures in the field of social security. Demands for basic reforms had been voiced in the Labour Conferences for many years, and the Government had assured the tripartite conferences that it would take early steps for review and reform.

Labour legislation is regarded as "a most dynamic institution. From a simple restraint on child labour in 1881, labour legislation in India has become an important agency of the State for the regulation of working and living conditions of workers, as indicated by the rising number and variety of labour Acts. This rapid development of labour legislation is an integral part of the modern social organisation."[1] "Like slave labour in ancient times, serf relics of all of which are still to be found in many backward countries, free labour is the direct result of growing industrialism and democracy, and labour legislation is the institution through which the State protects the interest, ameliorates the moral and material conditions, of the working classes."[2]

Labour is an item included in the Concurrent List in the Constitution, which implies that both Union and State Governments can legislate on this matter. However, State legislature cannot enact a law which is repugnant to an Act passed by the Parliament. The National Commission on Labour has observed that, in practice, however, the working of the Constitutional provisions have not created any difficulty in labour matters even at the time when Union-State relationship in other aspects of their respective functions had to undergo a severe strain.

BOX 19.2 : ILO DECLARATION ON FUNDAMENTAL PRINCIPLES AND RIGHTS AT WORK

The ILO declaration on Fundamental Principles and Rights at Work, adopted by the International Labour Conference in June 1998, declares *inter alia* that all Member States have an obligation to respect, to promote and to realise the principles concerning the fundamental rights which are the subject of those conventions, namely:

(*a*) freedom of association and the effective recognition of the right to collective bargaining

(*b*) the elimination of all forms of forced or compulsory labour;

(*c*) the effective abolition of child labour; and

(*d*) the elimination of discrimination in respect of employment and occupation.

The primary goal of the ILO today is to promote opportunities for women and men to obtain decent and productive work in conditions of freedom, equity, security and human dignity. The goal is not just the creation of jobs but the creation of jobs, of acceptable quality.

Government of India ratified Convention 122 on Employment and Social Policy in 1998. Article 1 of the Convention lays down:

(1) With a view to stimulating economic growth and development, raising levels of living, meeting manpower requirements, and overcoming unemployment and under-employment, each Member shall declare and pursue, as a major goal an active policy designed to promote full, productive and freely chosen employment.

(2) The said policy shall aim at ensuring that:

(a) There is work for all who are available for and seeking work.

(b) Such work is as productive as possible

(c) There is freedom of choice of the employment and the fullest possible opportunity for each worker to qualify for, and to use skill and the endowments in a job for which he is well suited, irrespective of race, colour, sex, religion, political opinion, national extraction or social origin.

(3) The said policy shall take due account of the State and the level of economic development and mutual relationships between employment objectives and other economic and social objectives, and shall be pursued by methods that are appropriate to national conditions and practices.

This convention was ratified by India. From the commitments of the Government of India, it can be deduced that the following rights of workers have been recognised as inalienable and must, therefore, accrue to every worker under any system of labour laws and labour policy. These are:

(a) Right to work of one's choice

(b) Right against discrimination

(c) Prohibition of child labour

(d) Just and humane conditions of work

(e) Right to social security

(f) Protection of Wages including right to guaranteed wages

(g) Right to redress of grievances

(h) Right to organise and form trade unions and Right to collective bargaining, and

(i) Right to participation in management.

The second NCL has observed regarding the above that one cannot overlook the fact that rights are also related to duties.

Principles of Labour Legislation

There are some cardinal principles of labour legislation.

Labour legislation should confirm to the socio-economic realities of the nation and ILO principles.

Social Justice: The principle of social justice demands that the State should afford protection to workers against harmful effects to their health, safety and morality, of their working conditions, as well as ensure a reasonable wage. But what is not sufficiently recognised and emphasised is that organised workers shall not be allowed to exercise their might to meet socially unjustifiable rights and hold public life at ransom.

Social Equity: The principle of social equity demands that the changes in the socio-economic and political conditions and environment should be appropriately absorbed into labour legislation from time-to-time.

International Uniformity: The International Labour Organisation (ILO) has been playing a very important role in ensuring uniformity in the labour legislation of different countries. The ILO helps in providing a common platform for men engaged in the field or industrial relations to study and understand the norms of social justice and social equity, applied to labour matters in different countries, and adapt them intelligently in their respective countries, with due regard for their own national economy. Most labour legislation in India is based on this principle.

National Economy: While formulating labour laws in respect of wages, working conditions, welfare, social security, etc., it is very important to bear in mind the general economic situation of the country.

BOX 19.3 : POSTULATES AND EVOLUTION OF LABOUR POLICY IN INDIA

The main postulates of labour policy operating in the country could be summed up as follows:

1. Recognition of the State, the custodian of the interests of the community, as the catalyst of 'change' and welfare programmes.
2. Recognition of the right of workers to peaceful direct action if justice is denied to them.
3. Encouragement to mutual settlement, collective bargaining and voluntary arbitration.
4. Intervention by the State in favour of the weaker party to ensure fair treatment to all concerned.
5. Primacy to maintenance of industrial peace.
6. Evolving partnership between the employer and employees in a constructive endeavour to promote the satisfaction of the economic needs of the community in the best possible manner.
7. Ensuring fair wage standards and provision of social security.
8. Cooperation for augmenting production and increasing 'productivity'.
9. Adequate enforcement of legislation.
10. Enhancing the status of the worker in industry.
11. Tripartite consultation.

The First Plan adumbrated these principles and they were reaffirmed in successive Plans.

In giving effect to them in practice, the accent has been on reciprocity and mutuality of obligations and recognition of workers' contribution to production and productivity. A subtle change in emphasis with regard to modes of settlement of disputes in successive Plans is also discernible. Legalistic approach is gradually yielding place to voluntary bilateral arrangements. Strengthening of trade unions to secure better labour-management relations has also been a part of this approach.

Courtesy: Report of the National Commission on Labour

CLASSIFICATION OF LABOUR LEGISLATION

V.V. Giri, (a veteran trade union leader who also adorned such positions as Union Minister of Labour and President of India), in his well-known book *Labour Problems in Indian Industry*, has classified the labour legislation in India under the following broad heads.[3]

> **There are a host of labour laws related different sections of the labour population, different sectors of economy, labour welfare and social security, specific labour matters and trade unions and industrial relations.**

I. *Laws Relating to Weaker Sections*

1. Children
2. Women

II. *Laws Relating to Specific Industries*

1. Factories and workshops
2. Mines and minerals
3. Plantations
4. Transport, namely: (*a*) Railways; (*b*) Seamen; (*c*) Ports and Docks; (*d*) Inland water transport; (*e*) Motor transport; (*f*) Air transport
5. Shops and commercial establishments
6. Contract labour
7. Construction Workers
8. Working journalists

III. *Laws Relating to Specific Matters*

1. Wages
2. Indebtedness
3. Social security: (*a*) Workmen's compensation; (*b*) maternity benefits; (*c*) retrenchment benefits; (*d*) provident fund and bonus schemes.
4. Bonus
5. Forced labour

IV. *Laws Relating to*

1. Trade unions
2. Industrial relations

Laws Relating to Weaker Sections

Laws relating to weaker sections cover conditions of employment of children and women.

The important legislative provisions with a bearing on the employment of children relate to minimum age of employment, working hours, health certification, employment on dangerous machines and the like. The Factories Act, 1948; the Mines Act, 1952; the Plantation Labour Act, 1951; the Employment of Children Act, 1938; the Shops and Establishments Act of various States, etc., regulate the minimum age of employment. To ensure the physical fitness of children, the Factories Act provides that children up to the age of 18 will be employed on the production of a health certificate which will be valid for one year only. The Factories Act, the Mines Act, the Plantation Labour Act, the Shops and Establishments Acts, etc., prescribe the maximum hours of work allowed to be assigned to children. The child labour (Prohibition and Regulation) Act, 1986 is limited in scope. It does not cover all occupations and processes where children are working. The Act covers only some hazardous occupations and processes. It excludes children working in family-based enterprises.

The legislative provisions for the protection and welfare of women workers are largely inspired by the ILO Conventions on:

1. Maternity Protection, 1919
2. Night Work, 1919
3. Underground Work, 1935
4. Equal Remuneration, 1951
5. Discrimination (Employment and Occupation), 1958

There are several laws to take care of problems/special needs of women and children in employment.

However, the actual wording of the enactments in India in which the protection is written draws heavily on the Indian experience. Maternity benefits are provided under the Employees' State Insurance Act and the Maternity Benefit Act, 1961. The other legislative measure for women relates to certain restriction on the lifting of weight, employment in hazardous occupations, provision for separate toilet facilities, rest rooms, creches, etc.

Laws Relating to Specific Industries

***Factories and Workshops*:** The Factories Act, 1948, which provides for the licensing, registration and inspection of factories, is meant to protect the interests of workmen, to ensure for them better conditions of work, and to prevent the employers from taking advantage of their weak bargaining power. It regulates the conditions of the employment of young persons and females, and provides for safe and healthy working conditions inside the factories.

The Industrial Employment (Standing) Orders Act, 1946, defines the rights and obligations of the employer and the workers in respect of recruitment, discharge, disciplinary action, holiday and leave, etc., with a view to reducing the friction between management and workers in industrial undertakings. The Act provides for the framing of standing orders in all industrial establishments (including factories, mines, railways, docks and plantations) employing 100 or more workers.

***Mines and Minerals*:** According to the definition of the term "mine" under the Indian Mines (Amendment) Act, 1959, mine includes all borings, bore holes, oil wells, shafts, quarries, open cast workings, railways, aerial ropeways, conveyors, tramways, slidings, workshops, power stations; etc., or any premises connected with mining operations and near or in the mining area. The Mines Act prohibits the employment of persons in a mine when its owner fails to comply with the notice of the Mines Inspectorate for remedying any matter connected with a mine which is dangerous to human life, limb or safety.

The Coal Mines (Conservation and Safety) Act, 1952, authorises the Central Government to take such measures as it deems proper or necessary for the maintenance of safety in coal mines or for the conservation of coal.

Other important laws in the field of mines and minerals are the Iron Ore Mines Labour Welfare Cess Act, 1961, Coal Mines Labour Fund Act, 1947, and Coal Mines Provident Fund and Bonus Schemes Act, 1948.

Plantations: The Plantation Labour Act, 1951, regulates the conditions of work of plantation workers and provides for their welfare. The Act, which applies to tea, coffee, rubber and cinchona plantations, may be applied by State Governments to other plantations also. The Act, amended in 1981, provided for compulsory registration of plantations.

***Transport*:** The working and service conditions of the employees of different transports are regulated by various laws, such as the Indian Railways Act, 1930; the Indian Merchant Shipping Act, 1973; the Indian Dock Labourers' Act, 1934; the Dock Workers (Regulation of Employment) Act, 1984; Marketing of Heavy Packages Act, 1951; Motor Vehicles Act, 1939; and Motor Transport Workers Act, 1961.

There are several laws pertaining to labour in specific segments/types of employment.

***Shops and Commercial Establishments*:** State Acts on shops and establishments broadly cover wage earners employed in shops, commercial establishments (including insurance and banking firms), restaurants, theatres, cinemas, and other places of public amusement. These Acts contain provisions related to opening and closing hours, hours of work, rest intervals, spread over, overtime rates and weekly holidays.

Contract Labour: Contract labour is generally employed for casual, seasonal or irregular work. The Contract Labour (Regulations and Abolition) Act, 1970, seeks to abolish the contract labour system in perennial operations and regulates it where the system cannot be abolished. The Act is implemented both by the Centre and States. In the Central sphere, contract labour has been prohibited for certain specified operations in coal, iron ore, limestone, dolomite and manganese mines, and in buildings owned or occupied by establishments under the Central Government.

The Act applies to every establishment which employs 20 or more workmen, and to every contractor who employs not less than 20 workers. The 2nd NCL has observed that this Act has many loopholes and as it does not apply to who does not employ less than 20 workers, if leads to manipulations.

In his Budget (2001-2002) speech, the Union Finance Minister observed that rigidities inherent in the existing legislation regarding Contract labour inhibit growth in employment in many service activities. Section 10 of the existing Act envisages prohibition of Contract labour in work/process/operation if the conditions set therein like perennial nature of job, etc., are fulfilled. Section 10 enables the Contract labour engaged in prohibited jobs to become direct employees of the principal employer. To overcome this difficulty and at the same time to ensure the protection to labour, it is proposed to bring an amendment to facilitate outsourcing of activities without any restrictions as well as to offer Contract appointments. It would not differentiate between core and non-core activities, and provide protection to labour engaged in outsourcing activities in terms of their health, safety, welfare, social security, etc. It would also provide for larger compensation based on last drawn wages as retrenchment compensation for every year of service. This proposal raised a lot of opposition.

Construction Labour: To a limited extent, the Workmen's Compensation Act, 1923; the Minimum Wages Act, 1948; the Employees State Insurance Act, 1948; the Contract Labour (Abolition and Regulation) Act, 1970, and Standing Instructions relating to casual labour applicable to the employing agencies apply to construction labour as well. It has, however, been noticed that these legislative enactments and standing orders do not cover safety at work and social security.

Working Journalists: The Working Journalists and Other Newspaper Employees (Conditions of Service) and Miscellaneous Provisions Act, 1955, regulates the conditions of service of working journalists and other persons employed in newspaper establishment. By a specific provision of this Act, the provisions of the Industrial Disputes Act with certain modifications have been applied to working journalists.

Laws Relating to Specific Matters

Wages: The two important enactments for wages are the Payment of Wages Act, 1936, and the Minimum wages Act, 1948.

The Payment of Wages Act, 1936, ensures that industrial workers receive payment of their wages at regular intervals and that no unauthorised deductions are made from their wages. This Act was amended in 2005 for enhancing the wage ceiling to ₹ 6,500/ month for applicability of the Act.

The Minimum Wages Act empowers the appropriate Government to fix the minimum rate of wages payable to workers employed in all scheduled employments, which include employments in any woollen, carpet-making or shawl-weaving establishment, rice mill, flour mill, dal mill, oil mill as well as employment under any local authority.

Bonus: In the past, bonus was regarded as an ex-gratia payment made by the employer to his workers to provide a stimulus for extra effort by them in the production process. Sometimes, it represented the desire of the employer to share with his workers the surplus generated by common endeavour and enterprise. However, later, bonus began to be looked upon as a "deferred wages" and the Payment of Bonus Act, 1965, by imposing a statutory liability upon the employer to pay bonus to the employees, has in effect accorded recognition to this view.

The Payment of Bonus Act applies to every factory as defined in the Factories Act, and to every other establishment in which 20 or more persons are employed on any day during an accounting year. Bonus is payable to employees drawing up to ₹ 3,500 per month. The second National Commission on Labour has recommended to raise the ceiling to ₹ 10,000.

Bonded Labour: The bonded labour system was abolished all over the country by the Bonded Labour System (abolition) Act, 1976. Under the Act, every bonded labourer stands freed and discharged from any obligation to render any bonded labour.

Laws Relating to Trade Unions and Industrial Relations

The law relating to the registration of trade unions and certain other matters is contained in the Trade Unions Act, 1926. The Act lays down the procedure for the registration of trade unions and defines very clearly their rights and liabilities. It specifies the objects on which trade union may spend its general funds and provides for the constitution of a separate fund for political purposes. Members of bonafide registered trade unions have been granted protection against various civil and criminal liabilities which they are likely to incur in promoting and safeguarding their legitimate interests. More information is provided in the chapter on Trade Unions.

The Trade Unions Act, 1926, the Industrial Disputes Act, 1947, and Industrial Employment (Standing Orders) Act, 1946, are the most important pieces of legislation covering employer-employee relations.

The various matters connected with industrial disputes are dealt with by the Industrial Disputes Act, 1947. The main objects of the Act are to secure industrial peace by preventing and settling disputes and to ameliorate the conditions of workmen in industry.

The Act specifies all those cases when a strike or a lockout shall be illegal and lays down the conditions necessary for the validity of lay-off and retrenchment of workers. It provides for the appointment of various conciliations authorities. The rights and powers of these authorities, the procedure of conciliation for the validity of settlements and awards have also been laid down by the Act. For details, see the chapter on Industrial Relations.

UNORGANISED SECTOR

The term 'unorganised labour' is defined as those workers who have not been able to organise themselves to pursue their common interests due to certain constraints like casual nature of employment, ignorance and illiteracy, small and scattered size of establishments, etc.

As per the survey carried out by the National Sample Survey Organisation in the year 2004-2005, of the total employment of 45.9 crore, around 2.6 crore (less 6 per cent) was in the organised sector and the balance 43.3 crore (nearly 95 per cent) workers in the unorganised sector. Out of 43.3 crore workers in the unorganised sector, 26.8 crore workers (about 62 per cent) were employed in agricultural sector, about 2.6 crore in construction work (about 6 per cent) and remaining in manufacturing and service.

Nearly 95 per cent of the employment in India is in the unorganised sector, more than 60 per cent of it being in the agricultural sector.

In order to take care of the social security and welfare of unorganized workers, tow-pronged strategy, i.e., legislative measures, and, implementation of welfare schemes and programmes have been followed so far. The legislative measures include the Minimum Wages Act, 1948, the Workmen's Compensation Act, 1923, the Maternity Benefit Act, 1961, the Bonded Labour System (Abolition) Act, 1970, the Contract Labour (Regulation and Abolition) Act, 1970, the Inter-State Migrant Workmen (Regulation of Employment and Conditions of Service) Act, 1979, the Building and Other

Construction Workers (Regulation of Employment and Conditions of Service) Act, 1996, etc. Mention about some of these laws have already been made in the preceding sections/chapter.

The Government has set up Welfare Funds for providing welfare measures to the beedi, non-coal mine and cine workers. The Funds are used to provide the financial assistance tot these workers for education of their children, recreation, medical and health facilities, construction of houses, etc. The Building and Other Construction Workers (Regulation of Employment and Conditions of Service) Act, 1996 also has provision for setting up of welfare Board/Fund by every State Government to provide welfare/social security measures to the construction workers. Some States, like Kerala, have constituted welfare funds for specific categories of workers in the unorganised sector.

BOX 19.4 : LABOUR REGULATIONS AND RIGIDITIES IN THE LABOUR MARKET

Almost all countries have labour laws and regulations to protect workers. These fall into five categories:

- Establishment and protection of workers' rights, including the right to associate and organize, the right to bargain collectively, and the right to engage in industrial action.
- Protection for vulnerable groups, including minimum working age requirements, equality of wages, and employment opportunities and special provisions for women.
- Establishment of minimum compensation for work, including minimum wages, minimum non-wage benefits, and overtime pay.
- Assurance of decent working conditions, including occupational health and safety provisions and maximum hours of work.
- Provision of income security, including social security, job security, severance pay, and public works.

World Development Report 1995 provides a detailed analysis of labour legislation and its effects and shows that not all labour laws achieve their intended objectives. The Report has suggested that labour laws in developing countries be simplified and focused on basic human rights and safety issues.

In developing countries excessively restrictive labour laws sometimes have the effect of benefiting a group of relatively well-off workers at the cost of limiting the employment of others (sometimes the majority) in the formal sector. In some countries labour laws have introduced significant rigidities into the labour market, with adverse consequences for production and growth.

An example is India, with 165 pieces of labour legislation. (World Bank, 2000, Zegha, 1998). Indian labour laws provide for a wide scope for initiating industrial disputes, long procedures for settlement of industrial disputes, inflexible provisions on change in conditions of service, and provisions enabling government interventions in areas such as layoff, retrenchment, and closures. The proliferation of labour laws is made worse by definitional complexities, making their interpretation even more difficult. There are 11 different ways of defining "wages", and the meaning of "worker", "employee", and "employed person" changes depending on the piece of legislation.

> Lack of clarity about the rights and obligations of employers and employees, litigiousness, and delays in settling disputes have consequently become key features in the application of India's labour laws. Most disputes take more than one year to settle, and 20 years is not infrequent. This legislative framework has impeded large-scale industrial restructuring, relocation, or exit — and hence entry into the formal sector — and even the relocation of labour within an enterprise and often even in the same city or town.
>
> *Courtesy: World Bank,* World Development Report, 2002.

SUMMARY

The nature of labour laws and the effectiveness of their implementation are an important dimension of the business environment.

Labour legislation should be based on the principle of social justice, social equity, international uniformity and national economy.

V.V. Giri has classified the labour legislation in India under the following broad heads:

1. *Laws Relating to Weaker Sections:* These laws cover conditions of employment of children and women.
2. *Laws Relating to Specific Industries:* These laws deal with conditions of employment in factories and workshops; mines and minerals; plantations; shops and commercial establishments; and transport, namely railways, seaman, ports and docks, inland water transport; motor transport and air transport. There are also laws pertaining to contract labour, construction workers, and working journalists.
3. *Laws Relating to Specific Matters:* This category of legislations include those dealing with payment of wages and minimum wages, indebtedness, bonus, bonded labour, and social security covering matters like workmen's compensation, maternity benefits, retrenchment benefits, provident fund and bonus schemes.
4. *Laws Relating to Trade Unions and Industrial Relations:* The Trade Unions Act lays down the procedure for the registration of trade unions and defines their rights and responsibilities. The various matters connected with industrial disputes are dealt with by the Industrial Disputes Act, 1947.

REFERENCES

1. Kuchhal, S.C., *The Industrial Economy of India,* Allahabad, Chaitanya Publishing Co., 1976, p. 445.
2. Das, R.K., *Principles and Problems of Indian Labour Legislation*, p. 1 (cited by Kuchhal, *ibid*., p. 445.)
3. Giri, V.V., *Labour Problems In Indian Industry*, Mumbai: Asia Publishing House, 1972, p. 137.

ANNEXURE 19.1

Second National Commission on Labour on Rationalisation of Labour Laws

According to the Second National Commission on Labour, existing set of labour laws should be broadly grouped into four or five groups of laws pertaining to: (i) industrial relations, (ii) wages, (iii) social security, (iv) safety, and (v) welfare and working conditions and so on. While the ultimate object must be to incorporate all such provisions in a comprehensive code, such a codification may have to be done in stages.

The Commission is of the view that the coverage as well as the definition of the term 'worker' should be the same in all groups of laws, subject to the stipulation that social security benefits must be available to all employees including administrative, managerial, supervisory and others excluded from the category of workmen and others not treated as workmen or excluded from the category of workmen.

The Commission observed that it is necessary to provide a minimum level of protection to Managerial and other (excluded) employees too, against unfair dismissals or removals. This has to be through adjudication by labour court or Labour Relations Commission or arbitration.

Central laws relating to the subject of Labour Relations are currently the Industrial Disputes Act, 1947, the Trade Unions Act, 1926 and the Industrial Employment (Standing Orders) Act, 1946. Mention must also be made of the Sales Promotion Employees (Conditions of Service) Act, 1976 and other specific Acts governing industrial relations in particular trades or employments. There are State level legislations too on the subject. We recommend that the provisions of all these laws be judiciously consolidated into a single law called the Labour Management Relations Law or the Law on Labour Management Relations. However, we would carve out a section of those workers who are employed in establishments with an employment size of 19 and below, for a different kind of dispensation. In view of our approach, we recommend the repeal of the Sales Promotion Employees (conditions of Service) Act, 1976 and other specific Acts governing industrial relations in particular trades or employments and also specific laws governing wage fixation in particular trades or employments, in the light of what we recommend later in respect of the law on wages. The general law on industrial relations and wages will apply to them.

The Commission recommend the enactment of a special law for small-scale units. We have come to the conclusion that the reasonable threshold limit will be 19 workers. Any establishment with workers above that number cannot be regarded as small. The composite law suggested by us for small enterprises has provisions for registration of establishments, (provisions pertaining to) securing safety, health and welfare of the workers, hours of work, leave, payment of wages, payment of bonus, compensation in case of lay-off, retrenchment and closure, resolution of individual and collective disputes of workers, etc. The law suggested by us also has provisions pertaining to social security. We are of the view that a composite law will not only protect the interests of the workers in these enterprises but will make it easier for the small enterprises to comply with the same.

The Commission adopted certain approaches in drafting the Law on Labour Management Relations.

Firstly, the Commission would prefer the gender neutral expression 'worker' instead of the currently used word 'workman' that we find in the Industrial Disputes Act and some other Acts.

Secondly, the law will apply uniformly to all such establishments.

Thirdly, we recognise that today the extent of unionisation is low and even this low level is being eroded, and that it is time that this trend was reversed and collective negotiations encouraged. Where agreements and understanding between the two parties is not possible, there, recourse to the assistance of a third party should as far as possible be through arbitration or where adjudication is the preferred mode, through labour courts and labour relations commissions of the type we propose later in this regard, and not Governmental intervention. A settlement entered into with a recognised negotiating agent must be binding on all workers.

Fourthly, we consider that provisions must be made in the law for determining negotiating agents, particularly on behalf of workers.

Fifthly, the law must provide for authorities to identify the negotiating agent, to adjudicate disputes and so on, and these must be provided in the shape of labour courts and labour relations commissions at the State, Central and national levels.

Sixthly, the Commission is of the view that changes in the labour laws be accompanied by a well defined social security package that will benefit all workers, be they in the 'organised' or 'unorganised' sector and should also cover those in the administrative, managerial and other categories which have been excluded from the purview of the term worker.

One of the most important steps that one needs to take in rationalising and simplifying the existing labour laws is in the area of simple common definitions of terms that are in constant use; such terms include 'worker', 'wages' and 'establishment'. By making the law applicable to establishments employing 20 or more workers, irrespective of the nature of the activity in which the establishment is engaged, we have avoided the need to define 'industry'. After examining all aspects of the question, we have come to the conclusion that the persons engaged in domestic service are better covered under the proposed type of umbrella legislation, particularly in regard to wages, hours of work, working conditions, safety and social security.

Likewise, the Commission defined establishment as a place or places where some activity is carried on with the help and cooperation of workers.

It is desirable to define two terms, 'wages' and 'remuneration', the former to include only basic wages and dearness allowance and no other for the purpose of contribution to social security and for calculations of bonus and gratuity and all other payments including other allowances as well as overtime payment together with wages as defined above will be 'remuneration'.

The Commission also discussed the question whether any distinction should be made between 'strike' and 'work stoppage' and came to the conclusion that the existing definition of 'strike' in the Industrial Disputes Act, 1947 may stand, "Go slow" and "work-to-rule" are forms of action which must be regarded as misconduct. Standing Orders and Provisions relating to unfair labour practices already include them and provide for action both in the case of "go slow" and "work-to-rule".

Term 'retrenchment' should be defined precisely to cover only termination of employment arising out of reduction of surplus workers in an establishment, such surplus having arisen out of one or more of several reasons.

☆☆☆

CHAPTER 20

LABOUR WELFARE AND SOCIAL SECURITY

LABOUR WELFARE

The National Commission on Labour observes that the concept of "welfare" is necessarily dynamic, bearing a different interpretation from country-to-country and from time-to-time, and even in the same country, according to its value system, social institutions, degree of industrialization and general level of social and economic development.[1] The Directive Principles of State Policy in our Constitution refer generally to the promotion of the welfare of the people. In its specific application to the working class, securing just and humane conditions of work has been highlighted, but what these actually imply cannot be specified in rigid terms for all times.

The ILO has defined broadly the scope of labour welfare

In its Resolution of 1947, the ILO defined Labour Welfare as "such services, facilities and amenities as adequate canteens, rest and recreation facilities, arrangements for travel to and from their houses, and such other services amenities and facilities as contribute to improvements in the conditions under workers are employed".[2]

The Governing Body of the ILO (Geneva, May-June, 1953) considered the subject and urged that it was essential to define precisely and closely the scope of labour welfare in view of the fact that it was a very wide subject, covered a very broad field and was not limited to any one industry or occupation. The ILO Recommendation No. 102 concerning the welfare for workers refers to:

- Facilities for food and meals in or near the undertaking;
- Rest and recreation facilities provided by the undertaking (excluding holiday facilities); and
- Transportation facilities to and from the place of work where ordinary public transport is inadequate or impractivable;[3]

The study team appointed by the Government of India in 1959 to examine the labour welfare activities then existing divided the entire range of these activities into three groups, *viz.*,

Labour welfare encompasses measures to ensure certain standards of basic comforts and working conditions.

1. Welfare within the precincts of an establishment; medical aid; creches, canteens supply of drinking water;
2. Welfare outside the establishment: provision for indoor and outdoor recreation, housing, adult education, visual instructions; and
3. Social security.

The Committee of Experts on Welfare Facilities for Industrial Workers convened by the ILO in 1963 divided welfare services into two groups – *(a)* within the precincts of the establishment, and *(b)* outside the establishment – but the total content of the activities was the same as that included in the three groups mentioned above.[4]

The classification adopted by the ILO is given below.[5]

Welfare and Amenities Within the Establishment

Minimum standards have been set by legislation in respect of working conditions

1. Latrines and urinals
2. Washing and bathing facilities
3. Creches
4. Rest shelters and canteens
5. Arrangements for drinking water
6. Arrangements for prevention of fatigue
7. Health service including occupational safety
8. Administrative arrangements within a plant to look after welfare
9. Uniforms and protective clothing
10. Shift allowance.

It is the employer's responsibility to provide facilities within the precincts of an establishment, as they form a part of working conditions. For many components of such welfare, legislation in the country has set certain minimum standards. Improvements upon them have been left to the employers.

The facilities within the precincts of the establishment are regulated by the Factories Act, 1948, the Plantation Labour Act, 1951; and the Mines Act, 1952.

The Factories Act makes it obligatory on the employer to provide:

1. Cool and clean drinking water; latrines and urinals; and washing and bathing facilities.
2. One first-aid box for every 150 employees.
3. Canteen in establishments which employ more than 250 workers.
4. Rest shelters or rest rooms and a suitable lunch room in all establishments employing 150 workers or more.
5. Creches in factory establishments employing more than 50 women.

The Factories Act also requires the factories employing 500 or more workers to appoint a Labour Welfare Officer to look after the welfare of the workers.

State Governments have been empowered to frame rules to prescribe standards and to grant exemptions, wherever considered necessary. They have laid down elaborate standards for all welfare amenities, keeping in view mainly the requirements of all workers.

The Mines Act, 1952, has laid down provisions for drinking water, conservancy, first aid (including a first-aid room in every mine, wherein more than 150 persons are employed) and creche (in every mine employing women). The Mines Rules provide that:

1. An ambulance room shall have to be maintained under the charge of a qualified medical practitioner assisted by qualified staff on every mine employing 500 or more persons;
2. A shelter shall be constructed for taking food and rest at every mine employing 150 or more persons on any one day of the previous calendar year, as also near loading places, workshops or open cast workings in mines employing 25 or more persons; and
3. A canteen is to be provided in every mine employing 250 or more persons.

Drinking water, conservancy, medical facilities, canteen, creche, recreational facilities, and provision of umbrellas, blankets and raincoats have been made statutory by the Plantations Labour Act, 1951. A canteen has to be set up on plantations with 150 workers or more and a creche where 50 or more women are employed.

Certain welfare facilities are provided to workers in ports and docks under the Dock Workers (Safety, Health and Welfare) Scheme, 1961, which applies to all major ports and docks in the country. Housing, education and recreation facilities are provided for port workers by the Port Trusts with the Port Trust Employees' Welfare Funds. All the Dock Labour Boards have constituted Labour Welfare Funds to provide amenities, including medical and recreation facilities, for dock workers. Welfare facilities for workers employed in the workshop located in port areas are provided under the Factories Act, 1948.

The Motor Transport Workers Act, 1961, provides for the welfare of motor transport workers and for the regulation of their working conditions. The various schemes in operation include canteens, restrooms, uniform hours of work and leave. The Act is administered by State Governments which have framed rules for its enforcement.

The bidi and cigar workers under the Bidi and Cigar Workers (Conditions of Employment) Act, 1966, and contract labour under he Contract Labour (Regulation and Abolition) Act, 1970, have also been provided with many of the facilities mentioned in the foregoing paragraphs.

Welfare Outside the Establishment

1. Maternity benefits
2. Social insurance measures, including gratuity, pension, provident fund and rehabilitation
3. Benevolent funds
4. Medical facilities, including programmes for physical fitness and efficiency, family planning and child welfare
5. Education facilities including adult education
6. Housing facilities;
7. Recreation facilities, including sports, cultural activities, library and reading room
8. Holiday homes and leave travel facilities
9. Workers' cooperatives, including consumers' cooperative stores, fair price shops and cooperative thrift and credit societies
10. Vocational training for dependants of workers;
11. Other programmes for the welfare of women, youth and children
12. Transport to and from the place of work

Welfare and amenities within the establishment are essential conditions and those outside the establishment are supplementary ones for improving labour welfare.

Welfare amenities outside the precincts of the establishment, such as medical, educational, recreational, housing and other facilities, are non-statutory in many cases. However, in plantations, the provisions of some of them is obligatory on the employer.

Large establishments now pay attention to the above facilities. A number of large industrial enterprises also provide transportation facilities to their employees.

The Government have been trying to see that all industrial establishments employing more than 300 workers set up consumers' cooperative stores and fair shops for their workers. A large number of industrial establishments have set up their own consumers' cooperative stores and fair price shops.

The importance of workers' education has been duly recognised by the Government. The Central Board for Workers' Education (CBWE), set up in 1958, is a tripartite body, consisting of representatives of Central and State Governments organizations of employers and workers and educationists. It is a registered society for the implementation of workers' education schemes with the following objectives.

1. To equip all sections of workers for their intelligent participation in the socio-economic development of the nation.

2. To promote among workers a greater understanding of the problems of their socio-economic environment, their responsibilities towards family and their rights and obligations as citizens, as workers in industry and as members and officials of their trade unions.
3. To develop leadership from among the rank and file of workers themselves.
4. To create strong, united and more responsible trade unions through enlightened members and better trained officials.
5. To strengthen democratic processes and traditions in the trade union movement.
6. To enable trade unions themselves to take over ultimately the functions of workers' education.

The scheme of workers' education needs improvement and strengthening

The CBWE, a tripartite society registered under the Societies Registration Act, 1860, implements the workers' education programmes at national, regional and unit/village levels. The focus of the education programmes is to create awareness among all sections of the working class about their rights and obligations for their effective participation in the socio-economic development of the country. The Board undertakes training programmes which cover workers from organised, unorganised, rural and informal sectors. Supervisory and managerial cadres are also covered through joint education programmes.

With headquarters at Nagpur, the Board has a network of regional and sub-regional centres spread throughout the country. It also has four zonal directorates at Delhi, Kolkata, Mumbai and Chennai monitor the activities of the regional centres. The Indian Institute of Workers Education at Mumbai was set up by the Board to conduct national level training programmes.

The V.V. Giri National Labour Institute (earlier known as National Labour Institute), an autonomous body under the Ministry of Labour, Government of India, is engaged in research pertaining to labour and training of labour administrators, trade unions, public-sector managers and other government functionaries concerned with labour. The Institute now pays attention on child labour also.

The National Safety Council was set up in March 1966. Its main function is to conduct seminars, organise film shows in factories, and distribute posters on the subject of safety.

Various schemes for the grant of National Safety Awards to factories, covered by the Factories Act, 1948, and ports have been instituted for good safety records. Each scheme consists of cash prizes and certificates of merit.

SOCIAL SECURITY

Modern Welfare States are expected to take care of the citizens from the "cradle to the grave". Resource constraints, however, do not permit many of them to completely accomplish this task. They, therefore, endeavour to look after the welfare of the individuals according to their capability. The Constitution of India, for instance, lays down that the

State shall, within the limits of its economic capacity and development, make effective provisions for securing public assistance in the event of unemployment, old age, sickness, and disablement.

As the International Labour Organisation (ILO) states, social security envisages that the members of a community shall be protected by collective action against social risks causing undue hardship and privation to individuals whose private resources can seldom be adequate to meet them. It covers, through an appropriate organisation, certain risks to which a person is exposed. These risks are such that an individual of small means cannot effectively provide for them by his own ability or foresight alone or even private combination with his colleagues.[6]

In the words of V.V. Giri, "social security measures have a two-fold significance for every developing country. They constitute an important step towards the goal of a Welfare State, by improving living and working conditions and affording the people protection against the uncertainties of the future. These measures are also important for every industrialisation plan, for not only do they enable workers to become more efficient but they also reduce the wastage arising from industrial disputes. The man-days lost on account of sickness and disability also constitute a heavy drain on the slender resources of the worker and on the industrial output of the country. Lack of social security impedes production and prevents the formation of a stable and efficient labour force. Social security is, therefore, not a burden, but a wise investment in the long-run."[7]

According to the 2nd NCL, social security should be considered as a fundamental human right and the commission recommend a system in which the State bears the responsibility for providing and ensuring an elementary or basic level of security, and leaves room for partly or wholly contributory schemes. This will mean that the responsibility to provide a floor will be primarily that of the State, and it will be left to individual citizens to acquire higher levels of security through assumption of responsibility and contributory participation.

Giri observes that "in modern times, the active participation of the State in social security has resulted in two distinct methods of solving the problem. The first method is that of social assistance, where the State or the local bodies step into ameliorate the distress caused by these contingencies to the population in general. In this method, there are generally no contributory conditions. In concrete terms, social assistance includes non-contributory benefits towards the maintenance of children, mothers, invalids, the aged, the disabled and others. It also includes unemployment assistance. Social assistance can, therefore, be defined as a device for providing benefits, like exemption from taxation or general revenues, to persons of small means in amounts sufficient to meet a minimum standard of needs. The second method is that of social insurance, to which the persons concerned, their employers and the State, make contributions and mainly out of these contributions, benefits necessary to prevent want during unemployment, sickness, old age and other contingencies are given as a right, subject to certain qualifying conditions. In other words, social insurance can be defined as a device to provide benefits as of right for persons of small earnings, in amounts which combine the contributive efforts of the insured with subsidies from the employer and the State.

"The social insurance approach has grown from the system of friendly societies, which developed in Western countries and particularly in the United Kingdom during the last three centuries. The social assistance approach is the outcome of the Poor Laws, which also developed in these countries at the same time. In fact, in the United Kingdom, where social security is available to the entire population from the cradle to the grave, the main approach is that of social insurance, and persons are entitled to benefits by virtue of compulsory contributions. Those who are qualified or can no longer get such benefits, are looked after by measures of social assistance.

"Present-day developments show that social insurance and social assistance are moving closer to one another. In fact, they even meet and combine as, *for example*, in New Zealand and Denmark, where it is difficult to say whether social insurance or social assistance predominates. Such countries have adopted a national system of social securities.

"To be equitable, measures of social assistance should provide for the population as a whole. The extent to which this can be done will depend on the level of national income; and in a developing country, this cannot be adequate. Measures of social insurance, on the other hand, depend very much more on the capacity of the individual industry. As such, it can be introduced in phases; first in more prosperous industries and later in less prosperous ones. In a country like India, where it is impossible at present to provide social security for the whole population, the main approach has to be that of insurance".[8]

Legislative Enactments

There are some important legislative enactments in India for the provision of social security. These enactments may be broadly classified into two categories:

- Acts that provide security in cases of employment injury, maternity and sickness.
- Acts that cover the risks of old age and unemployment.

The following three Acts come under the first category

1. The Workmen's Compensation Act, 1923.
2. The Maternity Benefits Act, 1961.
3. The Employees' State Insurance Act, 1948.

The Acts that come under the second category are:

1. The Employees' Provident Fund and Miscellaneous Provisions Act, 1952
2. The Coal Mines Provident Fund, Family Pension and Bonus Act, 1948
3. The Payment of Gratuity Act, 1972
4. The Industrial Disputes Act, 1947.

Workmen's Compensation

The Workmen's Compensation Act, 1923, amended several times, applies to workmen who are employed in factories, mines, plantations, transport and construction work, railways and certain hazardous occupations. The Central and State Governments are empowered to extend the scope of the Act to any class of persons whose occupations are considered hazardous. Workers covered by the Employees' State Insurance Scheme are not entitled to benefits under the Workmen's Compensation Act.

The 2nd NCL has recommended that the Workmen's Compensation Act should be converted from an employers' liability scheme to a social insurance scheme, its coverage should be progressively extended to more employments and classes of employees, and the restrictive clauses in Schedule II of the Act should be removed.

The Act provides for the payment of compensation by employers to workmen and their dependents for personal injury caused by accidents arising out of and in the course of employment and for death or disablement as a result of contracting certain occupational diseases. The amount of compensation depends on the nature of the injury and the average monthly wages and age of the workmen. Compensation for death is payable to the dependents of workmen. The minimum and maximum rates of compensation payable for death and disablement have been fixed and is subject to revision from time-to-time. The Act is administered by State Governments through Commissioners for Workmen's Compensation. The Commissioners are entrusted with the settling of disputed claims, the disposal of claims for injuries resulting in death; and the revision of the periodic payments.

Maternity Benefits

The Maternity Benefit Act, 1961, enacted with a view to achieving uniformity in matters relating to maternity protection, applies to all factories, mines and plantations, except to those to whom the Employees' State Insurance Act applies.

The 2nd NCL has recommended that so far as the organised sector is concerned, the existing provisions for maternity benefit should be extended so as to be applicable to all women workers.

The Maternity Benefit Acts provide for the payment of cash maternity benefit for certain periods before and after confinement, and grant of leave and other facilities to women employees, on conditions prescribed in these Acts. The qualifying period of service shall be eighty days during a span of 12 months. The benefit is payable for a maximum period of 12 weeks. Apart from the Central Maternity Benefit Act, 1961, which permits the payment of a medical bonus, some State Acts include additional benefits, such as free medical aid, maternity bonus, provision of creches and additional rest intervals. In order to safeguard the interests of pregnant women workers, both the Central and State Acts provide that such women shall not be dismissed; nor can a woman worker be discharged during the period of maternity leave.

The administration of the Acts in all the States is the responsibility of factory inspectorates. Whereas in the Coal Mines, the Coal Mines Welfare Commissioner is in charge of it, the Director General of Mines Safety is in charge of mines other than coal.

Employees' State Insurance Scheme

The Employees' State Insurance Act, 1948, applies in the first instance to all non-seasonal factories run with power and employing 10 or more persons and factories run without power and employing 20 or more persons. Under the enabling provisions contained in the Act, the Act is being extended by the State Governments to new classes of establishments, namely shops, hotels, restaurants, cinemas, including preview theatres, road motor transport undertakings, and newspaper establishments employing 20 or more persons.

The ESI scheme applies only to persons whose aggregate remuneration does not exceed ₹ 6,500 per month.

An insured person, entitled to benefits under this scheme, is not eligible to claim similar benefits under the Workmen's Compensation Act and the State Maternity Benefit Act.

The benefits provided by the ESI scheme are:

1. Free medical treatment (including specialised services such as cardiological and pathological services) in cases of sickness and employment injury.
2. Free maternity care for women employees. The maternity benefit is admissible for 12 weeks, of which not more than 6 weeks may precede the expected date of confinement.
3. In the case of employment injury disabling the employee for more than seven days, a cash disablement benefit, which is roughly half the employee's wages for the duration of the disability, is allowed.
4. In the case of total permanent disablement, a life pension equal to about half the employee's wages, and in the case of partial but permanent disablement, a proportion of the amount that may fall due as life pension.
5. If the injury proves fatal, the half-wage benefit takes the form of a pension for the family or dependants of the deceased.

The scheme is financed out of a fund built from contributions collected from employees and employers and grants from the Central and State Governments.

The Act is administered by a Corporation in which employers, employees, the medical profession, the Central and State Governments and Parliament are represented. A Medical Benefit Council functions in an advisory capacity. A standing committee of the Corporation is responsible for general supervision, but executive responsibility at headquarters lies with the Director-General.

To secure cooperation of all levels, regional boards and local committees have been set up, on which are representatives of labour, employers, State Governments and the Corporation. In order to settle disputes speedily, the Act provides for the setting up of Employees' Insurance Courts by State Governments.

Provident Fund

While provident fund schemes were common in some government employments and with enlightened employers, the first legislative measure to cover industrial workers was the Coal Mines Provident Fund and Bonus Schemes Act, 1948. Though in the initial years the Act ran into opposition, both from employers and workers, after sometime the misgivings on both sides were dispelled, and the Act got off to a good start.

> The 2nd NCL has recommended that the PF Act be made applicable to all classes of establishments, subject to necessary exceptions and that the employment threshold should be brought down to 10 immediately, to 5 during the next 3-5 years, and to one within a short timeframe thereafter.

Encouraged by the success of the Coal Mines Provident Fund Scheme and faced with the persistent demand made to the Central Government for the extension of similar benefits to workers employed in other industries, the Employees' Provident Fund and Miscellaneous Provisions Act was passed in 1952. (Since 1971, it is known as the Provident Funds and Family Pension Fund Act).

The Act provides insurance against old age, retirement, discharge, retrenchment or death of the workers. It is against these risks that the schemes guarantee the necessary protection to workers and their dependants. The Act and the scheme extend to the whole of India. It applies to factories and establishments falling under any notified industry employing 20 or more persons.

To become eligible for membership of the Fund, a worker must have completed one year's continuous service, or worked for 240 days during a period of 12 months.

The employees have to contribute at the rate 6¼ per cent of the basic wage, dearness allowance and retaining allowances, if any, including the cash value of food concessions given to them. The employers too, have to contribute at the same rate. Workers, if they so desire, can contribute more, subject to a maximum of 8¼ per cent. With effect from January 1, 1963, the statutory rate of provident fund contribution has been raised to 8 per cent in respect of certain industries/classes of establishments employing 50 or more persons in a few specified industries.

The scheme is administered by a Central Board of Trustees, consisting of the representatives of the Central and State Governments, employers and workers. There are a number of regional offices, each under a regional commissioner. There are also regional committees, whose function is to advise the Central Board.

Lay-off and Retrenchment Compensation

The Industrial Disputes Act of 1947 was amended several times, provide for the payment of compensation in the event of lay-off, retrenchment, closure and transfer of undertakings.

Workers, employed in any factory, mine or plantation having an average daily employment of 50 or more where the work done is not of an intermittent or seasonal character, are entitled to compensation for lay-off, provided that they have put in the prescribed qualifying service in the preceding twelve calendar months.

A workman laid-off is entitled to get compensation according to the following rules:

1. A workman laid-off will be paid compensation by the employer for all the days during which he is so laid-off except for such weekly holidays as may intervene.
2. The rate of compensation shall be equal to fifty per cent of the total basic wages and dearness allowance that would have been payable to him had he not been so laid-off.

3. A workman laid-off shall be entitled to compensation only when he is not a badli workman or a casual workman, Badli workman means a workman who is employed in an industrial establishment in the place of another workman whose name is borne on the muster rolls of the establishment. A badli workman shall cease to be regarded as such on the completion of one year of continuous service in the establishment.

Unlike the lay-off provision, the benefits of retrenchment compensation are applicable to all the workmen covered by the Act. No workman, who has been in continuous service in any industry for not less than one year, can be retrenched by an employer until one month's notice (or wages in lieu thereof) has been given to him in writing, indicating the reasons for the retrenchment. If the establishment employs not less than one hundred workers, the notice period shall be three months or wages for the period of notice. Retrenchment compensation is payable at the rate of 15 days' average pay for every completed year of service or any part thereof in excess of six months. In the event of bonafide closures or transfer of undertakings, compensation shall be payable to workers who loose employment in consequence of such closure or transfer. In the event of a change of ownership, such workers as have been re-employed on the terms and conditions which are not less favourable to them shall not be entitled to compensation.

Gratuity Scheme

The 2nd NCL has recommended that the Payment of Gratuity Act may be integrated with the EPF Act and converted into a social insurance scheme. This will ensure automatic extension of the Payment of Gratuity Act to all establishments to which the EPF Act applies.

The Payment of Gratuity Act, 1972 is applicable to factories, mines, oil fields, plantations, ports, railways, motor transport undertakings, companies, shops and other establishments. The Act provides for payment of gratuity at the rate of 15 days' wages for each completed year of service subject to a maximum of ₹ 3,50,000. In the case of seasonal establishment, gratuity is payable at the rate of seven days' wages for each season. The Act does not affect the right of an employee to receive better terms of gratuity under any award or agreement or contract with the employer.

In case of misconduct of the employee, which involves financial loss to the management, an amount equal to the loss directly suffered by the employer by reason of such misconduct is liable to be forfeited from the gratuity due to the employee. The Act also provides for the punishment of the employer who fails to pay gratuity to an employee. Thus, gratuity has now become a statutory service condition, and its quantum has no bearing on the size of the profit of the organisation or similar extraneous consideration.

Employees' Pension Scheme

This scheme was introduced for the industrial workers with effect from 16 November, 1995. Under the Scheme, pension at the rate of 50 per cent pay is payable to the employees on retirement/super-annuation on completion of 33 years' contributory service. A minimum 10 years' service is required for entitlement to pension. Depending upon the salary and service of the employee at the time of death the scheme also provides for grant of family pension ranging from ₹ 450 per month to ₹ 2,500 per month. In addition, children-pension at the rate of 25 per cent of widow pension subject to a minimum of ₹ 115 per child is also payable up to two children.

The schemes are financed by diverting a portion of the employers' and employees' contribution to the Employees' Provident Funds with an additional contribution by the Central Government.

SUMMARY

According to the ILO, *labour welfare* refers to "such services, facilities and amenities as adequate canteens, rest and recreation facilities, arrangements for travel to and from their houses, and such other services amenities and facilities as contribute to improvements in the conditions under workers are employed".

The labour welfare services may be divided into two groups – (a) within the precincts of the establishment, and (b) outside the establishment.

Welfare and amenities within the establishment include latrines, urinals and washing and bathing facilities; crèches; rest shelters and canteens; arrangements for drinking water; arrangements for prevention of fatigue; health service including occupational safety; administrative arrangements within a plant to look after welfare; uniforms and protective clothing; and shift allowance.

It is the employer's responsibility to provide facilities within the precincts of an establishment, as they form a part of working conditions. For many components of such welfare, legislation in the country has set certain minimum standards. Improvements upon them have been left to the employers.

The facilities within the precincts of the establishment are regulated by the Factories Act, 1948, the Plantation Labour Act, 1951; and the Mines Act, 1952.

Welfare outside the establishment include maternity benefits; social insurance measure; benevolent funds; medical facilities; education facilities including adult education; housing facilities; recreation facilities, including sports, cultural activities, library and reading room; holiday homes and leave travel facilities; workers' cooperatives; vocational training for dependants of workers; other programmes for the welfare of women, youth and children; transport to and from the place of work.

Welfare amenities outside the precincts of the establishment, such as medical, educational, recreational, housing and other facilities, are non-statutory in many cases. However, in plantations, the provisions of some of them is obligatory on the employer.

Social security is also a component of labour welfare. Social security envisages that the members of a community shall be protected by collective action against social risks causing undue hardship and privation to individuals whose private resources can seldom be adequate to meet them. The Constitution of India lays down that the State shall, within the limits of its economic capacity and development, make effective provisions for securing public assistance in the event of unemployment, old age, sickness, and disablement.

The legislative enactments in India for the provision of social security may be broadly classified into two categories: (1) Acts that provide security in cases of employment injury, maternity and sickness., and (2) Acts that cover the risks of old age and unemployment.

REFERENCES

1. Government of India, *Report of National Commission on Labour*, Manager of Publications, New Delhi, 1969, p. 111.
2. Cited by *Report of National Commission on Labour*, *ibid.*, p. 112.
3. *Ibid.*, p. 112.
4. *Ibid.*, p. 112.
5. *Ibid.*, p. 112.
6. ILO, *Approach to Social Security*, 1942, p. 80. (Cited by *Report of National Commission on Labour*, *ibid.*, p. 162.)
7. Giri, V.V., *Labour Problems in Indian Industry*, Asia Publishing House, Mumbai, 1972, p. 271.
8. *Ibid.*, pp. 270-271.

☆☆☆

CHAPTER 21

INDUSTRIAL RELATIONS

Industrial disputes is a serious problem that many democratic societies face. At a point of time an industrial relations problem may be confined to one firm, an industry, a sector, a locality/region or the whole nation. Industrial disputes sometimes have a cascading effect. Labour laws, policies and attitudes of political parties, characteristics of labour and trade unionists, policies and attitudes of industrialists and management, government policies and approaches, behaviour of general public, etc., all contribute in varying degrees to the industrial relations environment.

MEANING

The important Central laws relating to the subject of Labour Relations are the Industrial Disputes Act, 1947, the Trade Unions Act, 1926 and the Industrial Employment (Standing Orders) Act, 1946. There are State level legislations too on the subject. The 2nd NCL has recommended that the provisions of all these laws be judiciously consolidated into a single law called the Labour Management Relations Law or the Law on Labour Management Relations.

The term industrial relations is so broad that it is not amenable to a precise definition. We may, however, state that *the core of industrial relations is the various aspects of interactions between employer and employees, employees and employees, employers and employers, and between the State, employers and employees*. Professor Richardson observes: "How people get on together at their work, what difficulties arise between them, how their relations, including wages and working conditions, are regulated, and what organisations are set up for the protection of different interests – these are some of the main problems of industrial relations and indicate the wide scope of the subject".[1] Industrial relations are indeed "an integral aspect of social relations arising out of employer-employee interaction in modern industries, which are regulated by the State in varying degrees, in conjuncture with organised social forces and influenced by the existing institutions. This involves a study of the State, the legal system, and the workers' and employers' organisations at the institutional level; and of patterns of industrial organisation (including management), capital structure (including technology), compensation of the labour force, and a study of market forces — all at the economic level."[2]

Professor J.T. Dunlop of Harvard University views industrial relations in a very broad perspective.[3] According to him, industrial relations should not be taken as one which denotes union-management relations operating within the spectrum of industrial peace or conflict. On the other hand, it should be taken as one which is concerned with the larger subject of an industrial relations system which defines the role, status and the conduct of different groups of people who work together for productive purposes in an economy characterised by its peculiar social and economic conditions prevailing in a given technological, market and power context, giving rise to the creation of a body of rules to govern the interactions of the different groups of people involved therein. To quote him: "An industrial relations system at any one time in development is regarded as comprised of certain actors, certain contents, an ideology which binds the industrial relations system together; and a body of rules created to govern the actors at the workplace and work community".[4]

INDUSTRIAL DISPUTES

Meaning

"According to the Industrial Disputes Act, 1947, the term "industrial dispute" means any dispute or difference between employers and employers, or between employers and workmen, or between workmen and workmen, which is connected with the employment or non-employment, or the terms of employment or with the conditions of labour, of any person."

In the literature on industrial relations, the words dispute and conflict are used more or less as synonyms. However, there is a difference between unrest and dispute. Unrest is "psychological in nature and the disputes are concrete evidence of unrest. Disputes constitute open manifestations of the feeling of dissatisfaction, disputes are the overt expression."[5] Thus, as Dr. Nagaraju observes, industrial unrest "refers to the discontent or dissatisfaction lurking in the disturbed minds of labourers, about certain lapses at the workplace or about their wages or security of employment, etc. Labourers are always hopeful that their causes of discontent or unrest can be eliminated by their collective strength. Hence, they form their own organisation and resort to certain measures with which they try to gain their ends. Since industrial unrest involves questions of right or wrong and also affects every section of society, it thrusts itself upon the attention of the community and becomes a social problem. That is the reason why in all industrial conflicts, the public is viewed as an important factor."[6]

CAUSES OF INDUSTRIAL DISPUTES

There are a number of causes for industrial dispute. A dispute may be caused by any one or more of these many factors. Some of these factors are so intertwined that sometimes it is not possible to segregate and categorise them definitely. The common causes have been adumbrated below.

Conflict of Interests

Industrial disputes arise mostly from the conflicts of interests of employees and employers.

Needless to say, all disputes emerge from one or other type of conflict of interest. Though the employer and employees are integral parts of the same organisation, many a time the goals or strategies of each party are guided by its own vested interests, the interests of one affecting those of the other. As. Nagaraju points out[7], though there is a large area in which the interests of employers and employees are the same, there are at least three areas in which conflict is certain to occur.

First, there is the conflict of interests over the division of the total product of the industry. For instance, there are a number of instances of industrial disputes caused by the labour's demand for higher bonus on the ground that the enterprise has been making substantial profits. This is one instance of labour and capital coming into conflict on the issue of sharing what the enterprise mops up from the market.

Second, as Srivastava points out, there is the conflict between the humanitarian rights of the workers and the property rights of the employers.[8] Labour wants to have a healthy and pleasant working environment, including good behaviour of the supervisors. But if the employer, in his eagerness to maximise profits, does not care for the human factor, a conflict of interest is bound to arise.

Third, as Butler observes, there is a continuing conflict between the efficiency aspirations of the management and the security aspirations of the workers.[9] For instance, where rationalisation or automation leads to retrenchment of labour, it is likely to cause a dispute.

Economic Causes

In the developing countries, where the monetary rewards for work are meagre, economic causes are the most important source of industrial disputes. We have already hinted at a few of the economic causes under the "Conflict of Interests" dealt with above. We may now more specifically state the important economic causes of industrial disputes.

Wages: The demand for higher wages is one of the most important sources of industrial conflict. An examination of the causes of industrial disputes in India shows that in most of the years, in about one-third of the total number of disputes, the main issue was wages and allowances. The common reasons for a demand for higher wages and allowances are:

1. Workers may feel that their wages do not correspond to their output or the work they do, including the risks involved in the nature of their work.
2. Existing wages are insufficient to provide a reasonable standard of living.
3. Wages and allowances have not increased sufficiently to offset the increase in the cost of living
4. Wages and allowances may be lower than those of the workers in other comparable enterprises or industries.
5. Differences of income between industrial workers and the property-owning class and the differences in the distribution of wealth.
6. The feeling that the enterprise has the capacity to pay higher wages (even when the wages are comparatively better).

Bonus: Another important issue on which disputes crop up is bonus. Despite the Payment of Bonus Act, disputes over the rate of bonus, etc., have been common. Bonus has been the cause of a significant number of industrial disputes in India.

Economic Insecurity: Sometimes industrial disputes crop up following the demand of labour for economic security. The most important economic security for the worker is his job. It is, then, natural that labour should try its best to protect the job. It is the feeling of insecurity that leads labour into a strike against retrenchment and dismissals and for a permanent status for temporary workers. Particularly in countries where there is no social safety net, like unemployment insurance, the fear of job loss creates unrest. Industrial disputes are also caused by a demand for social security benefits.

> **The most common factors behind industrial disputes are monetary, job security, working conditions and labour welfare.**

Working Conditions and Labour Welfare

Workers have come to believe that they have a right to good working conditions. Working conditions include the length of the working day, the interval and frequency of leisure, physical work environment, including safety measures.

As stated in a previous chapter, the term labour welfare refers to such services, facilities and amenities, and adequate canteen, rest and recreation facilities, arrangements for travel to and from work and for the accommodation of workers employed at a distance from their houses, and such other services such as amenities and facilities that contribute to improvements in the conditions under which workers are employed.

Personnel Factors

Poor personnel administration may also cause industrial disputes. In the absence of effective personnel management, grievances and unrest, which can be solved at the incipient stage, may spark off a dispute. V.V. Giri observes: "The services of personnel officers

> **The role of personnel management in preventing dispute is not adequately appreciated.**

are called for only when a disputes arises, and their role prior to that is lost sight of While they are useful in solving disputes, they would be far more valuable in preventing the occurrence of a dispute, if their services are properly utilised. By regularly keeping themselves in touch with labour and interpreting to them the policies of the management and also apprising the employers of the possible reactions of labour to their various schemes, personnel officers would be able to restrict, to a great extent, the nature and number of disputes in the industries"[10].

Psychological Factors

As Patterson remarks: "There are human or psychological causes of labour conflict as well as material or market causes. A worker's satisfaction with the job is based only partly on his wages, hours of work or other conditions of employment. It is also based upon the extent to which he enjoys his work and feels that it is worthwhile."[11] Such psychological factors as denial of opportunity to the worker of satisfying his basic urge for self-expression, personal achievement and betterment may cause unrest and labour problems.

External Factors

External factors refer to those causes which are not directly connected with the industrial establishment. *For example*, if the workers of an establishment strike work in support of, or to express sympathy for, the strikers in some other establishment, it is an external factor.

One of the important external factors is the political factor. Labour may strike work to protest against certain legislative measures or government policies, to support certain social and political movements, or even to change a political regime.

INDUSTRIAL DISPUTES IN INDIA

The total number of man-days lost due to strikes and lockouts increased from 4.92 million in 1961 to 16.55 million in 1971 and 36.58 millions in 1981. In 1982, the number was 77.4 million and 44.3 million in 1983, including the man-days lost due to Bombay textile strike which were estimated at 44.2 million in 1982 and 19.3 million in 1983. In most years, a majority of the man-days were lost because of strikes. The number of man-days lost due to strikes and lockouts in 1991-92 was about 34 million and 19.2 million in 1994-95. In 2003, it was about 30.25 million, 29.66 million in 2005 and 20.32 million in 2006.

PREVENTION OF INDUSTRIAL DISPUTES

As prevention is better than cure, no effort should be spared to prevent the occurrence of industrial disputes. Preventive measures may be taken at the enterprise level and at the macro-level.

Employer-Employee Relations

At the enterprise level, a good personnel management and cordial employer-employee relationship contribute to industrial peace. The participation of labour in management, a good employer-employee communication system, a proper understanding of the situation by both the parties, mutual respect for each other's rights, a proper discharge of the responsibilities by both the parties, etc., are very important if conflicts and disputes are to be avoided. There should be proper procedure for the redressal of individual grievances so that they may not ultimately lead to disputes.

Tripartite Machinery

Certain general measures have been taken to prevent disputes and to promote industrial peace, such as the establishment of a number of tripartite bodies, the adoption of the Code of Discipline, and the Industrial Truce Resolution.

The term tripartite machinery refers to the various bodies, composed of representatives of employers, employees and the Government, set up for the promotion of industrial peace. The important tripartite bodies are the following:

1. The Indian Labour Conference which is concerned with such matters as the promotion of uniformity in labour legislation, in the procedures for the settlement of industrial disputes, etc.
2. The Standing Labour Committee, which considers all those matters referred to it by the Indian Labour Conference (ILC) or by the Central Government, including the suggestions of State Governments, employers and employees bearing on labour affairs.
3. The Industrial Committees, which discuss the specific problems of industries for which they have been set up, and submit their reports to the ILC, which coordinates their activities.
4. The Central Implementation and Evaluation Committees, which are concerned with the effective implementation of labour laws, awards, settlements, etc.
5. The Committee on Conventions, which examines the ILO conventions and recommendations, and explores the possibility or advisability of ratifying them and applying them to Indian conditions.

Code of Discipline and Industrial Truce Resolution

The central organisations of employers and workers adopted the Code of Discipline in 1958. To ensure better discipline in industry, the Code lays down that:

1. There shall be no strike or lockout without notice.
2. No unilateral action shall be taken in connection with any industrial matter.
3. The existing machinery for the settlement of disputes should be utilised with the utmost expedition.

4. Neither party will have recourse to coercion, intimidation and lockout.
5. They will avoid litigation, sit-down and stay-in strikes and lockouts.
6. No deliberate damage shall be done to plant and machinery.
7. Awards and agreements should be speedily implemented.
8. Any action which disturbs cordial industrial relations should be avoided.

The Industrial Truce Resolution, which was adopted in 1962, provides that there should be maximum recourse to voluntary arbitration, and envisages that all complaints pertaining to dismissal, discharge, victimisation and retrenchment of individual workmen, not settled mutually, should be settled by arbitration.

Works Committee

The ID Act lays down that the appropriate government may require the employer of every industrial establishment in which one hundred or more workers men are employed to constitute a Works Committee consisting of representatives of employers and workmen engaged in the establishment. The number of representatives of workmen on the Committee shall not be less than the number of representatives of the employer. The representatives of the workmen shall be chosen in the prescribed manner from among the workmen engaged in the establishment and in consultation with their trade union, if any.

It shall be the duty of the Works Committee to promote measures for securing and preserving amity and good relations between the employer and workmen and, to that end, to comment upon matters of their common interest or concern and endeavour to compose any material difference of opinion in respect of such matters. The 2nd NCL recommend that the Works Committee should be substituted by Industrial Relations Committee (IRC) to promote inhouse dispute settlement.

SETTLEMENT OF DISPUTES

There are statutory and non-statutory methods for the settlement of industrial disputes.

If the dispute can be settled by non-statutory methods, the employer-employee relations might continue to be cordial. Under statutory methods, the settlement is sometimes imposed rather than willingly accepted.

Sometimes, an amicable settlement may arise out of negotiation and discussion directly between management and employees. When this is not possible, a third party, like a Government representative, may mediate and try to bring the parties to a mutual agreement.

Voluntary Arbitration

V.V. Giri, who regarded compulsory adjudication as Enemy Number One of collective bargaining and industrial peace, had great faith in the virtues of arbitration on voluntary basis. The Code of Discipline adopted by the central organisations of employers and workers in 1958 and the Industrial Truce Resolution of 1962 stressed the significance of voluntary arbitration. The spirit of voluntary arbitration is to settle disputes mutually and without recourse to legal remedies, for "it is essentially the existence of a spirit of give-and-take amongst employers and workers which is a *sine qua non* for the maintenance of peace between the two parties".

The second NCL suggested that arbitration should become the accepted mode of determining disputes which are not settled by the parties.

The merits attributed to voluntary arbitration are:

1. It is less time-consuming.
2. It is less expensive than adjudication.
3. It avoids litigation which so often occurs in adjudication cases.
4. It promotes goodwill and confidence between the parties to the dispute.
5. The award of the voluntary arbitrator is generally accepted with better spirit than under compulsory arbitration.
6. It promotes collective bargaining and the democratic spirit.

SETTLEMENT OF DISPUTES UNDER THE INDUSTRIAL DISPUTES ACT

The statutory machinery for the settlement of industrial disputes has been provided by the Industrial Disputes Act, 1947, amended from time-to-time (significantly in 1982). The important authorities which constitute the machinery for the settlement of industrial disputes under the Act are described below.

Grievance Settlement Authority

The ID Act provides that every industrial establishment which employs 50 or more workers shall have a Grievance Settlement Authority (GSA) for the settlement of industrial disputes connected with any individual workman employed in the establishment.

When an industrial dispute connected with an individual workman arises in such an establishment, the workman or any trade union of workmen of which such workman is a member, may refer, in such manner as may be prescribed, such dispute to the GSA.

The GSA shall follow the prescribed procedure and complete the proceedings within the prescribed period.

No reference shall be made with respect to any such dispute to any other authority under the Act unless such dispute has been referred to the GSA and the decision of the GSA is not acceptable to either of the parties to the dispute.

Conciliation Officers

The ID Act provides for the appointment of conciliation officers by appropriate Government, charged with the duty of mediating in and promoting the settlement of the industrial dispute. (It may be stated, generally, that in respect of industrial disputes concerning a Central Government establishment, the appropriate government is the Central

Government, and in most other cases the State Governments concerned is the appropriate government).

A conciliation officer may be appointed for a specified area, or for specified industries in a specified area, or for one or more specified industries, either permanently or for a limited period.

According to the 2nd NCL, to make conciliation effective, it is necessary to improve the status and competence and calibre of conciliation officers through proper recruitment, training and placement. A. Labour and Judicial Service can be formed.

Where any industrial disputes exists or is apprehended, the conciliation officer may (or where the dispute relates to a public utility service and a notice for strike or lockout has been given in accordance with the provisions of the Act, the conciliation officer *shall*) hold conciliation proceedings in the prescribed manner.

If a settlement of the dispute or of any of the matters in dispute is arrived at, the conciliation officer shall send a report of it to the appropriate Government (or an officer authorised in this behalf by the appropriate Government), together with a memorandum of the settlement signed by the parties to the dispute.

If no such settlement is arrived at, the conciliation officer shall report the reasons on account of which, in his opinion, a settlement could not be arrived at. If, on a consideration of the such a report by the conciliation officer, the appropriate Government is satisfied that there is a case for reference to a Board of Conciliation, Labour Court, Tribunal or National Tribunal, it may make such a reference. Where the appropriate Government does not make such a reference, it shall record and communicate to the parties concerned its reasons thereof.

Board of Conciliation

The ID Act provides that the appropriate Government may, as occasion arises, constitute a Board of Conciliation to promote the settlement of an industrial dispute.

The Board shall consist of a chairman and two or four other members, as the appropriate Government thinks fit. The chairman shall be an independent person and the other members shall be persons appointed in equal numbers to represent the parties to the dispute, and any person appointed to represent a party shall be appointed on the recommendation of that party. However, if any party fails to make a recommendation as aforesaid within the prescribed time, the appropriate Government shall appoint such persons as it thinks fit to represent that party.

Where a dispute has been referred to a Board, it shall, without delay, investigate the dispute do all such things as it thinks fit for the purpose of inducing the parties to come to a fair and amicable settlement of the dispute.

If the settlement of a dispute or of any of the matters in dispute is arrived; the Board shall send a report thereof to the appropriate Government, together with a memorandum of the settlement signed by the parties to the dispute.

If no such settlement is arrived at, the Board shall report the reasons on account of which, in its opinion, settlement could not be arrived at its recommendations for the termination of the dispute. If, on the receipt of such a report, the appropriate Government does not make a reference to a Labour Court, Tribunal or National Tribunal, it shall record and communicate the parties concerned its reasons thereof.

Courts of Inquiry

The ID Act provides that the appropriate Government may, as occasion arises, constitute a Court of Inquiry to inquire into any matter appearing to be connected with or relevant to an industrial dispute.

A Court may consist of one independent person or of such number of independent persons as the appropriate Government may think fit and where a Court consists of two or more members, one of them shall be appointed as the Chairman.

A Court shall inquire into the matters referred to it and report thereon to the appropriate Government ordinarily within a period of six months from the commencement of its inquiry.

Labour Courts

The appropriate Government may constitute one or more Labour Courts to adjudicate industrial disputes relating to any matter specified in the Second Schedule and to perform such other functions as may be assigned to them under the Act. A Labour Court shall consist of one person only to be appointed by the appropriate Government. (The Second Schedule covers matters such as issues related to Standing Orders, discharge or dismissal of workers, illegality or otherwise of strikes and lockouts withdrawal of any customary benefit).

Tribunals

The appropriate Government may constitute one or more Industrial Tribunals to adjudicate an industrial dispute relating to any matter, whether specified in the Second Schedule or Third Schedule, and to perform such other functions as may be assigned to them under this Act. A Tribunal shall consist of one person only to be appointed by the appropriate Government. (The Third Schedule covers matters such as wages, bonus, allowances and certain other benefits, certain working conditions, discipline, rationalization, retrenchment and closure of establishment).

National Tribunals

The Central Government may, by notification in the Official Gazette, constitute one or more National Industrial Tribunals to adjudicate an industrial dispute which, in the opinion of the Central Government, involve questions of national importance or are of such a nature that industrial establishments situated in more than one State are likely to be interested in, or affected by, such disputes. A National Tribunal shall consist of one person only to be appointed by the Central Government. The Central Government may, if it so thinks fit, appoint two persons as assessors to advise the National Tribunal in the proceedings before it.

Duties of Labour Courts, Tribunals and National Tribunals: Where an industrial dispute has been referred to a Labour Court, Tribunal or National Tribunal for adjudication, it shall hold its proceedings expeditiously and shall within the period specified in the order referring such industrial dispute, or within the further period extended under the provisions of the Act, submit its award to the appropriate Government.

Reference and Awards

Where the appropriate Government is of the opinion that any industrial dispute exists or is apprehended, it may at any time refer the dispute or any matter appearing to be connected with it to the concerned authority.

Where an industrial dispute has been so referred to the concerned authority, the appropriate Government may prohibit the continuance of any strike or lockout in connection with such dispute which may be in existence on the day of reference.

There is also a provision in the Act for voluntary reference of disputes to arbitration if the employer and the workman agree to that.

The award of the concerned authority on the dispute shall be in writing and shall, within a period of thirty days from the date of its receipt by the appropriate Government, be published in such manner as the appropriate Government thinks fit. (*Award* "means an interim or final determination of any industrial dispute or of any question relating thereto by any Labour Courts, Industrial Tribunal and National Industrial Tribunal and includes an arbitration award" made under this Act).

An award shall become enforceable on the expiry of thirty days from the date of its publication. However, the appropriate Government may declare that the award shall not become enforceable on the expiry of the said period of thirty days if it thinks that it will be expedient so to do on public grounds affecting national economy or social justice. Where such a declaration has been made, the appropriate Government may, within ninety days from the date of the publication of the award, make an order rejecting or modifying the award, and shall, on the first available opportunity, lay the award, together with a copy of the order, before the State legislature or Parliament, as the case may be.

Prohibition of Strikes and Lockouts

The Act prohibits strikes and lockouts in public utilities without sufficient notice as specified in the Act. It also prohibits strikes and lockouts during the pendancy of proceedings relating to the dispute before the concerned authority and a certain specified period after that. Further, strikes and lockouts are prohibited during any period in which a settlement or award is in operation in respect of any of the matters covered by the settlement of the award.

Where a strike or lockout in pursuance of an industrial dispute has already commenced and is in existence at the time of the reference of the dispute to the authority, the continuance of such strike or lockout shall not be deemed to be illegal, provided that such strike or lockout was not at its commencement in contravention of the provisions of this Act and the continuance thereof was not prohibited under the Act. Further, a lockout declared in

BOX 21.1 : NATIONAL COMMISSION ON LABOUR ON STRIKES

The second National Commission on Labour in its Report observed that strike could be called only by the recognised negotiating agent and that too only after it had conducted a strike ballot amongst all the workers, of whom at least 51 per cent support the strike. Correspondingly, an employer will not be allowed to declare a lockout except with the approval at the highest level of management except in cases of actual or grave apprehension of physical threat to the management or to the establishment. The appropriate government will have the authority to prohibit a strike or lockout by a general or special order and refer for adjudication the issue leading to the strike/lockout. The general provisions like giving of notice of not less than 14 days, not declaring a strike or lockout over a dispute which is in conciliation or adjudication and so on will be incorporated in the law. In this context we also recommend that an illegal strike or illegal lockout should attract similar penalties. A worker who goes on an illegal strike should lose three days wages for every day of illegal strike, and the management must pay the worker wages equivalent to three days wages per day of the duration of an illegal lockout. The union which leads an illegal strike must be derecognised and debarred from applying for registration or recognition for a period of two or three years.

The Commission also discussed the question whether any distinction should be made between 'strike' and 'work stoppage' and came to the conclusion that the existing definition of 'strike' in the Industrial Disputes Act, 1947 may stand, "Go slow" and "work-to-rule" are forms of action which must be regarded as misconduct. Standing Orders and Provisions relating to unfair labour practices already include them and provide for action both in the case of "go slow" and "work-to-rule".

Driving the dispute into the realm of law and order, and using the strong arm of the.State to convert industrial disputes into matters for the police or the law and order enforcement machinery is not to the advantage of the workers, and perhaps to that of the industry as well.

There are some industries or services where the effects of industrial action create situations which threaten the lives and normal and essential needs and activities of the vast majority. One's liberty has to be seen in the light of the equal right that everyone else has to demand and enjoy liberty. Social intervention thus becomes justified and necessary to protect the interests of all concerned. The Commission has, therefore, recommended that in the case of socially essential services like water supply, medical services, sanitation, electricity and transport, when there is a dispute between employers and employees in an enterprise, and when the dispute is not settled through mutual negotiations, there may be a strike ballot as in other enterprises, and if the strike ballot shows that 51 per cent of workers are in favour of a strike, it should be taken that the strike has taken place, and the dispute must forthwith be referred to compulsory arbitration (by arbitrators from the panel of the Labour Relations Commission (LRC), or arbitrators agreed to by both sides).

The Commission also discussed the question whether any distinction should be made between 'strike' and 'work stoppage' and came to the conclusion that the existing definition of 'strike' in the Industrial Disputes Act, 1947 may stand, "Go slow" and "work-to-rule" are forms of action which must be regarded as misconduct. Standing Orders and Provisions relating to unfair labour practices already include them and provide for action both in the case of "go slow" and "work-to-rule".

The Commission has recommended the withdrawal of the Essential Services Maintenance Act.

consequence of an illegal strike or a strike declared in consequence of an illegal lockout shall not be deemed to be illegal.

The Act also provides that no person shall knowingly expend or apply any money in direct furtherance or support of any illegal strike or lockout. Any person who violates this shall be punishable with imprisonment for a term which may extend to six months, or with fine up to ₹ 1,000 or both.

Other Important Provisions of the Act

The Industrial Disputes Act lays down the conditions of lay-off and retrenchment; the right of workmen laid-off for compensation; the procedure for closing down an undertaking; the compensation for workmen in the event of the closure and transfer of undertakings; and penalties for illegal strikes and lockouts, instigation, breach of settlement or award, disclosing confidential information, closure without notice and other offences.

The Act also lays down that no employer or workmen or a trade union shall commit any unfair labour practice. Any person who commits any unfair labour practice shall be punishable with imprisonment for a term which may extend to six months or with fine which may extend to ₹1,000, or both.

While presenting the Union Budget 2001-2002, the Finance Minister made the following observation. Some existing provisions in the Industrial Disputes Act have made it almost impossible for industrial firms to exercise any labour flexibility. The Government is now convinced that some change is necessary in this legislation. Chapter VB of the ID Act stipulates that employers in specified industrial establishments must obtain prior approval of the appropriate government authority for effecting lay-off, retrenchment and closure, after following the prescribed procedure. It is proposed that these provisions may now apply to industrial establishments employing not less than 1,000 workers instead of 100. The requirement of compensation will be increased from 15 days to 45 days for every completed year of service. The enhancement of compensation would act as a deterrent on employers to take recourse to lay-off, retrenchment and closure in a routine manner.

SUMMARY

The term industrial relations covers the various aspects of interactions between employer and employees, employees and employees, employers and employers, and between the state, employers and employees.

"Many a time industrial relations are far from satisfactory and industrial disputes are not uncommon. According to the Industrial Disputes Act, 1947, the term "industrial dispute" means any dispute or difference between employers and employers, or between employers and workmen, or between workmen and workmen, which is connected with the employment or non-employment, or the terms of employment or with the conditions of labour, of any person."

Though there is a large area in which the interests of employers and employees are the same, there are at least three areas in which conflict is certain to occur. First, there is the conflict of interests over the division of the total product of the industry. Second, there is the conflict between the human rights of the workers and the property rights of the employers.

Third, there is a continuing conflict between the efficiency aspirations of the management and the security aspirations of the workers.

The important issues causing industrial disputes are Economic (wages, bonus, economic insecurity – fear of loss of job), and working conditions and labour welfare. External factors like political reasons, sympathy to workers in other establishments, etc., may also cause labour problems. In the absence of effective personnel management, grievances and unrest, which can be solved at the incipient stage, may spark-off a dispute. Sometimes psychological factors also cause industrial relations problem.

Prevention is better than cure. There are several measures that may be taken at the enterprise level and at the macro-level to prevent the occurrence of industrial disputes.

At the enterprise level, a good personnel management and cordial employer-employee relationship, and a proper system for the redressal of individual grievances contribute to industrial peace.

Certain general measures have been taken to prevent disputes and to promote industrial peace, such as the establishment of a number of tripartite bodies, the adoption of the Code of Discipline, and the Industrial Truce Resolution.

The ID Act provides for the constitution of a Works Committee consisting of representatives of employers and workmen in every industrial establishment in which one hundred or more workers men are employed to promote measures for securing and preserving amity and good relations between the employer and workmen.

There are a number of authorities under the Industrial Disputes Act to deal with industrial disputes. They are Conciliation Officers, Board of Conciliation, Court of Enquiry, Labour Court, Industrial Tribunal and National Industrial Tribunal.

The Industrial Disputes Act prohibits strikes and lockouts in public utilities without sufficient notice as specified in the Act. It also prohibits strikes and lockouts during the pendancy of proceedings relating to the dispute before the concerned authority and a certain specified period after that. Further, strikes and lockouts are prohibited during any period in which a settlement or award is in operation in respect of any of the matters covered by the settlement of the award.

The Act lays down the conditions of lay-off and retrenchment; the right of workmen laid-off for compensation; the procedure for closing down an undertaking; the compensation for workmen in the event of the closure of undertakings; and penalties for illegal strikes and lockouts, instigation, breach of settlement or award, disclosing confidential information, closure without notice and other offences.

The Act also lays down that no employer or workmen or a trade union shall commit any unfair labour practice.

REFERENCES

1. Richardson, J.H., *An Introduction to Industrial Relations* (Cited by Nagaraju, S., *Industrial Relations System in India*, Chugh Publications, Allahabad, 1981, p. 1.)
2. Singh, V.B., *Climate for Industrial Relations* (cite in C.B. Mamoria, *Personnel Management*, Himalaya Publishing House, Bombay, 1982, p. 754.
3. For details of Dunlop's Model of Industrial Relations System and its application at a regional level in India, see Nagaraju, S., *Industrial Relations System in India, op. cit.*

4. Cited by S. Nagaraju, *ibid.*, p. 2.
5. Nagaraju, S., *ibid.*, p. 2, 3.
6. *Ibid.*, p. 24.
7. *Ibid.*, p. 24.
8. Srivastava, K.N., *Industrial Peace and Labour in India*, (Cited by Nagaraju, *ibid.*, p. 26).
9. Butler, A.D., *Labour Economics and Labour Institutions* (Cited by Nagaraju, *ibid.*, p. 26).
10. Giri, V.V., *Labour Problems in Indian Industry*, Asia Publishing House, Bombay, 1972, p. 121.
11. Cited by Nagaraju, *op. cit.*, p. 30.

ANNEXURE 21.1

SCHEDULES TO THE INDUSTRIAL DISPUTES ACT, 1947
THE FIRST SCHEDULE

INDUSTRIES WHICH MAY BE DECLARED TO BE PUBLIC UTILITY SERVICES UNDER SUB-CLAUSE (VI) OF CLAUSE (N) OF SECTION 2

1. Transport (other than railways) for the carriage of passengers or goods, by land or water.
2. Banking.
3. Cement.
4. Coal.
5. Cotton textiles.
6. Foodstuffs.
7. Iron and Steel.
8. Defence establishments.
9. Service in hospitals and dispensaries.
10. Fire Brigade Service.
11. India Government Mints.
12. India Security Press.
13. Copper Mining.
14. Lead Mining.
15. Zinc Mining
16. Iron Ore Mining.
17. Service in any oilfield.
18. Service in the Uranium Industry.
19. Pyrites Mining Industry.
20. Security Paper Mill, Hoshangabad.
21. Service in the Bank Note Press, Dewas.
22. Phosphorite Mining.
23. Magnesite Mining.
24. Currency Note Press.
25. Manufacture or production of mineral oil (crude oil), motor and aviation spirit, diesel oil, kerosene oil, fuel oil, diverse hydrocarbon oils and their blends including synthetic fuels, lubricating oils and the like.
26. Service in the International Airports Authority of India.
27. Industrial establishment, manufacturing or producing nuclear fuel and components, heavy water and allied chemicals, and atomic energy.

THE SECOND SCHEDULE

MATTERS WITHIN THE JURISDICTION OF LABOUR COURTS (*SECTION 7*)

1. The propriety or legality of an order passed by an employer under the standing orders.
2. The application and interpretation of standing order.
3. Discharge or dismissal of workmen including reinstatement of, or grant of relief to, workmen wrongfully dismissed.
4. Withdrawal of any customary concession or privilege.
5. Illegality or otherwise of a strike or lockout.
6. All matters other than those specified in the Third Schedule.

THE THIRD SCHEDULE

MATTERS WITHIN THE JURISDICTION OF INDUSTRIAL TRIBUNALS (*SECTION 7A*)

1. Wages, including the period and mode of payment.
2. Compensatory and other allowances.
3. Hours of work and rest intervals.
4. Leave with wages and holidays.
5. Bonus, profit sharing, provident fund and gratuity.
6. Shift working otherwise than in accordance with standing orders.
7. Classification by grades.
8. Rules of discipline.
9. Rationalisation.
10. Retrenchment of workmen and closure of establishment.
11. Any other matter that may be prescribed.

THE FOURTH SCHEDULE

CONDITIONS OF SERVICE FOR CHANGE OF WHICH NOTICE IS TO BE GIVEN (*SECTION 9A*)

1. Wages, including the period and mode of payment.
2. Contribution paid, or payable, by the employer to any provident fund or pension fund or for the benefit of the workmen under any law for the time-being in force.
3. Compensatory and other allowances.
4. Hours of work and rest intervals.
5. Leave with wages and holidays.
6. Starting, alteration or discontinuance of shift working otherwise than in accordance with standing orders.
7. Classification by grades.
8. Withdrawal of any customary concession or privilege or change in usage.

9. Introduction of new rules of discipline, or alteration of existing rules, except in so far as they are provided in standing orders.
10. Rationalisation, standardization or improvement of plant or technique which is likely to lead to retrenchment of workmen.
11. Any increase or reduction (other than casual) in the number of persons employed or to be employed in any occupation or process or department or shift, not occasioned by circumstances over which the employer has no control.

THE FIFTH SCHEDULE

UNFAIR LABOUR PRACTICES [SECTION 2(RA)]

I. On the Part of Employers and Trade Unions of Employers

1. To interfere with, restrain from, or coerce, workmen in the exercise of their right to organise, form, join or assist a trade union or to engage in concerted activities for the purposes of collective bargaining or other mutual aid or protection, that is to say —
   (*a*) threatening workmen with discharge or dismissal, if they join a trade union;
   (*b*) threatening a lockout or closure, if a trade union is organised;
   (*c*) granting wage increase to workmen at crucial periods of trade union organisation, with a view to undermining the efforts of the trade union at organisation.
2. To dominate, interfere with or contribute support, financial or otherwise, to any trade union, that is to say,
   (*a*) an employer taking an active interest in organising a trade union of his workmen; and
   (*b*) an employer showing partiality or granting favour to one of several trade unions attempting to organise his workmen or to its members, where such a trade union is not a recognised trade union.
3. To establish employer sponsored trade unions of workmen.
4. To encourage or discourage membership in any trade union by discriminating against any workman, that is to say,
   (*a*) discharging or punishing a workman, because he urged other workmen to join or organise a trade union;
   (*b*) discharging or dismissing a workman for taking part in any strike (not being a strike which is deemed to be an illegal strike under this Act);
   (*c*) changing seniority rating or workmen because of trade union activities;
   (*d*) refusing to promote workmen of higher posts on account of their trade union activities;
   (*e*) giving unmerited promotions to certain workmen with a view to creating discord amongst other workmen, or to undermine the strength of their trade union;
   (*f*) discharging office-bearers or active members of the trade union on account of their trade union activities.

5. To discharge or dismiss workmen —
   (*a*) by way of victimisation;
   (*b*) not in good faith, but in the colourable exercise of the employer's rights;
   (*c*) by falsely implicating a workman in a criminal case on false evidence or on concocted evidence;
   (*d*) for patently false reasons;
   (*e*) on untrue or trumped up allegations of absence without leave;
   (*f*) in utter disregard of the principles of natural justice in the conduct of domestic enquiry or with undue haste;
   (*g*) for misconduct of a minor technical character, without having any regard to the nature of the particular misconduct or the past record or service of the workman, thereby leading to a disproportionate punishment.
6. To abolish the work of a regular nature being done by workmen, and to give such work to contractors as a measure of breaking a strike.
7. To transfer a workman *mala fide* from one place to another, under the guise of following management policy.
8. To insist upon individual workmen, who are on a legal strike to sign a good conduct bond, as a precondition to allowing them to resume work.
9. To show favouritism or partiality to one set of workers regardless of merit.
10. To employ workmen as "badlis", casuals or temporaries and to continue them as such for years, with the object of depriving them of the status and privileges of permanent workmen.
11. To discharge or discriminate against any workman for filing charges or testifying against an employer in any enquiry or proceeding relating to any industrial dispute.
12. To recruit workman during a strike which is not an illegal strike.
13. Failure to implement award, settlement or agreement.
14. To indulge in acts of force or violence.
15. To refuse to bargain collectively, in good faith with the recognised trade unions.
16. Proposing or continuing a lockout deemed to be illegal under this Act.

II. On the Part of Workmen and Trade Unions of Workmen

1. To advise or actively support or instigate any strike deemed to be illegal under this Act.
2. To coerce workmen in the exercise of their right to self-organisation or to join a trade union or refrain from joining any trade union, that is to say—
   (*a*) for a trade union or its members to picketing in such a manner that non-striking workmen are physically debarred from entering the workplaces;
   (*b*) to indulge in acts of force or violence or to hold out threats of intimidation in connection with a strike against non-striking workmen or against managerial staff.

3. For a recognised union to refuse to bargain collectively in good faith with the employer.
4. To indulge in coercive activities against certification of a bargaining representative.
5. To stage, encourage or instigate such forms of coercive actions as wilful, "go-slow", squatting on the work premises after working hours or "gherao" of any of the members of the managerial or other staff.
6. To stage demonstrations at the residence of the employers or the managerial staff members.
7. To incite or indulge in wilful damage to employer's property connected with the industry.
8. To indulge in acts of force or violence or to hold out threats of intimidation against any workman with a view to prevent him from attending work.

☆☆☆

CHAPTER 22

TRADE UNIONS

Trade unions are very important, sometimes very critical, environment of business. While responsible trade unions would be beneficial to the workers, business and the society, irresponsible trade unions could be harmful to all.

MEANING

Under the Trade Unions Act, the expression trade union includes both employers' and workers' organisations.

> **Under the Indian Trade Unions Act, the definition of Trade Unions is very broad; workers' union is just one of the different forms of Trade Unions**

According to he Indian Trade Unions Act, 1926, a "Trade union means any combination, whether temporary or permanent, formed primarily for the purpose of regulating the relations between workmen and employers, or between workmen and workmen, or between employers and employers, or for imposing restrictive conditions on the conduct of any trade or business, and includes any federation of two or more trade unions". The Act does not, however, affect:

1. Any agreement between partners as to their own business.
2. Any agreement between an employer and those employed by him as to such employment.
3. Any agreement in consideration of the sale of the goodwill of a business or of instruction in any profession, trade or handicraft.

The term trade union, however, is commonly used to refer to the organisation of workers formed to protect their rights and enhance their welfare. In this chapter, the discussion is limited to the organisation of workers. According to V.V. Giri, "trade unions are voluntary organisations of workers formed to promote and protect their interests by collective action".[1] A trade union "must possess definite aims; its members must be welded together in a united front for the good of the whole group rather than for the promotion of any selfish individual interests; and it must, to be effective, take on a definite and permanent form of organisation through which it strives to accomplish its goal".[2]

Functions of Trade Unions

Trade unions are intended to protect the rights and enhance the welfare of the members in particular and of the working class in general. According to the National Commission on Labour (NCL), the important functions of the trade unions are:[3]

1. To secure for workers fair wages.
2. To safeguard security of tenure and improve conditions of service.
3. To improve opportunities for promotion and training.
4. To improve working and living conditions.
5. To provide for educational, cultural and recreational facilities.
6. To cooperate in and facilitate technological advance by broadening the understanding of workers of its underlying issues.
7. To promote identity of interests of the workers with their industry.
8. To offer responsive cooperation in improving levels of production and productivity, discipline and high standard of quality.
9. To promote individual and collective welfare.

Social Responsibilities of Trade Unions

It is not uncommon that the organised might of the trade unions holds public life to ransom as pressure tactics to serve their purpose, throwing civil rights and liberties to the winds. While the unions have the right to fight for their legitimate rights, it is high time they realised that they have no right to misuse their organised might to deny the unorganised innocent public their legitimate rights.

Trade unions are expected to be socially responsible and responsive to the social conditions and demands.

As the NCL observes, it is imperative that unions keep the well-being and progress of the community constantly before them even in the midst of their endeavours to help the working class. Unions have a stake in the success of the national plans for economic development, since these are formulated and implemented as much for maximising production as for distributing the product in an equitable manner. Unions have to adapt themselves to changing social needs, and rise above the divisive forces of caste, religion and language. In this context, some important social responsibilities of trade unions appear to be in the field of:[4]

1. Promotion of national integration;
2. Generally influencing the socio-economic policies of the community through active participation in their formulation at various levels; and
3. Instilling in their members a sense of responsibility towards industry and the community.

According to Giri, "the scope of trade unions should not be confined merely to the workers' demands, but should include the inculcation in the workers of a sense of discipline and responsibility, an appreciation of their moral responsibility to do a fair day's work for a fair day's wages. The unions should make every worker understand fully, first, his duties and responsibilities and then, his rights and privileges. This means that the objects of a trade union should be such as to instill in the individual worker a spirit of self-reliance, toleration and cooperation. In fact, in a society which is well set on the road to socialism and in which the workers' claim to proper wages and good working conditions receives constant attention, the worker has substantial responsibilities which he should fully understand and discharge. Socialism requires the establishment of an industrial democracy, which in turn calls for discipline on the one hand and sincere and efficient work on the other."[5]

TRADE UNION MOVEMENT IN INDIA

Though the trade union movement in India had its germination in the last quarter of the nineteenth century, it was only in the first quarter of the twentieth century that the trade union movement, as it is understood today, took its birth. N.M. Lokhande, who was a factory worker in Bombay, is regarded as the founder of the organised labour movement in India.

Factors Which Contributed to Growth

As Giri observes,[6] the following factors helped the growth of trade union movement of India:

1. World War I: Though the labour movement in India began about a century ago; it was only from the end of the First World War (1914-1918) that it gathered momentum. Giri points out that both economic and political conditions alike contributed to the new awakening. Prices had shot up during the war and there had been no corresponding increase in the wages, though the employers had amassed fantastic profits. In the political field, new ideas were in the air. The Indian National Congress had formulated its demand for immediate self-government. All this was reflected in considerable labour unrest, one of the features of the nineteen twenties. These conditions led, inevitably, to the formation of a large number of trade unions throughout the country.[7]

Several developments within and outside the country fostered the trade union movement in India

2. Influence of Political Leaders: The early stages of the development of trade union movement in India owe a lot to the contributions of some political leaders, social reformers and philanthropists. "The mass movement started by Lokamanya Tilak, Annie Besant and later by Mahatma Gandhi caused ripples in the trade union movement. In particular, the non-cooperation movement launched by Gandhiji during 1919-21 and the espousal by him of the cause of the peasants and industrial labour had a profound impact on the working class. Gandhiji was also greatly responsible for giving a reorientation to the labour movement by establishing the Ahmedabad Textile Labour Association, which had, as its main plank, the settlement of trade disputes by negotiations and peaceful methods before resorting to direct action."[8]

3. The ILO: The establishment of the International Labour Organisation, of which India was a founder member, prompted the formation of trade unions in India. In choosing its nominees to the International Labour Conference, held annually, the Government had to consult the organisations of the workers and employers to represent their interests. This led to the establishment of the All India Trade Union Congress as the central body of workers, representing the various trade unions affiliated to it.

4. The Russian Revolution: The success of the Russian revolution gave an impetus to the labour movement because of the feeling it generated that the solidarity of the working class could achieve great things.

5. The Trade Unions Act: The Indian Trade Unions Act, passed in 1926, is landmark in the history of trade union movement in India because this Act gave trade unions a legal status and immunity to its officers and members against civil and criminal liability for concerted action.

Some Important Developments

As indicated earlier, it was only after the First World War that the trade union movement in India gathered momentum. The widespread labour unrest in the immediate post-war period led to the formation of a number of trade unions in different industries on a permanent basis. In 1920, the All-India Trade Union Congress (AITUC) was established to co-ordinate and guide the activities of the individual unions and to express their views on the general policy matters and programmes affecting labour. As Giri observes, the foundation of the AITUC marked the first recognition of the common interest of labour throughout the country, and it gave a great fillip to the rapid formation of unions in different parts of the country and in industries, big and small.

In addition to the rights conferred on the registered unions by the Act, their registration enhanced the status of unions in the eyes of the public as well as the employers. In this process, even unregistered unions benefited, and the movement as a whole gained greater confidence of workers.

The conflicts between the moderates and leftists within the All-India Trade Union Congress resulted in a split in the organisation in 1929, with the leftists capturing the Congress. The break away group formed the All-India Trade Union Federation "with a realistic policy, programme and objectives".

The early nineteen thirties were an unfavourable period for the trade union movement. Apart from the serious economic depression which the country had been passing through,

Gandhiji's civil disobedience movement, launched in 1930, had diverted the attention of the political leaders of India from the trade union movement. The second split in the All-India Trade Union Congress occurred in 1931, resulting in the formation of a new organisation called the Red Trade Union Congress which, in the next year, united with the parent organisation. The All-India Trade Union Federation and the railway unions joined the National Trade Unions Federation which came into existence in 1933, with a view to foregoing unity in the trade union movement. The National Trade Union Federation, which claimed a larger membership than the AITUC, and the AITUC merged together in 1938.

BOX 22.1 : IMPACT OF POLITICAL AND SOCIAL FORCES

The National Commission On Labour in its Report (1969) has made the following observation.

Forming of trade unions and the shaping of their activities by the political workers and their philosophy, were not entirely unknown in the past. They have acquired new dimensions with the advent of Independence and the environment which the political system has operated in or has created for itself. Though unions are apparently free from organisational ties with political parties, the association of many unions/federations with politics through ideology and leadership cannot be denied. Such ties have led to fragmentation of unions, to inter-union and intra-union rivalries, and some confusion in the minds of the rank and file of workers.... A demand for freeing unions from political influence is gaining ground and assertions about their autonomous character in relation to their ideological political partners are frequently made.

A major change on the social side has been brought about by the Hindu Code with its two important components: the Hindu Succession Act, 1955, and the Hindu Marriage Act, 1956. The first gave women equal rights with men in the matter of succession to and holding of property; the second struck at the root of polygamy and provided for divorce with alimony and maintenance. The joint family system is losing its hold, more particularly in urban areas where provision for social security by the State is encouraging nuclear families; because of the growth of nuclear families, demand for improvement of social security provisions is also gaining in strength.

The period of the Second World War (1939-45) was again a bad time for the trade union movement in India. The unity in the movement that was secured before the war did not last long. Differences arose on the question of the attitude of labour towards the war. The attitude of the communists in the AITU swung in favour of the Russian involvement in the war. In the early days of the war, the communists were opposed to the war effort of the British Government because the USSR had been in the opposite camp with Germany. A section of labour leaders, who supported the war effort of the British Government, led by the radical democratic leader, M.N. Roy, seceded from the All-India Trade Union Congress and formed a separate central organisation called the Indian Federation of Labour. The Federation, which had the support of the Government, also gained strength and the support of a large number of trade unions. In many industries, rival unions were formed by those who did not subscribe to the view that workers should assist the British in their war efforts.

When Hitler and Stalin fell out and the Soviet Union changed over to the side of the Allies, the communists in India changed their attitude too, and at the behest of the Secretary of the British Communist Party, lent support to the war efforts.

The nationalist elements in the All-India Trade Union Congress, however, followed the lead of the Indian National Congress, and most of them were arrested and detained for a long time. Their absence from the trade union field enabled the leaders of the Indian Federation of Labour to strengthen their hold on the workers and the communist leaders to dominate the All-India Trade Union Congress. Even though the official outlook of the AITUC was one of neutrality, there were different groups in it having different views on the war.

The pattern of trade union movement in India was influenced by developments in the political scenario.

Because of the sharp increase in the cost of living and the failure of the employers to appreciate the workers' demands, there was widespread labour unrest. The Government used the Defence of India Rules and prohibited strikes and lockouts, and referred industrial disputes for conciliation and adjudication. However, the deteriorating economic condition of the workers made the latter conscious of the need for making organised efforts to secure relief. This gave a fillip to the trade union movement, and there was a marked increase, both in the number of unions and of organised workers, by the end of the war. The two central organisations, namely, the All-India Trade Union Congress and the Indian Federation of Labour, actively strove to organise workers in different industries; but the absence of nationalist trade union leaders from the field and the general national outlook of the people operated as a negative factor.

The strained economic conditions following the war and the partition of the country at the time of its independence increased the number of the unemployed and made the plight of the workers very miserable, resulting in widespread labour unrest. There was a feeling on the part of the nationalist-minded trade union leaders, when they came out of jails, that the trade union movement was in a most unorganised manner and that steps should be taken to re-establish the unity which had been noticeable in the thirties. The All-India Trade Union Congress was in the grip of the communists; and the Indian Federation of Labour, because of the patronage it had received from the British, was suspect in the eyes of the people. The Indian National Trade Union Congress (INTUC) was, therefore, started in 1947 under the patronage of the Indian National Congress. In the next year, the Hind Mazdoor Sabha (HMS) was formed by the Praja Socialist Party, and the United Trade Union Congress (UTUC) was formed in the following year by some radicals.

The trade union movement in India after independence has become highly politicised, so much so that conflicts in the political parties and political alliances and realignments have had their impact on the trade unions as well. Splits in political parties have usually led to splits in the trade unions related to the parties concerned. Thus, for instance, the split in the communist party and the emergence of the Communist Party of India (Marxists) led to a split in the AITUC and the formation of the Centre of Indian Trade Unions (CITU) by the CPI(M). The successive splits in the Indian National Congress and other political parties have had similar effects.

Limitations and Problems of Trade Unionism in India

The trade union movement in India suffers from a number of limitations and problems. Important among them are the following:

1. Limited Representation: Trade unions encompass only a small portion of the total workforce of the country. The extent of unionisation is very limited in the unorganised sectors; particularly in agriculture. However, in some places like Kerala, irresponsible trade unionism sometimes is a curse of the agricultural sector.

2. Small-size and Increasing Number: There has been an increase in the number of trade unions. One reason for this increase has been the break-up of the existing unions into two or more fractions. Besides, new small unions have been taking birth. The small size of unions poses problems of weak financial and administrative position, weakening of collective bargaining power, inter-union rivalry, difficulty in establishing employer-employee rapport, etc.

3. Multiplicity of Unions: The multiplicity of unions has become a very serious problem. As indicated above, the ever-increasing number of unions reduces the average size of the unions, so much so that, in many a situation, no single union has an absolute majority support of the workers. Even when a single union can claim majority, the existence of a number of other unions create serious problems for it. The multiplicity of unions weakens the collective bargaining strength of labour. It also makes employer-employee negotiations and the settlement of issues very difficult. The ideal of "one union for one industry" is likely to remain a dream for a very long time to come.

The Trade Union movement in India suffers from a number of problems arising mostly from the socio-economic and political conditions and attitudes of Trade Union leaders and employers.

4. Inter-union and Intra-union Rivalries: Inter-union rivalries are a corollary of the multiplicity of unions. Instances of one union trying to beat another union even at the expense of the interests of labour are not uncommon. Inter-union rivalries tend to be intense when the different unions subscribe to different political ideologies, or when they are controlled by mutually opposing political parties. Such rivalries often undermine the effectiveness of collective bargaining and lead to industrial unrest. Sometimes, intra-union rivalries create problems. The personal aspirations of the members, personality conflicts, personal rivalries, etc., are among the causes of intra-union rivalries.

5. Political Infiltration: Politicisation is a serious problem afflicting trade unionism in India. The major trade unions of India – the Indian National Trade Union Congress (INTUC), the All-India Trade Union Congress (AITUC), the Centre of Indian Trade Unions (CITU), the United Trade Union Congress (UTUC), etc., have political affiliations. Indeed, each political party tries to have its own trade union. As a corollary of this, political rivalries are extended to trade unions. Split in the political parties and political rivalries may have impact on the trade union also. The politicisation of the trade unions many a time leads to a situation wherein the trade unions become tools in the hands of political parties.

As Giri observes, "the introduction of politics in to the trade union movement and its domination by leaders of political parties have shattered the unity and strength of the trade union movement in the country. The Indian trade union movement has, therefore, become organisationally weak and, as an institution, it may not be able to effectively promote and protect the interests of the workers, unless and until unions are scientifically managed, placing the genuine economic interests of the workers uppermost in their plan of action."[9]

6. Outside Leadership: True, in the early stages of the growth of trade unionism in India, outside leadership made very significant contributions. In the past, such leaders were, by and large, dedicated to the cause of labour. But, today the situation appears to be different. It seems that, today, for many outside leaders trade unions are a means to their personal ends. Outside leadership causes a number of problems like inter-union rivalries, misdirection and misuse of trade union movement, etc.

7. Meagre Funds: Because of the low income of the Indian working class and the small number of members, the funds of the unions are very meagre. Financial constraints come in the way of having full-time officials, organisation and administration, so that it is very difficult to properly organise and sustain strikes and to undertake welfare activities for the members and their dependants, etc.

8. Low Income: The low income of the workers is a negative factor in the growth of trade unions. Because of their low income, workers may feel it difficult to regularly subscribe to the unions. As a result, they may hesitate to join a union. As the Indian workers have a hand-to-mouth existence, he is not able to strike work for a long time.

9. Illiteracy: Illiteracy and lack of education of the workers hinder the growth of the trade union movement because workers are often unable to appreciate, and contribute to, the positive role of trade unionism. This also encourages outside leadership. The ignorance and indifference of workers may result in lack of proper control of the leadership and misdirection.

10. Lack of Integrity: Lack of integrity and dedication on the part of trade union leaders is a major drawback of trade unionism in India. Leaders deceiving workers in the negotiations with the employer, misusing their position and funds, using the union for vested interests, etc., are not uncommon. These lead to the disillusionment of workers, so that they may even backout of the union.

11. Unhealthy Attitude of Employers: Many employers in India still regard trade unions as something very bad. There is lack of appreciation of the positive role of trade unions. Many employers are accused of trying to foster disunity among the workers, encouraging inter-union rivalries, disintegrating unions and resorting to unfair practices to weaken trade unionism.

REGULATION OF TRADE UNIONS – THE TRADE UNIONS ACT

Trade unions in India are regulated by the *Indian Trade Unions Act, 1926,* amended from time-to-time.

Registration of Unions

> **The Trade Unions Act lays down the procedure for the registration of trade unions and their rights and liabilities.**

Any seven or more members of a trade union may, by subscribing their names to the rules of the trade union and otherwise complying with the provisions of this Act with respect to registration, apply for the registration of the trade union under this Act. Every application for the registration of a trade union shall be made to the Registrar, and shall be accompanied by a copy of the rules of the trade union, and provide all other particulars required by the Act.

The Act lays down that the following Acts, namely: The Societies Registration Act 1960; The Cooperative Societies Act, 1912; and The Companies Act, 1956, shall not apply to any registered trade union, and that the registration of any such trade union under any such Act shall be void.

Rights and Responsibilities of Registered Unions

The Act lays down the rights and liabilities of registered trade unions. Some of the important rights and liabilities of the registered unions are:

1. The general funds of a registered union shall not be spent on any other objects than those specified in the Act.

   A registered union may constitute a separate fund from contributions separately levied for or made to that fund, from which payments may be made for the promotion of the civil and political interests of its members, in furtherance of any of the objects specified in the Act.
2. No office-bearer or member of a registered trade union shall be liable to punishment under Sub-section (2) of Section 120-B of the Indian Penal Code in respect of any agreement made between the members for the purpose of furthering any such object of the trade union as is specified in Section 15, unless the agreement is an agreement to commit an offence.
3. No suit or other legal proceeding shall be maintainable in any civil court against any registered trade union or any office-bearer or member thereof in respect of any act done in contemplation or furtherance of a trade dispute to which a member of the trade union is a party on the ground only that such an Act induces some other person to break a contract of employment, or that it is an interference with the trade, business or employment of some other person or with the right of some other person to dispose of his capital or of his labour as he wills.

   Further, a registered trade union shall not be liable in any suit or other legal proceeding in any civil court in respect of any tortious act done in contemplation or furtherance of a trade dispute by an agent of the trade union, if it is proved that such person acted without the knowledge of, or contrary to express instructions given by, the executive of the trade union.

4. The account books of a registered trade union and the list of members thereof shall be open to inspection by an office-bearer or member of the trade union at such times as may be provided for in the rules of the trade union.
5. A person shall be disqualified for being chosen as, and for being a member of, the executive or any other office-bearer of a registered trade union if: (a) he has not attained the age of eighteen years; (b) he has been convicted by a court in India of any offence involving moral turpitude and sentenced to imprisonment, unless a period of five years has elapsed since his release.
6. Not less than one-half of the total number of office-bearers of every registered trade union shall be persons actually engaged or employed in an industry with which the trade union is connected. However, the appropriate Government may, by a special or general order, declare that the provisions of this section shall not apply to any trade union or class of trade unions specified in the order.
7. Any registered trade union may, with the consent of not less than two-thirds of the total number of its members and subject to the provisions of Section 25, change its name.
8. Any two or more registered trade unions may become amalgamated together as one trade union with or without the dissolution or division of the funds of such trade unions or either or any of them, provided that the votes of at least one-half of the members of each or every such trade union entitled to vote are recorded, and that at least sixty per cent of the votes recorded are in favour of the proposal.
9. When a registered trade union is dissolved, notice of the dissolution signed by seven members and by the secretary of the trade union shall, within fourteen days of dissolution, be sent to the Registrar, and shall be registered by him if he is satisfied that the dissolution has been effected in accordance with the rules of the trade union, and the dissolution shall have effect from the date of such registration. Where the dissolution of a registered trade union has been registered and where its rules do not provide for the distribution of the funds of the union on dissolution, the Registrar shall divide the funds among the members in such manner as may be prescribed.
10. A registered trade union shall send to the Registrar a properly audited annual statement of all receipts and expenditure in the prescribed form within the prescribed time. Along with this, a statement showing all the changes in the office-bearers made by the union during the year and a copy of the rules of the union corrected up to the date of despatch should also be sent.
11. A copy of every alteration made in the rules of a registered trade union shall be sent to the Registrar within fifteen days of the making of the alteration.
12. For the purpose of examining the documents of a registered union, as specified in the Act, the Registrar, or any officer authorised by him, may, at any reasonable time, inspect the certificate of registration, account books, registers and other

documents relating to the trade union at its registered office or may require their production at such place as he may specify in this behalf; but no such place shall be at a distance of more than ten miles from the registered office of the trade union.

Amendments to Trade Unions Act

The Trade Unions Act was amended with effect from January 9, 2002. Accordingly:

First, no trade union of workmen shall be registered unless at least 10 per cent or 100, whichever is less, of workmen engaged or employed in the establishment of industry with which it is connected are members of such trade union on the date of making application for registration. However, in no case shall a union be registered without a minimum strength of seven workmen.

Secondly, a registered trade union shall at all times continue to have not less than 10 per cent or 100 members whichever is less, subject to a minimum of seven persons engaged or employed in the establishment or industry with which is connected, as its members.

Thirdly, all office bearers of a registered trade union, except not more than one-third of the total number of office bearers or five, whichever is less shall be persons actually engaged or employed in the establishment or industry with which the trade union is connected.

It is also provided that the employees who have been retired or have been retrenched shall not be construed as outsiders for the purpose of holding an office in the trade union concerned. This provision was specifically included at the behest of trade union leaders who had appeared before the Parliamentary Standing Committee on Labour and Welfare, to which the Bill had been referred for examination.

An aggrieved trade union may even go for an appeal before Industrial Tribunal/Labour Court in case of non-registration or for restoration of registration.

BOX 22. 2 : SECOND NATIONAL COMMISSION LABOUR ON TRADE UNIONS

Coming to the question of it would have been desirable if the Trade Union Act, 1926, had also provided for a ceiling on the total number of trade unions of which an 'outsider' can be a member of executive bodies. Amendments made in Section 4 recently appear to disentitle workers in the unorganised sector from getting their trade unions registered. To overcome this difficulty, a specific provision may be made to enable workers in the unorganised sector to form trade unions, and get them registered even where an employer-employee relationship does not exist or is difficult to establish; and the proviso stipulating 10% of membership shall not apply in their case.

A question was raised whether the right to registration as Trade Unions should be confined to organisations of workers only or employer's organisations should also enjoy this right as provided in the existing provisions. We have come to the conclusion that the present system of eligibility for registration may continue. All benefits which accrue to workers as a result of collective bargaining do not distinguish between those who are members of Trade Unions and those who are not. A worker who is not a member of any Trade Union will have to pay an amount equal to the subscription rate of the negotiating agent or the highest rate of subscription of a union out of the negotiating college. The amounts collected on this account may be credited to a statutory welfare fund.

Any such dispute, which currently goes under the appellation of inter-union or intra-union rivalries, should be capable of being resolved by reference of the dispute to the labour court having jurisdiction, either *suo moto* or by one or both the disputing parties or by the State.

Federations of trade unions as also Central organisations of trade unions and federations should be covered within the definition of trade union and be subject to the same discipline as a primary trade union. The same dispensation will apply to employers' organisations and employees' organisations.

The Commission does not favour craft-based or caste-based organisations of workers or employees or employers. An unregistered organisation shall not be entitled to any privileges, immunities, and rights.

Other provisions of the Trade Unions Act, 1926 including the provision to set up a separate political fund may be allowed to continue and appropriately included in the proposed integrated law. However, care must be taken to ensure that the general funds of trade unions are not used for political purposes.

SUMMARY

Trade unions are voluntary organisations of workers formed to promote and protect their interests by collective action. As V.V. Giri has advised, the scope of trade unions should not be confined merely to the workers' demands, but should include the inculcation in the workers of a sense of discipline and responsibility, an appreciation of their moral responsibility to do a fair day's work for a fair day's wages.

The trade union movement, as it is understood today, took birth in India in the first quarter of the twentieth century and it was only from the end of the First World War (1914-1918) that it gathered momentum. Both economic and political conditions alike contributed to the new awakening. Prices had shot up during the war and there had been no corresponding increase in the wages, though the employers had amassed fantastic profits. The widespread labour unrest in the immediate post-war period led to the formation of a number of trade unions in different industries on a permanent basis. The early stages of the development of trade union movement in India owe a lot to the contributions of some political leaders, social reformers and philanthropists. The non-cooperation movement launched by Gandhiji during 1919-21 and the espousal by him of the cause of the peasants and industrial labour, in particular, had a profound impact on the working class. The success of the Russian revolution gave an impetus to the labour movement because of the feeling it generated that the solidarity of the working class could achieve great things.

The establishment of the International Labour Organisation, of which India was a founder member, also encouraged the formation of trade unions in India.

An important landmark in the history of trade union movement in India was the passing of the Trade Unions Act, 1926, which gave trade unions a legal status and immunity to its officers and members against civil and criminal liability for concerted action. This Act deals with the registration of trade unions and their rights and responsibilities. It also seeks to ensure that the funds of the registered unions are properly utilised.

Almost all major political parties, and even many small parties, have trade unions affiliated to them. The trade union movement in India after independence has become highly politicised, so much so that conflicts in the political parties and political alliances and realignments have had their impact on the trade unions as well.

The trade union movement in India suffers from a number of limitations and problems such as limited representation, small-size and increasing number of trade unions, multiplicity of unions, inter-union and intra-union rivalries, political infiltration, meagre funds, illiteracy of workers, lack of integrity and dedication on the part of many trade union leaders, unhealthy attitude of employers and so on.

REFERENCES

1. Giri, V.V., *Labour Problems in Indian Industry*, Asia Publishing House, Mumbai, 1972, p. 1.
2. Gorden, Watkins, and Paul, Dodd, A., *Labour Problems* (Cited by Giri, *Ibid.*, p. 1).
3. Giri, *op. cit.*, p. 70.
4. *Ibid.*, p. 4.
5. *Ibid.*, p. 4.
6. *Ibid.*, p. 5
7. *Ibid.*, p. 10.

☆☆☆

CHAPTER

23

WORKERS' PARTICIPATION IN MANAGEMENT

MEANING

Though the concept of workers' participation in management has become very popular, it is very difficult to define it clearly, for there are various forms and levels of participation, ranging from the role of workers limited to making suggestions on certain matters which are not very important to active involvement in decision-making and administration.

As the International Institute of Labour Studies remarks, "the participation results from practices which increase the scope for employees' share of influence in decision-making at different tiers of the organisational hierarchy with concomitant assumption of responsibility".[1] We should hasten to add here the apt remark of group of practising managers that "workers' participation in management is involvement of workers only in such areas of activities of the enterprises where they can make some positive contribution".[2] If the workers' mental and emotional involvement in decision-making and execution of programmes should be substantial, workers' participation may be defined as a "principle of ensuring industrial democracy through mutual understanding, faith, trust and cooperation of workers and managements by establishing an effective communication system for attaining the wholehearted involvement of each worker in the area of his competence and concern with a view to maximising results in regard to the achievement of the organisational goals and individual well-being".[3]

The extent of WPM varies very widely from making suggestions on certain matters to complete management of an enterprise.

However, as mentioned earlier, the form and extent of workers' participation in management varies widely. In some cases, it is limited to making suggestions on certain matters, whereas, at the other extreme, workers are represented on the Board of Directors so that they are a part and parcel of decision-making and administration; in some cases, even the whole management of the enterprise is vested in the workers.

Objectives

The objectives of workers' participation in management may vary from country-to-country and from enterprise-to-enterprise. However, the various objectives may be listed as follows.

1. To promote industrial peace
2. To promote industrial democracy
3. To give due recognition to the personality of the workers
4. To safeguard the interest of workers
5. To regulate the self-centred actions of the capitalists
6. To give a social orientation to the business
7. To ensure the best utilisation of the human resources
8. To improve employee morale
9. To satisfy workers' urge for self-expression
10. To improve industrial productivity.

Problems and Limitations

Workers' participation in management, however, poses certain problems and has some limitations.

1. Workers may not be competent enough to understand and appreciate the managerial aspects of the enterprise. This is particularly so in developing countries.
2. It has been argued that workers are more bothered about labour welfare and the like than about the growth, dynamics and challenging problems of the enterprise.
3. It is possible that the workers' representative in the management may be an outsider – a politician or a trade union leader. To that extent, the "real" participation or involvement of the workers is limited.
4. The possibility of the workers' representative on the Board falling in line with the capitalists against the interests of the workers cannot be completely ruled out.
5. The worker-management collaboration may sometimes turn against the interest of society. The capitalist may get the support of labour to exploit the consumers. Labour may lend its support to the capitalist in this respect if it can also share the enlarged cake.

Forms of Participation

As mentioned earlier, the forms and levels of labour participation in management may vary widely between enterprises. The nature of participation depends on a number of factors, such as the socio-political attitudes and situation, the attitude of management and labour, labour-management relations, the relative strengths of labour and management, the peculiarities of the industry or enterprise, etc. Further, "there could be various forms of managerial decisions in social, personnel and economic matters which have an impact on the workforce of an enterprise. Some decisions, especially economic ones, can be taken only at the higher level where basic policies are decided. There are also some decisions at the middle and lower levels concerning the formulation and execution of policies, especially in the area of social and personnel matters."[4] Accordingly, "workers' participation in management will have to be at different levels and in different forms. Workers may be given an opportunity to influence or take part in managerial decisions at the higher level through their representatives on Supervisory Boards or the Board of Directors or through Work Councils. Participation may also be at lower levels at which workers are given some authority to plan and take decisions about their work, like job-enrichment, job-enlargement, delegation, etc. Workers may participate in managerial decisions through collective bargaining. They may also participate informally through the participative style of supervision. Some consider that workers' participation in ownership is also a form of participation. However, it has to be realised that participation in the result of an enterprise through profit sharing or some schemes does not, in the real sense mean participation in management."[5]

> **WPM can be at different levels and different forms, ranging from lower levels to Board level.**

The common forms of workers' participation in management are the following:

Collective Bargaining: It is common to decide certain matters, especially those which have direct economic significance for workers, on the basis of collective bargaining. The growth of trade unionism, the workers' awareness of their rights and strength, and the recognition of the importance of negotiations by labour and management have contributed to the growth of collective bargaining. Some of the common subject matters of collective bargaining are wages, bonus, working conditions, and welfare matters.

Joint Consultation: The functions of joint bodies, comprising representatives of the management and employees, may range from decision-making on some issues to merely advising the management as consultative bodies. Joint consultation as a form of WPM is common in countries like India and Britain. The essential features of the Joint Management Council in India are the following:

(a) The Council is entitled to be consulted on certain specified matters.

(b) In some others, the management is expected to share information with the Council, and, in a set of functions, administrative responsibilities have to be given to it.

Though the Joint Management Councils/Committees have been tried in some countries, they have, generally, "not been found effective". There is a certain amount of lack of clarity of objectives. Moreover, being advisory or consultative bodies, neither the management nor the workers take them seriously. Often, they merely work as forums where workers and management freely vent their complaints and grievances without solving them. Some consider that unless these joint committees are vested with powers to take binding decisions, they will remain ineffective. There are others who feel that such joint committee should not be given authority to take decisions on such issues as are normally the concern of the management. In such a case, joint management committees would be accused of shedding their advisory role and becoming a kind of management body instead; and no sooner does Committee become managerial, there would be need for a new consultative body.[6]

Joint Decision-Making and Administration: For the purpose of joint decision-making and administration, the workers are represented on the Board of Directors. Sometimes, the worker representative's role is limited to participating in decision-making; but the actual execution of the programmes is the responsibility of the management. In the area of joint administration, however, workers and management share the responsibility and power of execution. In India, the scheme of worker-directors has been introduced, both as a statutory arrangement in nationalised banks as well as voluntary one in selected Central public enterprises. As Virmani observes, though "legally the workers' representative on the Board may have all the rights and obligations like the other members of the Board, his ability to participate in managerial decision-making, to a large extent, will depend on his quality, his knowledge of company affairs, his educational background, his level of understanding and also on the number of worker representatives on the Board. Most of the decisions in which the workers are interested are normally made at the lower levels of management."[7]

Complete Control of Management: In some cases, like the system of self-management in Yugoslavia, workers have complete control over the management of the enterprises. Under the system in Yugoslavia, the workers have the option to influence all the decisions taken at the top level; but in actual practice, the Board and the top management team assume a fairly independent role in taking policy decisions for the enterprise, especially on economic matters. The system of complete control of management cannot, obviously, fit into a capitalistic system. A potential danger of complete control of management by the workers is that, like capitalists, the workers might try to maximise their benefits even at the expense of the consumers or society.

Workers' Participation in Share Capital: As the Sachar Committee observes, workers' participation in equity and in management are in some sense inter-related from the point of view of attaining the ultimate goal of co-partnership in industry. In favour of the workers' participation in share capital, it has been said that, besides giving them a sense of dignity and status as co-partners, equity participation secures for them a share in the company's future prosperity while holding out promises for improved industrial relations and steady growth of internal finances for the company's operations. It has also been said that the improved performance of industry and harmonious industrial relations pave the way for the ultimate gain of the community as well as the State.

The majority view of the Sachar Committee was that in all future issues of shares by the companies, they should reserve a portion of new shares, say, about 10 to 15 per cent., exclusively for the workers, to be called workers' shares. These shares in the first instance must be offered to the existing shareholders or to the public.[8]

It may be noted that several private enterprises, particularly in the IT sector, in India have introduced employee's stock option scheme (ESOP) to attract and retain talented people and many employees have become multi-millionaires thanks to the appreciation of the stock prices.

WORKERS' PARTICIPATION SCHEMES IN INDIA

> **In the discussion on WPM in the India labour Conference, while workers wanted 50 per cent representation at the Board level, employers wanted to confine it to only one representative.**

The Government of India is of the view that, at the enterprise level, workers' participation in management should become an integral part of the industrial relations system to serve as an effective instrument of modern management, and that it should be made a vehicle for transforming the attitudes of both employers and workers with a view to establishing a cooperative culture which may help in building a strong, self-confident and self-reliant country with a stable industrial base.

The Directive Principles of State Policy, enshrined in the Indian Constitution, lays down that "the State shall take steps, by suitable legislation or in any other way, to secure the participation of workers in the management of undertakings, establishments or other organisations engaged in any industry" (Article 43A). Some of the Five Year Plan documents and industrial policy statements have also mentioned the importance of labour participation in management.

Various measures have been tried in India to promote workers' participation. Starting with the limited scheme of statutory Works Committees, voluntary arrangements were made in the form of joint management councils, the scheme of worker-directors, both as statutory arrangements in nationalised banks as well as a voluntary one is selected Central public enterprises; and voluntary schemes of workers' participation in the manufacturing/mining industries introduced in 1975 and in commercial and service organisations in the public sector introduced in 1977.

Works Committees/Joint Committees

The Industrial Disputes Act, 1947, provides for the setting up of a Works Committee, consisting of representatives of management and employees, in every undertaking employing 100 or more workmen "to promote measures for securing and preserving amity and good relations between the employer and workmen and, to that end, to comment upon matters to their concern and endeavour to compose any material difference of opinion in respect of such matters". The representatives of the workmen, whose number shall not be less than the number of representatives of the employer, are to be chosen from among the workmen engaged in the establishment and in consultation with their recognised trade union, if any.

The usefulness of the Works Committees as a channel for joint consultation and the need for strengthening and promoting this institution was stressed in the labour policy statements in the successive Plans. The legal requirement and encouragement given by the Government led to the setting up of works committees in a number of undertakings. The Works Committees, however, have not proved effective. The vagueness in the legal definition of the scope and functions of the Committees was a major reason for this ineffectiveness. To remedy to this defect, the Indian Labour Conference in 1956 drew up an illustrative list of items which Works Committees would normally deal with, and a list of items which would be beyond their scope.

The items which Works Committees would normally deal with include consultation on:

1. The conditions of work, such as ventilation, lighting, temperature and sanitation, including latrines and urinals.
2. Amenities, such as drinking water, canteens, dining rooms, rest rooms, medical and health services.
3. Safety and accident prevention, occupational diseases and protective equipment.
4. Adjustment of festivals and national holidays.
5. Administration of welfare and fine funds.
6. Educational and recreational activities.
7. Implementation and review of decisions arrived at in the meetings of Works Committees.

The items specifically excluded were discussion on:

1. Wages and allowances.
2. Bonus and profit-sharing bonus.
3. Rationalisation and matters connected with the fixation of the work load.
4. Matters connected with the fixation of a standard labour force.
5. Programmes of planning and development.
6. Matters connected with retrenchment and lay-off.
7. Victimisation for trade union activities.
8. Provident fund, gratuity schemes and other retirement benefits.
9. Quantum of leave, and national and festival holidays.
10. Incentive schemes.
11. Housing and transport services.

> **WPM through Works Committees has not been successful because of the method of constitution of WCs and the functions assigned to them.**

In spite of these clarifications, the Works Committees have not, generally, proved very successful.

Reasons for Failure

In the evidence before the National Commission on Labour (NCL), State Governments expressed the view that the advisory nature of the recommendations, vagueness regarding their exact scope and functions, inter-union rivalries, union opposition, reluctance of employers to utilise such media, etc., have rendered Works Committees ineffective. The employers' associations have attributed the failure of Works Committees to factors like inter-union rivalries, union antipathy, and the attitude of members (workers' wing) in trying to raise in the Committee discussions extraneous issues. According to the unions, conflict between the Works Committees and the unhelpful attitude of the employers had generally led to their failure.

> **A number of factors have contributed to the failure of Works Committees.**

Suggestions

The NCL indicated that the effectiveness of these committees will depend on the following factors.

1. A more responsive attitude on the part of the management.
2. Adequate support from unions.
3. A proper appreciation of the scope and functions of the Works Committees.
4. Wholehearted implementation of the recommendations of the Works Committees.
5. Proper coordination of the functions of the multiple bipartite institutions at the plant level.

Joint Management Councils

The Scheme of joint management councils (JMCs) is based on a draft prepared by the tripartite committee appointed by the 15th Session of the Indian Labour Conference, as subsequently modified by two tripartite national seminars on the subject held in 1958 and 1960.

Objectives: The main objectives in the establishment of JMCs were:

1. To promote cordial relations between management and workers.
2. To build-up understanding and trust between management and workers.
3. To effect a substantial increase in productivity.
4. To secure better welfare and other facilities for workers.
5. To train the workers to understand and to share the responsibilities of management.

Functions: The essential features of the scheme of JMC are:

1. The Council is entitled to be consulted on certain specified matters.
2. In some others, the management is expected to share information with the Council.

3. In a set of functions, administrative responsibilities have to be given to it.

(*a*) The Councils would be consulted by the management on such matters as:

1. The administration of Standing Orders and their amendment, when needed.
2. Retrenchment
3. Rationalisation
4. Closure, reduction in, or cessation of operations.

(*b*) The Council/Councils would also have the right to receive information, to discuss and to give suggestions on:

1. The general economic situation of the concern.
2. The state of the market, production and sales programmes.
3. The organisation and general running of the undertaking.
4. The circumstances affecting the economic position of the undertaking.
5. The methods of manufacture and work.
6. The annual balance sheet and profit and loss statement and connected documents and explanation.
7. Long-term plan for expansion, redeployment.
8. Such other matters as may be agreed to.

(*c*) The Councils would be entrusted with administrative responsibility in respect of:

1. Administration of welfare measures.
2. Supervision of safety measures.
3. Operation of vocational training and apprenticeship schemes.
4. Preparation of schedules of working hours and breaks and of holidays.
5. Payment of rewards for valuable suggestions received from the employees.
6. Any other matter.

JMCs have different roles in respect of different categories of matters.

(d) All matters, *e.g.*, wages, bonus, etc., which are subjects for collective bargaining, are excluded from the scope of the Council/Councils. In short, the creation of new rights as between employers and workers should be outside the jurisdiction of the Management Council. Individual grievances are also excluded for its/ their scope.

Shop/Departmental Councils and Joint Councils

In October 1975, the Government announced a model scheme for workers' participation in management. This scheme, meant for implementation in all manufacturing and mining enterprises employing 500 or more workers, envisaged shop councils at shop/departmental levels and a joint council at the enterprise level.

The two councils were to have an equal number of representatives of the employers and employees. The representatives of the workers on the councils were to be nominated by the management, in consultation with the union, from amongst the workers actually engaged in the enterprises. All decisions of a Shop Council should be on the basis of consensus and not be a process of voting, provided that either party might refer the unsettled matters to the Joint Council for consideration. Every decision of the shop council is to be implemented within a month, unless otherwise provided in the decision itself.

The main functions of the Shop Council are to help management in achieving production targets, improving productivity, assist in maintaining general discipline in the shop, attend to physical conditions of working, welfare and health measures, and to ensure a proper flow of adequate two-way communication between the management and the workers, particularly on matters relating to production schedules and the progress in achieving the targets.

The main functions of the Joint Council are fixation of productivity norms, dealing with the unresolved problems referred to it by the Shop Councils, awarding of rewards for creative suggestions from workers, ensuring optimum use of raw materials, ensuring the quality of finished products, etc.

The issues thrown up by the working of the scheme of 1975 were discussed at a tripartite labour conference held in May 1977. On the recommendations of the conference, a Committee on Workers' Participation in Management and Equity, consisting of representatives of Central organisations of employers and trade unions of some of the States and professional institutions of management, was appointed in September 1977. The report of the Committee submitted to the Government showed that a majority of the members favoured adoption of a three-tier system of participation, *viz,* at the corporate level, at the plant level and at shop-floor level. The Committee laid down the detailed functions of the various councils at shop, plant and corporate levels. It commended that the workers' representatives on the participation forums should be optional. Further, it recommended that an organisation be set up, both at the Centre and in the States, to monitor the implementation of the scheme and review its working.

The Government introduced in 1983 a new and comprehensive scheme for the workers' participation in Central public sector undertaking. The State Governments have been requested to introduce it in their enterprises and the private sector has also been encouraged to introduce the scheme.

The issue of WPM was discussed by the Indian Labour Conference in November 1986 and the conference agreed in principle to the implementation of the scheme of workers' participation in public, private and cooperative sectors.

BOX 23.1 : IMPERATIVES OF WORKERS' PARTICIPATION IN MANAGEMENT

There is overwhelming evidence to suggest that wherever the system has been introduced the enterprises and the economy as a whole have shown tremendous growth. Workers and the management have to join together to not only sort out their day-to-day problems, but build up confidence in each other, improve work culture, ensure the introduction of new technology, improve production processes, achieve production targets, smoothen retrenchment and welcome introduction of new technologies, to make the enterprises capable of standing up to global competition.

Our efforts made in this regard during more than half century underline the extreme importance of a cooperative approach. Almost all the economically advanced nations have worked out their own variants of industrial cooperation and co-determination. All of them have found systems of participatory management useful and beneficial for efficiency, and for creating the atmosphere necessary to meet the demands of competitiveness.

It has also improved human relations which has led to improved industrial relations.

Content of work has undergone a sea change in many essential processes and all production processes are no longer carried out under one roof. The knowledge worker has taken the place of the old unskilled worker. Collective excellence, it has been found, depends very much on cooperation, voluntary vigilance and coordination

India cannot be an exception to this state of affairs in the age of new technology.

Globalisation will accentuate and accelerate this process. It will, therefore, make it necessary for us to reach higher levels of participatory activity. With globalisation the time has come when we cannot leave the question of participative management to be determined by the management or the trade unions. We believe therefore, that the time has come for the Government to enact a law to provide for participatory forums at all levels keeping in mind the necessity to ensure that the responsibility and freedom to take managerial decisions are not fragmented to the detriment of the enterprise, the social partners or society at large.

(Adopted from the Report of the National Commission on Labour, 2002)

SUMMARY

Although the concept of workers' participation in management is very popular, there is no unanimity of opinion as to what should it exactly be. Indeed, the form and extent of workers' participation in management varies widely. In some cases, it is limited to making suggestions on certain matters, whereas, at the other extreme, workers are represented on the Board of Directors so that they are a part and parcel of decision-making and administration; in some cases, even the whole management of the enterprise is vested in the workers. However, in India the general view seems to be that "workers' participation in management is involvement of workers only in such areas of activities of the enterprises where they can make some positive contribution".

The various objectives of workers' participation in management include promotion of industrial peace and industrial democracy; safeguarding of the interests of workers; satisfying workers' urge for self-expression; improving employee morale; regulating the self-centred actions of the capitalists and giving a social orientation to the business, etc.

There are several problems in realising a meaningful workers' participation in management. Workers may not be competent enough to understand and appreciate the managerial aspects of the enterprise; they may be more bothered about labour welfare and the like than about the growth, dynamics and challenging problems of the enterprise. If the workers' representative in the management is an outsider – a politician or a trade union leader – the "real" participation or involvement of the workers is limited. There is also possibility of collusion between the workers' representatives and the capitalists.

The common forms of workers' participation in management are summarized in Figure 23.1.

IMPORTANT FORMS OF WPM

Collective Bargaining

Common subject matters of collective bargaining include wages, bonus, working conditions, and welfare matters.

Joint Consultation

The functions of joint bodies, comprising representatives of the management and employees, may range from decision-making on some issues to merely advising the management as consultative bodies.

Complete Control of Management

Under this system, the workers' representatives are involved in all the decisions taken at the top level.

Workers' Participation in Share Capital

ESOP is growing in popularity. This ensures participation in management by the virtue of and to the extent of shareholding.

Joint Decision-Making and Administration

For the purpose of joint decision-making and administration, the workers are represented on the Board of Directors. Sometimes, the worker representative's role is limited to participating in decision-making; but the actual execution of the programmes is the responsibility of the management. In the area of joint administration, however, workers and management share the responsibility and power of execution.

Fig. 23.1: Forms of Workers' Participation in Management

Various measures have been tried in India to promote workers' participation. Starting with the limited scheme of statutory Works Committees, voluntary arrangements were made in the form of joint management councils, the scheme of worker-directors, both as statutory arrangements in nationalised banks as well as a voluntary one is selected Central public enterprises; and voluntary schemes of workers' participation in the manufacturing/ mining industries and in commercial and service organisations in the public sector. Figure 23.2 gives summary view of the schemes of workers' participation in management in India.

WPM SCHEMES IN INDIA

Works Committees/Joint Committees

The Works Committees, which is statutory requirement in undertaking employing 100 or more workers, consisting of representatives of management and employees, may be consulted on matters related to the working conditions and labour welfare. A number of matters such as wages and allowances; bonus; provident fund, gratuity schemes and other retirement benefits; rationalization; retrenchment and lay-off, planning and development are specifically excluded from the scope of these committees.

Joint Management Councils

JMC (1) is entitled to be consulted on certain specified matters. (2) In some others, the management is expected to share information with the Council. (3) In a set of functions, administrative responsibilities have to be given to it. The Councils would be consulted by the management on such matters as administration of Standing Orders and their amendment, retrenchment, rationalization, closure/reduction in, operations. Matters of collective bargaining and individual grievances are also excluded from their scope.

Shop/Departmental Councils and Joint Councils

Both the Councils shall have an equal number of representatives of the employers and employees. The main functions of the Shop Council are to help management in achieving production targets, improving productivity, assist in maintaining general discipline in the shop, attend to physical conditions of working, welfare and health measures, and to ensure a proper flow of adequate two-way communication between the management and the workers, particularly on matters relating to production schedules and the progress in achieving the targets.

The main functions of the Joint Council are fixation of productivity norms, dealing with the unresolved problems referred to it by the Shop Councils, awarding of rewards for creative suggestions from workers, ensuring optimum use of raw materials, ensuring the quality of finished products, etc.

ESOP

Now many organizations, particularly in IT sector, have Employees' Stock Option Scheme.

Fig. 23.2: Schemes of Workers' Participation in Management in India.

REFERENCES

1. Cited by Michael, V.P., *Industrial Relations in India and Workers' Participation in Management*, Himalaya Publishing House, Bombay, 1970, p. 168.
2. Cited by Michael, V.P., *Ibid*., p. 168.
3. Michael, V.P., *Ibid*., p. 169.
4. Virmani, B.R., *Workers' Participation in Management*, The Macmillan Co. of India Ltd., 1978, p. 9.
5. *Ibid*., p. 9.
6. *Ibid*., pp. 13-14.
7. *Ibid*., p. 9-11.
8. Government of India, *Report of the High Powered Committee on Companies and MRTP Acts*, Manager of Publications, Govt. of India, New Delhi, 1978, p. 93.

☆☆☆

CHAPTER 24

EXIT POLICY

With the new economic policy which would pave way for economic restructuring, *Exit Policy* has become a widely debated subject in India.

Exit policy refers to the policy regarding the retrenchment of the surplus manpower resulting from restructuring of industrial units or the workers becoming unemployed by the closure of sick units. The exit policy in its wider context covers the policy for the compensation for the employees who leave the organisation and the measures for their rehabilitation also.

NEED FOR EXIT POLICY

Surplus manpower is a major problem of many industrial units in India. In other words, the industrial sector too is characterised by *disguised unemployment.* (There is disguised unemployment if some labour employed in an enterprise can be withdrawn without adversely affecting the production. This concept was originally used to describe the situation which exists in the agricultural sector of the developing countries.) This problem is very rampant in the public sector. The private sector also seriously suffers from this problem.

An exit policy is often required to facilitate corporate restructuring and to redeploy/reemploy workers.

In the seller's market which existed in India under the protected economic system, the high costs of surplus manpower employed by the companies could be passed on to the consumers by way of high prices. However, survival in a competitive system demands cost efficiency improvement and cost reduction in every possible way. It may become necessary not only to get rid of the surplus manpower under the existing technology but also to cut the labour force size further due to modernization. In some cases, it may also become necessary to give up some of the lines of business to maintain or improve the health of the enterprise. Thus, some of the measures which industrial undertakings take to improve the competitiveness and to ensure survival would render a part of the existing manpower unemployed. If the enterprises do not take such measures in time, it may even ultimately lead to the closure of the units throwing all the workers unemployed.

There are also a large number of unviable sick units, both in the public and private sectors. There is no economic and social justification for their continuation. Those who argue that the State should run the sick units fail to recognise the fact that the society will have to bear the cost of the huge losses these units make and that amount could be invested elsewhere for generation of productive employment or for enhancing the social welfare.

If the required restructuring to improve competitiveness and the closure of unviable sick units are not allowed, the whole economy would become sick in due course. There are, therefore, no options.

The new economic policy may create unemployment at the enterprise level in a large number of cases. It does not, however, mean that NEP would increase the total unemployment in the economy. Contrary to that, it would help increase the total employment. In fact, a deviation from the old policy was a must even to maintain the existing level of employment in the long-run.

Technology is becoming more and more labour saving. Technological developments are making several industries which in the past were labour intensive more and more capital intensive. Countries which do not adapt themselves to the changing environment would ultimately see their employment shrinking.

Technological developments which increase productive efficiency are affecting employment in many organisations all over the world. Down-sizing the manpower is inevitable due to other reasons also. The multinational giant IBM which has assiduously followed a cardinal philosophy of non-retrenchment for a very long time has been compelled to give up this policy. Modernisation or restructuring may lead to job cuts at the enterprise level. But will this mean a fall in total employment or only a change in the pattern of employment generation? The evidence from other countries suggests the latter. Had this not been so, the level of unemployment would have been highest in Japan where the rate of technological change is the swiftest. Instead, it is the lowest, with Germany only a step behind.

One of the major failures of Indian system has been the inability to recognise the implications of technological developments. The unpragmatic employment protection policies have created many long-term problems. "Experience the world over suggests that modernisation can work only if labour is trimmed sharply. Modern looms need only one-fifth the labour that obsolete ones do. If a company cannot shed labour, modernisation will saddle it with both high capital costs and high labour costs, a recipe for bankruptcy. Indeed, the inability of the Indian firms to tailor their workforce to the level of capital employed has been an important reason why firms have not modernised. This rigidity in the labour market has also meant that the Indian labour, contrary to popular belief, is not at all cheap. The Japanese have pointed this out often, saying that while it may be cheap in the first round of investment, thereafter it becomes expensive because swift capital-labour adjustment are just not possible."

It is high time that India corrected the growth defeating policy of protecting the existing jobs at high social costs. Employment generation by the industrial sector depends, *inter alia,* on the dynamism of the industrial sector.

EXTENT OF OVERMANNING

A large member of the people employed in the industrial and other sectors of India is surplus. However, there is no reasonably accurate estimate of the extent of the surplus of the manpower employed.

Many industrial enterprises and other organisations in India are overburdened by huge excess manpower.

The overmanning has two dimensions, *viz.*, the surplus even with the existing technology employed by the enterprises and the surplus that will emerge if the existing technology is replaced by modem technology.

In many cases, the Indian industry uses more labour than those in other countries even when the technology used is the same. *For example*, the Aditya Birla group uses the same textile machinery in India that it does in its other plants in South-east Asia. But it takes just two workers to process 100 kgs. of yarn in Indonesia and three in Philippines and Thailand; in India, Birla's Grasim Industries needs seven people for the same job. This made the labour cost of processing 100 kgs. of yarn in India 14 times more than it in Indonesia.[1]

Use of obsolete technology causes very high labour costs. The use of obsolete technology makes cost of production very high in India in several cases. For instance, while it took a South Korean worker 11 hours to make a tonne of steel, his counterpart in TISCO would take two days. With vintage factories, some of which were more than 75 years old, ACC produced 475 tonnes of cement per worker while Gujarat Ambuja produced 2,000 tonnes per head.

By estimating the number of workers in sick public and private sector units, Sudipto Mundle arrived at a figure of 2.4 million surplus manpower in the industrial sector in India. Assuming the same level of redundancy in government employment (18 per cent), Mundle has assumed for estimating the surplus in public sector companies, *Business Today* estimated that 1.8 million of the total of over 10 million government staff, including administrative staff and workers in departmental undertakings (like railways, telecom, etc.), was excess.

According to Pramod Verma, even without technological change, it should have been possible to reduce labour by five to seven per cent which meant between 13 and 18 lakh people and if technology was upgraded, the organised sector would lose another 25 lakh jobs.

A study by the Textile Ministry had estimated that there was 80,000 surplus workers in the National Textile Corporation (44 per cent of total employment). There was a surplus of about 50,000 workers in Coal India and this figure could be much higher once the technology for underground mining was upgraded. Besides, the Singareni Collieries which had been referred to the BIFR, had about one lakh workers.

A study by Mrityunjaya Athreya, conducted in 1987, revealed that the Steel Authority of India (SAIL) had a surplus of 80,000 workers.

At least 50 per cent of the workers of the State Road Transport undertakings were estimated to be surplus. The same may be true of State Electricity Boards.

The figures given above give some indication of the extent of the alarming overmanning of the Indian economy.

VRS AND GOLDEN HANDSHAKE

The problem of excess manpower is particularly serious in the public sector.

It is necessary to dispense with the excess manpower for improving the health of an organisation. If this is not done, the excess labour could cause industrial sickness.

A popular method to trim the manpower is the voluntary retirement scheme (VRS). Under the VRS, employees who have attained forty years of age or ten years of service would seek voluntary retirement. The minimum benefits under this scheme would be forty-five days emoluments for each completed year of service before normal date of retirement or the monthly emoluments at the time of retirement multiplied by the remaining months of service before the normal date of service, whichever is less. The benefits would be in addition to the amount that has accrued to the Provident Fund as per the rules or to the Gratuity fund whichever is applicable.

Some companies offer very attractive package of benefits to the employees who would opt for VRS. Such schemes are often referred to as golden handshake scheme. While the golden handshake scheme offered by some companies in the past worked very well, the offers made by some other companies failed to elicit the required response from the employees. An important reason for this was said to be the higher expectations workers began to entertain as the concept of golden handshake became popular. The VRS offered by some banks like the SBI and Canara Bank in 2001 have got very high response.

A number of companies have already reduced their work force by VRS. These VRSs have taken different forms. In fact, the process of getting rid of the excess labour started in several companies much before the economic reforms ushered in India.

The ACC had brought down its workforce from 25,000 to 16,000 in 10 years. Between 1987 and early 1993, SAIL got rid of 17,000 workers through its VRS and by 2,000 another 57,000 were estimated to retire.

The VRS takes different forms. While in SRF Ltd., the VRS cost was a low ₹ 25,000 to one lakh per head, in Hindustan Geigy it was about ₹ 4.4 lakh per head on an average. The absolute limit set by the Government is ₹ 5 lakh.

One possible drawback of the VRS is that the efficient employees would leave the company while the inefficient may stay back; the efficient ones would be hopeful of alternatives outside while the inefficient may not be very optimistic.

The NTC had offered looms at subsidised rates to the workers under the VRS package. They are also offered sheds for housing the looms and marketing facilities to sell their production. Between November 1992 and March 1993, 25,000 NTC workers had accepted VRS. Road Transport firms can offer buses to the employees under the VRS.

Between April 1997 and March 1999, the central public undertakings reduced their manpower by over one lakh.

NATIONAL RENEWAL FUND

A very important step taken by the Central Government to benefit the workers affected by industrial restructuring, modernisation or closure of the unit was the establishment of the National Renewal Fund which was operationalised in 1992. The objectives of the NRF are the following:

1. To provide assistance to firms to cover the cost of retraining and redeployment of employees arising as a result of modernisation and technological upgradation of existing capacities and from industrial restructuring.
2. To provide funds for compensation to employees affected by restructuring or closure of industrial units, both in the public and private sectors.
3. To provide funds for employment generation schemes in the organised and unorganised sectors in order to provide social safety net for labour.

The NRF is administered by the Department of Industrial Development. The first set of cases taken up by the Department were those relating to the National Textile Corporation.

The NRF was proposed to have a corpus of ₹ 2,000 crore which would be contributed by three sources; ₹ 200 crore as budgetary support (the 1991-92 Budget earmarked this amount); ₹ 1,000 crore from the disinvestment of public sector undertaking's shares and ₹ 800 crore from the World Bank.

The NRF was proposed to have two parts. The first part is the Employment Generation Fund, which would provide resources to approved employment schemes in the organised sectors. The second part is the National Renewal Grant Fund to meet the compensation and training expenditures of retrenched workers.

The World Bank has offered (in February 2001), to fund Government of India's downsizing plan, estimated to cost a minimum of ₹ 5,000 crore, provided the Government is willing to settle for a young bureaucracy.

CONCLUSION

Although a full-fledged, detailed exit policy has not yet been formulated, the establishment of the National Renewal Fund is very important step. This is indeed a clear indication of the appreciation of the need for modernisation, restructuring and even closure of units in inevitable cases and that if these measures render workers unemployed the right policy is not to resist such measures but to retrain and redeploy the workers to the extent possible.

Schemes like NRF should not be made completely dependent on the national exchequer. A scheme for regular contribution to such a fund by the companies and workers should be designed and implemented.

As mentioned earlier many companies and organisations all over the world, one time or the other, have faced the problem of surplus manpower. It was reported that the Chinese Government had decided to bring about sweeping changes in the Central Government structure causing a 20 per cent cut in the number of government employees. India cannot afford to be blind towards hard realities. Organisations should be allowed and facilitated to swiftly respond to environmental realities to enable them to become efficient and competitive.

The workers have a lot of apprehension about the very term exit policy. One of the important objectives of an exit policy is to protect the interests of the workers. However, instead of educating the workers about it, the trade unions and politicians seem to be causing unnecessary fears in the minds of the workers. It is pointed out that "the exit policy on which the union bosses are currently declaiming pertains to their own impending exit and not that of the common worker. It is almost a certainty that the average retrenched blue-collared person will get a fair deal by way of compensation, retraining and redeployment."

In fact, "the biggest loser of not having an exit policy is the labour because the legitimate interests of labour are protected only when there is a legal closure of a sick mill. In a situation of a sick unit not functioning and not legally closed, workers may remain years together without employment, wages and not getting their legitimate dues. One may therefore, argue that "if properly implemented, it is the most pro-labour policy imaginable."

There is however, a growing realisation among the workers of a need to increase productivity to survive the domestic and foreign competition; if firms do not shed the excess manpower all the workers would sink with the firm. While in some companies the unions cooperate with the VRS, in several companies they have strongly opposed. In a number of cases the workers defied the call of the unions to boycott the VRS.

The response of the workers to the VRS may depend upon the attractiveness of the scheme, their assessment of the future of the enterprise, etc. In 1989, when the Hindustan Lever (HLL) lifted its year long lockout at its Sewree plant in Bombay, more than 550 workers availed of the VRS. But in 1992 when the HLL offered another Scheme to retire 500 workers, only nine of them accepted it. Recent offers of VRSs many organizations have evoked very good response.

SUMMARY

Exit policy refers to the policy regarding the retrenchment of the surplus manpower resulting from restructuring of industrial units or the workers becoming unemployed by the closure of sick units. The exit policy in its wider context covers the policy for the compensation for the employees who leave the organisation and the measures for their rehabilitation also.

The economic liberalization has made exit policy highly important because of restructuring of enterprises and closure of units.

Surplus manpower is a common problem of the private as well as the public sectors in India. In a globally competitive environment no organization can survive with large surplus human resource. It is, therefore, necessary to have an appropriate exit policy to make the transition smooth.

There is a feeling that exit policy is something anti-labour. The fact, however, is that the biggest loser of not having an exit policy is the labour. It is argued that "if properly implemented, it is the most pro-labour policy imaginable".

A popular method to trim the manpower is the voluntary retirement scheme (VRS). Some companies offer very attractive package of benefits to the employees who would opt for VRS. Such schemes are often referred to as golden handshake scheme. One possible drawback of the VRS is that the efficient employees would leave the company while the inefficient may stay back; the efficient ones would be hopeful of alternatives outside while the inefficient may not be very optimistic.

A very important step taken by the Central Government to benefit the workers affected by industrial restructuring, modernisation or closure of a unit was the establishment of the National Renewal Fund (NRF) with a view to (1) providing assistance to firms to cover the cost of retraining and redeployment of employees arising as a result of modernisation and technological upgradation of existing capacities and from industrial restructuring; (2) providing funds for compensation to employees affected by restructuring or closure of industrial units, both in the public and private sectors; (3) providing funds for employment generation schemes in the organised and unorganised sectors in order to provide social safety net for labour.

The workers have a lot of apprehension about the very term exit policy. One of the important objectives of an exit policy is to protect the interests of the workers. However, instead of educating the workers about it, the trade unions and politicians seem to be causing unnecessary fears in the minds of the workers.

REFERENCE

1. The statistics quoted in this sub-section and in the next are from Neeraj Kaushal and Shekhar Gosh, "Axing 4 million Jobs" and Shekhar Gosh, "Painless Fair-well", *Business Today*, April 22-May 6, 1993.

☆☆☆

CHAPTER 25

PLANNING IN INDIA

The pattern of economic development in India is very significantly affected by Government planning. The direction of the development pattern of the various sectors and the relative priorities within each sector are determined by the Five Year Plans. The scope and prospects of different industries and other businesses, therefore, depend, to a very large extent, on the development planning.

THE PLANNING MACHINERY

Planning Commission

The Planning Commission was set up in March 1950, by a Resolution of the Government of India, with the following functions:

- To make an assessment of the material, capital and human resources of the country, including technical personnel, and investigate the possibilities of augmenting such of these resources as are found to be deficient in relation to the nations's requirements.
- To formulate a plan for the most effective and balanced utilisation of the country's resources.

> **The Planning Commission plays a major role in the formulation of Five Year Plans.**

National Development Council

A number of Committees and Commissions are also working under or associated with the Planning Commission. One of the most important among them is the National

Development Council (NDC). The NDC is presided over by the Prime Minister and is composed of Union Cabinet Ministers, Chief Ministers of States and Union Territories and Members of the Planning Commission. The other Union and State Ministers may also be invited to participate in the deliberations of the Council. The Secretary of the Planning Commission acts as Secretary of the NDC, and the Commission is expected to provide such administrative and other support as may be necessary. The main functions of the NDC are:

1. To prescribe guidelines for the formulation of the National Plan including the assessment of the resources for the plan.
2. To consider the National Plan as formulated by the Planning Commission.
3. To consider important questions of social and economic policy affecting national development.
4. To review the working of the plan from time-to-time and to recommend such measures as are necessary for achieving the aims and targets set out in the National Plan, including measures to secure the active participation and cooperation of the people, improve the efficiency of the administrative services, ensure the fullest development of the less advanced regions and sections of the community, and through sacrifice borne equality by all the citizens, build-up resources for national development.

> **The role of the NDC signifies the federal and democratic nature of the Indian planning.**

From the functions mentioned above, it is quite obvious that the NDC has a decisive role in the formulation and follow-up of the execution of the National Plan.

NITI Aayog

With effect from January 1, 2015, the Planning Commission was replaced by NITI Aayog (National Institution for Transforming India).

Functions

(*a*) To evolve a shared vision of national development priorities sectors and strategies with the active involvement of States in the light of national objectives.

(*b*) To foster cooperative federalism through structured support initiatives and mechanisms with the States on a continuous basis, recognising that strong States make a strong nation.

(*c*) To develop mechanisms to formulate credible plans at the village level and aggregate these progressively at higher levels of government.

(*d*) To ensure, on areas that are specifically referred to it, that the interests of national security are incorporated in economic strategy and policy.

(*e*) To pay special attention to the sections of our society that may be at risk of not benefitting adequately from economic progress.

(*f*) To design strategic and long-term policy and programme frameworks and initiatives, and monitor their progress and their efficacy. The lessons learnt through monitoring and feedback will be used for making innovative improvements, including necessary mid-course corrections.

(*g*) To provide advice and encourage partnerships between key stakeholders and national and international like-minded think tanks, as well as educational and policy research institutions.

(*h*) To create a knowledge, innovation and entrepreneurial support system through a collaborative community of national and international experts, practitioners and other partners.

(*i*) To offer a platform for resolution of inter-sectoral and inter-departmental issues in order to accelerate the implementation of the development agenda.

(*j*) To maintain a state-of-the-art Resource Centre, be a repository of research on good governance and best practices in sustainable and equitable development as well as help their dissemination to stakeholders.

(*k*) To actively monitor and evaluate the implementation of programmes and initiatives, including the identification of the needed resources so as to strengthen the probability of success and scope of delivery.

(*l*) To focus on technology upgradation and capacity building for implementation of programmes and initiatives.

(*m*) To undertake other activities as may be necessary in order to further the execution of the national development agenda, and the objectives mentioned above.

Comments

There does not appear to be any rationale for the replacement of the Planning Commission by the NITI. It is the result of the Narendra Modi government's eagerness to condemn the old system for the sake of it. The earlier BJP-led government did not feel it necessary to dismantle the Planning Commission.

The Planning Commission was a better organisation than the NITI Aayog. The Planning Commission was a more focused organisation with a clear role, unlike the new organisation which with a gamut of roles and functions over a wide spectrum can result in confusions and conflicts.

One of the criticisms of the Planning Commission by the advocates of the new regime is that under the old system the States did not have a role. The NDC described above makes it clear that it is not a correct view.

The view that liberalisation has made national planning irrelevant is not right. National planning is very much relevant for India. The right thing would have been to reform the Planning Commission appropriately.

In short, national planning continues to be very important for the nation and NITI Aayog is a wrong substitute for the Planning Commission.

State Plans

State Plans account for about one half of the total outlay of the Government under a Five Year Plan. The subjects that come under State jurisdiction include such vital sectors of development as agriculture, small industries, irrigation and power, roads and road transport, and education and social services.

A successful implementation of major national policy objectives calls for an organisation at the State level which can coordinate effectively and provide guidance to local democratic bodies, and take a wider view of development than is generally possible for individual departments. The States have Planning Boards and Departments which coordinate the work of other departments for the preparation of development plans, and present reports on the execution of State Plans. State Planning generally receives directions from a committee of the State Cabinet and is supported by the State Statistical Bureau.

FORMULATION OF THE PLAN[1]

The preparation of a Five Year Plan is usually spread over a period of two to three years. The first stage is the consideration of the general approach to the formulation, involving an examination of the state of the economy, an appraisal of past trends in production, and the rate of growth in relation to the long-term view of the economy. Preliminary conclusions on these and related matters are submitted by the Commission to the Central Cabinet and to the National Development Council. On their approval, these are published in the form of a document and circulated widely for countrywide debate.

Formulation of the Five Year Plan is an elaborate exercise involving several stages.

The second stage consists of studies which are intended to lead to a consideration of the physical content of the plan. While these studies proceed, the Planning Commission constitutes groups for each sector, composed of its own specialists and those of Ministers and non-official experts, which review the situation in their respective fields and make the assumptions to be made in the formulation of the plan, and indicate the targets of production to be achieved.

While preliminary documents are being debated throughout the country, the Commission holds detailed discussions with the Union Ministers, State Governments and Union Territories at the highest level. The Consultative Committee of Members of Parliament on Planning keeps in close touch with plan formulation constantly by periodic meetings and informal discussions.

On the basis of the preliminary studies undertaken by the groups and discussions with the various interests, the Commission presents the main features of the plan under formulation in the form of a draft plan, which is discussed in detailed by the Cabinet and is placed again before the National Development Council. With the approval of the Council, the Draft Plan is published for public consideration and countrywide debate.

The comments and suggestions on the Draft Plan offered by Members of Parliament and people from different walks of life are taken into consideration in the preparation of the final document of the plan. This document, prepared by the Planning Commission, outlines the objectives, policies and programmes of the plan. It is once again submitted to the Cabinet and the National Development Council.

With such modifications as the National Development Council might suggest, the document is presented to Parliament for final approval.

What has been described above is the system that prevailed until the formulation of the 12th FY Plan (2012-17). As stated above, the NITI Aayog replaced this system.

REVIEW OF THE PLANS

The era of planned development dawned in India with the launching of the First Five Year Plan on April 1, 1951. The process of implementation of Five Year Plans was, however, interrupted in 1966, after the completion of the Third Five Year Plan by the end of March 1966. The Fourth Plan, which should have, in normal course, commenced in April 1966 did not get off on schedule due to some problems during the Third Plan which seriously disrupted the development process, like the aggressions by China and Pakistan and the severe drought in the country, particularly in the last year of the Third Plan, 1965-66, (and also the year that followed) resulting in fall in income, sharp rise in prices and fall in savings; serious balance of payments problems which led to the devaluation of the Rupee by 36.5 per cent in June 1966, etc.

> **The time horizon of Five Year Plan was disrupted several times due to economic adversities and political reasons.**

The Fourth Five Year Plan was put-off by three years. The intervening period between the Third and the Fourth Plans (*i.e.,* 1966-67 to 1968-69) had Annual Plans. This period is referred to by some people as Plan Holiday.

The political change at the Central Government led to a premature end to the Fifth Five Year Plan. The new Government, headed by *Janata* party, which assumed power in 1977, terminated the Fifth Plan at the end of the fourth year, *i.e.,* in March 1978 instead of March 1979 and formulated a Draft Five Year Plan for 1978-83.

The *Janata* Government also introduced the concept of *Rolling Plan*. Under the rolling plan, when one year elapses another year is added to the planning horizon so that we will always have a 'Five Year Plan'. The main advantage claimed for the rolling plan is that plan performance can be reviewed and targets revised on the basis of the changing situation. However, the success of rolling plan in a country like India is constrained by the non-availability of up to date data needed for such revisions.

The fall of the *Janata* Government also led to the end of the Five Year Plan formulated by them. The Congress Government which came to power in 1980 terminated the Five Year Plan formulated by the previous Government at the end of its second year and formulated a Five Year Plan for 1980-85 (the Sixth Plan). On the completion of the Sixth Plan, the Seventh Five Year Plan was launched on April 1, 1985. The Eighth Plan was launched only in 1992. The Ninth Plan (1997-2002) commenced on time. So are the next two plans.

Objectives

The main objectives of the Indian plans have been:

- Proper utilization of the national resources in accordance of the national priorities and fast development of the economy.
- Alleviation and ultimate removal of unemployment and poverty.
- Improvements in the standard of living in general.

The avowed objectives of planning like rapid increase in income, generation of employment, social or redistributive justice, self-reliance, etc., are obviously means to achieve the objectives or aspects of the objectives mentioned above.

There were some variations in the development priorities through Five Year Plans.

There have been changes in the priorities of development and emphasis on objectives through the plans. *For example*, the development priority shifted from agriculture in the First Plan to basic and heavy industries in the Second Plan. The Third Plan recognised the importance of export promotion and the Fourth Plan emphasised self-reliance as an objective of development. *Growth with Social Justice* has been receiving added emphasis since the Fifth Plan. The Fifth Plan, which realised that a *direct attack on poverty* was necessary for rapid eradication of poverty, formulated a specific package of programmes, known as the *minimum needs programme*, to improve the living conditions of the poor and these programmes have been continued, with modifications, in the subsequent plans.

A significant step-up in the rate of growth of the economy, strengthening the redistributive bias of the public policies and services in favour of the poor were among the major objectives of the Sixth Plan. The focus of the Seventh Plan was on food, work and productivity.

Special schemes for improving the living conditions of the poor were introduced since the Fifth Plan.

The Eighth Plan (1992-97) launched at a time of momentous changes in the world and India sought to carry the competitive stimulus of the economic reform process further and gave much greater emphasis on private initiative in industrial development. This Plan was indicative in nature. It concentrated on building a long-term strategic vision of the future and set forth the priorities of the nation. While for the public sector, the Plan went into the details examining the alternatives and identifying the specific projects in various sectors, for the rest of the economy it worked out sectoral targets and tended to provide promotional stimulus to the economy to grow in the desired direction. The Plan recognised "human development" as the core of all developmental effort. The priority sectors that were identified to contribute towards realisation of this goal were health, education, literacy and basic needs, including drinking water, housing and welfare programmes for the weaker sections.

BOX 25.1 : NEW ENVIRONMENT, NEW ROLE

In line with the changed circumstances, we have redefined the role of the Planning Commission. From a highly centralised planning system, we are gradually moving towards indicative planning. Through clear prioritisation of goals, efforts will be made to reduce the bottlenecks, making higher rates of growth possible. If each sector can clearly visualise what is expected of it, then it can gear up to meet the set target. Through the instrument of indicative planning, it will be possible to provide a clear picture of the effects on the entire economy of any change in governmental policy.

The Planning Commission will play an integrative role and help in the development of a holistic approach to the policy formulation in critical areas of development. The Planning Commission will play a mediatory and facilitating role for managing the change smoothly and creating a culture of high productivity and efficiency in the Government.

In addition to the resource allocation role, the Planning Commission will concern itself with resource mobilisation for development as well as with efficient utilisation of the funds. The key to efficient utilisation of resources lies in the creation of appropriate self-managed organisations at all levels. In this area, the Planning Commission will play a systems change role and provide internal consultancy for developing better systems.

– Pranab Mukherjee, Deputy Chairman, Planning Commission, in the *Preface* to the Eighth Plan (1992-97).

The focus of the Ninth Plan was *growth with social justice and equality*. It gave priority to agriculture and rural development with a view to generating adequate employment and eradication of poverty. The other objectives included acceleration of growth with stability; ensuring food and nutritional security for all, particularly the vulnerable sections of the society; providing certain basic minimum facilities and services to all; population control; ensuring environmental sustainability; empowering women and socially disadvantaged groups; promoting people's participation in the development process, etc.

The Tenth Five Year Plan (2002-2007) emphasized the need to incorporate the quality parameter of the development objective. It was underlined that economic growth cannot be the only objective for national planning and indeed over the years, development objectives were being defined not just in terms of increases in GDP or per capita income but more broader in terms of enhancement of human well-being. This includes not only an adequate level of consumption of food and other types of consumer goods but also access to basic social services especially education, health, availability of drinking water and basic sanitation. It also includes the expansion of economic and social opportunities for all individuals and groups and greater participation in decision-making. The Tenth Plan, therefore, sought to set suitable targets in these areas to ensure significant progress towards improvement in the quality of life of all people. The Plan established specific and monitorable targets for a number of key indicators of human development.

TWELFTH FIVE YEAR PLAN (2012-2017)

Vision

The broad vision and aspirations which the Twelfth Five Year Plan (2012-17) seeks to fulfill are reflected in the subtitle: **Faster, Sustainable, and More Inclusive Growth**. The simultaneous achievement of each of these elements is regarded critical for the success of the Plan.

Objectives and Targets

The multi-dimensional objectives are reflected in the adoption of 25 monitorable targets in the Twelfth Plan of which growth of GDP is only one. The other targets cover the many features of development which measure inclusiveness and sustainability. Individual states have also been encouraged to set state-specific targets in the same areas.

Twenty-five core indicators that are listed below reflect the vision of rapid, sustainable and more inclusive growth:

Economic Growth

1. Real GDP Growth Rate of 8.0 per cent.
2. Agriculture Growth Rate of 4.0 per cent.
3. Manufacturing Growth Rate of 10.0 per cent.
4. Every State must have an average growth rate in the Twelfth Plan preferably higher than that achieved in the Eleventh Plan.

Poverty and Employment

5. Head-count ratio of consumption poverty to be reduced by 10 percentage points over the preceding estimates by the end of Twelfth Five Year Plan.
6. Generate 50 million new work opportunities in the non-farm sector and provide skill certification to equivalent numbers during the Twelfth Five Year Plan.

Education

7. Mean Years of Schooling to increase to seven years by the end of Twelfth Five Year Plan.
8. Enhance access to higher education by creating two million additional seats for each age cohort aligned to the skill needs of the economy.
9. Eliminate gender and social gap in school enrolment (that is, between girls and boys, and between SCs, STs, Muslims and the rest of the population) by the end of Twelfth Five Year Plan.

Health

10. Reduce IMR to 25 and MMR to 1 per 1,000 live births, and improve Child Sex Ratio (0-6 years) to 950 by the end of the Twelfth Five Year Plan.
11. Reduce Total Fertility Rate to 2.1 by the end of Twelfth Five Year Plan.
12. Reduce undernutrition among children aged 0-3 years to half of the NFHS-3 levels by the end of Twelfth Five Year Plan.

Infrastructure, Including Rural Infrastructure

13. Increase investment in infrastructure as a percentage of GDP to 9 per cent by the end of Twelfth Five Year Plan.
14. Increase the Gross Irrigated Area from 90 million hectare to 103 million hectare by the end of Twelfth Five Year Plan.
15. Provide electricity to all villages and reduce AT&C losses to 20 per cent by the end of Twelfth Five Year Plan.
16. Connect all villages with all-weather roads by the end of Twelfth Five Year Plan.
17. Upgrade national and state highways to the minimum two-lane standard by the end of Twelfth Five Year Plan.
18. Complete Eastern and Western Dedicated Freight Corridors by the end of Twelfth Five Year Plan.
19. Increase rural tele-density to 70 per cent by the end of Twelfth Five Year Plan.
20. Ensure 50 per cent of rural population has access to 40 lpcd piped drinking water supply, and 50 per cent *gram panchayats* achieve Nirmal Gram Status by the end of Twelfth Five Year Plan.

Environment and Sustainability

21. Increase green cover (as measured by satellite imagery) by 1 million hectare every year during the Twelfth Five Year Plan.
22. Add 30,000 MW of renewable energy capacity in the Twelfth Plan.
23. Reduce emission intensity of GDP in line with the target of 20 per cent to 25 per cent reduction over 2005 levels by 2020.

Service Delivery

24. Provide access to banking services to 90 per cent Indian households by the end of Twelfth Five Year Plan.
25. Major subsidies and welfare related beneficiary payments to be shifted to a direct cash transfer by the end of the Twelfth, Plan, using the *Aadhar* platform with linked bank accounts.

PERFORMANCE OF THE PLANS

Although the Plans have, by and large, failed to achieve the targets and shortfalls are conspicuous in several areas, India has made, undoubtedly, very significant progress. With about 30 per cent of the population still below the poverty line, India is one of the largest industrial powers in the world and has the third largest stock of scientific manpower.

When compared to the modest targets, the performance of the First Plan was satisfactory. In the Fifth, Sixth, Seventh and Eighth Plans, the actual growth rates slightly exceeded the targets. Growth rates in other Plans lagged behind the targets– moderately to substantially. See Table 25.3.

TABLE 25.2 : INDIA'S GROWTH PERFORMANCE DURING THE PLANS

Sl. No.		Target	Actual
1	First Plan (1951-56)	2.1	3.60
2	Second Plan (1956-61)	4.5	4.21
3	Third Plan (1961-66)	5.6	2.72
4	Fourth Plan (1969-74)	5.7	2.05
5	Fifth Plan (1974-79)	4.4	4.83
6	Sixth Plan (1980-85)	5.2	5.54
7	Seventh Plan (1985-90)	5.0	6.02
8	Eighth Plan (1992-97)	5.6	6.68
9	Ninth Plan (1997-02)	6.5	5.5
10	Tenth Plan (2002-07)	8.0	7.2*
11	Eleventh Plan (2007-12)	90	79

* Estimate

Source: Government of India, *India 2005* (publications Division, Ministry of Information and Broadcasting) and Planning Commission, Government of India, *Towards Faster and More Inclusive Growth – An approach to the 11th Five Year Plan*, December, 2006.

To solve the basic problems, the additional number of children to be educated, the additional number of people to be provided with medical facilities and so on during one Five Year Plan in India is more than what most nations have done over centuries.

It is common to criticize the Indian Planning for its failures, pointing out the magnitude of poverty, unemployment, housing problem, etc., prevailing today despite over five decades of planning. The total population of only a few countries like China and the USA is more than the size of the Indian population below the poverty line. Similarly, the number of people unemployed in India is larger than the labour force of many countries; the number of households in India without satisfactory housing is larger than the total number of households in most countries. In fact, the number being added to the Indian population during a decade is larger than the total population in most of the countries. All these highlight the gigantic task facing a poor nation. It is, therefore, not right to view the prevalence of certain problems of large magnitude only as a reflection of the failure of the planning; they should also be viewed as an alarming problem of the magnitude which no other country in the world, except perhaps China, faces.

It goes to the credit of India that it achieved steady growth, albeit moderate, throughout the planning period of the last five-and-a-half-decades, without serious social catastrophes, unlike in China where an estimated more than 30 million people, mostly peasants, died in the Great famine during 1959-62.[4] It may be noted that in 1978, the year in which China started the economic reforms, the per capita income of India was higher than that of China. Although the growth rate of the Indian economy has been poor in comparison with those of several South East Asian countries, India is one among the countries whose per capita income in the early 1990s was higher than ever before. Over much of the period since 1980 to early 1990s, economic decline or stagnation affected about 100 countries, reducing the incomes of more than a quarter of the world's population. In 70 of these countries, average incomes in the early 1990s were less than they were in 1980 and in 43 countries less than they were in 1970. Among the 48 low human development countries, India is the only country whose annual growth in per capita income was above 1.5 per cent during the period 1960-1993.

> **India achieved more or less steady economic growth throughout the planning period of the last five-and-a-half-decades, unlike the case of most of the developing countries.**

The human tragedy of the 1959-62, the biggest in the economic history of any nation, is a telling reflection of the palpable failures of the Chinese system to usher in social justice and to ensure the basic necessity of life to a large section of its citizens. According to the estimates of the Chinese government, there were about 260 million people – a third of the rural population — below the poverty line in China in 1978.[5] The faster economic growth that was made possible by the economic liberalisation had the result of reducing the number of rural poor from 260 million in 1978 to 97 million by 1985. The Chinese economic growth began to accelerate in the second half of the 1980s mainly because of the massive investments in the industrial sector and the thrust on export growth. However, economic disparities and poverty tended to rise. By 1989, the number of rural poor increased to 103 million. Educational achievements also faltered.[6]

Despite many odds, significant progress was made in almost all important spheres. Of course, it would have been possible to achieve better results with better planning, more efficient implementation of the programmes and pragmatic policies.

In the Foreword to the Seventh Five Year Plan, Prime Minister Rajiv Gandhi observed: "Planning has given us a strong base for building a modern, self-reliant industrial economy. Indian industry today is highly diversified, producing a wide range of products, many embodying a high level of technology. The public sector has commanding presence and has played a pioneering role in many areas. We have a broad entrepreneurial base and ample technological and managerial manpower. But some weakness have also become evident. Much of our industry suffers from high cost. There is inadequate attention to quality. In many areas we are working with technology that is obsolete. We have reached a watershed in our industrial development, and in the next phase we must focus on overcoming these problems. Our emphasis must be on greater efficiency, reduction of cost and improvement of quality. This calls for absorption of new technology, greater attention to economies of scale and greater competitions." It may be noted that efforts are being made in these directions.

SUMMARY

The planning system is an important business environment because the direction of the development pattern of the various sectors and the relative priorities within each sector are determined by the Five Year Plans.

The Plans are drawn up by the Planning Commission in accordance with the guidelines given by the National Development Council (NDC) which is presided over by the Prime Minister and is composed of Union Cabinet Ministers, Chief Ministers of States and Union Territories and Members of the Planning Commission. The NDC has a decisive role in the formulation and follow-up of the execution of the National Plan. Its role signifies the federal and democratic nature of the Indian planning.

The States also have their on Plans. State jurisdiction include such vital sectors of development as agriculture, small industries, irrigation and power, roads and road transport, and education and social services. The States have Planning Boards and Departments which co-ordinate the work of other departments for the preparation of development plans, and present reports on the execution of State Plans. State Planning generally receives directions from a committee of the State cabinet and is supported by the State Statistical Bureau.

Following the, economic liberalisation, a shift in the planning strategy has taken place. In the past, planning envisaged a dominant role for the public sector with massive investments in basic and heavy industries. Since the Eighth Plan, the private sector began to gain greater significance and from a highly centralised planning system we are gradually moving towards indicative planning

The main objectives of the Indian plans have been proper utilization of the national resources in accordance of the national priorities and fast development of the economy; alleviation and ultimate removal of unemployment and poverty, and improvements in the standard of living in general. The avowed objectives of planning like rapid increase in income, generation of employment, social or redistributive justice, self-reliance etc. are obviously means to achieve the objectives or aspects of the objectives mentioned above.

There have, however, been changes in the priorities of development and emphasis on objectives through the plans. For example, the development priority shifted from agriculture in the First Plan to basic and heavy industries in the Second Plan. The Third Plan recognised the importance of export promotion and the Fourth Plan emphasised self-reliance as an objective of development. *Growth with Social Justice* has been receiving added emphasis since the Fifth Plan. The Fifth Plan, which realised that a *direct attack on poverty* was necessary for rapid eradication of poverty, formulated a specific package of programmes, known as the *minimum needs programme*, to improve the living conditions of the poor and these programmes have been continued, with modifications, in the subsequent plans. A significant step-up in the rate of growth of the economy, strengthening the redistributive bias of the public policies and services in favour of the poor were among the major objectives of the Sixth Plan. The focus of the Seventh Plan was on food, work and productivity. The Eighth sought to carry the competitive stimulus of the economic reform process further and gave much greater emphasis on private initiative in industrial development. The Plan recognised "human development" as the core of all developmental effort.

The focus of the Ninth Plan has been described as *Growth with Social Justice and Equity.* The development strategy for the future has been formulated against the emerging new economic environment in which private sector has a greater role than in the past.

The Ninth Plan has set a target of 6.5 per cent. Annual growth for GDP, an industrial growth rate of 8.2 per cent, agricultural growth rate of 3.9 per cent and export growth rate of 11.8 per cent per annum.

The poverty ratio has been expected to come down from about 29 per cent in 1996-97 to 18 per cent by the end of the Ninth Plan, less than 10 per cent by 2006-07 and less than 5 per cent by 2011-12.

Indian Plans have, by and large, failed to achieve the targets and shortfalls are conspicuous in several areas. The long-term average annual growth rate of the economy was only about 3.5 per cent and of the per capital income about 1.5 per cent. There has, however, been an acceleration of the growth rates since the Sixth Plan.

Despite many odds, significant progress was made in almost all important spheres. Of course, it would have been possible to achieve better results with better planning, more efficient implementation of the programmes and pragmatic policies.

It is common to criticise the Indian planning for its failures, pointing out the magnitude of poverty, unemployment, housing problem, etc., prevailing today despite over five decades of planning. It is, however, not right to view the prevalence of certain problems of large magnitude only as a reflection of the failure of the planning; they should also be viewed as alarming problems of the magnitude which no other country in the world, except perhaps China, faces.

As Prime Minister Rajiv Gandhi observed, "Planning has given us a strong base for building a modern, self-reliant industrial economy. Indian industry today is highly diversified, producing a wide range of products, many embodying a high level of technology. The public sector has commanding presence and has played a pioneering role in many areas. We have a broad entrepreneurial base and ample technological and managerial manpower. But some weakness have also become evident. Much of our industry suffers from high cost. There is inadequate attention to quality. In many areas we are working with technology that is obsolete. We have reached a watershed in our industrial development, and in the next phase we must focus on overcoming these problems. Our emphasis must be on greater efficiency, reduction of cost and improvement of quality. This calls for absorption of new technology, greater attention to economies of scale and greater competitions.

REFERENCES

1. Adopted from "How a Plan is Formulated", *Yojana*, August 15, 1980, p. 45.
2. Planning Commission, Government of India, *Towards faster and more inclusive Growth – An approach to the 11th Five Year Plan*, December, 2006, p. 2.
3. *Ibid.*, p. 71.
4. UNDP, *Human Development Report 1997*, Oxford University Press, New York, 1997, p. 49.
5. *Ibid.*, p. 49.
6. *Ibid.*, p. 49.

☆☆☆

CHAPTER 26

GATT/WTO AND GLOBAL LIBERALISATION

National economic and business policies as well as international economic relations and development patterns are influenced by international economic organisations like World Bank, International Monetary Fund (IMF) and World Trade Organisation (WTO).

The global business environment is very significantly influenced by the World Trade Organisation (WTO) principles and agreements. They also affect the domestic environment. For example, India has had to substantially liberalise imports, including almost complete removal of quantitative import restrictions. The liberalisation of imports implies that domestic firms have to face an increasing competition from foreign goods. Liberalisation of foreign investment can result in growing competition from local outfits of MNCs.

These liberalisations, on the other hand, also provide new opportunities for Indian firms as the foreign markets become more open for exports and investments. Further, the liberalisation enables Indian firms to seek foreign equity participation and foreign technology. This could help them to expand their business or improve competitiveness. The liberalisation also facilitates global sourcing by Indian firms so that they can improve their competitiveness. Indian suppliers can benefit from global sourcing by foreign firms. Firms will have to be efficient and dynamic to survive the global competition. Inefficient firms may go out of business.

Consumers stand to benefit significantly from the liberalisation. But indiscriminate liberalisation and unfair competition will be harmful.

GATT

An understanding of the General Agreement on Tariffs and Trade (GATT), the predecessor of WTO, will help understand the WTO better.

The Bretton Woods Conference of 1944 which recommended the establishment of the IMF and World Bank had also recommended the establishment of an International Trade Organisation (ITO). Although the IMF and World Bank were established in 1946, because of objections that its enforcement provisions would interfere with the autonomy of domestic policy making, the ITO charter was never ratified. Instead the GATT, which had been drawn up only as an interim agreement to fill the gap until the ITO charter was ratified, became the framework for international trading system since 1948. The international trading system since 1948 was, at least in principle, guided by the rules and procedures agreed to by the signatories to the GATT which was an agreement signed by the contracting nations which were admitted on the basis of their willingness to accept the GATT disciplines.

The GATT was transformed into a World Trade Organisation (WTO) with effect from January, 1995. Thus, after about five decades, the original proposal of an International Trade Organisation has taken shape as the WTO. The WTO which is a more powerful body than the GATT has an enlarged role than the GATT.

India is one of the founder members of the IMF, World Bank, GATT and the WTO.

Objectives

The primary objective of GATT was to expand international trade by liberalising trade so as to bring about all-round economic prosperity. The Preamble to the GATT mentioned the following as its important objectives:

1. Raising the standard of living.
2. Ensuring full employment and a large and steadily growing volume of real income and effective demand.
3. Developing full use of the resources of the world.
4. Expansion of production and international trade.

GATT embodied certain conventions and general principles governing international trade among countries that adhere to the agreement. The rules or conventions of GATT required that:

1. Any proposed change in the tariff, or other type of commercial policy of a member country should not be undertaken without consultation of other parties to the agreement.
2. The countries that adhere to GATT should work towards the reduction of tariffs and other barriers to international trade, which should be negotiated within the framework of GATT.

GATT Principles

For the realisation of its objectives, GATT adopted the following principles. These principles are applicable to WTO.

1. *Non-discrimination:* The principle of non-discrimination requires that no member country shall discriminate between the members of GATT in the conduct of international trade. To ensure non-discrimination, the members of GATT agree to apply the principle of most favoured nation (MFN) to all import and export duties. This means that "each nation shall be treated as well as the most favoured nation." As far as quantitative restrictions are permitted, they too, are to be administered without favour.

However, certain exceptions to this principle are allowed. For instance, GATT does not prohibit economic integration such as free trade areas or customs union, provided the purpose of such integration is "to facilitate trade between the constituent territories and not to raise barriers to the trade of other parties." The GATT also permits the members to adopt measures to counter dumping and export subsidies. However, the application of such measures shall be limited to the offending countries.

2. *Prohibition of Quantitative Restrictions:* GATT rules seek to prohibit quantitative restrictions as far as possible and limit restrictions on trade to the less rigid tariffs. However, certain exceptions to this prohibition are granted to countries confronted with balance of payments difficulties and to developing countries. Further, import restrictions were allowed to apply to agricultural and fishery products if domestic production of these articles was subject to equally restrictive production or marketing controls.

3. *Consultation:* By providing a forum for continuing consultation, it sought to resolve disagreements through consultation. So far, eight rounds of trade negotiations were held under the auspices of the GATT. Each round took several years. The Uruguay Round, the latest one, took more than seven years to conclude, as against the originally contemplated more than four years. This shows the complexity of the issues involved in the trade negotiations.

Evaluation of GATT

One of the principal achievements of GATT was the establishment of a forum for continuing consultations. "Disputes that might otherwise have caused continuing hard feelings, reprisals, and even diplomatic rupture have been brought to the conference table and compromised."

GATT could achieve considerable trade liberalisation. There were, of course, several exceptions.

Agricultural trade was clearly an exception to the liberalisation. Far from becoming freer, trade in agriculture became progressively more distorted by the support given to farmers (which took the form of severe barriers to imports, and subsidies to exports) in the industrial nations.

GATT achieved substantial trade liberalisation. But sectors which would have significantly benefited developing countries, like agriculture and textiles, were not liberalised.

Similarly, another exception was textiles. Trade in textiles was restricted by the Multifibre Arrangement (MFA). Under the MFA, imports of textile items to a number of developed countries were restricted by quotas.

The progressive liberalisation of trade, however, suffered a setback since 1974, Although the elimination of Tariff Barriers continued, even the developed countries have substantially increased non-tariff barriers since then. The collapse of the Bretton Woods system in the early 1970s and the oil crisis made matters very difficult for many countries, both developing and developed, and as a result of these, demands for protection increased dramatically. The developing country exports have been hit very hard by the NTBs, as pointed out earlier in this chapter.

Further, the exports of developing countries gained significantly less from the GATT Rounds than did exports of the industrial nations. The trade liberalisation has been confined mostly to goods of interest to the developed countries. In case of agricultural commodities, not only was that there was no liberalisation, but also there was an increase in protection. Manufactured products of interest to developing countries like textiles and clothing, footwear, etc. were subject to increasing non-tariff barriers. While the developed countries enjoyed a more liberalised trading environment, the growing NTBs severely affected the exports of developing countries. Ironically, the developed countries have been increasing the protectionism when the developing countries have been liberalising. This is indeed a sad commentary on the GATT and other multilateral organisations.

WTO

The eighth Round of the multilateral trade negotiations (MTNs) held under the auspices of the GATT is popularly known Uruguay Round (UR) because it was launched in Punta del Este in Uruguay, a developing country, in September 1986. The UR, which paved the way for the establishment of the WTO (replacing the GATT), was by far the most far-reaching MTN, because it ushered in, for the first time, measures for liberalisation of international capital flows, trade in services and a new regime of intellectual property rights (IPRs). In short, it set the stage for substantial global economic liberalisations with far-reaching implications – economic, business and social.

GATT AND WTO

Following the UR Agreement, GATT was converted into a formal international organisation called World Trade Organisation (WTO) with effect from January 1, 1995.

The situation, after the coming into effect of WTO may be described as the GATT is dead, long live the GATT.

Under the old system, there were two GATTs: (i) GATT, the Agreement — *i.e.,* the agreement between contracting parties (governments) setting out the rules for conducting international trade; and (ii) GATT, the Organisation — an international organisation created to facilitate discussions and administration related to the Agreement (ad hoc, though, continued to exist until the establishment of the WTO). GATT, the organisation, ceased to exist with the establishment of WTO; GATT the agreement, which always dealt with (and still does) trade in goods, continues to exist, in amended form, as part of the WTO alongside two new agreements, viz., General Agreement on Trade in Services (GATS) and General Agreement on Trade Related Aspects of Intellectual Property Rights (TRIPs). The old text is now called 'GATT 1947' and the updated version is called 'GATT 1994'. In short, the WTO is GATT plus a lot more.

TABLE 26.1: DIFFERENCE BETWEEN GATT AND WTO

GATT	WTO
GATT was ad hoc and provisional.	WTO and its agreements are permanent.
GATT had contracting parties.	WTO has members.
GATT system allowed existing domestic legislation to continue even if it violated a GATT agreement.	WTO does not permit this.
GATT was less powerful, dispute settlement system was slow and less efficient, its ruling could be easily blocked.	WTO is more powerful than GATT, dispute settlement mechanism is faster and more efficient, very difficult to block the rulings.

WTO Agreements

The WTO endeavours to ensure that trade is as fair as possible and as free as practicable by negotiating rules and abiding by them. The WTO's rules — the agreements — are the result of negotiations between the members.

GATT is now the WTO's principal rule-book for trade in goods. The Uruguay Round also created new rules for dealing with trade in services, relevant aspects of intellectual property, dispute settlement and trade policy reviews. Through these agreements, WTO members operate a non-discriminatory trading system that spells out their rights and their obligations. Each country receives guarantees that its exports will be treated fairly and consistently in other countries' markets. Each promises to do the same for imports into its own market. The system also gives developing countries some flexibility in implementing their commitments.

Goods: Trade in goods was the concentration of GATT until the Uruguay Round negotiations. From 1947 to 1994, GATT was the forum for negotiating lower customs duty rates and other trade barriers; the text of the General Agreement spelt out important rules, particularly non-discrimination.

Since 1995, the updated GATT has become the WTO's umbrella agreement for trade in goods. It has annexes dealing with specific sectors such as agriculture and textiles, and with specific issues such as state trading, product standards, subsidies and actions taken against dumping.

Services: Banks, insurance firms, telecommunications companies, tour operators, hotel chains and transport companies looking to do business abroad can now enjoy the same principles of freer and fairer trade that originally only applied to trade in goods.

These principles appear in the new General Agreement on Trade in Services (GATS). WTO members have also made individual commitments under GATS stating which of their services sectors they are willing to open to foreign competition, and how open those markets are.

Intellectual Property: The WTO's intellectual property agreement amounts to rules for trade and investment in ideas and creativity. The rules state how copyrights, patents, trademarks, geographical names used to identify products, industrial designs, integrated circuit layout designs and undisclosed information such as trade secrets — "intellectual property" — should be protected when trade is involved.

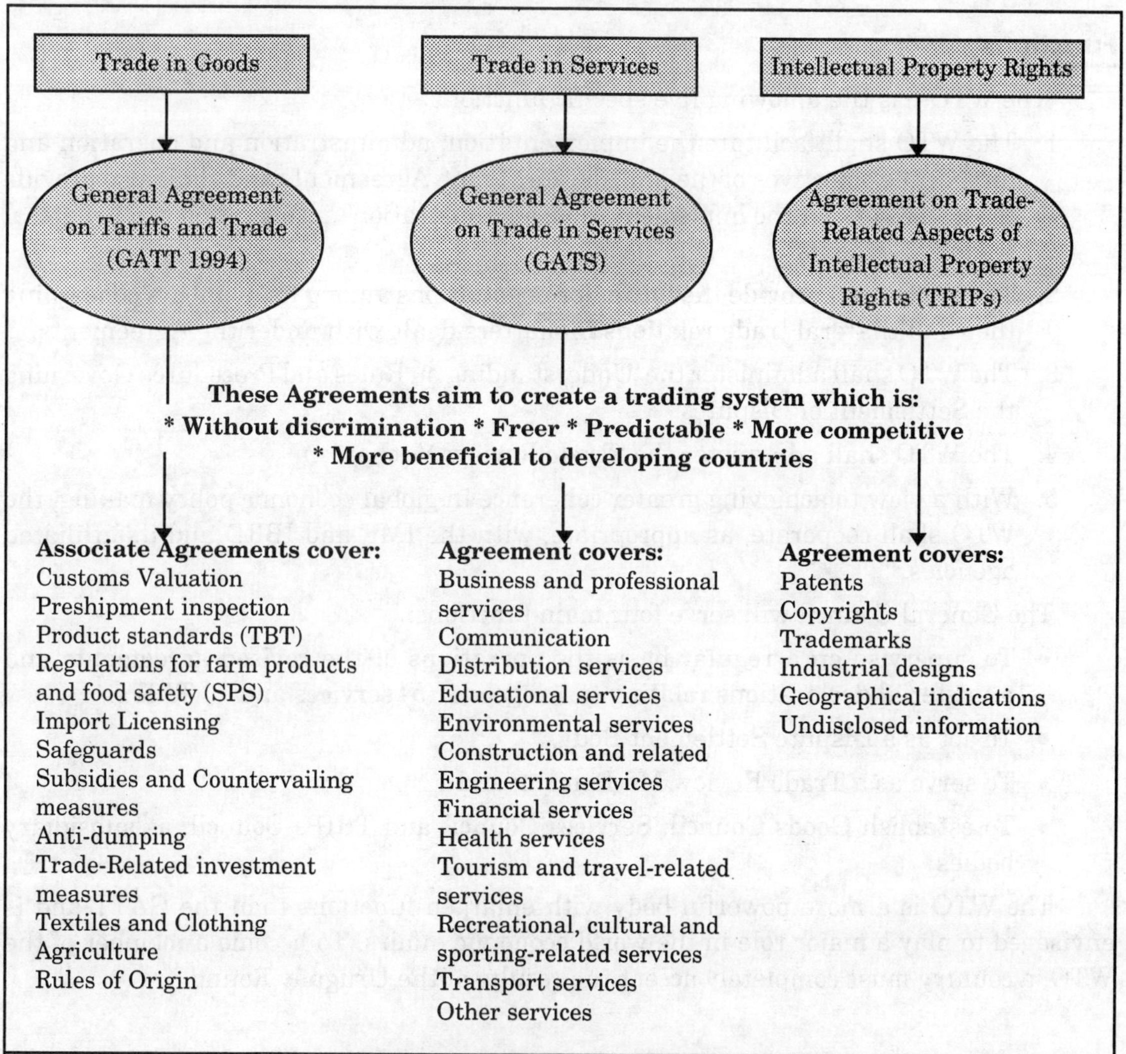

Fig. 26.1: WTO and World Trading System

Dispute Settlement: The WTO's procedure for resolving trade quarrels under the Dispute Settlement Understanding is vital for enforcing the rules and therefore for ensuring that trade flows smoothly. Countries bring disputes to the WTO if they think their rights under the agreements are being infringed. Judgements by specially-appointed independent experts are based on interpretations of the agreements and individual countries' commitments.

Policy Review: The Trade Policy Review Mechanism's purpose is to improve transparency, to create a greater understanding of the policies that countries are adopting, and to assess their impact. Many members also see the reviews as constructive feedback on their policies.

All WTO members must undergo periodic scrutiny, each review containing reports by the country concerned and the WTO Secretariat.

Functions

The WTO has the following five specific functions.

1. The WTO shall facilitate the implementation, administration and operation and further the objectives of the Multilateral Trade Agreements and shall also provide the framework for the implementation, administration and operation of plurilateral trade agreements.
2. The WTO shall provide the forum for negotiations among its members concerning their multilateral trade relations in matters dealt with under the Agreements.
3. The WTO shall administer the 'Understanding on Rules and Procedures Governing the Settlement of Disputes.'
4. The WTO shall administer the 'Trade Review Mechanism.'
5. With a view to achieving greater coherence in global economic policy making, the WTO shall cooperate, as appropriate, with the IMF and IBRD and its affiliated agencies.

The General Council will serve four main functions:

- To supervise on a regular basis the operations of the revised agreements and ministerial declarations relating to: (*a*) goods, (*b*) services and (*c*) TRIPs.
- To act as a Dispute Settlement Body.
- To serve as a Trade Review Mechanism; and
- To establish Goods Council, Services Council and TRIPs Council, as subsidiary bodies.

The WTO is a more powerful body with enlarged functions than the GATT and is envisaged to play a major role in the world economic affairs. To become a member of the WTO, a country must completely accept the results of the Uruguay Round.

IMPACT OF WTO

Impact of WTO on the economy is similar to the impact of liberalisation of foreign investment and trade.

Liberalisation of trade in goods has paved the way for more liberalisation of trade in goods. The implication of this is that consumers and business firms can source from the preferred source anywhere in the world. Competition in the goods market has the following effects:

- Increases consumer choice
- Puts downward pressure on price
- Quality improvement
- Better service including pre- and after-sales services.

Import competing industries face severe competition necessitating:

- Efficiency and quality improvements
- Cost reduction
- Improvement of services
- R&D and innovation

Firms which will not be able to survive the competition will be vanished.

The **General Agreement on Trade in Services (GATS):** The General Agreement on Trade in Services which extends multilateral rules and disciplines to services and provides for liberalisation of trade in services, including education, financial services, telecommunications, transport, audio visual, tourism, and professional services, as well as movement of workers. This will have both favourable and unfavourable effects as in liberalisation in other cases.

Trade Related Investment Measures (TRIMs): Another important area of WTO agreement pertains to TRIMs. TRIM refers to certain conditions or restrictions imposed by a government in respect of foreign investment in the country. TRIMs were widely employed by developing countries.

The Agreement on TRIMs provides that no contracting party shall apply any TRIM which is inconsistent with the WTO Articles. An illustrative list identifies the following TRIMs as inconsistent.

1. Local content requirement (*i.e.*, a certain amount of local inputs be used in products)
2. Trade balancing requirement (*i.e.*, imports shall not exceed a certain proportion of exports)
3. Trade and foreign exchange balancing requirements
4. Domestic sales requirements (*i.e.*, a company shall sell a certain proportion of its output locally).

The Agreement requires the notification of all WTO-inconsistent TRIMs and their phasing out within two, five and seven years by industrial, developing and least developed countries respectively. Transition period can be extended for developing and least developed countries if they face difficulties in eliminating TRIMs.

A number of TRIMs were employed in India prior to the liberalisation ushered in 1991 and many of them have been phased out since then.

Trade Related Aspects of Intellectual Property Rights (TRIPs): One of the most controversial outcomes of the UR is the Agreement on Trade Related Aspects of Intellectual Property Rights.

Intellectual Property Rights may be defined as "information with a commercial value". IPRs have been characterised as a composite of "ideas, inventions and creative expression" plus the "public willingness to bestow the status of property" on them and give their owners the "right to exclude others from access to or use of protected subject matter."

Under the WTO, TRIPs covers seven intellectual properties:

1. Copyright and related rights
2. Trade mark
3. Geographical indications
4. Industrial designs
5. Patents
6. Layout designs (topographics) of integrated circuits
7. Undisclosed information.

The TRIPs Agreement provides for legal protection of IPRs. Countries need to take effective measures for protection of IPRs.

The Patent protection stipulations brought in by the UR and implemented by the WTO has come in for scathing criticism in the developing countries because it harms the interests of the developing countries and benefits the MNCs with technological might. The Indian Patents Act was amended to make it WTO compliant. Now, we have both product and process patent compared to only process patent in the past, very adversely affecting the Indian pharmaceutical industry. The patent period now is 20 years compared to 14 earlier. There is a strong feeling that the more stringent patent regulation provides opportunity for multinationals to exploit the market, charging exorbitant prices, making the plight of poor patients more miserable.

Figure 26.2 provides a schematic summary view of the favourable impact of WTO on the economy.

India's gain from the trade liberalisation will be much less than that of many other developing countries, such as the South East Asian economies and China, because India's share in the world trade is very low (less than one per cent) and her foreign trade-GDP ratio is very low.

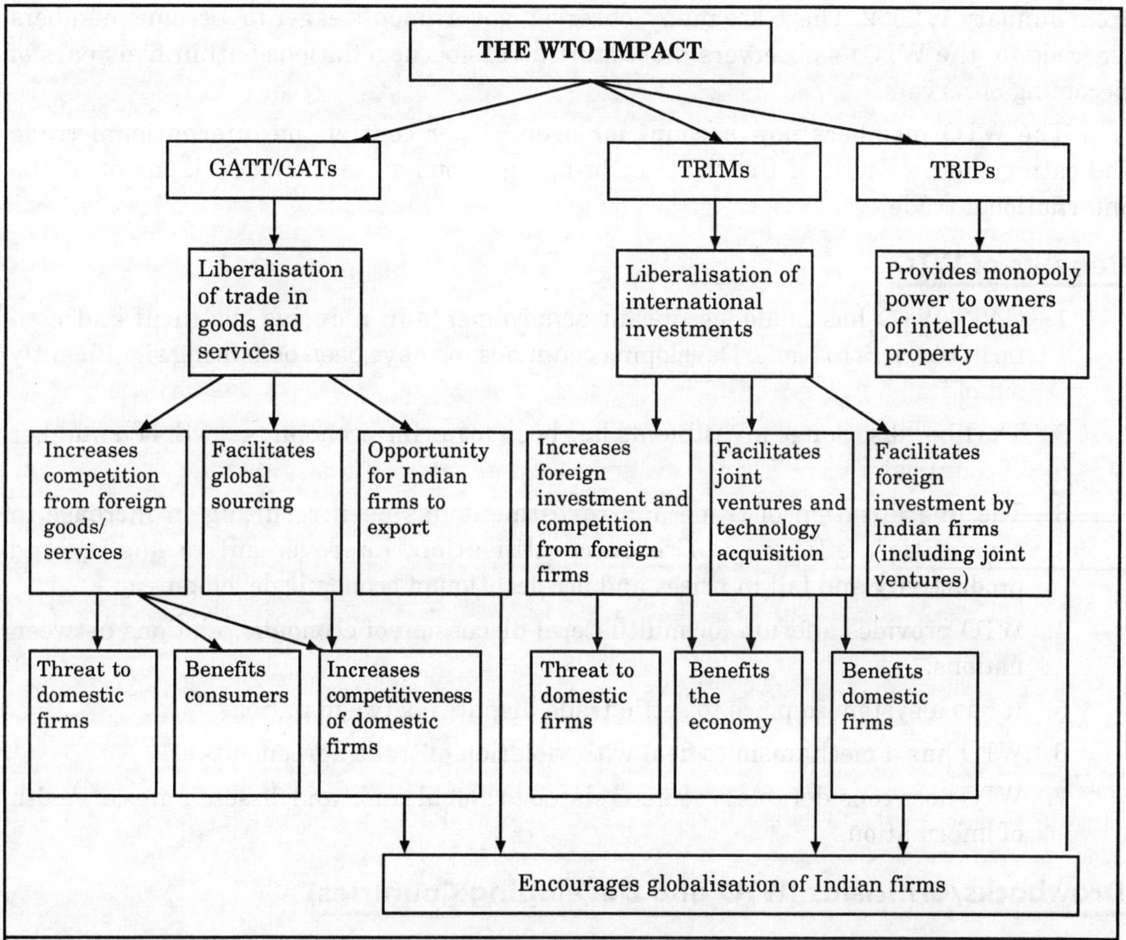

Fig. 26.2: The WTO Impact

EVALUATION OF WTO

WTO has come to ply a very important role in the global, and thereby, national economies. National economic policies are significantly influenced by the principles, policies and agreements of WTO. Because of this, there are severe criticisms against WTO, particularly in the developing countries. In fact, WTO has both positive and negative impacts.

The growing acceptance of GATT/WTO, despite the shortcomings, is evinced by the increase in the number of member countries. When the GATT was signed in 1947, only 23 nations were party to it. The Uruguay Round was signed in 1994 by 125 national governments. The membership of the WTO stood at 164 at the end of October 2016. It is interesting to note that the People's Republic of China, which was one of the original signatories of the GATT quit it in the late 1940s following the assumption of power by the communist party, but got admitted to the WTO, after a prolonged negotiations, with effect from January 1, 2002. There are many 'observer' governments eager to become members ("accede to" the WTO) – observers must start accession negotiations within five years of becoming observers.

The WTO members now account for over 97 per cent of the international trade indicating the potential of the WTO in bringing about an orderly development of the international trade.

Benefits of WTO

1. GATT/WTO has made significant achievements in reducing the tariff and non-tariff barriers to trade. Developing countries too have been benefiting significantly out of it.
2. The liberalisation of investments has been fostering economic growth of a number of countries.
3. The liberalisation of trade and investment has been resulting in increase in competition, efficiency of resource utilisation, improvement in quality and productivity and fall in prices and acceleration of economic development.
4. WTO provides a forum for multilateral discussion of economic relations between nations.
5. It has a system in place to settle trade disputes between nations.
6. WTO has a mechanism to deal with violation of trade agreements.
7. WTO does considerable research related to global trade and disseminates a wealth of information.

Drawbacks/Criticisms (WTO and Developing Countries)

As mentioned above, the WTO has been subjected to a number of criticisms. Important drawbacks criticisms include the following:

1. Negotiations and decision making in the WTO are dominated by the developed countries.
2. Many developing countries do not have the financial and knowledge resources to effectively participate in the WTO discussions and negations.
3. Because of the dependence of developing countries on the developed ones, the developed countries are able to resort to arms-twisting tactics.
4. Many of the policy liberalisations are done without considering the vulnerability of the developing countries and the possible adverse effect on them.
5. The WTO has not been successful in imposing the organisation's disciplines on the developed countries.

The developing countries have, in general, been getting a raw deal from the WTO.

It may also be noted that it has become a trend to blame WTO even for matters for which it is not responsible.

It is necessary that the developing countries do their homework properly before they go to the negotiating table, stand united to protect their common interests and formulate and implement strategies to combat the threats and to take advantage of the opportunities of the emerging world order.

Table 26.2 lists ten advantages of WTO and ten misunderstandings about WTO, as given in the WTO's website. It may be noted that there is some element of truth in some of the points.

TABLE 26.2: ADVANTAGES AND DISADVANTAGES OF WTO

The Ten Benefits	*The Ten Misunderstandings*
1. The system helps promote peace	1. The WTO dictates policy
2. Disputes are handled constructively	2. The WTO is for free trade at any cost
3. Rules make life easier for all	3. Commercial interests take priority over development ...
4. Freer trade cuts the costs of living	4. ... and over the environment
5. It provides more choice of products and qualities	5. ... and over health and safety
6. Trade raises incomes	6. The WTO destroys jobs, worsens poverty
7. Trade stimulates economic growth	7. Small countries are powerless in the WTO
8. The basic principles make life more efficient	8. The WTO is the tool of powerful lobbies
9. Governments are shielded from lobbying	9. Weaker countries are forced to join the WTO
10. The system encourages good government	10. The WTO is undemocratic

WTO AND INDIA

The sub-section *Drawbacks / Criticisms (WTO and Developing Countries)* given above is applicable to India as well.

The WTO faces scathing criticisms in India. Many politicians and others have argued that India should withdraw from the GATT. Many of the criticisms are either baseless or due to lack of knowledge of the international trading environment, and misinformation, or are just meant to oppose the government by the opposition parties.

It is true that WTO mostly benefits the developed countries. The criticism that WTO functioning is influenced by the vested interests of MNCs. That does not mean that developing countries like India are losing — only that their gain is limited as compared to that of the developed countries.

Accepting the demand of some of the critics, that India should withdraw from the WTO will be a great blunder that the nation can commit. By being a part of WTO, India enjoys the most favoured nation (MFN) status with all the other members of the WTO. Opting out of the system would mean an infinitely laborious task of entering into bilateral negotiations with each and every one of the trading partners which would amount to "having one's arms twisted bilaterally by the US, the EC and Japan, turn by turn, on everything from intellectual property rights to NPT, human rights and environmentally clean technologies for packaging." It may be noted at this juncture that China got readmitted to the system after a long wait and lobbying.

One major controversy is the agricultural subsidies. Much hue and cry have been raised in India about this factor. However, it needs to be mentioned that the WTO agreements would not adversely affect India's agricultural subsidies and its agriculture exports. Other developing countries would also largely benefit because of the lowering of the agricultural protection by the developed countries, in spite of the fact that the wish of the developing countries that the major Western nations would totally drop subsidies for their producers, substantially lower tariffs, and open markets did not materialise.

According to Government of India, the Market Access Agreements signed by India with the USA and EU will result in additional export earnings of around ₹ 1100 crores in the initial years and the additional access achieved will get magnified in the second and third phases of integration of the textiles trade with the multinational trade system and will provide larger earnings during these periods

However, India's gain will be much less than those of several other developing countries like China and the newly industrialised economies because : (i) India's share in the world trade is very low and (ii) The foreign trade-DGP ratio of India is low. The gain will also depend on the rate of growth of India's exports.

India has taken several measures to comply with UR agreements, including amending the Patent law. There is a strong view that the present patent regime imposed by the WTO is biased in favour of developed countries and MNCs and are detrimental to the interests of India and other developing countries.

[Readers are requested to update the information visiting WTO website.]

SUMMARY

The principles and Agreements of WTO have very significant impact on the business environment. Figure 26.1 provides a bird's eye view of the important impacts.

The salient features of the Uruguay Round Agreement are given below:

1. The Uruguay Round substantially expanded the scope of multilateral trade negotiation by including services, intellectual property rights (TRIPs) and trade related aspects of investment measures (TRIMs), as against only goods in the past.
2. With effect from January 1, 1995, GATT (which was temporary an *ad hoc*) was replaced by a permanent organisation, the WTO.
3. WTO is GATT plus a lot more. Under the GATT, there was only one major agreement—GATT. Under the WTO, there are agreements related to three major areas—GATT, GATs and TRIPs.
4. WTO is a more powerful and effective organisation than GATT. It has a more effective dispute settlement mechanism.

5. The Uruguay Round Agreement seeks to liberalise trade in manufactures by enlarging tariff bindings, reducing tariffs and removing tariffs.
6. A significant achievement of the UR is the measures to liberalise trade in agriculture, which was a highly protected sector, particularly in the developed countries. These measures are tariffication, tariff bindings, tariff cuts and reduction in subsidies and domestic support.
7. All member countries are required to adopt product patent (as also process patent). India had only process patent for drugs, food and chemical substances for which the patent period was 7 years and 14 years for other products. Under the WTO regime, the patent period for all products is 20 years.
8. As under GATT, under WTO also developing countries, particularly least developed countries, are accorded a number of concessions and favours. Their liberalisation requirements are lower and they are allowed longer period to fulfil the liberalisation commitments. The WTO also calls upon the developed nations to grant special preferences to imports from developing countries. There are also some committees under the WTO to look after the interests and special needs of the developing countries.
9. There is a general complaint that the fruits of the liberalisation accrue mostly to the developed countries. It is pointed out that the industrialised countries, which make up only 20 per cent of the membership, will appropriate about 70 per cent of the additional income generated by the implementation of the UR agreements. The losers, mostly in Africa and Caribbean, are some of the poorest countries in the world. The developed countries gain substantially because of their higher level of participation in trade and because of the fact that significant part of liberalisations has been in respect of goods of interest to them. Liberalisation of trade in textiles, by phasing out MFA, however, will substantially benefit the developing countries.
10. Even after all UR concessions are fully implemented by the industrialised countries, significant trade barriers in the form of high tariff peaks (exceeding 12 per cent but in some cases reaching or exceeding 300 per cent) will continue to affect many exports from developing countries. The removal of such barriers needs to be given high priority. There are several other areas of critical importance to the developing countries.
11. Developing countries are terribly disadvantaged due to the *participation gap*.
12. India has taken several measures to comply with the TRIPs Agreement. These include amendments to some laws and new legislations.
13. Estimates of India's possible gain from the trade liberalisation vary very wide — between $2 billion and $7 billion a year. Although the liberalisation of trade in textiles will benefit the developing countries, India's gain will depend a lot on her competitive strength *vis-a-vis* other textile exporters.

India's gain from the trade liberalisation will be much less than that of many other developing countries, such as the South East Asian economies and China, because India's share in the world trade is very low (less than one per cent) and her foreign trade-GDP ratio is very low.

(More elaborate and illustrative treatment of WTO is available in the new edition of the author's *International Business* – Prentice Hall of India).

☆☆☆

CHAPTER

27

FOREIGN INVESTMENT

Foreign investment has been playing a very important role in the industrial development in particular and economic development in general, globally.

> **There has been a spurt in the foreign investment to different countries, triggered by the economic liberalisation, particularly in the developing and erstwhile communist/ socialist countries.**

The economic liberalisations that swept across the world, particularly since the late 1980s, have very significantly changed the environment for international private financial flows. At the same time, the surging international capital flows, in its turn, are substantially impacting the business environment. The massive flow of international investment has resulted in a substantial increase in their role in global production, employment generation and trade. The ratio of world FDI inward stock to world GDP increased from about 5 per cent in 1980 to 1 about 23 per cent in 2005. As renowned management guru Peter Drucker in his *Managing For the Future* observers, "increasingly world investment rather than world trade will be driving the international economy. Exchange rates, taxes, and legal rules will become more important than wage rates and tariffs."[1]

BOX 27.1 TYPES OF FOREIGN INVESTMENT

Broadly, there are two types of foreign investment, *viz.*, foreign direct investment (FDI) and foreign portfolio investment (FPI).

Foreign direct investment (FDI) refers to investment in a foreign country where the investor retains control over the investment. It typically takes the form of starting a subsidiary, acquiring a stake in an existing firm or starting a joint venture in the foreign country. Direct investment and management of the firms concerned normally go together. If the investor has only a sort of property interest in investing the capital in buying equities, bonds, or other securities abroad, it is referred to as portfolio investment. That is, in the case of portfolio investments, the investor uses his capital in order to get a return on it, but has no much control over the use of the capital. Foreign portfolio investment (FPI), thus, is investment by individuals, firms, or public bodies (like governments or government organisations) in financial instruments (such as stocks and government bonds).

FDI may take the form of:

- Greenfield investment, i.e., establishing an entirely new enterprise in the foreign market.
- M&A, *i.e.*, merging or acquiring an existing firm in the foreign country. In recent years, cross-border M&A has been the major driver of FDI.

There are mainly two routes of portfolio investments in India, viz., by Foreign Institutional Investors (FIIs) like mutual funds and through Global Depository Receipts (GDRs), American Depository Receipts (ADRs) and Foreign Currency Convertible Bonds (FCCBs).

GDRs/ADRs and FCCBs are instruments issued by Indian companies in the foreign markets for mobilising foreign capital by facilitating portfolio investment by foreigners in Indian securities. Since 1992, Indian companies, satisfying certain conditions, are allowed to access foreign capital markets by Euro issues.

UNCTAD's *World Investment Report* defines foreign direct investment (FDI) as an investment involving a long-term relationship and reflecting a lasting interest and control by a resident entity in one economy (foreign direct investor or parent enterprise) in an enterprise resident in an economy other than that of the foreign direct investor (FDI enterprise or affiliate enterprise or foreign affiliate). FDI implies that the investor exerts a significant degree of influence on the management of the enterprise resident in the other economy. Such investment involves both the initial transaction between the two entities and all subsequent transactions between them and among foreign affiliates, both incorporated and unincorporated. FDI may be undertaken by individuals as well as business entities.

The ownership level required in order for a direct investment to exist is 10 per cent of the voting shares.

There are two related but different measures of FDI: FDI *flows* and FDI *stock*. FDI flows

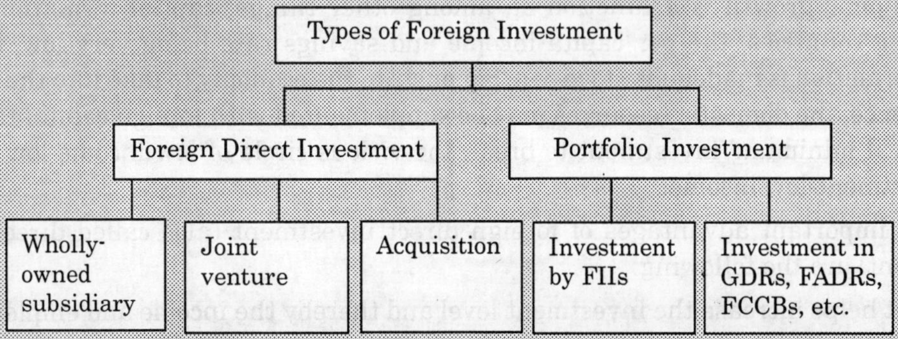

refer to the new FDI during a specified period while the FDI stock measures the total amount of that exists at a point in time. These stocks are the sums of past flows of FDI. *Flows of FDI* comprise capital provided (either directly or through other related enterprises) by a foreign direct investor to an FDI enterprise, or capital received from an FDI enterprise by a foreign direct investor. FDI has three components: equity capital, reinvested earnings and intra-company loans.

According to the World Bank, foreign direct investment is net inflows of investment to acquire a lasting management interest (10 per cent or more of voting stock) in an enterprise operating in an economy other than that of the investor. It is the sum of equity capital, re-investment of earnings, other long-term capital, and short-term capital, as shown in the balance of payments.

FDIs are governed by long-term considerations because these investments cannot be easily liquidated. Hence, factors like long-term political stability, government policy, industrial and economic prospects, etc., influence the FDI decision. However, portfolio investments, which can be liquidated fairly easily, are influenced by short-term gains. Portfolio investments are generally much more sensitive than FDIs. Direct investors have direct responsibility with the promotion and management of the enterprise. Portfolio investors do not have such direct involvement with the promotion and management. Direct investment refers to investment in a foreign country where the investor retains control over the investment. A direct investment typically takes the form of a foreign firm starting a subsidiary or taking over control of an existing firm in the country in question. Direct investment and management go together. If, however, the investor has only a sort of property interest in investing the capital funds in buying equities, bonds, securities or depositing with commercial banks abroad, it is referred to as portfolio investment. That is, in the case of portfolio investment, the investor lends his capital in order to get return on it, but has no control over the use of the capital.

SIGNIFICANCE AND ROLE OF FDI

Foreign capital played an important role in the early stages of industrialisation of most of the advanced countries of today like the countries of Europe (including Russia) and North America. Though the problems of development of the developing countries of today are not very much similar to those faced by the advanced countries, there is a general view that foreign capital, if properly directed and utilised, can assist the development of the developing countries.

Economic growth is a function of, among other things, capital formation. In the developing countries, the per capita income and savings rate being very low, domestic capital formation is inadequate to give a 'big push' to the economy to take it to the 'take-off' stage. Hence, the domestic resources may be supplemented with foreign capital to achieve the 'critical minimum' investment to break the vicious circle of low income-low savings-low investment-low income.

The important advantages of foreign direct investment (also called direct foreign investment) are the following:

1. It helps increase the investment level and thereby the income and employment in the host country.
2. Foreign investment may increase the tax revenue of the government.
3. Direct foreign investment facilitates transfer of technology to the recipient country.

4. It may kindle a managerial revolution in the recipient country through professional management and the employment of highly sophisticated management techniques.
5. Foreign capital may enable the country to increase its exports and reduce import requirements.
6. Foreign investments may stimulate domestic enterprise because, to support their own operations, the foreign investors may encourage and assist domestic suppliers and consuming industries.
7. Foreign investment may also help increase competition and break domestic monopolies.
8. If foreign investment improves the quality and reduces the cost of inputs, that would benefit the domestic industry.

FDI can accelerate economic growth, generate employment, improve BoP, kindle technological and managerial revolutions and boost government revenues.

FDI and Production Linkages

The contribution of FDI to sustainable economic development of the host countries depends to a large extent on the production *linkages* between foreign affiliates and domestic firms. Such linkages can take the form of *backward, forward or horizontal.*

Backward linkages exist when foreign affiliates acquire goods or services from domestic firms, and *forward linkages* when foreign affiliates sell goods or services to domestic firms. *Horizontal linkages* involve interactions with domestic firms engaged in competing activities. Linkages, broadly defined, can also involve non-business entities like universities, training centres, research and technology institutes, export promotion agencies and other official or private institutions.[2]

The extent to which foreign affiliates establish backward linkages with domestic suppliers is usually measured by the local content of production or local sourcing by foreign affiliates, although, for many reasons, however, these measures may not accurately reflect the magnitude of backward linkages with domestic firms.

Studies show that in selected developed host countries, affiliates source between 10 and 20 per cent of their inputs locally (i.e., supplied by domestic or foreign-owned suppliers). In *developing* countries, the share of locally-sourced inputs by foreign affiliates varies by industry and region[3] (For more information on FDI and production linkages, see the author's *International Business*–PHI Learning).

Trade and Investment

Foreign trade and foreign direct investment (FDI)are mutually influential. While some of the FDIs increase international trade, some decrease trade.

FDI in the natural resource sectors, including plantations, in developing countries increase trade. FDIs in several other sectors also increase international trade.

While on the one hand investment increases trade, as stated above, on the other hand foreign production by FDI substitutes foreign trade in many cases. Due to factors like foreign exchange problems, desire to generate employment and accelerate the pace of economic development foreign investment is encouraged by national governments across whole spectrum of political ideologies and development levels. The policies of many developing countries strongly prefer foreign investment (for import substitution) to imports.

Due to the protectionism and some other factors, large amounts of FDI have been taking place in the developed countries leading to substitution of foreign production for foreign trade. The regional integration schemes also tend to increase such investments to substitute production for trade.

It may also be pointed out that, to a considerable extent such FDIs are made possible by the past trade; the funds generated by trade are ploughed back to investment in the foreign markets. The massive foreign investments made by the Japanese companies since the mid-1980s deserves a special mention in this context.

> **While some FDIs may reduce trade by import substitution, some FDIs encourage trade by generating exportable surplus, etc.**

While the international investment replaces international trade in certain products, it may generate trade in some other products. That about one-third of the world trade in manufactures is intra-company trade is an indication of the investment-trade linkage. In case of China, which has been making stupendous growth of exports, more than half the total exports are said to be generated by foreign funded enterprises.

FACTORS AFFECTING INTERNATIONAL INVESTMENT

International investments are influenced by a number of factors. See Box 27.2 and the sub-section *Host-country Economic Determinants*.

BOX 27.2: 12 COMMANDMENTS OF FOREIGN DIRECT INVESTMENT

1. *Stable, predictable macroeconomic policy.* Companies must have the confidence that the economy in which they make an investment will be managed in a competent and predictable way. Simply stated, investors must believe that the rules of the game will not change in the middle of a contest.
2. *An effective and honest government.* An investor must be able to rely upon the integrity of the host government and its ability to maintain law and order.
3. *A large and growing market.* The size and potential for growth of a country's domestic market, especially the purchasing power of its customers, are key. Companies do not seek to invest in a market where there is little potential to make a profit.
4. *Freedom of activity in the* market. The strength of the competition, as well as the degree of government (theirs and ours) interference to entering a country's market, are important factors. The freer the market, the more attractive it becomes as an investment site for international investors.
5. *Minimal government regulation.* The cost of government regulation and intervention in the affairs — and profits — of private companies must be kept to a minimum.

6. *Property rights and protection.* Private property must be protected. The likelihood that a company's real or intangible (patents, copyrights, etc.), property will be stolen must be avoided.

7. *Reliable "infrastructure".* The ability to consummate transactions and get products and services to market is also critical. Whether it be reliable transportation, power generation, insurance and accounting services, a competent financial system or other basic factors, investments cannot yield a sufficient or reliable financial return without them.

8. *Availability of high-quality factors of production.* While the investor brings capital, technology and management to the table, the quality of the indigenous workforce and the availability of local raw materials are also key ingredients in the recipe for success.

9. *A strong local currency.* The local currency must retain its value. If you make an investment in dollars and then the local assets (valued in the local currency) are devalued, you have lost part — or possibly all — of your original dollar-based investment.

10. The *ability to remit profits, dividends and interest.* If you cannot get your money out of the country, why invest?

11. *A favourable tax climate.* Although tax incentives geared to attract initial investments are important, a company's final investment decision is usually based on how a country's taxation will affect the normal operating environment once the venture is off the ground.

12. *Freedom to operate between markets.* A company must be able to source goods and services from its operating unit in one market in order to serve other markets or to maximize its global efficiency by trading among its operating entities in different countries to "round out" its product-lines.

Courtesy: John D Sullivan, "Prospering in the Global Economy", *Economic Reform Today*, No. 1, 2000.

Host Country Economic Determinants

Traditionally, the economic determinants of inward FDI have been grouped, for analytical convenience, into three clusters, each of them reflecting the principal motivations of investing in foreign countries: ***resources seeking; market seeking*** and ***efficiency seeking.***

Resources

Historically, the most important motivation of FDI has been the exploitation of natural resources. Dunning points out that in the nineteenth century, much of the FDI by European, United States and Japanese firms was promoted by the need to secure an economic and reliable source of minerals, primary products for the investing industrialising nations of Europe and North America. Up to the eve of the Second World War, about 60 per cent of the world stock of FDI was in natural resources. The post-war period, particularly since the 1960s and 1970s, witnessed a decline in the share of natural resources in the FDI. Besides the decline in the importance of the primary sector in world output, this decline was caused by factors such the development of the indigenous enterprises in this sector. In a number of developing economies the public sector came to play an important role in the resources based industries. Public sector efforts also included equity or technical collaborations with MNCs.[4]

Figure 27.1 presents, in a little different way, the important factors which affect foreign investment. An explanation of this is available in the author's *International Business* (PHI Learning).

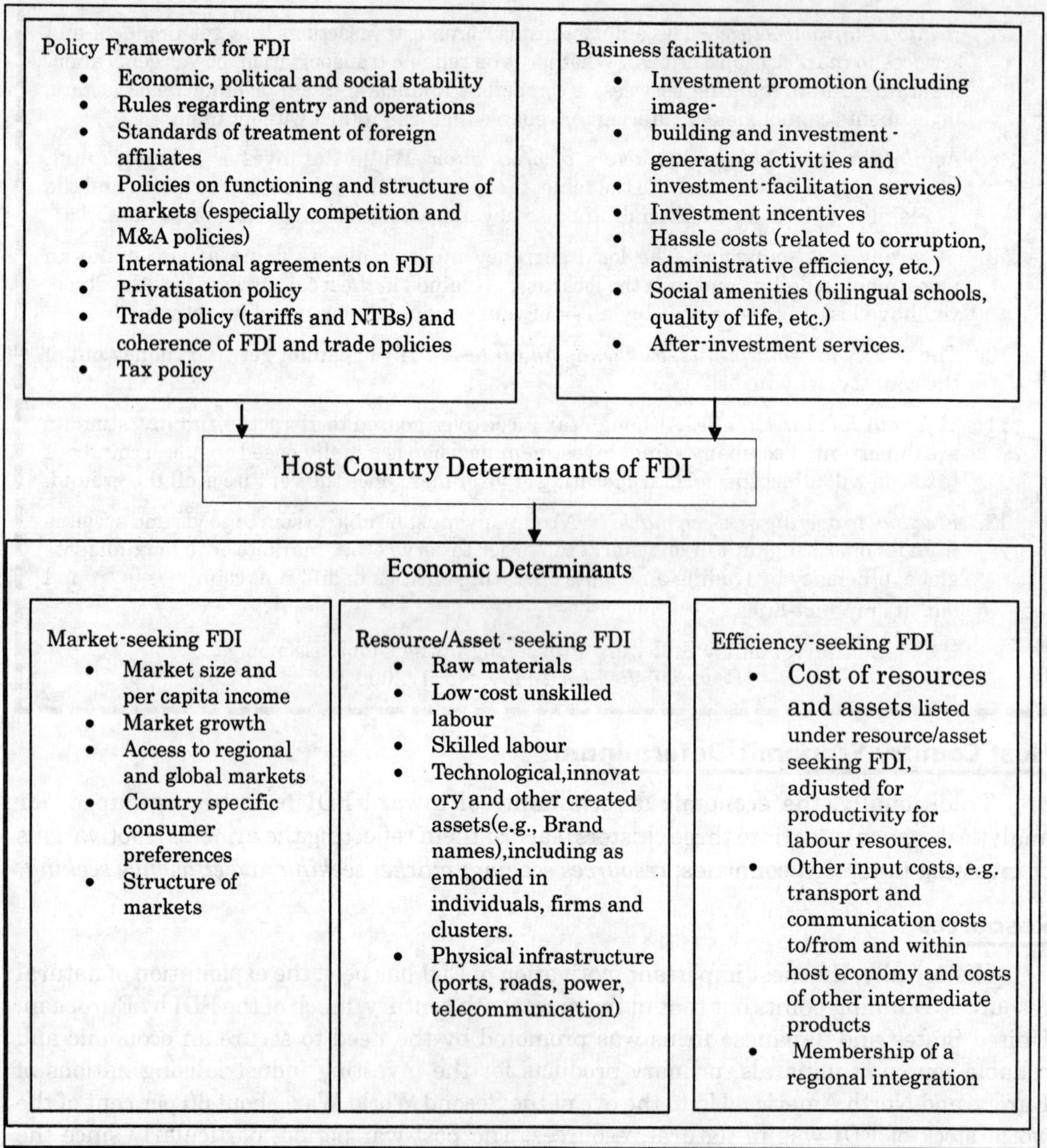

Fig. 27.1: Host Country Determinants of FDI (Reproduced from: UNCTAD, *World Investment Report*, 1998).

Although, the share of the primary sector in FDI has declined, there has been a substantial increase of the FDI in this sector in absolute terms. The FDI stock in the primary sector of developed countries increased more than five-fold between 1975-1990, while in the developing countries it increased more than six fold. According to the *World Investment Report 1998*, though declining in importance, the availability of natural resources is still a determinant of FDI and continues to offer important possibilities for inward investment in resource-rich countries. Natural resources still explain much of the inward FDI in a number of countries, developing (e.g., countries in sub-Sahara, Africa), developed (e.g., Australia) and countries in transition (Azerbaijan, Kiazakhistan and Russian Federation).[5]

Markets

FDIs in the primary sector is mostly resource seeking.

Another important traditional determinant of FDI has been market seeking. Markets protected from international competition by high tariffs or quotas triggered *tariff jumping* FDI. Dunning points out that market access became the predeterminant motive for investing in the manufacturing sector of developed countries between the two World Wars and of developing countries in the 1960s and 1970s, during the heyday of import substitution industrialisation. This motive was paramount, for example, in the wave of United States investments in Europe, especially in the United Kingdom, during the early post-war period and in Japanese investments in the United States after the mid-1980s, following voluntary export restrictions and the possibility of further protectionist measures in the automobile industry.[6]

It is very relevant to note here that the largest market in the world, the US is the largest recipient of FDI, followed by China, a huge market by the size of the economy, population and very high economic growth rate. As UNCTAD points out, some of the largest national markets remain unmatched in size by the largest regional markets or even by entire continents. For example, the market of the European Union during most of its existence has been smaller than the United States market; the market of the African continent (without South Africa) is smaller than that of Republic of Korea; and the combined markets of the 14 Central and Eastern European countries are smaller than the market of Brazil.[7]

The lion's share of FDI flow to the developing countries goes to the larger markets with comparatively good infrastructure and political stability in general.

Recent FDIs in many developing countries has been mostly market seeking.

The growing importance of the service sector has also been resulting in increasing FDI because of the fact that most services are not tradable and, therefore, the only way to deliver them to foreign markets is through establishment abroad. However, the highly regulated nature of the services sector has been a deterrent to the FDI flow in its full potential.

Efficiency

Another important motivation of FDI is efficiency seeking. Low cost of production, deriving mostly from cheap labour, is the driving force of many FDIs in developing countries. Export processing zones have been developed by developing countries mostly to take advantage of the efficiency seeing FDI flows.

Low cost of production is an important attraction of developing countries.

It may be noted that the presence of any of the three determinants mentioned above alone need not attract FDI. For example, even if a country has natural resources or abundance of cheap labour, FDI would not take place in the absence of required infrastructural facilities to develop the industry or trade. Besides, several other factors like the political environment, government policies, bureaucratic culture, social climate, etc., are also important determinants of FDI.

LIMITATIONS AND DANGERS OF FOREIGN CAPITAL

The following criticisms are levelled against foreign capital:

1. Private foreign capital tends to flow to the high profit areas rather than to the priority sectors.
2. The technologies brought in by the foreign investor may not be adapted to the consumption needs, size of the domestic market, resource availabilities, stage of development of the economy, etc.
3. Through their power and flexibility, the multinational corporations can evade or undermine national economic autonomy and control, and their activities may be inimical to the national interests of particular countries.
4. Foreign investment, sometimes, have unfavourable effect on the Balance of Payments of a country because when the drain of foreign exchange by way of royalty, dividend, etc., is more than the investment made by the foreign concern.
5. Foreign capital sometimes interferes in the national politics.
6. Foreign investors sometimes engage in unfair and unethical trade practices.
7. Foreign investment in some cases leads to the destruction or weakening of small and traditional enterprises.
8. Sometimes foreign investment can result in the dangerous situation of minimizing/eliminating competition and the creation of monopolies or oligopolistic structures.
9. FDI can also potentially displace domestic producers by preempting their investment opportunities.
10. The evolution of private capital flows, characterised by fluctuations (which are sometimes violent), suggests that they are not a reliable source of financing for development, partly because portfolio equity flows are very volatile and because financial liberalization has led to an increase in short-term speculative flows. Moreover, private capital flows, including FDI, are concentrated in a small number

of emerging-market economies, while most low-income and least developed countries, which are the most dependent on external financing, receive no or very small amounts of such flows.

Foreign investment, unless properly directed and regulated, will have several limitations and harmful effects.

11. Often, several costs are associated with encouraging foreign investment. Meier observes[8] that these costs may arise from special concessions offered by the host country, adverse effects on domestic saving, deterioration in the terms of trade, and problems of balance of payments adjustment.
    (*a*) The incentives (including tax concessions) services and facilities which the governments of the host countries offer to encourage foreign investment have opportunity cost and the opportunity cost tends to be very high in developing countries. The competition between countries and provinces to woo foreign investment make matters worse.
    (*b*) Foreign investment might also affect the recipient country's commodity terms of trade through structural changes associated with the pattern of development that results from the capital inflow. If the foreign capital causes an increase in the exportables to such an extent of resulting in a deterioration in the terms of trade, the rise in real income of the country will be less than that in output, and the worsening terms of trade may be considered another indirect cost of the foreign investment. Whether the terms of trade will turn against the capital-receiving country is problematical depending on various possible changes at home and abroad in the supply and demand for exports, import substitutes, and domestic commodities. It is unlikely, however, that private foreign investment would cause any substantial deterioration in the terms of trade. In fact private foreign investment can help bring about a favourable structural change in the countries foreign trade.
    (*c*) The servicing of foreign debt capital, both public and private, can cause balance of payments problems. Further, as has already been indicated above, repatriation of profits can also cause problems.

PRECONDITIONS FOR ATTRACTING FDI

The United Nations Economic Commission for Asia and Far East has drawn up the following list of conditions that have to be met if foreign capital is to be attracted to underdeveloped countries.

1. Political stability and freedom from external aggression
2. Security of life and property
3. Reasonable opportunities for earning profits
4. Prompt payment of fair and transferable compensation in case of nationalisation of foreign owned enterprise

5. Guarantee of the possibility of remittance of profits, dividends and interest, as well as of a reasonable depreciation allowance on the capital invested
6. Facilities for immigration and employment of foreign technical and administrative personnel
7. A system of taxation that does not impose a crushing burden on private enterprise
8. Freedom from double taxation
9. Absence of vexatious controls
10. Non-discriminatory treatment of foreigners in the administration of existing controls
11. Absence of competition between State-owned enterprises and private foreign capital
12. A general spirit of friendliness toward foreign investors.

GROWTH AND DISPERSION OF FDI

Trends in Magnitude of Flows

FDI flows are affected by economic conditions and several other factors like government policies and regulations.

Following the sweeping changes in the economic policy, foreign investment has been surging in many countries. Although foreign direct investment flows had their ups and downs, the stock of FDI has increased tremendously overtime. Between 1982 and 2000, foreign direct investment (FDI) inflows and outflows increased from $57 billion and $37 billion respectively to $ 1,271 billion and $ 1,150 billion respectively. After reaching its peak in 2000, the FDI inflows experienced a decline in the next three years. In 2003, inflows and outflows were $560 billion. However, after declining in 2001 and 2002, cross-border M&As slightly in 2003 and reached $ 612 billion of 51. Thus, in 2003, the FDI flows were less than half of the peak levels of 2000. The 2001 decline was the first drop in inflows since 1991 and outflows since 1992. The dramatic increases in cross-border M&As led to record flows in 1999 and 2000. Behaviour of cross-border M&As made its contribution to the decline in the FDI too. The FDI flows have grown significantly and reached the peak in inflow of $ 1,979 billion and outflow of $ 2,147 billion in 2007.[9]

Consequent to the global economic meltdown, the inflows and outflows declined in 2008 and 2009. Global FDI flows rose modestly in 2010, mainly due to higher flows to developing countries. However, FDI inflows in 2010 ($ 1,244 billion) was about 37 per cent lower than the peak of 2007 and 15 per cent below the pre-crisis (2005-07) average.

Developing and transition economies, which proved relatively immune to the global turmoil in 2008, were not spared in 2009 but did better than developed countries. After six years of uninterrupted growth, FDI flows to developing countries declined by 24 per cent in 2009.

Global FDI witnessed a modest, though uneven, recovery in 2010. Developing and transition economies in 2010 absorbed 52 per cent of FDI and they generated nearly 29 per cent of the outflows. The economic liberalisation in many countries, including the erstwhile communist countries and countries which still claim to be communist or socialist like the People's Republic of China, should be expected to enlarge the FDI flows in future.

TABLE 27.1: PERCENTAGE DISTRIBUTION OF FDI FLOWS

Country Grouping	*FDI Inflows*				*FDI Outflows*			
	2012	*2013*	*2014*	*2015*	*2012*	*2013*	*2014*	*2015*
Developed economies	39	39	41	55	63	61	61	72
Developing economies	55	54	56	43	33	32	35	26
Transition economies	6	7	3	2	4	7	5	2

***Source*:** UNCTAD, *World Investment Reports* of different years.

Directional Trends

The major chunk of the FDI flows have taken place between the developed countries. For nearly three decades till the early 1990s, about three-quarters of the FDI have gone to the developed countries. Nearly two-thirds of the flows were between the countries of the *Triad* — the US, the European Community and Japan. However, as noted above, in recent years the trend has changed – the shares of the developing and transition economies in both FDI inflows and outflows have increased significantly.

In developing countries, FDI is concentrated in a small number of them. Table 27.1 shows the distribution of FDI between different categories of countries.

The share of developing countries in global FDI flows has increased significantly, reaching nearly 52 per cent of inflows and 29 per cent of the outflows in 2010.

An examination of the investment pattern of the major sources of FDI shows that they, generally, had a regional bias in their investment in the developing countries. The US investments were largely in Latin America. Japan's investments went mostly to the Asian neighbours. There has, however, been some significant changes in the Japanese investments recently. Much of the United Kingdom's investment has gone to the Commonwealth nations, and France had a favour for countries with past colonial ties, mainly Africa.

It has also been observed that direct investment is concentrated in particular economic sectors. For instance, investment by UK and German firms has been mainly in manufacturing, while US and Japanese investment, although more evenly spread over the major economic sectors, has a bias towards manufacturing and primary industries; within manufacturing direct investment has been made mainly in transportation equipment, chemicals and machinery (which includes electronics).

The vast expansion of the investment opportunities across the world should be expected to encourage some changes in the directional pattern of the foreign investment flows.

Sectoral Trends

> **The shares of the different sectors in the FDI are, to a large extent, a reflection of their shares in the economy, the services sector accounting for the substantial part.**

Although, FDI has grown overtime in all three economic sectors — primary, manufacturing and services — the sectoral composition has undergone significant changes with marked shift towards services.

Primary Sector: The primary sector's share in world FDI *stock* decreased from 9 per cent in 1990 to 7 per cent in 2009. Within the primary sector, mining, quarrying and petroleum dominate with over 90 per cent of the inward FDI stock. In 2014, the primary sector accounted for just 7 per cent of the global FDI inward stock.

Manufacturing Sector: The share of manufacturing in global FDI stock worldwide fell from 42 per cent in 1990 to 28 per cent in 2009. Manufacturing FDI is increasingly geared to more capital and knowledge-intensive activities because of two developments. There has been a decline in labour-intensive manufacturing in general, and the share of traditional manufacturing employment has also steadily declined. Technological changes leading to increasing replacement of labour by capital and knowledge has been a key element in the decline of labour-intensive FDI in manufacturing. Secondly, firms in more and more countries, especially developing countries, have developed their own ownership-specific advantages based on different factor endowments, particularly low-cost labour, *vis-à-vis* developed countries. In 2014, the manufacturing sector accounted for 27 per cent of the global FDI inward stock.

Services Sector: During the period 1990-2002, while the global FDI stock in the primary sector nearly doubled and in the manufacturing sector increased nearly three-fold, in the services sector it more than quadrupled. As a result of more rapid growth in this sector than in the other sectors, services accounted for about 64 per cent of the global stock of inward FDI in 2014, compared to less than one-half in 1990 and only one-quarter in the early 1970s. Services sector continues to capture a large share of FDI.

CROSS-BORDER M&As AND FDI

Cross-border mergers and acquisitions (M&As) has been the key driver of global FDI since the late 1980s. A very significant aspect of the recent FDI surge is that it is triggered to a large extent by cross-border M&As. For instance, the total value of cross-border M&As with value of over $ 1 billion each alone accounted for three-fourths of the value of global FDI inflows in 2000 when the FDI reached the hitherto peak level. After the downturn in FDI during 2001-2003, the growth in FDI flows was also driven by cross-border M&As activity, which expanded in scope across countries and sectors. Its strong growth and a record number of mega deals (i.e., deals with a transaction value of over $1 billion) pushed the value of total cross-border M&As to a record $1,637 billion in 2007 when the FDI inflows reached peaked to $1,833 billion. Similarly, most of the drop in FDI in 2008 and 2009 was due to a substantial decrease in M&As deals

> **A substantial part of FDI emerge from cross-border M&As and the volume of FDI flows fluctuate in tandem with the value of such deals.**

rather than Greenfield operations. The number of cross-border M&As transactions declined by 34 per cent (65 per cent in terms of value), compared with a 15 per cent decline in greenfield projects.

Cross-border mergers and acquisitions *(M&As)* involve FDI in a host country by merging with or acquiring an existing local firm. In the latter case, the acquisition involves an equity stake of 10 per cent or more. The share of FDI accounted for by cross-border M&As is difficult to determine, since data sets are not directly comparable. First, the value of cross-border M&As includes funds raised in local and international financial markets. *Second*, FDI data are reported on a net basis, using the balance-of-payments concept, while data on cross-border M&As purchases or sales report only the total value of the transaction. Finally, payments for cross-border M&As are not necessarily made in a single year but may be spread over a longer period.[10]

As an UN report points out, one recent feature is that M&As among large or dominant TNCs, resulting in even larger TNCs, seem to impel other major TNCs to move towards restructuring or making similar deals with other TNCs. The pharmaceutical, automobile, telecommunications and financial industries are typical example of industries in which such concentration can be observed. This trend significantly changes the industry structure. In the automobile industry, for example, the total number of major automobile makers may well decline to 5-10 by 2010, from the 1998 figure of 15. In the pharmaceutical industry, many markets are now controlled by a small number of firms. In both these industries, there have been a string of M&As. Major M&As in the pharmaceuticals include Glaxo-SmithKline Beecham, Pfizer Warner Lambert and Hoechst-Rhone.

The trend towards M&As is also accelerating the sale of non-core operations or affiliates by firms and the acquisition of similar operations from other firms (of divisions or affiliates, or firms that have similar businesses). This indicates a strategic shift by TNCs to focus on their core activities. Unlike in the 1980s, there were fewer deals among unrelated. In addition to strategic considerations of firms, liberalization and deregulation are the other main factors behind the dramatic increases in M&As in both developed and developing countries.

Developed countries account for the lion's share of the mega mergers. However, an upward trend in M&As sales by developing countries and countries in transition is noticeable. Among developing countries, majority M&As sales in South, East and South-east Asia have been increasing recently, in particular after the 1997 financial crisis. Latin America and Central and Eastern Europe also recorded significant increases in M&As sales.

There has been a substantial shift towards services in cross-border M&As as it became a widely used mode of TNC entry in such service industries as banking, telecommunications and water. While, in the late 1980s services accounted for less than 40 per cent of global cross-border M&As, their share rose around 60 percent in the recent period.

The liberalisation and deregulation of several vital industries in many countries across the world have given an impetus to cross-border M&As in both developed and developing countries. Increasing M&As in the service sector in general and financial industries in particular reflect the impact of liberalisation. Privatisation has been a very important stimulant to M&As. Banking, finance, insurance and telecommunication industries have been witnessing a spate of M&As. Cross-border M&As contributed significantly to the surge in FDI in 2015.

IMPORTANT TRENDS IN FDI INFLOW TO DEVELOPING COUNTRIES

There was, an increase in the FDI flows to the developing countries. The economic liberalisations in the developing countries have helped increase the FDI to them. During 2003-06, the share of developing countries in the global FDI ranged between 26 and 39 per cent. Even while the level of FDI inflow to developing countries rise, the fluctuations in the FDI flows to developed economies affect the share of developing countries. In 2010, FDI inflows to developing and emerging economies crossed 50 per cent of the total.

FDI in developing countries has been larger than official inflows for every year since 1993. It was 10 times larger than bilateral official development assistance (ODA) in 2000; this contrasts with the latter half of the 1980s, when the two were about equal. Recently also FDI has accounted for about 90 per cent of the total financial flows to developing countries.

Within the group of the developing countries, the relatively developed among them get the lion's share of the FDI. Very little FDI has taken place in low income economies leaving exceptions like China and India. In most cases, this has been due to the small size of the domestic market and other adverse factors like poor infrastructure, lack of skilled labour, etc.

Although the FDI flow to the developing countries has increased substantially, the lion's share is concentrated in a handful of the countries which are the better off among them.

There has been a jumb in the FDI inflows to the developing countries. Their share in FDI inflows has also increased substantially and was more than half of the global total in 2013 and 2014, but in 2015, 55 per cent went to developed countries.

The lion's share of the FDI flows to the developing countries has been cornered by two regions, viz., East Asia and the Pacific and Latin America while Sub-Saharan/Africa, and Middle East and North Africa got very low shares. The least developed countries get only an insignificant share of FDI inflow to developing countries and less than one per cent of the world FDI inflows.

One traditional attraction of foreign investment, viz., cheap labour, is becoming less important. Foreign investment today is not merely for exploitation of local resources. Foreign companies today evaluate the market potential and production and related facilities and their efficiencies, *inter alia*, for investment decision-making. Countries with large and growing markets, fairly developed infrastructures and efficient input supplies, conducive trade policies, favourable political environment, required type of manpower supplies, etc., rank high for investment. An encouraging government policy alone is not sufficient. China has been able to attract huge FDI because its economic growth for quite sometime now has been very good, it is one of the largest potential markets in the world, because of the statist policy of until recently it is virtually a virgin market for many products, the labour force is 'disciplined' by the State and China has favourable political and bureaucratic environment. Although India is not as attractive as China in terms of the above factors, its potential is enormous.

OUTWARD FDI FROM DEVELOPING COUNTRIES

FDI outflows from developing economies have been significantly increasing, reflecting the recognition of firms that in a globalising world economy, they need a portfolio of locational assets to be competitive internationally. In fact, Countries like Malaysia, the Republic of Korea and Singapore already have an established track record and some others such as Chile, Mexico and South Africa have become players relatively recently. Countries like Brazil, China and India are at the take-off stage. Their investments span all sectors and country groups and involve complex as well as simple industries. Annual FDI outflows from developing countries have grown very faster since the early 1990s. However, even in recent years, only about 15 per cent of the global FDI outflows originate from the developing economies. Negligible until the beginning of the 1990s outward FDI from developing and emerging economies was 29 per cent of the world total in 2010.

FDI flows between from developing countries seems to be growing faster than from developing countries to developed countries. The growing importance of South-South FDI indicates that developing countries are more financially integrated with one another than was previously believed. Thus, a typical developing country has access to more sources of investment than before. This is particularly important for small economies, as TNCs from the South, because of their comparative advantages, tend to invest in countries with similar or lower levels of development than their home countries.

There has been a substantial rise in outward FDI from developing countries.

BOX 27.3 : OUTWARD FDI FROM THE BRIC COUNTRIES

Rapid economic growth at home, high commodity prices, and FDI liberalization in host countries have been feeding a boom in outward investment from BRIC (Brazil, Russia, India, China).

- As in the case of developed countries, outward FDI from BRIC has been boosted by rising volumes of cross-border M&As. For example, between 2000 and 2009, Indian firms finalized 812 deals abroad, Chinese firms finalized 450, Brazilian firms finalized 190, and Russian firms finalized 436. Some of these deals were valued at more than $1 billion.

TNCs from BRIC share a number of common features:

- They have developed various ownership-specific advantages that allow them to be competitive in foreign markets as well as in their own markets. In organizing their expansion abroad, Brazilian, Chinese, Indian and Russian TNCs alike have sought to establish portfolios of locational assets as increasingly important sources of their international competitiveness.
- Initially, firms from BRIC expanded mainly into their own region, often into countries with which they had close cultural links. A growing number of TNCs have ventured further a field, however, in search of new markets and resources. India's FDI stock in emerging markets, for example, used to be concentrated in Asia, which accounted for 75 per cent of the total in the mid-1990s. By 2008, India's FDI flows to outside of Asia had increased to 61 per cent.
- A large number of TNCs from BRIC are motivated by strategic considerations rather than by short-term profitability, reflecting the role of state-owned enterprises in the outward FDI of the group. The majority of Chinese TNCs, for example, are state-owned, and some Brazilian, Indian and Russian TNCs are also state-controlled (Petrobras, ONGC Videsh and Gazprom, for instance).
- Many of the TNCs headquartered in BRIC have become truly global players, as they possess – among other things – global brand names, management skills and competitive business models. Some of them, ranked by foreign assets, are: CITIC (China), COSCO (China), Lukoil (Russian Federation), Gazprom (Russian Federation), Vale S.A. (Brazil), Tata (India) and ONGC Videsh (India).
- Supportive government policies have backed the rise of BRIC's outward FDI. The adoption, in the early years of the new millennium, of China's "go global" policy successfully encouraged domestic enterprises to invest globally. Brazil, India and the Russian Federation also want to create global players through incentives (e.g., creating national champions in the Russian Federation and in Brazil, and further liberalization of foreign exchange regimes in India).

Source: Adopted from UNCTAD, *World Investment Report, 2010.*

FDI IN INDIA

The flow of direct foreign investment to India has been comparatively limited because of the type of industrial development strategy and the very cautious foreign investment policy followed by the nation.

Direct foreign investment (private) in India was adversely affected by the following factors.

1. The public sector was assigned a monopoly or dominant position in the most important industries and, therefore, the scope of private investment, both domestic and foreign, was limited.
2. When the public sector enterprises needed foreign technology or investment, there was a marked preference for the foreign government sources.

3. Government policy towards foreign capital was very selective. Foreign investment was normally permitted only in high technology industries in priority areas and in export oriented industries.
4. Foreign equity participation was normally subject to a ceiling or 40 per cent, although exceptions were allowed on merit.
5. Payment of dividends abroad, repatriation of capital, etc., as well as inward remittances were subject to stringent laws like the Foreign Exchange Regulation Act (FERA), 1973. These discouraged foreign investment.
6. Corporate taxation was high and tax laws and procedures were complex.
7. These factors either limited the scope of or discouraged the foreign investment in India.

Government Policy

Government of India's policy towards foreign capital technology during the pre-liberalisation era was highly restrictive.

The following paragraphs give a very brief account of Government of India's policy towards foreign capital and technology. First, the salient features of the policy followed till the economic liberalisation introduced in July 1991 are given. This is followed by an account of the new policy.

India was following a very restrictive policy towards foreign capital and technology. Foreign collaboration was permitted only in fields of high priority and in areas where the import of foreign technology was considered necessary. In other areas, import of technology was considered on merits if substantial exports were guaranteed over a period of 5 to 10 years and if there were reasonable proposals for such exports. The government had issued lists of industries where:

(*a*) (*i*) Foreign investment may be permitted.

(*ii*) Only foreign technical collaboration (but no foreign investment) may be permitted.

(*b*) No foreign collaboration (financial or technical) was considered necessary.

The government policy on foreign equity participation was, thus, selective. Such participation had to be justified with regard to factors such as the nature of technology involved, whether it would promote exports which might not otherwise take place and the alternative terms available for securing the same or similar technological transfers. Foreign equity participation was limited to 40 per cent, although exceptions were allowed on merit. The foreign share capital was to be by way of cash without being linked to tied imports of machinery and equipment or to payments for know how, trade marks, brand names, etc.

Technical collaborations were to be considered on the basis of annual royalty payments which were linked with the value of actual production. The percentage of royalty was dependent on the nature of technology. Whenever possible, the payment of fixed amount of royalty per unit of production was preferred. Royalty payments were limited to a period of 5 years.

The *Foreign Exchange Regulation Act* (FERA), 1973, served as a tool for implementing the national policy on foreign private investment in India. The FERA empowered the Reserve Bank of India to regulate or exercise direct control over the activities of foreign companies and foreign nationals in India. A foreign company was defined as one (other than a banking company) which was not incorporated in India or in which non-resident interest was more than 40 per cent or any branch of such a company.

According to the FERA, non-residents (including Indian citizens), foreign citizens resident in India and foreign companies required the permission of the RBI to accept appointment as agents or technical management advisers in India, of any person or company, or permit the use of their trade marks.

The trading, commercial and industrial activities in India of persons resident abroad, foreign citizens in India and foreign companies were regulated by the FERA. They had to obtain permission from the RBI for carrying on in India any activity of a trading, commercial or industrial nature; opening branches/offices or other places of business in India' acquiring any business undertaking in India; and purchasing shares of Indian companies.

RBI had given general permission for certain matters. For example, general permission was granted to foreign companies to acquire or hold any immovable property in India which was necessary for, or incidental to, any activity undertaken by them with the permission of the RBI.

The New Policy

Since 1991, the foreign investment policy has been progressively liberalised and the liberalisation trend continues.

The Industrial policy statement of July 24, 1991, which observes that while freeing the Indian economy from official controls, opportunities for promoting foreign investment in India should also be fully exploited has liberalised the Indian policy towards foreign investment and technology.

As pointed out earlier, in the pre-liberalisation era, foreign equity participation was restricted normally to 40 per cent and foreign investment and technology agreements needed prior approval. As against this, the new policy has allowed majority foreign equity with automatic approval in a large number of industries. The Modi government goes on liberalising more and more the foreign investment. Many sectors which were the exclusive reserve of the public sector is now open for foreign investment.

TABLE 27.2: INDIA: FDI INFLOWS AND OUTFLOWS

(Billions of dollars)

Type of FDI Flow	*2005-2007 (Pre-crisis annual average)*	*2010*	*2011*	*2012*	*2013*	*2014*	*2015*
Inward	17.77	27.43	36.19	24.20	28.20	34.4	44.2
Outward	11.50	15.93	12.46	8.49	1.68	11.8	7.5

Source: UNCTAD, *World Investment Report, 2014 and 2016.*

TABLE 27.3: INDIA: FDI AS A PERCENTAGE OF GROSS CAPITAL FORMATION					
Type of FDI Flow	*1955-2005 Annual Average*	*2007*	*2008*	*2009*	*2016*
Inward	3.2	6.3	9.6	8.4	7.0
Outward	0.8	4.4	4.4	3.6	1.2
Source: UNCTAD, *World Investment Report, 2010 and 2016.*					

TABLE 27.4: INDIA: FDI STOCK AS PERCENTAGE OF GDP					
Type of FDI Flow	*1995*	*2007*	*2008*	*2009*	*2015*
Inward	1.5	8.8	9.6	12.9	13.5
Outward	0.1	3.7	4.9	6.1	6.6
Source: UNCTAD, *World Investment Report, 2010 and 2016.*					

The political stability and further foreign investment liberalisations resulted in a substantial increase in foreign investment in India in recent years. In 2015, India was the 10th largest recipient of FDI.

FII INVESTMENTS

The Indian stock market was opened up to FII investment in 1992-93 and since then there has been a significant increase in the portfolio investment by FIIs.

The Regulations on Foreign Institutional Investors, which were notified on November 14, 1995, contains various provisions relating to definition of FIIs, eligibility criteria, investment restrictions, procedures of registration and general obligations and responsibilities of FIIs.

According to the Regulations, FIIs may invest only in:

(*a*) Securities in the primary and secondary markets including shares, debentures and warrants of companies listed on a recognised stock exchange in India, and

(*b*) Units of schemes floated by domestic mutual funds including Unit Trust of India, whether listed on a recognised stock exchange or not.

Joint ventures between a variety of domestic and foreign securities firms have been approved in the stock broking, merchant banking, assets management and other non-bank financial services sectors. The overall effect of FII investment and financial joint ventures has been the introduction of international practices and systems to the Indian Securities industry.

FIIs are permitted to invest in a company upto an aggregate of 24 per cent of equity, which can be increased to 40 per cent subject to approval by the Board of Directors and a Special Resolution of the General Body.

Foreign portfolio investments today play an important role in the Indian stock market.

In 1996-97, Government liberalised the FII investment policy, allowing them to invest in unlisted companies and in corporate and Government securities.

FOREIGN INVESTMENT BY INDIAN COMPANIES

Until 1991, Indian companies made very little investment abroad. Although Government of India's policy had been one of encouraging foreign investment by Indian companies, subject to certain conditions, several factors like the domestic economic policy and the domestic economic situation were deterrents to foreign investment by Indian companies.

By restricting the areas of operation and growth, the government policy seriously constrained the potential of Indian companies to make a foray into the foreign countries through investment. Added to this was the attraction of the protected domestic market which was, in many cases, a seller's market and this made the Indian companies to ignore the foreign markets.

An UNCTAD report observes that India also stands out among Asian investors, not so much because of its recent and significant increase in outward FDI and because of its potential to be a large outward investor, but because of the new trend set by some of its information technology (IT) firms. Most Indian outward FDI is in manufacturing (about 55 per cent), but non-financial services also account for a significant share (25 per cent). FDI in IT services in particular has begun to grow rapidly. The growing technological capabilities of Indian firms and their rising exports, particularly in IT services and pharmaceuticals, are driving the FDI growth. Access to markets, distribution networks, foreign technology and strategic assets such as brand names, are the main motivations. Securing natural resources is also becoming an important driver for FDI in the oil and gas industries and mining.

India's outward FDI has increased substantially in recent years. A significant part of it is the result of foreign acquisitions.

The most important destination for Indian FDI has been the United States, accounting for nearly one-fifth of its total outward flows since the mid-1990s to 2003, followed by the Russian Federation (with 18 per cent) due mainly to acquisitions in the oil and gas industries. Overall, however, about half of total Indian outward FDI has gone to other developing countries.

Strategic M&As have been finding favour with corporate India too. M&As by Indian companies involving foreign firms fall into three categories, viz., acquisition of foreign firms, acquisition of MNC affiliates in India and acquisition of foreign brands.

Foreign investment, both in greenfield enterprises and mergers and acquisitions (M&As), is clearly a part of the globalisation strategy of many Indian companies. Recently, there has been a spurt in FDI by Indian companies, reaching about $ 18 billion in 2008.

In light of the economic liberalisation and the growing competition at home, many Indian companies have been planning for a major thrust abroad. The investment limits for automatic clearance are too small and there is an urgent need for a substantial upward revision.

India has been gaining increasing global attention because of significant foreign acquisitions by Indian companies.

EVALUATION OF THE NEW FDI POLICY AND ITS IMPACT

Although the liberalisation has increased the inflow of foreign capital to India, until recently it had been at a low level; it had been no where near the annual target of $10 billion set by the Government many years ago. However, recently, there has been a substantial hike in the FDI inflow, crossing $ 40 billion in 2008. It however, declined, impacted by the global economic crisis, to $ about 35 billion.

Items like reinvested earnings used to be excluded from the estimation of FDI in India. However, in June 2003 Government has aligned the methodology of compilation of FDI with the international best practices. The revised definition includes three categories of capital flows under FDI: equity capital, reinvested earnings and other direct capital. Previously, the data on FDI reported in the balance of payments statistics used to include only equity capital. The revised estimates of FDI in India as per the new definition give a much high figures.

There are many ardent critics of foreign investment and technology. Foreign investment and technology is not without problems. However, the opening up of the economies of a number of nations for foreign companies and the several measures they have taken to woo foreign companies are a clear indicators of the positive contribution foreign capital and technology can make.

Inward and outward FDIs play a very significant role in the corporate and economic development of India.

The new policy of Government of India is, of course, much better than the old policy. However, in comparison with the business environment in many other countries, India still is not very attractive in the eyes of foreign companies, despite the large and growing Indian market. India indeed is regarded as one of the most difficult places to do business. Now that many countries are competing to lure the foreign capital and technology, the choice is indeed very wide for the foreign firms.

One important criticism of the liberalisation of foreign investment has been that foreign investment would take place mostly in non-priority sectors. However, lion's share of the foreign investment in India since the liberalisation has gone to priority sectors. Now several of the priority industries, including the infrastructural sector, which were earlier exclusively reserved for the public sector is opened to foreign investment. From January 1991 to March

2004, the following sectors/industries accounted for about 70 per cent of the FDI: Electrical equipment (including computer software and electronics); telecommunications; energy; transportation; services sector; chemicals (other than fertilisers); food and food processing; metallurgical industries; textiles and hotels and tourism. During 2009-10, FDI was mainly channeled into the manufacturing sector (22.9 per cent), followed by the construction sector (15.7 per cent), financial services and real estate sector (9.8 per cent each).

Past data shows that there is high degree of regional concentration of FDI. Five States – Maharashtra, Delhi, Tamil Nadu, Karnataka and Gujarat accounted for a disproportionately large share of the FDI inflows.

Country-wise, investments routed through Mauritius remained the largest component of gross FDI inflows to India during 2009-10, followed by Singapore and the USA.

Although there is a lot of talk about the procedural simplification, foreign companies still find the procedures very perplexing and unbearably time-consuming. China's FDI procedures are easier, and decisions can be taken rapidly. According to a Government of India publication, China has more flexible labour laws, a better labour climate and better entry and exit procedures for business. A confidence tracking survey in 2002 indicated that China was the top FDI destination, displacing the United States for the first time in the investment plans of the TNCs surveyed. India came 15th. Recently India's ranking has improved very significantly.

India is now regarded as one of the attractive destinations for FDI.

Also see the section *Evaluation of the Industrial Policy Liberalisation* in chapter 3 for the impact of the new FDI policy.

SUMMARY

Encouraged by the favourable business environment fostered by the global liberalisation, the international private capital flows have been increasing rapidly. Cross-border M&As have been the major driver of the recent surge in the FDI.

Foreign capital now contributes a significant share of the domestic investment, employment generation, industrial production and exports in a number of economies, including China.

Broadly, there are the following two types of foreign investment: (1) Foreign direct investment (FDI) where the investor has control over/participation in the management of the firm. (2) Portfolio investment the investor has only a sort of property interest in investing the capital in buying equities, bonds, or other securities abroad. In the case of portfolio investments, the investor uses his capital in order to get a return on it, but has no much control over the use of the capital. The major portfolio investment in the Indian capital market is by the foreign institutional investors (FIIs).

Broadly there are three economic motives of FDI, viz., resources seeking (e.g.; exploiting the natural resources of the host country); market seeking (i.e., to exploit the market opportunities of the host countries) and efficiency seeking (like low cost of production deriving from cheap labour).

The presence of any (or even all) of these determinants alone need not attract FDI. Several other factors like the political environment, government policies, bureaucratic culture, social climate, infrastructural facilities, etc., are also important determinants of FDI.

Although the international capital flows to the developing countries have increased substantially in the last one decade or so, they are still predominantly between the developed countries. A small number of countries account for the lion's share of the international capital inflows to the developing world.

Although India has substantially liberalised its foreign investment policy, the FDI inflows had been much below the targets. India had not been getting even one-tenth the size of FDI flow to China. Even the cumulative FDI flow to India between 1991 and 2007 was less the annual flow to China. Bureaucratic problems, certain unfavourable government attitudes, poor infrastructure, labour factors, high input costs, etc., are regarded as the major reasons.

Recently, there has been a spurt in the inward and outward FDI flow in respect of India.

REFERENCES

1. Peter, Drucker, F., *Managing For the Future,* Butterworth-Heinemann Ltd., Oxford, 1992, p. 35.
2. Cited by UNCTAD, *World Investment Report*, 2001, Bookwell, New Delhi, 2001, p. 127.
3. *Ibid.*, 134.
4. UNCTAD, *World Investment Report, 1998*, United Nations, New York, 1998, p. 113.
5. *Ibid.*, 113.
6. *Ibid.*, 113.
7. *Ibid.*, 113.
8. Gerald, Meier, M., "Benefits and Costs of Private Foreign Investment" in Leading Issues in Economic Development, Oxford University Press, Singapore, 1971, pp. 296-308.
9. The data related to foreign investment cited in this chapter are mostly from the various *World Investment Reports* of the UNCTAD. It may be noted that there may be differences in the data provided by different source.
10. UNCTAD, *World Investment Report, 2004* and *2007*.

☆☆☆

CHAPTER

28

DEVELOPMENT AND REGULATION OF FOREIGN TRADE

Government of India has taken a number of measures for the orderly development of the foreign trade in accordance with the national priorities and interests. Foreign trade is closely monitored and regulated by several measures undertaken under the Foreign Trade (Development and Regulation) Act, 1992. The Foreign Trade Policy (earlier known as the Exim Policy) announced under this Act sets out government's approach to trade development and regulation.

REGULATION OF FOREIGN TRADE

Control of foreign trade in India dates back to the early years of the Second World War. Import Control was introduced in 1940 as a war time measure under the Defence of India Rules with the primary objective of conserving the foreign exchange resources and restricting physical imports so as to reduce the pressure on the limited available shipping space. Initially, the import of only 68 commodities, mainly consumer goods, were brought under control. Subsequently, with the increasing pressure on the foreign exchange resources, import control was extended to other commodities as well.

The emphasis of trade policy and regulation in the past was on import control to conserve foreign exchange.

After the end of the war, the Defence of India Rules lapsed and hence in September 1946, the Emergency Provisions (Continuance) Ordinance, 1946, was promulgated to continue the import trade control. This was ultimately replaced by the Imports and Exports (Control) Act, 1947, which came into force with effect from 25th March, 1947. This Act gave the Government enormous powers of control over the foreign trade of India. This imports and exports was controlled by the Government under the Imports (Control) Order and Exports (Control) Order issued under this Act. The Imports and Exports (Control) Act, 1947, was replaced by the Foreign Trade (Development and Regulation Act), 1992 (FTDRA).

Besides the FTDR Act, there are some laws which control the trade in certain items. For instance, the export of antiquities is regulated under the Antiquities and Art Treasures Act, 1972; export of coffee is regulated by the Coffee Board under the Indian Coffee Act 1942; export of tea is regulated under Tea Act, 1953, etc. The export and import currency notes, bank notes and coins have been controlled by the Reserve Bank of India under the Foreign Exchange (Regulation) Act, 1973 (FERA).

The major concern of Government in the past was restriction of imports with a view to controlling the trade deficit and protection of domestic industries against foreign competition. Imports were, therefore, very much restricted by prohibition of imports of many items, import licensing, very high import duties and foreign exchange restrictions. The foreign trade policy was characterised by the overtone of negativism.

The Foreign Trade (Development and Regulation) Act, 1992

This Act which replaced the Imports and Exports (Control) Act, 1947, came into force on 19th June, 1992.

> **The change from the Imports and Exports (Control) Act to the Foreign Trade (Development and Regulation) Act marks a positive shift in emphasis from trade control to trade development and regulation.**

No export or import shall be made by any person except in accordance with the provisions of this Act, the orders and rules made under this Act and the export and import policy.

Objective: The objective of the Act is to *provide for the development and regulation of foreign trade by facilitating imports into, and augmenting exports from India and for matters connected therewith or incidental thereto.*

Main Provisions: The main provisions of the FTDR Act are the following:

Development and Regulation: The FTDRA empowers the Central Government to make provision for the development and regulation of foreign trade by facilitating imports and increasing exports.

Prohibition and Restriction: The Act also empowers the Central Government to make provision for prohibiting, restricting or otherwise regulating the import or export of goods as and when required. All goods which are so regulated under this sub-section shall be deemed to be goods the import or export of which has been prohibited under Section 11 of the Customs Act, 1962, and all the provisions of that Act shall have effect accordingly.

It may be noted that it is according to this sub-clause that the Government has provided for negative lists of exports and imports in the Exim policy.

Exim (Foreign Trade) Policy : The Act lays down that the Central Government may, from time-to-time, formulate and announce the export and import policy and may also amend that policy. The Policy is now called the Foreign Trade Policy.

Director General of Foreign Trade: The Act provides for the appointment by the Central Government, of a Director General of Foreign Trade for the purpose of this Act. The DGFT shall advise the Central Government in the formulation of the export and import policy and shall be responsible for carrying out that policy. [The corresponding authority under the Imports and Exports (Control Act), 1947, was called the Chief Controller of Imports and Exports (CCIE)]

Importer-exporter Code Number: The Act lays down that no person shall make any import or export except under an Importer-exporter Code (IEC) Numbers granted by the DGFT or the Officer authorised by him in his behalf.

The Director General is empowered to suspend or cancel the Importer-exporter Code Number granted to any person if there is valid reason to do so, like contravention of law relating to Central excise or customs or foreign exchange or having conducted import/ export in a manner gravely prejudicial to the trade relations of India with any foreign country or in a way detrimental to the interests of the country.

Issue and Suspension/Cancellation of Licence: The Director General or any other Officer authorised under this Act is empowered to suspend or cancel a licence issued for export or import of goods in accordance with this Act for good and sufficient reasons, after giving the licence holder a reasonable opportunity of being heard.

Imports and exports are regulated under the FTDRA.

Search, Inspection and Seizure: Where any contravention of any condition of the licence of authority under which any goods are imported is suspected or made, any person authorised by the Central Government may search, inspect and seize such goods, documents, things and conveyances subject to such requirements and conditions as may be prescribed.

Penalty for Contravention: Where any person makes or abets or attempts to make any export or import in contravention of any provisions of this Act or any rules or orders made under this Act or the policy, he shall be liable to a penalty not exceeding one thousand rupees or five times the value of the goods involved, whichever is more.

FOREIGN TRADE POLICY 2015-20

Government of India had been announcing Five Year **Export-Import Policy (Exim Policy)**. Since 2004, it is known as **Foreign Trade Policy (FTP)**. Anew Foreign Trade Policy should have come into effect on April 1, 2014 on the expiry of the FTP 2009-14. However, a new Policy was announced only on April 1, 2015, nearly a year after the Narendra Modi Government assumed office, as the new Government needed time to recast the Policy.

While unveiling the Policy for 2015-20, Commerce Minister Nirmala Sitharaman stated that it is in line with the initiatives 'Make in India', 'Digital India' and 'Skill India' announced by the government earlier. There will be a mid-term review of the Policy, compared to the past practice of annual reviews.

Salient Features

Some of the salient features of the Foreign **Trade Policy 2015-20** are outlined below.

Objective

According to the Commerce Minister, the FTP 2015 -20 aims at making the country a bigger player in global trade by improving the business environment and simplifying trade transactions in the wake of trade facilitation agreement of the World Trade Organization. It seeks to provide a stable and sustainable policy environment for foreign trade in merchandise and services and to promote diversification of India's export basket.

Export Growth Targets

The *FTP 2015-20* aims at almost doubling the merchandise exports of India from $466 billion in 2013-14 to $900 billion by 2019-20, by raising India's share in world exports from 2 per cent to 3.5 per cent during this period.

Simplification and Restructuring of Reward Schemes

The FTP for 2015-20 has restructured existing incentive schemes and introduced certain new schemes.

Earlier, there were five different schemes (Focus Product Scheme, Market Linked Focus Product Scheme, Focus Market Scheme, Agri Infrastructure Incentive Scrip, VKGUY) for rewarding merchandise exports with different kinds of duty scrips with varying conditions (sector-specific or actual user only) attached to their use. Now, all these schemes have been merged into a single scheme, namely Merchandise Export from India Scheme (MEIS) and there would be no conditionality attached to the scrips issued under the scheme.

Rewards for eligible export of goods to notified markets under MEIS shall be payable as percentage of realised FOB value (in free foreign exchange). The debits towards basic customs duty in the transferable reward duty credit scrips would also be allowed adjustment as duty drawback. Earlier, only the additional duty of customs/excise duty/service tax was allowed adjustment as CENVAT credit or drawback, as per Department of Revenue rules.

The current Policy has replaced the earlier scheme known as Served From India Scheme (SFIS) with Service Exports from India Scheme (SEIS). SEIS shall apply to 'Service Providers located in India' instead of 'Indian Service Providers'. Thus, SEIS provides for rewards to all service providers of notified services, who are providing services from India, regardless of the constitution or profile of the service provider.

Incentives under MEIS and SEIS have been extend to units located in SEZs also.

For the first time, exports by e-commerce firms will be provided incentives while under the MEIS.

New Trade Promotion Agency

Apart from the existing Board of Trade, a Council for Trade Development and Promotion will be set up comprising representatives from States and Union Territories.

Status Holders

For a long time, the Government has been recognising large exporters as Status Holders and given special treatment and privileges to facilitate their trade transactions, in order to reduce their transaction costs and time. (Also see *Export Houses and Trading Houses* in chapter 42).

The current Policy has changed the nomenclature of Export House, Star Export House, Trading House, Star Trading House, Premier Trading House certificate to One, Two, Three, Four, Five Star Export House. The criteria for export performance for recognition of status holder have been changed from Rupees to US dollar earnings. The new criteria is as under:-

TABLE 28.1: CATEGORIES OF EXPORT HOUSE

Status Category	*Export Performance FOB/FOR (as converted) Value (in US $ million) during current and previous two years*
One Star Export House	3
Two Star Export House	25
Three Star Export House	100
Four Star Export House	500
Five Star Export House	2000

New Initiatives for EOUs, EHTPs and STPs

According to the Foreign Trade Policies of the past, units undertaking to export their entire production of goods (except permissible domestic tariff area [DTA]) were permitted under Export Oriented Unit (EOU) Scheme, Electronic Hardware Technology Park (EHTP), Software Technology Park (STP) Scheme, Bio-Technology Park (BTP) Scheme for manufacture of goods including repair, remaking, reconditioning, reengineering and rendering of services. The **FTP 2015-20** has modified these schemes. Important modifications include the following, among others:

(*a*) EOUs, EHTPs and STPs are allowed to share infrastructural facilities among themselves. This will enable units to utilise their infrastructural facilities in an optimum way and avoid duplication of efforts and cost to create separate infrastructural facilities in different units.

(*b*) Inter-unit transfer of goods and services are allowed among EOUs, EHTPs, STPs and BTPs. This will facilitate group of those units which source inputs centrally in order to obtain bulk discount. This will reduce cost of transportation, other logistic costs and result in maintaining effective supply chain.

(*c*) EOUs are allowed facility to set up Warehouses near the port of export. This will help in reducing lead time for delivery of goods and will also address the issue of unpredictability of supply orders.

(*d*) STP units, EHTP units and software EOUs are allowed the facility to use all duty free equipment/goods for training purposes. This will help these units in developing skills of their employees.

Boost to 'Make in India'

To encourage domestic production, Export Obligation (EO) for domestic procurement under EPCG scheme has been reduced from 90 per cent of the normal export obligation (6 times at the duty saved amount) to 75 per cent, in order to promote domestic capital goods manufacturing industry.

Further, it is proposed to give higher level of rewards to products with high domestic content and value addition, as compared to products with high import content and less value addition.

The government also extended tax breaks to exporters of defence, pharma and environment-friendly products. The government will focus on branding India's products for which campaigns would be started soon in sectors including pharma and engineering. Traditional exports like handloom alongside yoga in services would also be promoted.

Evaluation

The Narendra Modi government took one year to do required homework for a new five year Foreign Trade Policy instead of coming out with a new Policy (which was due in April 2014) in a hurry soon after coming to power. Considerable thought has gone in to the making of the new Policy. However, it may be said that the new Policy reflects the general trend of the past of rationalising existing export promotion schemes and introducing new ones zeroing in the emerging business environment.

Although catchy terms of the favour of the present government such as 'Make in India', 'Digital India' and 'Skill India' are used in the Policy, they are more or less extensions of initiatives of the past. Indeed, every successive Policy has been a step forward from the previous Policy. It is true of the Foreign Trade Policy 2015-20 too. The endeavours towards procedural simplification and digitalisation have been carried further forward by the current Policy.

The Policy document evinces a serious homework. The success of the policy in achieving the objectives will depend on the efficiency of the implementation. The foreign trade environment in particular and the business environment in general being characterised by frequent changes and, some times, even turbulence, the Policy should be amenable to needed flexibility. In this context, the replacement of the Annual Review by Mid-term Review may not be appreciated by everybody.

Exports of India had been growing faster than the world average and as a result, India's share in global exports had been rising. But for more than a year after the announcement of the FTP 2015-16, there was a decline in India's exports. In 2015, the decline was about 17 per cent. The share of India in global exports declined from 1.7 per cent in 2014 to 1.6 in 2017 against the ambition of raising it to 3.5 per cent by 2020. In short, the FTP 2015-20 has not succeeded in boosting India's exports; on the other hand, the picture that has emerged is highly disappointing.

SPECIAL ECONOMIC ZONES

The Concept of SEZs

Special Economic Zones (SEZs) are conceived as a means to promote exports and economic development by providing quality infrastructure, reducing procedural hassles and providing a level playing field *vis-a-vis* the foreign countries. They are specifically delineated duty-free enclaves, deemed as foreign territory for the purposes of trade operations and application of duties and tariffs. According to Government of India's policy, SEZs can be set up for the manufacture of goods and the rendering of services, production, processing, assembling, trading, repair, remaking, reconditioning, re-engineering. Units for generation/ distribution of power can also be set up in the SEZs. Goods going into the SEZ area from the Domestic Tariff Area (DTA) are treated as deemed exports and goods coming from the SEZ area into DTA are treated as if the goods are being imported. The existing export promotion zones have been converted into SEZs.

As a RBI Report[1] observes, the economic rationale for establishing Special Economic Zones (SEZs) is not clearly laid down in trade theory. It is, however, obvious that these Zones can be justified either on considerations of equity where a less developed area is accorded special tax and non-tax benefits or on considerations of efficiency, where a region has a spatial advantage in terms of costs. SEZ, as an institutional measure, supports the economic policy shift from import substitution to export promotion with a view to promoting export-led growth to facilitate larger incomes and employment. For these reasons, a large number of countries have taken initiatives to set up SEZs over the last half century or so. India followed suit in recent years, with a view to improve its competitive position.

SEZs are special enclaves delineated from DTA providing facilities and special considerations for industrial development with emphasis on export development.

SEZs exist in more than a hundred countries, socialist and capitalist, developed and developing, with differing nomenclatures and have done so for many decades. In some countries, EPZs have close variants like Free Trade Zones (FTZs) or Free Economic Zones (FEZs).

The Evolution of SEZs in India

With the establishment of the Kandla Free Trade Zone (KAFTZ) in 1965 with the triple objective of earning foreign exchange, generating more employment in the backward areas of Kutch and fuller utilisation of the facilities provided by the Kandla port, India became the first Asian country to experiment with Export Processing Zone (EPZ), the forerunner of today's Special Economic Zones (SEZs) which are conceived as growth engines that can boost manufacturing, augment exports and generate employment. (The term free trade zone in the name of KFTZ was a misnomer — it was indeed an export processing zone). The second EPZ of India, the Santa Cruz Electronics Export Processing Zone (SEEPZ), was set up in 1974. While the KFTZ was a multi-product zone, SEEPZ was an exclusive zone for electronic products. Four more export processing zones were set up later in the country at Chennai, Cochin, Noida (UP) and Falta (West Bengal) and they commenced exports during the Seven Plan (1985-86). Later, an EPZ was established at Visakhapatnam. All these seven were Central Government projects. Later Government of India permitted private enterprises and State Governments to set up EPZs/SEZs. 12 such zones (besides the 7 Central Government ones) were operational before the coming into effect of the SEZ Act, 2005. All these were very small in size, both geographically and in terms of investment and exports. Their tardy progress was also due, to a large extent, to the policy and procedural hurdles.

SEZ Policy and Act

The success of the Chinese SEZs has encouraged people in India to think big. With a view to overcoming the shortcomings experienced on account of the multiplicity of controls and clearances, absence of world-class infrastructure and an unstable fiscal regime, and aiming at attracting larger foreign investments in India, a Special Economic Zones (SEZs) Policy was announced by Government of India in April 2000. The principal intention of this policy was to make SEZs an engine for economic growth supported by quality infrastructure complemented by an attractive fiscal package, both at the Centre and the State level, with the minimum possible regulations.

> **Although India was the first Asian country to set up an EPZ in 1965, the progress of EPZs/SEZs was very tardy for a very long time. The SEZ Policy announced in 2000 and SEZ Act, 2005, have given a boost to the growth of SEZs.**

SEZs in India functioned from 1.11.2000 to 09.02.2006 under the provisions of the Foreign Trade Policy and fiscal incentives were made effective through the provisions of relevant statutes. To instill confidence in investors and signal the Government's commitment to a stable SEZ policy regime and with a view to impart stability to the SEZ regime thereby generating greater economic activity and employment through the establishment of SEZs, a comprehensive Special Economic Zones Act was passed by Parliament in May, 2005. The SEZ Act, 2005, supported by SEZ Rules, came into effect from 10th February, 2006, providing for drastic simplification of procedures and for single window clearance on matters relating to Central as well as State Governments.

The main objectives of the SEZ Act are:

- Generation of additional economic activity.
- Promotion of exports of goods and services.
- Promotion of investment from domestic and foreign sources.
- Creation of employment opportunities.
- Development of infrastructure facilities.

The SEZ Policy and Act have been introduced with the expectation that they will trigger a large flow of foreign and domestic investment in SEZs, in infrastructure and productive capacity, leading to generation of additional economic activity and creation of employment opportunities.

The SEZ Act, 2005, envisages key role for the State Governments in Export Promotion and creation of related infrastructure. A Single Window SEZ approval mechanism has been provided through a 19 member inter-ministerial SEZ Board of Approval (BoA). The applications duly recommended by the respective State Governments/UT Administration are considered by this BoA periodically. All decisions of the Board of approvals are with consensus.

The SEZ Rules provide for different minimum land requirement for different class of SEZs. Every SEZ is divided into a processing area where alone the SEZ units would come up and the non-processing area where the supporting infrastructure is to be created.

Table 28.2: Phases of Evolution of SEZs in India

1965-2000	Export Processing Zones	Central Government Projects
2000 -2006	Special Economic Zones Guided by Exim Policy	State Government and Private Zones Permitted
2006 onwards	SEZs Governed by SEZs Act, 2005	State Government and Private Zones Permitted

Advantages, Incentives and Facilities Offered to the SEZs

The SEZ Rules provide for:

- Simplified procedures for development, operation, and maintenance of the Special Economic Zones and for setting up units and conducting business in SEZs;
- Single window clearance for setting up of an SEZ;
- Single window clearance for setting up a unit in a Special Economic Zone;
- Single window clearance on matters relating to Central as well as State Governments;
- Simplified compliance procedures and documentation with an emphasis on self-certification.

The incentives and facilities offered to **the units** in SEZs for attracting investments into the SEZs, including foreign investment include:

- Duty free import/domestic procurement of goods for development, operation and maintenance of SEZ units
- 100% Income Tax exemption on export income for SEZ units under Section 10AA of the Income Tax Act for first 5 years, 50% for next 5 years thereafter and 50% of the ploughed back export profit for next 5 years.
- Exemption from minimum alternate tax under Section 115JB of the Income Tax Act.

- External commercial borrowing by SEZ units up to US $ 500 million in a year without any maturity restriction through recognized banking channels.
- Exemption from Central Sales Tax.
- Exemption from Service Tax.
- Single window clearance for Central and State level approvals.
- Exemption from State sales tax and other levies as extended by the respective State Governments.

The major incentives and facilities available to **SEZ developers** include:

- Exemption from customs/excise duties for development of SEZs for authorized operations approved by the BOA.
- Income Tax exemption on export income for a block of 10 years in 15 years under Section 80-IAB of the Income Tax Act.
- Exemption from minimum alternate tax under Section 115JB of the Income Tax Act.
- Exemption from dividend distribution tax under Section 115-O of the Income Tax Act.
- Exemption from Central Sales Tax (CST).
- Exemption from Service Tax (Section 7, 26 and Second Schedule of the SEZ Act).

Evaluation of EPZs

Globally, SEZs present a mixed picture of performance. Although India is one of the first developing nations to experiment with the idea of special zones, its scorecard until recently has been far from satisfactory.

Some Global Observations

While, globally, there are a few zones like the Jebel Ali Free Zone (JAFZ), Dubai, which are regarded as shining examples, there are many unsatisfactory cases. Set up in 1985 as a component of the Jebel Ali port, JAFZ has helped cement Dubai as the key hinterland destination for the Gulf. JAFZ which has emerged as a regional distribution or manufacturing base for about 1,500 global companies is regarded as one of the world's most successful free zones. Several factors have contributed to the success of JAFZ, besides the quality of the infrastructure and services and global linkages this zone provides. It permits 100 per cent foreign ownership; 100 per cent repatriation of capital and profits; there are no corporate taxes for 15 years; there is no personal income tax, nor any consumption taxes; no policy or obligation for local hire; no currency restrictions or any exchange control.

Special Economic Zones, where even 100 per cent foreign investment is allowed, has been among the measures taken in the People's Republic of China to increase exports and accelerate economic development. Encouraged by the success story of Jebel Ali and the big-bang Chinese experiences, a number of developing countries have pinned great hopes in EPZs/EOUs as a means to increase export, achieve transfer of technology, inter-industry linkages, employment generation and economic development. The achievement of the objectives, however, have been limited in several developing countries.

The achievement of the objectives of SEZs has been limited in many countries.

One of the objectives of SEZs is facilitation of transfer of technology. However, MNCs have not been enthusiastic to effect transfer of technology. It is mostly the assembly stage of production that is located/relocated to the EPZs; the R&D and technology-oriented pre-assembly stage of production being done in the developed countries. Further, there has not been scope for forward linkages as the entire output is meant for exports. The scope for backward linkages has been very limited because of heavy reliance on imports for inputs. According to an ILO report, while many zone-operating countries had anticipated that the low-skilled processing and assembling of imported parts would be a necessary, but temporary, first step up the ladder towards higher value-added manufacturing, only a few such as Malaysia, Mauritius and Singapore, managed to develop domestic export industries on the basis of EPZ investment. The generally high import intensity of the exports of EOU/EPZ units limit the net foreign exchange earnings. The report said that "it is a regrettable feature of many zones that both male and female workers are trapped in low-wage and low-skill jobs". It noted that the workforce in EPZs worldwide is usually female in majority and in certain activities, notably textiles, garment manufacturing and electronics assembly, women account for 90 per cent or more of the workers.

The report said that the generous incentives and low costs to entry attract simple processing industries to invest in the zones. Such companies often lack professional management, particularly in human resources management. They also tend to be reluctant to invest in new skills, technology or productivity improvements. The labour-intensive nature of much of the processing and assembly work meant that enterprises compete largely on the basis of price. The report concluded that "labour relations and human resource development remain two of the most problematic aspects of zone functioning". The principal author of the report, Auret Van Heedren, said "the frequent absence of minimal standards and poor labour-management relations have predictable outcomes, such as high labour turnover, absenteeism, stress and fatigue, low rates of productivity, excessive wastage of materials and labour unrest which are still too common".

The Indian Scenario

As has already indicated, the Indian picture has not been very bright. When it has reached the threshold of making a leap forward it is mired in a host of political/administrative and developmental debates, controversies, conflicts and confusions.

The SEZ Act has given a Philip to the growth of SEZs in India. At the end of 2016, the number notified SEZs was 348. In addition to the notified SEZs, there are a large number of SEZs which have received formal approvals (33) and in principle approvals (155). Most of the SEZs, however, are small size; only a few are of more than 1,000 hectares in size.

The benefits derived from SEZs are evident from the investment, employment, exports and infrastructural developments additionally generated. The total investments in SEZs as *on* 30th September, 2016, amounted to more than ₹ 4,06,690 crore. Out of this, the incremental investment in SEZs notified under the SEZ Act was more than ₹ 1,61,700 crore.

The employment generated in the SEZs as on 30th September, 2016, was 16,88,337 persons. The incremental employment generated in the SEZs notified under the Act is 13,59,766 persons. According to government sources, At least double this number obtains indirect employment outside the SEZs as a result of the operations of SEZ units. This is in addition to the employment created by the developer for infrastructure activities.

As Table 28.3 shows, until 2006-07 the share of SEZs in the total exports was negligible, but there has been a significant improvement and in 2010 – 11 SEZs contributed nearly 30 per cent of India's exports. In 2015-16, exports from SEZs amounted to ₹ 4,67,337 crore.

TABLE 28.3: SEZS EXPORTS AND INDIA'S TOTAL EXPORTS: A COMPARISON

	Exports from SEZs		*Exports from India*		*Share of SEZs Exports in Total Exports*
	Value (₹ crore)	*Growth (%)*	*Value (₹ crore)*	*Growth (%)*	
2003-04	13,854	39.0	2,93,367		4.7
2004-05	18,314	32.2	3,75,340	27.9	4.9
2005-06	22,840	24.7	4,56,418	21.6	5.0
2006-07	24,615	51.6	5,71,779	25.3	6.1
2007-08	66,638	92.5	6,55,863	14.7	10.2
2008-09	99,689	49.668	8,40,755	28.2	11.9
2009-10	2,20,711	121.4	8,45,534	0.6	26.1
2013-14	4,94,077	4.0	19,05,011	16.7	25.9

Source: Government of India, *Economic Survey,* (different years).

Issues and Concerns

The rationale of SEZ in an era of progressive liberalization and its social justification are questioned. For example, while renowned development economist Jagadish Bhagawati feels that there is no need to establish SEZs at this stage of post-liberalisation, Raghuram Rajan, IMF's chief economist, holds that India, with its huge fiscal deficit, can ill-afford such huge revenue loss accruing from the scheme.[2]

The Finance Ministry has estimated revenue loss of over ₹ 102,000 crore on the SEZ account for 2006-2010, 54 per cent of it being on account of direct tax concessions. According to industrialist Rahul Bajaj, SEZs provide incentives disproportionate to the incremental benefits to the economy. The Reserve Bank of India (RBI), in a recent annual report, cautioned that SEZs could aggravate the uneven pattern of development by pulling out resources from the less developed areas. Rather than promoting new business ventures, SEZs will merely attract investment that would have come in anyway. Fiscal and monetary giveaways are more likely to generate incentives in no way conducive to economic growth.[3] Mr. C.J. Mathew, Development Commissioner, Cochin Special Economic Zone, however, presents a different perspective: If the tax that is foregone is computed in gross terms, it would appear that the country is a loser. This calculation fails to take into account that universally indirect taxes should not be incorporated in the export product. The existence of various export schemes, implemented by the customs authorities as well as rebates and drawback granted to exporters is in pursuance of this axiom. A calculation of the net duty foregone would shed light on the truth. Income tax benefits accorded are no different from investment allowance already existing and, in any case, is for a limited period. In the past, the State has collected taxes for putting up infrastructure including industrial infrastructure. The delivery systems not having proved satisfactory, it is time to implement this alternative model: do not tax the developer who puts up infrastructure and thus reduces the burden on the governance system.[4]

There are several serious social, economic, environmental and political issues and concerns related to SEZs.

The Department of Commerce has defended the scheme having an avowed objective of SEZs facilitating $5 billion of FDI inflows by end-2007, creating employment for 5,00,000 by end-2007, in addition to 1.5 million indirect jobs outside the zones, besides fixing the country's infrastructure.[5]

Another major issue pertains to exemption of the SEZs from several laws of the country. In this context, C J Mathew points out that contrary to all presumptions, all laws, except the tax laws, are applicable in an SEZ. There is no separate policy system. Labour laws are to be enforced in the zones as they are enforced elsewhere. It is a myth that unions do not exist in zones and that strikes are outlawed. In all zones, we have trade unions who carry on the useful tasks of shop floor negotiations and collective bargaining. Strikes have also occurred in SEZs in the manner that they have occurred in industrial and commercial establishments elsewhere.[6]

The problems/issues that have stemmed up from the approval of a large number of new SEZs within a short period and issues that have emerged related to land acquisitions have led the SEZ regime to a state of flux. There has even been a feeling that no more new SEZs be permitted or should at least be frozen for sometime.

While any policy should be reasonably and logically flexible, Government and various political parties appear to be very much confused as to what is a right policy in respect of SEZ and land acquisitions. One of the serious concerns is the conversion of agricultural land into SEZ and the farmers interests. It may be pointed out here that the total land area required for the SEZs which have received formal approval and SEZs which have received in principle approval so far forms only a very negligible percentage of the total land area and agricultural land of India. However, care needs to be taken to avoid large displacement of farmers.

Mathew observes that much of the controversy regarding the land conversion has been made of local responses at Nandigram and Panvel; without trivializing these movements, it must also be emphasized that the reports in the media have not touched upon the basic issues: archaic compensation systems and utilization of surplus land. Acquisitions are made by the State not just for SEZs but for all kinds of activity. The sole difference is the inclusion of a private investors who is perceived to be a beneficiary. There is need for a land acquisition system that goes beyond public purpose as prescribed in the ancient Land Acquisition Act. The consent acquisition statute of Karnataka is worth emulating not just for promoting SEZs but for all industrial activity.[7]

While it has been felt that the SEZs as a component of the development strategy can make a significant impact only if large size SEZs come up in different parts of the country, the current Government thinking appears to be taking a reverse direction. Mr. Kamal Nath, the Union Minister for Commerce and Industry had earlier announced that multi-product SEZs should have a minimum area of 1,000 hectares and service sector SEZs must have an area of 100 hectares or more. There were proposals for SEZs of vast spread. There was a report, for example, of a proposal for a SEZ of 20,0000 acres in Gurgaon. However, the report of a committee set up earlier under the chairmanship of BJP leader Murli Manohar Joshi recommended that the maximum permissible land area for multi-product SEZs coming up on cultivable land be 2,000 hectares and for zones to be set up on wastelands it be 5,000 hectares. The committee also recommended that "land for the zones should be taken on lease by developers and there should not be transfer of ownership". The meeting of the Group of Ministers on April 5, 2007 fixed the ceiling on land at 5,000 hectares. However, State Governments can reduce this even further. A comprehensive rehabilitation policy to provide employment to at least one person from each displaced family was also proposed.

Another key decision by the Government recently was to reduce the amount of land available with an SEZ developer for undertaking activities like malls, shopping areas, school and hospitals. Earlier the minimum processing area (for core industrial activity) was 35 per cent of the total land size, with a provision for reducing this to 25 per cent in multi-product zones. This rule has now been changed to a fixed and uniform 50 per cent for all types of zones (sector specific and multi-product). This would ensure greater use of the SEZ area for core economic activity and reduce the flexibility for commercial exploitation.

CONCLUSION

India did not give the special zones scheme a real thrust under the controlled regime when it had much more relevance than today. The belated attempt, inspired by the Chinese experience, to make the SEZ a major vehicle of export growth in particular and economic development in general has given rise to several vital socio-economic and political debates and conflicts. Several political parties show the usual confusion and populist summersaults. Farmers agitations related to land acquisitions are sought to be put-off with iron fist, resulting in several deaths leading to social unrest and political issues. SEZs cannot have a justification if it is not an integral part of the national development strategy. The relevance and rationale of SEZs in an environment characterised by increasing global liberalisation is debatable. What is really needed is a hassle free and conducive policy and procedural environment for the appropriate development of all sectors linked to rational effective utilisation of national resources in accordance with the national priorities.

AN EVALUATION OF EXPORT PROMOTION MEASURES

The success of export promotion measures should be judged by the growth of exports and the dynamism of the export sector.

No doubt, India's total exports have been growing and the export sector has achieved some diversification and sophistication. However, the achievements have been, as noted earlier, far below the requirements and potentials and have been very poor in comparison with those of several developing countries. Thus, export development measures in India have not been successful in producing the needed results. The infrastructure for international marketing is not efficient enough.

An effective export promotion should compensate for the disadvantages of the national exporters and should make the export business profitable enough to lure entrepreneurs to this sector and achieve the ultimate objective of boosting the exports.

The general feeling is that the export promotion regime in India has not succeeded in achieving these objectives.

It has also been pointed out that one of the drawbacks of the export incentives regime in India is that it is largely transparent in character.

"While foreign buyers have sharp eyes for them, these constitute an eye sore for the governments particularly of the industrialised importing countries. The importer try to grab these incentives almost in their entirety on the pretext of growing competition, thus depriving the Indian exporters of the benefits of the promotional measures. In fact, these tend to create an unsatiable urge for more and more incentives in extent and magnitude. On the other hand, the governments of the developed countries viewing these as subsidies invoke the provisions of the anti-dumping and countervailing duty laws. The effectiveness and purposiveness of incentives thus lie in their non-transparent character. This could be possible only by devising a policy framework with inherent and inbuilt, albeit latent, promotional incentives."[8]

A major factor necessitating large incentives is the structural weakness and high cost of the Indian economy. It is, therefore, necessary to remove these handicaps to reduce the needs for the exogenous incentives. Further, the institutional inadequacies and procedural complexities and delays need to be urgently attended to. Absence/lack of dynamism and innovativeness in policies, procedures, product development and marketing continue to hamper India's export development.

REFERENCES

1. RBI, *Report on Currency and Finance, 2001-02*.
2. Raghu, Dayal, "Special Economic Zones: How to Make a Success of Them", *The Hindu Business Line*, 6 July, 2007.
3. *Ibid*.
4. C.J. Mathew, "SEZs: Engines of Growth", *Erudition – The Albertian Journal of Management*, September *2007*.
5. Raghu, Dayal, *op. cit*.
6. C.J. Mathew, *op. cit*.
7. *Ibid*.
8. Verma, M.L., *Foreign Trade Management in India* (New Delhi: Vikas Publishing House, 1988), pp. 72-73.

☆☆☆

CHAPTER 29

FOREIGN EXCHANGE MANAGEMENT ACT

Foreign exchange transactions were regulated in India by the Foreign Exchange Regulations Act (FERA), 1973. This Act also sought to regulate certain aspects of the conduct of business outside the country by Indian companies and in India by foreign companies.

The FERA was widely described as a draconian and obnoxious law. Following the economic liberalisation ushered in 1991, some amendments to the FERA were effected in 1993.

The main objective of FERA, framed against the background of severe foreign exchange problem and the controlled economic regime, was conservation and proper utilisation of the foreign exchange resources of the country.

There was a lot of demand for a substantial modification of FERA in the light of the ongoing economic liberalisation and improving foreign exchange reserves position. Accordingly, a new Act, the Foreign Exchange Management Act (FEMA), 1999, replaced the FERA.

The FEMA, which came into effect from January 1, 2000, extends to the whole of India and also applies to all branches, offices, and agencies outside India, owned or controlled by a person resident in India.

Objectives

The objectives of FEMA are:

- To facilitate external trade and payments.
- To promote the orderly development and maintenance of foreign exchange market.

Dealing in Foreign Exchange, etc.

FEMA regulates dealings is foreign exchange and payments to and from persons outside India.

Section 3 of FEMA imposes restrictions on dealings in foreign exchange and foreign security and payments to and receipts from any person outside India. Accordingly, except as provided in terms of the Act, or with the general or special permission of the Reserve Bank, no person shall—

(*a*) deal in any foreign exchange or foreign security with any person other than an authorised person;

(*b*) make any payment to or for the credit of any person resident outside India in any manner;

(*c*) receive otherwise through an authorised person, any payment by order or on behalf of any person resident outside India in any manner;

(*d*) enter into any financial transaction in India as a consideration for or in association with acquisition or creation or transfer of a right to acquire, any asset outside India by any person.

Further, save as otherwise provided in this Act, no person resident in India shall acquire, hold, own, possess or transfer any foreign exchange, foreign security or any immovable property situated outside India.

Holding of Foreign Exchange, etc.

Save as otherwise provided in this Act, no person resident in India shall acquire, hold, own, possess or transfer any foreign exchange, foreign security or any immovable property situated outside India.

Current Account Transactions

FEMA permits dealings in foreign exchange through authorised persons for current account transactions. However, the Central Government can impose reasonable restrictions in public interest.

Capital Account Transactions

Any person may sell or draw foreign exchange to or from an authorised person for a capital account transaction permitted by the Reserve Bank in consultation with the Central Government.

The Reserve Bank may, however, without prejudice to the generality of this, prohibit, restrict or regulate the following:

(*a*) transfer or issue of any foreign security by a person resident in India;

(*b*) transfer or issue of any security by a person resident outside India;

(*c*) transfer or issue of any security or foreign security by any branch, office or agency in India of a person resident outside India;

(*d*) any borrowing or lending in foreign exchange in whatever form or by whatever name called;

(*e*) any borrowing or lending in rupees in whatever form or by whatever name called between a person resident in India and a person resident outside India;

(*f*) deposits between persons resident in India and persons resident outside India;

(*g*) export, import or holding of currency or currency notes;

(*h*) transfer of immovable property outside India, other than a lease not exceeding five years, by a person resident in India;

(*i*) acquisition or transfer of immovable property in India, other than a lease not exceeding five years, by 'a person resident outside India';

(*j*) giving of a guarantee or surety in respect of any debt, obligation or other liability incurred —

1. by a person resident in India and owed to a person resident outside India; or
2. by a person resident outside India.

A person resident in India may hold, own, transfer or invest in foreign currency, foreign security or any immovable property situated outside India if such currency, security or property was acquired, held or owned by such person when he was resident outside India or inherited from a person who was resident outside India.

A person resident outside India may hold, own, transfer or invest in Indian currency, security or any immovable property situated in India if such currency, security or property was acquired, held or owned by such person when he was resident in India or inherited from a person who was resident in India.

The Reserve Bank may prohibit, restrict, or regulate establishment in India of a branch, office or other place of business by a person resident outside India, for carrying on any activity relating to such branch, office or other place of business.

The Reserve Bank shall not impose any restriction on the drawal of foreign exchange for payments due on account of amortisation of loans or for depreciation of direct investments in the ordinary course of business.

Export of Goods and Services

1. Every exporter of goods shall—

   (*a*) furnish to the Reserve Bank or to such other authority a declaration as specified, containing true and correct material particulars, including the amount representing the full export value or, if the full export value of the goods is not ascertained at the time of export, the value which the exporter, having regard to the prevailing market conditions, expects to receive on the sale of the goods in a market outside India;

(*b*) furnish to the Reserve Bank such other information as may be required by the Reserve Bank for the purpose of ensuring the realisation of the export proceeds by such exporter.

For the purpose of ensuring that export value of the goods is received without any delay, the Reserve Bank may direct any exporter to comply with such requirements as it deems fit.

Every exporter of services shall furnish to the Reserve Bank or to such other authorities a declaration as specified, containing the true and correct material particulars in relation to payment for such services.

Realisation and Repatriation of Foreign Exchange

Where any amount of foreign exchange is due or has accrued to any person, he shall take all reasonable steps to realize and repatriate it to India within the time and in the manner prescribed by the RBI. Several exemptions are, however, granted to this clause.

Contravention and Penalties

Under this chapter, penalty for any kind of contravention under this Act is liable to a penalty up to thrice the amount involved where it is quantifiable or up to ₹ 2 lakh where it is not quantifiable and where such contravention is continuing one, further penalty which may extend to five thousand rupees for every day after the first day during which the contravention continues. This provision is in total contrast to the respective provision in the erstwhile FERA which provided for imprisonment and no limit on fine. Under FEMA, a person will be liable to civil imprisonment only if he does not pay the fine within 90 days from the date of notice and that too after formalities of show cause notice and personal hearing. If he does not respond to the notice, there can be a warrant of arrest.

Administration of the Act

The FEMA has assigned an important role to the Reserve Bank of India in the administration of this Act. The rules, regulations and norms pertaining to several sections of the Act are to be laid down by the RBI, in consultation with the Central Government.

The RBI has an important role in the administration of FEMA.

The Act requires the Central Government to appoint as many officers of the Central Government as Adjudicating Authorities for holding inquiries pertaining to contravention of the Act. There is also a provision for appointing one or more Special Directors (Appeals) to hear appeals against the order of the Adjudicating Authorities. The Central Government shall also establish an Appellate Tribunal for Foreign Exchange to hear appeals against the orders of the Adjudicating Authorities and the Special Director (Appeals).

The FEMA provides for the establishment, by the Central Government, of a Director of Enforcement with a Director and such other officers or class of officers as it thinks fit for taking up for investigation the contraventions under this Act.

FERA and FEMA — A Comparison

Important differences between FERA and FEMA have been summed up as follows:[1]

1. In FEMA, only the specified acts relating to foreign exchange are regulated, while in FERA, anything and everything that has to do with foreign exchange was controlled. Also, the aim of FEMA is facilitating trade as against that of FERA, which was to prevent misuse. In other words, the theme of FERA was : 'everything that is specified is under control'. While the theme of FEMA is : 'everything other than what is expressly covered is not controlled'. Thus, there is a lot of deregulation.
2. FEMA is a much smaller enactment — only 49 sections as against 81 of FERA.
3. In the process of simplification, many of the "laid downs" of the erstwhile FERA have been withdrawn.
4. Many provisions of FERA like the ones relating to blocked accounts, Indians taking up employment abroad, employment of foreign technicians in India, contracts in evasion of the act, vexatious search, culpable mental state ,etc., have no appearance in FEMA.

SUMMARY

The Foreign Exchange Management Act (FEMA), 1999, replaced the Foreign Exchange Regulations Act (FERA), 1973, which regulated the foreign exchange transactions in India and which sought to control certain aspects of the conduct of business outside the country by Indian companies and in India by foreign companies.

The FEMA, which came into effect from January 1, 2000, extends to the whole of India and also applies to all branches, offices, and agencies outside India, owned or controlled by a person resident in India.

The objectives of FEMA are to facilitate external trade and payments; and to promote the orderly development and maintenance of foreign exchange market.

The Reserve Bank of India is assigned an important role in the administration of this Act.

The FEMA empowers the Central Government to impose restrictions on dealings in foreign exchange and foreign security and payments to and receipts from any person outside India.

The Act imposes restrictions on persons resident in India on acquiring, holding or owning foreign exchange, foreign security and immovable property abroad and, on transfer of foreign exchange or security abroad.

The FEMA lays down that all dealings in foreign exchange or foreign security and all payments from outside the country to India shall be made only through authorised persons, except with the general or special permission of the Reserve Bank. The Act also prohibits any payment outside India except with the general or special permission of the Reserve Bank.

The FEMA permits dealings in foreign exchange through authorised persons for current account transactions. However, the Central Government can impose reasonable restrictions in public interest.

Any person may sell or draw foreign exchange to or from an authorised person for a capital account transaction permitted by the Reserve Bank. However, the Act empowers the RBI to impose a number of restrictions on capital account transactions.

The FEMA permits a person resident in India to hold, own, transfer or invest in foreign currency, foreign security or any immovable property situated outside India if such currency, security or property was acquired, held or owned by such person when he was resident outside India or inherited from a person who was resident outside India. Also, a person resident outside India may hold, own, transfer or invest in Indian currency, security or any immovable property situated in India if such currency, security or property was acquired, held or owned by such person when he was resident in India or inherited from a person who was resident in India.

The Reserve Bank is empowered by this Act to prohibit, restrict, or regulate establishment in India of a branch, office or other place of business by a person resident outside India, for carrying on any activity relating to such branch, office or other place of business. However, the RBI shall not impose any restriction on the drawal of foreign exchange for payments due on account of amortisation of loans or for depreciation of direct investments in the ordinary course of business.

The Act requires the exporters to furnish to the Reserve Bank or to such other authority certain details regarding the exports.

For the purpose of ensuring that export value of the goods is received without any delay, the Reserve Bank may direct any exporter to comply with such requirements as it deems fit.

Where any amount of foreign exchange is due or has accrued to any person, he shall take all reasonable steps to realize and repatriate it to India within the time and in the manner prescribed by the RBI. Several exemptions are, however, granted to this clause.

Under this chapter, penalty for any kind of contravention under this Act is liable to a penalty up to thrice the amount involved where it is quantifiable or up to ₹ 2 lakh where it is not quantifiable and where such contravention is continuing one, further penalty which may extend to five thousand rupees for everyday after the first day during which the contravention continues. This provision is in total contrast to the respective provision in the erstwhile FERA which provided for imprisonment and no limit on fine. Under FEMA, a person will be liable to civil imprisonment only if he does not pay the fine within 90 days from the date of notice and that too after formalities of show cause notice and personal hearing. If he does not respond to the notice, there can be a warrant of arrest.

An important difference between FERA and FEMA is that while in FEMA, only the specified Acts relating to foreign exchange are regulated, in FERA, anything and everything that has to do with foreign exchange was controlled. Also, the aim of FEMA is facilitating trade as against that of FERA, which was to prevent misuse. In other words, the theme of FERA was: 'everything that is specified is under control'. While the theme of FEMA is: 'everything other than what is expressly covered is not controlled'. Thus, there is a lot of deregulation.

REFERENCES

1. Chinubhai R. Shah and Komal Parikh, "FERA to FEMA: A Journey from Forbidden Lands to Semi-open Pastures", *Chartered Secretary*, May 2000, pp. A175:590-2.

ANNEXURE 29.1

DEFINITIONS

The meaning of some of the important terms used in FEMA are given below.

Foreign Exchange

Foreign exchange means foreign currency and includes —

(*i*) Deposits, credits and balances payable in any foreign currency,

(*ii*) Drafts, travellers' cheques, letters of credit or bills of exchange, expressed or drawn in Indian currency but payable in any foreign currency,

(*iii*) Drafts, travellers' cheques, letters of credit or bills of exchange drawn by banks, institutions or persons outside India, but payable in Indian currency.

Foreign Currency

Foreign currency means any currency other than Indian currency.

Foreign Security

Foreign security means any security, in the form of shares, stocks, bonds, debentures or any other instrument denominated or expressed in foreign currency and includes securities expressed in foreign currency, but where redemption or any form of return such as interest or dividends is payable in Indian currency.

Person

Person includes —

(*i*) An individual,

(*ii*) A Hindu undivided family,

(*iii*) A company,

(*iv*) A firm,

(*v*) An association of persons or a body of individuals, whether incorporated or not,

(*vi*) Every artificial juridical person, not falling within any of the preceding sub-clauses, and

(*vii*) Any agency, office or branch owned or controlled by such person.

Person Resident in India

Person resident in India means —

(*i*) A person residing in India for more than one hundred and eighty-two days during the course of the preceding financial year but does not include —

(A) a person who has gone out of India or who stays outside India, in either case —

(*a*) for or on taking up employment outside India, or

(*b*) for carrying on outside India a business or vocation outside India, or

(c) for any other purpose, in such circumstances as would indicate his intention to stay outside India for a uncertain period.

(B) a person who has come to or stays in India, in either case, otherwise than —

(a) for or on taking up employment in India, or

(b) for carrying on in India a business or vocation in India, or

(c) for any other purpose, in such circumstances as would indicate his intention to stay in India for an uncertain period.

(ii) Any person or body corporate registered or incorporated in India,

(iii) An office, branch or agency in India owned or controlled by a person resident outside India,

(iv) An office, branch or agency outside India owned or controlled by a person resident in India.

Person Resident Outside India

Person resident outside India means a person who is not resident in India.

Service

Service means service of any description which is made available to potential users and includes the provision of facilities in connection with banking, financing, insurance, medical assistance, legal assistance, chit fund, real estate, transport, processing, supply of electrical or other energy, boarding or lodging or both, entertainment, amusement or the purveying of news or: other information, but does not include the rendering of any service free of charge or under a contract of personal service.

Authorised Person

Authorised person means an authorised dealer, money changer, offshore banking unit or any other person for the time-being authorised under the Act to deal in foreign exchange or foreign securities.

Currency

Currency includes all currency notes, postal notes, postal orders, money orders, cheques, drafts, travellers' cheques, letters of credit, bills of exchange and promissory notes, credit cards or such other similar instruments, as may be notified by the Reserve Bank.

Current Account Transaction

Current account transaction means a transaction other than a capital account transaction and without prejudice to the generality of the foregoing such transaction includes—

(i) Payments due in connection with foreign trade, other current business, services, and short-term banking and credit facilities in the ordinary course of business,

(ii) Payments due as interest on loans and as net income from investments,

(ii) Remittances for living expenses of parents, spouse and children residing abroad, and

(iv) Expenses in connection with foreign travel, education and medical care of parent, spouse and children.

☆☆☆

CHAPTER 30

CORPORATE SOCIAL RESPONSIBILITY AND TRIPLE BOTTOM LINE

Social responsibility of business traditionally refered to what the business does, over and above the statutory requirement, for the benefit of the society. The word *responsibility* connotes that the business has some moral obligations to the society.

The term *corporate citizenship* is also commonly used to refer to the moral obligations of business to the society. This implies that, just as individuals, corporates are also integral part of the society and that their behaviour shall be guided by certain social norms.

Recently, there have been some very important government initiatives to foster the social commitment of the business. In July 2011, the Ministry of Corporate Affairs, Government of India, brought out a set of *National Voluntary Guidelines on Social, Environmental and Economic Responsibilities of Business* to be adopted by all categories of enterprises, including SMEs. The Guidelines prefer the use of responsible business to corporate social responsibility. With the incorporation of CSR in the Companies Act, 2013, India claims to have become the first nation to make spending towards corporate social responsibility mandatory.

Corporate Social Responsibility (Corporate Citizenship), a concept popular in the last several decades, has been attracting growing discussion. In the meantime, the idea of ***Triple Bottom Line*** **(also known as 3 Ps)** has been growing in popularity. With the incorporation of CSR in the Companies Act, 2013, the term social responsibility has come to assume a new dimension in India

WHAT ARE CSRS?

Social responsibility of business has been traditionally understood as what a firm does, over and above the statutory requirement, for the benefit of the society. The term social responsibility connotes that a firm has some moral obligation to the society (particularly because of the reasons described in the sub-section *The Rationale*). With the Companies Act, 2013, making CSR mandatory for certain categories of companies on the basis of net-worth/turnover/net profit, CSR can be regarded as a voluntary contribution to societal welfare by companies only when the CSR expenditure exceeds the mandatory requirement.

The European Commission defines CSR as "the responsibility of enterprises for their impacts on society" and observes that to completely meet their social responsibility, enterprises "should have in place a process to integrate social, environmental, ethical human rights and consumer concerns into their business operations and core strategy in close collaboration with their stakeholders."

The WBCSD defines CSR as "the continuing commitment by business to contribute to economic development while improving the quality of life of the workforce and their families as well as of the community and society at large." Another simple definition is that it is "the responsibility of enterprises for their impacts on society." The United Nations Industrial Development Organisation (UNIDO) has defined corporate social responsibility (CSR) as a management concept whereby companies integrate social and environmental concerns in their business operations and interactions with their stakeholders. CSR is a way in which companies achieve a balance of economic, environmental and social imperatives. This definition is akin to the Triple-Bottom-Line Approach.

H.S. Singhania classifies the nature of the social responsibility of business into two categories.

- The manner in which a business carries out its own business activity.
- The welfare activity that it takes upon itself as an additional function.

The first involves the acceptance of the fact that business is not merely a profit-making occupation but a social function which involves certain duties, and requires that appropriate ethics are followed. For example, a business must obey all the laws, even when they are disagreeable; it should produce the maximum goods of good quality, ensure smooth supplies at competitive prices, pay taxes, shun malpractices, pay a fair wage to employees and a reasonable dividend to shareholders. It is also the duty of a business to undertake new investment and promote the dispersal of economic activity through ancillarisation and the setting up of industries in backward areas so as to spread enterprise and take employment to the doorsteps of labour. In addition to its commercial activity, business also plays a role in promoting social welfare activity, even directly.[1]

THE RATIONALE

There has been a growing acceptance of the plea that business should be socially responsible in the sense that the business enterprise, which makes use of the resources of society and depends on society for its functioning, should discharge its duties and responsibilities in enhancing the welfare of the society of which it is an integral part.

The operations of business enterprises affect a wide spectrum. The resources they make use of are not limited to those of the proprietors and the impact of their operations is felt also by many a people who are in no way connected with the enterprises. The shareholders, the suppliers of resources, the consumers, the local community and society at large are affected by the way an enterprise functions. Hence, a business enterprise has to be socially very responsive so that a social balance may be struck between the opposing interests of these groups. Further, business and other economic activities have been causing serious damage to the natural ecosystem which needs to be prevented and remedied.

More than six-and-a-half decades ago, Goyder argued: "Industry...can no longer be regarded as a private arrangement for enriching shareholders. It has become a joint enterprise in which workers, management, consumers, the locality, Government and trade union officials all play a part. If the system which we know by the name private enterprise is to continue, some way must be found to embraçe many interests which go to make up industry in a common purpose."[2] Later, in 1978, while delivering the C.C. Desai Memorial Lecture, he reiterated his plea that if the corporation has to function effectively, it has to be accountable to the public at large; and he sought to equate the suggestion of a responsible company with the trusteeship concept advocated by Gandhiji, the aim of which was to ensure that private property was used for the common good. The declaration issued by the international seminar on the social responsibility of business held in India in 1965 also co-related the Gandhian concept of trusteeship with the social responsibility of business as "responsibility to customers, workers, shareholders and the community."[3]

The *Report of the High-Powered Expert Committee on Companies and MRTPA Acts* (Sachar Committee), appointed by Government of India has expressed similar view: "If the plea of the companies that they are performing a social purpose in the development of the country is to be accepted, it can only be judged by the test of social responsiveness shown to the needs of the community by the companies. The company must behave and function as a responsible member of society, like any other individual. It cannot shun moral values, nor can it ignore actual compulsions. The real need is for some focus of accountability on the part of the management which is not limited to shareholders alone. In modern times, the objective of business has to be the proper utilisation of resources for the benefit of others."[4]

CSR TO TBL

As indicated earlier, terms TBL and 3Ps are gaining mare popularity over CSR. However, they are, in essence, not significantly different from CSR and social audit.

The view that there shall be a holistic approach to evaluating the outcomes of the operations of business enterprises and other organisations is a long standing one. Although the usage triple bottom line or its rhythmic expression profit, people and planet – the triple P – is of recent origin, the basic idea behind it has been there in the intellectual domain for a long time.

The concept of TBL, consisting of the *triple Ps* – people, planet, profit – holds that a company's responsibility lies with the stakeholders, i.e., to those who are influenced, either directly or indirectly, by the actions of the firm, not merely with the shareholders. In other words, it is a reflection of the stakeholder theory according to which the business entity should be used as a vehicle for coordinating stakeholder interests, instead of maximising shareholder (owner) profit.

In the currently popular nomenclature Triple P, *People* is often linked to corporate social responsibility (CSR), and another P is in place to represent the environment. Social responsibility in a broader perspective encompasses planet too and as such the People and Planet are akin to the social responsibility of business.

At its broadest, the term TBL is used to capture the whole set of values, issues and processes that companies must address in order to minimise any harm resulting from their activities and to create economic, social and environmental value. This involves being clear about the company's purpose and taking into consideration the needs of all the company's stakeholders — shareholders, customers, employees, business partners, governments, local communities and the public.

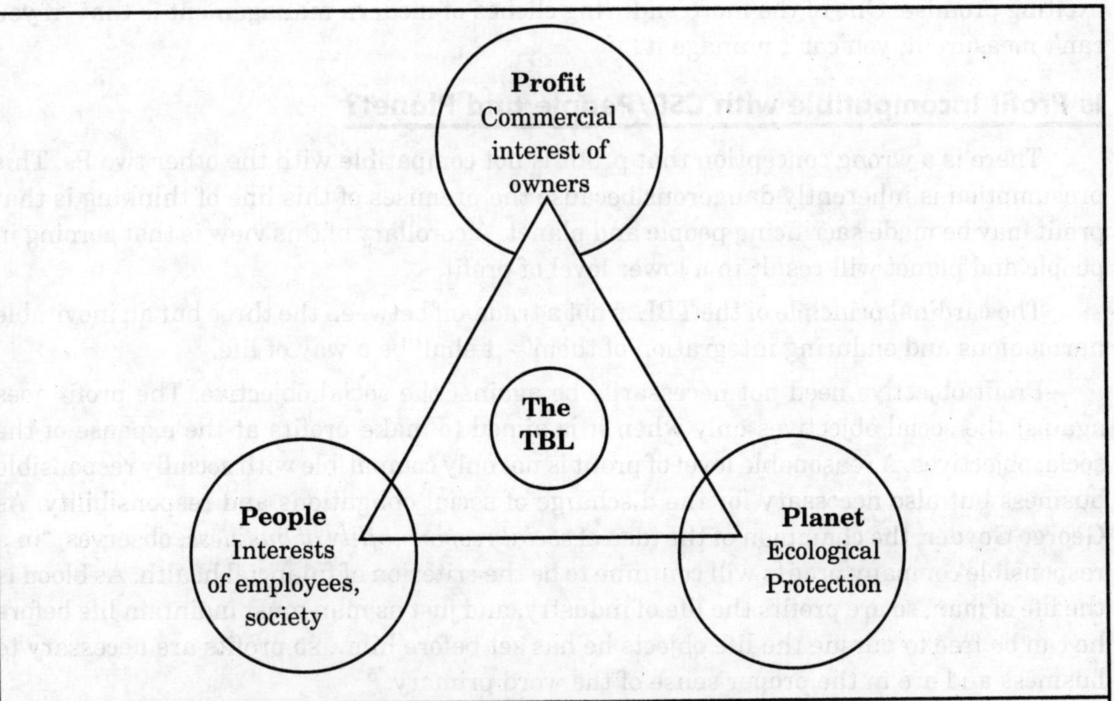

Fig. 30.1: The Components of TBL

The above descriptions clearly indicate that the accounting framework of TBL incorporates the social and environmental dimensions of the performance of an organisation, besides the traditional financial performance. The connotation of the TBL, thus, is that companies should be preparing three different (and quite separate) bottom lines:

- The traditional bottom line of the *profit and loss account.*
- The bottom line of a company's *people account* — a measure in some shape or form of how socially responsible then organisation has been in its operations.
- The bottom line of the company's *planet account* — a measure of how environmentally responsible it has been.

Is TBL a New/Better Idea?

The view that there shall be a holistic approach to evaluating the outcomes of the operations of business enterprises and other organisations is a long standing one. Although the usage triple bottom line or its rhythmic expression profit, people and planet – the triple P – is of recent origin, the basic idea behind it has been there in the intellectual domain for a long time. In short, *Triple Bottom Line*, or *Triple P* is not a new idea; it is old wine in new bottle.

The apparent novelty of 3BL lies in its supporters' contention that the overall fulfillment of obligations to communities, employees, customers, and suppliers (to name but four stakeholders) should be measured, calculated, audited and reported – just as the financial performance of public companies has been for more than a century. This is an exciting promise. One of the more enduring clichés of modern management is that "if you can't measure it, you can't manage it.

Is Profit Incompatible with CSR/People and Planet?

There is a wrong conception that profit is not compatible with the other two Ps. This presumption is inherently dangerous because the premises of this line of thinking is that profit may be made sacrificing people and planet. A corollary of this view is that zeroing in people and planet will result in a lower level of profit.

The cardinal principle of the TBL is not a trade-off between the three but an inevitable harmonious and enduring integration of them – it shall be a way of life.

Profit objective need not necessarily be against the social objective. The profit goes against the social objectives only when it is aimed to make profits at the expense of the social objectives. A reasonable level of profit is not only compatible with socially responsible business but also necessary for the discharge of social obligations and responsibility. As George Goyder, the champion of the idea of *social responsibility of business*, observes, "in a responsible company profits will continue to be the criterion of financial health. As blood is the life of man, so are profits the life of industry, and just as man must maintain life before he can be free to pursue the life objects he has set before him…so profits are necessary to business and are in the proper sense of the word primary."[5]

The Sachar Committee supports this view: "A profit is still a necessary part of the total picture, but it is not the primary purpose. This implies that the claims of various interests will have to be balanced, not on the narrow ground of what is best for the shareholders alone but from the point of view of what is best for the community at large. The company must accept its obligation to be socially responsible and to work for the larger benefit of the community."[6]

In short, a reasonable level of profit is necessary to enable a company to pursue the social objectives.

It is possible that adoption of the *triple P* principle will help companies in enhancing the profit in some cases. For example, the triple R – reduce, reuse, recycle – can lead to cost reduction. Similarly, use of new materials, technologies etc. as part of the green movement can also have similar effects.

Further, consumer preference for green products is increasing. Many consumers are willing to pay a premium for such products.

It is pointed out that the following business-based arguments support the concept of TBL:[7]

- **Reaching untapped market potential:** TBL companies can find financially profitable niches which were missed when money alone was the driving factor. Examples include:
  1. Adding ecotourism and geotourism to an already rich tourism market. Developing profitable methods to assist existing NGOs with their missions such as fundraising, reaching clients, or creating networking opportunities with multiple NGOs
  2. Providing products or services which benefit underserved populations and/or the environment which are also financially profitable.
- **Adapting to new business sectors:** Since many business opportunities are developing in the realm of social entrepreneurialism, businesses hoping to reach this expanding market must design themselves to be financially profitable, socially beneficial and ecologically sustainable or fail to compete with those companies who do design themselves as such. For example, Fair Trade and Ethical Trade companies require ethical and sustainable practices from all of their suppliers and service providers. A business which is planning to work with Fair Trade or Ethical Trade companies must design their business model to be TBL.

People and Planet may be antagonistic to the unscrupulous businessmen. However, they will have to fall in line when the expected moral and social commitment will become a legal obligation.

Limitations

A major difficulty in implementing TBL is accurately measuring the people and planet impacts. There is also no unanimity about the factors to be assessed. Monetisation of people and planet impact is too difficult a task. How do we assign monetary values to the species that are extinct or endangered or weather and climatic changes. Although several indices have been developed for the measurement, they all suffer from several limitations. The application of the TBL by businesses, non-profits and governments are motivated by the principles of economic, environmental and social sustainability, but differ with regard to the way they measure the three categories of outcomes. Proponents who have developed and applied sustainability assessment frameworks like the TBL encountered many challenges, chief among them, how to make an index that is both comprehensive and meaningful and how to identify suitable data for the variables that compose the index. The Genuine Progress Indicator (GPI), for example, consists of 25 variables that encompass economic, social and environmental factors. Those variables are converted into monetary units and summed into a single, dollar-denominated measure

Further, for many, TBL is mere a fad than a sincere and committed philosophy. The **adoption of 3BL rhetoric by a number of very prominent multinationals without traditions** of support for green and CSR principles is a more curious phenomenon. Perhaps, it should not be wholly surprising that prominent on this list are some firms trying to shake off recent reputations for decidedly irresponsible business practices or aloof management structures – firms like Shell and BP, British Telecom, AT&T and Dow Chemical. Of course, mind-set changes are possible. But, sometimes they may be eye washes or defensive tactics. There are also large organisations, such as Wal-Mart and McDonald's, which show green initiative but at the same time is unethical to 'people'.

CSR MODELS

Kash Rangan, Lisa A. Chase, Sohel Karim in an HBR Working Paper (2012) entitled "Why Every Company Needs a CSR Strategy and How to Build It" present the three models mentioned below.

Philanthropic Giving

By and large, this was the CSR model of the early days which is very common even today. It takes the form of money devoted for noble purpose like donations, directly to the beneficiaries, or through intermediaries like a charitable organisation. It emanates primarily out of the values, beliefs and convictions of the founders of the company and the top echelons.

This is a CSR model that has been globally popular. In India, a number of companies have been active in this kind of CSR. However, Tata Steel stands out. Not only that the company had a dedicated CSR approach since the very beginning, but also later it amended its Articles of Association to incorporate its social and moral responsibilities to the consumers, employees, shareholders, society and the local community." In 1980, "the company caused an independent audit to examine and report whether, and the extent to which, the company has fulfilled the objectives contained in its Articles of Association.

Reengineering the Value Chain

This refers to situations such as process reengineering or some other innovation which benefit the society and the company. For example, a new or improved process which will serve an important need of the society cost and performance effectively. This model neatly fits in to the "shared value" framework in which the corporation seeks to co-create economic and social value. For example, Walmart has undertaken corporate-wide supply chain initiatives both in response to pressure from environmental activists and as a profit-driven effort to reduce operating costs, partnering with environmental conservation organizations like the World Wildlife Fund.

Transforming the Ecosystem

The third CSR domain is emblematic of wide scale and disruptive change to a corporation's business model that puts the priority first on craftin a solution to a societal problem, which would then lead to financial returns in the longer run. This is a fundamental departure from the incremental and self-interested change of Reengineering the Value Chain initiatives that are focused primarily on increasing profits. In this third theatre, the company attempts to create societal value by significantly addressing a critical social or environmental need that is within its business reach, but that may not return immediate business profits. Unlike the first and second CSR domains, corporate endeavors within the third domain may not emerge from the company's core competencies, but may require the corporation to fundamentally change its business model and develop new skills and strategies.

Kash Rangan *et al*. points out hat within this third domain the corporation creates a radically new ecosystem solution that may be outside its core business interests, and that is fundamentally disruptive to the existing value chain. CSR efforts in this domain are not incremental or cautious, but require strategic risk-taking and a focus on long-range rather than short-term economic gains. For this reason, third domain CSR is most effectively undertaken by companies who have scale, diversified.

Indian CSR Models

All the three models described above prevail in India too. However, recently a new model, which we may call **government directed model**, has been put in place by the *National Voluntary Guidelines on Social, Environmental and Economic Responsibilities of Business* and the *Companies Act, 2013* described in the previous sub-section.

THE EMERGING SCENARIO

A large number of business enterprises — multinationals to small ones — now use 3BL terminology in their press releases, annual reports and other documents. Most of the big accounting firms are now using the concept approvingly and offering services to help firms that want to measure, report or audit their two additional "bottom lines". Similarly, there is now a sizable portion of the investment industry devoted to screening companies on the basis of their social and environmental performance, and many of these explicitly use the language of 3BL. Governments, government departments and political parties (especially Green parties) are also well represented in the growing documentation of those advocating or accepting 3BL "principles". For many NGOs and activist organisations, 3BL seems to be pretty much an article of faith.

The popularity of the TBL concept made the businessmen and society more concerned about the adverse impacts of economic activities in general and of large business enterprises in particular. Now, there is even clamor for social reporting, in several cases just for the sake of it. There have been several endeavours to develop criteria and framework for social reporting. The Global Reporting Initiative is an important institution in this area. It originated as a project of the Coalition for Environmentally Responsible Economies (CERES) and the United Nations Environment Program (UNEP) in late 1997 and become an independent institution at the end of 2002. This initiative was recognised at the UN World Summit on Sustainable Development. The aim of the guidelines issued by this organisation is to enable companies and other organisations to prepare comparable TBL reports on their economic, environmental and social performances. The GRI is also working with several industries to apply a multi-stakeholder model to develop industry specific supplements to the core Guidelines.

The UN Global Compact, has proposed to principles of CSR. UN Global Compact is an international initiative proposed in 2000 by former UN Secretary General Kofi Annan to call for stronger corporate social responsibility in the four areas of human rights, labour, environment and anti-corruption, and ten principles in respective areas. *National Voluntary Guidelines on Social, Environmental and Economic Responsibilities of Business* announced by the Government of India in 2011 resemble these principles.

It is observed that there are a number of corporations that have long prided themselves on their traditions of social responsibility and good corporate citizenship.

It may be mentioned here that several Indian companies have been publishing social audit report, CSR report, sustainability report, etc. Some companies have been very quick to respond to the *National Voluntary Guidelines*.

CSR: THE INDIAN PERSPECTIVE

Two recent developments have accorded a new perspective to CSR in India.

In 2011, the Central Government brought out a set of *National Voluntary Guidelines on Social, Environmental and Economic Responsibilities of Business* and certain provisions were incorporated in the Companies Act, 2013, requiring every company with certain level of turnover/profit to draw up a CSR Policy and earmark a certain portion of the profit for CSR activities.

Government Guidelines

In July 2011, the Ministry of Corporate Affairs, Government of India, brought out a set of *National Voluntary Guidelines on Social, Environmental and Economic Responsibilities of Business* to be adopted by all categories of enterprises, including SMEs. The Guidelines prefer the use of responsible business to corporate social responsibility. The Principles and Core elements laid down in the Guidelines are required to be integrated in the business policies, strategies and business processes emanating from the core business purpose of an enterprise. These Government guidelines and TBL, in essence, connote more or less the same as the broad perspective of CSR.

Nature and Significance of the Guidelines

These Guidelines are not prescriptive in nature, but are based on practices and precepts that take into account the realities of Indian business and society as well as global trends and best practices adapted to the Indian context. It urges businesses to embrace the "triple bottom line" approach whereby its financial performance can be harmonised with the expectations of society, the environment and the many stakeholders it interfaces with in a sustainable manner.

The Guidelines have been articulated in the form of nine Principles with the Core Elements to actualise each of the principles. A reading of each Principle, with its attendant Core Elements, should provide a very clear basis for putting that Principle into practice.

Principle 1: Businesses should conduct and govern themselves with Ethics, Transparency and Accountability.

Principle 2: Businesses should provide goods and services that are safe and contribute to sustainability throughout their life cycle.

Principle 3: Businesses should promote the well-being of all employees.

Principle 4: Businesses should respect the interests of, and be responsive towards all stakeholders, especially those who are disadvantaged, vulnerable and marginalised.

Principle 5: Businesses should respect and promote human rights.

Principle 6: Business should respect, protect, and make efforts to restore the environment.

Principle 7: Businesses, when engaged in influencing public and regulatory policy, should do so in a responsible manner.

Principle 8: Businesses should support inclusive growth and equitable development.

Principle 9: Businesses should engage with and provide value to their customers and consumers.

Companies are required to disclose their compliance to these principles.

Companies Act 2013 and CSR

With the Companies Act, 2013. (which replaced the Companies Act, 1956), it has become mandatory for certain specified categories of companies to spend a certain percentage of the profit on CSR.

Categories of Companies

Clause 135 of the Companies Act, 2013, pertaining to the CSR are applicable to any company having net worth of 500 crore or more, or turnover of 1,000 crore or more or net profit of 5 crore or more during any financial year.

CSRC and CSRP

Such companies as mentioned above shall constitute a Corporate Social Responsibility Committee (CSRC) consisting of three or more directors, including at least one independent director.

The CSRC shall formulate and recommend to the Board, a Corporate Social Responsibility Policy (CSRP) which shall indicate the activities to be undertaken by the company as specified in Schedule VII of the Act. The Committee shall recommend the amount of expenditure to be incurred on these activities. The Committee shall also monitor the CSR Policy of the company from time to time. The Board of Directors shall disclose in its report the contents of the CSR Policy as approved by the Board considering the recommendations made by the CSR Committee, and shall also place it on the company's website, if any.

Expenditure on CSR

In every financial year, the company shall spend at least two per cent of the average net profits of the company during the three immediately preceding financial years. Although the Companies Act, 2013, mandates companies to spend 2 per cent of their net profit on CSR, there are companies which spend a much higher proportion on CSR. Tata Steel, for example, has been spending 5 to 7 per cent of the profit after tax for this purpose.

CSR Activities

According to Schedule VII, the activities which may be undertaken under the CSR Policy relate to:

1. eradicating extreme hunger and poverty;
2. promotion of education;
3. promoting gender equality and empowering women;
4. reducing child mortality and improving maternal health;
5. combating human immuno deficiency virus, acquired immune deficiency syndrome, malaria and other diseases;
6. ensuring environmental sustainability;

7. employment enhancing vocational skills;
8. social business projects;
9. contribution to the Prime Minister's National Relief Fund or any other fund set up by the Central Government or the State Governments for socio-economic development and relief and funds for the welfare of the Scheduled Castes, the Scheduled Tribes, other backward classes, minorities and women; and
10. such other matters as may be prescribed.

It is also laid down that the company shall give preference to the local area and areas around it where it operates, for spending the amount earmarked for Corporate Social Responsibility activities.

Comments

The Ministry Corporate Affairs has estimated that some 12,000 companies would come under CSR ambit and in the first year of the application of the Act the eligible companies would spend about ₹ 5,000 crore (compared to its initial projection of more than ₹ 10,000 crore).

CSR has been practiced by companies in a big way in the developed economies like the United States where several reputed universities have been substantially funded by corporates. In India too, a number of companies and business houses have commendably contributed to social causes. The Companies Act 2013 is set to give a new dimension to CSR activities. Although the Companies Act, 2013, mandates companies to spend 2 per cent of their net profit on CSR, there are companies which spend a much higher proportion on CSR. Tata Steel, for example, has been spending 5 to 7 per cent of the profit after tax for this purpose. As indicated under the section Social Audit in India, the credit for conducting the social audit in India can, perhaps, be attributed to TISCO (Tata Steel). The Triple Bottom Line philosophy has been imbibed by many companies. For example, ITC "defines Corporate Governance as a systemic process by which companies are directed and controlled to enhance their wealth-generating capacity. Since large corporations employ a vast quantum of societal resources, ITC believes that the governance process should ensure that these resources are utilised in a manner that meets stakeholders' aspirations and societal expectations. This belief is reflected in the company's deep commitment to contribute to the "triple bottom line", namely the conservation and development of the nation's economic, social and environmental capital."

SOCIAL AUDIT

Meaning

One important issue related to social responsibility of business is how to evaluate the social performance. In other words, *social audit is a tool for evaluating how satisfactorily a company has discharged its social responsibilities. Social audit enables the public as well as the company to evaluate the social performance of the company.*

Bauer and Fenn Jr. define social audit as "a commitment to systematic assessment of and activities on some meaningful, definable domain of the company's activities that have social impact." According to Ahmed Belkaoui, "social audit much like the financial audit — is an identification and examination of the activities of the firm in order to assess, evaluate, measure and report their impact on the immediate social environment." In other words, social audit involves:

1. Identification of the firm's activities having potential social impact;
2. Assessment and evaluation of the social costs and social benefits of such activities;
3. Measurement of the social costs and benefits; and
4. Reporting, that is, presenting in a proper format and manner, the social performance of the firm.

Dr. Clark C. Abt, in his book *Audit for Management,* suggests that a Social Audit should, as far as possible, be approximated to an ordinary commercial audit; that this should be based on a social balance sheet with a "credit" side and "debit" side. He calls them "inputs" and "outputs" or "costs" and "benefits" so far as the social balance sheet is concerned. After suggesting that every "input" and "output" must be measured in monetary terms, he points out that the basic purpose of a business corporation is to maximise the financial return, earned on its financial investment plus the amount of social return on its social investment. To make rational investment decisions in social areas, it is necessary to know the social costs and if we are to assess them by the same measures as of financial investment, this must be expressed in dollar terms. He further asserts that, sooner or later, the social balance sheet must become a mandatory part of the normal commercial balance sheet of the company.

Objectives and Benefits of Social Audit

1. The basic objective of social audit is to evaluate the social dimensions of the performance of the company.
2. Another principal objective which follows the objective mentioned above is to take measures to improve the social performance of the company on the basis of the feedback provided by the social audit.
3. Social audit increases the public visibility of the organisation.
4. If the social audit reveals a socially commendable performance of the company, it will help boost the public image of the company.

Methods of Social Audit

There is no single universally agreed upon method of social auditing. Some of the important methods of social audit developed by different people or organisations are given below.

(i) Social Process Audit

The aim of the social process audit, also known as Programme management audit, is to develop an internal management information system that will allow management to create and administer the social programmes in a better way. This involves the determination of the objectives of the social programmes and a social cost benefit analysis of the programmes with a view to determining whether these objectives have been met.

(ii) Financial Statement Format Audit

Under the financial statement format audit, the social information is presented in the conventional financial statement format, *i.e.*, balance sheet and/or income statement.

(iii) Macro-Micro Social Indicator Audit

The macro-micro social indicator audit attempts to evaluate the micro indicators (i.e., the company's performance) against a set of macro indicators such as national policies.

(iv) Constituency Group Audit

Under this audit, the preference and attitudes of various constituencies (like employees, creditors, suppliers and customers) are identified and measured and the firm's performance is evaluated against the criteria developed for each group.

(v) Partial Social Audit

Partial social audit evaluates any particular aspects of social performance like energy conservation or ecological preservation.

(vi) Comprehensive Audit

Comprehensive audit attempts to evaluate the total performance of the organisation including social performance.

(vii) Corporate Rating Approach

In contradistinction to the audits mentioned above, this is an external evaluation of the company's performance by public groups like consumer organisations, social welfare organisations or media.

Given below is the format of social reporting used by the Cement Corporation of India.

Obstacles to Social Audit

Social audit encounters a number of problems. The important obstacles are:

1. Being a relatively new concept, social audit is yet to gain wide appreciation and acceptance.
2. Being a relatively new concept, a clear and generally well accepted methodology for conducting the social audits is not available.
3. There is no agreement as to the items to be included for social audit.

4. It is very difficult, and in several cases even impossible, to quantify the social costs and benefits of different activities or items.
5. There may be resistance within the company to social audit because of the time, effort, and difficulty involved in the task.
6. There may also be resistance because of the fear of a dismal or unsatisfactory picture that may be presented by the social audit.

As the Committee set up by the Tata Iron and Steel Company Limited (TISCO) to conduct the Social Audit of the TISCO points out, though social audits have been undertaken in a number of countries, principally in the USA (to which the practice owes its origin), Japan, the UK and one or two other Western countries, the subject has not yet attained the status of a science. There is no agreement, much less unanimity, among its most ardent proponents, particularly as to its basic principles or its true objectives. It is only a child of the last decade, during which there has been a growing concern about the environment and the problems of pollution, consumer protection, worker' safety and equal employment opportunities. Melvin Anshen, Professor of Public Policy and Business Responsibility at the Graduate School of Business, Columbia University, and an eminent authority on the subject, remarks that "the social audit has been described as an idea whose time has come but which isn't ready to be taken off the drawing board and put to work".

Social Audit in India

Although the idea of social audit originated in the United States about half a century ago, it is only recently that it received serious attention of corporations even in the advance countries.

The first comprehensive social audit in India was conducted by the TISCO in 1980. It was conducted by the Social Audit Committee appointed by the Board of Directors of the company "to examine and report whether, and the extent to which, the company has fulfilled the objectives contained in Clause 3A of its Articles of Association regarding its social and moral responsibilities to the consumers, employees, shareholders, society and the local community." The report of the Committee was a glowing tribute to the endeavours of the company in the discharge of its social and moral obligations to the various segments of the society.

Several companies have been making social reporting in their annual reports.

The High Powered Expert Committee on Companies and MRTP Acts (Sachar Committee) observes that the acceptance of the concept of social responsibility must be reflected in the information and disclosures that the company makes available for the benefit of its various constituents — shareholders, creditors, workers and the community — and has suggested that a provision may be made in the Companies Act that every company shall give a social report which will indicate and quantify, in as precise and clear terms as possible, the various activities relating to social responsibility which have been carried out by the company in the previous year. The Committee has further suggested that it is possible that a company may be required to alter its Memorandum with respect to the objects of the company so as to carry out its activities as an obligation to the concept of social responsibility.[8] It should be pointed out here that the TISCO had, in 1970, voluntarily incorporated in its Articles of Association its social and moral responsibilities to the consumers, employees, shareholders, society and the local people.

ARGUMENTS FOR AND AGAINST SOCIAL INVOLVEMENT

While there is a lot of appreciation of the idea of social responsibility of the business, there are also people who argue that social involvement of business has certain negative aspects.

The important arguments for and against the social involvement of business are given below.

Arguments for Social Involvement Business

1. Business which survives using the resources of the society has a responsibility to the society.
2. Business which is an integral part of the social system has to care for the varied needs of the society.
3. Business which is resourceful has a special responsibility to the society.
4. Social involvement of business would foster a harmonious and healthy relationship between the society and business to the mutual benefit of both.
5. Social responsibilities like recycling of waste may have favourable financial effects.
6. Social involvement may discourage additional government regulation and intervention.
7. Social involvement may create a better public image for the company which may help it in attracting customers, efficient personnel and investors.

Arguments against Social Involvement of Business

1. Business should confine to its own business. There are government and social organisations to carry out social activities.
2. Involvement in social activities could adversely affect the economic health of a business enterprise. It may be noted that the expenditures on social welfare has been imposing severe burden on TISCO.
3. If the cost of the social involvement of the business is ultimately passed on to the consumers, there is no point in exalting the social involvement of business. Sometimes there could even be a net loss to the society because of the high cost of the corporate sector undertaking such activities.
4. Many companies involve themselves in social activities because of the tax exemptions on the income spent on special social purposes.

5. If the social involvement of a business enterprise causes an increase in the price of its products, it could affect its competitiveness both in the domestic and international markets.
6. Social involvement of business could lead to an increase in the dominance or influence of business over the society.

SUMMARY

The rationale of the concept of social responsibility is that industry "can no longer be regarded as a private arrangement for enriching shareholders. It has become a joint enterprise in which workers, management, consumers, the locality, Government and trade union officials all play a part. If the system which we know by the name private enterprise is to continue, some way must be found to embrace many interests which go to make up industry in a common purpose."

It is argued that a company has a number of social responsibilities to the employees, shareholders, consumers and the community.

Social responsibility of business is advocated on the ground that the resources it makes use of are not limited to those of the proprietors and the impact of their operations is felt also by many a people who are in no way connected with the enterprises. The shareholders, the suppliers of resources, the consumers, the local community and society at large are affected by the way an enterprise functions. Hence, a business enterprise has to be socially very responsive so that a social balance may be struck between the opposing interests of these groups. Further, companies which have huge resources at their disposal have a moral responsibility to care for the society. Besides, discharge of social responsibilities will be in the company's own interest, because it will help build up good rapport with the society and Government and improve employee morale and industrial relations.

However, there are also arguments against the social involvement of business. It will affect the financial health of companies, it may lead to attempt to dominate the community's affairs, the costs of social involvement may be passed on to the consumers by price increase, for many companies it is a tax saving gimmick, so goes the arguments.

A social audit enables the public as well as the company to evaluate the social performance of the company. The "social audit — much like the financial audit — is an identification and examination of the activities of the firm in order to assess, evaluate, measure and report their impact on the immediate social environment."

There is no single universally agreed upon method of social auditing. Some of the important methods of social audit developed by different people or organisations include social process audit, financial statement format audit, macro-micro social indicator audit, constituency group audit, partial social audit, comprehensive audit, and corporate rating approach.

REFERENCES

1. See H.S. Singhania, "The Pace-Setters", *The Economic Times,* August 3, 1980.
2. George Goyder, *The Future of Private Enterprise: A Study in Responsibility* (Oxford: Basil Blackwell, 1951), p. 1.
3. Government of India, *Report of the High-Powered Expert Committee on Companies and MRTP Acts* (New Delhi : Controller of Publications, August 1978), p. 95.

4. *Ibid*.
5. Goyder, *op. cit.*
6. Government of India, *op. cit.*
7. Wikipedia, *The Free Encyclopedia.*

☆☆☆